Sports Law

Aspen College Series

Sports Law
Governance and Regulation, 2E

Matthew J. Mitten
Professor of Law and Director, National Sports Law Institute
Marquette University Law School

Timothy Davis
John W. & Ruth H. Turnage Professor of Law
Wake Forest University School of Law

Rodney K. Smith
Distinguished Professor of Practice and
Director, Sports Law and Business Program
The Sandra Day O'Connor College of Law, Arizona State University

Kenneth L. Shropshire
David W. Hauck Professor
Wharton School, University of Pennsylvania

Barbara Osborne
Associate Professor
University of North Carolina at Chapel Hill

Published by Wolters Kluwer in New York.

Wolters Kluwer Legal & Regulatory Solutions U.S. serves customers worldwide with CCH, Aspen Publishers, and Kluwer Law International products. (www.WKLegaledu.com)

To contact Customer Service, e-mail customer.service@wolterskluwer.com, call 1-800-234-1660, fax 1-800-901-9075, or mail correspondence to:

Wolters Kluwer
Attn: Order Department
PO Box 990
Frederick, MD 21705

Printed in the United States of America.

3 4 5 6 7 8 9 0

ISBN 978-1-4548-6978-8

Library of Congress Cataloging-in-Publication Data

Names: Mitten, Matthew J., 1959- author. | Davis, Timothy, 1954- author. | Smith, Rodney K., author. | Shropshire, Kenneth L., author. | Osborne, Barbara, author.
Title: Sports law / Matthew J. Mitten, Professor of Law and Director, National Sports Law Institute Marquette University Law School; Timothy Davis, John W. & Ruth H. Turnage Professor of Law Wake Forest University School of Law; Rodney K. Smith, Professor of Practice and Director, Center for Sports Law and Policy Thomas Jefferson School of Law; Kenneth L. Shropshire, David W. Hauck Professor Wharton School, University of Pennsylvania; Barbara Osborne, Associate Professor University of North Carolina at Chapel Hill;.
Description: Second edition. | New York : Wolters Kluwer, 2016. | Series: Aspen college series | Includes bibliographical references and index.
Identifiers: LCCN 2015046483 | ISBN 9781454869788 (alk. paper)
Subjects: LCSH: Sports–Law and legislation–United States. | LCGFT: Casebooks.
Classification: LCC KF3989 .M58 2016 | DDC 344.73/099–dc23 LC record available at http://lccn.loc.gov/2015046483

About Wolters Kluwer Legal & Regulatory Solutions U.S.

Wolters Kluwer Legal & Regulatory Solutions U.S. delivers expert content and solutions in the areas of law, corporate compliance, health compliance, reimbursement, and legal education. Its practical solutions help customers successfully navigate the demands of a changing environment to drive their daily activities, enhance decision quality and inspire confident outcomes.

Serving customers worldwide, its legal and regulatory solutions portfolio includes products under the Aspen Publishers, CCH Incorporated, Kluwer Law International, ftwilliam.com and MediRegs names. They are regarded as exceptional and trusted resources for general legal and practice-specific knowledge, compliance and risk management, dynamic workflow solutions, and expert commentary.

To Bob Berry,
our friend and colleague

Summary of Contents

Contents

Chapter 4: Legal Relationships Between the University and Student-Athletes   113

Contractual and NCAA Regulatory Dimensions   113

Chapter 5: Gender Equity Issues in Athletics   147

Chapter 12: Professional Sports Labor Law and Labor Relations   371

Chapter 14: Olympic and International Sports Issues   441

Preface

Second Edition

To provide users of our book with the most current and comprehensive sports law and governance text available, we have revised and updated the second edition of our book to include discussions of the most recent legal and governance developments affecting youth, interscholastic, intercollegiate, Olympic, and professional sports that have occurred since our first edition was published in 2012. The sports industry, at all levels, has experienced significant and rapid change in that time period. That change is captured in this text. This edition includes a number of recent legal decisions and new materials regarding developments in governance that reflect the increasing complexity of problems arising in the sports industry. This edition, therefore, includes materials reflecting changes in governance at the professional level (e.g., issues like "Deflategate" and governance within the National Football League (NFL)) and the new governance structure of the National Collegiate Athletic Association (NCAA). We have updated historical sections of the book as well, to give students a feel for the magnitude of those changes. The Second Edition also includes refined problems and notes that are designed to encourage students to wrestle with the kinds of legal and governance problems that are arising and will hereafter arise within the industry. With input from thoughtful users of the First Edition, we have been able to add new material without unduly expanding the length of the text. As such, the text can still be effectively used in either a two- or three-credit course. With users' comments and based on our own use of the text, we have reorganized and, where necessary, consolidated materials. We trust that you will find this Second Edition to be an excellent text for the study of sports law and governance. We welcome your continuing comments regarding the text. Please feel free to contact any of us with your comments and suggestions for improving the book: Matt Mitten (matt.mitten@marquette.edu), Tim Davis (davistx@wfu.edu), Barbara Osborne (bosborne8@nc.rr.com), Ken Shropshire (shrop@wharton.upenn.edu), and Rod Smith (Rodney.K.Smith@asu.edu).

First Edition

This book, which is adapted from three of the authors' widely used law school text, is designed to introduce undergraduate and graduate students to the various and often differing legal frameworks regulating high school, college, professional, and Olympic sports competition along with important, contemporary topics such as gender and racial equity; health, safety, and risk management; and intellectual property issues in sports. It provides an overview of the significant historical, economic, and sociological issues affecting the development of the laws regulating sports at each level of competition, as well as common sports-related legal issues. The book, which is intended for use as the text in either a two- or three-credit-hour undergraduate or graduate sports law course in sports management or other program, covers a wide variety of contemporary sports law issues of interest to future sports administrators, executives, and business managers, as well as coaches and other sports industry personnel. It has been carefully designed and written to provide undergraduate and graduate professors and students with a comprehensive, multipurpose text that gives a balanced perspective regarding a multitude of legal and regulatory issues that frequently arise in interscholastic, intercollegiate, professional, and Olympic sports industries.

This book begins by providing an introduction to the study of sports law and a brief overview of the U.S. legal system, as well as guidance on how to effectively use the case method to facilitate and enhance learning. In Chapters 2–4, 11–12, and 14, the book covers the internal governance systems for high school, college, professional, and Olympic sports, respectively. These chapters also cover the primary bodies of public law (e.g., private association, constitutional, antitrust, and labor law) that shape, regulate, and constrain each internal governance system. The remaining chapters cover various topics raising legal issues of significance in more than one of the amateur or professional sports industries: coaches' contracts (Chapter 10); gender equity (Chapter 5); racial equity (Chapter 6); health, safety, and risk management (Chapter 7); and intellectual property (Chapter 9).

This text uses the case method, which involves the study of illustrative legal disputes resolved by courts through the litigation process, and establishes a body of legal precedent regulating various aspects of the sports industry. This method of learning is designed to encourage students to engage in critical thinking by identifying the legal issues in each case, the parties' respective arguments, and the court's ruling and rationale for its decision. It stimulates the development of a dialogue between the professor and students (and frequently among students as well). It also facilitates students' understanding of the laws regulating the sports industry. In addition to the illustrative cases (which have been edited substantially), each chapter provides explanatory material, notes, questions, and review problems designed to enable students to understand how basic legal doctrines apply to problems arising in the sports context. Ideally, students can then use this knowledge to identify sports industry legal issues and to understand how they are likely to be resolved.

In addition to helping students develop an understanding of the legal framework regulating high school, college, professional, and Olympic sports and other sports-related legal issues, a sports law course provides several important educational benefits. It exposes students (some of whom may be considering law school) to several different bodies of law and provides them with a general understanding of numerous laws — knowledge that may be useful in future careers other than in the sports industry. In addition, sports law deals with broader issues that merit deeper study and reflection, such as the role of sports in our culture and whether current laws effectively promote appropriate, ethical, and just practices and behavior in the amateur and professional sports industries. We hope that our book encourages thoughtful consideration of these and other important sports-related issues.

ACKNOWLEDGMENTS

Second Edition

Professor Mitten thanks Lori Shaw (Marquette Law School Class of 2016) for her helpful review of and comments on various chapters and the glossary.

Professor Davis thanks Wake Forest University School of Law for its generous research support and Alan Bowie (Wake Forest School of Law Class of 2017) for his assistance.

Professor Osborne thanks the University of North Carolina Law School for providing research support and UNC law students Tyler O'Hara and Anna Finger for their research assistance.

Professor Smith thanks Dean Douglas Sylvester for his continuing support, and Devin Tarwater (Sandra Day O'Connor College of Law at Arizona State University 2015) and Krizia Verplancke and Blake Wilkie (Sandra Day O'Connor College of Law 2016 and 2017, respectively). He also thanks students J. Leigh Hawley and Jon Drago for their helpful review during the production process.

First Edition

Professor Mitten thanks Erica Reib (Marquette Law 2011) for her helpful review of and comments on various draft chapters and Chris Kaminski (Marquette Law 2013) for his assistance in preparing the glossary.

Professor Davis thanks Wake Forest University School of Law for its generous research support and the following Wake Forest students for their research assistance: Justin Bell, Thailer Buari, and Nathan Harrill.

Professor Shropshire wishes to thank students who recently participated in his sports law course at Penn for their helpful comments.

Professor Osborne thanks the University of North Carolina Law School for providing research support and UNC law student Scott Holder for his research assistance.

Professor Smith appreciates the support offered by Dean Rudy Hasl and Associate Dean Eric J. Mitnik.

We also thank the following reviewers, whose insightful comments helped shape this text: Jan Blade, Delaware State University; Sandra Defebaugh, Eastern Michigan

University; Gil Fried, University of New Haven; Michael Gentile, Niagara University; Richard Hunter, Seton Hall University; Paul Klein, Duquesne University; William Nowlan, Lasell College; Marissa Pollick, University of Michigan; Jessie C. Roberson, Ohio University; and Ellen M. Zavian, George Washington University.

Matthew J. Mitten
Timothy Davis
Rodney K. Smith
Kenneth L. Shropshire
Barbara Osborne
December 2015

An Introduction to the Study of Sports Law

Should sports law be recognized as an independent substantive area of the law such as torts, contracts, or employment law? As the following excerpt reveals, scholars have debated this question.

WHAT IS SPORTS LAW?[1]

A. The Traditional View: "Sports Law" Does Not Exist

The traditional view is that sports law represents nothing more than an amalgamation of various substantive areas of the law that are relevant in the sports context. According to this perspective, the term *sports law* is a misnomer, given that sport represents a form of activity and entertainment that is governed by the legal system in its entirety. Adherents to the traditional perspective argue that "sports law simply entails the application of basic legal precepts to a specific industry" that are drawn from other substantive areas of the law. Consequently, no separately identifiable body of law exists that can be characterized as sports law.

B. The Moderate Position: "Sports Law" May Develop into a Field of Law

Other commentators have begun increasingly to question the traditional view that no corpus of law exists that can be characterized as an independent field of law called "sports law" . . . . [Some] have staked out what represents a middle ground. Professor Kenneth Shropshire acknowledges that developments, such as state and federal

---

[1] This excerpt was originally published at Timothy Davis, 11 MARQ. SPORTS L. REV. 211 (2001). All citations to authority have been omitted.

legislation impacting sports (for example, state statutes regulating sports agents, and federal statutes such as Title IX), suggest a "growing sports-only corpus" of law.

Professor Burlette Carter argues that sports law is in the midst of an exciting, yet challenging, transformative process. According to Professor Carter, this process parallels the increased focus by law schools on sports and the growing significance of sports regulation to participants, organizations, and communities. She believes that these developments will better shape the contours of this emerging field of study. This, in turn, will eventually transform sports law from "a course without a corpus" to a widely recognized independent substantive area of law.

C. "Sports Law": A Separate Field of Law

Others argue that sports law currently exists as a field of law. Adherents to this view emphasize the growing body of case and statutory law specific to the sports industry as evidence of the existence of a separately identifiable body of law. Pointing to the increasing body of judicial and legislative law specific to sports, Professor [Simone] Gardiner argues:

> It is true to say that [sports law] is largely an amalgam of interrelated legal disciplines involving such areas as contract, taxation, employment, competition and criminal law but dedicated legislation and case law has developed and will continue to do so. As an area of academic study and extensive practitioner involvement, the time is right to accept that a new legal area has been born — sports law.

Commentators also propose that references to sports law as merely an amalgamation of various other substantive areas of the law ignore an important present-day reality — very few substantive areas of the law fit into separate categories that are divorced from, and independent of, other substantive areas of the law. Doctrinal overlap exists not only within sports law, but within other areas of law as well. According to Professor Carter, "the field of sports law has moved beyond the traditional antitrust and labor law boundaries into sports representation and legal ethics, sports and corporate structure, sports and disability, sports and race, sports and gender, sports and taxation, international issues in sports law, and numerous other permutations."

Proponents of the sports law designation and those sympathetic to the view also argue that reticence to recognize sports law as a specific body of law may reflect attitudes regarding the intellectual seriousness of sports. In this regard, they emphasize the tendency to marginalize the study of sports rather than treat it as any other form of business. The intellectual marginalization of sport has been attributed, in part, to the belief that social relations extant in sports were not deemed proper subjects for reconstruction into legal relationships. Thus, private and public law were considered "inappropriate [mechanisms for] controlling the social norms of sport." The competing and increasingly predominant view, however, casts sports as a significant economic activity suitable, like other big businesses, to regulation, whether it be internal or external.

In the end, whether sports law is recognized as an independent field of law may turn on the perceptions of those who practice, teach, and engage in scholarship related to sports law. Professor Carter asks that we consider the following:

> But what makes a field a field? The answer is that a field becomes a field not because it is inherently so but because in our public legal dealings we shape it as such, defining the concepts and legal norms that will prevail uniquely in that context. It becomes a field because enough people with power on all sides are so affected by it to require some special treatment of it in the law.

Regardless of the position that is adopted regarding the "what is sports law" debate, most would agree that matters arising in the sports law context implicate diverse substantive areas of law. Whether or not sports law is a separate field of law, a reflection of substantive law related to the sports industry, or some combination, the vast array of substantive legal topics presented in a basic Sports Law course can sometimes prove surprisingly challenging. To enjoy and ultimately excel in this area, it will be helpful for you to have an introduction to legal basics.

Sports law involves both public and private law. Public law can be broadly described as the law that governs the relationships between the government and individuals, as well as the relationships between individuals that directly affect society. Constitutional law, administrative law, and criminal law are areas of public law that intersect with sports law. Private law governs the relationships between individuals (or corporations); sports law applications include contracts, torts, and the law of private associations. However, you will learn that distinctions in law are rarely clear. Public and private law often intersect in areas such as labor and antitrust. For undergraduate and graduate students interested in working in some capacity in the amateur or professional sports industries, this introduction will help you better understand the legal landscape and will aid you in your work with lawyers, who should be consulted whenever you deal with legal issues.

FUNDAMENTALS OF THE LEGAL SYSTEM

The United States has a federalist government, which means power is shared between the national and state (and local) governments. The basic operating principles for the federal and state governments are embodied in the Constitution. The federal Constitution identifies the fundamental rights of citizens of the United States and delineates limits on the government's ability to interfere with those rights. The federal Constitution applies to all states, and is preeminent; states may grant additional rights, but they may not limit rights that the federal Constitution guarantees. Constitutional cases are based on the interpretation of state constitutions or the federal Constitution. Federal laws that are inconsistent with the U.S. Constitution are invalid — in our legal hierarchy, constitutional provisions are the most significant. That is what is meant when it is said that the U.S. Constitution is the law of the land. State laws that are inconsistent with the state or federal constitutions are also held to be unconstitutional and invalid.

The foundation of the federal government is based upon a balance of power between the executive, legislative, and judicial branches. Each of these branches is a source of law. The executive branch is the President of the United States. The President is ultimately responsible for implementing and enforcing federal laws, through executive orders and through the regulations set forth by the administrative agencies. For example, the U.S. Department of Education promulgates Title IX regulations dealing with gender discrimination under the auspices of administrative legal authority that provides part of the substantive basis of sports law. The President also appoints the heads of the federal agencies, who also serve on the President's cabinet.

The legislative branch is responsible for writing, debating, and passing bills. Demonstrating balance of power, bills only become law when the President has signed them. If the President vetoes a bill, Congress has the ability to vote to override the veto.

The role of the judicial branch is to interpret the Constitution or legislation. Balance of power is demonstrated through judicial interpretation of legislation (statutes) or regulations (regulatory materials developed by administrative or regulatory bodies). In these instances, judicial decisions often involve interpreting or determining the applicability and reach of a given regulation or piece of legislation. The judiciary also creates law, known as the common law, through the precedent established in case decisions. The concepts of common law and precedent will be discussed later in this chapter.

State governments are organized similarly. The state constitution embodies the principles upon which the state government operates. Balance of power exists within each state, with the governor of each state representing the executive branch and enforcing the law, state representatives to the legislature who enact the law, and the state (and local) judiciary interprets the law.

There are also local and regulatory decision-making bodies that make law. County governments and school districts, for example, regularly promulgate laws that may provide the grist for a decision in the sports area. High school and collegiate athletic associations may also pass and enforce regulations that provide the basis for decisions in the sports law area.

JURISDICTION AND THE FEDERAL AND STATE COURT SYSTEMS

In the United States, there are two dominant court systems — the federal courts and the state courts. Jurisdiction is the power of the court to hear and determine the outcome of a case. A court establishes this power because of the subject matter of the case or the parties who are involved. Subject matter jurisdiction refers to the particular category of the case, for example, a dispute involving land or the right to use a corporate logo. Personal jurisdiction refers to the court's power over the various parties to the case.

Cases in the federal court system or the state courts may involve civil law or criminal law. Disputes between public or private parties are civil law matters which are decided on a preponderance of the evidence standard. Criminal law involves acts that are harmful to society as a whole, so the government represents the people in putting forward a case against a criminal defendant. The government must prove that the defendant committed the crime beyond a reasonable doubt.

Broadly too, particularly in sports law–related cases, parties will seek remedies in "law" or "equity." A remedy at law is primarily one where money damages are sought as a means of compensating the injured party. For example, if a coach feels that he or she is owed an additional salary payment, money would resolve that issue and constitute a remedy at law. However, if a team wanted to retain a coach with special skills or keep him or her from coaching for another team, that would require an equitable remedy, including a court's issuance of an order of specific performance or an injunction. Specific performance would be an order for the coach to continue coaching, and the injunction would bar the coach from coaching another team.

A. Federal Courts

The federal court system is established by Article III of the U.S. Constitution and consists of three levels. At the trial level, the federal courts are divided into 94 districts, with at least one district in each state, the District of Columbia, and Puerto Rico. District courts have original jurisdiction over cases involving federal issues, issues that are based on the U.S. Constitution, federal legislation, regulations, treaties, or cases arising in states that implicate other states and their citizens and residents. Federal judges are nominated by the President, confirmed by the U.S. Senate, and typically serve for life. Decisions of the district court may be appealed to the appropriate circuit court. The federal court of appeals is organized into 12 regional circuits plus a court of appeals for the Federal Circuit. The circuit courts also hear appeals of decisions by the federal administrative agencies. Typically, a panel of three judges hears the arguments on appeal and renders a decision. Parties that are not satisfied may appeal to the Supreme Court, which has discretionary jurisdiction; it selects which cases it will hear. The highest court within the federal judiciary, the Supreme Court consists of nine justices, including the Chief Justice. A Supreme Court decision is final unless there is a constitutional amendment to overturn its decision, Congress alters the Court's decision by changing the law, or the Supreme Court overturns its own decision through a decision in a later case.

B. State Courts

State court systems are established by the state constitution of their respective state. State cases, in turn, involve state issues, issues that are based on state legislation, regulation, and the provisions of that state's constitution. State court systems are also typically three-tiered systems with a trial court, appellate court, and a court of final decision. The names of the appellate level courts vary by state, so a Court of

Appeals in one state may be the Supreme Court of another. Because state courts have unique jurisdiction, a party that is not satisfied with the final decision in a state court may not appeal to the federal court. One exception is when there is some conflict between state and federal law such as state constitutional provisions that are inconsistent with federal constitutional law or that deprive citizens and residents of other states of their federal constitutional rights. Judges in the state courts may be elected or appointed, depending upon state law.

C. Tax and Other Specialized Courts

There are other specialized courts and decision makers at the state, federal, and international levels. For example, there are specialized tribunals or courts that decide cases in particular areas of law such as tax. Those specialized tribunals exist at the state and federal levels, and sometimes even at the local and international levels.

While the government legislates, and the judiciary enforces the laws that regulate the sports industry, the majority of regulation occurs within the sports industry. Most sport organizations belong to a league or association that establishes rules for membership and competition. Community recreation and sport programs, as well as some high school athletics associations, are considered state actors (see Chapter 2). However, the National Collegiate Athletic Association (NCAA) (Chapter 3), the U.S. Olympic Committee and national sport governing bodies (Chapter 14), and professional sports leagues (Chapter 11) are all considered private organizations. Generally, courts give tremendous deference to sports organizations to govern their own affairs and create and enforce their own rules. Under the principle of limited judicial review, the courts will intervene in a sport organization's affairs only if the association's rules: (1) violate constitutional rights (when the association is considered a state actor); (2) violate basic notions of fairness or public policy (for private associations); (3) exceed the scope of the association's authority; (4) violates one of the association's own rules; or (5) are applied unreasonably or arbitrarily and capriciously. Generally, the court will not review the merits of a rule, or whether there is a better way for the organization to achieve the same goal.

CIVIL PROCEDURE

The term *procedure* refers to the mechanics of the legal process. Procedure varies between the civil court system and the criminal law system. Although criminal activity occurs within the sport industry, the overwhelming majority of sport law issues fall within the civil law. Civil procedure is the legal method, including rules of practice, which must be strictly adhered to in order to advance through the legal process. This section provides a quick overview of the Federal Rules of Civil Procedure.

The succession of events constituting civil procedure includes complaint, service, answer, discovery, motions, trial, judgment, and appeal. The complaint is the formal legal document that lists the pleadings, or claims, that the plaintiff is bringing forth against the defendant. The purpose of the complaint is to provide notice to the defendant and the court as to the nature of the claims that are asserted. Service is the delivery of a legal document, such as a pleading or complaint, to the adverse party in a legal action. Completion of service requires strict adherence to the rules of the court of that jurisdiction. Upon completion of service, the defendant is subject to the rules of the court in resolving the issue. The defendant must file a formal answer to the complaint; the answer must address all of the allegations in the complaint, whether confirmed or denied, and include any defenses or counterclaims that the defendant will assert. After the answer has been properly filed, the parties may advance to discovery or file motions with the court. The defendant may file a motion to dismiss based on inadequacy of the pleadings. In that case, a court will determine whether or not the basic outline for a case has successfully been set forth by the plaintiff. If not, a court may dismiss the action.

Assuming the case proceeds, discovery is the process of sharing information between the parties. Interrogatories, written questions for the opposing parties, may be submitted. Similarly, depositions, statements of potential witnesses, may be acquired either orally or in writing. Oral depositions are made under oath, with representatives of both parties present and having the opportunity to cross-examine while the procedure is recorded and/or transcribed. The parties may also request additional information and documents from the opposing party. The purpose of discovery is for all parties to share information to achieve a fair and just resolution.

Either party, or sometimes both parties, may submit a motion for summary judgment. In this situation, the court will apply the law to the facts of the case in the light most favorable to the nonmoving party to determine whether the motion is granted or denied.

Should the case proceed to trial, the parties are required to follow the rules of the court in presenting evidence to support their positions. The trial may be heard by a judge, called a *bench trial,* or by a jury. Civil trials most commonly have six citizens serve on a jury. Throughout the trial, there may be additional motions made by either party. At the end of a bench trial, the judge will render a decision. In a jury trial, the judge will provide the jury with the rules of law upon which they are required to make their decision.

If a party, plaintiff or defendant, loses in a lower court, that party may have a right to appeal. An appeal involves a right by one or both of the parties to contest the legal ruling that was reached at the preceding stage of the litigation process. Generally, appellate courts are quite deferential to the findings of fact made by the trial court because the trial court actually hears the testimony of the witnesses and can evaluate their credibility firsthand. The appellate court does not hear new witnesses or review new evidence — it merely addresses whether there was an error in procedure or in application of the law that adversely affected the outcome of the trial. The appellate court may affirm the lower court decision, overturn the decision of the lower court and render a new decision, or remand the matter back to the lower court with instructions. A party may appeal an appellate court decision. However, the highest court in the process, often called the *supreme court,* is unlikely to hear the case unless there are conflicting decisions among the appellate court districts at the state level or among the various circuit courts at the federal level, or unless the case presents a significant legal issue.

USING THE CASE METHOD TO STUDY LAW

The study of law in American law schools is primarily done via the case method, although non-case law and policy-related materials often complement the cases. This book is designed in a manner that takes full advantage of pedagogy based on the study of cases and related materials and problems, which strengthen students' thinking and analytical skills. Going forward, you will read a case or a series of cases on a given topic. For example, in focusing on antitrust law in baseball, the first major or seminal case in the United States was *Federal Baseball Club of Baltimore, Inc. v. National League of Professional Baseball Clubs*, 259 U.S. 200 (1922). By proceeding, often chronologically, through a series of cases, culminating in a study of the latest cases, students learn how law develops. This method also assists students in applying the law and strengthens their capacity to anticipate future legal developments.

A. Common Law

Part of what the case method requires you to do is to bring together the meaning of the cases and to develop the law through the synthesizing of the cases, with each case building on the foundation of prior cases. Through this process, one comes to understand what cases and commentators refer to as the "common law."

1. Precedent

In applying case law, there is little more powerful than a supporting precedent, or a case that provides support for your position. *Precedent* is a holding, or ruling of a court, that establishes authority for the disposition of future similar cases. Ideally, litigants and their attorneys are thrilled to uncover a Supreme Court case addressing exactly the same facts and legal questions that comprise their situation. When they do so, there is often little need to proceed (however, this does not happen often). If one cannot find a Supreme Court decision directly on point, the next best option may be some other highly respected federal or state court with a ruling similar to your matter. Lower courts are to follow the decisions of higher courts within their jurisdiction. In the federal judiciary, district courts must adhere to the decisions of the Court of Appeals for their circuit or distinguish their case from other previously decided cases. Other circuit court or even state court decisions provide influential or persuasive authority. In this search for precedent, lawyers know that cases with slight factual variations can be supportive as well. For example, if you have a case involving an injury to a soccer player and find a case where the facts are similar but the sport is rugby, that case may be strong precedent in your case, unless you can distinguish soccer from rugby in a manner that would persuade a court that the cases should be treated differently as a legal matter.

2. How to Brief a Case

Whether you are reading a case assigned in this text or cases that you find while engaged in a legal research project, briefing each case will help you to better understand the legal issues as well as how the law develops. Every brief should include the following elements: case name and citation, named parties, legal issue(s), key facts, legal rationale, and holding(s).

The case name generally identifies the plaintiff (the person who has filed a lawsuit) and the defendant (the party against whom the lawsuit has been initiated). Typically, the plaintiff's name is on the left and the defendant on the right, although these are sometimes transposed. The numbers and letters after the case name identify the reporter where a written copy of the case decision is published. Historically, law students would have gone to the law library, located the appropriate reporter (the abbreviation in the middle), then found the volume (the first numbers listed) and opened it to the correct page (the numbers after the designated reporter). When using digital legal search engines such as Lexis or Westlaw, you just type in the citation, and the case is delivered right to your computer screen. The name of the court that wrote the decision and the year the case was decided are included in parentheses after the case citation. It is important to note which court (state or federal) and level of court for precedent purposes. It is also helpful to order your cases in chronological order, as well as by jurisdiction to see how the law develops.

Next, you should identify the plaintiffs and the defendants. All parties are not always included in the case name.

It is often helpful to identify the legal issue, or issues, in the case by posing them in the form of a question. The legal issue is the question of law that the court is deciding. Identifying the legal question is important, as you may find a case that has facts very similar to your own situation, but the court makes a decision on a legal question that is irrelevant to you. This case would not provide strong precedent.

Many students confuse the legal issue with the facts. The key facts include only the information that is necessary for the court to address the legal issue. Some judges will provide extensive background information and paint a lovely backdrop for the case. However, for briefing purposes, it is useful to pare down all of this information to just the facts that come into play in order for the court to make a decision.

The rationale section identifies the various legal theories that the court examines in order to reach a decision. Using an outline format is helpful in this section of the brief. First, identify the legal theory or legislation that the court uses. Next, define that area of law or explain the statute. Finally, show how the court applies the facts of the case to the legal definition. Some cases may address only a single area of the law, while more complex litigation may address a dozen or more legal theories. The key words identified prior to the cases in this text will often help you to identify the key legal theories addressed. If you are reading other cases, you can look at the keynotes (literally identified by a key-shaped symbol) in Westlaw or the headnotes in Lexis. The rationale section of the brief really helps you to identify and digest how the common law develops. It will also assist you in building legal explanations or arguments if you are researching a legal topic. One additional tip — if you are briefing cases for a legal research paper, it is helpful to identify the page number in the case where you found the information in your brief. The page numbers can be found in brackets (for example, [413]) as you are reading the case. This will save you significant time in tracking down your citations for your legal paper.

The final element of the case brief is the holding, or decision of the court. There should be a holding for every legal issue that you have identified. The holding is critically important because it establishes precedent.

The following case provides you with the opportunity to brief a case, as well as learn a little about civil procedure and tort law.

KEY TERMS **In reviewing the following materials, note the definition and meaning of the following terms:**

- Answer
- Appeal
- Assumption of risk
- Complaint
- Deposition
- Discovery
- Interrogatories
- Negligence
- Recklessness
- Summary judgment

Savino v. Robertson
273 Ill. App. 3d 811 (1995)

JUDGES: Justice McCormick delivered the opinion of the court: Scariano, P.J., and DiVito, J., concur.

[*812] Plaintiff John Savino brought a negligence action against defendant Scott Robertson after plaintiff was struck and injured in the eye by a hockey puck shot by defendant. The trial court granted defendant's subsequent motion for summary judgment, but allowed [*813] plaintiff to amend the complaint to allege that defendant's conduct was willful and wanton. Upon another motion by defendant, the trial court granted summary judgment in favor of defendant on the amended complaint. On appeal from both orders, plaintiff raises the following issues for our consideration: (1) whether a plaintiff must plead and prove willful and wanton conduct in order to recover for injuries incurred during athletic competition; and (2) whether there was a genuine issue of material fact as to whether defendant's conduct was willful and wanton in injuring plaintiff. We affirm.

Plaintiff and defendant were teammates in an amateur hockey league sponsored by the Northbrook Park District. Plaintiff and defendant also had met in various "pick-up" games prior to playing in the Northbrook league, but they were neither friends nor enemies. On April 20, 1990, plaintiff and defendant were warming up prior to a game. During warm-up, teams skate around and behind their goal on their half of the ice. Plaintiff was on the ice, "to the right of the face-off circle in front of the net." Defendant shot a puck that missed the goal and hit plaintiff near the right eye. Plaintiff lost 80% vision in that eye.

On September 11, 1990, plaintiff filed a one-count complaint against defendant alleging that defendant was negligent and failed to exercise ordinary care in shooting the puck. Specifically, plaintiff alleged that defendant (a) failed to warn plaintiff that he was going to shoot the puck toward plaintiff; (b) failed to wait until a goalie was present before shooting the puck; (c) failed to warn others that he was shooting the puck; (d) failed to follow the custom and practice of the Northbrook Men's Summer League which required the presence of a goalie at the net before shooting; and (e) failed to keep an adequate lookout.

Defendant filed his answer to the complaint and, after interrogatories and discovery depositions were taken, defendant moved for summary judgment. . . . Defendant argued that he was entitled to judgment as a matter of law because plaintiff alleged ordinary negligence. To be entitled to relief for injuries incurred during athletic competition, defendant argued, plaintiff had to plead and prove willful and wanton conduct or conduct done in reckless disregard for the safety of others. The trial court granted defendant's motion for summary judgment and denied plaintiff leave to amend count I of the complaint. Upon reconsideration, the trial court granted plaintiff leave to file an amended complaint to allege a count II based on willful and wanton conduct.

Defendant filed his answer to plaintiff's subsequent amended complaint and the parties engaged in discovery as to count II of that [*814] complaint. Defendant later filed another motion for summary judgment. Defendant argued that, due to plaintiff's admission that his injury was caused by an accident, plaintiff's case presented no genuine issue of material fact with regard to defendant's alleged willful and wanton conduct. Defendant further argued that plaintiff could not show that defendant's action was anything more than an ordinary practice shot normally taken during warm-up sessions.

Plaintiff, on the other hand, argued in his response to defendant's motion that ordinary negligence should be the standard applied to his case rather than willful and wanton conduct, because, since the hockey game had not officially begun, he was not a participant at the time of his injury. Plaintiff attached the affidavit of Thomas Czarnik, a hockey coach at Deerfield High School, to his response. According to Czarnik, it was the custom of amateur hockey leagues to wait until the goalie was present in the net before any practice shots were taken.

Defendant also took Czarnik's deposition. In that deposition, Czarnik described himself as a 15-year acquaintance of plaintiff. . . . Czarnik further stated that he had been a hockey player since childhood and had coached various youth hockey organizations. The Northbrook Hockey League played what was known as "non-check" hockey. Non-check meant non-collision. However, there was still bodily contact in non-check hockey and, in Czarnik's opinion, hockey, regardless of the type, is a contact sport. Czarnik had no knowledge of the rules and usages of the Northbrook Hockey League and had no firsthand knowledge of the incident.

Czarnik also stated that he had seen players in adult hockey leagues take shots at open goals, that is, goals without a goalie present, during the warm-up period and that he had taken shots at open goals. According to Czarnik, the warm-up period was a part of the game of hockey even though the players are not technically playing a game. Czarnik considered plaintiff's injury an accident.

Defendant attached excerpts of Czarnik's deposition in support of his reply to plaintiff's response to the motion for summary judgment. Defendant argued that Czarnik's responses demonstrated that plaintiff could not show, as a matter of law, that defendant's conduct was willful or wanton. Defendant also contended that Czarnik was not a proper expert to render an opinion in this case, given his lack of familiarity with adult hockey leagues and lack of knowledge of the rules and usages of the Northbrook Summer Men's Hockey League. The trial court granted defendant's motion for summary judgment. **[*815]** Plaintiff now appeals from both orders of the trial court granting summary judgment in favor of defendant.

Our review of the trial court's grant of summary judgment is *de novo.* The granting of summary judgment is proper when the pleadings, depositions, and affidavits show that no genuine issue of material fact exists and the moving party is entitled to judgment as a matter of law. In determining whether summary judgment is proper, the court must construe the evidence in a light most favorable to the non-movant and strongly against the movant.

Plaintiff first argues that he should not have been required to plead willful and wanton conduct in this case because he was not actually "playing" the game of hockey at the time his injury occurred, but rather was participating in the warm-up practice.

The seminal case on this issue is *Nabozny v. Barnhill* (1975), 31 Ill. App. 3d 212 . . . . In *Nabozny,* the plaintiff was the goalkeeper for a teenage soccer league and the defendant was a forward from an opposing team. The game's rules prevented players from making contact with the goalkeeper while he is in possession of the ball in the penalty area. During the game, the ball was passed to the plaintiff while he was in the penalty area. The plaintiff fell onto his knee. The defendant, who had been going for the ball, continued to run towards the plaintiff and kicked the plaintiff in the head, causing severe injuries. The trial court directed a verdict in favor of the defendant, holding that as a matter of law the defendant was free from negligence (owed no duty to the plaintiff) and that the plaintiff was contributorily negligent.

In reversing the trial court, the *Nabozny* court held that when athletes engage in organized competition, with a set of rules that guides the conduct and safety of the players, then "a player is charged with a legal duty to every other player on the field to refrain from conduct proscribed by a safety rule." The court then announced the following rule:

> It is our opinion that a player is liable for injury in a tort action if his conduct is such that it is either deliberate, wilful, or with a reckless disregard for the safety of the other player so as to cause injury to that player, the same being a question of fact to be decided by a jury.

[*816] Illinois courts have construed *Nabozny* to hold that a plaintiff-participant injured during a contact sport may recover from another player only if the other's conduct was wilful or wanton. Plaintiff contends, however, that decisions subsequent to *Nabozny* have misconstrued the court's holding in that case. According to plaintiff,

Nabozny is to be applied only to conduct during a game because *Nabozny* "involved an injury that occurred during a game and therefore, it implicitly recognizes a distinction with pre-game injuries."

Illinois has enacted a modified comparative fault statute. (*735 ILCS 5/2-1116* (West 1992).) The enactment of this statute, however, has no effect on express assumption of risk, where a plaintiff expressly assumes the dangers and risks created by the activity or a [*817] defendant's negligence, or on primary implied assumption of risk, where a plaintiff knowingly and voluntarily assumes the risks inherent in a particular situation or a defendant's negligence.

In the case at bar, we believe that plaintiff was no less a participant in a team sport merely because he was engaged in "warm-up" activities at the time of his injury. However, assuming *arguendo* that we were to view plaintiff's action using an ordinary negligence standard, we must find that plaintiff knowingly and voluntarily assumed the risks inherent in playing the game of hockey. Plaintiff's own testimony bears out this fact. Plaintiff was an experienced hockey player, playing from the time he was eight years old. He had played in organized adult leagues for approximately 10 years prior to his accident. Plaintiff testified that while it was "customary" for players to wait for a goalie to be present prior to taking practice shots, in his experience he had seen players take shots at open nets. There was no written rule against taking shots at open nets. Plaintiff was also aware, at the time he stepped onto the ice, that there was a risk of being hit with a puck during "warm-ups." Indeed, according to plaintiff, that risk "always" existed. Nonetheless, plaintiff chose not to wear a protective face mask, since it was not required, even though in his estimation 65–70% of his teammates were wearing protective masks during "warm-up" and despite the inherent risk of being hit with a puck, irrespective of the goalie's presence at the net. Based on plaintiff's testimony, we believe that plaintiff voluntarily consented, understood, and accepted the dangers inherent in the sport or due to a co-participant's negligence.

As we have stated, we believe that the distinction plaintiff raises, between the "warm-up" and the actual commencement of the game, to be illusory. Hockey is a contact sport. It is not made less so merely because the participants are "warming up" prior to the commencement of the game. Proof of ordinary negligence will not sustain an action against defendant in this case, merely because plaintiff alleges a violation of a rule. Moreover, the evidence suggests that defendant here did not violate the customs and rules of the league. In addition to plaintiff's testimony, plaintiff's witness Czarnik and teammate Steve Marcordes testified that players may be hit by pucks during "warm-up" and during the game . . . Marcordes, unlike Czarnik, was familiar with the customs and usages of the Northbrook [*818] league, so much so that plaintiff testified that he considered Marcordes a "player-coach." Marcordes also testified that it was common for players to take shots at an open net during warm-up.

We find no reason to abandon the well-established precedent of this court, and that of a majority of jurisdictions, that a participant in a contact sport may recover for injury only where the other's conduct is wilful or wanton or in reckless disregard to safety. There are a number of reasons justifying the application of this standard to sports-related injury cases. First, the risk of injury accompanies many informal contact sports. Thus, wilful and wanton or reckless conduct allows the court to gauge what is and is not permissible conduct under the circumstances. Second, as the court recognized in *Nabozny,* courts must strike a balance between "the free and vigorous participation in sports" and the protection of the individual from reckless or intentional conduct. Third, we believe that the practical effect of applying an ordinary negligence standard would be to open a legal pandora's box, allowing virtually every participant in a contact sport, injured by another during a "warm-up" or practice, to bring an action based on the risks inherent in virtually every contact sport. This is exactly the type of result the courts have sought to avoid. . . . [*820] It is undisputed that plaintiff and defendant were teammates in an organized hockey league. There were rules and usages. Reviewing the evidence in a light most favorable to plaintiff, there appears to be no genuine issue of material fact that practice shots were often taken at an open net and such was the custom of the team.

For the foregoing reasons, we affirm both orders of the circuit court granting summary judgment in defendant's favor.

Affirmed.

QUESTIONS

1. How did the court in *Savino* determine whether granting summary judgment is proper?
2. What cases did the court use as precedent in this decision?
3. What legal theories are identified? How are these theories explained?
4. How would you "brief" this case?
5. Provide an example of a future case where this case might serve as a precedent.
6. How was precedent used to determine the outcome of this case?

Regulating Interscholastic (High School) and Youth Athletics

2

INTRODUCTION: THE RISE OF THE REGULATION OF INTERSCHOLASTIC AND YOUTH ATHLETICS AT THE STATE, NATIONAL, AND INTERNATIONAL LEVELS

A. Historical Overview

A Detroit high school football team existed in 1888, and by 1892, a Detroit high school baseball team traveled to Ann Arbor for an interscholastic game. In late 1895 and early 1896, educators in Wisconsin met to discuss interscholastic athletics and the formation of an association for governance purposes. After the formal organization of the Wisconsin Interscholastic Athletic Association, state athletic associations proliferated throughout the United States, and the National Federation of State High School Associations was formed in 1923.

Participation in interscholastic athletics has grown steadily. For the past two decades, the number of high school students participating in interscholastic athletics has increased, although current economic challenges are causing schools to consider either slowing growth or actually cutting opportunities for participation in interscholastic athletics. Approximately 7.5 million students are currently involved in interscholastic athletics.

Youth athletics has also proliferated at all levels. A broad array of associations govern youth athletics in the United States, ranging from local park and recreational organizations and YMCAs to national associations such as Little League baseball (*http://www.littleleague.org/Little_League_Online.htm*), American Youth Soccer Association (AYSO; *http://www.ayso.org/aboutayso/What_is_AYSO_.htm#.Vc1auflVikp*), and Pop Warner football (*http://www.popwarner.com/About_Us/orgchart.htm*). The Amateur Athletic Union (AAU) has also become increasingly involved in youth athletics. See *http://image.aausports.org/codebook/article_I.pdf* (Article I of the Constitution of the AAU). The National Football League (NFL) formed USA Football in an effort to improve coaching in youth football at the interscholastic and nonscholastic levels (see *http://usafooball.com/coach#* for a discussion of the role of the NFL with youth coaches). Youth athletics in other countries are often overseen by governmental entities (see, e.g., *http://www.sport.gov.tt/* for the national governing body in Trinidad). With concerns rising regarding head and related injuries, as well as other health and safety issues at all levels, governmental bodies are becoming more involved in regulating and exercising increasing oversight in this area.

Increases in participation and the competitiveness in our culture have spawned significant regulation. State and youth associations have also developed increasingly sophisticated and elaborate regulations to govern youth athletics. State and federal legislation will continue to affect interscholastic and youth athletics, with courts playing a role in overseeing the operation of interscholastic and youth athletics.

B. Interscholastic and Youth Athletics Regulatory Structure, Governance, and Administrative Processes

Interscholastic athletics is largely regulated under the rules formulated by public and private high schools that are members of state athletic associations. Youth athletics, in turn, is generally governed by entities that are wholly private (nonpublic) in nature. The presence of public schools in state athletic associations often raises issues of whether the association is public, and hence subject to more judicial scrutiny, or private in nature. Rules governing the playing of the game and participation by boys and girls in interscholastic athletics are adopted by athletic associations at the statewide level. Occasionally, conferences or other groups of schools on a regional basis may adopt rules as well. At the interscholastic level, school boards and local school officials may also adopt rules that will apply to participation in interscholastic athletics. The courts may intervene to deal with disputes, particularly if the governing or state athletic association is deemed to be public. Some state legislatures have been willing to intervene and enact laws pertaining to some aspects that apply to both interscholastic and youth athletics, particularly health and safety issues.

Actions by youth-governing bodies, state athletic associations, conferences and regional bodies, school districts, school officials, and coaches may be challenged in court. In this chapter, we examine cases that will provide the reader with a sense of how courts (and occasionally legislative bodies) act with regard to interscholastic and youth athletics. If the governing body is determined to be acting in a public capacity, it will be held to higher judicial accountability. Courts, on the other hand, are very deferential to actions taken by private associations, such as nearly all nonscholastic youth athletic associations (e.g., Pop Warner football or Little League baseball), largely permitting them to govern themselves. State-level athletic associations, local school districts, and individual high schools are subject to more oversight, but the courts generally defer to such entities. Courts, nevertheless, have long been reluctant to get involved in academic decisions made by those who are directly involved in overseeing or governing schools from the kindergarten through 12th grade levels. Courts, as you will note, generally consider participation in athletics to be a privilege and not a right and provide those who oversee interscholastic and youth athletics with broad authority or deference. Courts often see schools and those who directly govern the activities of schoolchildren as extensions of the home and parents and are reluctant to substitute a court's wisdom for that of school officials and parents, even though they are much more willing to get involved in matters involving public institutions.

JUDICIAL REGULATION OF INTERSCHOLASTIC AND YOUTH ATHLETICS

KEY TERMS
- Dictum
- Entwinement
- National Collegiate Athletic Association (NCAA)
- State action

The majority of interscholastic athletics programs operate within public schools, raising the issue of "state action." The rights enumerated in the U.S. Constitution protect against state or governmental action, but not against private action. A government official must recognize a person's federal constitutional rights, but nongovernmental officials or persons acting privately are not required to do so. For example, a court may recognize a right to speak in a public place, but it will not generally extend that right to speak in private contexts. In these materials, we examine whether a state high school athletic association is a state actor for federal constitutional law purposes. Athletic associations are generally considered to be private associations made up of public and private schools in the interscholastic athletics context. Nevertheless, their actions are often so closely related to state or government action that courts must decide whether an athletic association is a state actor for constitutional purposes. If the athletic association is a state or government actor, then it has to act in a manner that respects the constitutional rights of sports participants.

We begin by exploring what is often the threshold question of whether an association or individual is acting on behalf of the state. We also examine several rules and regulations established by a state athletic associations, local school districts, or high schools that deal with student-athletes' eligibility to participate in interscholastic sports, including cases challenging mandatory drug testing and asserting claims alleging infringement of free speech, association, and religious rights.

A. State Action

In the early nineteenth century, prior to the Civil War, the Bill of Rights (the first ten amendments to the U.S. Constitution) were held to apply only as against federal action. There were state constitutional provisions that applied at the state level, but the Bill of Rights — including the First Amendment rights of freedom of speech and religion — applied only against the national or federal government. They were not applicable at the state or private level. After the Civil War, which dealt in part with states' rights, the Civil Rights Amendments (Amendments 13 to 15 to the U.S. Constitution) were adopted and ratified. The Fourteenth Amendment, which secured equal protection of law against state action (government action at any level) subsequently came to be read, in a series of cases, to provide that rights included in the first ten amendments (the Bill of Rights) were applicable against state officials or those acting in a governmental capacity at the state or local level. This clause-by-clause or right-by-right determination is referred to as *incorporation,* meaning the incorporation of each of the rights included in the Bill of Rights as against government action at any level. The reason why this is referred to as "state action" is that the Fourteenth Amendment used the language "state action" when it secured the right of equal protection of law to all citizens.

A prerequisite to bringing a claim alleging infringement of a federal constitutional right is that the deprivation of the right occurred as the result of state action. The Fourteenth Amendment to the U.S. Constitution, under which the Bill of Rights have been made applicable to the states, limits enforcement of those rights to cases in which the right has been deprived or limited by a state actor (someone acting on behalf of the state or in some public capacity). If an educational institution or state interscholastic sports association is deemed to be a state actor, it is held to a higher level of judicial accountability than it would be if it were not deemed to be a state actor. State actors are held accountable under the U.S. and state constitutions — private associations generally are not. The *Brentwood I* and *II* cases, discussed *infra,* effectively illustrate this dynamic between state action (the actions of associations that are held to be state actors) and substantive constitutional claims.

The question of whether a state athletic association is a state actor was a troublesome issue for many years, with lower courts reaching differing conclusions on this point. In 2001, however, in a 5-4 decision in *NCAA v. Tarkanian*, 488 U.S. 179 (1988), the United States Supreme Court held that the National Collegiate Athletic Association (NCAA) is not a state actor. It was not clear, however, whether state interscholastic associations would be considered state actors for purposes of the enforcement of constitutionally protected rights, because the decision in the *Tarkanian* case dealt with the NCAA. The issue of whether a state interscholastic athletic association is a state actor was raised before the Supreme Court in *Brentwood v. Tennessee Secondary School Athletic Assn.*, 531 U.S. 288 (2001) (*Brentwood I*).

The *Brentwood I* decision raises the question of whether the Tennessee Secondary School Athletic Association (TSSAA) is a state actor. The Court had to resolve this issue before it could examine the claim that the TSSAA had deprived individuals of their constitutional rights of due process and freedom of speech. As you read *Brentwood I,* do not worry about the underlying substantive constitutional issue regarding recruitment and free speech, because those issues cannot be addressed until the court determines whether the high school athletics association is a state actor subject to constitutional requirements. State action cases are often quite fact specific, with courts closely examining the facts to determine whether the association is effectively acting as a state or governmental actor. As you read *Brentwood I,* think of the outcome-determinative facts (the facts that influenced the decision). The Court is closely divided, 5-4, in the *Brentwood* and the *Tarkanian* cases. As you read the *Brentwood I* case, think of facts that might cause the Court to decide differently and hold that a state association or other entity is not a state actor subject to actions by individuals or groups seeking enforcement of their constitutional rights.

You will note, as you read the *Brentwood I* case, that five of the nine (a mere majority) justices on the United States Supreme Court agreed that the TSSAA is a state actor. To reach this decision, the five justices in the majority had to distinguish the TSSAA from the NCAA, which the Supreme Court had held not to be a state or government actor required to provide protection for the constitutional rights of student-athletes and others affected by the NCAA's decisions. As you read the majority and the dissenting opinions, think about whether the court is right. With a change in the makeup of the Court, it is possible that a majority of the Court would agree with the dissenting opinion, which would result in a future decision holding that no state athletic associations are state actors subject to the constraints of the Constitution. Reflect as well on the implications of an association being held to be a state actor in subsequent cases.

Brentwood Academy v. Tennessee Secondary School Athletic Association
531 U.S. 288 (2001)

Justice SOUTER delivered the opinion of the Court.

[Editors' note: We have intentionally retained the discussion of the *Tarkanian* decision in this case, which deals with intercollegiate athletics, believing that "state action" should be considered jointly with high school and intercollegiate sports issues. It is important to remember that interscholastic athletic associations have often been held to be state actors, and therefore subject to constitutional restrictions, while the NCAA has not been determined to be a state actor. As you read, think about why the NCAA is not a state actor, but state athletic associations often are.]

The issue is whether a statewide association incorporated to regulate interscholastic athletic competition among public and private secondary schools may be regarded as engaging in state action when it enforces a rule against a member school. The association in question here includes most public schools located within the State, acts through their representatives, draws its officers from them, is largely funded by their dues and income received in their stead, and has historically been seen to regulate in lieu of the State Board of Education's exercise of its own authority. We hold that the association's regulatory activity may and should be treated as state action owing to the pervasive entwinement of state school officials in the structure of the association, there being no offsetting reason to see the association's acts in any other way.

I

. . . [I]n *Tarkanian* . . . we found no state action on the part of the NCAA. We could see, on the one hand, that the university had some part in setting the NCAA's rules, and the

Supreme Court of Nevada had gone so far as to hold that the NCAA had been delegated the university's traditionally exclusive public authority over personnel. But on the other side, the NCAA's policies were shaped not by the University of Nevada alone, but by several hundred member institutions, most of them having no connection with Nevada, and exhibiting no color of Nevada law. Since it was difficult to see the NCAA, not as a collective membership, but as surrogate for the one State, we held the organization's connection with Nevada too insubstantial to ground a state action claim.

But dictum in *Tarkanian* pointed to a contrary result on facts like ours, with an organization whose member public schools are all within a single State. "The situation would, of course, be different if the [Association's] membership consisted entirely of institutions located within the same State, many of them public institutions created by the same sovereign."

B

Just as we foresaw in *Tarkanian*, the "necessarily fact-bound inquiry," leads to the conclusion of state action here. The nominally private character of the Association is overborne by the pervasive entwinement of public institutions and public officials in its composition and workings, and there is no substantial reason to claim unfairness in applying constitutional standards to it. . . .

[T]o the extent of 84% of its membership, the Association is an organization of public schools represented by their officials acting in their official capacity to provide an integral element of secondary public schooling. There would be no recognizable Association, legal or tangible, without the public school officials, who do not merely control but overwhelmingly perform all but the purely ministerial acts by which the Association exists and functions in practical terms. . . .

To complement the entwinement of public school officials with the Association from the bottom up, the State of Tennessee has provided for entwinement from top down. State Board members are assigned *ex officio* to serve as members of the board of control and legislative council, and the Association's ministerial employees are treated as state employees to the extent of being eligible for membership in the state retirement system. . . .

The entwinement down from the State Board is therefore unmistakable, just as the entwinement up from the member public schools is overwhelming. Entwinement will support a conclusion that an ostensibly private organization ought to be charged with a public character and judged by constitutional standards; entwinement to the degree shown here requires it.

The judgment of the Court of Appeals for the Sixth Circuit is reversed, and the case is remanded for further proceedings consistent with this opinion.

It is so ordered.

Justice THOMAS, with whom The Chief Justice, Justice SCALIA, and Justice KENNEDY join, dissenting.

We have never found state action based upon mere "entwinement." The majority's holding — that the Tennessee Secondary School Athletic Association's (TSSAA) enforcement of its recruiting rule is state action — not only extends state-action doctrine beyond its permissible limits but also encroaches upon the realm of individual freedom that the doctrine was meant to protect. I respectfully dissent.

Commonsense dictates that the TSSAA's actions cannot fairly be attributed to the State, and thus cannot constitute state action. The TSSAA was formed in 1925 as a private corporation to organize interscholastic athletics and to sponsor tournaments among its member schools.

The State of Tennessee did not create the TSSAA. The State does not fund the TSSAA and does not pay its employees. In fact, only 4% of the TSSAA's revenue comes from the dues paid by member schools; the bulk of its operating budget is derived from gate receipts at tournaments it sponsors. The State does not permit the TSSAA to use state-owned facilities for a discounted fee, and it does not exempt the TSSAA from state taxation. No Tennessee law authorizes the State to coordinate interscholastic athletics or empowers another entity to organize interscholastic-athletics on behalf of the State. The only state pronouncement acknowledging the TSSAA's existence is a rule providing that the State Board of Education permits public schools to maintain membership in the TSSAA if they so choose.

[T]he State of Tennessee has never had any involvement in the particular action taken by the TSSAA in this case: the enforcement of the TSSAA's recruiting rule prohibiting members from using "undue influence" on students or their parents or guardians "to secure or to retain a student for athletic purposes."

Because I do not believe that the TSSAA's action of enforcing its recruiting rule is fairly attributable to the State of Tennessee, I would affirm [the decision by the lower court holding that the TSSAA is not a state actor].

QUESTIONS

Justice Souter and the majority hold that the TSSAA is a state actor because "[t]he nominally private character of the Association is overborne by the pervasive entwinement of public institutions and public officials in its composition." Do you agree with Justice Souter and the majority, or with Justice Thomas? Why? Can you develop other persuasive arguments not made here? What constitutes sufficient "entwinement" for an association to be held to be a state actor under Justice Souter's test? Does that test clearly articulate a basis on which interscholastic athletic associations can know whether or not they are state actors? Why did the TSSAA aggressively resist being held to be a state actor?

NOTES

Analysis and vulnerability of *Brentwood*. The 5-4 decision in *Brentwood* may be overruled or limited in a subsequent case for three reasons: (1) The case is fact specific, and a subsequent case may have facts that are less supportive of a holding that the state association is a state actor; (2) the entwinement (and other tests for that matter) offered by the Supreme Court are confusing and do not make it easy to determine whether an association is a state actor; and (3) there has been a shift in the membership of the Court, with Justice Souter and others leaving and being replaced by new justices (these new justices may align with the dissenters in *Brentwood* and vote to overrule or limit the holding in the case).

The courts in Tennessee continue to rely on the general reasoning in the *Brentwood* case. In *City Press Communs., LLC v. Tenn. Secondary Sch. Ath. Ass'n*, 447 S.W.3d 230, 2014 Tenn. App. LEXIS 256, 2014 WL 1778191 (Tenn. Ct. App. 2014), the court extended the reasoning in the *Brentwood* case in holding that the TSSAA acted as a government agency and therefore was required to produce records under the Tennessee Public Records Act.

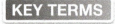 **KEY TERMS**
- Due process
- Speech rights (freedom of speech)

Having held in *Brentwood I* that the TSSAA is a state actor, in *Tennessee Secondary School Athletic Assn. v. Brentwood Academy*, 127 S. Ct. 2489 (2007) (*Brentwood II*), the Court considered the merits of the plaintiff high school's federal constitutional law challenges to the TSSAA's anti-recruiting rule on free speech and due process grounds. Brentwood argued that it had a free speech right to send a letter seeking to recruit a potential student to attend and play for Brentwood. The First Amendment of the U.S. Constitution states that "Congress [which has been broadly interpreted to include government generally] shall make no law . . . abridging the freedom of speech. . . ." This provision has been read broadly to protect the freedom of expression in its many forms. Written communications such as letters are protected as a form of speech. In the case, however, the Court declines to find that Brentwood's freedom of speech was abridged.

The Court also examines whether Brentwood was denied due process. The due process clause of the Fourteenth Amendment to the U.S. Constitution provides that no state shall "deprive any person of life, liberty, or property without due process of law." Due process has been interpreted as requiring that a state or government actor afford certain procedures ("due process") before it deprives a person of certain interests: life, liberty, or property. If a person's liberty or property interest is affected by a decision, that party must be afforded fair process, which is generally defined as notice of the fact that his or her interest may be affected or deprived by a decision and a fair hearing prior to that deprivation. In the interscholastic sports context, students and their parents have unsuccessfully asserted that they have a protectable interest or right to participate in interscholastic athletics, which would trigger the due process requirement. However, they have been able, on occasion, to assert that due process is triggered because they have a property interest in the possibility of earning a scholarship.

Tennessee Secondary School Athletic Association v. Brentwood Academy (Brentwood II)
127 S. Ct. 2489 (2007)

Justice STEVENS delivered the opinion of the Court with respect to Parts I, II-B, III, and IV, concluding:

I

[Editors' note: With one judge dissenting, the Court of Appeals held that the TSSAA's anti-recruiting rule is a content-based regulation of speech that is not narrowly tailored to serve its permissible purposes. It also concluded that the TSSAA Board improperly considered *ex parte* evidence during its deliberations, thereby violating Brentwood's due process rights.]

The First Amendment protects Brentwood's right to publish truthful information about the school and its athletic programs. It likewise protects the school's right to try to persuade prospective students and their parents that its excellence in sports is a reason for enrolling. But Brentwood's speech rights are not absolute. . . .

II [Speech]

Brentwood made a voluntary decision to join TSSAA and to abide by its anti-recruiting rule. Just as the government's interest in running an effective workplace can in some circumstances outweigh employee speech rights, so too can an athletic league's interest in enforcing its rules sometimes warrant curtailing the speech of its voluntary participants. . . .

We need no empirical data to credit TSSAA's common-sense conclusion that hard-sell tactics [in a letter] directed at middle school students could lead to exploitation, distort competition between high school teams, and foster an environment in which athletics are prized more highly than academics. . . . [T]he First Amendment does not excuse Brentwood from abiding by the same anti-recruiting rule that governs the conduct of its sister schools. To hold otherwise would undermine the principle, succinctly articulated by the dissenting judge at the Court of Appeals, that "[h]igh school football is a game. Games have rules."

III [Due Process]

The decision to sanction Brentwood for engaging in prohibited recruiting was preceded by an investigation, several meetings, exchanges of correspondence, an adverse written determination from TSSAA's executive director, [and] a hearing before the director and an advisory panel composed of three members of TSSAA's Board of

Directors. During the investigation, Brentwood was notified of all the charges against it. At each of the two hearings, Brentwood was represented by counsel and given the opportunity to adduce evidence. No evidence offered by Brentwood was excluded.

Even accepting the questionable holding [of the Sixth Circuit] that TSSAA's closed-door deliberations were unconstitutional, we can safely conclude that any due process violation was harmless beyond a reasonable doubt. . . .

QUESTIONS

1. Is the fact that the students were generally younger than 18 critical to the decision (i.e., if the letter came from a college coach, might it be protected speech)? Should impressionable young people be shielded from recruiting efforts? Do parents have a role in insulating their children from recruiting efforts? Should students have access to the information contained in such a letter to help them make important decisions in their lives?
2. The court held that Brentwood (the school) had a right or interest in the writing and sending of its letter (speech) and was entitled to due process. It then held that Brentwood had been afforded due process by the TSSAA. Why? This case is a good example of how little process (i.e., notice and a fair hearing) must be offered to satisfy due process in such cases.

B. Eligibility Issues

KEY TERMS
- Arbitrary and capricious
- Common law
- Equal protection
- State constitution
- Transfer rules

The remainder of this chapter deals with substantive issues that have been raised by student-athletes and participants in youth sports and their parents challenging the nature of associational and institutional governance of interscholastic and youth athletics. The principal cases consider eligibility issues arising out of the application and enforcement of transfer, outside competition, good conduct, maximum age, personal appearance and grooming, and home school rules. Other cases address mandatory random drug testing and alleged infringement of student-athletes' federal constitutional rights to freedom of expression and religion. There is also a discussion of efforts to regulate youth athletics, particularly with regard to health and safety issues. Think about the different types of rules and actions typically challenged by young athletes and their parents. Also, consider what the appropriate role of legislative and government administrative bodies should be in protecting young people participating in athletics. As you read these materials, think about the following question:

Are courts and legislative and administrative bodies too deferential to state athletic associations, individual educational institutions, and youth organizations involved in governing younger athletes?

The Sport and Development Organization refers to evidence that supports the argument that an opportunity to participate in interscholastic and youth athletics may merit legal protection in some form. They note:

> Sport and physical education is fundamental to the early development of children and youth and the skills learned during play, physical education and sport contribute to the holistic development of young people. Through participation in sport and physical education, young people learn about the importance of key values such as:
>
> * honesty,
> * teamwork,
> * fair play,
> * respect for themselves and others, and
> * adherence to rules.
>
> It also provides a forum for young people to learn how to deal with competition and how to cope with both winning and losing. These learning aspects highlight the impact of physical education and sport on a child's social and moral development in addition to physical skills and abilities. *http://www.sportanddev.org/en/learnmore/sport_education_and_child_youth_development2/healthy_development_of_children_and_young_people_through_sport/*

Studies have also found that "female and male students who participate in high school team sports through the 12th grade have a school-based identity that correlates to positive academic performance (e.g., an increased 12th-grade GPA and an increased probability of being enrolled in college full time at age 21). This highly positive finding is consistent with prior research evidencing that sports participation, relative to participation in other extracurricular activities such as student government and academic clubs, is "linked to lower likelihood of school dropout and higher rates of college attendance." Matthew J. Mitten and Timothy Davis, *Athlete Eligibility Requirements and Legal Protection of Sports Participation Opportunities*, 8 Va. Sports and Entertainment L.J. 71, 113 (2009).

Consider whether athletic participation is of sufficient importance that it should be protected as a constitutional matter as you read the following materials, which deal with rules established by interscholastic associations and youth organizations. Associations, organizations, and schools promulgating rules governing youth athletics must follow those rules. Occasionally, a court will intervene when a governing body does not follow its own rules. A recent Mississippi case demonstrates the importance of following rules established by a school or school district. In *Miss. High Sch. Activities Ass'n v. R.T.*, 163 So. 3d 274, 2015 Miss. LEXIS 229 (Miss. 2015), the Mississippi Supreme Court held that once a school decides to create a sports program and establish eligibility rules, it must follow those rules and may be held accountable when it does not do so. The court added that young athletes are among the intended beneficiaries of high school athletic programs and the rules that govern them. Courts will largely defer to sports governing bodies in administering or interpreting their rules, but they may not refuse to follow their own rules.

1. Transfer Rules

High school athletes often challenge transfer rules and regulations adopted by state athletic associations. Transfer rules limit the eligibility of student-athletes to participate immediately in interscholastic competition after they move from one school to another. A common type of transfer rule renders a student-athlete who transfers from one high school to another within the same school district without a corresponding change in his or her parents' residence ineligible to engage in interscholastic competition for a period of time — often as long as an entire school year.

The *Carlberg* case illustrates how courts have resolved a variety of federal and state law legal challenges to transfer rules. While reading this case, consider the purposes for which transfer rules are adopted. Reasons typically cited in support of transfer rules include deterring the recruitment of student-athletes (i.e., protecting student-athletes from the pressure and harassment of zealous coaches and fans that might ensue from unregulated recruiting) and affording academics a higher priority than athletics.

In cases involving transfer and other eligibility rules, athletes often argue that the regulation is being applied in an arbitrary and capricious manner, thereby denying them due process of law or violating the law of private associations. In most cases, courts are quite deferential to athletic associations and organizations, in part because they (judges) do not generally believe that it is wise for them to substitute their judgment for that of educators and others who devote their lives to ensuring that interscholastic and youth athletic programs are wisely administered.

In many cases, young athletes claim that they are being denied equal protection. Equal protection claims are based on the Fourteenth Amendment to the U.S. Constitution, which provides that no citizen shall be denied equal protection of the law. As the court notes in *Carlberg*, parties are likely to succeed if they can argue that they have not been treated equally in a case involving a right or if they are members of a class or group that has historically been treated unequally. For example, if the distinction is based on a racial classification (what the courts refer to as a "suspect class"), courts will closely or strictly scrutinize the rule and are likely to find it to be unconstitutional unless it is supported by a compelling interest or reason and is being applied in the least restrictive manner possible. Girls (gender) are part of another class that receives heightened but not strict scrutiny (what is sometimes referred to as "intermediate scrutiny"). As to gender-based classifications, the courts seek to determine whether there is a substantial purpose of the regulation (a less stringent requirement than the compelling interest standard used in race). Thus, gender-based regulations are examined (scrutinized) closely, but are more likely to be found to be acceptable than race-based classifications. Courts recognize that associations and regulatory bodies must draw distinctions in making and enforcing general rules that do not raise issues of racial or gender-based discrimination, so all other distinctions need only be supported by a rational reason or basis. Some even argue that obese participants should be protected. See *The Obese and the Elite: Using Law to Reclaim School Sports,* 2015 Okla. L. Rev. 383.

Indiana High School Athletic Association v. Carlberg
694 N.E.2d 222 (Ind. 1997)

SULLIVAN, Justice.

After attending Brebeuf Preparatory School as a freshman (where he swam on the varsity swim team), Jason Carlberg, who lives with his parents near Indianapolis, transferred to Carmel High School for academic reasons. The Indiana High School Athletic Association ("IHSAA") is a voluntary association of public and private high schools that adopts and enforces rules regarding eligibility and similar matters related to interscholastic athletic competition. Applying Rule 19 (the "Transfer Rule"), the IHSAA determined that Carlberg transferred for nonathletic reasons without a change of permanent residence by his parents or guardians. [Editors' note: Under the terms of the rule, he was not permitted to participate on a varsity athletic team.]

After exhausting available administrative remedies, including a hearing before the IHSAA Executive Committee, which denied his appeal, Carlberg alleged, *inter alia*, that application of the Transfer Rule violated his constitutional rights under the due process and equal protection clauses of the Fourteenth Amendment of the U.S. Constitution, and was arbitrary and capricious in violation of Indiana common law. . . .

In its appeal to the Indiana Supreme Court, the IHSAA argued that the Transfer Rule is subject to the rule of limited judicial interference in the affairs of private voluntary membership associations. . . .

[Editors' note: After holding that the IHSAA is a state actor, the court dealt with Carlberg's asserted due process right and found that Carlberg had been given a sufficient hearing. Regarding his equal protection claim, the court held that "[a]bsent a burden upon the exercise of a constitutionally protected right (none is at stake here) or creation of a suspect class (none is alleged here), the general standard of review of state action challenged under the equal protection clause is the rational basis test." It found that the Transfer Rule's objectives of preserving the integrity of interscholastic athletics, preventing recruiting, and school transfers for athletic reasons are legitimate and concluded that the Transfer Rule is rationally related to achieving these goals.]

We find resolution of challenges to IHSAA rules and enforcement actions well within the ambit of Indiana common law. Our state constitution specifically recognizes that "knowledge and learning" are "essential to the preservation of a free government" and so mandates a statewide system of free public education. We believe athletics are an integral part of this constitutionally-mandated process of education. . . .

The substantial educational benefits derived from interscholastic athletics, together with the rationale that underlies the determination that IHSAA decisions constitute "state action," help explain why Indiana courts have been so willing to adjudicate disputes between the IHSAA and parties aggrieved by the association's decisions.

The rule in Indiana is that courts exercise limited interference with the internal affairs and rules of a voluntary membership association: A voluntary association may, without direction or interference by the courts, for its government, adopt a constitution, by-laws, rules and regulations which will control as to all questions of discipline, or internal policy and management, and its right to interpret and administer the same is as sacred as the right to make them. . . .

The provisions of the IHSAA Transfer Rule at issue in this case apply to a student who changes schools without a corresponding change of residence by the student's parents. Such a student may participate as a member of a junior varsity or freshman team at his or her new school unless the transfer was either primarily for athletic reasons or as a result of undue influence. However, such a student may not participate in interscholastic athletics as a member of a *varsity* athletic team during the first 365 days after enrollment unless (i) the student meets one of the special criteria set forth in Rule 19-6.1 or (ii) is declared eligible under the IHSAA "Hardship Rule."

Carlberg agrees that he changed schools without a corresponding change of residence by his parents and that none of the special criteria of Rule 19-6.1 nor the Hardship Rule apply. For its part, the IHSAA acknowledges that the transfer was neither for primarily athletic reasons nor as a result of undue influence. Carlberg argues that the IHSAA acted arbitrarily and capriciously when it enforced the Transfer Rule against him where it was undisputed that his transfer was neither primarily for athletic reasons nor as a result of undue influence.

"Arbitrary and capricious" is a narrow standard of review and the reviewing court may not substitute its judgment for the judgment of the IHSAA. The rule or decision will be found to be arbitrary and capricious "only where it is willful and unreasonable, without consideration and in disregard of the facts or circumstances in the case, or without some basis which would lead a reasonable and honest person to the same conclusion."

We do not find the IHSAA decision that Carlberg was ineligible for varsity athletics for 365 days following his transfer to be "willful and unreasonable, without consideration and in disregard of the facts or circumstances in the case, or without some basis which would lead a reasonable and honest person to the same conclusion." First, there is no contention that the IHSAA failed to publicize its interpretation of the rule or failed to apply consistently its interpretation of the rule.

Second, by establishing objective standards for eligibility "governing residence and transfer," including the provision allowing for only limited eligibility upon a transfer not accompanied by a parental change of residence, Rule 19(c) acts as a deterrent to athletically motivated transfers.

Third, the operation of the rule does not sweep too broadly in its proscription. While it is true that some students who change schools neither primarily for athletic reasons nor as a result of undue influence are denied varsity eligibility for one year, conducting a factual inquiry into the motivation for every transfer would impose a considerable burden on both the IHSAA and its member schools. . . .

[Editors' note: Having found that the IHSAA's application of the transfer rule to Carlberg was neither arbitrary nor capricious, the court next considered whether the IHSAA possessed the authority to enforce the transfer rule. The court concluded:

> The IHSAA does not derive its authority directly from the legislature but instead from a delegation of authority from member schools. As such, the analysis with respect to the three factors that concern authorizing legislation is conducted best by examining the challenged rule's consistency with the IHSAA's purpose in general and the purpose of the Transfer Rule in particular.

The IHSAA exists "to encourage, regulate, and give direction to wholesome amateur interschool athletic competition between schools who are members." To further this purpose, the IHSAA Articles and By-Laws mandate that it "determine qualifications of individual contestants . . . and provide written communications to establish standards for eligibility." We find authority to take such action, and to delegate that authority to the IHSAA, to be within the powers granted Indiana public school corporations by the legislature. We further find Rule 19-6.2 to fall within the scope of, to be consistent and harmonious with, and not to expand or vary this authority.]

DICKSON, Justice, concurring and dissenting.

I am convinced that the trial court was correct in finding the IHSAA's attempts to apply its Transfer Rule . . . to be arbitrary and capricious and thus improper. . . .

[T]he arbitrariness of the IHSAA's application of its rule becomes apparent in the present case: A rule purporting to limit athletically-motivated transfers and promote education as the primary value of school in fact punishes a student whom the IHSAA found did *not* transfer for an athletic reason and where the uncontradicted evidence points only to academic reasons for the transfer. Common sense instructs that application of the Transfer Rule to limit Jason's opportunities for participation would be blatantly arbitrary and capricious. The trial court was correct in making such a finding. . . .

NOTES

1. Arbitrary and capricious. Courts are disinclined to overrule discretionary decisions made by interscholastic sports associations and youth organizations. They do so only when they find that the association has acted in an arbitrary and capricious manner. The majority opinion in *Carlberg* is illustrative of the deference given — the reluctance to find that the association acted in an arbitrary and capricious manner. The dissenting judge is less willing to defer and would have found the transfer rule, as applied in this case, to be arbitrary and capricious. Should courts be deferential in these cases? As you consider the following cases and materials, think of what kinds of decisions by an association might be considered to be arbitrary and capricious. Remember as a matter of practice that, given that courts are typically quite deferential to associations, the hearing before the association is critical — a student who wishes to transfer must persuade the association to waive their rule or apply it in a manner that permits the transfer, or must uncover material that would cause courts to be concerned with the reasons offered by the association for its prohibition.

2. State constitutional issues. State constitutional provisions may be interpreted as providing the student-athlete with more (but not less) protection than that offered under the federal constitution, in terms of equal protection and other protected rights (e.g., association, education, free exercise, free speech, and privacy). In *Indiana High*

School Athletic Assn., Inc. v. Avant, 650 N.E.2d 1164 (Ind. App. 1995), the court acknowledged that the Indiana state constitution provided a higher level of protection to the student-athlete than is afforded under the federal equal protection clause.

Problem 2-1

Issues related to student-athlete transfers between school districts and schools arise with some frequency. As a member of a committee asked to make recommendations regarding transfer rules what, if any, kinds of rules and guidelines would you recommend the association consider adopting?

2. Outside Competition Rules

Students have also challenged outside competition rules — rules that limit competition in a sport outside the interscholastic athletics context. For example, in *Letendre v. Missouri State High School Athletics Assn.*, 86 S.W.3d 63 (Mo. App. 2002), a 15-year-old swimmer, with a goal of swimming competitively and ultimately participating on her high school's swim team, sought to enjoin the Missouri State High School Activities Association (MSHSAA) from enforcing an outside competition rule that prohibited students from competing on both a school and a nonschool team in the same sport during the school team's season. The student claimed that the rule violated equal protection. She claimed that the rule was irrational (lacked a rational basis) because it was "internally inconsistent in that it did not affect those who wished to participate in non-athletic activities both in and outside of school; it did not affect those who participated in one sport in school and another sport outside of school; and it did not apply to athletes who participated in national or Olympic development competitions during a sport season." The court rejected her claim, noting that the association had a rational basis for a general rule that limited students from participating in the same sport at the same time on two different teams.

The court in *Letendre* concluded its opinion with a statement that explains why courts are often disinclined to substitute their judgment for that of an athletic association:

> While we might personally believe that a better rule could be drafted, one that would allow a student athlete who is getting good grades, such as Claire, to compete simultaneously on both her school and non-school swim teams, the law does not permit us to interject our personal beliefs in the name of the Constitution. Claire's constitutional challenges must fail because by-law 235 is rationally related to the MSHSAA's purpose of drafting rules that protect the welfare of the greatest number of high school athletes possible.

Courts have uniformly rejected legal challenges to "outside competition" rules, even if the rule applies only to certain sports and prohibits participation in the same sport outside the time period for interscholastic competition in that sport. To comply with the Amateur Sports Act of 1978's objective of furthering the development of Olympic sports (see Chapter 14, *infra*), however, "outside competition" rules generally provide waivers to enable high school students to try out and qualify for spots on U.S. Olympic teams.

Courts will seek to ensure that the athletic association is following its own rules — if it fails to follow its own rules, the court will generally intervene and require that the rules be followed.

QUESTION

Do you agree that high school athletic governing bodies should have broad authority to effectively prohibit students' participation in competitive club sports as a condition of participating in interscholastic athletics? Given the rising importance of competitive youth sports opportunities outside the interscholastic context, should courts and governing bodies be more willing to find ways to facilitate outside competition?

3. Good Conduct Rules

KEY TERMS
- Eighth Amendment (cruel and unusual punishment)
- Hearsay
- Liberty interest
- Procedural due process
- Property interest
- Substantive due process
- Temporary restraining order

Individual high schools and governing bodies generally have broad authority to discipline and impose sanctions (such as the loss of their athletic eligibility or limitations on their ability to participate) on young athletes who engage in conduct that is considered inappropriate. Good conduct rules vary, but they all prohibit a range of activities, which can include the consumption and use of drugs, tobacco, and alcohol; violations of the law; and conduct that violates community norms of appropriate behavior. Student-athletes who are punished for violating good conduct rules have asserted various legal challenges with limited success. Courts afford considerable, albeit not complete, deference to schools and governing bodies to use good conduct rules to regulate participant behavior. While courts have been very deferential as to rules regulating conduct at the school, questions have been raised regarding the nature and scope of their authority to promulgate rules governing off-campus behavior and the extent to which the association or school has legitimate interests in regulating such conduct. We have previously introduced procedural due process and related issues, but this case examines such issues in greater depth.

Brands v. Sheldon Community School
671 F. Supp. 627 (N.D. Iowa 1987)

[Editors' note: The student, a member of his school's wrestling team, amassed a nearly perfect record in four years of competition and is a defending state champion, attracting the attention of the media and college coaches. After hearing from students and others regarding allegations that the student had been involved in sexual intercourse with a 16-year-old student at a party in a home, the principal concluded that the student had been involved in actions detrimental to the best interests of the school district and had "committed a breach of discipline by engaging in conduct which interfered with the maintenance of school discipline and by engaging in behavior which was antagonistic to the rights of (name redacted) to attain her education." As a result of this determination, the principal declared the student to be ineligible to participate in the sectional, district, and state wrestling tournaments. The parents appealed to the superintendent, who granted the parents' request for a closed hearing before the school board. The board heard from the student and others and deliberated for several hours. At the close of those deliberations, the board made extensive findings of fact in upholding the disciplinary action taken in the case. The student sought a temporary restraining order and a preliminary injunction permitting him to participate in the state wrestling tournament. The trial court granted a temporary restraining order. The school district appealed.

The court first rejected plaintiff's Fourteenth Amendment equal protection claim because he had not "alleged that he was treated differently because of his race, ethnicity, gender, or any other suspect classification, and his interests in wrestling or receiving a college scholarship are not among the small set of rights fundamental enough to warrant separate protection under the equal protection clause." Likewise, the Eighth Amendment claim was flatly rejected because school discipline did not constitute cruel and unusual punishment, with the court recognizing that the Eighth Amendment is reserved to deal with severe forms of punishment.]

Procedural Due Process

The majority of the plaintiff's complaints . . . are most relevant to his right to procedural due process. To consider those complaints, however, the Court must first find that the plaintiff is being deprived of liberty or property by the defendant. If not, no procedural protections were "due" to the plaintiff under the Constitution.

The Supreme Court has consistently held that the existence of a protected liberty or property interest does not depend upon the seriousness of the loss the plaintiff would suffer as a result of the government's action.

A clear majority of courts addressing this question in the context of interscholastic or intercollegiate athletics has found that athletes have no legitimate entitlement to participate. One court has stated that "a student's interest in participating in a single year of inter-scholastic athletics amounts to a mere expectation rather than a constitutionally protected claim of entitlement."

[Another] court recognized a property interest where . . . the plaintiff's "continued status as a member of the . . . football team during his last year was very important to

[his] development educationally and economically in the future." . . . When scholarships are awarded at the discretion of a college coach, and such discretion has not yet been exercised, no property interest in the receipt of a scholarship can exist, and the plaintiff cannot invoke his expectation that he would earn a scholarship at the state tournament in order to claim a property interest in wrestling there.

If any property interest of the plaintiff is involved in this case, it is a property right created by the defendant's own Disciplinary Policy and Administrative Rules. When a government must follow mandatory laws or regulations which limit its discretion to make a decision in any way or for any reason, those laws or regulations can create a property right which is deprived if those regulations are not followed. However, the plaintiff was not deprived of this right because [the school followed its rules].

Even if this Court were to recognize a protected interest in participation, the Court is satisfied that the plaintiff received all process due to him. The plaintiff and his mother were notified of the charges against him and were told of opportunities for appeal. . . . The plaintiff was given an opportunity to explain his side of the story to the principal prior to the suspension. . . . He was given a five- to six-hour evidentiary hearing within ten days of the initial suspension, which was also early enough to permit the Board to reverse the administration's decision before the plaintiff would be precluded from participating in the state tournament. . . .

As long as a decision rests upon "some evidence," due process may have been satisfied. Hearsay which has a "rational probative force" can constitute substantial evidence, which is a higher standard than "some evidence."

In this case, there appears to be little or no evidence in the hearing record directly contradicting the Board's hearsay-based finding that the plaintiff "as well as three other male youths engaged in multiple acts of sexual intercourse with a sixteen-year-old female student of the Sheldon Community School District. . . ."

Substantive Due Process

The plaintiff can show that his right to substantive due process was denied if the Board's decision was arbitrary or capricious; or if it violated one of the substantive due process rights such as the right to privacy, which cannot be deprived no matter how much procedural protection is used.

The Court is persuaded that the Board's decision was not arbitrary or capricious. The Board's objectives were legitimate. . . .

The Board's findings indicate that it was not merely trying to impose its moral standard upon the plaintiff; the Board found that his acts injured another student and disrupted the school. These are legitimate school board concerns. Moreover, the school has not regulated the plaintiff as a student; by revoking his eligibility without suspending or expelling him, it has regulated him as a representative of the school, and has chosen a sanction which limits his ability to represent the school without limiting his basic rights as a student. For these reasons, the Court finds that whatever right the plaintiff has to sexual privacy . . . was not violated in this case, and the last possible ground for finding a likelihood that his substantive due process rights were violated is rejected.

QUESTIONS

1. Does a school district or a youth organization have a legitimate interest in regulating student-athlete behavior outside school or the playing field? What kinds of rules, if any, should be promulgated to regulate student-athlete and youth behavior outside school or competition?

2. Consistent with *Brands*, courts generally find that student-athletes do not possess a property interest in athletic participation that requires procedural due process. Notwithstanding the general rule that no such interest exists, *Brands* and other courts have developed an exception to the general rule. What are the contours of the exception recognized in *Brands*?

NOTES

1. One area in which due process issues often arise involves actions by disciplinary bodies to take away championships. For example, lawyers have challenged Little League International's decision to take away Jackie Robinson West's Little League 2014 United States championship on procedural, not substantive, grounds. The plaintiffs in that case do not deny that they had ineligible players on the roster. Rather, they are primarily questioning the procedures and timing of Little League International's decision.

2. ***A less deferential approach.*** In *Scott v. Oklahoma Secondary School Activities Association,* 2013 OK 84 (Oct. 2013), the court found that the Oklahoma Secondary School Activities Association (OSSAA) had acted in an arbitrary and capricious manner in sanctioning a student athlete without clearly indicating which rules the student athlete had violated, particularly where those sanctions involved monetary penalties. The majority in *Scott* argued for a less deferential judicial view than has prevailed in the past:

> Competition in sports is more than a mere passing enjoyment for students. Particularly in rural areas, athletic teams are the glue which holds the community together. The college and post-college careers of student athletes often have their genesis at the secondary school level, and for some provide the only path to higher education. The OSSAA wields too much control over their future to be allowed to act in an arbitrary and capricious manner in applying its rules. It must be reasonable, it must be conscientious, and it must be fair. From now on, we trust, it will be.

It will be interesting to see whether this far less deferential approach will be followed by other jurisdictions. The Oklahoma Supreme Court's recognition of the importance of athletics to communities and student athletes is also worthy of note and may be a step in the direction of recognizing that participation in sports is more than a mere privilege that is subject to judicial deference to association and institutional decisions that implicate student athletes and coaches. Courts and legislative bodies may become less deferential to governing bodies. They have been very deferential under a participation in sports as a privilege model (the historic approach). Under a heightened sensitivity to participation in sports as more than a mere privilege evidenced in *Scott,* courts and legislative bodies may become more willing to intervene. Should they?

4. Age Rules

KEY TERMS
- Competitive advantage
- Waiver rule

Most governing bodies impose rules that prohibit athletes from engaging in competition at a prescribed age. Age limitations are generally accepted on the ground that governing bodies have a legitimate or reasonable interest in limiting participation by older and often stronger and more physically and mentally mature athletes. Courts do so on the ground that such participation will give the older athlete a competitive advantage. Athletes may seek a waiver of such a rule, but if the governing body refuses to grant the waiver, courts will generally defer to the association in such cases.

The *Cruz* case that follows, however, illustrates an instance in which a court was willing to intervene based on federal laws prohibiting disability discrimination. As you read the case, think of the reasons why the court declined to defer to the association.

Cruz v. Pennsylvania Interscholastic Athletic Association, Inc.
157 F. Supp. 2d 485 (E.D. Pa. 2001)

BUCKWALTER, District Judge.

[Editors' note: Luis Cruz was a 19-year-old public school special education student who was educable mentally retarded in his fourth year at Ridley High School, a recipient of federal funding. He had played several sports in his first three years at Ridley High School, including football, wrestling, and track. Because he was a student with a disability, Luis Cruz was educated in accordance with an individualized education program (IEP), pursuant to the federal Individuals with Disabilities Education Act (IDEA). As a "non-graded" student, Luis Cruz was not enrolled in a particular numerical grade. "His window of opportunity to participate in high school instruction and sports at an earlier age was limited and he did not have comparable opportunities as non-special education children, since due to his intellectual limitations he entered elementary school between ages eleven and twelve, rather than at the customary younger age, and then stayed an additional two years over the regular education students."

The defendant was the Pennsylvania Interscholastic Athletic Association, Inc. (P.I.A.A.), a Pennsylvania nonprofit membership corporation composed of most public and many private high schools in Pennsylvania, for a total of approximately 1,350 schools. A purpose of P.I.A.A. is to develop and apply rules regulating interscholastic athletic competition among its members. The P.I.A.A.'s "Age Rule" provided, "A pupil shall be ineligible for interscholastic athletic competition upon attaining the age of nineteen years, with the following exception: If the age of 19 is attained on or after July 1, the pupil shall be eligible, age-wise, to compete through that school year."

A school was required to forfeit a contest for using an ineligible coach or contestant. P.I.A.A. rules permitted students to participate in eight semesters of interscholastic sports; however, Cruz had been permitted to participate in only six semesters. The director of special education services observed that he still needed the remaining two semesters of interscholastic sports activities to interact with peers and adults, familiarize himself with demands and responsibilities, and develop interpersonal skills that would help him maintain employment after high school. Participation in these activities was vital to the development of his self-esteem and self-confidence. Although there was a provision for waiving either the eight-semester or transfer rules, with the key issue usually being "athletic intent," there was no waiver provision for the age rule. This was only the second time that the P.I.A.A. had received a request for a waiver of this rule by a student with an IEP.]

The purposes of [the age rule] are: (1) to protect high school athletes of customary age from the dangers and unfairness of participation with those who are older and thus perhaps physically larger, stronger, and more mature and experienced; (2) to limit the possibility that the team with the over-age student will gain an unfair competitive advantage over opponents; (3) to have available the maximum number of team positions for high school athletes who are of customary age for students in high school; and (4) to maintain uniformity of standards with regard to the age of participants. . . .

[Editors' note: According to Bradley Cashman, the P.I.A.A.'s executive director, the age rule did not provide for any waivers because it would be an overly burdensome task to evaluate competitive advantage in individual cases. An assessment of whether the student would "skew the overall competitiveness of the particular activity," or whether the student would constitute a competitive advantage, would have to be looked at not only sport by sport, but individual by individual. This would be a very difficult, complex, and burdensome assessment involving many variables, including both objective and subjective elements.]

P.I.A.A. estimates that it would have to significantly increase the size of its staff, doubling or tripling it, in order to perform assessments of whether a student would "skew the overall competitiveness of the particular activity" or whether the student would constitute a competitive advantage.

Luis Cruz is not a "star" player in any of his interscholastic sports. Luis Cruz has been included in the football program for an inclusive experience. He is a marginal player and appeared in football games on a very limited basis such as a few kickoffs where the performance apparently was not critical. At the same time, the non-special education students of Ridley High School are attempting to be inclusive. They have rallied around him, as he is a "great team player."

Luis Cruz is not more experienced than other players. In fact, he is less experienced and therefore has played football only on a very limited basis. [H]e is five foot three inches tall and weighs 130 pounds. . . . [His participation therefore presents] no safety threat to others or competitive advantage in the situation presented here. Also, again, there is no "cut" policy on the football squad, so Luis Cruz is not replacing any other student who would otherwise have an opportunity to play.

Luis Cruz has "good basic skills" in wrestling, but there are "a lot of better wrestlers than him." He is not a safety risk factor, but he may have a competitive advantage based on his outstanding dual meet record.

In track, where there is also a no-cut policy, Luis Cruz is not a fast runner, does not displace other students, has no competitive advantage, and represents no safety risk. He runs a minute behind qualifying time in the mile. He has been unable to earn points in dual meets and would only place by default.

[Editors' note: The court ruled that the P.I.A.A violated a federal statute, the Americans with Disabilities Act (ADA), which is discussed more fully in Chapter 8.]

It is clear from the findings of fact that Luis Cruz would not fundamentally alter the nature of the competition in football and track and that the modification of the age rule is necessary for him to be able to play in interscholastic competition in those two sports. What is more difficult to assess is whether the modification is reasonable. Initially, that involves a determination as to whether the age rule is essential to the P.I.A.A. sports program. . . .

It now seems clear that a rule is essential to a program unless it can be shown that the waiver of it would not fundamentally alter the nature of the program.

This determination must be made on an individual basis. The court has looked at the specific facts applicable to Luis Cruz in reaching its conclusion stated earlier in this opinion. In doing so in this case, it is clear that Luis Cruz playing on the football team and track team would not fundamentally alter the nature of P.I.A.A. interscholastic competition.

P.I.A.A. argues that requiring it to develop a waiver system which would assess whether an over-age student would have a competitive advantage over opponents in a given sport would be unreasonable, as it would require complex fact-finding as well as extremely difficult judgments about leadership skills, motivational abilities, physical maturity, benefits of experience, quickness, agility, strength, and sport-specific abilities which are extremely difficult to measure. . . .

In light of the other waivers which the P.I.A.A., through district committees, routinely considers, namely transfer and 8 term waivers (some of which require the determination of athletic intent), and in view of the apparent ability of the P.I.A.A. to make what must be very difficult decisions in those waiver cases, I do not believe that an age waiver rule would put an undue burden on the P.I.A.A. The statistics to date suggest that there may not be many occasions for the age waiver to be requested. . . .

[Editors' note: The court issued the following order: "(1) Defendant is restrained and prohibited from application and enforcement of its by-law as to age ineligibility with respect to Luis Cruz, unless done so pursuant to a waiver rule which provides for an individual evaluation of him. (2) Thus, as to any interscholastic sports in which Luis Cruz wishes to participate, the defendant must entertain an application for waiver of its by-laws as to age ineligibility rules pursuant to procedures that it establishes. (3) Failure to adopt such waiver procedures in a timely manner as to Luis Cruz will result under this opinion in his being eligible to participate in interscholastic football and track for the 2001–2002 school year."]

QUESTIONS

1. What is the rationale for imposing an age limitation on participation in a sport? Will older, more experienced, players necessarily have a competitive advantage? Do older players subject younger players to an increased likelihood of being injured or harmed? Should a general rule furthering such interests keep an athlete from participating if he or she does not constitute a competitive advantage or does not increase the threat of injury to other athletes?

2. Why did the association refuse to adopt a waiver provision as a part of its age limitation? Is the court's requirement that the association adopt and act on such a waiver appropriate, or is the court exceeding its authority? Should courts mandate the drafting of certain rules by a legislative body or association?

Problem 2-2

A young girl who is 13 years old has been promoted to the 12th grade because of high academic performance. She is 5'5" tall and weighs 123 pounds. She wants to participate in varsity lacrosse. Her parents are supportive and join in their daughter's belief that participation in athletics provides a student with character-building opportunities. The association has a rule that provides that students must be 14 to participate in sports that involve physical contact. The coach and the team do not want the girl to participate, fearing that she will cause them to be less aggressive in their play. As principal, you are going to meet with the young girl and her parents. What will you say as a legal and practical matter?

5. Grooming Rules

Courts have dealt with cases involving grooming rules. Most cases involving the validity of personal appearance and grooming rules arose during the turbulent period of time from 1965 to 1975 in the United States. These cases often raise claims based on the constitutional right of expression, which is grounded in the First Amendment. In *Tinker v. Des Moines Independent Community Sch. Dist.*, 393 U.S. 503 (1969), a public school dress code prohibited students from wearing black armbands. Finding that the prohibition violated the students' First Amendment rights, the Supreme Court concluded:

> The school officials banned and sought to punish petitioners for a silent, passive expression of opinion, unaccompanied by any disorder or disturbance on the part of petitioners. There is here no evidence whatever of petitioners' interference, actual or nascent, with the schools' work or of collision with the rights of other students to be secure and to be let alone. Accordingly, this case does not concern speech or action that intrudes upon the work of the schools or the rights of other students.

The subject continues to arise today, and appearance and grooming rules have been challenged on the ground that they are arbitrary and capricious. In *Davenport v. Randolph County Bd. of Educ.*, 730 F.2d 1395 (11th Cir. 1984), two student-athletes challenged a grooming policy that required that they be clean shaven, contending that the policy was unconstitutional because it was arbitrary and unreasonable to require 14- and 15-year-old adolescents to shave in order to participate in high school athletics. The court noted that in the high school environment, there is "a per se rule that [grooming regulations] are constitutionally valid," on the ground that grooming regulations are a reasonable means of furthering a school board's undeniable interest in teaching hygiene, instilling discipline, asserting authority, and compelling uniformity. The court acknowledged, however, that if the plaintiffs had provided medical evidence of a medical condition that made shaving harmful, they might not be subject to the rule.

Courts generally defer to schools regarding appropriate grooming rules. However, some courts have been less deferential. See, e.g., *Holsapple v. Woods*, 500 F.2d 49 (7th Cir. 1974) (a student's right to wear hair at any length or in any desired manner is an ingredient of personal freedom protected by the U.S. Constitution); *Gorman v. St. Raphael's Academy*, 2002 WL 31455570 (R.I. Super. Ct.) (academy's regulation of the hair of male students is arbitrary and capricious because it bears no rational relation to the legitimate mission statement of the school, nor does it in any way inhibit or enhance the learning process or order and discipline of the school). For a recent court decision refusing to defer in a hair-length case on the basis of gender discrimination, see *Hayden v. Greensburg Community School Corp.*, 743 F.3d 569 (7th Cir. 2014), in which the court noted: "The [plaintiffs] are entitled to judgment on their Title IX claim for the same reasons we have already discussed with respect to the equal protection claim . . . The hair-length policy is applied only to the boys team, with no evidence concerning the content of any comparable grooming standards applied to the girls team." There was a strong dissent in the *Hayden* case that would have deferred to the school. Should courts be deferential in grooming cases? Should hair-length or related cases be subject to gender discrimination claims?

6. No-Pass, No Play Rules

Eligibility rules commonly referred to as "no-pass, no-play" rules were initially promulgated in the early 1980s as state legislatures, athletic associations, and individual institutions sought to strike an appropriate balance between participation in academics and athletics. No-pass, no-play rules are designed to condition participation in extra-curricular activities, including sports, on students achieving a certain academic performance. The first no-pass, no-play statute, which was enacted in Texas, provided:

> A student, other than a mentally retarded student, enrolled in a school district in this state shall be suspended from participation in any extracurricular activity sponsored or sanctioned by the school district during the grade reporting period after a grade reporting period in which the student received a grade lower than the equivalent of 70 on a scale of 100 in any academic class.

No-pass, no-play rules have been controversial as a policy matter, and questions have been raised regarding whether they achieve their ultimate objective — better academic performance. Opponents of the rules argue that they may increase the number of students who simply drop out of school because the one thing that keeps them there — participation in athletics — has been taken away. Such rules, however, are generally held to be legally acceptable unless they are being applied inappropriately.

Students deemed ineligible to participate in interscholastic sports have challenged the legality of no-pass, no-play rules on equal protection and due process grounds. Starting from the premise that participation in extracurricular activities is neither a fundamental right nor an infringement on the rights of a suspect or protected class, courts have applied a rational basis test in addressing equal protection challenges. The application of such a standard almost invariably leads them to conclude that no-pass, no-play rules are rationally related to their intended goals because they are designed to further academic objectives. Similarly, courts have rejected due process challenges to no-pass, no-play rules because a student's interest in participating in extracurricular activities is not a protected property or liberty interest.

QUESTIONS

1. Since no-pass, no-play rules are generally upheld by courts, the critical issue is whether an association should adopt such a rule and what its terms should be. These policy issues are raised at the state legislative, associational, and institutional levels. An institution, for example, may create more (but not less) stringent standards. As a member of a school board, would you favor increasing the required GPA from the 2.0 required by the state athletic association to a 2.25 within your school district?
2. Would it make a difference to you if your school district did a study and discovered that athletes with a 2.25 average are 25 percent more likely to graduate from high school than athletes who maintain the minimal 2.0 average?

7. Exclusion of Homeschooled Students from Athletic Participation

In two important cases, courts have addressed the issue of the eligibility of home-schooled students to participate in extracurricular sporting activities. In *Jones v. West Virginia State Board of Education*, 622 S.E.2d 289 (W. Va. 2005), plaintiffs sought to have their 11-year-old child, whom they homeschooled, try out for the Mannington Middle School wrestling team. The West Virginia Secondary School Activities Commission (WVSSAC) denied their request on the ground that only full-time students were permitted to participate in interscholastic athletics. Plaintiffs filed a complaint seeking declaratory, equitable, and injunctive relief. The trial court found in favor of plaintiffs and entered the injunction.

On appeal, the West Virginia Supreme Court addressed three issues: (1) Did the WVSSAC breach a statutory duty by not allowing homeschoolers to participate in interscholastic athletics? (2) Did the WVSSAC violate the West Virginia equal protection rights of homeschool children by prohibiting them from participating in interscholastic athletics? (3) Did the WVSSAC breach its duty to promulgate reasonable rules and regulations by implementing a total ban on allowing home-schooled children to participate in interscholastic athletics?

The court held in favor of the WVSSAC on all three issues. With respect to the alleged breach of a statutory duty, the court held that the plain language of the relevant statute imposed an obligation on the school superintendent to provide assistance and resources to the person providing the homeschool instruction (here, the student's mother). The statute, however, did not require that resources, including interscholastic athletics, be provided to the homeschooled student himself.

The court also held that the WVSSAC did not violate plaintiffs' equal protection rights. In reaching this conclusion, the court first found that participation in interscholastic athletics is neither a fundamental nor a constitutional right under the West Virginia constitution. Consequently, any classification affecting participation in interscholastic athletics will be upheld as long as it is rationally related to a legitimate state interest. Among the several grounds offered by defendant as providing a rational basis for excluding homeschooled children, the court focused on two as offering sufficient justification: "(a) promoting academics over athletics, and (b) protecting the economic interests of the county school systems." With respect to the former, the court examined the grade requirements for participating in extracurricular activities. It found that homeschooled children are graded on different standards than public school children and that converting such grades would impose a burden on the school district. Moreover, the different grading standards would impede the ability of school officials to maintain the academic standards required for participation in interscholastic sports. The court noted that a parent could withdraw an underperforming student from the public school system and homeschool him or her to retain the student athlete's eligibility.

As it relates to protecting the economic interests of the county school system, the court emphasized that money is apportioned to schools based on attendance in class. According to the court, requiring counties to spend limited funds to support athletic participation of homeschooled students (from whom no funds are allocated) would create a financial burden. Finally, the court held that the WVSSAC did not breach its duty to promulgate reasonable rules and regulations. Even though homeschooled students are totally banned from interscholastic athletics participation, the court held it is not arbitrary and capricious because it is rationally related to the two legitimate state purposes discussed above.

In *Reid v. Kenowa Hills Public Schools*, 680 N.W.2d (Mich. Ct. App. 2004), the court similarly resolved a homeschooled student's challenge to a rule of the Michigan High School Athletic Association (MHSAA) providing that only students enrolled in school for at least 20 hours may participate in extracurricular sports.

QUESTIONS

1. Given the growth of the homeschool movement in the United States, it is likely that this issue will be raised in both judicial and legislative arenas. Should courts require schools to permit homeschooled athletes to participate in interscholastic athletics? As a matter of policy, should homeschool students be permitted by governing bodies to participate in athletic competition?

2. What reasons favor such a policy, and what reasons can be raised in opposition to it? Would your answer change at all if a homeschooled child desired to participate in tennis or golf, compared to one who wanted to participate in football?

NOTE

Approximately 30 states now have laws permitting homeschooled students to participate in interscholastic sports. These rules have been dubbed "Tim Tebow" laws, after Tim Tebow, who had been homeschooled, gained notoriety on the football field at the collegiate and professional levels. See *http://aol.sportingnews.com/nfl/story/2012-08-21/tim-tebow-new-york-jets-quarterback-law-home-schooled-students-south-carolina*. Not surprisingly, success on the part of homeschooled students has been primarily legislative in nature, not through litigation. Given the growth of the home-school movement in the United States, and its power in the lobbying and legislative senses, it is likely that legislative success at the state level will continue.

C. First and Fourth Amendment Issues

The cases in the prior sections often raised constitutional questions: procedural due process (adequate notice and a fair hearing are required when a liberty or property interest is implicated); substantive due process (infringement of a privacy or personal autonomy right or acting in an arbitrary and capricious manner); and denial of equal protection of the law (singling out an individual or identifiable group for differential treatment). Additional constitutional claims also arise out of alleged violation of First Amendment privacy, freedom of speech and religion rights, and Fourth Amendment protections against unreasonable searches and seizures.

1. Drug Testing

KEY TERMS
- Clearly erroneous
- Privacy interest
- Search and seizure
- Suspicionless
- Warrant

Like society at large, drug use pervades all levels of athletic competition, including competition among high school athletes. The National Federation of State High School Associations does not require that high schools develop a drug-testing program for athletes. Nevertheless, some high school districts throughout the country recently have implemented random drug-testing programs that require students to consent to testing as a condition of being eligible to participate in interscholastic athletics. These policies vary by individual school district, with testing done for illegal recreational drugs, such as marijuana, and performance-enhancing drugs, such as anabolic steroids, the use of which is a growing problem among high school athletes.

Prior to 1995, lower federal courts were split on whether drug testing of high school athletes by public schools violates the Fourth or Fourteenth Amendment, as unreasonable searches or violations of due process, respectively.

In the following case, the United States Supreme Court considered whether suspicionless random drug testing of high school athletes is constitutional.

Vernonia School District 47J v. Acton
515 U.S. 646 (1995)

Justice SCALIA delivered the opinion of the Court.

[Editors' note: The Student Athlete Drug Policy adopted by School District 47J in the town of Vernonia, Oregon, authorized random urinalysis drug testing of students who participated in the district's school athletics programs. Drugs had not been a major problem in Vernonia schools. In the mid- to late-1980s, however, teachers and administrators observed a sharp increase in drug use. Students began to speak out about their attraction to the drug culture, and to boast that there was nothing the school could do about it. Along with more drugs came more disciplinary problems.

Student athletes were among the leaders of the drug culture. This caused the district's administrators particular concern since they believed that drug use increased the risk of sports-related injury. Expert testimony at the trial confirmed the deleterious effects of drugs on motivation, memory, judgment, reaction, coordination, and performance. The high school football and wrestling coach witnessed a severe sternum injury suffered by a wrestler, and various omissions of safety procedures and misexecutions by football players, all attributable in his belief to the effects of drug use.

Initially, the district responded to the drug problem by offering special classes, speakers, and presentations designed to deter drug use. However, the drug problem persisted. Ultimately, the district adopted a Student Athlete Drug Policy (Policy) at a meeting, which parents in attendance gave their unanimous approval.

The school board approved the Policy for implementation in the fall of 1989. Its expressed purpose was to prevent student athletes from using drugs, to protect their health and safety, and to provide drug users with assistance programs.

The Policy applied to all students participating in interscholastic athletics. Students wishing to play sports were required to sign a form consenting to the testing and obtain the written consent of their parents. Athletes were tested at the beginning of the season for their sport. In addition, once each week of the season, the names of the athletes were placed in a "pool" from which a student, with the supervision of two adults, blindly drew the names of 10 percent of the athletes for random testing. Those selected are notified and tested that same day, if possible. Students to be tested entered an empty locker room accompanied by an adult monitor of the same sex and provided a urine sample. After the sample was produced, it was given to the monitor, who checked it for temperature and tampering and then transferred it to a vial.

The samples were sent to an independent laboratory, which routinely tested them for amphetamines, cocaine, and marijuana. Other drugs, such as lysergic acid diethyamide (LSD), could be screened at the request of the district, but the identity of a particular student did not determine which drugs will be tested. The laboratory's procedures were 99.94 percent accurate. If a sample tested positive, a second test was administered as soon as possible to confirm the result. If the second test was negative, no further action was taken. If the second test was positive, the athlete's parents were notified, and the school principal convened a meeting with the student and his parents, at which the student was given the option of (1) participating for six weeks in an assistance program that included weekly urinalysis, or (2) suffering suspension from athletics for the remainder of the then current season and the next athletic season. The student was then retested prior to the start of the next athletic season for which he or she was eligible. The Policy stated that a second offense resulted in automatic imposition of option (2); a third offense resulted in suspension for the remainder of the then current season and the next two athletic seasons.

In the fall of 1991, respondent James Acton, then a seventh grader, signed up to play football at one of the district's grade schools. He was denied participation, however, because he and his parents refused to sign the testing consent forms. The Actons filed suit, seeking declaratory and injunctive relief from enforcement of the Policy on the grounds that it violated the Fourth and Fourteenth Amendments to the United States Constitution and Article I, §9, of the Oregon Constitution.]

II

In [a prior case,] we held that state-compelled collection and testing of urine, such as that required by the Policy, constitutes a "search" subject to the demands of the Fourth Amendment.

As the text of the Fourth Amendment indicates, the ultimate measure of the constitutionality of a governmental search is "reasonableness." [W]hether a particular search meets the reasonableness standard "'is judged by balancing its intrusion on the individual's Fourth Amendment interests against its promotion of legitimate governmental interests.'" Where a search is undertaken by law enforcement officials to discover evidence of criminal wrongdoing, this Court has said that reasonableness generally requires the obtaining of a judicial warrant. Warrants cannot be issued, of course, without the showing of probable cause required by the Warrant Clause. But a warrant is not required to establish the reasonableness of *all* government searches; and when a warrant is not required (and the Warrant Clause therefore not applicable), probable cause is not invariably required either. A search unsupported by probable cause can be constitutional, we have said, "when special needs, beyond the normal need for law enforcement, make the warrant and probable-cause requirement impracticable."

We have found such "special needs" to exist in the public school context. There, the warrant requirement "would unduly interfere with the maintenance of the swift and informal disciplinary procedures [that are] needed," and "strict adherence to the requirement that searches be based upon probable cause" would undercut "the substantial need of teachers and administrators for freedom to maintain order in the schools." The school search we approved in [a prior case], while not based on probable cause, *was* based on individualized *suspicion* of wrongdoing. As we explicitly acknowledged, however, " 'the Fourth Amendment imposes no irreducible requirement of such suspicion,'?" We have upheld suspicionless searches and seizures to conduct drug testing [in some other contexts].

III

The first factor to be considered is the nature of the privacy interest upon which the search at issue intrudes. . . . Central, in our view, to the present case is the fact that the subjects of the Policy are (1) children, who (2) have been committed to the temporary custody of the State as schoolmaster. . . .

Fourth Amendment rights . . . are different in public schools than elsewhere; the "reasonableness" inquiry cannot disregard the schools' custodial and tutelary responsibility for children. For their own good and that of their classmates, public school children are routinely required to submit to various physical examinations, and to be vaccinated against various diseases. . . . Particularly with regard to medical examinations and procedures, therefore, "students within the school environment have a lesser expectation of privacy than members of the population generally."

Legitimate privacy expectations are even less with regard to student athletes. School sports are not for the bashful. They require "suiting up" before each practice or event, and showering and changing afterwards. Public school locker rooms, the usual sites for these activities, are not notable for the privacy they afford.

There is an additional respect in which school athletes have a reduced expectation of privacy. By choosing to "go out for the team," they voluntarily subject themselves to a degree of regulation even higher than that imposed on students generally. In Vernonia's public schools, they must submit to a preseason physical exam, they must acquire adequate insurance coverage or sign an insurance waiver, maintain a minimum grade point average, and comply with any "rules of conduct, dress, training hours and related matters as may be established for each sport by the head coach and athletic director with the principal's approval." [S]tudents who voluntarily participate in school athletics have reason to expect intrusions upon normal rights and privileges, including privacy.

IV

Having considered the scope of the legitimate expectation of privacy at issue here, we turn next to the character of the intrusion that is complained of. . . . Under the District's Policy, male students produce samples at a urinal along a wall. They remain fully clothed and are only observed from behind, if at all. Female students produce samples in an enclosed stall, with a female monitor standing outside listening only for sounds of tampering. These conditions are nearly identical to those typically encountered in public restrooms, which men, women, and especially schoolchildren use daily. Under such conditions, the privacy interests compromised by the process of obtaining the urine sample are in our view negligible.

The other privacy-invasive aspect of urinalysis is, of course, the information it discloses concerning the state of the subject's body, and the materials he has ingested. In this regard it is significant that the tests at issue here look only for drugs, and not for whether the student is, for example, epileptic, pregnant, or diabetic. Moreover, the drugs for which the samples are screened are standard, and do not vary according to the identity of the student. And finally, the results of the tests are disclosed only to a limited class of school personnel who have a need to know; and they are not turned over to law enforcement authorities or used for any internal disciplinary function.

V

Finally, we turn to consider the nature and immediacy of the governmental concern at issue here, and the efficacy of this means for meeting it. . . .

That the nature of the concern is important — indeed, perhaps compelling — can hardly be doubted. Deterring drug use by our Nation's schoolchildren is at least as important as enhancing efficient enforcement of the Nation's laws against the importation of drugs, or deterring drug use by engineers and trainmen [two prior cases in which drug testing was found to be constitutional]. School years are the time when the physical, psychological, and addictive effects of drugs are most severe. . . . And of course the effects of a drug-infested school are visited not just upon the users, but upon the entire student body and faculty, as the educational process is disrupted. . . . Finally, it must not be lost sight of that this program is directed more narrowly to drug use by school athletes, where the risk of immediate physical harm to the drug user or those with whom he is playing his sport is particularly high. Apart from psychological effects, which include impairment of judgment, slow reaction time, and a lessening of the perception of pain, the particular drugs screened by the District's Policy have been demonstrated to pose substantial physical risks to athletes. . . .

We are not inclined to question — indeed, we could not possibly find clearly erroneous — the District Court's conclusion that "a large segment of the student body, particularly those involved in interscholastic athletics, was in a state of rebellion," that "[d]isciplinary actions had reached 'epidemic proportions,'?" and that "the rebellion was being fueled by alcohol and drug abuse as well as by the student's misperceptions about the drug culture." . . .

VI

Taking into account all the factors we have considered above — the decreased expectation of privacy, the relative unobtrusiveness of the search, and the severity of the need met by the search — we conclude Vernonia's Policy is reasonable and hence constitutional.

We caution against the assumption that suspicionless drug testing will readily pass constitutional muster in other contexts. The most significant element in this case is the first we discussed: that the Policy was undertaken in furtherance of the government's responsibilities, under a public school system, as guardian and tutor of children entrusted to its care. . . .

Justice O'CONNOR, with whom Justice STEVENS and Justice SOUTER join, dissenting.

The population of our Nation's public schools, grades 7 through 12, numbers around 18 million. By the reasoning of today's decision, the millions of these students who participate in interscholastic sports, an overwhelming majority of whom have given school officials no reason whatsoever to suspect they use drugs at school, are open to an intrusive bodily search. . . . I find unreasonable the school's choice of student athletes as the class to subject to suspicionless testing — a choice that appears to have been driven more by a belief in what would pass constitutional muster (indicating that the original program was targeted at students involved in any extracurricular activity) than by a belief in what was required to meet the District's principal disciplinary concern. . . . [I]t seems quite obvious that the true driving force behind the District's adoption of its drug testing program was the need to combat the rise in drug-related disorder and disruption in its classrooms and around campus. I mean no criticism of the strength of that interest. On the contrary, where the record demonstrates the existence of such a problem, that interest seems self-evidently compelling. . . . And the record in this case surely demonstrates there was a drug-related discipline problem in Vernonia of "'epidemic proportions.'" The evidence of a drug-related sports injury problem at Vernonia, by contrast, was considerably weaker. . . .

Having reviewed the record here, I cannot avoid the conclusion that the District's suspicionless policy of testing all student athletes sweeps too broadly, and too imprecisely, to be reasonable under the Fourth Amendment.

QUESTIONS

1. Why does the *Acton* majority uphold suspicionless testing of high school athletes for recreational drug use?

2. Would suspicion-based drug testing accomplish high school administrators' legitimate objectives equally well without intruding on students' privacy rights? Should student-athletes be singled out?

NOTES

1. *Acton* extended. In *Board of Education of Indep. Sch. Dist. No. 92 of Pottawatomie County v. Earls*, 536 U.S. 822 (2002), the Supreme Court upheld the constitutionality of mandatory suspicionless drug testing of all students participating in high school extracurricular activities. The only consequence of a positive test for illegal drugs was to limit the student's privilege of participating in extracurricular activities; it did not result in the imposition of any other discipline or have any academic consequences. If the suspicionless search resulted in discipline in the form of suspension or expulsion from school, do you think the Court would have found in favor of the students?

2. State constitutions. Although the Court approves mandatory drug testing for students desiring to participate in extracurricular activities under the Fourth Amendment of the U.S. Constitution, such policies may still face challenges under state constitutional provisions. In *York v. Wahkiakum*, 178 P.3d 995 (Wash. 2008), the Washington supreme court considered the constitutionality of a school district's blanket suspicionless random drug testing program for student-athletes. Although the court acknowledged that the district's drug testing policy did not violate the Fourth Amendment of the U.S. Constitution, it concluded that the Washington state constitution provided a higher level of protection. It held that the district's drug testing policy violated a provision of the state constitution that provides, "No person shall be disturbed in his private affairs, or his home invaded, without authority of law." Other state courts have refused to interpret their state constitutions more broadly and have upheld suspicionless searches.

Problem 2-3

School districts are not required to have drug testing policies in place for students, athletes, or others. They are, however, permitted to do so under the circumstances outlined in the *Acton* case. As a policy matter, would you support such a policy? What kinds of facts might persuade you that such a policy is necessary? What would it have to look like to be legally acceptable after *Acton*?

2. Freedom of Speech and Association

KEY TERMS	• Freedom of speech
	• Retaliation

Previously, in discussing grooming rules, we introduced the concept of freedom of expression. In those cases, we noted that the courts often defer to athletic associations and schools even though First Amendment rights are implicated. In the following materials, we explore this concept in greater depth.

The First Amendment of the United States Constitution, together with many similar provisions in state constitutions, protects against government limitations of the right to speak (freedom of expression), to assemble (freedom to associate), and to share information through print and other media (freedom of the press). In the *Wildman* case, the court examines whether a school acted appropriately in disciplining a student athlete for distributing a letter that criticized her coach. As you will see, the court acknowledges that the student has a right of expression that is implicated in the case but goes on to hold that the school's discipline was appropriate.

Wildman v. Marshalltown School District
249 F.3d. 768 (8th Cir. 2001)

BRIGHT, Circuit Judge.

Wildman argues that the First Amendment prevents the school from disciplining her for distributing a letter which was a personal communication to other students containing her personal expression. Both parties agree that, students do not "shed their constitutional rights to freedom of speech or expression at the schoolhouse gate." [A prior Supreme Court decision] involved an attempt by high school students to wear black armbands on school property to symbolize their protest against the Vietnam War. The Supreme Court struck down school authorities' efforts to discipline this expression of opinion (suspending the students from school until they would come back without their armbands) and stated that "undifferentiated fear or apprehension of disturbance is not enough to overcome the right to freedom of expression."

However, this right to express opinions on school premises is not absolute. It is well within the parameters of school officials' authority to prohibit the public expression of vulgar and offensive comments and to teach civility and sensitivity in the expression of opinions. . . .

Marshalltown had in place a handbook for student conduct, as well as a Marshalltown Bobcat Basketball Handbook, drafted by Coach Rowles and distributed to Wildman and her teammates at the start of the season. Both handbooks indicated that disrespect and insubordination will result in disciplinary action at the coach's discretion. . . .

Wildman admits that her speech contained one profane word but contends that because there was no specific evidence of a material disruption of a school activity, her speech is protected. We disagree with the claim of protection. . . .

The school did not interfere with Wildman's regular education. A difference exists between being in the classroom, which was not affected here, and playing on an athletic team when the requirement is that the player only apologize to her teammates and her coach for circulating an insubordinate letter.

This suit does not present a case like [a prior case cited by Wildman, in which] the football coach asked the player to apologize to the football team for reporting to the police and to school authorities a hazing incident in which the player was assaulted in the high school locker room by a group of his teammates, forcibly restrained, and bound to a towel rack with adhesive athletic tape.

In contrast, Wildman's letter, containing the word "bullshit" in relation to other language in it and motivated by her disappointment at not playing on the varsity team, constitutes insubordinate speech toward her coaches. Here, in an athletic context void of the egregious conduct which spurred the football player's speech about the hazing incident in [a prior case protecting such speech], no basis exists for a claim of a violation of free speech.

III. Conclusion

Accordingly, we affirm the [dismissal] of Wildman's claim of alleged violation of her rights under the Free Speech Clause of the First Amendment.

QUESTIONS

1. The court rejected the student-athlete's free speech claim. On what ground did they do so? Do you agree? Why or why not? The court states that "[t]he parties could have achieved with minimal creativity and flexibility a solution more amicable or less humiliating to the student." What could they have done? What would you recommend in a similar context?

2. In the fall of 2013, a high school football player and wrestler in Minnesota sued his school, which had suspended him indefinitely from participation in athletics for sending the following message to a fellow student regarding an upcoming football practice on his Twitter account: "Im boutta drill my 'teammates' on Monday." The school believed the message to be a threat. The student argued that it was just his way of saying that he would be aggressive in football practice. The student was not permitted to participate in football and initially was not permitted to wrestle either. The student, who had a chance of obtaining a wrestling scholarship at the collegiate level, eventually dropped the suit when the school permitted him to wrestle as part of a settlement worked out during mediation. In another case, *Bell v. Itawamba Cnty. Sch. Bd. (http://www.ca5.uscourts.gov/opinions/pub/12/12-60264 -CV0.pdf)*, the court held that a school board in Mississippi violated a student's First Amendment free speech rights when it suspended the student for posting a rap song accusing two coaches of sexual harassment, without providing any evidence that the posting was in fact disruptive. In a partial dissent, Judge Rhesa Hawkins argued that the majority's decision was "absurd," particularly in light of recent school shootings, which ought to provide school districts with broad latitude in addressing language by a student that they found to be threatening or harassing. Was the statement in the Minnesota case a threat? Do you agree with the majority of the dissent in the Mississippi case? How would you have handled such matters if you represented the school district? Is mediation helpful in such cases?

3. A Texas state appellate court recently held that a school principal did not violate the Texas wiretapping statute by surreptitiously recording a high school basketball coach's comments at the end of the game and during halftime, because the coach did not have a reasonable expectation of privacy in that context. The court treated the coach the same way that it would treat any other teacher or educator and held that "society is not willing to recognize that a public school educator — whether a teacher or a coach — has a reasonable expectation of privacy in his or her instructional communications and activities, regardless of where they occur, because they are always subject to public dissemination and generally exposed to the public view." *Long v. State of Texas*, 8th Dist. Ct. of App. 08-13-00334-CR (June 30, 2015). Should coaches be treated like other public educators for privacy purposes? What privacy rights should a coach-teacher have?

3. Freedom of Religion

The First Amendment of the U.S. Constitution and similar amendments in many state constitutions mandate that government or state actors "make no laws respecting an establishment of religion" or "prohibiting the free exercise [of religion]." Laws respecting an establishment of religion are prohibited because government should not establish or prefer one religion over another. Free exercise, in turn, recognizes that the right of individuals to freely exercise their religious conscience is a right that should be protected against state action. Free exercise and establishment issues may arise in the context of interscholastic sports under either federal or state constitutions. For example, religious students may argue that being scheduled to participate in athletics on a religious holiday or day of worship recognized in their religious faith violates their right to freely exercise their religion. Athletic associations and others, in turn, may argue that scheduling athletic events to accommodate religious concerns does not violate a student's right to freely exercise her religion because the student does not have to participate. Associations also argue that accommodating a religious student, by changing their schedule, may constitute an establishment of religion — a preference for one religion over another. The wearing of yarmulkes, crosses, or other religious symbols in competition has also raised free exercise issues and establishment issues. Students argue that their faith requires that they wear the symbol, but associations argue that the wearing of such religious symbols may increase the likelihood of injury or may give the appearance that the association or institution is endorsing that religious exercise. Another way in which religious liberty issues often arise is when students desire to pray in a public context.

a. Free Exercise Issues

In *Menora v. Illinois High School Ass'n*, 683 F.2d 152 (5th Cir. 1980), the court upheld a rule that forbade student-athletes from wearing hats or other headwear (with the sole exception of a headband no wider than two inches) while playing basketball against a claim that this rule infringed on the religious freedom of Orthodox Jews who sought to wear yarmulkes during play. Despite dealing with a serious free exercise claim, the court accepted the association's assertion that the rule preserved the safety of players by ensuring that a player would not trip over a yarmulke that had fallen from a player's head.

In *Walsh v. Louisiana High School Athletic Association*, 616 F.2d 152 (5th Cir. 1980), the court upheld a transfer rule against a claim that it burdened a student's free exercise of religion rights. The parents sought to have their children educated in Lutheran schools, as a matter of faith, and argued that the transfer rule prohibiting their children from participating for a period of time in interscholastic athletics infringed their free exercise rights. The court found that the burden on free exercise was minimal and held that it did not constitute a legally cognizable infringement because the transfer provision was religiously neutral, generally applicable, and did not distinguish between private and parochial schools.

Prior to *Employment Division v. Smith*, 494 U.S. 872 (1990), in which Justice Scalia, writing for a majority of the Supreme Court, rejected the strict scrutiny (compelling interest) test that the Court had previously used to deal with religious liberty cases and held that neutral laws of general applicability — laws that do not intentionally discriminate against religion or religious exercise — are not subject to free exercise limitations under the free exercise clause of the First Amendment of the U.S. Constitution. It should be noted, however, that statutory or regulatory accommodations of religious exercise are permissible. Athletic associations may create rules that accommodate the free exercise of religion. It is clear, for example, that associations may permit transfers on religious grounds. Indeed, that is one of the lessons of *Employment Division v. Smith*—such matters are largely left to the democratic or regulatory process at the state and federal levels. Furthermore, a student may argue for a religious accommodation or exemption under a state constitutional right of free exercise provision, which may be interpreted to provide broader rights than similar provisions under the U.S. Constitution.

More than 20 states have reacted negatively to Justice Scalia's weakening of the free exercise test and have passed state statutes that are designed to ensure that religious exercise receives a higher level of protection or scrutiny. In those states, or in states in which the state constitution is interpreted to provide more protection for religious exercise, it is more likely that religious exercise on the part of students will be protected.

QUESTIONS

1. The First Amendment offers little protection to parents, student-athletes, or coaches unless they can establish they are actually being discriminated against on religious grounds or can persuade a regulatory or legislative body to provide them with an accommodation. Do you agree with the judicial precedent making it very difficult to assert successfully the infringement of a religious liberty right in this context?
2. Given that a plaintiff now has to establish that he or she has actually been discriminated against on religious grounds to prevail in a free exercise case, what kind of proof might be presented to establish such a claim?
3. It is very difficult to prove religious discrimination because people seldom acknowledge that they have discriminated. Should the burden be on the plaintiff to prove discrimination?

NOTE

Religious Freedom Restoration Act (RFRA). The United States Supreme Court held that the Religious Freedom Restoration Act (RFRA), which was passed in an effort to restore the strict scrutiny test in free exercise cases, is unconstitutional. The RFRA, however, has been held to be constitutional in the federal context. In *Gonzales v. O Centro Espirita Beneficiente Uniao do Vegetal*, 546 U.S. 418 (2006), the Supreme Court, with Chief Justice Roberts writing for the Court, applied the compelling state interest test of RFRA in the federal, as opposed to state, context and held that a religious organization was entitled to a preliminary injunction against federal governmental efforts to curtail its access to a hallucinogenic sacramental tea, *hoasca*. This decision in the federal context may evidence a willingness on the part of the Supreme Court to recognize religious liberty claims in other contexts as well.

Similarly, under state constitutions, state courts have been willing to extend greater protection for religious liberty than that articulated by Justice Scalia and the Court in *Employment Division v. Smith*. Courts, therefore, occasionally have been willing to recognize free exercise rights on the part of institutions, students, and coaches. In a case out of New York, the court granted an injunction allowing a high school lacrosse player the right to participate despite his refusal for religious reasons to get a required tetanus vaccination. In another case, a court found that the school board erred in applying a *de minimis* test when it refused to accommodate a request made by an Adventist school to adjust a basketball tournament schedule to enable students to avoid having to choose between participating in athletics on their Sabbath and refusing to play.

Problem 2-4

A coach at a high school removed a student athlete from his team for insubordination because the student had asked her teammates to join with her after the game in a prayer. Every member of the team attended, and the girl prayed for the team and also prayed that "coach will be blessed to be able to do a better job of coaching us as a team." The student and her parents are meeting with you, as the school superintendent, and have asked you to reinstate her on the team. What would you do?

b. Establishment Clause Issues

The First Amendment provides that "Congress shall make no law respecting an establishment of religion. . . . " This provision prohibits state actors from engaging in activities that might be considered to have the effect of establishing a religion. One issue that regularly arises is the question of whether prayers may be offered prior to, or as a part of, interscholastic *athletic* events sponsored by public schools. In the *Santa Fe Independent School Dist. v. Doe*, 530 U.S. 290 (2000), the United States Supreme Court held that a public school district's policy permitting student-led, student-initiated prayer at football games violated the establishment clause of the First Amendment.

QUESTIONS

1. The majority in the *Santa Fe* case indicated that religious activities may still occur in the interscholastic athletics context if a public school's or state high school's athletics association (determined to be a state actor) is not viewed as sponsoring or endorsing the religious activity. What activities might be appropriate? If the captain of a public high school team led his team in prayer without the participation or knowledge of the coach, would that be permissible? What if an athlete were injured and his teammates spontaneously knelt in prayer around him? If a school's mascot is the crusaders or the saints, should the school be prohibited from using that name on establishment grounds?

2. Cases involving prayer by high school student-athletes and coaches often raise free speech, free exercise, and establishment clause issues. Students often argue, for example, that they have a (free exercise and speech) right to pray. When students make such an argument, however, the offering of such prayers often raise establishment clause issues because the prayers appear to be endorsed, preferred, or supported by public schools or officials. How should the tension between the student's free exercise and expression rights be balanced with the need to avoid establishing a religion?

Problem 2-5

A coach at a public high school has been bringing players together regularly for a prayer before practice and competition. Does the coach's act violate the Establishment Clause? Given that it is likely that the coach's action violates the Establishment Clause, are there other possible ways in which religious interests of coaches and players can or should be accommodated or recognized in the public interscholastic context? For example, could the coach have the students pause for a moment of silence?

D. Review of Game Results

With the increasing use of instant replay to confirm or overrule on-the-field decisions by referees, judicial reconsideration of on-the-field decisions by referees where instant replay is not in use may become more common. While it is likely that courts will continue to be deferential to state athletic associations and governing bodies in their handling of such incidents, cases of this sort raise interesting legal and moral issues, as evidenced by a recent case in Oklahoma. With 64 seconds remaining in the Oklahoma playoff game in November 2014, Douglass High School took a 25-20 lead over Locust Grove. The receiver for Douglass High caught a short pass and ran more than 50 yards to the end zone. Video depicted a Douglass coach running excitedly along the sideline, appearing to unintentionally bump one of the referees. The referee threw a flag and invalidated the touchdown. Under association rules, however, the violation is minor, calling for a 5-yard penalty to be assessed on the extra-point attempt or the ensuing kickoff. Locust Grove went on to win the game.

The Oklahoma Secondary School Activities Association later apologized to Douglass High, labeling the referees' mistake "inexcusable." Nevertheless, the association found that state and national bylaws do not permit protesting the outcome of a game because of an official's error on the field. Oklahoma City public school officials disagreed and are seeking in court to have some of or all the game replayed. Questions of racism were also raised by fans from Douglass High, an inner-city school with a team made up predominantly of players of color.

Judge Bernard M. Jones II, serving on the District Court in Oklahoma City, initially issued a temporary restraining order, prohibiting Locust Grove from playing its scheduled semifinal playoff game. The Oklahoma City school district supported Douglass High, arguing that fairness justified overruling a correctable mistake. Brandon Carey, general counsel for Oklahoma City public schools, argued that the Douglass case was unique because the district was not questioning the judgment of the referee; rather, it was seeking relief in an instance in which the referee made a mistake based on his misunderstanding of the penalty prescribed by the rule. Judge Jones ultimately denied the district's request to have all or part of an Oklahoma high school football playoff game replayed after a critical mistake by the referees negated a late touchdown. Judge Jones noted that he was aware of no precedent allowing a court to order the replay of a high school football game, and expressed concern that there was no way to ensure that a replay would be fair to both teams because the conditions of the disputed contest could not be replicated. The judge expressed concern that a "slippery slope of solving athletic contests in court instead of on campus will inevitably usher in a new era of robed referees and meritless litigation due to disagreement with or disdain for decisions of gaming officials." Judge Jones added that the referees' error "could be considered by many as a tragedy," but deferred to the association given that both teams agreed to be bound by the rules of the state high school activities association. School officials declined to appeal the decision.

See Cliff Brunt, Oklahoma Judge Says Disputed High School Game Won't Be Replayed, Associated Press, *http://www.varsitykansas.com/2014/12/11/74398/oklahoma-judge-says-disputed-high.html.*

QUESTIONS

Does fairness dictate that the game be replayed? If the court intervened, does the case involve a slippery slope that would lead to inappropriate litigation and judicial oversight of referees' decisions or is the district right in asserting that this is a unique case that warrants judicial intervention? Did the high school association make the right decision? Should Locust Grove have agreed to replay the game or permit Douglass High to go on to play in the state championship, in the interest of teaching the athletes a lesson in good sportsmanship? If you represented Locust High or its school district, what would you do? How would you communicate your decision to the athletes and the student body as a whole? Can you conceive of an instance in which the court should intervene? If the referee acted out of racial bias, as some argued, should his erroneous call be overruled by the association, the court, or Locust Grove? How would one prove racial bias?

E. Health and Safety Issues in Youth and Interscholastic Sports

Unlike state athletic associations, most youth governing bodies are not state actors and do not have to provide constitutional protections to their participants. The exception would be youth recreational bodies that are public in nature. Therefore, courts generally are even more deferential to the decisions of private governing bodies, like Pop Warner, USA Football, AYSO, and the AAU, than they are to public governing bodies, like many high school athletic associations. Nevertheless, courts and legislative bodies do oversee some activities of youth athletic governing bodies. In particular, they get involved in health and safety issues. Indeed, courts have long held private entities responsible for torts or personal injuries that they caused through negligence or otherwise. Personal injury law is discussed in detail in Chapters 7 and 8.

As more attention has been directed to health and safety issues — particularly serious head injuries at all levels — it is not surprising that governing entities, courts, and legislative bodies are exercising more authority in those areas in an effort to limit or prevent injuries. This is all the more true in the case of youth sports, where the participants are not as physically developed. The governing bodies themselves regularly take action to protect the health and safety needs of their participants, in the form of playing and related rules. For example, in an effort to limit head injuries and to ensure that participants and their parents that youth football is safe, USA Football has initiated an expansive program entitled "Heads-up Football," which is designed to protect against injuries of all kinds through safety rules and training for coaches. In creating and implementing those rules and training, USA Football and the NFL have teamed with the Centers for Disease Control (CDC). See *http://usafootball.com/coach*.

Head injury cases are proliferating at all levels. There are serious concerns regarding head injuries on the part of younger athletes in particular because studies have confirmed that such injuries have a greater impact on younger brains. There are also concerns that younger people are more impressionable and less able to decide whether they should decline to play for health and safety reasons. It is not surprising, therefore, that schools and governing bodies are facing litigation involving injuries to young participants. In *Limones v. Sch. Dist.*, 161 So. 3d 384 (Fla. 2015), the Florida Supreme Court reiterated that schools have a common law duty to adequately supervise student athletes. The court noted that the school's duties "regarding athletic activities include: 1. Providing adequate instruction, 2. Supplying appropriate equipment, 3. Reasonably selecting or matching athletes, 4. Properly supervising the event, and 5. Utilizing appropriate post injury efforts to protect against aggravation." With the increased knowledge regarding health and safety issues, it is likely that the common law duty will be enforced with greater stringency. But see *Mehr v. FIFA*, 2015 WL 4366044 (N.D. Cal.) (dismissing negligence claims against worldwide, national, and state soccer governing bodies because "[p]laintiffs have alleged no basis for imputing to any defendant a legal duty to reduce the risks inherent in the sport of soccer, or to implement any of the 'Consensus Statement' guidelines or concussion management protocols, and have alleged no facts showing that any defendant took any action that increased the risks beyond those inherent in the sport").

In an Illinois case filed in 2015, *Bukal v. Illinois High School Association*, plaintiffs are seeking to change concussion policies along with improved management and handling of head injuries. This lawsuit seeks to require medical doctors to be on the sidelines of high school sporting events, and to force the governing body, the Illinois High School Association (IHSA), to cover the costs of medical examinations for high school football players back to 2002. Although the IHSA denies that the new implementations are a response to the lawsuit, they have adopted a "Play Smart. Play Hard" initiative, which establishes a council to review current procedures and concussion management best practices. The IHSA argues, as other governing bodies surely would as well, that requiring doctors on staff would create a "have-have not" situation in which less affluent schools would be substantially burdened in an economic sense, which would lead to the dissolution of their football programs. Should the Illinois lawsuit prevail, attorneys might invoke similar strategies in other states. Even if the case is ultimately unsuccessful, the push for stronger safety procedures and protocols is likely to grow.

In the fall of 2015, Florida became the first state to require high school athletes to complete a course on concussions before they are allowed to compete in interscholastic sports. Coaches have been required to take similar online courses, which are free, for five years. Under the new rule, once a player completes the course, his or her parent or parents are required to sign a compliance form on behalf of their child. Participants receive a certificate of completion that remains on file with their coach. The Florida High School Athletic Association (FHSAA) will randomly check to confirm that certificates have been filed for every player on a team. If coaches fail to provide a certificate for every player on their team, the coach will be suspended until every team member completes the course. The rule applies to both noncontact and contact sports.

Legislative bodies are also involved in this area. In 2011, Wisconsin passed an act related to "concussions and other head injuries sustained in youth athletic activities," and the Pennsylvania legislature passed the Safety in Youth Sports Act. In July 2014, the California legislature passed more specific legislation, the Cooley Bill, to protect youth football players by restricting contact practices. That bill restricts schools and coaches to two contact football practices per week in California. It also provides that no contact practice may exceed 90 minutes in length and limits the head impact sustained by middle and high school age participants in an effort to ensure that the incidence of injuries is lessened and players do not return from head injuries too quickly. In January 2015, California passed an additional statute requiring schools that offer athletic programs to remove any athlete suspected of sustaining a concussion for the rest of that day's activities and mandating that the athlete be examined by a licensed health care provider in order to return to play. If a participant has been determined to have sustained a concussion, he or she will be subject to a concussion protocol consisting of a seven-day period of monitoring and testing under the guidance of the licensed health care provider. Participants are also required to submit a head injury form at the beginning of each season as a baseline. Other states and youth organizations may adopt similar statutes or rules as litigation and media attention continue to increase in response to schools and governing bodies that fail to take precautions against foreseeable injuries, and as efforts like those in California have the effect of raising the standard of care.

In 1997, Congress passed the Volunteer Protection Act in an effort to ensure that volunteers would be protected against liability in certain cases, in an effort to ensure that people would continue to volunteer to coach and work in youth athletics. Acts of that sort evidence the tension that is present in this area. On the one hand, there is a desire to protect young participants from injury. On the other hand, there is a recognition that subjecting volunteers (coaches and other personnel) to liability will make it more difficult to provide opportunities for young people to participate in athletics. How those tensions are balanced will have a major impact on youth sports and have to be handled as decisions are made by governing organizations, courts, and legislative bodies.

QUESTIONS

If you were serving as a member of a board of directors of a governing organization, would you recommend adding new health and safety rules and protocols? Do such rules increase the standard of care and make it more likely that the organization and its members will be held to a higher duty of care (i.e., do such actions potentially increase liability)? Do such rules increase the costs for members and participants? If costs increase, is it possible or likely that opportunities to participate may decrease? Do you think the Florida rule requiring the taking of a course by participants was adopted, in part, to protect the school district? Does it protect the school district?

NCAA Internal Governance of Intercollegiate Athletics and Legal Limits

3

INTRODUCTION

This chapter examines the governing authority of the National Collegiate Athletic Association (NCAA) and federal and state law limitations thereon. This chapter begins with a brief overview of the NCAA's general history and its internal governance system, particularly its rules enforcement processes. It then addresses how various federal and state laws, including federal antitrust and civil rights statutes as well as state contract and private associations law, affect the NCAA's regulatory authority. It does not discuss the intersection with Olympic and other "amateur" sports in detail.

A BRIEF HISTORY: NCAA GOVERNANCE OF INTERCOLLEGIATE ATHLETICS

The NCAA includes over 1,000 colleges and universities organized into three divisions based on the nature of their intercollegiate athletic programs. Division I (D-I) offers full athletic scholarships to many of its athletes and is the highest level of competition in most sports; Division II (D-II) also offers athletic scholarships and competes at an intermediate competitive level; and Division III (D-III) does not offer athletic scholarships and is the lowest and most student-centered competitive level. The discussion in this chapter focuses on the most competitive level of competition within the NCAA—namely, D-I. With the passage of so-called autonomy legislation in 2015, five power conferences were given autonomy within the NCAA governance in the form of additional legislative authority, effectively creating another decision-making tier.

There are other associations engaged in the regulation of intercollegiate athletics. The National Association of Intercollegiate Athletics (NAIA) includes more than 360 colleges and universities and conducts numerous national championships. It is also developing programs designed to enhance the experience of student-athletes, including their Champions of Character program that encourages schools to take actions designed to develop character traits among student-athletes. The National Christian College Athletic Association (NCCAA) was incorporated to provide an association for Christ-centered collegiate institutions that are committed to athletic competition as an integral component of education, evangelism, and encouragement. The United States Collegiate Athletic Association (USCAA), another smaller national organization, was organized for the purpose of holding national championships in a number of sports for very small schools. The National Junior College Athletic Association (NJCAA) is made up of more than 500 junior and community colleges throughout 24 regions in the United States that sponsor men's and women's intercollegiate athletic teams, which compete for national championships in three divisions, based on levels of competitiveness. California also has a community college athletic association that governs athletics within California. These collegiate athletic associations have rules and standards by which its member schools are governed and through which student-athletes' participation is regulated, but the focus of this chapter is on the NCAA. Although the rules and governance structures differ among the various national associations that govern intercollegiate athletics, much of what you will learn by examining how the NCAA is legally regulated is relevant to all of these governing bodies.

Students, with some faculty oversight, initially were the major force in running intercollegiate athletics. With the deaths of 18 intercollegiate football players in 1905, President Theodore Roosevelt invited university officials to participate in a White House Conference to review football rules. These efforts to reform football rules led to the formation of a Rules Committee and the formation of the Intercollegiate Athletic Association, which in 1910 was renamed the NCAA.

Interest in intercollegiate sports and attendant increases in commercialization led the highly respected Carnegie Foundation for the Advancement of Education to issue, in 1929, a significant report regarding intercollegiate athletics, which concluded:

> [A] change of values is needed in a field that is sodden with the commercial and the material and the vested interests that these forces have created. Commercialism in college athletics must be diminished and college sport must rise to a point where it is esteemed primarily and sincerely for the opportunities it affords to mature youth.

After the Depression and World War II, with a dramatic increase in access to higher education on the part of all segments of society, largely through government support for returning military personnel to cover the costs of attending college, public interest in intercollegiate athletics expanded significantly. Commercial pressures intensified with the advent of television, the presence of radio in the vast majority of homes in the United States, and the broadcasting of major sporting events. These factors, coupled with a series of gambling scandals and recruiting excesses, caused the NCAA to promulgate additional rules, resulting in an expansion of its governance authority. In 1948, the NCAA enacted the so-called Sanity Code, which was designed to "alleviate the proliferation of exploitive practices in the recruitment of student-athletes."

To enforce the rules in the Sanity Code, the NCAA created the Constitutional Compliance Committee. Neither the Sanity Code with its rules nor the Constitutional Compliance Committee with its enforcement responsibility was particularly successful because the only possible sanction was expulsion, which was so severe that enforcement of the rules was ineffectual.

Two other developments in the 1950s contributed to the transformation of the NCAA into a major regulatory body: (1) Walter Byers became executive director of the NCAA and personally contributed to strengthening the NCAA and its enforcement division; and (2) the NCAA negotiated its first contract to televise intercollegiate football, valued in excess of $1 million, opening the door to increasingly lucrative future television contracts.

In the coming decades, the NCAA gained broader enforcement power but found itself caught between two critiques. On the one hand, it was criticized for responding inadequately to the increased commercialization of intercollegiate athletics, with all its attendant excesses. On the other hand, it was criticized for unfairly exercising its regulatory authority.

In difficult economic times for higher education in the 1980s, presidents increasingly found themselves caught between the pressures applied by influential members of boards of trustees and graduates, who often demanded winning athletic programs, and faculty, who feared the rising commercialization of athletics and its impact on academic values and their institutions' budgets. In the mid-1980s, the presidents became increasingly involved in the governance of intercollegiate athletics through the NCAA, taking some of the power away from athletics directors and faculty representatives who had previously largely controlled governance of intercollegiate athletics.

In 1984, in *NCAA v. Board of Regents of the University of Oklahoma*, 468 U.S. 85 (1984), the U.S. Supreme Court held that the NCAA television plan for D-I football violated federal antitrust law. This decision ultimately gave birth to the Bowl Championship Series (BCS).

In 1989, the Knight Commission, with support in the form of a $2 million grant from the Knight-Ridder newspaper chain, recommended a series of significant reforms that included more presidential involvement and control. The Knight Commission has also become a major force in offering reform recommendations on a periodic basis. The presidents, with guidance from groups like the Knight Commission, began to become increasingly concerned with cost containment and ensuring that academic values continue to be central to the governance of intercollegiate athletics. However, the pressure to produce income largely through the revenue-producing sports of football and men's basketball (and at some institutions, other sports produce revenue as well) has made it difficult to ensure academic values. Nevertheless, the presidents and others have been successful in implementing some reforms that are helping to increase graduation rates of student-athletes participating in the major revenue-producing sports. (See the discussion of academic reform initiatives in Chapter 3.)

With the challenge of budgetary issues associated with achieving gender equity in intercollegiate athletics and proliferating expenses in athletics during difficult economic times, presidents' efforts to gain further control of the NCAA's governance process intensified and resulted in restrictions within the NCAA, giving presidents primary control of legislative and administrative processes within the NCAA and conferences. These efforts, in turn, have led to the consolidation of the most profitable athletics programs into large, major conferences.

The last two decades of the twentieth and the first decade of the twenty-first centuries have been active ones for the NCAA. With the meteoric rise in television and related revenues, the commercialization of intercollegiate athletics continued to grow at a pace that placed significant strain on institutions and the NCAA. These commercial pressures, together with rapidly increasing costs and a budgetary crisis related to a downturn in the economy, have affected both public and private institutions. These challenges make it more difficult to maintain a viable enforcement process and a level playing field while ensuring that student-athletes continue to have an opportunity to obtain an education. Those pressures, coupled with the rise of presidential involvement in the governance of intercollegiate athletics and increasing media attention directed toward issues related to the governance of intercollegiate athletics, have led to major efforts to implement academic reform. Presidential involvement, as evidenced by the hiring of Mark Emmert, former president of the University of Washington, continues. Emmert's hiring has been balanced by increasing involvement on the part of athletics personnel, as evidenced by the hiring of Oliver Luck, a former athletics director at a Power 5 conference member institution, to serve as executive vice president of regulatory affairs reporting directly to President Emmert. After being named as President, Emmert emphasized that his priorities would be to protect "student-athlete well-being and the collegiate model." Issues regarding student welfare and fairness to student-athletes have, indeed, become very significant, although not always in the manner or intensity anticipated by President Emmert.

President Emmert has supported increasing financial aid for student-athletes, worked to develop a commercially successful playoff structure in big-time collegiate football, raised concerns regarding graduation rates and compensation for student-athletes, and drawn increased attention to health and safety for student-athletes. In a controversial act, President Emmert worked in concert with the Executive Committee of the NCAA in 2012 to impose very significant sanctions on Penn State University for the alleged failure of their football coach and president, together with other university officials, to exercise institutional control and deal openly with a sex abuse accusation against a former assistant football coach associated with the university. He also has had to deal with a major academic fraud scandal at the University of North Carolina, an internationally respected academic institution and prominent member of the NCAA.

The NCAA's Committee on Infractions and the Infractions Appeals Committee have also significantly increased sanctions for violations of NCAA rules by members at the highly commercialized D-I level. Under Emmert's leadership, the NCAA also had to acknowledge serious problems within the NCAA's enforcement system as a result of inappropriate investigative actions in a case involving the University of Miami and as a result of criticism raised in other high-profile cases. Those efforts have given rise to a major revamping of the enforcement system.

Questions regarding the NCAA and its values persist, as academic and commercial (i.e., revenue-related) tensions create new crises on a regular basis. Those crises, in turn, contribute to continuing demands for reform within the NCAA.

QUESTIONS

1. If calls for reform, which are common in the media, are not grounded in a sense of the historical development of the regulatory rubric governing intercollegiate athletics, are they likely to be successful?
2. Is President Emmert right when he asserts that highly commercialized athletics programs can and must be consistent with academic values and student-athlete well-being?

NCAA REGULATORY AUTHORITY AND PROCESSES

KEY TERMS
- Committee on Infractions (COI)
- Infractions Appeals Committee (IAC)
- Lack of institutional control
- Order to show cause
- Unethical conduct

A. NCAA: History of Regulation and the Rules Infractions Process

The NCAA is an association of colleges and universities that develops rules and regulations for the governance of intercollegiate athletics among those member institutions. Those rules and regulations are the product of legislation that is generally developed and proposed by member institutions and committees within the NCAA, which are made up of representatives from member institutions. Full-time employees of the NCAA assist in executing and enforcing those rules.

In 1954, to ensure fairness and a level playing field in intercollegiate athletics, the NCAA formed the Committee on Infractions (COI) to interpret NCAA rules and impose penalties on member institutions for rules violations. Concerns were frequently raised regarding the allegedly unfair manner in which the COI imposed sanctions against member institutions and others, such as coaches, for NCAA rules violations. For example, in the late 1970s, Jerry Tarkanian asserted that the NCAA and its COI violated his federal due process rights by finding him guilty of NCAA rules violations and effectively requiring his termination as coach of the University of Nevada, Las Vegas (UNLV) men's basketball team, despite a UNLV internal investigation finding that he had not violated any NCAA rules. In a 1988 landmark decision, *NCAA v. Tarkanian*, 488 U.S. 179 (1988), the U.S. Supreme Court held that the NCAA is not a state actor, freeing it from having to comply with federal constitutional requirements such as providing due process in its rules enforcement proceedings. In other words, the NCAA does not have to provide constitutionally mandated procedural due process safeguards in its investigative or rules enforcement process to its member institutions and others defending themselves in proceedings before the COI. (*Tarkanian* is discussed in Chapter 1 in comparison to the *Brentwood Academy I* case, in which the Supreme Court ruled that a state high school athletic association is a state actor and subject to federal constitutional limitations.)

After *Tarkanian*, NCAA member institutions continued to be concerned about the need for greater procedural due process in NCAA rules enforcement proceedings. A Special Committee to Review the National Collegiate Athletic Association Enforcement and Infractions Process (Review Committee) was formed to evaluate the NCAA's rules enforcement process. In 1991, the Review Committee issued a report that included a series of recommended reforms designed to ensure that the NCAA operated in a more timely, fair, and consistent manner. For both political and fairness reasons, the NCAA voluntarily adopted most of these recommendations, which provide institutions and others indirectly subject to the NCAA's regulatory authority (e.g., coaches) with enhanced procedural due process protections. In 1993, the NCAA created the Infractions Appeals Committee (IAC), whose function is to review the COI's findings and sanctions, which was one of the Review Committee's recommendations. Working collectively, the COI, IAC, Management Council, conferences, and member institutions and their personnel play the critical role in fulfilling the mission of the NCAA enforcement program, which is summarized in Bylaw 19, at pages 313-335 in the 2014-2015 *NCAA Manual*. Bylaw 19.01.1, on page 313, sets forth the mission of the infractions program:

> It is the mission of the NCAA infractions program to uphold integrity and fair play among the NCAA membership, and to prescribe appropriate and fair penalties if violations occur. One of the fundamental principles of the infractions program is to ensure that those institutions and student-athletes abiding by the NCAA constitution and bylaws are not disadvantaged by their commitment to compliance. The program is committed to the fairness of procedures and the timely resolution of infractions cases. The ability to investigate allegations and penalize infractions is critical to the common interests of the Association's membership and the preservation of its enduring values.

Bylaw 19.01.2, in turn, provides that "The infractions program shall hold institutions, coaches, administrators, and student-athletes who violate the NCAA constitution and bylaws accountable for their conduct, both at the individual and institutional levels." Id. at page 313.

As a result, in part, of criticism leveled against the NCAA for mishandling the University of Miami investigation and for perceived unfairness, or unequal treatment, in its enforcement processes, the NCAA adopted a major reform of the enforcement and penalty structure by moving to four, rather than two, levels or categories of violations.

A series of helpful figures and graphic summaries of the infractions penalty structure and guidelines appear on pages 331-333, including a very helpful summary of the recently adopted four-level penalty structure that can found in Bylaws 19.1.1

(Level I Violation: Severe Breach of Conduct), 19.1.2 (Level II Violation: Significant Breach of Conduct), 19.1.3 (Level III Violation: Breach of Conduct), and 19.1.4 (Level IV Violation: Incidental Violations). Also see *http://www.ncaa.org/enforcement ?division=d1* for a discussion of the substance of the new infractions structure. For a discussion of the penalties for violations at the various levels, see *http://www.ncaa.org/ sites/default/files/Figure19-1.pdf.*

The following excerpts from reported decisions of the IAC are illustrative of procedural and substantive issues that often arise in the NCAA rules enforcement process. Given the nature of these cases, it is clear that institutions need to develop educational, monitoring, and compliance programs for athletic department personnel, coaches, student-athletes, and others who deal with the detailed rules and regulations that govern intercollegiate athletics. These cases were decided under the former two-level enforcement system (i.e., major and minor infractions). As you read the cases, think about how they might be decided differently under the new four-level enforcement structure.

B. Institutional Violations of NCAA Rules and Sanctions

In the enforcement process, the COI and the IAC have the authority to impose penalties on NCAA member institutions for rules violations by institutional personnel (e.g., athletics administrators, coaches, boosters) and student-athletes. Two important issues that arise in the infractions process are whether the conduct and activities of the institution demonstrate a lack of institutional control or a failure to monitor compliance with NCAA rules.

The following decisions and discussion provide illustrative examples of a university's lack of institutional control or failure to monitor that resulted in violations of NCAA extra benefits, amateurism, ethical conduct, and/or academic integrity rules.

University of Southern California Infractions Appeals Committee Report No. 323
May 26, 2011

[Editors' note: The COI found that the University of Southern California (USC) had acted in a manner evidencing a lack of institutional control relating to impermissible inducements, extra benefits, and exceeding staff limits. In a separate proceeding, the COI also found that a coach had engaged in unethical conduct. According to the COI's report, "The general campus environment surrounding the violations troubled the committee." The COI indicated that the university failed to heed clear warning signs, did not have proper controls in place to monitor rules compliance, failed to regulate access to locker rooms and practice facilities, and in some instances failed to be proactive in investigating concerns.

Between 2004 and 2005, a former star (elite) football student-athlete and his family members formed a partnership with two individuals to create a sports agency. After that agreement was entered into, the student-athlete and his family asked for and received substantial financial assistance from the partners of the agency. The receipt of those benefits rendered the student-athlete ineligible to play in intercollegiate athletics. Early in 2006, one of the agency partners contacted an assistant football coach asking for assistance in convincing the student-athlete to adhere to his agreement with the agency. The assistant coach, however, failed to notify university compliance staff of this potential violation and thereafter provided false and misleading information to the NCAA's enforcement staff, which ultimately resulted in the COI finding that the coach had violated ethical conduct rules. The former football student-athlete and his family and friends received benefits from another sports marketing agency during 2005–2006. The former football student-athlete, who went on to play professional football, refused to cooperate fully with the NCAA's investigation.

The case also included multiple impermissible inducements from a sports agent or representative to a former star (elite) basketball student-athlete and his family and friends. The former head men's basketball coach, the assistant men's basketball coach, an institutional compliance staff member, a faculty athletics representative, and the athletics director all knew that this representative had previously committed two separate NCAA violations. Nevertheless, they did not take steps to monitor the relationship between the player and the representative.

The COI concluded that the football program violated coaching staff limit rules by hiring a consultant who analyzed video footage, attended practices, and discussed his observations with the coach. The COI also found that a former tennis student-athlete used an athletics department long-distance access code to make 123 unauthorized international telephone calls valued at over $7,000.

The COI acknowledged the difficulty that attends investigating matters involving violation of amateurism rules. In determining the penalties to be imposed, the COI considered the university's self-imposed penalties but felt that they were inadequate given the gravity of the violations.

The penalties imposed by the COI included four years of probation, public reprimand and censure, a two-year postseason ban for football, a one-year postseason ban for men's basketball, vacation of regular and postseason wins for all three involved sports, scholarship reductions for football and men's basketball, recruiting restrictions for men's basketball, a $5,000 penalty, forfeiture of $206,200 in revenue from the 2008 NCAA Division I Men's Basketball Championship, and limitations for the access granted to boosters and on-university personnel to team charters, practices, locker rooms, and so forth. The COI also mandated that the university dissociate itself from three boosters, including former football and men's basketball student-athletes.

On appeal, the university raised the following issues: reduction of the penalties on the ground that they "are not supported by the facts and are excessive" and that some of the COI's findings of violations "are contrary to the evidence, based upon facts that do not constitute a violation and compromised by a procedural error."]

Findings of Violations

The institution argues the following with respect to findings of violations:

- *The finding of unethical conduct is "contrary to the evidence, based on incompetent evidence and compromised procedural error. . . ."*

While this argument was included in the institution's appeal, [it lacks standing] to appeal that finding since it was made against the institution's former football coach and not the institution itself.

- *The [COI] "erred in concluding that the [sports marketers] were representatives of USC's athletic interests. . . ."*

The institution specifically takes issue with the [COI's] findings that [the sports marketers] "became representatives of USC's athletics interests by hiring three USC student-athletes" and that "summer positions were created exclusively for USC student-athletes." The [COI] "weighed conflicting evidence" and ultimately concluded that the internship at least initially was created exclusively for student-athletes of the institution. [Citations to record omitted throughout.]

We are persuaded that there is sufficient evidence to support the [COI's] conclusions regarding these issues and find no basis on which to reverse the pertinent findings.

- *The [COI's] finding of lack of institutional control "should be set aside because some of the facts found by the committee did not constitute a violation of NCAA rules, and the committee failed to consider a number of factors."*

One of the institution's principal arguments regarding this point is that the [COI] based its finding of lack of institutional control on a "heightened duty" to monitor elite student-athletes, and that "NCAA bylaws do not set forth any 'heightened duty' standard, nor do they differentiate between 'elite' athletes and other student-athletes." However, we do not see the COI's statements as establishing a new or different standard not permitted by the applicable bylaws. Rather, we note the COI's explanation that "high profile athletes at a high profile program are at greater risk and need to be more vigilantly monitored," and its corollary conclusion that at this institution the "resources committed to compliance were inadequate. . . ."

[W]e find no basis on which to reverse the COI's finding of lack of institutional control. More particularly, but without limitation, there was evidence sufficient to permit the COI to determine that the institution had devoted inadequate resources to its compliance program, especially when the institution had devoted inadequate resources to its compliance program especially when the institution learned that problems with the compliance program were developing.

Penalties

The institution argues that penalties imposed by the COI were excessive and to that extent constituted an abuse of discretion. More specifically, the institution argues that

(a) the COI "has imposed significantly lesser sanctions in major infractions cases based on similar violations"; (b) "abused its discretion in imposing a two-year post-season ban and drastic scholarship reductions in football for violations in this case"; and (c) "the scholarship reductions are excessive, particularly when considering their unintended impact."

The committee (IAC) stated in the Alabama State case as follows:

> An abuse of discretion in the imposition of a penalty occurs if the penalty: (1) was not based on a correct legal standard or was based on a misapprehension of the underlying substantive legal principles; (2) was based on a clearly erroneous factual finding; (3) failed to consider and weigh material factors; (4) was based on a clear error of judgment, such that the imposition was arbitrary, capricious, or irrational; or (5) was based in significant part on one or more irrelevant or improper factors. . . .

Guided by that standard, we find no abuse of discretion in the imposition of either the two-year postseason ban or the grants-in-aid reduction. We note in particular the COI's recognition that this was the institution's sixth major infractions case involving football, and that the institution had last been before the COI in June 2001, fewer than four years before the violations which occurred in this case. Thus, the institution was a "repeat-violator" under Bylaw 19.5.2.3 and therefore at risk for enhanced penalties set forth in Bylaw 19.2.5.2.3.2. As the COI stated in response to the institution's appeal:

> Although the COI ultimately chose not to impose any of the enhanced penalties, it noted that "stiff sanctions are warranted in light of the serious violations found by the subcommittee and the fact that the institution is a "repeat violator." Those stiff penalties are particularly warranted because the school failed to take to heart the lessons it should have learned in 2001.

Thus, we believe that the penalties imposed make clear to the institutions the message which the COI intended to convey:

> Similar strong penalties will be meted out to institutions that do [not] take the problem of sports agents and their runners seriously. It is not enough for the institutions simply to educate student athletes about the dangers of unscrupulous agents. Schools must have appropriate staff and procedures in place to combat this significant problem. An institution that does not foster a climate of compliance on its campus should expect serious consequences.

In reaching this decision, [the IAC] closely considered both the institution and the COI's substantial arguments regarding the application to this case of prior decisions of both the COI and [IAC]. Indeed, we have recognized since the University of Mississippi (May 1, 1995) case that a "factor of particular significance in considering an appeal of penalties is the review and analysis of the penalty or penalties imposed when compared with the penalty or penalties imposed in other cases with similar characteristics. However, we also stated in the 2002 University of Alabama case that "the COI must have latitude in tailoring remedies to the particular circumstances involved in each case and that the universe of relevant cases is not static, but evolving." Given this latitude afforded the COI, there is no basis on which to conclude that the COI departed from prior decisions, much less to any impermissible extent.

The institution placed particular reliance on the COI's decision in the 1996 Florida State case, arguing that the case "illustrates how the COI historically has penalized universities for amateurism violations." While the institution's observations regarding the case may be correct, we also make clear that the principle of guidance from prior decisions is not an unyielding directive. It is instead a matter of considered judgment to be applied along with all other factors which this committee has recognized should guide the COI and IAC. And, one very important factor in the application of that principle, and in determining the extent to which a prior decision should guide a present decision, is change in the matters to which the decisions of the COI and IAC are directed. The COI should not be strictly bound to a decision made fifteen years earlier, when the circumstances of intercollegiate athletics were qualitatively different than those which presently obtain. This, of course, does not mean that prior decisions provide no restraint on or guidance to the COI and IAC, or that insignificant changes in the environment in which NCAA member institutions operate can justify ignoring those prior decisions. It means only that the guidance provided by prior decisions is, and always has been, a matter of judgment. In this case, we cannot say that the COI improperly exercised that judgment.

QUESTIONS

1. The USC case involved violations of amateurism rules regulating student-athletes' relationships with agents or representatives (boosters). Is the amateurism principle consistent with the operation of highly commercialized intercollegiate athletics in major revenue-producing sports (generally football and men's basketball) at schools like USC? The NCAA permits institutions to pay student-athletes a cash stipend in addition to tuition, room and board, fees, and books to cover the full cost of attendance at the university. Does the adoption of such legislation constitute recognition on the part of the NCAA that student-athletes should be "paid more"? Is the possibility of graduation (along with payment of the full cost of attendance) sufficient compensation for student-athletes in revenue-producing sports, or should they receive additional cash payments?

2. The NCAA and conferences require that institutions demonstrate that they are exercising adequate institutional control over their athletics programs. What did USC do (or fail to do) that constituted a lack of institutional control? What can be done to ensure that there is sufficient institutional control?

3. In the concluding paragraphs of its opinion, the IAC discusses the role of precedent (i.e., prior decisions) regarding penalties. How much reliance may an athletic administrator place on decisions of the IAC and COI? What is the impact of this lack of certainty on the operation of athletics programs? Does this indicate

that the NCAA is now committed to imposing more stringent sanctions? If so, what is its objective in doing so?

4. Bylaw 6.4.2, on page 42 of the 2014-2015 *NCAA Manual*, provides that an institution is responsible for actions taken by boosters, donors, or other individuals associated with the athletics program. USC was held responsible for the actions of certain "representatives" — individuals associated with the athletic department. In 2002, the IAC upheld strong sanctions against the University of Alabama (which like USC was a repeat violator) for the actions of certain individuals in using inducements (money) to try to recruit athletes to the university. In the Southern Methodist University (SMU) case, involving a repeat offender and decided in 1987, the NCAA imposed what has been referred to as the "death penalty" for SMU's football program, shutting it down for two years, which effectively decimated the program for many years. The COI and the IAC declined to impose the death penalty in the USC or Alabama case, even though in each one, the university was a repeat offender involved in major infractions. Why do you think the NCAA declined to impose the death penalty in these cases? When should it consider the imposition of the death penalty?

5. In the public infractions report of December 20, 2011, in a case concerning The Ohio State University (Ohio State), the COI acknowledged that the university "was diligent in its efforts to monitor and track awards and other items provided to football student-athletes," but it went on to find that "[t]he institution failed to monitor the representative [booster,] including his interaction with and employment of football student-athletes." The COI added that the "failure to monitor" constituted an "aggravating factor in imposing [major] competition restrictions," which justified a one-year ban from participation in a football bowl game. The COI referred to the Alabama infractions decision in 2002 and reiterated that "favored access and insider status creates both a greater university obligation to monitor and a greater university responsibility for any misconduct in which such individuals engage." Jim Tressel, Ohio State's tremendously successful head coach, was also pressured to resign based on his ethical misconduct in failing to cooperate in the NCAA's investigation. (Ironically, the coach was shortly thereafter named president of Youngstown State University, a D-I member institution.) The USC and Ohio State cases make it clear that failure to monitor will result in costly sanctions for the most competitive and commercially lucrative programs. What can be done in such cases to ensure that adequate monitoring is in place?

6. On February 27, 2008, the Division II (D-II) IAC determined that Lane University failed to detect and report NCAA rules violations even after numerous letters of inquiry, an investigation, and evidence that infractions were occurring. Even though this was the first major infractions case for the university, the athletic director had all his athletic duties terminated, and any institution hiring him within four years would be required to show cause why it should not be penalized for permitting him to work in athletics during this period (a four-year order to show cause). *Lane* evidences a willingness by the NCAA, at all levels, to hold athletics and other university personnel responsible for the failure to cooperate and investigate.

THE PENN STATE UNIVERSITY CASE

On November 17, 2011, NCAA President Emmert wrote a letter to Penn State President Rodney Erickson in which he stated, in pertinent part:

> As we have discussed, on November 5, 2011, the NCAA first learned about allegations of sexual abuse of young boys occurring in the athletic facilities of Pennsylvania State University, perpetrated by a former assistant head football coach. Further, at the same time the NCAA learned that these alleged acts occurred over two decades and that individuals with present or former coaching responsibilities may have been aware of this behavior. The recount of these tragic events in the Grand Jury Report is deeply troubling, and if true, individuals who were in a position to monitor and act upon learning of potential abuses appear to have been acting starkly contrary to the values of higher education, as well as the NCAA. I am writing to notify you that the NCAA will examine Penn State's exercise of institutional control over its intercollegiate athletics program, as well as the actions, and inactions, of relevant responsible personnel. . . .

President Emmert then stated the NCAA constitutional and bylaw provisions requiring institutional control, monitoring, and ethical conduct and asked for Penn State's response to the following questions:

1. How has Penn State and/or its employees complied with the Articles of the [NCAA] Constitution and bylaws [implicated in this case];
2. How has Penn State exercised institutional control over the issues identified in and related to the Grand Jury Report? Were there procedures in place that were or were not followed? What are the institution's expectations and policies to address conduct that has been alleged in this matter upon discovery by any party?
3. Have each of the alleged persons to have been involved or have notice of the issues identified in and related [to this matter] behaved consistent with principles and requirements governing ethical conduct and honesty? If so, how? If not, how?
4. What policies and procedures does Penn State have in place to monitor, prevent, and detect the issues identified in [this case,] or to take disciplinary or corrective action if such behaviors are found?" . . .

Penn State responded by hiring the law firm of Judge Louis Freeh, a former FBI director, to investigate the matter. In compiling that report, Freeh's law firm and those working with them interviewed 430 university and other individuals and reviewed over 3.5 million e-mails and documents. The Freeh report concluded, "Our most saddening finding is the total disregard [by Penn State officials] for the safety and welfare of [the abuse] victims."

Rather than engaging in further investigation or hearings, President Emmert and the leadership of the NCAA stated that the Freeh report chronicled "an unprecedented failure of institutional integrity leading to a culture in which a football program was held in higher esteem than the values of the institution, the values of the NCAA, the values of higher education, and most disturbingly the values of human decency."

It also pressured the university to enter into a consent decree pursuant to the findings of the Freeh report, which imposed a $60 million sanction on the university (a sum equal to the average gross annual revenue generated by the football program). That penalty was to be placed in an endowment to support national programs designed to prevent child sexual abuse. The sanctions also included a four-year postseason ban from college football and included a vacating of all the team's wins from 1998 through 2011, which were to be reflected in the record of its legendary coach Joe Paterno. Other penalties included a reduction in scholarships. In addition, Penn State was placed on probation and required to enter into an Athletics Integrity Agreement, which mandated the appointment of an independent Athletics Integrity Monitor who would provide regular reports to the NCAA. Former U.S. Senator George Mitchell was appointed to serve as the first monitor.

In an effort to avoid potentially stronger sanctions to their football program, including the possibility of the death penalty, and in an effort to demonstrate their commitment to the values shared with other NCAA members, Penn State cooperated with the NCAA and quickly agreed to the consent decree. From the outset, concerns were raised regarding the propriety of the consent decree and the authority of the NCAA to sanction Penn State for actions related to the child abuse scandal. President Emmert responded to such criticism by stating, "We cannot look to NCAA history to determine how to handle circumstances so disturbing, shocking, and disappointing . . . As the individuals charged with governing college sports, we have a responsibility to act. These events should serve as a call to every single school and athletics department to take an honest look at its campus environment and eradicate the 'sports are king' mindset that can so dramatically cloud the judgment of educators."

Some scholars expressed concerns regarding whether the NCAA overstepped its authority and failed to comply with its own rules in disciplining Penn State. See, e.g., Matthew J. Mitten, *The NCAA's Unprecedented Disciplinary Action Against Pennsylvania State University: Its Coercive Means Don't Justify the Laudable Ends, But Is There A Legal Remedy?*, 41 Pepp. L. Rev. 321 (2014). Lawsuits were filed on behalf of Coach Paterno, who had died of cancer during the aftermath of the consent decree. Monitoring reports from Senator Mitchell found that Penn State had moved effectively to deal with the underlying cultural problems that had contributed to the university's cover-up or failure to disclose matters related to the child abuse accusations. Armed with those findings — and, no doubt, in response to continuing criticism — the NCAA began the process of lifting the sanctions, beginning with the scholarship limitations and then moving to the postseason ban, in part due to a recognition that such limits harmed student-athletes who bore no responsibility for Penn State's handling of the matter.

In an apparent response to the Penn State consent decree, the Commonwealth of Pennsylvania enacted the Institution of Higher Education Monetary Penalty Endowment Act, mandating that the fine assessed against Penn State be paid to the treasury of Pennsylvania. A suit was filed by the Commonwealth under the Act to require the NCAA to comply with this requirement. A series of embarrassing e-mails written by NCAA personnel were released late in the fall of 2014, as the Commonwealth of Pennsylvania's case was proceeding to trial. On January 16, 2015, as part of a settlement in the lawsuit brought by Pennsylvania, the NCAA entered into a new consent decree with Penn State University that reinstated the wins vacated in the prior consent decree and stipulated the following (*http://www.ncaa.org/about/resources/ media-center/news/ncaa-reaches-proposed-settlement-corman-lawsuit*):

- Penn State agree[d] to commit a total of $60 million to activities and programs for the prevention of child sexual abuse and the treatment of victims of child sexual abuse.
- Penn State acknowledge[d] the NCAA's legitimate and good-faith interest and concern regarding the [child sex abuse] matter.
- Penn State and the NCAA would enter into a new Athletics Integrity Agreement (with the concurrence of the Big Ten) that includes best practices with which the university [was] committed to comply and that provides for the university to continue to retain the services of Sen. George Mitchell and his firm to support the university's activities under the Athletics Integrity Agreement and in the areas of compliance, ethics, and integrity.

QUESTIONS

1. It has been argued that the NCAA did not have any authority to intervene in a case involving sexual abuse of young boys by a former coach. Proponents of this position argue that it should have been left to the legal system, which found the coach guilty of multiple counts. Opponents of the action also argue that the NCAA acted improvidently when it did not follow its own hearing and investigative processes, instead choosing to simply rely on the Freeh report, which had been commissioned by Penn State. Do you agree? Was it wise for the NCAA to act promptly? Why do you think it did so? Should the NCAA have intervened? What repercussions would the NCAA potentially have suffered if they failed to intervene in this high-profile case? Can it be argued that Penn State did, in fact, seek to receive some competitive advantage (or at least avoid a major disadvantage) by covering up the child abuse scandal?
2. The sanctions in this case were "unprecedented." Do you think they were excessive? It has been reported that the NCAA leadership seriously considered the suspension of the football program (the death penalty). Should they have invoked the death penalty?
3. The USC, Ohio State, and Penn State cases appear to be evidence that the NCAA is taking a much stronger role in sanctioning infractions occurring at institutions with commercially successful and well-known football and athletic programs. Why is it doing this?

The Penn State, USC, and Ohio State cases involved major coaches, who were also penalized by removal from their coaching positions. In the Penn State case, other university personnel, including the athletics director and president were removed from their positions by the university. The following section examines the sanctioning of coaches and other personnel in more detail.

THE UNIVERSITY OF MIAMI CASE

On October 22, 2013, the COI issued its decision in a high-profile case involving the University of Miami that had garnered significant public attention, particularly because the NCAA enforcement staff had improperly obtained information in handling the case. The NCAA's investigator had collaborated with a lawyer, who agreed to obtain testimony, under oath, from a witness in a separate judicial matter. That witness had refused to cooperate in the NCAA's investigation. The NCAA is unable to force a witness to testify under oath, so it used this rather surreptitious method to obtain testimony related to its investigation of the University of Miami. NCAA President Mark Emmert acknowledged that the manner in which that evidence was obtained was "shocking." In evaluating the facts and imposing sanctions, the NCAA further noted that, "the [Committee on Infractions] only considered information obtained appropriately during the investigative process and presented at the hearing. . . . [The case involved serious violations of NCAA rules] including 18 general allegations of misconduct with 79 issues within those allegations. These were identified through an investigation that included 118 interviews of 81 individuals. Additionally, the committee had the responsibility of determining the credibility of individuals who submitted inconsistent statements and information provided by a booster who is now in federal prison. In reaching its conclusions, the committee found, in most instances, corroboration through supporting documentation and the statements of individuals other than the booster." See *University of Miami Lacked Institutional Control, Resulting in a Decade of Violations,* NCAA.com, Oct. 22, 2013, *http://www.ncaa.org/about/resources/media-center/press-releases/university-miami-lacked-institutional-control-resulting-decade-violations.*

In sanctioning Miami, the COI also acknowledged that the university had cooperated in the investigation and had self-imposed major sanctions, including bowl and league championship bans. After concluding that the university "lacked institutional control" for over a decade in many of its programs by failing to monitor a major booster, coaches, and student-athletes, the COI censured and then sanctioned the university with three years of probation, a loss of 12 scholarships (9 in football and 3 in basketball), and numerous other lesser sanctions applicable to men's football, basketball, baseball, and track and field, as well as women's swimming and diving, basketball, soccer, track and field, rowing, and tennis. Two former assistant football coaches and one assistant basketball coach received two-year show cause orders. Even the former associate athletics director for compliance received a letter of admonishment. The COI's decision can be found at *http://www.ncaa.org/about/resources/media-center/press-releases/university-miami-lacked-institutional-control-resulting-decade-violations.* Miami's president criticized the severity of the decision, despite the fact that the COI maintained that the ill-gotten evidence had not been used.

The COI was criticized for inconsistency in applying its sanctions after the Miami case. In an ESPN report on the decision, USC's athletics director, Pat Haden, for example, is quoted as having responded to the COI's decision by stating, "[w]e have always felt that our penalties were too harsh. This decision only bolsters that view."

Andrea Adelson, *No Bowl Ban for Miami Hurricanes,* ESPN.com, Oct. 23, 2013, *http://espn.go.com/college-sports/story/_/id/9861775/miami-hurricanes-avoid-bowl-ban-lose-nine-scholarships-part-ncaa-sanctions.*

The problems in the *Miami* case led to a major shake-up in the enforcement staff at the NCAA, which slowed the enforcement process. The *Miami* decision also may have contributed to the move to make changes in the enforcement process itself. In July 2014, at the same time that the autonomy legislation was gaining momentum and President Emmert was appearing before the Senate Commerce Committee defending the actions of the NCAA in the handling of enforcement matters and other issues, Bob Bowlsby, commissioner of the Big 12 Conference, attacked the NCAA enforcement process, stating, "Enforcement is broken . . . The infractions committee hasn't had a hearing in almost a year [since the decision in the University of Miami case], and I think it's not an understatement to say that cheating pays presently. If you seek to conspire to certainly bend the rules, you do it successfully and probably do not get caught on most occasions." See *Big 12 Commissioner Blasts Lack of NCAA Enforcement,* Insider Higher Education, July 22, 2014, *http://www.insidehighered.com/quicktakes/2014/07/22/big-12-commissioner-blasts-lack-ncaa-enforcement.* Jonathan Duncan, who had recently been hired to direct the NCAA's enforcement division after the improprieties in the University of Miami case, responded, "We don't pretend to be able to catch every violation in a given year. [But] the people who violate rules will be found out, and we will report them back to the committee on infractions." Duncan added that there could be more than 20 major infraction cases heard during the coming year. *NCAA Enforcement Chief Fires Back,* ESPN.com, July 24, 2014, *http://espn.go.com/college-football/story/_/id/11256975/ncaa-enforcement-director-jonathan-duncan-defends-investigators.* See Timothy Davis & Christopher Todd Hairston, *Majoring in Infractions: The Evolution of the National Collegiate Athletic Association's Enforcement Structure,* 92 Oregon L. Rev. 979 (2014) (discussing changes to the NCAA's enforcement processes).

QUESTIONS

What lessons can be learned from the Miami decision? Is the NCAA facing a near-impossible task in trying to effectively regulate highly commercialized intercollegiate sports?

THE UNIVERSITY OF NORTH CAROLINA CASE

On March 12, 2012, the COI determined that the University of North Carolina, Chapel Hill (UNC) was responsible for multiple violations, including academic fraud, involving a former coach and a former tutor, who had been involved in working with student-athletes. Both were found to have engaged in unethical conduct, including failure to cooperate. The university was also penalized with a one-year postseason ban, reduction of 15 football scholarships, vacating of records, and three years of probation. After that decision was rendered, new and extremely serious allegations of academic fraud involving thousands of students, many of whom were student-athletes, over an 18-year period began to surface, due initially to revelations disclosed to the media. In response to those reports, in June 2014, the NCAA released a statement indicating that it had reopened its investigation of UNC. One year later, the NCAA issued a notice of allegations to the University of North Carolina, noting, "It is important to remember the following information about the NCAA members' rules on academic misconduct:

- "An NCAA member school is responsible for determining if violations of its academic standards occurred.
- "Schools are responsible for the quality of the degree programs offered for all students, including student-athletes. Generally, academic issues are managed first and foremost by the faculty member in the classroom, second by that faculty member's department head, next by their dean, then the provost, and finally the president or chancellor. NCAA rules do not address course curriculum, rigor, or content.
- "Ultimately, member schools must determine if the courses for which they are giving credit and the degrees they are awarding meet the academic standards of the school and its overall mission.
- "While schools are in the best position to determine compliance with academic standards on campus, the enforcement staff will consider if other infractions occurred.
- "These might include violations of progress toward degree requirements, extra benefit rules or ethical conduct obligations. Any alleged violation of NCAA rules would be investigated and decided through the formal infractions process." See *NCAA Sends Notice of Allegations to University of North Carolina, http://www.ncaa.org/about/resources/media-center/news/ncaa-sends-notice-allegations-university-north-carolina*.

The university hired an independent investigator who found that, in fact, thousands of students received credit for fraudulent or fake classes. He also found that counselors had directed student-athletes into the classes in an effort to keep them eligible. The university fired four employees and disciplined five others, and it can be anticipated that more actions will be taken. On August 14, 2015, UNC disclosed additional violations in women's basketball and men's soccer and submitted its report to the NCAA enforcement staff. The new violations in women's basketball involved the providing of improper assistance by a tutor, whereas, the soccer violations involved recruiting violations.

When finally resolved by the NCAA enforcement process, the UNC case will be a major, perhaps historic, case. It is already influencing policy regarding the handling of academic matters. While current NCAA rules permit some involvement in academic matters on the part of the association, that role is limited. However, the academic misconduct charges against UNC have raised new concerns for the NCAA. In part as a result of the nature and extent of academic misconduct issues raised in the North Carolina case, the NCAA responded at the D-I level by directing the

Committee on Academics to consider how the NCAA should respond to issues of academic misconduct. On June 26, 2015, the NCAA announced that its Committee on Academics, in collaboration with the Committee on Infractions and the Legislative Committee, recommended new legislative proposals that will set "expectations for athletics staff and student-athletes [and] define academic misconduct and impermissible academic assistance." The NCAA stated "The proposal . . . strives to strike the appropriate balance between the sentiment that there should be significant deference to member campuses on issues related to academic misconduct and the belief that the NCAA must ensure a consistent national approach in certain circumstances." See *Division I to Consider Tougher Academic Integrity Policies, http://www.ncaa.org/about/resources/media-center/news/division-i-consider-tougher-academic-integrity-policies.* The legislative proposals recommended by the joint committee would extend the power of the Committee on Infractions to some academic matters that have previously been handled at the institutional level. The proposed legislation, which has not been adopted, defines impermissible academic assistance as:

- "Substantial academic assistance to a student-athlete not generally available to the school's students or not expressly authorized by other Division I rules that causes the student to be declared eligible, receive aid, or earn an Academic Progress Rate point.
- "Creating an academic exception for a student-athlete to improve a grade, earn credit, or meet a graduation requirement that is not generally available to the rest of the student body and that causes the student to be declared eligible, receive aid, or earn an Academic Progress Rate point falsely."

It can be anticipated that the debate regarding these proposals, which could hold athletics and academic personnel responsible under NCAA rules for involvement in academic misconduct that has traditionally been handled at the institutional level, will be closely scrutinized by member institutions. Under the proposed rules, the NCAA would play a significant role in some "academic" matters that have historically been the sole responsibility of institutions.

QUESTIONS

Should the NCAA get involved in academic matters of this sort? Why might institutions oppose such legislation? Why do you think the NCAA has decided to enter this area? What penalties or sanctions do you believe should be self-imposed by UNC or imposed by the COI?

C. Individual Responsibility for NCAA Rules Violations and Sanctions

In addition to penalties assessed against institutions for lack of institutional control and other infractions, institutions, conferences, and ultimately the COI can fashion penalties to deal with NCAA rule violations by coaches and other personnel. Bylaw 10.1 addresses "unethical conduct" on the part of a student-athlete or staff member (coach, professor, tutor, student manager, etc.). It generally notes that failure to cooperate in an investigation, involvement in academic fraud, providing extra benefits, dishonesty, and inappropriate interaction with an agent constitute possible examples of unethical conduct. Under Bylaw 11.1.1, a head coach is presumed to be responsible for the actions of all institutional staff members who report to the coach, directly or indirectly. A head coach is required to promote an atmosphere of compliance within his or her program and must monitor the activities of all institutional staff members involved with the program who report, directly or indirectly, to the coach.

A seminal IAC decision involved Coach Clem Haskins, the head men's basketball coach at the University of Minnesota. The COI found that Haskins had engaged in myriad violations of NCAA rules, and their response illustrates the kinds of penalties that can result when a coach or other member of the athletics department engages in actions that violate NCAA rules. Haskins ultimately lost his coaching position and effectively was precluded from coaching at an NCAA member institution in the future. Other members of the athletics department were also removed from their positions as a part of the university's efforts to demonstrate it had taken adequate corrective efforts in response to its investigation of facts related to possible NCAA rules violations.

Former Head Men's Basketball Coach University of Minnesota, Twin Cities Public Infractions Appeals Committee Report

April 6, 2001

[Editors' note: The COI found major infractions consisting of (1) academic fraud — from 1994 to 1998, a secretary prepared coursework consisting of typing, composing papers, completing homework assignments, and preparing take-home exams for at least 18 men's basketball student-athletes; (2) provision of extra benefits — from the 1994–1995 through the 1998–1999 academic years, the men's basketball coaching staff provided substantially discounted rates at a local hotel for parents and friends of men's basketball student-athletes, and the head coach and other basketball coaches provided cash payments to men's basketball student-athletes; (3) improper recruiting inducements — the head coach invited a prospective student-athlete to his home for dinner; and (4) supplement pay provisions — the head coach made monthly car lease payments for the academic counselor without the knowledge of university administrators. The COI found that the head coach violated the principle of ethical conduct by "(1) committing the violations alleged against him in this report; (2) providing false and misleading information during interviews with the university and NCAA enforcement staff; and (3) directing the four men's basketball student-athletes named in the Pioneer Press to give false and misleading information to the university regarding their involvement in the academic fraud." It also found that the head coach committed a secondary violation.]

IV. Penalties Imposed by the Committee on Infractions

The Committee on Infractions imposed additional penalties because of the seriousness of the violations and "because they involved the active complicity of the head coach and because they involved a men's basketball program for which the university previously had been cited for a failure of institutional control." [Editors' note: The penalties imposed included vacating postseason tournament team and individual records from 1994–1998 and reconfiguring the university's records to so reflect the change, as well as ordering the former head coach and academic advisor and any member institution that might employ them within a seven-year period to appear before the COI to determine whether they or the institution should be subjected to NCAA show cause procedures, "which could limit athletically-related duties of the head coach and academic advisor at any such institution for a designated period. . . . "]

a. Access to pertinent documents during the investigation.

[Editors' note: Coach Haskins alleged that the NCAA denied him access to certain documents — principally, audiotapes of witness interviews. Articulating the governing standard as whether the former head coach could prove that he was denied "reasonable access" to these materials, the IAC rejected the former coach's argument.]

b. Contact between the NCAA and federal law enforcement authorities.

[Editors' note: The IAC also rejected Haskins's argument that the COI prejudiced him by not delaying the hearing to permit him to introduce evidence of an internal NCAA memorandum of conversations between a member of the COI's enforcement staff and federal officials, including FBI agents. The former head coach did not show how this conversation was related, directly or indirectly, to any of the findings of the case.]

c. Participation in the hearing by the former head coach's attorney alone.

[Editors' note: Relying on language in its bylaws, the IAC rejected Haskins's assertion that he was not obligated to attend the hearing so long as his attorney appeared before the COI. "There is no provision for appearance by attorneys alone."]

2. Academic Integrity

The most serious charges against the former head coach are those that he knew of the secretary's fraudulent assistance to student-athletes. The findings of the Committee on Infractions bear repeating here:

> The numerous violations found by the committee are among the most serious academic fraud violations to come before it in the past 20 years. The violations

were significant, widespread and intentional. More than that, their nature — academic fraud — undermined the bedrock foundation of a university and the operation of its intercollegiate athletics program. By purposeful acts of commission, and, through the absence of effective oversight, serious acts of omission, these violations damaged the academic integrity of the institution.

[Editors' note: The IAC next summarized the facts that demonstrated that Coach Haskins knew the secretary was preparing work for student-athletes. These findings included the coach's $3,000 payment to the secretary; the secretary's constant and open contact with student-athletes (including her attendance at study halls), of which the former head coach could not have been ignorant; her own admissions that she told the former head coach that she was assisting the student-athletes; his caution to her that the papers she was writing "can't be too good"; his apology to her after a student-athlete had admitted to the associate director of athletics that she was giving him academic assistance; another student-athlete's statement that he told the former head coach that the secretary was working with him on coursework; evidence that the secretary's assistance to student-athletes was common knowledge in the basketball program; and evidence that the former head coach tightly controlled the academic counselor and indeed "all aspects of the men's basketball program." The IAC agreed with the COI that the evidence satisfactorily established, both directly and indirectly and by permissible inference from the circumstances, the former head coach's knowing involvement in academic fraud.]

d. An objective standard of knowledge of academic fraud.

It is not at all clear that Bylaw 10.1 requires actual knowledge of academic fraud and thus precludes a finding of unethical conduct against an individual who should have known of fraud. The bylaw states that unethical conduct "may include, but is not limited to" actual knowledge of the academic fraud. This at least leaves open the possibility that an objective standard may be applied.

We believe that the objective, "should have known" standard may well be appropriate to assess the responsibility of a person, such as the head coach of an athletics program, who is expected to know what those in the program are doing. To conclude otherwise would be to encourage coaches or others in similarly responsible positions to close their eyes and ears to what is happening in areas for which they are accountable.

A head coach's responsibility goes beyond merely acting upon academic fraud that comes to his attention. A coach should take reasonable steps to see that it does not happen in the first place. . . .

3. Unethical Conduct

The Committee . . . concluded that "the evidence is not fully consistent," but it found that the clear weight of the evidence showed that the former head coach attempted to influence young men to provide false and misleading information and, in doing so, violated NCAA standards of ethical conduct. . . . The Committee on Infractions' finding in this regard is not clearly contrary to the evidence presented to the Committee.

B. Whether the Penalties Imposed by the Committee Are Excessive or Inappropriate and Should Be Set Aside

The former head coach's argument is based on a number of factors, including his age, his belief that the penalty "essentially prohibits [him] from ever being able to coach at an NCAA institution again," the fact that previous cases have imposed shorter periods, the fact that the Committee on Infractions imposed lesser penalties in this case on others who were involved and his assertion (which we have rejected) that the evidence failed to establish his "knowing" violation of NCAA rules.

We have considered all these factors carefully, and we have also considered, independent of the former head coach's arguments, whether the penalty was either "excessive" or "inappropriate" based on all the evidence and circumstances.

We affirm the penalty. . . . The most severe penalties are appropriate when the academic mission of the university has been compromised. The former head coach was not the only one who bears responsibility for the damage; as the Committee on Infractions' report demonstrates, others in the program, and Minnesota itself, also failed in their responsibilities. The former head coach's appeal is the only one before us. We have no doubt that his conduct, fully established by the evidence in this case, justifies the penalty imposed.

QUESTIONS

1. The university's new president responded by seeking the resignations of athletics administrators and coaches as part of the institution's corrective efforts made prior to the hearing before the COI. Why did he take this strong action? Was he responding to institutional control issues? Was he seeking scapegoats in an effort to placate the NCAA?
2. The COI and IAC clearly doubted Haskins's credibility. Why? Was it a mistake for Haskins to refuse to appear before the COI?

OTHER CASES INVOLVING COACHES

On April 29, 2011, the IAC upheld severe sanctions against a former assistant football coach for USC, including findings that the assistant coach had engaged in unethical conduct, had violated amateurism legislation, and had failed to report knowledge of NCAA violations. Given the significance of these findings, including the COI's determination that the coach's denials were not credible, the IAC upheld the COI's imposition of a one-year order to show cause period during which his activities as a coach would be restricted in terms of recruiting and interactions with recruits. It also required the assistant coach to attend a rule seminar.

On June 23, 2005, in a very strongly worded decision regarding Baylor University, the COI issued show-cause orders for the former head coach (ten years), an assistant coach (seven years), and two former assistant coaches (five years). Baylor had self-imposed significant penalties, but even that effort was stiffened by the committee. As in the *Baylor* case, the COI has imposed severe limitations on the capacity of coaches to continue coaching at NCAA universities in a number of other cases. These limits run from a short period of time (one to two years) up to the seven to ten years noted in the *Haskins* and *Baylor* cases. In less significant cases, the COI also will suspend coaches, as it did when it suspended Syracuse University's men's basketball coach for nine games for failing to promote an atmosphere of compliance and monitor his staff. See *http://www.ncaa.org/sites/default/files/Syracuse%20Final %20Public%20Infractions%20Decision%20%28Corrected%29.pdf.*

A significant question arises as to whether the NCAA should follow the lead of professional leagues and punish athletes for off-the-field conduct. During the fall of 2015, issues arose regarding the penalization of student-athletes for off-the-field behavior. The University of Georgia, for example, worked with the NCAA and held its star running back out of four games (or 30 percent of the season) for accepting more than $3,000 in cash from multiple individuals for autographed memorabilia and other items over a two-year period. In another case that garnered wide national attention, a former Heisman Trophy winner and star football player at Florida State University was suspended by his football coach for only *one-half* of a game for a series of major off-the-field activities, including theft and a very serious continuing allegation of sexual assault. The student-athlete also played baseball at Florida State and had previously been suspended for three games by his baseball coach for the same offenses. Should coaches be given wide latitude in deciding whether to suspend a player? Should that be left to the Faculty Athletics Committee, as is done at some institutions? What kinds of pressures exist in such a case? Should the NCAA get involved in such matters, given that it may be difficult for institutions to act against their own interest by sitting a very valuable player? If the NCAA gets involved, what should the nature of that involvement be?

Recent cases make it very clear that universities must closely monitor their coaches and athletic programs, and head coaches must closely monitor the activities of their assistant coaches, under a liberal standard presuming that head coaches know what their assistants are doing. In a case involving Ohio State, decided in December 2011, the IAC joined the COI in voicing its concern that "the former coach became aware of [serious] violations and decided not to report the violations to the institution, the Big Ten Conference or the NCAA." In that case, Ohio State was cited for failing to adequately monitor its program for compliance purposes. The university also pressured their head football coach to resign for unethical behavior (he had failed to cooperate with the NCAA in its investigation). Ohio State went on to develop a comprehensive, state-of-the-art model for monitoring compliance.

QUESTIONS

1. Is this move to hold coaches accountable for rules compliance by limiting or ending their careers appropriate? Should head coaches be held responsible for the acts of assistant coaches? If so, under what standard (actual knowledge, constructive knowledge, or a presumption of knowledge)? Should coaches also be held responsible by their institutions for low graduation rates of their student-athletes?

2. Should university presidents be held responsible for the operation of their athletic departments, as well as the conduct of coaches and other personnel?

NOTES

The NCAA has penalized university personnel other than coaches for violations of NCAA rules. For a recent case in which a math professor received a five-year order to show cause for completing coursework for student-athletes, see *http://www.ncaa.org/sites/default/files/Weber%20State%20University%20Infractions%20Decision%20PUBLIC.PDF.*

Problem 3-1

As a director of compliance at a major D-I university, you have been asked by the athletic director to prepare a short memorandum indicating what lessons you have learned from the cases discussed in these materials. In particular, she wonders what you would recommend to avoid the institutional control problems that resulted in severe penalties to USC and the unethical conduct in coaching violations that led to Coach Haskins being given an order to show cause that resulted in his being prevented from coaching at the D-I level in the future. What should the university do to minimize the likelihood that it and its coaches will be subject to severe NCAA penalties like those imposed on USC and Coach Haskins?

LEGAL LIMITS ON NCAA REGULATORY AUTHORITY

As previously discussed, in *NCAA v. Tarkanian*, the Supreme Court ruled that the NCAA is a private association rather than a state actor; therefore, it is not subject to the legal requirements of the U.S. Constitution. However, the NCAA must comply with its contractual obligations to its member institutions and their student-athletes who are third-party beneficiaries of this contractual relationship, according to *Bloom v. NCAA, infra.* In addition, the NCAA's rules, agreements, and decisions must comply with applicable federal and state civil rights laws, as well as the law of private associations and antitrust law.

A. Federal and State Civil Rights Law

Virtually all public and private universities receive some federal funds and therefore must comply with federal civil right statutes such as Title IX and the Rehabilitation

Act of 1972. As the following case illustrates, this does not necessarily mean that the NCAA is subject to these federal laws.

 **KEY TERMS**
- Civil Rights Restoration Act
- Deference
- Performance-enhancing drugs

NCAA v. Smith
525 U.S. 459 (1999)

Ginsburg, Justice.

This case concerns the amenability of the National Collegiate Athletic Association (NCAA or Association) to a private action under Title IX of the Education Amendments of 1972. . . . Title IX proscribes sex discrimination in "any education program or activity receiving Federal financial assistance."

Renee M. Smith sued the NCAA under Title IX alleging that the Association discriminated against her on the basis of her sex by denying her permission to play intercollegiate volleyball at federally assisted institutions. . . . Dues payments from recipients of federal funds, we hold, do not suffice to render the dues recipient subject to Title IX. . . .

I

[Editors' note: Smith received her bachelor's degree from one institution in two and a half years and attended graduate school at another institution, where she sought to participate in intercollegiate volleyball. She was not permitted to do so, under an NCAA rule that permitted students to use their athletic eligibility at the institution where they received their undergraduate degree if they were pursuing a graduate degree at the same institution. The same rule, however, did not permit students to participate in intercollegiate athletics at other institutions where they might be pursuing their graduate education. Smith sought a waiver of the rule, as permitted under the rule, but the NCAA refused to grant it. Smith challenged the application of this rule to her on the ground that the NCAA granted more waivers to male than female student-athletes and, therefore, violated Title IX, which limits discrimination based on gender.]

The NCAA moved to dismiss Smith's Title IX claim on the ground that the complaint failed to allege that the NCAA is a recipient of federal financial assistance. In opposition, Smith argued that the NCAA governs the federally funded intercollegiate athletics programs of its members, that these programs are educational, and that the NCAA benefited economically from its members' receipt of federal funds. . . .

II

Under the Civil Rights Restoration Act of 1987 (CRRA), 102 Stat. 28, 20 U.S.C. §1687, a "program or activity" includes "all of the operations of . . . a college, university, or other postsecondary institution, or a public system of higher education . . . any part of which is extended Federal financial assistance." . . . Thus, if any part of the NCAA received federal assistance, all NCAA operations would be subject to Title IX.

We have twice before considered when an entity qualifies as a recipient of federal financial assistance. In *Grove City College v. Bell*, we held that a college receives federal financial assistance when it enrolls students who receive federal funds earmarked for educational expenses. Finding "no hint" that Title IX distinguishes "between direct institutional assistance and aid received by a school through its students," we concluded that Title IX "encompass[es] *all* forms of federal aid to education, direct or indirect."

Entities that receive federal assistance, whether directly or through an intermediary, are recipients within the meaning of Title IX; entities that only benefit economically from federal assistance are not.

Unlike the earmarked student aid in *Grove City*, there is no allegation that NCAA members paid their dues with federal funds earmarked for that purpose. At most, the Association's receipt of dues demonstrates that it indirectly benefits from the federal assistance afforded its members. This showing, without more, is insufficient to trigger Title IX coverage. . . .

III

Smith, joined by the United States as *amicus curiae*, presses two alternative theories for bringing the NCAA under the prescriptions of Title IX. First, she asserts that the NCAA directly and indirectly receives federal financial assistance through the National Youth Sports Program NCAA administers. Second, Smith argues that when a recipient cedes controlling authority over a federally funded program to another entity, the controlling entity is covered by Title IX regardless whether it is itself a recipient. . . .

We do not decide in the first instance issues not decided below. . . .

For the reasons stated, we conclude that the Court of Appeals erroneously held that dues payments from recipients of federal funds suffice to subject the NCAA to suit under Title IX. Accordingly, we vacate the judgment of the Third Circuit and remand the case for further proceedings consistent with this opinion.

QUESTION

Should the NCAA be subject to Title IX, in a broader sense, and should dues payments from recipients of federal funds suffice to subject the NCAA to a suit under Title IX?

B. Drug Testing and Privacy

As a condition of participating in intercollegiate athletics, student–athletes are required to provide written consent to random drug testing for substances prohibited by the NCAA during NCAA championship competitions and out–of–season testing programs. The NCAA's list of banned substances includes performance-enhancing drugs such as anabolic steroids, stimulants (e.g., cocaine and amphetamines), and certain illegal recreational drugs such as marijuana and heroin. In effect, a student-athlete's compliance with the NCAA's drug testing program, which has been alleged to violate his or her civil rights protected by state law, is a condition of eligibility to compete in intercollegiate athletics. In *Brennan v. Board of Trustees for University of Louisiana Systems*, 691 So. 2d 324 (La. App. 1997), the court was deferential in upholding the NCAA's drug-testing program against a claim that the privacy right of the student-athlete should be protected. The *Brennan* court rejected the plaintiff's indirect challenge to the NCAA's drug-testing program, even though it includes recreational and not just performance-enhancing drug use.

The sanction generally imposed on a student-athlete who tests positive for a banned substance is ineligibility to participate in any intercollegiate sports for one year and loss of one season of eligibility. (Athletes ineligible to participate in Olympic or international sports competition for violating the World Anti-Doping Code also are ineligible to participate in NCAA intercollegiate sports during the period of their suspension.) The student-athlete, in conjunction with his or her institution, has the right to appeal the finding of a positive drug test to the NCAA's Committee on Competitive Safeguards and Medical Aspects of Sports. That committee may reduce the penalty based on the student-athlete's relative degree of fault for a doping violation. After a hearing, the committee may reduce the length of the student-athlete's suspension to one-half of the season of competition in the particular sport or determine that no suspension is appropriate based on extenuating circumstances.

In January 2015, the Committee on Competitive Safeguards and Medical Aspects of Sports recommended extensive changes to the NCAA's drug-testing policies. These include more testing for performance-enhancing substances, based on research showing that their usage drops significantly when student-athletes believe they have at least a 30 percent chance of getting caught; and the development of a new deterrence model for recreational drug use (e.g., marijuana, alcohol, and opiates) that focuses on NCAA and member university educational programs instead of testing for usage of these substances. Those proposals have not been adopted yet and will be considered at the D-I, D-II, and D-III levels.

QUESTIONS

Does the NCAA have a valid justification for testing adult student-athletes for the usage of recreational drugs that are not performance enhancing? Should the NCAA recognize the student-athlete's right of privacy and restrict its drug testing accordingly? If so, how should it do so?

C. Contract and Private Association Laws

Courts generally are deferential to the NCAA regarding its interpretation and enforcement of its own rules and regulations, particularly its student-athlete eligibility rules. As you read the following case, consider whether such judicial deference is warranted in this context and results in a fair and principled resolution of the issues.

<table>
<tr><td>**KEY TERMS**</td><td>

- Arbitrary and capricious
- Confidentiality
- Declaratory and injunctive relief
- Good faith and fair dealing
- Restitution rule
- Standing
- Subpoena
- Third-party beneficiary
</td></tr>
</table>

Bloom v. NCAA
93 P.3d 621 (Colo. App. 2004)

DAILEY, J.

I. Background

Bloom, a high school football and track star, was recruited to play football at CU [the University of Colorado]. Before enrolling there, however, he competed in Olympic and professional World Cup skiing events, becoming the World Cup champion in freestyle moguls. During the Olympics, Bloom appeared on MTV, and thereafter was offered various paid entertainment opportunities, including a chance to host a show on Nickelodeon. Bloom also agreed to endorse commercially certain ski equipment, and he contracted to model clothing for Tommy Hilfiger.

Bloom became concerned that his endorsements and entertainment activities might interfere with his eligibility to compete in intercollegiate football. On Bloom's behalf, CU first requested waivers of NCAA rules restricting student-athlete endorsement and media activities and, then, a favorable interpretation of the NCAA rule restricting media activities.

The NCAA denied CU's requests, and Bloom discontinued his endorsement, modeling, and media activities to play football for CU during the 2002 fall season. However, Bloom instituted this action against the NCAA for declaratory and injunctive relief, asserting that his endorsement, modeling, and media activities were necessary to support his professional skiing career, something which the NCAA rules permitted.

Bloom requested that the NCAA restrictions be declared inapplicable, and that the NCAA and CU be enjoined from applying them, to activities originating prior to his enrollment at CU or wholly unrelated to his prowess as a football player.

IV. Standing

[Editors' note: The court first addressed the NCAA's assertion that Bloom lacked standing to pursue either his contract claims or his arbitrary and capricious argument.]

Courts are reluctant to intervene, except on the most limited grounds, in the internal affairs of voluntary associations. . . . Even then, it would appear that a plaintiff must ordinarily allege an invasion of some type of civil or property right to have standing.

Here, Bloom is not a member of the NCAA, and he does not have a constitutional right to engage in amateur intercollegiate athletics at CU. Nor does he assert any property interest in playing football for CU.

However, to the extent Bloom's claim of arbitrary and capricious action asserts a violation of the duty of good faith and fair dealing that is implied in the contractual relationship between the NCAA and its members, his position as a third-party beneficiary of that contractual relationship affords him standing to pursue this claim.

In sum, we conclude that Bloom has third-party beneficiary standing to pursue what in essence are two claims for violation of his contractual rights.

V. Probability of Success

[In asserting that he is entitled to injunctive relief,] Bloom contends that the trial court erred in assessing the probability of success on his contract claims. We disagree.

A. Interpretation of NCAA Bylaws

In interpreting a contract, we seek to give effect to the intent and the reasonable expectations of the parties. . . . To determine the intent and expectations of the parties, we view the contract in its entirety, not in isolated portions . . . and we give words and phrases their plain meaning according to common usage.

Bloom relies on NCAA Bylaw 12.1.2, which states that "[a] professional athlete in one sport may represent a member institution in a different sport." He asserts that, because a professional is one who "gets paid" for a sport, a student-athlete is entitled to earn whatever income is customary for his or her professional sport, which, in the case of professional skiers, primarily comes from endorsements and paid media opportunities.

We recognize that, like many others involved in individual professional sports such as golf, tennis, and boxing, professional skiers obtain much of their income from sponsors. We note, however, that none of the NCAA's bylaws mentions, much less explicitly establishes, a right to receive "customary income" for a sport.

Unlike other NCAA bylaws, the endorsements and media appearance bylaws do not contain any sport-specific qualifiers. In our view, when read together, the NCAA bylaws express a clear and unambiguous intent to prohibit student-athletes from engaging in endorsements and paid media appearances. . . .

The clear import of the bylaws is that, although student-athletes have the right to be professional athletes, they do not have the right to simultaneously engage in endorsement or paid media activity and maintain their eligibility to participate in amateur competition. And we may not disregard the clear meaning of the bylaws simply because they may disproportionately affect those who participate in individual professional sports. . . .

Thus, even if the bylaws were viewed as ambiguous, the record supports the trial court's conclusion that the bylaws would ultimately be interpreted in accordance with the NCAA's and its member institutions' construction of those bylaws.

B. Application of Bylaws to Bloom

The U.S. Supreme Court has recognized the NCAA as "the guardian of an important American tradition, namely, amateurism in intercollegiate athletics."

Under that tradition, "college sports provided an important opportunity for teaching people about character, motivation, endurance, loyalty, and the attainment of one's personal best — all qualities of great value in citizens. In this sense, competitive athletics were viewed as an extracurricular activity, justified by the university as part of its ideal objective of educating the whole person."

The NCAA's "Principle of Amateurism" states:

> Student-athletes shall be amateurs in an intercollegiate sport, and their participation should be motivated primarily by education and by the physical, mental and social benefits to be derived. Student participation in intercollegiate athletics is an avocation, and student-athletes should be protected from exploitation by professional and commercial enterprises.

The NCAA's purpose, in this regard, is not only "to maintain intercollegiate athletics as an integral part of the educational program," but also to "retain a clear line of demarcation between intercollegiate athletics and professional sports."

Similar concerns underlie the NCAA's prohibition on paid entertainment activity. Paid entertainment activity may impinge upon the amateur ideal if the opportunity were obtained or advanced because of the student's athletic ability or prestige, even though that activity may further the education of student-athletes such as Bloom, a communications major.

In this case, Bloom presented evidence that some of his acting opportunities arose not as a result of his athletic ability but because of his good looks and on-camera presence. However, the record contains evidence that Bloom's agent and the Tommy Hilfiger company marketed Bloom as a talented multi-sport athlete, and a representative from a talent agency intimated that Bloom's reputation as an athlete would be advantageous in obtaining auditions for various entertainment opportunities. . . .

Under these circumstances, we perceive no abuse of the trial court's discretion in failing to fault the NCAA for refusing to waive its rules, as requested by CU, to permit Bloom "to pursue any television and film opportunities while he is a student-athlete at CU."

Bloom also asserts that the NCAA is arbitrary in its application of the endorsement and media bylaws. He notes that, while the NCAA would bar him from accepting commercial endorsements, it will allow colleges to commercially endorse athletic equipment by having students wear the equipment, with identifying logos and insignias, while engaged in intercollegiate competition. But the trial court determined, and we agree, that this application of the bylaws has a rational basis in economic necessity: financial benefits inure not to any single student-athlete but to member schools and thus to all student-athletes, including those who participate in programs that generate no revenue.

Bloom further argues that the NCAA is arbitrary in the way it applies its bylaws among individual students. Bloom presented evidence that, in one instance, a student-athlete was permitted to make an unpaid, minor appearance in a single film. But the NCAA could rationally conclude that this situation was different: Bloom did not seek permission to make an unpaid appearance in one specific instance; he wanted to take advantage of any number of television and film opportunities, and he wanted to be paid. . . .

Bloom has thus failed to demonstrate any inconsistency in application which would lead us to conclude that the NCAA was arbitrarily applying its rules.

Finally, we are not convinced that the NCAA treated Bloom unfairly in the manner in which it denied the requests to waive or interpret its rules. . . .

For these reasons, we agree with the trial court that Bloom failed to demonstrate a reasonable probability of success on the merits.

QUESTIONS

1. Why did the court hold that the NCAA's application of its endorsement and media bylaws was not arbitrary and capricious? As is true of other private associations, courts afford considerable deference to the NCAA in enforcing its rules and regulations. Notwithstanding the policy of judicial deference, courts will intervene into the affairs of private associations when the association has acted in violation of its own rules, regulations, and policies. Courts are also less inclined to defer to the NCAA in litigation involving the courts and the federal government.

2. In *NCAA v. Lasege*, 53 S.W.3d 77 (Ky. 2001), the Supreme Court of Kentucky ruled in favor of the NCAA, which had prohibited Muhammad Lasege, a University of Louisville basketball player, from participating in intercollegiate sports. Prior to his matriculation at Louisville, Lasege played basketball in Russia under a professional contract and engaged in other conduct that the NCAA found to be in violation of its amateurism rules. Ruling on the athlete's claim that the NCAA acted arbitrarily and capriciously when it declared him ineligible, the Kentucky Supreme Court held that

   a ruling is arbitrary and capricious only where it is "clearly erroneous, and by 'clearly erroneous' we mean unsupported by substantial evidence." Here, the NCAA's ruling has strong evidentiary support—Lasege unquestionably signed contracts to play professional basketball and unquestionably accepted benefits.

The *Lasege* court also validated the NCAA rule that permits the organization to seek restitution from its member institutions as a result of rules violations such as those that Louisville committed when it allowed Lasege to play. The Indiana Supreme Court noted the tensions that arise in restitution cases:

   Undeniably, the Restitution Rule imposes hardship on a school that, in compliance with an order of a court which is later vacated, fields an ineligible player. On the other hand, use of an ineligible player imposes a hardship on other teams that must compete against the teams fielding ineligible players. While schools will contend that [it] is unfair when they have to forfeit victories earned with an ineligible player on the field because they complied with a court order, competing schools will reply that it is unfair when they have to compete against a team with an ineligible student athlete because a local trial judge prohibited the school or the IHSAA from following the eligibility rules.

Courts have upheld the restitution rule. Do you agree with the courts?

D. Federal Antitrust Law

The purpose of federal antitrust law is to preserve a competitive marketplace that furthers consumer welfare by resulting in lower prices, better products, and more efficient methods of production than would occur absent vigorous economic competition. Antitrust law provides an important limit on the NCAA's regulatory authority; thus, college sports administrators need to have a basic understanding of this complex area of federal law.

Despite the more-than-100-year history of the NCAA's national governance of college sports through the collective action of its members, federal antitrust law has only recently had a significant role in regulating the NCAA. There was virtually no antitrust litigation challenging the NCAA's rules, enforcement activities, or other conduct prior to the early 1970s, when the financial rewards for fielding winning big-time football and basketball programs escalated as public demand for intercollegiate sports viewing and television revenues skyrocketed. Since then, there have been several antitrust suits against the NCAA and its member universities asserting that their conduct unreasonably restrains trade to some party's economic detriment.

Today's economic realities have reshaped the idealistic student-athlete model of intercollegiate athletics for sports such as NCAA D-I men's basketball and Football Bowl Subdivision (FBS) football (formerly Division I-A) because the tremendous popularity of these sports creates a substantial revenue-generating capacity that has been exploited by television for the benefit of schools that sponsor these sports. This trend toward commercialism in big-time football and men's basketball has continued until today, and intercollegiate athletics is now a multibillion-dollar industry. In recent years, the NCAA has sought to capitalize on the popularity of its members' athletic programs and enable university athletic departments to increase their revenues. For example, the NCAA has increased the maximum allowable number of football games during a season, stimulated conference expansion by permitting championship games to be played by conferences with 12 or more members, and certified new postseason football bowl games. Beginning in 2011, the NCAA also increased to 68 the total number of teams participating in its popular "March Madness" postseason basketball tournament, which culminates in the Final Four championship round. In January 2015, a four-team D-I FBS national championship playoff system, which generated substantial public interest and will generate billions of dollars in media and sponsorship revenues, made its debut.

The current economic realities of intercollegiate sports have spawned an athletics arms race, as big-time programs engage in a spending spree to compete for the substantial monetary rewards that come with winning. This economically induced and often insatiable desire to win has led to a corresponding proliferation of NCAA rules violations, along with enforcement actions and sanctions against member universities for their misconduct. Membership in the NCAA is unquestionably an economic necessity if a school desires to participate in big-time intercollegiate athletics. Nonmembers cannot compete in NCAA championship events, do not have the prestige and visibility to consistently attract a large number of quality athletes to their programs, and do not generate the substantial economic revenues from gate receipts and television contracts that NCAA schools do. Perhaps because there is no viable existing alternative, some universities whose individual economic interests have been harmed by NCAA regulations and rules enforcement actions have resorted to antitrust litigation.

Many NCAA rules and regulations are specifically directed toward and indirectly govern players, coaches, boosters, and alumni, even though these parties are not members of the NCAA and lack effective representation in the NCAA's rule-making and enforcement process. Thus, in governing the association's affairs, the NCAA effectively possesses and exercises significant regulatory power over persons without a voice or vote, often to their economic detriment. As illustrated by the following cases, antitrust suits against the NCAA have been brought by coaches, student-athletes, competing athletics governing bodies, television broadcasters, and others whose economic interests have been allegedly adversely affected by the NCAA's pervasive regulation of intercollegiate athletics.

1. Nature and Scope of Antitrust Limits on NCAA Regulatory Authority

Federal antitrust litigation against the NCAA generally has been brought under §1 of the Sherman Act (15 U.S.C. §1), which provides that "[e]very contract, combination . . . or conspiracy in restraint of trade or commerce" is illegal. The NCAA also is subject to §2 of the Sherman Act (15 U.S.C. §2), which prohibits monopolization or attempts to monopolize trade or commerce, although litigation asserting §2 claims against the NCAA historically has been unsuccessful. See, e.g., *Association of Intercollegiate Athletics for Women v. NCAA*, 735 F.2d 577 (D.C. Cir. 1984) (rejecting allegation that the NCAA unlawfully used its monopoly regulatory power over men's intercollegiate sports to facilitate its entry into the regulation of women's intercollegiate sports and to force the Association of Intercollegiate Athletics for Women, a competing national governing body, out of existence).

The NCAA has no blanket exemption from the federal antitrust laws merely because it is a nonprofit organization whose members are predominantly colleges and universities with educational objectives. In *Hennessey v. NCAA*, 564 F.2d 1136 (5th Cir. 1977), the Fifth Circuit observed that "[w]hile the participating athletics [*sic*] may be amateurs, intercollegiate athletics in its management is clearly business, and big business at that." *Id.* at 1150. The court concluded, "While organized as a non-profit organization, the NCAA and its member institutions are, when presenting amateur athletics to a ticket-paying, television-buying public, engaged in a business venture of far greater magnitude than the vast majority of 'profit-making' enter-prises." *Id*. at 1149, n. 14.

The NCAA's general business activities and regulation of intercollegiate athletics clearly are national in scope. For example, the NCAA conducts national champion-ships in most men's and women's intercollegiate sports and sells the national television broadcasting and other media rights to these events, which are business activities sat-isfying the Sherman Act's jurisdictional requirement that conduct alleged to violate the antitrust laws affect interstate trade or commerce.

The collective adoption and enforcement of NCAA rules by its member uni-versities, as well as other agreements concerning the production, marketing, and regulation of intercollegiate athletics, is considered concerted action for purposes of §1 of the Sherman Act. As a result, virtually all NCAA rules and agreements among NCAA members are potentially subject to antitrust challenge. However, §1's broad statutory language has been judicially interpreted to prohibit only unrea-sonable restraints of trade in economic terms.

The following 1984 Supreme Court decision considers how the federal antitrust laws limit the NCAA's regulatory authority and establishes the legal framework for determining whether an NCAA rule or agreement unreasonably restraints trade benefits or harms college sports fans.

2. Case Law

KEY TERMS
- Anticompetitive effects
- Horizontal restraint (e.g., price-fixing, output limitations)
- Illegal per se rule
- Input market
- Output market
- Procompetitive justification
- "Quick look" rule of reason
- Rule of reason

NCAA v. Board of Regents of the University of Oklahoma
468 U.S. 85 (1984)

Justice STEVENS delivered the opinion of the Court.

The University of Oklahoma and the University of Georgia contend that the National Collegiate Athletic Association has unreasonably restrained trade [in violation of §1 of the Sherman Act] in the televising of college football games. . . .

With the exception of football, the NCAA has not undertaken any regulation of the televising of athletic events. . . .

[Editors' note: In separate agreements, the NCAA granted the American Broadcasting Company (ABC) and the Columbia Broadcasting System (CBS) each the right to telecast 14 regular-season football games in accordance with certain "ground rules." Each network agreed to pay a specified "minimum aggregate compensation to the participating NCAA member institutions" during the four-year period in an amount that totaled $131,750,000. The plan also contained "appearance requirements" and "appearance limitations" that pertained to each of the two-year periods that the plan was in effect. The basic requirement imposed on each of the two networks was that it must schedule appearances for at least 82 different member institutions during each two-year period. Under the appearance limitations, no member institution was eligible to appear on television more than a total of six times and more than four times nationally, with the appearances to be divided equally between the two carrying networks. The number of exposures specified in the contracts also set an absolute maximum on the number of games that could be broadcast. It limited the total amount of televised intercollegiate football and the number of games that any one team could televise. No NCAA member university was permitted to make any sale of television rights except in accordance with the basic plan.

Some years ago, five major conferences, together with major football-playing independent institutions, organized the College Football Association (CFA). The original purpose of the CFA was to promote the interests of major football-playing schools within the NCAA structure. The Universities of Oklahoma and Georgia, respondents in this case, were members of the CFA. Beginning in 1979, CFA members began to advocate that colleges with major football programs should have a greater voice in the formulation of football television policy than they had in the NCAA. They developed an independent television plan and entered into a 1981 contract with the National Broadcasting Company (NBC) that would have permitted a greater number of its members' games to be televised, and would have increased the overall football television revenues realized by CFA members. In response, the NCAA publicly announced that it would take disciplinary action against any CFA member that complied with the CFA-NBC contract, which would apply to other sports as well as football. Although respondents obtained a preliminary injunction against the NCAA's threatened disciplinary action, most CFA members were reluctant to enter into the proposed contract with NBC and the agreement was never consummated.]

II

There can be no doubt that the challenged practices of the NCAA constitute a "restraint of trade" in the sense that they limit members' freedom to negotiate and enter into their own television contracts. . . . In that sense, however, every contract is a restraint of trade, and as we have repeatedly recognized, the Sherman Act was intended to prohibit only unreasonable restraints of trade.

It is also undeniable that these practices share characteristics of restraints we have previously held unreasonable. The NCAA is an association of schools which compete against each other to attract television revenues, not to mention fans and athletes. As the District Court found, the policies of the NCAA with respect to television rights are ultimately controlled by the vote of member institutions. By participating in an association which prevents member institutions from competing against each other on the basis of price or kind of television rights that can be offered to broadcasters, the NCAA member institutions have created a horizontal restraint — an agreement among competitors on the way in which they will compete with one another. A restraint of this type has often been held to be unreasonable as a matter of law. Because it places a ceiling on the number of games member institutions may televise, the horizontal agreement places an artificial limit on the quantity of televised football that is available to broadcasters and consumers. By restraining the quantity of television rights available for sale, the challenged practices create a limitation on output; our cases have held that such limitations are unreasonable restraints of trade. Moreover, the District Court found that the minimum aggregate price in fact operates to preclude any price negotiation between broadcasters and institutions, thereby constituting horizontal price fixing, perhaps the paradigm of an unreasonable restraint of trade.

Horizontal price fixing and output limitation are ordinarily condemned as a matter of law under an "illegal per se" approach because the probability that these practices are anticompetitive is so high; a per se rule is applied when "the practice facially appears to be one that would always or almost always tend to restrict competition and decrease output." *Broadcast Music, Inc. v. Columbia Broadcasting System, Inc.*, 441 U.S. 1, 19-20, 99 S.Ct. 1551, 1562, 60 L.Ed.2d 1 (1979). In such circumstances a restraint is presumed unreasonable without inquiry into the particular market context in which it is found. Nevertheless, we have decided that it would be inappropriate to apply a per se rule to this case. This decision is not based on a lack of judicial experience with this type of arrangement, on the fact that the NCAA is organized as a nonprofit entity, or on our respect for the NCAA's historic role in the preservation and encouragement of inter-collegiate amateur athletics. Rather, what is critical is that this case involves an industry in which horizontal restraints on competition are essential if the product is to be available at all.

As Judge Bork has noted: "[S]ome activities can only be carried out jointly. Perhaps the leading example is league sports. When a league of professional lacrosse teams is formed, it would be pointless to declare their cooperation illegal on the ground that there are no other professional lacrosse teams." R. Bork, *The Antitrust Paradox* 278 (1978). What the NCAA and its member institutions market in this case is competition itself — contests between competing institutions. Of course, this would be completely ineffective if there were no rules on which the competitors agreed to create and define the competition to be marketed. A myriad of rules affecting such matters as the size of the field, the number of players on a team, and the extent to which physical violence is to be encouraged or proscribed, all must be agreed upon, and all restrain the manner in which institutions compete. Moreover, the NCAA seeks to market a particular brand of football — college football. The identification of this "product" with an academic tradition differentiates college football from and makes it more popular than professional sports to which it might otherwise be comparable, such as, for example, minor league baseball. In order to preserve the character and quality of the "product," athletes must not be paid, must be required to attend class, and the like. And the integrity of the "product" cannot be preserved except by mutual agreement; if an institution adopted such restrictions unilaterally, its effectiveness as a competitor on the playing field might soon be destroyed. Thus, the NCAA plays a vital role in enabling college football to preserve its character, and as a result enables a product to be marketed which might otherwise be unavailable. In performing this role, its actions widen consumer choice — not only the choices available to sports fans but also those available to athletes — and hence can be viewed as procompetitive. . . .

III

Because it restrains price and output, the NCAA's television plan has a significant potential for anticompetitive effects. The findings of the District Court indicate that this potential has been realized. The District Court found that if member institutions were free to sell television rights, many more games would be shown on television, and that the NCAA's output restriction has the effect of raising the price the networks pay for television rights. Moreover, the court found that by fixing a price for television rights to all games, the NCAA creates a price structure that is unresponsive to viewer demand and unrelated to the prices that would prevail in a competitive market. And, of course, since as a practical matter all member institutions need NCAA approval, members have no real choice but to adhere to the NCAA's television controls. . . .

[The] NCAA television plan on its face constitutes a restraint upon the operation of a free market, and the findings of the District Court establish that it has operated to raise prices and reduce output. Under the Rule of Reason, these hallmarks of anticompetitive behavior place upon petitioner a heavy burden of establishing an affirmative defense which competitively justifies this apparent deviation from the operations of a free market. We turn now to the NCAA's proffered justifications. . . .

V

Throughout the history of its regulation of intercollegiate football telecasts, the NCAA has indicated its concern with protecting live attendance. This concern, it should be noted, is not with protecting live attendance at games which are shown on television; that type of interest is not at issue in this case. Rather, the concern is that fan interest in a televised game may adversely affect ticket sales for games that will not appear on television. . . . Under the current plan, games are shown on television during all hours that college football games are played. The plan simply does not protect live attendance by ensuring that games will not be shown on television at the same time as live events.

There is, however, a more fundamental reason for rejecting this defense. The NCAA's argument that its television plan is necessary to protect live attendance is not based on a desire to maintain the integrity of college football as a distinct and attractive product, but rather on a fear that the product will not prove sufficiently attractive to draw live attendance when faced with competition from televised games. At bottom the NCAA's position is that ticket sales for most college games are unable to compete in a free market. The television plan protects ticket sales by limiting output — just as any monopolist increases revenues by reducing output. By seeking to insulate live ticket sales from the full spectrum of competition because of its assumption that the product itself is insufficiently attractive to consumers, petitioner forwards a justification that is inconsistent with the basic policy of the Sherman Act. "[T]he Rule of

Reason does not support a defense based on the assumption that competition itself is unreasonable."

VI

Petitioner argues that the interest in maintaining a competitive balance among amateur athletic teams is legitimate and important and that it justifies the regulations challenged in this case. We agree with the first part of the argument but not the second.

Our decision not to apply a per se rule to this case rests in large part on our recognition that a certain degree of cooperation is necessary if the type of competition that petitioner and its member institutions seek to market is to be preserved. It is reasonable to assume that most of the regulatory controls of the NCAA are justifiable means of fostering competition among amateur athletic teams and therefore procompetitive because they enhance public interest in intercollegiate athletics. The specific restraints on football telecasts that are challenged in this case do not, however, fit into the same mold as do rules defining the conditions of the contest, the eligibility of participants, or the manner in which members of a joint enterprise shall share the responsibilities and the benefits of the total venture.

The NCAA does not claim that its television plan has equalized or is intended to equalize competition within any one league. The plan is nationwide in scope and there is no single league or tournament in which all college football teams compete. There is no evidence of any intent to equalize the strength of teams in Division I-A with those in Division II or Division III, and not even a colorable basis for giving colleges that have no football program at all a voice in the management of the revenues generated by the football programs at other schools.

The interest in maintaining a competitive balance that is asserted by the NCAA as a justification for regulating all television of intercollegiate football is not related to any neutral standard or to any readily identifiable group of competitors.

The television plan is not even arguably tailored to serve such an interest. It does not regulate the amount of money that any college may spend on its football program, nor the way in which the colleges may use the revenues that are generated by their football programs, whether derived from the sale of television rights, the sale of tickets, or the sale of concessions or program advertising. The plan simply imposes a restriction on one source of revenue that is more important to some colleges than to others. There is no evidence that this restriction produces any greater measure of equality throughout the NCAA than would a restriction on alumni donations, tuition rates, or any other revenue-producing activity. At the same time, as the District Court found, the NCAA imposes a variety of other restrictions designed to preserve amateurism which are much better tailored to the goal of competitive balance than is the television plan, and which are "clearly sufficient" to preserve competitive balance to the extent it is within the NCAA's power to do so. And much more than speculation supported the District Court's findings on this score. No other NCAA sport employs a similar plan, and in particular the court found that in the most closely analogous sport, college basketball, competitive balance has been maintained without resort to a restrictive television plan.

Perhaps the most important reason for rejecting the argument that the interest in competitive balance is served by the television plan is the District Court's unambiguous and well-supported finding that many more games would be televised in a free market than under the NCAA plan. The hypothesis that legitimates the maintenance of competitive balance as a procompetitive justification under the Rule of Reason is that equal competition will maximize consumer demand for the product. The finding that consumption will materially increase if the controls are removed is a compelling demonstration that they do not in fact serve any such legitimate purpose.

VII

The NCAA plays a critical role in the maintenance of a revered tradition of amateurism in college sports. There can be no question but that it needs ample latitude to play that role, or that the preservation of the student-athlete in higher education adds richness and diversity to intercollegiate athletics and is entirely consistent with the goals of the Sherman Act. But consistent with the Sherman Act, the role of the NCAA must be to preserve a tradition that might otherwise die; rules that restrict output are hardly consistent with this role. Today we hold only that the record supports the District Court's conclusion that by curtailing output and blunting the ability of member institutions to respond to consumer preference, the NCAA has restricted rather than enhanced the place of intercollegiate athletics in the Nation's life. Accordingly, the judgment of the Court of Appeals is Affirmed.

Justice WHITE, with whom Justice REHNQUIST joins, dissenting.

Although some of the NCAA's activities, viewed in isolation, bear a resemblance to those undertaken by professional sports leagues and associations, the Court errs in treating intercollegiate athletics under the NCAA's control as a purely commercial venture in which colleges and universities participate solely, or even primarily, in the pursuit of profits. Accordingly, I dissent. . . .

The NCAA, in short, "exist[s] primarily to enhance the contribution made by amateur athletic competition to the process of higher education as distinguished from realizing maximum return on it as an entertainment commodity." *Association for Intercollegiate Athletics for Women v. NCAA*, 558 F. Supp. 487, 494 (DC 1983), *aff'd*, 236 U.S.App.D.C. 311, 735 F.2d 577 (1984). In pursuing this goal, the organization and its members seek to provide a public good — a viable system of amateur athletics — that most likely could not be provided in a perfectly competitive market. See *Hennessey v. NCAA*, 564 F.2d 1136, 1153 (CA5 1977). "Without regulation, the desire of member institutions to remain athletically competitive would lead them to engage in activities that deny amateurism to the public. No single institution could confidently enforce its own standards since it could not trust its competitors to do the same." Note, *Antitrust and Nonprofit Entities*, 94 Harv. L. Rev. 802, 817–818 (1981). The history of intercollegiate athletics prior to the advent of the NCAA provides ample support for this conclusion. By mitigating what appears to be a clear failure of the free market to serve the ends and goals of higher education, the NCAA ensures the continued availability of a unique and valuable product, the very existence of which might well be threatened by unbridled competition in the economic sphere.

In pursuit of its fundamental goal and others related to it, the NCAA imposes numerous controls on intercollegiate athletic competition among its members, many of which "are similar to those which are summarily condemned when undertaken in a more traditional business setting." Weistart & Lowell, *supra*, at §5.12.b. Thus, the NCAA has promulgated and enforced rules limiting both the compensation of student-athletes and the number of coaches a school may hire for its football and basketball programs; it also has prohibited athletes who formerly have been compensated for playing from participating in intercollegiate competition, restricted the number of athletic scholarships its members may award, and established minimum academic standards for recipients of those scholarships; and it has pervasively regulated the recruitment process, student eligibility, practice schedules, squad size, the number of games played, and many other aspects of intercollegiate athletics. One clear effect of most, if not all, of these regulations is to prevent institutions with competitively and economically successful programs from taking advantage of their success by expanding their programs, improving the quality of the product they offer, and increasing their sports revenues. Yet each of these regulations represents a desirable and legitimate attempt "to keep university athletics from becoming professionalized to the extent that profit making objectives would overshadow educational objectives." *Kupec v. Atlantic Coast Conference*, 399 F. Supp. 1377, 1380 (MDNC 1975). Significantly, neither the Court of Appeals nor this Court questions the validity of these regulations under the Rule of Reason.

Notwithstanding the contrary conclusion of the District Court and the majority, . . . I do not believe that the restraint under consideration in this case — the NCAA's television plan — differs fundamentally for antitrust purposes from the other seemingly anti-competitive aspects of the organization's broader program of self-regulation. The television plan, like many of the NCAA's actions, furthers several complementary ends. Specifically, the plan is designed "to reduce, insofar as possible, the adverse effects of live television . . . upon football game attendance and, in turn, upon the athletic and related educational programs dependent upon the proceeds therefrom; to spread football television participation among as many colleges as practicable; to reflect properly the image of universities as educational institutions; to promote college football through the use of television; to advance the overall interests of intercollegiate athletics; and to provide college football television to the public to the extent compatible with these other objectives." More generally, in my view, the television plan reflects the NCAA's fundamental policy of preserving amateurism and integrating athletics and education. . . .

QUESTIONS

1. The Supreme Court's majority characterizes the NCAA's restrictions on televised college football games as commercial activity subject to Sherman Act scrutiny. They conclude that NCAA members "compete against each other to attract television revenues, not to mention fans and athletes," and are economic competitors. By contrast, in his dissent, Justice White, who played college football at CU and finished second in the 1937 Heisman Trophy balloting, emphasizes the "essentially non-economic nature of the NCAA's program of self regulation" and asserts that the majority erroneously characterizes intercollegiate athletics "as a purely commercial venture in which . . . universities participate solely, or even primarily, in the pursuit of profits."

Tom McMillen, a former All-American college basketball player at the University of Maryland and also a Congressman, argues that *Board of Regents* was wrongly decided because "the NCAA's loss of monopoly broadcast power [has led] to an escalating competition for money among schools." McMillen supports Justice White's dissent, arguing that "the NCAA monopoly 'fosters the goal of amateurism by spreading revenues among various schools and reducing the financial incentives towards professionalism.'" Tom McMillen, *"Whizzer" White Had It Right When It Came to TV Money*, NCAA News, May 27, 2002, at 4. Do you agree or disagree?

2. To determine whether an agreement unreasonably restrains trade, courts historically have applied either per se or rule of reason analysis. The objective of either standard is "to form a judgment about the competitive significance of the restraint," although the respective application of these tests is quite different. Restraints deemed to be predominantly anticompetitive, as a matter of law or fact, are found to be unreasonable and thus illegal under the antitrust laws. Under the per se rule, certain restraints are conclusively presumed to be illegal as a matter of law because of their significant adverse effects on competition and lack of redeeming procompetitive virtues. Under the rule of reason, the anticompetitive effects of the challenged restraint are balanced against its procompetitive effects on a case-by-case basis, considering the specific facts introduced into evidence by the parties.

Although the Supreme Court notes that agreements among industry competitors to fix prices and limit output generally are illegal per se, why does it analyze the legality of the NCAA's television plan (an output restriction raising the price networks paid for television rights) under the rule of reason? What procompetitive justifications justify NCAA rules and regulation, and why did the *Board of Regents* majority reject them as defenses to an antitrust challenge to the NCAA's television plan?

The federal antitrust laws are intended to ensure that consumers receive the benefits of a competitive marketplace. Have college football fans benefited from judicial invalidation of the NCAA's college football television plan? How much impact has the decision in the *Board of Regents* case had on the commercialization of college football?

• • • • • • • • •

Although *Board of Regents* determined that the NCAA may not limit the total number of televised college football games or fix the price of broadcasting rights, this case did not rule that groups of NCAA universities are prohibited from jointly selling television or other media rights to college football games. Today, college football television contracts often are negotiated and entered into by athletic conferences on behalf of their member universities, a collective business practice that generally does not violate the antitrust laws. Some independent schools, like Notre Dame and Brigham Young University, enter into their own agreements with broadcasters.

The *Board of Regents* case considered the validity of NCAA rules that restrain the intercollegiate athletics output market (e.g., a limit on the total number of televised college football games), whose adverse effects on consumer welfare are readily apparent. Next, we consider the validity of NCAA rules limiting competition among universities in the input market for the resources necessary to produce intercollegiate sports such as the services of coaches and student-athletes.

In *Law v. NCAA*, 134 F.3d 1010 (10th Cir. 1998), a federal appellate court ruled that fixed maximum salaries for D-I "restricted-earnings" basketball coaches established by an NCAA bylaw (the REC Rule) violated §1. Characterizing coaching services as a necessary input to produce intercollegiate athletic competition, the court analyzed the legality of this restraint under the same legal standard that *Board of Regents* applied to NCAA restraints on the output market.

The *Law* court described the rule of reason standard for evaluating the net competitive effects of a challenged collective restraint of trade as follows:

> Courts have imposed a consistent structure on rule of reason analysis by casting it in terms of shifting burdens of proof. Under this approach, the plaintiff bears the initial burden of showing that an agreement had a substantially adverse effect on competition. If the plaintiff meets this burden, the burden shifts to the defendant to come forward with evidence of the procompetitive virtues of the alleged wrongful conduct. If the defendant is able to demonstrate procompetitive effects, the plaintiff then must prove that the challenged conduct is not reasonably necessary to achieve the legitimate objectives or that those objectives can be achieved in a substantially less restrictive manner. Ultimately, if these steps are met, the harms and benefits must be weighed against each other in order to judge whether the challenged behavior is, on balance, reasonable.

Id. at 1019.

Applying the "quick look" rule of reason, the court ruled that capping the salaries of restricted-earnings coaches below the level that free market competition previously had established is horizontal price-fixing, with clear anticompetitive effects that were not justified by any countervailing procompetitive benefits. It concluded that "[t]he NCAA's cost containment justification is illegitimate because . . . [r]educing costs for member institutions, without more, does not justify the anticompetitive effects of fixing the price of coaches' salaries." The court found "no evidence that limits on restricted-earning coaches' salaries would be successful in reducing deficits, let alone that such reductions were necessary to save college basketball" from being destroyed by overspending. While recognizing that the NCAA's need to ensure competitive balance in intercollegiate athletics is a valid procompetitive justification, the court determined that the NCAA had not proved that "the salary restrictions enhance competition, level an uneven playing field, or reduce coaching inequities" among its member schools. It observed that this restriction "does not equalize the overall amount of money Division I schools are permitted to spend on their basketball programs," and there is "no reason to think that the money saved by a school on the salary of a restricted-earnings coach will not be put into another aspect of the school's basketball program, such as equipment or even another coach's salary, thereby increasing inequity in that area."

The coaches whose economic interests were adversely affected by the REC Rule (including those coaching sports other than basketball) ultimately won a jury verdict of $22.3 million, which, with mandatory tripling of damages under the Sherman Act, resulted in a total award of $66.9 million from the NCAA. The NCAA ultimately agreed to pay $54.5 million to settle this lawsuit, and the court awarded approximately $20 million in attorneys' fees and costs to plaintiffs' attorneys. See *Law v. NCAA*, 108 F. Supp. 2d 1193 (D. Kan. 2000) (approving revised settlement plan as fair, reasonable, and adequate).

By contrast, courts generally have ruled that NCAA student–athlete eligibility rules are a noncommercial form of regulation that do not violate antitrust laws.

Smith v. NCAA
139 F.3d 180 (3d Cir. 1998)

GREENBERG, Circuit Judge.

[Editors'note: Renee M. Smith appealed the district court's order dismissing her complaint for failure to state a claim and denying her motion for leave to amend her complaint. She alleged that the NCAA's promulgation and enforcement of a bylaw prohibiting a student-athlete from participating in intercollegiate athletics while enrolled in a graduate program at an institution other than the student-athlete's undergraduate institution violated §1 of the Sherman Act. Her allegations that this conduct violated Title IX are discussed in Chapter 5. At some point after this case was decided in its favor, the NCAA repealed this bylaw and student-athletes now are permitted to participate in intercollegiate athletics as a graduate student at an institution other than the one from which he or she earned an undergraduate degree.]

II. Facts and Procedural History

Smith graduated from high school in the spring of 1991 and enrolled in St. Bonaventure University the following fall, where she participated in Division I athletics. Smith played intercollegiate' volleyball for St. Bonaventure during the 1991–92 and 1992–93 athletic seasons. By her choice, Smith did not participate in intercollegiate volleyball for St. Bonaventure during the 1993–94 season.

Smith graduated from St. Bonaventure in two and one half years. Thereafter, she enrolled in a postbaccalaureate program at Hofstra University, and then in 1995 she enrolled in a second postbaccalaureate program at the University of Pittsburgh. St. Bonaventure did not offer either of these postbaccalaureate programs. . . .

The NCAA denied Smith eligibility to compete for Hofstra and the University of Pittsburgh in the 1994–95 and 1995–96 athletic seasons, respectively, based upon Bylaw 14.1.8.2 in the NCAA Manual (the "Postbaccalaureate Bylaw"). The Postbaccalaureate Bylaw provides that a student-athlete may not participate in intercollegiate athletics at a postgraduate institution other than the institution from which the student earned her undergraduate degree. Both Hofstra and the University of Pittsburgh applied to the NCAA for a waiver of the bylaw with respect to Smith, but the NCAA denied both requests. Smith was, however, in good academic standing and in compliance with all other NCAA eligibility requirements for the 1994–95 and 1995–96 athletic seasons.

III. Discussion

A. Sherman Act Claim

Count I of Smith's complaint alleges that the NCAA, in promulgating and enforcing the Postbaccalaureate Bylaw, violated section 1 of the Sherman Act because the bylaw unreasonably restrains trade and has an adverse anticompetitive effect. As we have indicated, the district court dismissed this claim for failure to state a claim upon which relief could be granted, holding that "the actions of the NCAA in refusing to waive the Postbaccalaureate Bylaw and allow the Plaintiff to participate in intercollegiate athletics is not the type of action to which the Sherman Act was meant to be applied." Smith argues that the district court erred in limiting the application of the Sherman Act to the NCAA's commercial and business activities. We disagree. . . .

The Supreme Court addressed the applicability of the Sherman Act to the NCAA in [*Board of Regents*], holding that the NCAA's plan to restrict television coverage of inter-collegiate football games violated section 1. The Court discussed the procompetitive nature of the NCAA's activities such as establishing eligibility requirements as opposed to the anticompetitive nature of the television plan. Yet, while the Court distinguished the NCAA's television plan from its rule making, it did not comment directly on whether the Sherman Act would apply to the latter.

Although insofar as we are aware no court of appeals expressly has addressed the issue of whether antitrust laws apply to the NCAA's promulgation of eligibility rules, *cf. McCormack v. National Collegiate Athletic Assn*, 845 F.2d 1338, 1343 (5th Cir. 1988) (assuming without deciding that the NCAA's eligibility rules were subject to antitrust scrutiny and holding that the "no-draft" and "no-agent" rules do not have an anticom-petitive effect), many district courts have held that the Sherman Act does not apply to the NCAA's promulgation and enforcement of eligibility requirements. *See Gaines v. National Collegiate Athletic Assn*, 746 F. Supp. 738, 744-46 (M.D. Tenn. 1990) (holding that antitrust law cannot be used to invalidate NCAA eligibility rules, but noting in dicta that the "no-agent" and "no-draft" rules have primarily procompetitive effects); *Jones v. National Collegiate Athletic Assn*, 392 F. Supp. 295, 303 (D. Mass. 1975) (holding that antitrust law does not apply to NCAA eligibility rules).

We agree with these courts that the eligibility rules are not related to the NCAA's commercial or business activities. Rather than intending to provide the NCAA with a commercial advantage, the eligibility rules primarily seek to ensure fair competition in intercollegiate athletics. Based upon the Supreme Court's recognition that the Sher-man Act primarily was intended to prevent unreasonable restraints in "business and commercial transactions," and therefore has only limited applicability to organizations which have principally noncommercial objectives, we find that the Sherman Act does not apply to the NCAA's promulgation of eligibility requirements . . .

For the foregoing reasons, we will affirm the district court's dismissal of appellant's Sherman Act claim. . . .

NOTES

1. Student-athlete eligibility rules. The *Smith* case illustrates that courts are reluctant to find that eligibility rules for student-athletes have anticompetitive effects and presume, without detailed legal or factual analysis, that such rules are necessary to preserve amateurism, academic values, or competitive balance in intercollegiate athletics; therefore, they do not violate the Sherman Act. See also *Banks v. NCAA*, 977 F.2d 1081 (7th Cir.), *cert. denied*, 508 U.S. 908 (1992) (rejecting claim that NCAA "no-draft" and "no-agent" rules are anticompetitive restraints that reduce economic competition among universities for college football players' services). After *Smith*, the NCAA changed its rules to permit student-athletes who graduate before their four years of eligibility is exhausted to participate in intercollegiate athletics at another institution as a graduate student

In *Board of Regents*, the Supreme Court recognized that NCAA schools compete against each other to attract student-athletes to their intercollegiate athletic programs. Uniform eligibility rules both define and limit the nature and scope of competition among NCAA members for student-athletes' services. Scholars contend that these rules should be characterized as commercial activity with their respective net competitive effects individually analyzed under the rule of reason rather than presumed not to violate federal antitrust law. See, e.g., Daniel E. Lazaroff, *The NCAA in Its Second Century: Defender of Amateurism or Antitrust Recidivist?*, 83 Or. L. Rev. 329 (2007); Matthew J. Mitten, *University Price Competition for Elite Students and Athletes: Illusions and Realities*, 36 S. Tex. L. Rev. 59 (1995). Do you agree?

In a recent opinion, the 9th Circuit Court of Appeals wrestled in the context of antitrust law with issues related to amateurism, student compensation at the most competitive and commercial levels in the NCAA:

O'Bannon v. NCAA
2015 WL 5712106 (9th Cir.)

BYBEE, Circuit Judge:
. . . For more than a century, the National Collegiate Athletic Association (NCAA) has prescribed rules governing the eligibility of athletes at its more than 1,000 member colleges and universities. Those rules prohibit student-athletes from being paid for the use of their names, images, and likenesses (NILs). The question presented in this momentous case is whether the NCAA's rules are subject to the antitrust laws and, if so, whether they are an unlawful restraint of trade.

After a bench trial and in a thorough opinion, the district court concluded that the NCAA's compensation rules were an unlawful restraint of trade. It then enjoined the NCAA from prohibiting its member schools from giving student-athletes scholarships up to the full cost of attendance at their respective schools and up to $5,000 per year in deferred compensation, to be held in trust for student-athletes until after they leave college. As far as we are aware, the district court's decision is the first by any federal court to hold that any aspect of the NCAA's amateurism rules violate the antitrust laws, let alone to mandate by injunction that the NCAA change its practices.

We conclude that the district court's decision was largely correct. Although we agree with the Supreme Court and our sister circuits that many of the NCAA's amateurism rules are likely to be procompetitive, we hold that those rules are not exempt from antitrust scrutiny; rather, they must be analyzed under the Rule of Reason. Applying the Rule of Reason, we conclude that the district court correctly identified one proper alternative to the current NCAA compensation rules — *i.e.,* allowing NCAA members to give scholarships up to the full cost of attendance — but that the district court's other remedy, allowing students to be paid cash compensation of up to $5,000 per year, was erroneous. We therefore affirm in part and reverse in part. . . .

III

A. *Board of Regents* Did Not Declare the NCAA's Amateurism Rules "Valid as a Matter of Law"

We consider, first, the NCAA's claim that, under *Board of Regents,* all NCAA amateurism rules are "valid as a matter of law." . . .

[T]he NCAA contends that any Section 1 challenge to its amateurism rules must fail as a matter of law because the *Board of Regents* Court held that those rules are presumptively valid. We disagree.

The *Board of Regents* Court certainly discussed the NCAA's amateurism rules at great length, but it did not do so in order to pass upon the rules' merits, given that they were not before the Court. Rather, the Court discussed the amateurism rules for a different and particular purpose: to explain why NCAA rules should be analyzed under the Rule of Reason, rather than held to be illegal per se. . . .

What is more, even if the language in *Board of Regents* addressing amateurism were *not* dicta, it would not support the tremendous weight that the NCAA seeks to place upon it. The Court's opinion supports the proposition that the preservation of amateurism is a legitimate procompetitive purpose for the NCAA to pursue, but the NCAA is not asking us to find merely that its amateurism rules are procompetitive; rather, it asks us to hold that those rules are essentially exempt from antitrust scrutiny. Nothing in *Board of Regents* supports such an exemption. To say that the NCAA's amateurism rules are procompetitive, as *Board of Regents* did, is not to say that they are automatically lawful; a restraint that serves a procompetitive purpose can still be invalid under the Rule of Reason if a substantially less restrictive rule would further the same objectives equally well. *See Bd. of Regents,* 468 U.S. at 101 n. 23 ("While as the guardian of an important American tradition, the NCAA's motives must be accorded a respectful presumption of validity, it is nevertheless well settled that good motives will not validate an otherwise anticompetitive practice."). . . .

In sum, we accept *Board of Regents'* guidance as informative with respect to the procompetitive purposes served by the NCAA's amateurism rules, but we will go no further than that. The amateurism rules' validity must be proved, not presumed.

B. The Compensation Rules Regulate "Commercial Activity"

The NCAA next argues that we cannot reach the merits of the plaintiffs' Sherman Act claim because the compensation rules are not subject to the Sherman Act at all. The NCAA points out that Section 1 of the Sherman Act applies only to "restraint[s] of trade or commerce," 15 U.S.C. §1, and claims that its compensation rules are mere "eligibility rules" that do not regulate any "commercial activity."

This argument is not credible. Although restraints that have no effect on commerce are indeed exempt from Section 1, the modern legal understanding of "commerce" is broad, "including almost every activity from which the actor anticipates economic gain." Phillip Areeda & Herbert Hovenkamp, *Antitrust Law: An Analysis of Antitrust Principles and Their Application*, ¶ 260b (4th ed. 2013). That definition surely encompasses the transaction in which an athletic recruit exchanges his labor and NIL rights for a scholarship at a Division I school because it is undeniable that both parties to that exchange anticipate economic gain from it. . . .

IV

Like the district court, we follow the three-step framework of the Rule of Reason: "[1] The plaintiff bears the initial burden of showing that the restraint produces significant anticompetitive effects within a relevant market. [2] If the plaintiff meets this burden, the defendant must come forward with evidence of the restraint's procompetitive effects. [3] The plaintiff must then show that any legitimate objectives can be achieved in a substantially less restrictive manner." *Tanaka v. Univ. of S. Cal.*, 252 F.3d 1059, 1063 (9th Cir. 2001).

A. Significant Anticompetitive Effects Within a Relevant Market

[T]he district court made the following factual findings: (1) that a cognizable "college education market" exists, wherein colleges compete for the services of athletic recruits by offering them scholarships and various amenities, such as coaching and facilities; (2) that if the NCAA's compensation rules did not exist, member schools would compete to offer recruits compensation for their NILs; and (3) that the compensation rules therefore have a significant anticompetitive effect on the college education market, in that they fix an aspect of the "price" that recruits pay to attend college (or, alternatively, an aspect of the price that schools pay to secure recruits' services). These findings have substantial support in the record. . . .

B. Procompetitive Effects

[T]he NCAA offered the district court four procompetitive justifications for the compensation rules: (1) promoting amateurism, (2) promoting competitive balance among NCAA schools, (3) integrating student-athletes with their schools' academic community, and (4) increasing output in the college education market. The district court accepted the first and third and rejected the other two. . . .

[The] district court found, and the record supports that there is a concrete procompetitive effect in the NCAA's commitment to amateurism: namely, that the amateur nature of collegiate sports increases their appeal to consumers. We therefore conclude that the NCAA's compensation rules serve the two procompetitive purposes identified by the district court: integrating academics with athletics, and "preserving the popularity of the NCAA's product by promoting its current understanding of amateurism." *O'Bannon,* 7 F.Supp.3d at 1005.17 . . .

C. Substantially Less Restrictive Alternatives

The third step in the Rule of Reason analysis is whether there are substantially less restrictive alternatives to the NCAA's current rules. We bear in mind that — to be viable under the Rule of Reason — an alternative must be "virtually as effective" in serving the procompetitive purposes of the NCAA's current rules, and "without significantly increased cost." . . .

The district court identified two substantially less restrictive alternatives: (1) allowing NCAA member schools to give student-athletes grants-in-aid that cover the full cost of attendance; and (2) allowing member schools to pay student-athletes small amounts of deferred cash compensation for use of their NILs.18 *O'Bannon,* 7 F.Supp.3d at 1005–07. We hold that the district court did not clearly err in finding that raising the grant-in-aid cap would be a substantially less restrictive alternative, but that it clearly erred when it found that allowing students to be paid compensation for their NILs is virtually as effective as the NCAA's current amateur-status rule.

1. *Capping the permissible amount of scholarships at the cost of attendance*

. . . All of the evidence before the district court indicated that raising the grant-in-aid cap to the cost of attendance would have virtually no impact on amateurism: Dr. Mark Emmert, the president of the NCAA, testified at trial that giving student-athletes scholarships up to their full costs of attendance would not violate the NCAA's principles of amateurism because all the money given to students would be going to cover their "legitimate costs" to attend school. Other NCAA witnesses agreed with that assessment. *Id.* at 983. Nothing in the record, moreover, suggested that consumers of college sports would become less interested in those sports if athletes' scholarships covered their full cost of attendance, or that an increase in the grant-in-aid cap would impede the integration of student-athletes into their academic communities. . . .

A compensation cap set at student-athletes' full cost of attendance is a substantially less restrictive alternative means of accomplishing the NCAA's legitimate procompetitive purposes. And there is no evidence that this cap will significantly increase costs; indeed, the NCAA already permits schools to fund student-athletes' full cost of attendance. The district court's determination that the existing compensation rules violate Section 1 of the Sherman Act was correct and its injunction requiring the NCAA to permit schools to provide compensation up to the full cost of attendance was proper.

2. *Allowing students to receive cash compensation for their NILs*

In our judgment, however, the district court clearly erred in finding it a viable alterative to allow students to receive NIL cash payments untethered to their education expenses. . . .

We cannot agree that a rule permitting schools to pay students pure cash compensation and a rule forbidding them from paying NIL compensation are both *equally* effective in promoting amateurism and preserving consumer demand. Both we and the district court agree that the NCAA's amateurism rule has procompetitive benefits. But in finding that paying students cash compensation would promote amateurism as effectively as not paying them, the district court ignored that not paying student-athletes is *precisely what makes them amateurs.*

Having found that amateurism is integral to the NCAA's market, the district court cannot plausibly conclude that being a poorly-paid professional collegiate athlete is "virtually as effective" for that market as being as amateur. Or, to borrow the Supreme Court's analogy, the market for college football is distinct from other sports markets and must be "differentiate[d]" from professional sports lest it become "minor league [football]." *Bd. of Regents,* 468 U.S. at 102. . . .

The difference between offering student-athletes education-related compensation and offering them cash sums untethered to educational expenses is not minor; it is a quantum leap. Once that line is crossed, we see no basis for returning to a rule of amateurism and no defined stopping point; we have little doubt that plaintiffs will continue to challenge the arbitrary limit imposed by the district court until they have captured the full value of their NIL. At that point the NCAA will have surrendered its amateurism principles entirely and transitioned from its "particular brand of football" to minor league status. *Bd. of Regents,* 468 U.S. at 101–02. . . . We thus vacate that portion of the district court's decision and the portion of its injunction requiring the NCAA to allow its member schools to pay this deferred compensation.

V

We vacate the district court's judgment and permanent injunction insofar as they require the NCAA to allow its member schools to pay student-athletes up to $5,000 per year in deferred compensation. We otherwise affirm. . . .

THOMAS, Chief Judge, concurring in part and dissenting in part:

I largely agree with all but one of the majority's conclusions. I respectfully disagree with the majority's conclusion that the district court clearly erred in ordering the NCAA to permit up to $5,000 in deferred compensation above student-athletes' full cost of attendance.

I

. . . There was sufficient evidence in the record to support the award. The district court's conclusion that the proposed alternative restraint satisfied the Rule of Reason was based on testimony from at least four experts — including three experts presented by the NCAA — that providing student-athletes with small amounts of compensation above their cost of attendance most likely would not have a significant impact on consumer interest in college sports. *O'Bannon,* 7 F.Supp.3d at 976–77, 983–84, 1000–01. It was also based on the fact that FBS football players are currently permitted to accept Pell grants in excess of their cost of attendance, and the fact that Division I tennis recruits are permitted to earn up to $10,000 per year in prize money from athletic events before they enroll in college. *Id.* at 974, 1000. The majority characterizes the weight of this evidence as "threadbare." I respectfully disagree.

The NCAA's own expert witness, Neal Pilson, testified that the level of deferred compensation would have an effect on consumer demand for college athletics, but that paying student-athletes $5,000 per year in trust most likely would not have a significant impact on such demand. He also testified that any negative impact that paying student-athletes might have on consumer demand could be partially mitigated by placing the compensation in a trust fund to be paid out after graduation. . . .

The majority also dismisses the testimony given by expert witness Dr. Daniel Rascher demonstrating that consumer interest in major league baseball and the Olympics increased after baseball players' salaries rose and professional athletes were allowed to compete in the Olympics. * * * Rascher also testified that consumer demand in sports such as tennis and rugby increased after the sports' governing boards permitted athletes to receive payment. *O'Bannon,* 7 F.Supp.3d at 977. . . .

The district court accepted the testimony of multiple experts that small amounts of compensation would not affect consumer demand, and then used the lowest amount suggested by one of the NCAA's experts. The district court was within its right to do so.

II

. . . The NCAA insists that consumers will flee if student-athletes are paid even a small sum of money for colleges' use of their NILs. This assertion is contradicted by the district court record and by the NCAA's own rules regarding amateurism. The district court was well within its right to reject it. Division I schools have spent $5 billion on athletic facilities over the past 15 years. The NCAA sold the television rights to broadcast the NCAA men's basketball championship tournament for 12 years to CBS for $10.8 billion dollars. The NCAA insists that this multi-billion dollar industry would be lost if the teenagers and young adults who play for these college teams earn one dollar above their cost of school attendance. That is a difficult argument to swallow. Given the trial evidence, the district court was well within its rights to reject it. . . .

QUESTIONS

1. Analyzing *O'Bannon*.   Should the NCAA's rules barring student-athletes from receiving a share of the licensing revenues generated from products using student-athletes' names, images, and likenesses violate §1? Is preservation of amateurism a legitimate procompetitive economic objective or merely a factor in determining whether these rules have a procompetitive effect? What issues do all three judges agree on and what is the issue upon which the two-judge majority disagrees with the dissenting judge? If the dissent prevailed on this issue, what would the implications be for NCAA member institutions playing at this level?

2. Value of a scholarship.   The value of a baccalaureate degree is generally substantial. See, e.g., *http://www.bls.gov/careeroutlook/2014/data-on-display/education-still-pays.htm* for a recent article indicating that the median weekly income for a high school graduate is $651 and $1,108 for a graduate with a bachelor's degree. If the NCAA became a minor league for the NFL and NBA, is it likely that most student-athletes would receive: 1) more compensation; 2) compensation at essentially the same level (with dollars being paid in cash compensation rather than as scholarships covering educational and living expenses); or 3) less valuable compensation? In allocating its limited resources, should the NCAA focus on increasing student-athletes graduation rates, particularly for FBS football players and Division I men's basketball players (as it has of late), or on increasing non-educational related compensation? What are the corresponding effects of either objective on athletes and its member institutions?

3. NCAA limits on number of scholarships.   In *Agnew v. NCAA*, 683 F.3d 328 (7th Cir. 2012), the Seventh Circuit distinguished between NCAA student-athlete eligibility rules, which courts generally rule are presumptively legal under *Board of Regents* as procompetitive means of fostering competition among amateur intercollegiate athletic teams, and other forms of NCAA regulation such as limiting the duration of athletic scholarships to one year and the total number of scholarships a university may award for a particular sport, which have adverse commercial effects on student-athletes and may be challenged as a violation of §1 of the Sherman Act. Observing that "[m]ost — if not all — eligibility rules . . . fall comfortably within the presumption of procompetitiveness afforded to certain NCAA regulations," the court explained that "the prohibition against multi-year scholarships, seem to be aimed at containing university costs, not preserving the product of college football, though evidence presented at a later stage could prove that the Bylaws are, in fact, key to the survival of the student-athlete and amateurism." *Id.* at 343. While this case was pending, but before it was decided by the Seventh Circuit, NCAA bylaws were amended to permit Division I universities to award multi-year athletic scholarships, which many of them now are doing.

Applying *Agnew*, in *Rock v. NCAA*, 2013 WL 4479815 (S.D. Ind.), a case involving a former FCS football player who sought damages for non-renewal of his athletic scholarship, the court ruled that an antitrust challenge to NCAA limits on the maximum number of Division I football scholarships its member universities could award (85 for FBS teams, and 63 for FCS teams) and former prohibitions against multi-year scholarships constitutes commercial activity subject to §1. The court determined Rock adequately alleged these NCAA bylaws had the requisite anticompetitive effects in a relevant market defined as "the nationwide market for the labor of Division I football student athletes" by "reduc[ing] the overall supply of football scholarships available to student-athletes thereby forcing them to accept far less compensation than they would have received for their labor." *Id.* at *3. It held he had standing to challenge both the FCS and FBS scholarship limits because of his allegation that "he would have received more scholarship offers, including from FBS teams," which he would have to prove at trial. *Id.* at *7.

4. Possible congressional intervention.   Given the high costs of complying with the *O'Bannon* ruling as well as the complexity and uncertainty associated with antitrust challenges to its student-athlete eligibility rules, the NCAA might seek a congressional exemption from antitrust law, which would permit the NCAA and its member institutions to spend the substantial revenues generated from intercollegiate athletics in other ways, including increased educational support for all student-athletes. If you were a member of Congress, what assurances or conditions would you require from the NCAA in exchange for the granting of an exemption immunizing its student-athlete eligibility rules from antitrust challenge?

5. Pending antitrust cases.   In *Jenkins v. NCAA*, a group of current and former Division I basketball and FBS football players allege the NCAA, Pacific 12 Conference, Big Ten Conference, Big Twelve Conference, Southeastern Conference, and Atlantic Coast Conference "earn billions of dollars in revenues each year through the hard work, sweat, and sometimes broken bodies of top-tier college football and men's basketball athletes who perform services for Defendants' member institutions in the big business of college sports. However, instead of allowing their member institutions to compete for the services of those players while operating their businesses, Defendants have entered into what amounts to cartel agreements with the avowed purpose and effect of placing a ceiling on the compensation that may be paid to these athletes for their services. Those restrictions are pernicious, a blatant violation of the antitrust laws, have no legitimate pro-competitive justification, and should now be struck down and enjoined." They assert this is "a patently unlawful price-fixing and group boycott arrangement" causing them to receive "less remuneration for their playing services than they would receive in a competitive market," which should be enjoined so that the free market can determine the economic value and components of athletic scholarships for Division I basketball and FBS football players. Considering *Board of Regents* and *O'Bannon*, do the antitrust laws prohibit NCAA universities from agreeing to any limits on the amount of economic compensation intercollegiate athletes may receive?

Legal Relationships Between the University and Student-Athletes

4

CONTRACTUAL AND NCAA REGULATORY DIMENSIONS

A. Introduction

An examination of the contractual nature of the relationship between student-athletes and their colleges and universities is an appropriate point of departure for studying the various dimensions of this relationship. To facilitate your understanding, we begin with a discussion of basic contract law principles.

KEY TERMS
- Breach
- Consideration
- Contract
- Damages
- Express contract
- Implied contract
- Modification
- Mutual assent
- Offer
- Promise
- Promissory estoppel

1. Contract Formation and Consideration

a. Mutual Assent

The law of contracts deals with promises and the legal effect of the promises that individuals or groups of individuals make to each other. A key term in the body of law known as contracts is a *promise*, which involves a person making a commitment to do or not to do something in the future. Another important term is *contract*, which is defined as "a promise or a set of promises for the breach of which the law gives a remedy, or the performance of which the law in some way recognizes as a duty." Restatement (Second) of Contracts §1. In other words, a "contract is simply an agreement, oral or written, that can be enforced in court." Katherine Currier and Thomas E. Eimermann, *Introduction to Paralegal Studies* 171 (4th ed. 2010).

Consider the following scenario. If a professor and student agree that the student will serve as his research assistant during the summer term at $10 per hour, they have entered into a contract. The professor promised to pay the student $10 per hour, and the student, in turn, promised to serve as the professor's research assistant. To reiterate, an enforceable contract resulted from their communication.

Often, one party to a contract is referred to as the *promisor* and the other as the *promisee.* The promisee is the party who seeks to enforce the promise. The promisor is the party who has allegedly refused to honor the promise. Thus, if the professor alleged that no contract existed, he would be the promisor and the student would be the promisee.

For an exchange of promises to create an enforceable contract, there must be (1) an agreement (mutual assent), which generally arises when one person makes an offer to another person who accepts the offer, and (2) consideration to support the promise. *Consideration* refers to something of legal value that is exchanged between the parties.

An *offer* is defined as a promise to do or not to do something conditioned on the other party's promising to do something in return or actually do what the offer requested. In order for a promise to give rise to an offer, it must specifically express an intention to enter into a contract if the other party accepts the offer. An *acceptance* is the expression of intent to enter into a contract on the terms set forth in the offer. An acceptance is effective only if communicated to the offeror by the person or persons to whom the offer was directed.

The offeror is said to be the *master* of the offer, in that he or she can specify the manner in which the offer can be accepted. Thus, if the offer specifies that it can only be accepted by performance, then the parties have entered into a unilateral contract. For example, suppose a woman promises to give a teenager $20 if the teenager climbs a flagpole within five minutes. The woman has created an offer for a unilateral contract. A unilateral contract will arise if the promisee, the teenager, climbs the flagpole within the five minutes allowed by the offer.

More commonly, however, the offer expressly or impliedly permits an acceptance by an exchange of promises. In the case of the research assistant, the professor made an offer to hire and pay the student at a certain rate in return for the student's promise to serve as his research assistant. The student's affirmative response constituted an acceptance of the offer and the two, the offer and the acceptance, combined to satisfy the mutual assent requirement of an enforceable contract. Assuming that consideration is present, the parties have entered into a bilateral contract, which arises pursuant to an exchange of promises.

Suppose that instead of accepting the professor's offer to work for $10 per hour, the student responded to the offer by stating, "I will not work for $10 but will work for you for $12 per hour." In this instance, no contract arises. The student has made a counteroffer that terminates the original offer made by the professor. In its place is a new offer made by the student, in which she offers to work in exchange for $12 per hour. If the professor says, "I accept," a contract has arisen pursuant to the terms of the student's contract.

b. Consideration and Promissory Estoppel

Consideration is present as follows: "A performance or return promise is bargained for if it is sought by the promisor in return for making his promise and is given by the promisee in exchange for that promise." *Restatement (Second) of Contracts* §71. In our scenario, the professor made the offer to the student seeking to induce her to promise to perform as his research assistant. At the same time, the student made the promise to perform in response to and seeking the promise from the professor to pay her $8 per hour. Therefore they exchanged something of value that each sought from the other.

A promise may give rise to a legal obligation even though there is no consideration to support the promise. The concept of promissory estoppel provides for the enforceability of a promise based on the justifiable reliance of the promisee on that promise. Therefore, if a person makes a promise with reason to know that the promisee is likely to rely on that promise, and the promisee does justifiably rely (changes his or her position), the promise is binding based on the promisee's reliance. Assume that the professor promised the student an unpaid summer research position. After the professor made the promise, the student received an offer for a paid internship with a company. In reliance on the professor's promise of an unpaid internship, the student rejected the offer of the firm. Subsequently, the professor reneged on his promise. The student could have a claim against the professor for promissory estoppel.

2. Modification

Parties often seek to change the terms of their agreement. When this occurs, they may seek to modify their contract. As was true of the original contract to which the parties agreed, a *modification* requires mutual assent (agreement to change the terms) and consideration. A lack of consideration will render the attempted modification unenforceable if the promisee's performance is no different than what it originally promised to do. The preexisting duty rule provides that "a promise to perform a preexisting obligation is not sufficient consideration in exchange for a promise by the other party." In our scenario, assume the professor originally agreed to pay and the student agreed to work for $10 per hour. The professor subsequently promised to pay the student $12 per hour. If the student is to perform the same services as originally agreed, the modification is ineffective due to a lack of consideration, and the professor's promise would be unenforceable if he later were to refuse to pay the student the increased amount. On the other hand, if the professor promised to pay the student $12 per hour because the nature of the services the student were to perform had changed, then consideration would be present and the modified contract would be enforceable. The student's duties under the modified agreement would be different from the duties that the student originally agreed to undertake.

3. Express and Implied Contracts

A distinction is sometimes made between an express contract and an implied contract. An *express contract* is simply one where the mutual assent arises from the words exchanged between the parties to the contract. An *implied contract* is one where the mutual assent arises from their conduct. Even though this distinction is sometimes made, it has no real legal significance. Returning to our scenario, assume that the professor and the student generally discuss but never expressly agree that the student will provide services at $10 per hour. Assume also that the student provides and the professor accepts her research services. They will have entered into an implied contract. If $10 per hour is the generally recognized rate for research assistant services at their university, the professor will more than likely be required to pay $10 per hour.

Even if mutual assent and consideration are present, circumstances may nevertheless bar the enforcement of the contract. Contract law recognizes defenses that will render a contract unenforceable. These defenses include misrepresentation, undue influence, duress, mistake, illegality, the statute of frauds (i.e., the agreement was not memorialized in a writing or record as required by law), and lack of capacity of one or both parties (i.e., at least one of the parties to the contract was mentally incompetent or a minor).

4. Performance, Breach, and Remedies

a. Breach

In our scenario, assume that the professor and student have entered into an enforceable contract. The student, who was to be paid on a weekly basis, works for three weeks, but the professor unjustifiably refuses to make any of the three payments due to the student. The professor has breached the contract. A breach occurs when there is nonperformance of a legal duty. Because a court would likely find that the professor's breach was a material breach, not only would the student be able to sue for damages (the payments due), she would also be entitled to discontinue her performance obligations under the contract.

A party may also commit a breach by anticipatory repudiation, which occurs when a party, before the time when its performance is due, unequivocally expresses an unwillingness or inability to perform the agreed-upon obligations. Assume that two weeks before she is to begin to work for the professor, the student tells the professor that she has decided to work at a company rather than for him. The student has anticipatorily repudiated the contract and unless the repudiation is properly retracted, the professor may sue the student for breach. In addition, the professor's obligation to pay the student is discharged.

b. Excuses for Nonperformance

A party's breach of a contract may be excused. The impossibility doctrine excuses a party's nonperformance where performance has become objectively impossible due to no fault of the promisor, and the promisor has assumed the risk of performing even if performance were to become impossible. Illness is considered a form of impossibility. Thus, if the student is incapacitated and unable to perform due to an illness, her nonperformance will be excused and her performance obligation will be discharged. A party's nonperformance will also be excused when its performance becomes impracticable or by frustration of purpose (where the underlying purpose of the contract is so defeated as to be worthless).

5. *Damages*

Where a party's nonperformance is unjustified, the other party is entitled to a remedy for breach. Contract damages seek to compensate the injured party for the actual loss from breach. The preferred remedy in American law is monetary relief. Requiring the breaching party to perform as promised, specific performance, is considered an extraordinary form of relief and will be awarded under limited circumstances.

Therefore in our scenario, assume that the student works, but the professor pays only part of the agreed-upon salary. The student would be entitled to damages, most likely measured by the difference between the promised payment and what was actually paid. So if the professor promised to pay the student a total of $800 but paid her only $600, the student would be entitled to recover $200 as damages.

Assume that the student unjustifiably refuses to work for the professor. Because this is a personal services/employment contract, the professor cannot seek specific performance, which would involve going to court and requesting that the court order the student to work for the professor. The professor would be entitled to monetary damages measured by the difference between what he promised to pay the student and the additional cost, if any, that he would be required to pay if he had to hire another student to perform the services of the breaching student.

In the above scenario, the nonbreaching party was awarded its expectation damages. We note, without discussion, that damages may also be measured based on protecting the nonbreaching party's reliance and restitution interests.

B. Contractual Aspects of the Student-Athlete and University Relationship

KEY TERMS
- National Letter of Intent
- One academic year in residence
- Statement of Financial Assistance

The contractual relationship between a student-athlete and his or her institution arises out of several documents, including the Statement of Financial Assistance, the National Letter of Intent (NLI), and university publications such as bulletins and catalogues. These documents largely define the nature of the obligations that student-athletes owe to their colleges or universities and the obligations that these educational institutions owe to their student-athletes.

1. Statement of Financial Assistance

Student-athletes who obtain athletic scholarships sign form documents commonly referred to as a Statement of Financial Assistance. Pursuant to a Statement of Financial Assistance, a college agrees to extend financial aid to student-athletes to the extent of tuition, fees, room, board, and books. The purpose of the financial aid award is to assist and enable student-athletes to pursue a program of study and to participate in the educational process of the institution. In exchange for the university's commitment, a student-athlete promises to attend a particular college and to participate in athletics. A student-athlete's right to continue to receive financial assistance is contingent on the athlete remaining academically eligible to participate in the institution's athletic program. Student-athletes also promise to comply with the rules and regulations of their institutions, athletic conferences (e.g., Atlantic Coast Conference (ACC) and Southeastern Conference (SEC)), and the athletic association (e.g., National Collegiate Athletic Association (NCAA)).

2. National Letter of Intent

The other key document that defines the student-athlete and university relationship is the National Letter of Intent (NLI). The purposes of the NLI include reducing and limiting recruiting pressure on student-athletes. See National Letter of Intent, *About the National Letter of Intent (NLI), http://www.nationalletter.org/aboutTheNli/index.html.*

Several implications flow from a prospective student-athlete signing a NLI. By signing an NLI, a prospective student-athlete agrees for a period of one year to attend the institution named in the NLI (hereinafter referred to as "named institution"). Thereafter, other institutions must cease all recruiting contacts with the student-athlete. Conversely, the named institution may freely contact the student-athlete. The NLI is not effective unless the student-athlete has received a promise in writing from the named institution to provide financial aid for an entire academic year. Assuming the student-athlete complies with NCAA financial aid eligibility requirements and is admitted to the named institution, the athlete is entitled to a scholarship for a minimum of one full academic year from the named institution. A student-athlete who fails to attend the named institution will be penalized by having to serve one academic year in residence at and losing one year of athletic eligibility to compete in all sports at the new institution in which he or she enrolls. Finally, a student-athlete's one-year commitment remains effective even if the coach for whom the athlete anticipated he or she would play leaves the named institution.

NLI provisions are available at *http://www.nationalletter.org/nliProvisions/index.html.* The following is a sampling of key provisions of the NLI.

THE NATIONAL LETTER OF INTENT

2. Financial Aid Requirement.   At the time I sign this NLI, I must receive a written offer of athletics financial aid applicable for the entire . . . academic year from the institution named in this document. The offer must list the terms, conditions, and amount of the athletics award. . . . In order for this NLI to be valid, my parent/legal guardian and I must sign the NLI and I must also sign the offer of athletics aid . . . prior to submission to the institution named in this document, and any other stated conditions must also be met. If the conditions stated on the financial aid offer are not met, this NLI shall be declared null and void. . . .

7. Letter Becomes Null and Void. This NLI shall be declared null and void if any of the following occur:

 a. Admissions Requirement. This NLI shall be declared null and void if the institution named in this document notifies me in writing that I have been denied admission or, by the opening day of classes in the fall . . . , has failed to provide me with written notice of admission, provided I have submitted a complete admission application. . . .

 b. Eligibility Requirements. This NLI shall be declared null and void if, by the opening day of classes in the fall . . . , I have not met (1) NCAA initial eligibility requirements; (2) NCAA, conference or institution's requirements for financial aid to student-athletes; (3) or the two-year transfer requirements, provided I have submitted all necessary documents for eligibility determinations.

QUESTIONS

1. Identify a requirement that must be satisfied before the NLI commits a student-athlete to a particular institution.
2. Identify a circumstance under which a student-athlete would no longer be bound to an institution by the NLI.
3. You are a student-athlete whose decision to sign with a particular institution is influenced by your desire to play for a certain coach. After you sign a NLI and before you arrive on campus, the coach leaves to work at another institution. Can you follow the coach to the new institution? What are the consequences of your doing so?
4. What principle that underlies the NLI program is reinforced by having student-athletes commit to an educational institution rather than to a coach? What are the pros and cons of this approach?

C. Student-Athlete Financial Aid and Other Benefits

1. NCAA Regulations Governing Contracts and Scholarships

In determining the terms of the athletic scholarship between a university and its student-athletes, it is important also to consider applicable NCAA regulations. NCAA Bylaw Article 15, which governs institutional financial aid to student-athletes, is particularly significant. From an association-wide perspective, Article 15 regulates how many scholarships an institution is allowed to give to student-athletes in a particular sport. For example, a football team is permitted to give more scholarships than a baseball team. (See 2012–13 NCAA Division I Manual, Bylaw 15.5.)

Article 15 also speaks to the specifics of the financial aid that institutions award to student-athletes. Pursuant to legislation the NCAA adopted in 1973, its rules restricted institutions to awarding to student-athletes one-year renewable athletic scholarships. Effective August 2012, NCAA amended legislation permits institutions to award multiyear scholarships. (See 2012–13 NCAA Division I Manual, Bylaw 15.3.3.1.) Because of its permissive nature, institutions have the discretion to award scholarships from one to up to four or five years. Since 2012, several institutions adopted policies stating that they would award multiyear scholarships. Representative institutions include Ohio State, Florida, Arizona State, South Carolina, UCLA, Oklahoma State, Kentucky, Clemson, Virginia, and Oregon. Jon Solomon, *Schools Can Give out 4-Year Athletic Scholarships, but Many Don't,* CBS Sports.com (Sept. 16, 2014), *http://www.cbssports.com/collegefootball/writer/jon-solomon/24711067/schools-can -give-out-4-year-scholarships-to-athletes-but-many-dont.*

Following the lead of individual institutions, three of the five autonomy conferences have adopted conference legislation pursuant to which their institutions will offer multiyear scholarships. The Big Ten led the way when it announced in October 2014 that its institutions would offer multiyear scholarships in all sports. The Big Ten policy also permits its institutions, consistent with NCAA financial aid rules effective in 2012, to award athletic aid to a student-athlete who returns to the school to complete his or her degree if his or her education was interrupted for a legitimate reason. See *2014–15 NCAA Division I Manual* §15.01.5.2; Big Ten, *Big Ten Acts to Support Student-Athlete Graduation,* BigTen.org (Oct. 8, 2014), *http://www.bigten.org/genrel/100814aaa.html.* The Pac-12 followed the Big Ten in adopting a policy to award multiyear scholarships in all sports and permitting a student-athlete to return to the institution and receive athletic aid. As it relates to athletic scholarships, the Big 12 has adopted conference legislation that is substantively the same as that of the Pac-12 and Big Ten.

NCAA regulations also strictly limit the circumstances under which an institution can cancel or reduce the amount of the athletic scholarship during the term of the scholarship. Suppose an athlete has been awarded a one-year athletic scholarship. If the athlete suffers an injury playing sports or practicing during that year, his or her scholarship cannot be canceled. On the other hand, the scholarship can be canceled if the athlete becomes ineligible to participate in intercollegiate athletics, voluntarily withdraws from athletic participation, or engages in serious misconduct warranting substantial disciplinary action. When the term of a scholarship expires, an institution has the discretion not to renew the scholarship for virtually any reason, including athletic performance–related reasons. Indeed, the NCAA provides the student-athlete little recourse to challenge the nonrenewal decision so long as the institution complies with the timeline articulated in NCAA regulations and the decision is made by the institution's financial aid authority. In such instances, the student-athlete must look to policies of his or her institution, which may provide additional protections including the process (e.g., a hearing) that the institution must follow before a scholarship can be canceled.

Changes adopted by the NCAA at its January 15, 2015, annual meeting restrict the ability of institutions to cancel athletic scholarships. Universities that comprise what are characterized as the "autonomy schools," consisting of institutions that are members of the Atlantic Coast Conference (ACC), Southeastern Conference (SEC), Pac 12, Big Ten, and Big-12, passed legislation that prevents schools and coaches from reducing or refusing to renew a student-athlete's scholarship based on a "student-athlete's athletics ability, performance, or contribution to a team's success . . . or [a]n injury, illness, or physical or mental medical condition. . . ." *2015–16 NCAA Division I Manual* at §15.3.4.3. These resolutions are particularly important in those instances in which an institution awards a multiyear scholarship to an athlete.

The autonomy schools also adopted legislation that redefines an athletic scholarship to encompass not only tuition, room, board, books, and fees, but also the incidental costs of attending college, such as transportation and miscellaneous personal expenses. The gap between how the NCAA traditionally defined an athletic scholarship and the true cost of attendance has been estimated at between $2,000 and $5,000 annually per student. The cost to colleges and universities of awarding true-cost-of-attendance scholarships has been estimated to range from $1 to $2.5 million per institution. The true-cost-of-attendance legislation is mandatory for autonomy schools but is permissive for non-autonomy schools. See *Id.* at §§15.02.5, 15.5.3.2.1.

The autonomy schools also passed legislation that permits a student-athlete to "borrow against future earnings to purchase so-called loss of value insurance — policies that can help athletes if an injury while playing college sports results in an athlete getting less money from a professional contract." *Id.* at §12.1.2.4.4. Finally, these schools passed a resolution in which they pledged to approve within two years changes to the rule that "[r]egulate time demands to ensure an appropriate balance between athletics participation and the academic obligations and opportunities presented to students generally . . . [and to e]nhance benefits provided to student-athletes in a manner that is reasonable and appropriate for supporting their needs within the collegiate model." NCAA Resolution R-2014-1.

QUESTIONS

1. Prior to 2012, what was the duration of a student-athlete's contract with his or her college? Beginning in 2012, may a university award a student-athlete a two-year athletic scholarship? May it award a four-year athletic scholarship?
2. Assume that an institution grants a student-athlete a one-year athletic scholarship. In the middle of the athlete's sport's season, the athlete's coach becomes dissatisfied with the athlete's athletic performance. At this point, may the coach cancel or reduce the amount of the athlete's scholarship because his or her performance has not met the coach's expectations?
3. What limitations, if any, are imposed on the discretion that institutions have to refuse to renew a student-athlete's scholarship? Does the discretion afforded institutions encourage particular forms of conduct by coaches?

4. Prior to 2015, what was the gap between the amount an athlete received from an athletic scholarship and the true cost of attendance? What is the estimated cost to universities to provide true-cost-of-attendance scholarships?
5. Beginning in 2015, are all universities required to provide true-cost-of-attendance scholarships to athletes?
6. Assume that a NFL draft-eligible athlete was a projected first-round draft pick entering his final season. During his last season, he suffers a severe injury causing him to go undrafted. Could he have done anything to protect his future earnings if he attended an autonomy school? What if he attended a school outside the "Power Five"?

NOTE

For additional discussions of the contractual aspects of the student-athlete/university relationship, see the following: Michael Cozzillio, *The Athletic Scholarship and the College National Letter of Intent: A Contract by Any Other Name*, 35 Wayne L. Rev. 1275 (1989); Louis Hakim, Note, *The Student-Athlete vs. the Athlete Student: Has the Time Arrived for an Extended-Term Scholarship Contract?*, 2 Va. J. Sports & L. 145, 165 (2000); Debra D. Burke & Angela J. Grube, *The NCAA Letter of Intent: A Voidable Agreement for Minors?*, 81 Miss. L.J. 265 (2011).

D. Defining the Scope of Institutional Obligations to Student-Athletes

KEY TERMS
- Breach of contract
- Duty of good faith
- Educational malpractice
- Reasonable academic progress

Litigation has ensued over the scope of the respective obligations that arise out of the student-athlete and university relationship. Colleges maintain that the primary contractual obligation they owe to their student-athletes is the provision of financial aid. Nevertheless, student-athletes have filed lawsuits urging courts to impose obligations on institutions that are not specifically articulated in the principal contract documents (i.e., Statement of Financial Aid and the NLI). Much of this litigation involves student-athletes' efforts to broaden the scope of the obligations their institutions owe to them. The following cases reveal, however, that courts have been very reluctant to expand the rights of student-athletes or to impose obligations on institutions beyond those duties expressly spelled out in the contract documents. *Taylor* addresses the fundamental obligations that result from the contractual relationship between student-athletes and their institutions. *Ross* focuses on the extent to which terms, other than those expressly delineated in the contract, should be incorporated into the student-athlete/university contract in order to promote the academic interests of student-athletes.

Taylor v. Wake Forest University
191 S.E.2d 379 (N.C. App. 1972)

CAMPBELL, Judge.

[Editors' note: Gregg Taylor, a student-athlete at Wake Forest University, and his father alleged that the university wrongfully terminated the athlete's football scholarship after he refused to participate in football because of his poor academic performance. Taylor's grade point average (GPA) for the first semester of his freshman year was 1.0 on a 4.0 scale. As a result of this poor academic showing, Taylor refused, and in fact was ineligible, to play football during the spring term of his freshman year. Taylor's second semester GPA improved to 1.9, which restored his academic eligibility to participate (at that time, Wake Forest required a 1.35 GPA after freshman year). He refused, however, to play football during his sophomore year. Following a hearing before the university's Faculty Athletic Committee, Wake Forest terminated Taylor's scholarship after his sophomore year because of his failure to participate in the football program. Taylor, who ultimately received a degree from Wake Forest, sought to recover expenses that he incurred in completing his junior and senior years at the university.]

Plaintiffs contend that . . . a jury should determine whether Gregg Taylor acted reasonably and in good faith in refusing to participate in the football program at Wake Forest when such participation interfered with reasonable academic progress.

The plaintiffs' position depends upon a construction of the contractual agreement between plaintiffs and Wake Forest. . . . [T]he position of the plaintiffs is that it was orally agreed between plaintiffs and the representative of Wake Forest that:

[I]n the achievement and athletic involvement, participation in athletic activities could be limited or eliminated to the extent necessary to assure reasonable academic progress.

And plaintiffs were to be the judge as to what "reasonable academic progress" constituted.

We do not agree with the position taken by plaintiffs. The scholarship application filed by Gregg Taylor provided:

I agree to maintain eligibility for intercollegiate athletics under both Conference and Institutional rules. Training rules for intercollegiate athletics are considered rules of the Institution, and I agree to abide by them.

Both Gregg Taylor and his father knew that the application was for "Football Grant-In-Aid or A Scholarship," and that the scholarship was "awarded for academic and athletic achievement." It would be a strained construction of the contract that would enable the plaintiffs to determine the "reasonable academic progress" of Gregg Taylor. Gregg Taylor, in consideration of the scholarship award, agreed to maintain his athletic eligibility and this meant both physically and scholastically. As long as his grade average equaled or exceeded the requirements of Wake Forest, he was maintaining his scholastic eligibility for athletics. Participation in and attendance at practice were required to maintain his physical eligibility. When he refused to do so in the absence of any injury or excuse other than to devote more time to studies, he was not complying with his contractual obligations.

The record disclosed that Wake Forest fully complied with its agreement and that Gregg Taylor failed to do so. . . . [S]ummary judgment was proper.

QUESTIONS

In *Taylor*, the court identified two requirements necessary for student–athletes to maintain their athletic eligibility. What are they? Do you view one as being more important than the other, or are they of equal importance?

Ross v. Creighton University
957 F.2d 410 (7th Cir. 1992)

RIPPLE, Circuit Judge.

[Editors' note: In the spring of 1978, Kevin Ross, a high school senior from an academically disadvantaged background, accepted an athletic scholarship to attend Creighton University and to play on its varsity basketball team. When he enrolled, Ross's academic level was far below that of the average Creighton student. Ross scored in the bottom-fifth percentile of college-bound seniors taking the American College Test, while the average freshman admitted to Creighton with him scored in the upper 27 percent.

During Ross's attendance at Creighton from 1978 until 1982, he maintained a D average and acquired 96 of the 128 credits he needed to graduate. Many of Ross's credits were in courses such as Marksmanship and Theory of Basketball, which did not count toward a university degree. Ross alleged that Creighton's Athletic Department advised him to take these courses and employed a secretary to read his assignments and prepare and type his papers. Ross also asserted that Creighton failed to abide by its promise to provide him with sufficient and competent tutoring. When he left Creighton, Ross had the overall language skills of a fourth grader and the reading skills of a seventh grader.

Ross filed a lawsuit asserting several claims, including a tort-based educational malpractice claim and a breach of contract claim. The district court granted the university's motion to dismiss all of Ross's claims and he appealed the decision. (See Chapter 7 for an overview of tort law principles.)

With respect to the educational malpractice claim, Ross asserted that Creighton owed a duty to educate him and breached its duty when it failed to do so. The appellate court agreed with the district court in dismissing Ross's educational malpractice claim.

The court identified several policy reasons, drawn from cases involving nonathlete students, for rejecting Ross's educational malpractice claim: (1) the lack of a satisfactory standard of care by which to evaluate educators since theories of education differ; (2) the inherent uncertainties about the cause and nature of damages because several factors (e.g., the student's attitude, motivation, temperament, past experience, and home environment) converge to affect the student's learning experience, which in turn makes it very difficult to establish that the teacher's conduct proximately caused a student's learning deficiency; (3) recognizing such a claim would create a flood of litigation, the sheer volume of which could overburden schools; and (4) an educational malpractice action would embroil the courts into overseeing the day-to-day operations of schools, which could implicate a university's academic freedom and autonomy.

Turning to Ross's breach of contract claims, the court stated he alleged that "Creighton agreed, in exchange for Mr. Ross' promise to play on its basketball team, to allow him an opportunity to participate, in a meaningful way, in the academic program of the University despite his deficient academic background." Ross alleged that Creighton breached its contract with him by failing to (1) "provide adequate and competent tutoring services," (2) "require [Ross] to attend tutoring sessions," and (3) afford Ross "a reasonable opportunity to take full advantage of tutoring services."]

The Contract Claims

There is no question, we believe, that Illinois would adhere to the great weight of authority and bar any attempt to repackage an educational malpractice claim as a contract claim. As several courts have noted, the policy concerns that preclude a cause of action for educational malpractice apply with equal force to bar a breach of contract claim attacking the general quality of an education. . . .

To state a claim for breach of contract, the plaintiff must do more than simply allege that the education was not good enough. Instead, he must point to an identifiable contractual promise that the defendant failed to honor. Thus, as was suggested in *Paladino*, if the defendant took tuition money and then provided no education, or alternately, promised a set number of hours of instruction and then failed to deliver, a breach of contract action may be available. *Paladino*, 454 N.Y.S.2d at 873. . . .

We read Mr. Ross' complaint to allege more than a failure of the University to provide him with an education of a certain quality. Rather, he alleges that the University knew that he was not qualified academically to participate in its curriculum. Nevertheless, it made a specific promise that he would be able to participate in a meaningful way in that program because it would provide certain specific services to him. Finally, he alleges that the University breached its promise by reneging on its commitment to provide those services and, consequently, effectively cutting him off from any participation in and benefit from the University's academic program. To adjudicate such a claim, the court would not be required to determine whether Creighton had breached its contract with Mr. Ross by providing deficient academic services. Rather, its inquiry would be limited to whether the University had provided any real access to its academic curriculum at all.

Accordingly, we must disagree respectfully with our colleague in the district court as to whether the contract counts of the complaint can be dismissed at the pleadings stage. . . . [W]e believe that the district court can adjudicate Mr. Ross' specific and narrow claim that he was barred from *any* participation in and benefit from the University's academic program without second-guessing the professional judgment of the University faculty on academic matters. . . .

Accordingly, the judgment of the district court is affirmed in part and reversed and remanded in part for proceedings consistent with this opinion. . . .

[Editors' note: Ross eventually settled his lawsuit for $30,000.]

QUESTIONS

1. In *Ross*, what reasons did the court articulate for refusing to recognize an educational malpractice claim? The reasons articulated by the court were drawn from cases not involving student-athletes. Was the court justified in relying on these reasons? Is the student-athlete's relationship with his or her university distinguishable from the nonathlete-student's relationship with his or her university?

2. Although the court rejected Ross's breach-of-contract claim to the extent it merely restated a tort claim for educational malpractice, what is the narrow exception to the general rule of no liability that the court recognized?

NOTES

1. Jackson v. Drake University.   Another leading case, *Jackson v. Drake University*, 778 F. Supp. 1490 (S.D. Iowa 1991), reveals the reluctance of courts to imply terms into the agreement as a means of expanding the obligations that a university owes to student-athletes. In *Jackson*, a basketball player alleged that the coaching staff of the men's basketball team engaged in improper conduct, such as failing to provide independent tutoring and adequate counseling and requiring him to turn in plagiarized work, which undermined the athlete's ability to play basketball and to succeed academically. According to Jackson, the coaching staff's conduct amounted to a breach of contract because "the express contract between him and Drake implicitly granted him the right to an educational opportunity and the right to play basketball for a Division I school." *Id.* at 1493. The court held that "the financial aid agreements do not implicitly contain a right to play basketball." *Id.* The court also refused to impose an obligation on Drake to provide Jackson with an educational opportunity.

2. UNC Litigation.   In *McAdoo v. UNC,* Civil Action No. 1:14-cv-935 (M.D. MC, filed Nov. 6, 2014), a former UNC scholarship basketball player sued the University of North Carolina at Chapel Hill (UNC), alleging that the university failed to "provide the promised legitimate education" but rather "systematically funneled its football student-athletes into a 'shadow curriculum' of bogus courses which never met and which were designed for the sole purpose of providing enrollees high grades." *Id.* at ¶ 1. McAdoo contends that UNC's actions facilitated student-athletes remaining academically eligible so that they could engage in intercollegiate athletics and thereby financially benefit the university. He asserts, "UNC has reaped substantial profits from football student-athletes' performance for the school, but it has not provided them a legitimate education in return." *Id.* at ¶ 4. According to McAdoo, the university's conduct gives rises to claims sounding in breach of contract, fraud in the inducement, and deceptive trade practices. *Id.* at ¶ 7. Subsequent to McAdoo filing his complaint, Rashanda McCants, a former UNC women's basketball player, and Kevin Ramsey, a former UNC football player, filed suit against UNC and the NCAA. In *McCants v. NCAA*, Case No. 15 cvs 1782 (N.C. Superior Ct., filed Jan. 22, 2015), plaintiffs allege that the NCAA and UNC failed to "safeguard and provide a meaningful education to scholarship athletes who agreed to attend UNC — and take the field — in exchange for academically sound instruction." *Id.* at ¶ 1.

3. Disclosure laws.   Student-athletes and their parents are often unaware of the terms and conditions of athletes' contracts with their schools. For example, many athletes and their parents incorrectly assume that scholarships are guaranteed for a four-year period so long as the athletes remain academically and athletically eligible. On September 30, 2010, Governor Arnold Schwarzenegger signed into law the California Student-Athletes' Right to Know Act, which requires university coaches who recruit athletes in California to disclose their institutional and the NCAA's policies regarding medical expenses, scholarship renewals, and transfers to other institutions. The goal of this act is to provide increased disclosure to student-athletes to help them make wise choices. Connecticut has adopted similar legislation. Other states are considering whether to adopt such legislation as well. *Laws Force Disclosure of Scholarships' Fine Print*, Yahoo Sports, June 25, 2011, *http://sports.yahoo.com/top/news?slug=txscholarships*. Is this wise public policy?

4. Rights arising from promises.   Although courts have been reluctant to imply terms into the student-athlete and university relationship, an express promise (written or oral) may be actionable. Bryan Fortay was a highly recruited high school quarterback. Influenced by its reputation as "Quarterback University," Fortay decided to attend and play football at the University of Miami. In his lawsuit, *Fortay v. Univ. of Miami*, 1994 U.S. Dist. Lexis 1865, Fortay maintained that his contract with Miami impliedly obligated the university to provide the guidance necessary to allow him to develop his football talents. A federal district court ruled that the NLI and other contract documents did not give rise to the alleged implied obligations. The district court ruled, however, that Fortay had alleged facts sufficient to support a breach of oral contract claim. These promises allegedly included representations that Miami would provide guidance that would enable Fortay to develop his football skills, that Miami would not recruit other quarterbacks, and that Fortay would be Miami's starting quarterback by his third year.

5. *Giuliani v. Duke University.*   The limits of a student-athlete's ability to rely on oral representations were recently addressed in *Giuliani v. Duke University*, 2010 WL 1292321 (M.D.N.C.) (March 30, 2010). Rod Myers, a former Duke golf coach, recruited plaintiff to play golf at the university. Plaintiff asserted that his decision to enroll at Duke was strongly influenced by Myers's promises of "lifetime access" to Duke's training facilities and the opportunity that would be afforded plaintiff to compete with his teammates to earn spots in NCAA tournaments. Following Coach Myers's unexpected death in spring 2007, Orin Vincent took over as head coach. On February 11, 2008, Vincent announced that he was immediately and indefinitely suspending plaintiff's eligibility to participate in Duke's athletic program. Plaintiff filed claims against Duke and Vincent asserting breach of contract, breach of the covenant of good faith and fair dealing, promissory estoppel, and tortuous interference with contract. In dismissing all of plaintiff's claims, the federal district court judge held that neither Myers's oral statements nor the provisions of the university's policy manuals were enforceable as binding contracts. For recent cases demonstrating courts' unwillingness to enforce oral promises, see *Hairston v. Southern Methodist University*, 441 S.W.3d 327 (Tex. App. 2013) (rejecting student-athlete alleging breach of a coach's oral promise of a scholarship); and *Eppley v. Univ. of Delaware*, 2015 WL 156754 (D. Del. Jan. 12, 2015) (in dismissing plaintiff's negligent misrepresentation claim against university, the court holds, assuming coach promised student-athlete an athletic scholarship for four years, her reliance was unjustified given the terms of the grant in aid and the NLI).

For commentary regarding these issues, see Timothy Davis, *Absence of Good Faith: Defining a University's Educational Obligation to Student-Athletes*, 28 Hous. L. Rev. 743, 783 (1991); Sean M. Hanlon and Ray Yasser, *J.J. Morrison and His Right of Publicity Lawsuit Against the NCAA*, 15 Vill. Sports & Ent. L.J. 241 (2008); and Jamie Y. Momura, *Refereeing the Recruiting Game: Applying Contract Law to Make the Intercollegiate Recruitment Process Fair*, 32 U. Haw. L. Rev. 275 (2009).

E. NCAA Academic Reform Initiatives

KEY TERMS
- Academic Progress Rate (APR)
- Clustering
- Initial eligibility standards
- Jock majors
- Satisfactory progress

1. NCAA Academic Reform Legislation

How likely is it that a Kevin Ross–type scenario will recur? NCAA rules seek, in part, to reduce the likelihood that a student-athlete will leave college after three or four years with the types of learning deficiencies experienced by Ross. These rules include "initial eligibility standards" and "satisfactory progress rules." With respect to the latter, NCAA rules require that, as a condition to eligibility for participation, student-athletes must enroll in classes that allow them to make progress toward obtaining a degree. Particularly pertinent NCAA bylaws in this regard include 14.4.3.1, "Fulfillment of Credit-Hour Requirements," and 14.4.3.2, "Fulfillment of Percentage of Degree Requirements."

The above-described and other "satisfactory progress rules" were a part of Division I (D-I) academic reforms enacted by the NCAA between 2002 and 2004. Another component of the NCAA's reform efforts were the significant revisions made to its initial eligibility rules; NCAA revised eligibility rules deemphasize standardized test scores (i.e., the SAT and ACT), place greater emphasis on high school grades, and increase the number of core course requirements. (The history of and changes to initial eligibility requirements are detailed in Chapter 6.)

Some academics and college administrators laud the revisions as likely to achieve their goal of improving graduation rates. Others, however, warn that the revised rules may have a negative impact on academic achievement. Some are concerned that more athletes will be steered toward "jock majors" — fields of study that allow student-athletes to "maneuver through the maze of academic requirements and remain eligible to compete." Welch Suggs, *Jock Majors*, Chron. Higher Educ., Jan. 17, 2003, at A33. As expressed by one commentator, "[T]he march toward tougher standards and, the NCAA hopes, higher graduation rates begs a crucial question, however: What do numbers matter if players are being sent into academic programs that won't give them a meaningful education or marketable skills?" *Id.* at A34. The clustering of players in particular majors is not a new phenomenon. Whether the revised standards will contribute to this practice is uncertain at this time. For a recent examination of clustering of majors by football players, see Paul Newberry, *Examining Football Player Majors*, USA Today, Sept. 5, 2011, *http://usatoday30.usatoday.com/sports/college/football/2011-09-05-1085948273_x.htm*. In April 2012, the NCAA D-I Board of Directors voted to increase initial academic standards, which will become effective in 2016. See NCAA, *New Eligibility Standards Start in 2016*, NCAA.com (Apr. 26, 2012), *http://www.ncaa.com/news/ncaa/article/2012-04-26/new-eligibility-standards-start-2016*. The new eligibility requirements create a higher academic standard for an incoming freshman. *Id.* In order to compete in intercollegiate athletics, students enrolling on August 1, 2016, and thereafter must: (1) earn at least a 2.3 GPA in core courses; (2) meet an increased sliding-scale standard (for example, an SAT score of 820 requires a 2.5 high school course GPA; and (3) successfully complete 10 of the 16 total required core courses before the start of their seventh semester in high school (7 out of the 10 courses must be successfully completed in English, math, and science). *Id.*

2. Academic Progress Rate

The NCAA adopted another component of its academic reform legislation with its 2004 approval of legislation that instituted a metric known as the *Academic Progress Rate (APR)*. The failure of a team to reach a certain numerical benchmark is likely to lead to the assessment of penalties including scholarship and recruiting restrictions and a team's loss of eligibility for postseason competition.

The impact of the APR on postseason play was realized in dramatic fashion when the NCAA declared that because of a low APR for the four-year period 2007–2008 through 2010–2011, the University of Connecticut men's basketball team, which in 2011 was the NCAA national champion, would be ineligible to participate in post-season play during the 2012–2013 season. Connecticut appealed the NCAA's penalty, arguing that its men's basketball team's APR for 2010–2011 and the first semester of 2011 were perfect. In April 2012, the NCAA rejected the university's appeal. For discussions of the APR, see Welch Suggs, *NCAA Weighs New Penalties for Academic Laggards*, Chron. Higher Educ., April 23, 2004, A42 (discussing the APR as NCAA's incentive/disincentive program); NCAA, *NCAA Backgrounder on Academic Reform*; Michelle B. Hosick, *Academic Success Stories Transcend Improved APRs*, NCAA News, June 9, 2010; and Michelle B. Hosick, *Division I Beginning Major APR Assessment*, NCAA News, June 9, 2010.

In August 2011, the NCAA Board of Directors voted to ban D-I teams with an APR below 930 from participating in the postseason. This ban applies to all NCAA tournaments and football bowl games. See Dana O'Neil, *Increase in Academic Cutline Approved*, ESPN.com (August 12, 2011), *http://espn.go.com/college-sports/story/_/id/6853878/ncaa-committee-approves-increase-apr-cutline*. There are additional punishments for violations of the new APR mandate, which are split into three levels. See NCAA, *Raising the Bar*, NCAA.com (May 27, 2015), *http://www.ncaa.org/about/resources/media-center/news/raising-bar*. Level-one penalties focus on practice restrictions, and teams must use the missed practice time to focus on academics. *Id.* Level-two penalties include the level-one penalty; a reduction of four hours of practice time from the season, to be replaced with academic activities; and the elimination of a nonchampionship season and spring football. Teams without nonchampionship seasons may face a reduced number of contests. *Id.* Level-three penalties include the level-one and level-two penalties and other potential penalties, such as additional practice and contest restrictions, coach-specific penalties (including game and recruiting restrictions), restricted access to practice for incoming students who fall below certain academic standards, restricted membership, and potential multiyear bans on postseason competition. Although overall APR numbers released over the past several years indicate positive trends, APRs posted for football and men's basketball and for low-resource institutions reveal some of the remaining challenges. Football and men's basketball together have shown improvement since APRs were first released but continue to post low multiyear D-I APRs. Low-resource institutions, many of which are also historically black colleges and universities (HBCUs), have posted low APRs, especially for their men's basketball teams.

In 2013–2014, the overall four-year APR increased by 2 points. The increase was heavily aided by substantial increases in the APRs for basketball and football. Men's basketball players earned a 961, which was up 4 points. The APR for football increased 5 points, to 956. Women's basketball increased 2 points to 975. NCAA, *Raising the Bar*, NCAA.com (May 27, 2015), *http://www.ncaa.org/about/resources/media-center/news/raising-bar*.

QUESTIONS

1. Which institutional body or bodies determines whether a student-athlete is making progress toward a degree?
2. Which institutional body or bodies determine if a student-athlete is academically eligible to participate in intercollegiate athletic competition?

3. Can you think of majors at your undergraduate institution in which a disproportionate number of student-athletes are enrolled? What makes these majors appealing to student-athletes? Would you consider them jock majors?

4. Under the current guidelines, student-athletes are required to make progress toward a degree. Should there be additional limitations as to what degrees student-athletes may pursue? Why or why not?

5. Do you think that the penalties for failing to meet the APR requirements will improve the quality of education for student-athletes? Or will it simply funnel more student-athletes into jock majors?

6. Why might football and men's basketball continue to post low multiyear D-I APRs in spite of the increased APR requirements?

F. Limited Scope of Constitutional Protections

KEY TERMS	• Contract rationale
	• Economic rationale
	• Fourteenth Amendment
	• Procedural due process
	• Promissory estoppel
	• Property interest or right
	• Scholarship rationale
	• Substantive due process

1. General Principles: What Is a Property Interest?

Under the U.S. Constitution, before a person is deprived of life, liberty, or property by "state action," procedural due process — adequate notice and a fair hearing — must be given. Substantive due process also provides a party with a means of determining whether a constitutionally protected substantive right has in fact been infringed. In such cases, (1) the plaintiff must establish the requisite "state action"; (2) the party must be a person; and (3) an interest in life, liberty, or property must be threatened or infringed. Then, the court must determine whether these property interests were violated without either procedural or substantive due process. The state action requirement (which is satisfied by a public university's conduct) is addressed at length in Chapter 2. In the case of student-athletes, coaches, or other personnel, the requirement that the party be a person is easily met. The major issue remaining generally is whether a property or liberty interest has been implicated.

The question of whether a student-athlete possesses a property or liberty interest most often arises where student-athletes, seeking to retain their athletic eligibility, challenge either NCAA or institutional eligibility determinations that terminate an athlete's ability to continue to engage in intercollegiate competition. In asserting these challenges, student-athletes claim that the Fourteenth Amendment protects against deprivation of property without due process.

One commentator states that student-athletes have most often advanced four theories in arguing that they possess a constitutionally protected property interest in sports eligibility. The four theories are the following:

- **Economic Rationale:** property interests in training for lucrative careers as professional athletes.
- **Educational Rationale:** athletic participation is a substantial part of the educational experience.
- **Scholarship Rationale:** loss of a scholarship deprives student-athlete of benefits—athletic, educational, and financial—that result from being awarded a scholarship in exchange for athletic participation.
- **Contractual Rationale:** the athlete university scholarship constitutes a contract that incurs benefits (e.g., right to participate in intercollegiate athletics) that cannot be deprived without due process.

Brian L. Porto, Note, *Balancing Due Process and Academic Integrity in Intercollegiate Athletics: The Scholarship Athlete's Limited Property Interest in Eligibility*, 62 Ind. L.J. 1151, 1158-59 (1987).

A leading case that rejected the economic rationale is *Colorado Seminary v. NCAA*, 417 F. Supp. 885 (D. Colo. 1976), *aff'd*, 580 F.2d 320 (10th Cir. 1978), wherein the court rejected plaintiffs' argument that a constitutionally protected property interest in athletic participation stems from the vital role college athletics play in providing a training ground for a career in professional sports. Notes one commentator, "Because so few former college athletes ever sign a professional contract, college athletes' economic interests in professional sports opportunities are speculative and not of constitutional dimensions." Porto, *supra*, at 1158.

Although a clear majority of courts have ruled that student-athletes possess no constitutionally protected interest in athletic competition, a few courts have not considered as too speculative the student-athlete's future economic interests. In *Behagen v. Int'l Conference of Faculty Representatives*, 346 F. Supp. 602 (D. Minn. 1972), the court took "judicial notice of the fact that, to many, the chance to display their athletic prowess in college stadiums and arenas throughout the country is worth more in economic terms than the chance to get a college education." *Id.* at 604.

Courts also have largely rejected the contract rationale as a basis for establishing a property interest in intercollegiate athletics participation. Arguing in support of the contractual rationale, one commentator writes, "The scholarship agreement is the sort of 'mutually explicit understanding,' . . . which supports a claim of entitlement to participate in intercollegiate athletics." Porto, *supra*, at 1168–1169.

The case that follows examines whether a student-athlete possesses a property interest in athletic participation. In reviewing the case, consider the rationales on which athletes rely in asserting the existence of a property interest.

2. A Property Interest in Athletic Participation?

Hysaw v. Washburn University of Topeka
690 F. Supp. 940 (D. Kan. 1987)

SAFFELS, Judge.

[Editors' note: This civil rights and breach of contract action arose out of allegations by several black football players that they were treated in a racially discriminatory manner by the university's coaching staff and administrations. The players, all of whom were awarded football scholarships for the 1986–1987 school year, alleged that promises of full scholarships had not been carried out; many also felt that their white teammates were favored by the coaching staff. Each player signed a financial aid agreement with Washburn. The written agreements did not promise that the plaintiffs would be allowed to play football for Washburn. A series of events transpired that culminated in the players boycotting team practices and the administration removing them from the football team. All of the players involved received the financial aid allocations promised them for the 1986–1987 school year.

In their lawsuit, the players alleged that their removal from the team violated constitutional rights, including their free speech, liberty, and property rights in violation of 42 U.S.C. §1983, violated 42 U.S.C. §1981, and breached their contracts with Washburn University. The university requested summary judgment on all of the plaintiffs' claims.]

. . . A. Property Rights

Plaintiffs . . . argue they held a property interest in contractual rights to play football for Washburn, and argue that by breaching their scholarship contracts the defendants have deprived them of a property right without due process.

Property rights "are created and their dimensions are defined by existing rules or understandings that stem from an independent source such as state law." [*Board of Regents v. Roth*, 408 U.S. 564, at 577 (1972).] Only after a protectable property interest has been established do we then determine whether due process was afforded.

Plaintiffs claim defendants deprived them of their contractual rights under the scholarship agreements to play football for Washburn University. However, plaintiffs have only established a property right in the scholarship funds. No deprivation of those funds took place. Plaintiffs had no other protectable property interest. "To have a property interest in a benefit, a person clearly must have more than an abstract need or desire for it. He must have more than a unilateral expectation of it. He must, instead, have a legitimate claim of entitlement to it." *Roth*, 408 U.S. at 577. Plaintiffs concede that the only source for their alleged property interest is their scholarship agreements. The court has determined that the only interests created by those agreements are interests in receiving scholarship funds. Any other terms plaintiffs attempt to read into those agreements are, without supporting evidence, no more than "unilateral expectations." The court will therefore grant defendants' summary judgment motion on this claim.

B. Liberty Interests

Plaintiffs Battle and Chapman next argue that defendants infringed upon their liberty interests in pursuing a college football career. This claim arises out of those plaintiffs' efforts to be recruited by the nearby Emporia State University football team after they were dismissed from the Washburn team. . . .

A due process claim is made out only if the liberty interest allegedly violated is protectable under the Constitution. Again we look to an independent source of law to determine whether plaintiffs held a legitimate interest in the right to pursue a college football career. Only if this right is a protected liberty right under state law have plaintiffs made out a Section 1983 violation.

The plaintiffs concede that no right to pursue a college football career exists under well-established Tenth Circuit law. . . . [D]amage to an individual's reputation by a state official is not enough to establish a due process violation. Something more must be shown; a tangible interest must be established. . . .

The court finds no tangible interest here. *Roth* held that defamatory comments made by a government employer which cast a cloud over an employee's future employment prospects could constitute a deprivation of liberty. Plaintiffs now ask this court to extend the holding in *Roth* to the present situation; in effect, they are asking the court to equate government employment with a football scholarship. The court is unwilling to take such a giant leap. While no constitutional right to a government job exists, the Supreme Court has noted that qualification for a government job is a "privileg[e] of first-class citizenship." *Anti-Fascist Committee v. McGrath*, 341 U.S. 123, 183, 95 L. Ed. 817, 71 S. Ct. 624 (1950) (J. Douglas, concurring). Plaintiffs have offered no reason why a right to pursue a collegiate athletic career should be afforded the same status, and the court likewise sees no reason to do so. . . .

III. Breach of Contract

The law in Kansas is well-established that when a written contract exists and its language is clear and unambiguous, the language controls. . . . Plaintiffs argue they were promised that they would be allowed to play football during the 1986–87 season. Yet the written scholarship contracts they signed make no indication of such promises. In fact, the only promises in those written contracts were that the players would receive money. Plaintiffs provide no other evidence, other than "understandings" and "expectations," that they were promised a position on the 1986 team. . . . Plaintiffs concede that they received all disbursements on time. Defendants therefore met all their obligations under the contracts. . . .

QUESTION

In *Hysaw*, the court concluded that plaintiffs only established a property right in the scholarship funds. What would have to be present in order for a plaintiff to establish a property right to play football?

NOTES

1. The absence of a property interest. The majority of courts continue to adhere to the principle articulated in *Hysaw* as illustrated by *Hart v. NCAA*, 550 S.E.2d 709 (W. Va. 2001). Hart, a fifth-year senior on the Appalachian State University wrestling team, sought to compete in a lower weight class than that in which he had previously competed. An NCAA regulation prevented wrestlers from competing in a weight class that differed from the class in which they had competed prior to a certain date. After the NCAA rejected plaintiff's request for a waiver of the regulation, he eventually filed a lawsuit asserting a denial of an opportunity to fulfill his scholarship contract and to compete in intercollegiate competition. The West Virginia Supreme Court ruled that "participation in interscholastic athletics . . . does not rise to the level of a constitutionally protected 'property' or 'liberty' interest. . . . " *Id.* at 86. See also *Hall v. NCAA*, 985 F. Supp. 782, 799 (N.D. Ill. 1997) ("there is no protected economic interest in an athletic scholarship because, while a college degree enhances one's ability to earn a livelihood, the lack of a scholarship does not prohibit a person from pursuing a college degree"); and *NCAA v. Yeo*, 171 S.W.3d 863, 869 (Tex. 2005) (rejecting a student-athlete's claim that she possessed a property or liberty interest under the Texas constitution because of her unique "reputation as a world-class athlete in home country of Singapore"); *Mattison v. E. Stroudsburg Univ.*, 2013 WL 1563656(M.D. Pa. 2013) (a college baseball player, who accepted sanctions delineated in a disciplinary notification for violations of school rules, including marijuana use, alleged the university's failure to notify him that he could also be suspended from baseball team violated his due process rights; in denying the player's request for a preliminary injunction, the court found that a student possesses no property interest in extracurricular or sporting activities, the university provided the athlete with "notice and a hearing," and the university was not required to provide plaintiff with notice of all potential penalties); but see *Hall v. Univ. of Minnesota*, 530 F. Supp. 104, 108 (D. Minn. 1982) (concluding because what was at stake for the student-athlete was his ability to obtain a no-cut contract with the NBA, "[t]he plaintiff would suffer a substantial loss if his career objectives were impaired").

2. Rules violations. Student-athletes have asserted claims alleging deprivation of a constitutionally protected property interest when universities revoke or refuse to renew athletes' scholarships because the athletes violated rules. In *Conard v. University of Washington*, 834 P.2d 17 (Wash. 1992), the University of Washington refused to renew the scholarships of two student-athletes who were involved in a series of incidents, including assaulting and threatening other students and vandalism; the university claimed this behavior violated football team rules. The athletes alleged they were entitled to their athletic scholarships for four to five years. They based this belief on what they characterized as the common understanding as to the duration of scholarships as set forth in the financial aid documents.

The Washington Supreme Court ruled against the plaintiffs, stating, "Unless a legitimate claim of entitlement to the renewal of plaintiffs' scholarships was created by the terms of the contract, by a mutually explicit understanding, or by substantive procedural restrictions on the part of the decisionmaker, plaintiffs have no constitutional due process protections." *Id.* at 22. The court concluded that plaintiffs' scholarships were only for one year and that none of the contract terms established any entitlement to renewal.

Problem 4-1

You serve as legal counsel to a legislative committee. One of the members of your committee has indicated that she wants you to draft legislation that would recognize a property interest in participation in intercollegiate athletics. The legislator is irate because her daughter was not permitted to try out for the football team at her public university. Her daughter believes that she could earn an athletic scholarship if she had the opportunity to demonstrate her ability as a kicker and that she could increase her future job opportunities by playing college football. When the legislator and her daughter asked the coach why she was not permitted to try out, the coach simply said he thought it was best. When he was pressed for further reasons, he simply said he did not want to offer any. When the legislator discussed the matter with her lawyer, he said it was unlikely that a court would review why her daughter was not being permitted to participate because she does not have a property interest that would trigger federal due process protection. Was the lawyer's advice correct? What advice would you have given to the legislator regarding the advantages and disadvantages of a law that would create a property interest in athletic participation?

G. Student-Athletes as Employees: Workers' Compensation

KEY TERMS
- Catastrophic injury insurance program
- Contract of hire
- National Labor Relations Act (NLRA)
- National Labor Relations Board (NLRB)
- Right to control
- Unions
- Workers' compensation

1. Workers' Compensation: General Principles

Workers' compensation laws, which are governed by state law, provide a simple and inexpensive method for workers to obtain compensation and medical expenses for work-related injuries or diseases. The theory of these laws is that industries should bear the burden of industrial accidents as a component of the cost of production. Under workers' compensation legislation, benefits are available to injured workers regardless of an employer's common law tort or other statutory liability. These laws, however, preclude employee tort actions against employers, and limit the amount of damages that can be recovered. Thus, employees waive tort claims against their employers in exchange for a simplified, but limited, recovery under workers' compensation laws.

Generally, a person injured while performing services for compensation is considered an employee if two elements are present: (1) an express or implied contract to hire, and (2) employee status. A contract to hire binds an employer to pay compensation to an employee who performs services, sets forth the place to perform such services and work to be performed, and sets the compensation for the performance of the work. Assuming the existence of a contract to hire, the inquiry shifts to whether the contract gives rise to an employer-employee relationship.

Courts often adopt one of the following standards to determine an employment relationship: (1) the right to control the details of the work test, or (2) the relative nature of the work test. The right to control test examines whether the employer possessed the right to control the manner, means, and details of the worker's performance. Factors that demonstrate the requisite right of control include the terms of the employment agreement, the actual exercise of control, the method of payment, the furnishing of equipment, and the right to terminate the worker. An alternative standard used by an increasing number of courts is the relative nature of the work test. Pursuant to this test, "employees are those who as a matter of economic reality are dependent upon the business to which they render service." Leo L. Lam, Comment, *Designer Duty: Extending Liability to Manufacturing for Violation of Labor Standards in Garment Industry Sweatshops*, 141 U. Pa. L. Rev. 623, 651 (1992). This test is likely to be satisfied where a worker performs tasks integral to the employer's regular business and does not provide an independent business or professional service vis-à-vis the employer. The principal consideration under the nature of the work test is the relationship between the services provided and the regular business of the alleged employer.

2. Student-Athletes and Workers' Compensation: Waldrep v. Texas Employers Insurance Association

Most states do not expressly include or exclude scholarship athletes from coverage under their respective workers' compensation statutes, nor do they provide a system of compensation for injured university athletes. Thus, courts must determine whether or not scholarship athletes are covered "employees."

Some early cases held that an injured intercollegiate athlete could recover workers' compensation benefits if he held a university job unrelated to athletics. See, e.g., *Van Horn v. Indus. Accident Comm'n*, 33 Cal. Rptr. 169 (Cal. Ct. App. 1963). After the *Van Horn* case, California amended its workers' compensation statute to expressly exclude student-athletes from its coverage. Other states that expressly exclude student-athletes from the definition of an employee for workers' compensation purposes include Hawaii, New York, Oregon, and Vermont. In contrast, Nebraska has established an administrative system for providing medical and disability benefits to injured university athletes. See, e.g., Neb. Rev. Stat. §85-106.05 (1999).

Courts now generally hold that athletes who suffer injuries while participating in intercollegiate athletics are not entitled to workers' compensation benefits. *Shephard v.*

Loyola Marymount Univ., 102 Cal. App. 4th 837 (Cal. App. 2 Dist. 2002) (rejecting student-athlete's argument that she was an employee for purposes of California Fair Employment and Housing Act); *Rensing v. Indiana State Univ. Bd. of Trustees*, 444 N.E.2d 1170 (Ind. 1983) (student-athletes not entitled to workers' compensation benefits).

A leading case in this regard is *Waldrep v. Texas Employers Insurance Association*, 21 S.W.3d. 692 (Tex. Ct. App. 2000). In 1972, Kent Waldrep agreed to play football for Texas Christian University (TCU). In exchange, TCU agreed to provide financial aid "to the extent of room, board, tuition, fees and $10.00 per month for incidentals. . . . " *Id.* at 696. In October 1974, while playing football for TCU against the University of Alabama, Waldrep sustained a severe injury to his spinal cord and was paralyzed below the neck. In 1991, Waldrep filed a workers' compensation claim for his injury. The Texas Workers' Compensation Commission awarded workers' compensation benefits to Waldrep. On an appeal of the commission's finding, a jury ruled in favor of TCU. Waldrep appealed this adverse result.

The Texas court of appeals framed the issue before it as "whether, for workers' compensation law purposes, a recipient of a scholarship or financial aid from a university" is an employee. In upholding the jury's judgment in favor of TCU, the appellate court considered: whether a contract of hire existed between Waldrep and TCU, and whether Waldrep was an employee for workers' compensation purposes under the right to control test.

Concluding there was evidence to support the jury's finding that no contract of hire arose, the court stated:

> It is undisputed that before Waldrep signed the Letter of Intent and Financial Aid Agreement, both he and TCU understood that his recruitment and future football career at TCU would be governed by and subject to the rules of the NCAA. . . . The record indicates that the NCAA's policies and rules in effect at that time exhibited a concerted effort to ensure that each school governed by these rules made certain that student-athletes were not employees. Indeed, the rules declared that the fundamental policy of the NCAA was " 'to maintain intercollegiate athletics as an integral part of the educational program and the athlete as an integral part of the student body, and, by so doing, retain a clear line of demarcation between college athletics and professional sports.'" Following its policy, the evidence reflects that the NCAA rules made the principle of amateurism foremost and established several requirements to ensure that the student-athlete would not be considered a professional. . . .

Id. at 699–700. The court also pointed to evidence (e.g., TCU never having placed Waldrep on its payroll) establishing that neither Waldrep nor TCU treated the financial aid Waldrep received as "pay" or "income."

With respect to the right of control, Waldrep argued that because the TCU football coaches exercised dominion over his college life, he was an employee. Rejecting Waldrep's argument, the court concluded:

> The record reflects that TCU *exercised* direction and control over all of the athletes in its football program, including non-scholarship players, while they were participating in the *football program*. Waldrep admitted that his high school coaches exercised the same type of control over his participation in sports as the coaches at TCU. Waldrep further

testified that he did everything that the coaches told him to do because he wanted to, because he loved the game, and because he wanted to be the best, not because he had to. The evidence is clear that TCU did not have the right to direct or control all of Waldrep's activities during his tenure at the school. The NCAA rules protected Waldrep's financial-aid award even if his physical condition prevented him from playing football for any reason. . . . Moreover, TCU could not simply cancel Waldrep's grant-in-aid based on his "athletic ability or his contribution to [the] team's success," or even, in certain circumstances, if he quit. *Id.*

The fact that the athletic department at TCU established practice and meeting times to be observed by those playing football does not establish that TCU had the *right* to direct and control all aspects of the players' activities while enrolled in the university. Waldrep's acceptance of financial aid from TCU did not subject him to any extraordinary degree of control over his academic activities.

Waldrep clearly presented evidence that TCU *exercised* direction or control over some of his activities while a student at the university. Perhaps the jury might have found this sufficient to prove that TCU had the *right* to direct the means or details of Waldrep's activities, but the jury declined to do so. . . .

Id. at 702.

QUESTIONS

For workers, what are the advantages and disadvantages of workers' compensation? According to the *Waldrep* court, what was the essence of Waldrep's and TCU's understanding regarding the nature of their relationship? What action might the Texas legislature have taken if the court had ruled in favor of Waldrep?

NOTE

Control. The *Waldrep* court concluded that even though the university "*exercised* direction and control over all of the athletes in its football program" (emphasis in original), TCU did not have the "right to direct or control all of Waldrep's activities during his tenure at the school." Moreover, Waldrep's participation in football "did not subject him to any extraordinary degree of control over his academic activities." Do you agree with the court's conclusion? Which factor seems most influential in the court's assessment that the requisite right to control for workers' compensation purposes is absent? In responding, consider the following comments taken from *University of Colorado v. Derdeyn*, 863 P.2d 929 (Colo. 1993), a drug-testing case that hinged in part on whether student-athletes have a lessened expectation of privacy:

CU's athletic director testified in relevant part that the NCAA sets limits on financial aid awards, playing seasons, squad size, and years of eligibility; that the NCAA requires that CU maintain records of each athlete's academic performance; that the "athletes that eat at training tables are football and men's basketball and the other athletes eat in the dorms or at their off-campus residences"; that some coaches within their discretion impose curfews; that athletes are required to show up for practice; that athletes are "advised . . . on what they should take for classes"; that "we have a required study hall in the morning and in the evening"; and that it is "fair to say that the athletes are fairly well regulated." A student athlete testified in relevant part that "Yes," "if you are an NCAA athlete, you have to keep a certain grade average," and "Yes," "if your grades drop below that average, then you are not eligible for competition."

Id. 940–41. For commentary, see Robert A. McCormick and Amy Christian McCormick, *Myth of the Student-Athlete: The College Athlete as Employee*, 81 Wash. L. Rev. 71 (2006); and Mark R. Whitmore, Note, *Denying Scholarship Athletes Worker's Compensation: Do Courts Punt Away a Statutory Right?*, 76 Iowa L. Rev. 763 (1991).

3. Student-Athlete Unionization

In *Northwestern University and College Athletes Players Association (CAPA)*, Case 13-RC-121359 (National Labor Relations Board Region 13, March 26, 2014), a regional office of the National Labor Relations Board (NLRB) found that scholarship football players at Northwestern University, who had not exhausted their athletic eligibility, are employees as defined by the National Labor Relations Act (NLRA), and therefore could decide whether to be represented for collective bargaining purposes (i.e., unionize). In reaching the result, the regional director deemed the grant-in-aid received by scholarship athletes as compensation. The ruling also focused on the control that Northwestern exercises over its scholarship football players.

The decision states that coaches and universities exercise extensive control over almost every aspect of the scholarship players' lives, including: (1) the preseason and in-season training regimes that dictate players' activities; (2) monitoring players' behavior and adherence to NCAA and team rules, which includes the power of coaches to discipline players for violations; (3) control over players' private lives that manifest either in restrictions or requiring players to obtain permission from coaches on matters ranging from players' making living arrangements, applying for outside employment, making posts on social media, using drugs and alcohol, and traveling off campus; and (4) making academic decisions. The ruling's characterization of student athletes as employees is antithetical to the NCAA's conceptualization of amateurism.

Northwestern appealed the ruling to the NLRB. Approximately a year after Northwestern University's appeal was filed, the five-member NLRB unanimously dismissed the football players' petition that they be recognized as employees for collective bargaining purposes. *Northwestern University and College Athletes Players Association (CAPA)*, Petitioner, 362 NLRB No. 167 (Aug. 17, 2015). According to the Board, "because of the nature of sports leagues (namely the control exercised by the leagues over the individual teams) and the composition and structure of [Football Bowl Subdivision] football (in which the overwhelming majority of competitors are public colleges and universities over which the Board cannot assert jurisdiction), it would not promote stability in labor relations to assert jurisdiction in this case. *Id*. at 3. After noting that Northwestern is the only private school in the Big Ten, the Board explained because many of Northwestern's competitors are public institutions, the Board would not possess the authority to assert jurisdiction over them. Thus, the Board's resolution of a labor issue involving one university and its player could have leaguewide ramifications for teams, most of which would be outside the Board's jurisdiction. "Consequently, 'it would be difficult to imagine any degree of stability in labor relations' if we were to assert jurisdiction in this single-team case." *Id.* at 5 (citing *The North American Soccer League*, Case 2–RC–17740 (June 30, 1978)). The Board also strongly suggested that exercising jurisdiction could upset the competitive balance. *Id.* at 4–5. The Board limited its decision to the Northwestern University football players, stating that it need not address "whether it might assert jurisdiction in another case involving grant-in-aid scholarship football players (or other types of scholarship athletes). . . . " *Id.* at 1.

It is important to note that the Board did not rule on whether college student-athletes are employees. In this regard, the Board stated that it reached its decision without deciding "whether the scholarship players are employees." *Id.* at 6.

QUESTIONS

If affirmed, how might the decision harm student-athletes? Would the decision transform the relationship between students and their universities? If so, how?

NOTE

In *Sackos v. NCAA*, Civil Action No. 1:14-CV-1710 WTL-MJD (S.D. Ind., filed Oct. 20, 2014), the plaintiff, a former female volleyball player at the University of Houston, alleged that the NCAA and its D-I universities conspired to violate the Fair Labor Standards Act by failing to pay D-I athletes at least the current federal minimum wage of $7.25 per hour for their athletic playing services, which constitute part-time employment because they "engage in non-academic performance for no academic credit in athletic competition" on behalf of their respective universities. Do you agree with the plaintiff's characterization of D-I student-athletes' playing services? If the court agrees that playing intercollegiate athletics constitutes part-time employment, what are the potential implications?

FIRST AMENDMENT RIGHTS IN INTERCOLLEGIATE ATHLETICS

A. Introduction

In addition to contract and other private causes of action, those associated with intercollegiate athletics may be able to assert constitutional rights in the intercollegiate context. Equal protection or equality rights as set forth in the Fourteenth Amendment to the U.S. Constitution and in state constitutional provisions, for example, are discussed in Chapter 5 (gender equity) and Chapter 6 (racial equity). Courts will only reach (decide) constitutional issues when a case cannot be decided on a private, nonconstitutional ground, such as a contract right.

As was the case in the interscholastic area (see Chapter 2), student-athletes, coaches, and others may raise issues regarding alleged violations of their rights under the First Amendment of the U.S. Constitution by state actors. In the *Tarkanian* case, discussed in Chapter 2, the Supreme Court held that the NCAA is not a state actor. The NCAA, therefore, is not obligated to afford coaches, students, and others their constitutional rights, including their First Amendment rights. Nevertheless, state universities and colleges may be obligated to do so. Lawsuits seeking to protect alleged infringement of such rights arise in a number of contexts.

In deciding those cases, courts consider the maturity of the student-athletes involved in determining whether rights have been infringed. High school or younger students are often treated differently than more mature college students. Secondary schools often act in an *in loco parentis* (in the place of the parent) capacity. High schools are, therefore, often afforded greater power to regulate the speech and expression of their students than is afforded to colleges and universities. As you read the following materials, reflect on how First Amendment and other constitutional standards may be different at the intercollegiate and interscholastic or high school levels.

First Amendment rights have been raised with respect to athletic department officials' and student-athletes' interaction with the media, as well as alleged violations of an athlete's freedom of religion by a public university. The materials in this section are only intended to be illustrative of the kinds of issues and analyses that arise and are not intended to be exhaustive in their treatment of the First Amendment area.

KEY TERMS

- Actual malice (knowing falsity, reckless disregard for the truth)
- Defamation
- Establishment clause
- Freedom of expression
- Free exercise clause
- Free speech
- *In loco parentis*
- Invasion of privacy
- Public figure
- Retaliation
- Truth as a defense

B. The First Amendment and the Media

Athletic administrators, coaches, and student-athletes often have conflicts with the broadcast and print media. With the public attention and commercialization of sports, it is not surprising that the media has extended its coverage into matters that might have been deemed, in other contexts, to be private in nature. For example, criminal accusations or other comments in the media that deal with the private lives of student-athletes and coaches may be given broad coverage in the media, particularly in the case of high-profile coaches, student-athletes, and administrators. High-profile administrators, coaches, and student-athletes receive less protection against incursions by the media into their private lives than most individuals do, under defamation law and the right of privacy, because they have been held to be public figures. If a high-profile administrator, coach, or student-athlete decides to pursue recovery for alleged defamatory falsehoods against the media, he or she must prove that the media acted with "actual malice," "knowing falsity," or "reckless disregard for the truth" in publishing a falsehood (truth is a defense in such cases) as required under applicable First Amendment case law. Such proof is not easy to muster, and it is clearly difficult for a high-profile athletic figure to recover if he or she is deemed to be a public figure.

The landmark Supreme Court case *Curtis Publishing Co. v. Butts*, 388 U.S. 130 (1967), arose from the accusations in a newspaper accusing Wally Butts, the athletic director at the University of Georgia, of attempting to "fix" a 1962 football game between the Universities of Georgia and Alabama. In a libel action filed in federal court, Butts sought $5 million compensatory and $5 million punitive damages. The jury returned a verdict for $60,000 in general damages and for $3 million in punitive damages. The trial court reduced the total to $460,000. In a strongly divided set of opinions, the Court held that the *New York Times* actual malice (knowing falsity or reckless disregard for the truth on the part of the media, in this case the Curtis Publishing Company) standard applied in the case of someone in the position of Athletic Director Butts.

Even though the public-figure status invoked in the *Butts* case makes it very difficult for someone in the position of Butts to prevail in a defamation action, the *Butts* and *Tarkanian* cases do provide a means by which a party might prevail — by proving that the media acted with reckless disregard, with full knowledge of the harm that is likely to result from the publication. In fact, Butts ultimately prevailed on just such a ground.

In *Bilney v. The Evening Star Newspaper Co.*, 406 A.2d 652 (Md. App. 1979), six members of the University of Maryland's men's basketball team sued two newspapers alleging invasions of privacy and intentional infliction of emotional distress. In finding that the athletes were public figures, the court stated as follows:

> The gravamen of their complaint, both in terms of the invasion of privacy and intentional infliction of mental distress counts, was that [the defendants] willfully, wrongfully, and maliciously invaded [and obtained the plaintiffs'] confidential University records and published private and privileged facts about their private lives.
>
> [The student-athletes] achieved the status of public figures solely by virtue of their membership on the University basketball team. Their possible exclusion from the team whether for academic or any other reason was therefore a matter of legitimate public interest. Had they quit the team or withdrawn from the University, the public would be entitled to ask and to speculate as to the reasons for such action. That the threat of exclusion was academically based does not lessen the legitimacy of the public interest. Appellants were not in the same posture as other students, whose scholastic standing, in its entirety, was purely of private concern; when their standing reached the point of

affecting their eligibility to play basketball for the University, the privacy of that status became somewhat attenuated. Publication of that eligibility-threatening status was not unreasonable and did not trample upon community mores. Having sought and basked in the limelight, by virtue of their membership on the team, appellants will not be heard to complain when the light focuses on their potentially imminent withdrawal from the team. We thus [hold] that, upon the undisputed evidence in this case, the publications in question did not constitute a tortious invasion of privacy.

Id. at 660.

QUESTIONS

1. Should coaches in revenue-producing sports be treated as public figures for defamation and privacy purposes, thereby permitting the media with broad latitude to write or broadcast about them? Should student-athletes in those sports be treated as public figures as well?
2. Do you agree with the decision in *Bilney*? Should presidents and other administrators at a university be considered public figures?

C. Religious Liberty Issues

As noted previously, religious liberty issues often arise in the interscholastic athletics context. Religious liberty issues are discussed in greater length in Chapter 2, which deals with interscholastic athletics. Similar issues arise at the intercollegiate level.

Some of the areas where it can be anticipated that religious liberties will be implicated in the intercollegiate athletic context include the following: (1) recognition of religious activity on the part of student-athletes, coaches, and athletic personnel; (2) accommodating the religious interests of competitors (e.g., coaches and conferences have been known to be sensitive to the religious interests of student-athletes and have rescheduled events and have relieved student-athletes of practice and other obligations so that they could exercise their religious conscience); and (3) accommodating religious institutions (e.g., a university that refuses to participate in athletic events on Sunday, which is the Sabbath for members of the Church of Jesus Christ of Latter-day Saints).

Courts have been reluctant to recognize rights of religious conscience by requiring institutions or associations to accommodate the religious conscience of administrators, coaches, and student-athletes. Nevertheless, although the NCAA, conferences, and coaches have often been willing to permit such accommodations, this is not always the case. The courts have indicated, however, a willingness to intervene to avoid discrimination against certain religious groups. It should be noted that proving religious discrimination is very difficult — few individuals admit to such discrimination.

QUESTIONS

1. Even though it is not subject to the constraints of the federal constitution because it is not a state actor (see *NCAA v. Tarkanian* in Chapter 1), the NCAA has exempted brief religious observances by student-athletes, including pausing to pray or express religious gratitude in the end zone after scoring a touchdown, from its general rule that prohibits players from celebrating or drawing attention to themselves on the football field. Some interscholastic associations have refused to exempt such activities from rules against celebration. Do you agree with this exemption? Does it prefer religion over other interests of student-athletes?

2. Student-athletes at the intercollegiate level are generally older and more mature than high school or interscholastic student-athletes. Does this distinction as to levels of maturity provide a legitimate basis for permitting more religion or religious exercise on the part of intercollegiate student-athletes than on the part of interscholastic athletes?

3. State constitutional or legislative (statutory) issues may arise regarding religious liberty and other rights. Remember, even if federal constitutional law does not require that the religious conscience of student-athletes be recognized, state constitutional law may do so.

Problem 4-2

You are the athletic director at a major state (public) university, and a Muslim student-athlete has asked to meet with you to discuss a dispute he has with his coach. The coach insists that student-athletes maintain a rigorous diet, which includes eating certain meals each day. The Muslim student wishes to follow his religious conscience and fast on certain days and avoid eating some of the meals prescribed by the coach. He also eats a more vegetarian diet than the high-protein fare established by the coach. Before the meeting, you call the coach, and he says that although he respects the student-athlete for his religious conviction, it is imperative that he eat with the team for health purposes and to maintain team morale. He is fearful that yielding to this student-athlete's religious beliefs would simply open a Pandora's box, permitting student-athletes to contrive all kinds of reasons for getting out of his strict dietary regimen. The coach also indicated that the diet was devised in conjunction with his trainer and is believed to maximize performance on the part of student-athletes. What do you say to the student-athlete and coach?

Gender Equity Issues in Athletics

INTRODUCTION

In this chapter, we explore issues related to gender equity in athletics. A brief history is followed by sections focusing on the development of the law in this area over the past four decades. Gender discrimination issues were first raised through equal protection claims, with additional regulation for school-based sports programs coming from Title IX of the Educational Amendments of 1972, 20 U.S.C. §1681, and the various regulations, policy interpretations, and other documents issued by the Office of Civil Rights (OCR) of the U.S. Department of Education (DOE). Increasing athletics participation opportunities for girls and women has introduced other gender-based legal issues, such as sexual harassment and pregnancy discrimination, to the world of sports. Although much of the focus on gender equity in athletics has centered on female participants, gender discrimination issues also exist for women who wish to work in sports, including as administrators, coaches, officials, and journalists.

HISTORICAL PERSPECTIVE

In the United States, progress toward gender equality in athletics has occurred, but it has been slow in coming. An invidious myth that women are not competitive and therefore not interested in sports has been perpetuated throughout American culture. Although Native American women participated in a variety of sports and competitive activities, European social customs and religious beliefs precluded female settlers in the United States from participating in athletics. The first girls' interscholastic athletic activity — gymnastics — was introduced at the Latin School for girls in Salem, Massachusetts in 1821, but women's participation in competitive athletics remained virtually invisible throughout the nineteenth century.

It was not until the 1920s that some of the cultural opposition to the involvement of women in athletics began to dissipate. In 1920, female swimmers became the first American women to be accorded full Olympic status. As the United States became more industrialized and increasing numbers of women entered the workforce, industrial league athletics programs became popular. Professional athletics opportunities for women developed in golf, tennis, and in barnstorming teams in basketball. During World War II, the All-American Girls Professional Baseball League was established. While some progress was made in creating opportunities for females to compete in sports, the cultural shift after World War II, which dictated that athletics participation was not appropriate for "ladies," stagnated these efforts. However, visionaries such as the Iowa Girls' High School Athletic Association established a statewide program in 1954 that placed girls on equal footing with boys in high school athletics.

In the late 1960s and early 1970s, women finally made significant strides in terms of their participation in competitive intercollegiate athletic events. In 1966, the first intercollegiate women's basketball tournament was played in Pennsylvania, and the Commission on Intercollegiate Athletics for Women (CIAW) was established in 1967. The CIAW was formed for the purpose of increasing participation by women in competitive sports, which led to the first women's national championship competition in 1969, in the sport of gymnastics. In 1971, the first national intercollegiate athletics association to govern women's sports, the Association for Intercollegiate Athletics for Women (AIAW), was formed, replacing the CIAW and offering seven national championships for women (it was not until 1982 that the NCAA began offering national championships for women in all three of its divisions).

The 1970s proved to be a historic decade in terms of increased participation by women in athletics in the United States. Title IX of the Education Amendments of 1972 was enacted by Congress to eliminate discrimination based on sex in educational programs or activities, and signed into law by President Richard M. Nixon on June 23, 1972. The legislation did not specifically mention athletics, but it did require the promulgation of regulations to achieve gender equity in educational opportunities.

The regulations, 34 C.F.R. §106.41,which became effective on July 21, 1975, provided significant momentum for increased participation for women in organized athletics at the interscholastic and intercollegiate levels. The regulations defined equal opportunity in athletics in two parts: equal accommodation and equal treatment. *Equal accommodation* measured whether the participation opportunities by selection of sports and levels of competitions reflected the interests and abilities of both sexes. *Equal treatment* examined whether male and female participants had similar access to a laundry list of program components including provision of equipment and supplies, locker rooms, practice and competitive facilities, medical and training facilities and services, housing and dining facilities and services, and travel and per diem allowances; scheduling of games and practice times; access to coaching and academic tutoring as well as compensation for coaches and tutors; and publicity. 34 C.F.R. §106.41(c). Expectations for compliance were incremental, with elementary schools given one year, middle and high schools given two years, and colleges and universities given three years to adjust their programs.

Political opponents immediately rallied in an effort to limit the scope of Title IX as applied to intercollegiate athletics with seven bills or resolutions unsuccessfully proposed between 1974 and 1977. The first was proposed by Senator John Tower of Texas, who attempted to exempt revenue-producing sports from Title IX regulation, as well as funds received from donations to athletics programs. The Tower Amendment was rejected in committee. 120 Cong. Rec. 15,322–15,323 (1974). Senator Jesse Helms of North Carolina was also opposed to Title IX, first attempting to disapprove of the regulations in their entirety, 121 Cong. Rec. 17,300 (1975), then introducing S. 2146 to prohibit the application of the regulations to athletics, "Prohibition of Sex Discrimination, 1975," Hearings Before the Senate Subcommittee on Education of the Committee on Labor and Public Welfare on S. 2106, 94th Cong., 1st Sess., Sept. 16–18, 1975, and finally reintroducing S. 2146 as S. 535 in 1977. All attempts failed in committee. Interestingly, Senator James McClure of Idaho tried to distinguish athletics programs from educational programs or activities by proposing an amendment that would limit Title IX requirements to "the curriculum or graduation requirements of the institutions." 122 Cong. Rec. 28136 (1976). In the House, Representative James O'Hara of Michigan twice attempted to propose bills that would have allowed schools to use money earned from a revenue-producing sport only on that sport, or first on that sport, regardless of gender inequities in the athletics program. 121 Cong. Rec. 21,685 (1975).

Meanwhile, a revolution was occurring on the courts and on the fields and tracks at schools across the country. By 1978, the number of female high school student-athletes grew from 300,000 to more than 2 million. Women's participation in intercollegiate athletics doubled from 32,000 participants in 1971 to more than 64,000 participants in 1977. Hundreds of complaints of gender discrimination were filed with the U.S. Department of Health, Education, and Welfare (HEW), while schools lamented that they were unsure about Title IX requirements for compliance. In response, HEW issued a policy interpretation in 1979 regarding the application of Title IX to athletics. 44 Fed. Reg. 71,413 et seq. The Policy Interpretation provided additional information regarding items to be measured to determine compliance with the regulations. Schools were particularly concerned with proving that they were effectively accommodating the interests and abilities of both male and female students.

The Policy Interpretation introduced a three-part test, allowing schools to choose any one of the following three ways to prove that they were providing equal participation opportunities:

(1) Whether intercollegiate level participation opportunities for male and female students are provided in numbers substantially proportionate to their respective enrollments; or

(2) Where the members of one sex have been and are underrepresented among intercollegiate athletes, whether the institution can show a history and continuing practice of program expansion which is demonstrably responsive to the developing interest and abilities of the members of that sex; or

(3) Where the members of one sex are underrepresented among intercollegiate athletes, and the institution cannot show a continuing practice of program

> expansion such as that cited above, whether it can be demonstrated that the interests and abilities of the members of that sex have been fully and effectively accommodated by the present program.

Although the three-part test has become what most people characterize as Title IX, for compliance purposes, it is only one of several provisions that measure the effective accommodation requirement. Overall compliance with Title IX as applied to athletics is measured by looking at all required program component areas and comparing the men's program as a whole to the women's program as a whole to determine whether disparities are substantial enough to be discriminatory.

Title IX is meant to be self-enforcing, meaning that schools are supposed to voluntarily comply with the law. The administrative process of Title IX enforcement is set forth in §88.71 of the Title IX regulation. Anyone who believes a school is not complying may file a complaint, and the OCR may also initiate periodic compliance reviews of colleges and universities. The Department has 90 days to conduct an investigation and inform the institution (and the complainant, if applicable) of its findings. If the investigation indicates that an institution is in compliance, the Department states this, and the case is closed.

For those institutions that are not in compliance, the Department outlines the violations found and provides an additional 90 days to resolve violations by obtaining a voluntary compliance agreement from the institution. According to the regulations, schools that are not in compliance may lose their federal funding. 45 C.F.R. 80.8–80.11 and 45 C.F.R. Part 81. However, no school has ever met that fate. Instead, the OCR works with the institution to create a plan that will correct the violation, with a specific timetable for reaching interim goals, as well as full compliance. When agreement is reached, the Department notifies the institution that its plan is acceptable. The Department then is obligated to review periodically the implementation of the plan.

A person who believes he or she is being discriminated against on the basis of sex does not have to file a complaint with the OCR and exhaust administrative options. In 1979, in *Cannon v. University of Chicago*, 441 U.S. 677, the Supreme Court held that although the legislation did not expressly empower an individual to bring a Title IX lawsuit, there was an implied private right to do so.

Responsibilities for enforcing Title IX shifted to the DOE's OCR in 1980, when the HEW was reorganized. One of the OCR's first official acts was to issue an interim investigators manual dealing with Title IX and athletics. In 1982, the OCR also issued *Guidance for Writing Title IX Intercollegiate Athletics Letters of Findings.* In spite of these enforcement guides, Title IX was not vigorously enforced during the 1980s. In 1984, in *Grove City College v. Bell*, 465 U.S. 555, the Supreme Court held that Title IX applied only to programs that benefited directly from federal funds. By mandating a program-specific tie to federal funding, the *Grove City* decision seriously limited the OCR's jurisdiction over university athletic programs, few of which receive federal funding. The Supreme Court had accomplished in one decision what politicians had been unable to do since the 1975 Regulations — eliminate athletics from Title IX requirements. Congress made its displeasure known by passing the Civil Rights Restoration Act, despite a veto effort. 20 U.S.C. §1687 (1988). This act mandates an institutionwide approach: All programs and activities sponsored by educational institutions that receive federal funds, including their athletics departments, are bound by the requirements of Title IX.

Typically, Title IX complainants (usually female student-athletes) were not involved in OCR investigations, and resolution of complaints may or may not have included provisions that would make the complainant whole. Litigants were limited to equitable relief until 1992, when the Supreme Court unanimously held in *Franklin v. Gwinnett County Public Schools*, 503 U.S. 60 (1992), that prevailing plaintiffs can recover monetary damages and attorneys' fees for intentional violations of Title IX. The *Gwinnett* decision, coupled with increased enforcement activity on the part of the OCR, contributed to a significant rise in the number of Title IX athletics cases. In 1992, the NCAA completed a gender equity study, which increased awareness of these issues and encouraged institutions to take appropriate action. Gender equity was also included as a component in the athletics certification process the NCAA instituted during the 1990s.

In 1994, Congress passed the Equity in Athletics Disclosure Act (EADA), 20 U.S.C. §1092(g), which requires all federally funded institutions of higher education to disclose information regarding their athletics programs. The first annual reporting date was October 1, 1996. EADA reports provide a source of information that has increased public awareness and constitutes a better evidentiary basis for quantifying gender inequities under the Title IX regulations.

In the early 2000s, Title IX was once again targeted politically, this time in the campaign promises of President George W. Bush to eliminate affirmative action and racial quotas. In 2002, the Secretary of Education, Rod Paige, created the Commission on Opportunity in Athletics to investigate whether Title IX is fair to both boys and girls. A total of 15 men and women, primarily representing the interests of major NCAA Division I (D-I) athletics programs, were assembled to hear testimony through four Town Hall meetings across the United States. The commission then filed a final report on February 28, 2003, with several recommendations. Unhappy with what they perceived as a politically tainted process, two commissioners filed a Minority Report voicing their concerns. Secretary Paige accepted both reports and publicly declared that the DOE would not act on any recommendation that did not have unanimous support.

However, on March 25, 2005, the DOE issued modified guidelines for determining compliance with the third prong of the OCR's three-part test. Under these guidelines, educational institutions could establish whether the athletic interests and abilities of the underrepresented gender have been effectively accommodated simply by administering an Internet or e-mail survey. Nonresponse was allowed to be interpreted as a lack of interest — a significant research flaw that was recognized by the National Collegiate Athletic Association (NCAA). The association urged the DOE to honor its prior commitments to strongly enforce the standards of long-standing Title IX athletics policies while also discouraging its own members from relying on an e-mail survey as the sole measure of women's interest in athletics. NCAA News Release, June 22, 2005. In July 2005, the powerful Senate Appropriations Committee in turn called on the DOE to rescind the guideline. The DOE, under President Bush, did not relent, but in April 2010, under President Barack Obama, the policy was finally withdrawn.

Private litigation and government enforcement activity under Title IX have resulted in increased athletic participation opportunities for women and increased equity in funding and resources. However, it is generally conceded that the goal of gender equity in athletics has not been fully achieved. Women continue to be underrepresented in intercollegiate athletics — approximately 44 percent of athletics participants are women — and male participation in interscholastic athletics is dramatically higher than female participation, although disparities vary tremendously state by state (see *The Next Generation of Title IX Athletics,* NWLC.com, June 2012). At all levels, female athletes still do not have access to equivalent athletic facilities, equipment, and other resources.

The following materials and problems present the legal, practical, and policy aspects of gender equity issues in connection with intercollegiate and interscholastic athletics. Title IX litigation regarding intercollegiate athletics has often focused on gender equity in terms of athletic participation opportunities, whereas the emphasis in interscholastic athletics litigation has focused on providing girls with access to equal sports facilities and other benefits of athletic participation. Nevertheless, all aspects of Title IX are fully applicable to all levels of interscholastic and intercollegiate sports, as well as high school and university intramural and recreational athletic programs.

GENDER-BASED EXCLUSION FROM A PARTICULAR SPORT

The first sports-related gender equity cases were brought by female students in the 1970s and 1980s seeking the opportunity to play an interscholastic sport traditionally offered only for males. Historically, boys have had a wider variety of sports to participate in than girls, particularly in contact sports. Even if there was no girls' team, athletic governing body or school district rules often prohibited girls from playing on boys' teams regardless of their ability level. The following case illustrates that courts generally held that such exclusion is illegal sex discrimination.

KEY TERMS
- Equal protection
- Intermediate scrutiny

Force v. Pierce City R-VI School District
570 F. Supp. 1020 (W.D. Mo. 1983)

ROBERTS, District Judge.

[Editors' note: Nichole Force, a 13-year-old female student enrolled in the eighth grade at Pierce City Junior High School in Missouri, sought an injunction that would have allowed her to compete for a place on the school's eighth-grade football team. She had already been involved to a considerable extent in athletics (swimming, diving, organized softball, organized basketball, and elementary school football) and had grown up with two brothers who excelled at football and who encouraged and helped her in her own athletic endeavors.

Pierce City Junior High School is a public school facility made up of the seventh, eighth, and ninth grades that sponsored an interscholastic athletics program. Boys could participate in football during the fall, basketball during the winter, and track during the spring. The corresponding sports for girls were volleyball, basketball, and track.

The boys' athletics coach for the school said he would let Nichole participate if school administration officials approved. However, school board members expressed concern over the potential precedent involved in granting her request (e.g., the possibility that boys would wish to participate on the girls' volleyball team and that high school girls might wish to play on the high school football team), the potential safety risk to a female competing in a contact sport with males, the administrative difficulties that might ensue (arrangements for locker room facilities, etc.), and that, at least as some board members understood it, the applicable provisions of Title IX and its regulations or Section 1.6 of the Missouri State High School Activities Association (MSHSAA) rules might be violated by permitting coeducational participation in a contact sport. The board voted unanimously to deny the request. While "they all agreed" Nichole would be a good football player and would have no problems playing, they also said that if she were permitted to play, the same allowance would have to be made for all other girls as well.

Nichole contended that this refusal to allow her an opportunity to play football was based solely on the fact that she was a female rather than a male and that this sex-based determination violated her right to the equal protection of the laws under the Fourteenth Amendment and 42 U.S.C. §1983.]

II. Discussion

The record makes clear, and I find, that defendants' refusal to grant plaintiff's request is the product of a gender-based classification. Stated simply, only males are permitted to compete for a place on the Pierce City Junior High School eighth grade football team. Since Nichole is a female, that opportunity is denied to her.

The principles which must govern in this situation are summarized in the opening passages of Section II of the Supreme Court's recent decision in *Mississippi University For Women v. Hogan*, 458 U.S., 102 S.Ct. 3331, 73 L.Ed.2d 1090 (1982). I can do no better than to quote those passages here:

> Because the challenged policy expressly discriminates among applicants on the basis of gender, it is subject to scrutiny under the Equal Protection Clause of the Fourteenth Amendment. Our decisions also establish that the party seeking to uphold a statute that classifies individuals on the basis of their gender must carry the burden of showing an "exceedingly persuasive justification" for the classification. The burden is met only by showing at least that the classification serves "important governmental objectives and that the discriminatory means employed" are "substantially related to the achievement of those objectives."

Although the test for determining the validity of a gender based classification is straightforward, it must be applied free of fixed notions concerning the roles and abilities of males and females. Care must be taken in ascertaining whether . . . the objective itself reflects archaic and stereotypic notions. Thus if the . . . objective is to exclude or "protect" members of one gender because they are presumed to suffer from an inherent handicap or to be innately inferior, the objective itself is illegitimate.

If the State's objective is legitimate and important, we next determine whether the requisite direct, substantial relationship between objective and means is present. The purpose of requiring that close relationship is to assure that the validity of the classification is determined through reasoned analysis rather than through the mechanical application of traditional, often inaccurate, assumptions about the proper roles of men and women. . . .

Defendants do not quarrel with the fact that the present case must be governed by these principles; indeed they candidly acknowledge that fact. They argue, rather, that in the circumstances shown here a gender-based classification fully satisfies those principles. To that end, they identify four "important governmental objectives" which are said to be at stake: (a) maximization of equal athletic educational opportunities for all students, regardless of gender; (b) maintenance of athletic educational programs which are as safe for participants as possible; (c) compliance with Title IX of the Educational Amendments of 1972 and the regulations thereunder; and (d), compliance with the constitution and by-laws of MSHSAA. According to defendants, there is a "substantial relationship" between each of these objectives and a gender based classification which would prevent any female from competing with males for a place on the Pierce City Junior High School eighth grade football team.

Defendants' suggestion with respect to the necessity of compliance with Title IX can, I think, be dealt with in relatively short order. There is in fact nothing whatsoever in Title IX, or in its implementing regulations (34 C.F.R. §106.41(b)), which would mandate the action defendants have taken here. To the contrary, Title IX's regulations leave each school free to choose whether co-educational participation in a contact sport will be permitted. Allowing Nichole Force to compete with males for a place on the Pierce City Junior High School eighth grade football team would no more violate those regulations than would refusing her that opportunity. Title IX simply takes a neutral stand on the subject.

Nor in my judgment can defendants' point regarding compliance with MSHSAA rules withstand scrutiny. A school can hardly validate an otherwise unconstitutional act (assuming for the moment that there is one here) by noting that it has agreed with other schools to commit that act. There can be no doubt, of course, that MSHSAA performs a valuable and needed service for the schools and citizens of this state. But its rules cannot transcend constitutional requirements, and a member school's adherence to those rules cannot make constitutional that which is not.

I accordingly reject defendants' "objectives" (c) and (d) as providing any sort of appropriate predicate for the action taken here. Defendants' first two points, however, have more meat to their bones, and are deserving of more detailed treatment. Each will be examined separately below.

A. Maximizing Participation in Athletics

One might wonder, at first blush, how denying all females the right to participate in a sport — which is the case here, since Pierce City eighth grade girls are not allowed to compete for a place on the only football team which might be available to them — will result in maximizing the participation of both sexes in athletics. And the short answer is that it probably does not. Defendants' argument in this regard, however, is sufficiently sophisticated to merit more than first blush treatment.

That argument proceeds on three interrelated theories. Defendants suggest, first, that males (as a class) will outperform females (as a class) in most athletic endeavors, given male size, speed, and greater ratio of lean body mass. That being so, the argument proceeds, the best way in which to encourage and maximize female participation in athletics is by providing separate male and female teams, where males compete only against males and females only against females, since otherwise males will dominate the competition and ultimately discourage female participation. Pursuant to this idea, defendants have established separate inter-scholastic athletic programs for the two sexes in the Pierce City secondary schools, with the fall season sport being football for males and volleyball for females. But if (second) Nichole Force is permitted to compete for a place on the football team, then other girls must be accorded the same privilege, and boys must be allowed to compete for positions on the volleyball team. When (third) that happens, the girls will lose their best athletes, the boys will come to dominate volleyball, and overall female participation will ultimately wither.

Based upon the expert testimony presented in this case, I am willing to accept the proposition that the average male, even at age 13, will to some extent outperform the average female of that age in most athletic events, although the matter may be open to some dispute. And I note, without being called upon to decide the issue, that a number of courts have held that the establishment of separate male/female teams in a sport is a constitutionally permissible way of dealing with the problem of potential male athletic dominance . . . . Beyond these two points, however, I am unable to accept defendants' argument.

The principal difficulty with the remaining portions of that argument, it seems to me, is that the various hypotheses used to bind it together are just that — hypotheses, and nothing more. There is, for example, no factual indication that the girls' eighth grade volleyball team will be blighted by the defection of its best players to the football field, if Nichole Force is allowed to play football. . . . [Even if this were the case,] the governmental interest in redressing past discrimination against women in athletics is sufficient to justify a regulation which excludes boys from participating on girls' teams, even though girls are allowed to compete on boys' teams. . . .

Each sport has its own relatively unique blend of requirements in terms of skills and necessary physical attributes, and each person, male or female, will for a variety of reasons probably find one or another sport more enjoyable and rewarding than others. In point of fact, volleyball is *not* football; and baseball is *not* hockey; and swimming is *not* tennis. Accordingly, if the idea is to "maximize educational athletic opportunities for all students, regardless of gender," it makes no sense, absent some substantial reason, to deny all persons of one sex the opportunity to test their skills at a particular sport. Of course there may be certain exceptional instances in which there is a "substantial reason" for such an exclusion, as for example where peculiar safety and equipment requirements demand it [boxing was used as an example] . . . or perhaps where excluding males is necessary to redress past inequality and to foster female participation. But those instances would, I think, be relatively rare, and would need to be factually established. And that is precisely where defendants' present argument fails, as far as the instant case is concerned.

I do not question the idea that maximizing the participation of both sexes in interscholastic athletic events is a worthy, and important, governmental objective. Nor do I question the sincerity of defendants' efforts in that regard. In the circumstances of this case, however, I must and do hold that the gender based classification used by defendants does not bear a sufficiently "substantial" relationship to that objective to withstand a constitutional challenge.

B. Safety

Neither do I question the fact that the "maintenance of athletic educational programs which are as safe for participants as possible" is an "important governmental objective." [However], the "safety" factor which defendants would utilize to prevent any female from playing eighth grade football — including those who could play safely — is not applied to males at all, even to those who could not play safely. All this tends to suggest the very sort of well-meaning but overly "paternalistic" attitude about females which the Supreme Court has viewed with such concern. . . . [T]here is an insufficient relationship between defendants' announced goal of "safety" and a rule which automatically excludes all eighth grade females from competing with eighth grade males for a place on a football team. That holding, I note, is consistent with the result reached by virtually every other court which has considered this same sort of "safety" argument in connection with male/female competition in contact sports. . . .

Conclusion

Nichole Force obviously has no legal entitlement to a starting position on the Pierce City Junior High School eighth grade football team, since the extent to which she plays must be governed solely by her abilities, as judged by those who coach her. But she seeks no such entitlement here.

Instead she seeks simply a chance, like her male counterparts, to display those abilities. She asks, in short, only the right to try.

I do not suggest there is any such thing as a constitutional "right to try." But the idea that one should be allowed to try — to succeed or to fail as one's abilities and fortunes may dictate, but in the process at least to profit by those things which are learned in the trying — is a concept deeply engrained in our way of thinking; and it should indeed require a "substantial" justification to deny that privilege to someone simply because she is a female rather than a male. I find no such justification here.

[Editors' note: The court enjoined defendants from refusing to allow Nichole Force to compete for membership on the Pierce City Junior High School eighth-grade interscholastic football team on the same basis that males are allowed to compete.]

QUESTIONS

1. What is the standard of review for a gender-based discrimination claim under equal protection?

2. In *Williams v. School District of Bethlehem, PA*, 998 F.2d 168 (3d. Cir. 1993), a boy asserted his right to participate on the girl's field hockey team. In a decision that dealt with Title IX (whether field hockey is a contact sport that would justify his exclusion) and constitutional issues, including a challenge under the state equal rights amendment, the court remanded the case for the trial court to determine whether there were physical differences between girls and boys that would justify excluding the boy. The appellate court directed the trial court to examine whether "boys are more likely to dominate the school's athletic program if admitted to the girls' teams."

   In *Force*, what justification did the court offer regarding a regulation that would exclude boys from participating on girls' teams, even though girls would be permitted to participate on boys' teams? Do you agree with the court's reasoning?

3. Both the Equal Protection Clause and Title IX's regulations permit "separate but equal" athletic teams in the same sport for both sexes. When there are "separate but equal" teams, in assessing equality one court noted, "There may be differences depending upon the effects of such neutral factors as the level of student interest and geographic locations. Accordingly, the standard should be one of comparability, not absolute equality." *Hoover v. Meiklejohn*, 430 F. Supp. 164, 170 (D. Colo. 1977).

   Why didn't Nichole Force assert a Title IX claim that she was being discriminated against by being prohibited from an activity (playing football) because of her sex? Title IX regulations §106.41(b) states:

   > A recipient may operate or sponsor separate teams for members of each sex where selection for such teams is based upon competitive skill or the activity involved is a contact sport. However, where a recipient operates or sponsors a team in a particular sport for members of one sex but operates or sponsors no such team for members of the other sex, and athletic opportunities for members of that sex have previously been limited, members of the excluded sex must be allowed to try-out for the team offered unless the sport involved is a contact sport. For the purposes of this part, contact sports include boxing, wrestling, rugby, ice hockey, football, basketball and other sports the purpose or major activity of which involves bodily contact.

4. In *Mercer v. Duke University*, 190 F.3d 643 (4th Cir. 1999), a case involving a challenge by a woman seeking to participate in intercollegiate football, the appellate court held:

   > Because appellant has alleged that Duke allowed her to try out for its football team (and actually made her a member of the team), then discriminated against her and ultimately excluded her from participation in the sport on the basis of her sex, we conclude that she has stated a claim under the applicable regulation, and therefore under Title IX. We take to heart appellees' cautionary observation that, in so holding, we thereby become "the first Court in United States history to recognize such a cause of action." . . . Where, as here, however, the university invites women

into what appellees characterize as the "traditionally all-male bastion of collegiate football," we are convinced that this reading of the regulation is the only one permissible under law.

Mercer stands for the proposition that once a woman has been permitted to participate in a contact sport like football, she cannot be removed from the team for reasons clearly unrelated to her ability as a player (Mercer was an accomplished kicker). On remand, Mercer was awarded $1 in compensatory damages and $2 million in punitive damages. On appeal, the punitive damage award was vacated. Nevertheless, Mercer was awarded approximately $350,000 in attorney fees.

Should women be permitted to participate in male contact sports? Private universities such as Duke are not state actors subject to federal equal protection claims, although state gender discrimination laws may apply. Title IX applies to any institution that receives any federal funding, regardless whether the institution is public or private. Is the refusal to permit girls from participating in contact sports paternalistic, particularly if they have the talent necessary to make the team?

5. Consider the similarities and differences between racial and gender equity issues in sport. The equal protection clause of the Fourteenth Amendment requires application of strict scrutiny in the racial context (racial distinctions can be drawn only when supported by a compelling state interest applied in the least restrictive manner). In the gender equity context, on the other hand, an intermediate equal protection standard (the government interest must be substantial, but not necessarily compelling, and the fit between the interest and the gender distinction has to be narrowly tailored but does not have to be the least restrictive means to the government's end) is all that is required, making it possible to distinguish on gender grounds in a manner that would be impermissible in the racial context. Ironically, the more permissive discrimination standard in the gender area has clearly been instrumental in increasing opportunities in athletics for women, while the more restrictive standard in the racial context has made it more difficult for the government to effectively address racial inequities in sports.

Problem 5-1

A 14-year-old girl wants to try out for the boys' wrestling team and is not interested in participating in any other sports. She is an exceptionally talented athlete who has regularly lifted weights for the past two years and is in excellent physical condition. Although she has no prior experience in wrestling, her dream is to one day earn a gold medal as a member of the U.S. Olympic women's wrestling team. No other girls at her high school are interested in wrestling. The team's coach has refused to allow "a girl to try out for a man's sport." If you were her parent, would you be willing to file a lawsuit on her behalf to challenge this decision? If you were the school's principal, how, if at all, would you counsel the coach?

EQUAL ATHLETIC PARTICIPATION OPPORTUNITIES, BENEFITS, AND TREATMENT

Although equal protection claims may also be asserted, Title IX is currently the law most frequently utilized to remedy gender discrimination in interscholastic and intercollegiate athletics. Despite numerous challenges, Title IX, its regulations, policy interpretations, and other guidance materials have been validated by every court that has tried these issues. The following case established the judicial framework that has been followed by every other court in assessing whether a college athletics program provides equal participation opportunities.

A. Accommodation

 **KEY TERMS**
- Effective accommodation
- Substantial proportionality
- Three-part test

Cohen v. Brown University
101 F.3d 155 (1st Cir. 1996), cert. denied, 520 U.S. 1186 (1997)

BOWNES, Senior Circuit Judge.

This is a class action lawsuit charging Brown University, its president, and its athletics director (collectively "Brown") with discrimination against women in the operation of its intercollegiate athletics program, in violation of Title IX. . . .

This suit was initiated in response to the demotion in May 1991 of Brown's women's gymnastics and volleyball teams from university-funded varsity status to donor-funded varsity status. Contemporaneously, Brown demoted two men's teams, water polo and golf, from university-funded to donor-funded varsity status. As a consequence of these demotions, all four teams lost, not only their university funding, but most of the support and privileges that accompany university-funded varsity status at Brown. . . .

I

Brown operates a two-tiered intercollegiate athletics program with respect to funding: although Brown provides the financial resources required to maintain its university-funded varsity teams, donor-funded varsity athletes must themselves raise the funds necessary to support their teams through private donations. The district court noted that the four demoted teams were eligible for NCAA competition, provided that they were able to raise the funds necessary to maintain a sufficient level of competitiveness, and provided that they continued to comply with NCAA requirements. The court found, however, that it is difficult for donor-funded varsity athletes to maintain a level of competitiveness commensurate with their abilities and that these athletes operate at a competitive disadvantage in comparison to university-funded varsity athletes. . . .

Brown's decision to demote the women's volleyball and gymnastics teams and the men's water polo and golf teams from university-funded varsity status was apparently made in response to a university-wide cost-cutting directive. . . .

Plaintiffs alleged that, at the time of the demotions, the men students at Brown already enjoyed the benefits of a disproportionately large share of both the university resources allocated to athletics and the intercollegiate participation opportunities afforded to student athletes. Thus, plaintiffs contended, what appeared to be the even-handed demotions of two men's and two women's teams, in fact, perpetuated Brown's discriminatory treatment of women in the administration of its intercollegiate athletics program. . . .

The district court . . . summarized the history of athletics at Brown, finding . . . that, while nearly all of the men's varsity teams were established before 1927, virtually all of the women's varsity teams were created between 1971 and 1977, after Brown's merger with Pembroke College. The only women's varsity team created after this period was winter track, in 1982.

In the course of the trial on the merits, the district court found that, in 1993–94, there were 897 students participating in intercollegiate varsity athletics, of which 61.87% (555) were men and 38.13% (342) were women. During the same period, Brown's undergraduate enrollment comprised 5,722 students, of which 48.86% (2,796) were men and 51.14% (2,926) were women. The district court found that, in 1993–94, Brown's intercollegiate athletics program consisted of 32 teams, 16 men's teams and 16 women's teams. Of the university-funded teams, 12 were men's teams and 13 were women's teams; of the donor-funded teams, three were women's teams and four were men's teams. At the time of trial, Brown offered 479 university-funded varsity positions for men, as compared to 312 for women; and 76 donor-funded varsity positions for men, as compared to 30 for women. In 1993–94, then, Brown's varsity program — including both university- and donor-funded sports — afforded over 200 more positions for men than for women. Accordingly, the district court found that Brown maintained a 13.01% disparity between female participation in intercollegiate athletics and female student enrollment. . . .

In computing these figures, the district court counted as participants in intercollegiate athletics for purposes of Title IX analysis those athletes who were members of varsity teams for the majority of the last complete season. . . .

The district court found from extensive testimony that the donor-funded women's gymnastics, women's fencing and women's ski teams, as well as at least one women's club team, the water polo team, had demonstrated the interest and ability to compete at the top varsity level and would benefit from university funding.

The district court did *not* find that full and effective accommodation of the athletics interests and abilities of Brown's female students would disadvantage Brown's male students.

II

Title IX . . . specifies that its prohibition against gender discrimination shall not "be interpreted to require any educational institution to grant preferential or disparate treatment to the members of one sex on account of an imbalance which may exist" between the total number or percentage of persons of that sex participating in any federally supported program or activity, and "the total number or percentage of persons of that sex in any community, State, section, or other area." 20 U.S.C.A. §1681(b) (West 1990). Subsection (b) also provides, however, that it "shall not be construed to prevent the consideration in any . . . proceeding under this chapter of statistical evidence tending to show that such an imbalance exists with respect to the participation in, or receipt of the benefits of, any such program or activity by the members of one sex."

Applying §1681(b), the prior panel held that Title IX "does not mandate strict numerical equality between the gender balance of a college's athletic program and the gender balance of its student body." The panel explained that, while evidence of a gender-based disparity in an institution's athletics program is relevant to a determination of noncompliance, "a court assessing Title IX compliance may not find a violation solely because there is a disparity between the gender composition of an educational institution's student constituency, on the one hand, and its athletic programs, on the other hand. . . . "

[A 1978 OCR] Policy Interpretation establishes a three-part test, a two-part test, and factors to be considered in determining compliance under 34 C.F.R. §106.41(c)(1) [which provides a non-exhaustive list of ten factors to be considered in determining whether equal athletics are available to both genders]. At issue in this appeal is the proper interpretation of the first of these, the so-called three-part test, which inquires as follows:

(1) Whether intercollegiate level participation opportunities for male and female students are provided in numbers substantially proportionate to their respective enrollments; or

(2) Where the members of one sex have been and are underrepresented among intercollegiate athletes, whether the institution can show a history and continuing practice of program expansion which is demonstrably responsive to the developing interests and abilities of the members of that sex; or

(3) Where the members of one sex are underrepresented among intercollegiate athletes, and the institution cannot show a continuing practice of program expansion such as that cited above, whether it can be demonstrated that the interests and abilities of the members of that sex have been fully and effectively accommodated by the present program.

44 Fed. Reg. at 71, 418.

The district court held that, "because Brown maintains a 13.01% disparity between female participation in intercollegiate athletics and female student enrollment, it cannot gain the protection of prong one." Nor did Brown satisfy prong two. While acknowledging that Brown "has an impressive history of program expansion," the district court found that Brown failed to demonstrate that it has "maintained a continuing practice of intercollegiate program expansion for women, the under-represented sex." . . . [T]he fact that Brown has eliminated or demoted several men's teams does not amount to a continuing practice of program expansion for women. As to prong three, the district court found that Brown had not "fully and effectively accommodated the interest and ability of the under-represented sex" to the extent necessary to provide equal opportunity in the selection of sports and levels of competition available to members of both sexes. . . .

IV

A

Title IX is not an affirmative action statute; it is an anti-discrimination statute, modeled explicitly after another anti-discrimination statute, Title VI. No aspect of the Title IX regime at issue in this case — inclusive of the statute, the relevant regulation, and the pertinent agency documents — mandates gender-based preferences or quotas, or specific timetables for implementing numerical goals.

Like other anti-discrimination statutory schemes, the Title IX regime permits affirmative action. In addition, Title IX, like other anti-discrimination schemes, permits an inference that a significant gender-based statistical disparity may indicate the existence of discrimination. Consistent with the school desegregation cases, the question of substantial proportionality under the Policy Interpretation's three-part test is merely the starting point for analysis, rather than the conclusion; a rebuttable presumption, rather than an inflexible requirement. In short, the substantial proportionality test is but one aspect of the inquiry into whether an institution's athletics program complies with Title IX. . . .

From the mere fact that a remedy flowing from a judicial determination of discrimination is gender-conscious, it does not follow that the remedy constitutes "affirmative action." Nor does a "reverse discrimination" claim arise every time an anti-discrimination statute is enforced. While some gender-conscious relief may adversely impact one gender — a fact that has not been demonstrated in this case — that alone would not make the relief "affirmative action" or the consequence of that relief "reverse discrimination." To the contrary, race- and gender-conscious remedies are both appropriate and constitutionally permissible under a federal anti-discrimination regime, although such remedial measures are still subject to equal protection review. . . .

Brown has contended throughout this litigation that the significant disparity in athletics opportunities for men and women at Brown is the result of a gender-based differential in the level of interest in sports and that the district court's application of the three-part test requires universities to provide athletics opportunities for women to an extent that exceeds their relative interests and abilities in sports. . . .

We view Brown's argument that women are less interested than men in participating in intercollegiate athletics, as well as its conclusion that institutions should be required to accommodate the interests and abilities of its female students only to the extent that it accommodates the interests and abilities of its male students, with great suspicion. To assert that Title IX permits institutions to provide fewer athletics participation opportunities for women than for men, based upon the premise that women are less interested in sports than are men, is (among other things) to ignore the fact that Title IX was enacted in order to remedy discrimination that results from stereotyped notions of women's interests and abilities.

Interest and ability rarely develop in a vacuum; they evolve as a function of opportunity and experience. The Policy Interpretation recognizes that women's lower rate of participation in athletics reflects women's historical lack of opportunities to participate in sports. . . . [T]here exists the danger that, rather than providing a true measure of women's interest in sports, statistical evidence purporting to reflect women's interest instead provides only a measure of the very discrimination that is and has been the basis for women's lack of opportunity to participate in sports. Prong three requires some kind of evidence of interest in athletics, and the Title IX framework permits the use of statistical evidence in assessing the level of interest in sports. Nevertheless, to allow a numbers-based lack-of-interest defense to become the instrument of further discrimination against the under-represented gender would pervert the remedial purpose of Title IX. We conclude that, even if it can be empirically demonstrated that, at a particular time, women have less interest in sports than do men, such evidence, standing alone, cannot justify providing fewer athletics opportunities for women than for men. Furthermore, such evidence is completely irrelevant where, as here, viable and successful women's varsity teams have been demoted or eliminated.

Finally, the tremendous growth in women's participation in sports since Title IX was enacted disproves Brown's argument that women are less interested in sports for reasons unrelated to lack of opportunity. . . .

Brown's relative interests approach is not a reasonable interpretation of the three-part test. This approach contravenes the purpose of the statute and the regulation because it does not permit an institution or a district court to remedy a gender-based disparity in athletics participation opportunities. Instead, this approach freezes that disparity by law, thereby disadvantaging further the under-represented gender. Had Congress intended to entrench, rather than change, the status quo — with its historical emphasis on men's participation opportunities to the detriment of women's opportunities — it need not have gone to all the trouble of enacting Title IX.

VII

Brown may achieve compliance with Title IX in a number of ways: It may eliminate its athletic program altogether, it may elevate or create the requisite number of women's positions, it may demote or eliminate the requisite number of men's positions, or it may implement a combination of these remedies. I leave it entirely to Brown's discretion to decide how it will balance its program to provide equal opportunities for its men and women athletes. I recognize the financial constraints Brown faces; however, its own priorities will necessarily determine the path to compliance it elects to take. . . .

Brown's proposed compliance plan stated its goal as follows: The plan has one goal: to make the gender ratio among University-funded teams at Brown substantially proportionate to the gender ratio of the undergraduate student body. To do so, the University must disregard the expressed athletic interests of one gender while providing advantages for others. The plan focuses only on University-funded sports, ignoring the long history of successful donor-funded student teams. . . .

Brown states that it "seeks to address the issue of proportionality while minimizing additional undue stress on already strained physical and fiscal resources."

The general provisions of the plan may be summarized as follows: (i) Maximum squad sizes for men's teams will be set and enforced. (ii) Head coaches of all teams must field squads that meet minimum size requirements. (iii) No additional discretionary funds will be used for athletics. (iv) Four new women's junior varsity teams — basketball, lacrosse, soccer, and tennis — will be university-funded. (v) Brown will make explicit a de facto junior varsity team for women's field hockey.

The plan sets forth nine steps for its implementation, and concludes that "if the Court determines that this plan is not sufficient to reach proportionality, phase two will be the elimination of one or more men's teams."

The district court found Brown's plan to be "fatally flawed" for two reasons. First, despite the fact that 76 men and 30 women participated on donor-funded varsity teams, Brown's proposed plan disregarded donor-funded varsity teams. Second, Brown's plan "artificially boosts women's varsity numbers by adding junior varsity positions on four women's teams." As to the propriety of Brown's proposal to come into compliance by the addition of junior varsity positions, the district court held:

> Positions on distinct junior varsity squads do not qualify as "intercollegiate competition" opportunities under the Policy Interpretation and should not be included in defendants' plan. . . . "[I]ntercollegiate" teams are those that "regularly participate in varsity competition." See 44 Fed. Reg. at 71,413 n.l. Junior varsity squads, by definition, do not meet this criterion. Counting new women's junior varsity positions as equivalent to men's full varsity positions flagrantly violates the spirit and letter of Title IX; in no sense is an institution providing equal opportunity if it affords varsity positions to men but junior varsity positions to women.

The district court found that these two flaws in the proposed plan were sufficient to show that Brown had "not made a good faith effort to comply with this Court's mandate." . . .

The district court ordered Brown to "elevate and maintain women's gymnastics, women's water polo, women's skiing, and women's fencing to university-funded varsity status. . . ."

We agree with the district court that Brown's proposed plan fell short of a good faith effort to meet the requirements of Title IX as explicated by this court in *Cohen II* and as applied by the district court on remand. . . .

It is clear, nevertheless, that Brown's proposal to cut men's teams is a permissible means of effectuating compliance with the statute. . . . [A]lthough the district court's remedy is within the statutory margins and constitutional, we think that the district court was wrong to reject out-of-hand Brown's alternative plan to reduce the number of men's varsity teams. After all, the district court itself stated that one of the compliance options available to Brown under Title IX is to "demote or eliminate the requisite number of men's positions." Our respect for academic freedom and reluctance to interject ourselves into the conduct of university affairs counsels that we give universities as much freedom as possible in conducting their operations consonant with constitutional and statutory limits.

Brown therefore should be afforded the opportunity to submit another plan for compliance with Title IX. . . . Accordingly, we remand the case to the district court so that Brown can submit a further plan for its consideration. In all other respects the judgment of the district court is affirmed. . . .

VIII

Affirmed in part, reversed in part, and remanded for further proceedings. . . .

QUESTIONS

1. As noted in *Cohen* and subsequent cases, a school can prove compliance with the participation opportunities requirement under Title IX by independently showing that they meet the requirements of any one prong of the three-part test. How did the *Cohen* court apply the substantial proportionality test?

2. There have been efforts to exclude intercollegiate football from this equation (i.e., only male sports other than football would count for purposes of the proportionality analysis). What are the advantages or disadvantages of this approach? Does this approach eliminate discrimination or perpetuate inequities?

3. In order to prove compliance with Title IX's effective accommodation requirement, a school may establish that it has a history and continuing practice of adding sports for the underrepresented gender, which is usually female student-athletes. Why did Brown University fail to prove compliance on this ground? The issue of a history of continuous expansion has been examined in subsequent cases. In those cases, and among commentators, it is understood that the expansion needs to be continual and, where possible, done according to a formal policy or plan. See *Boucher v. Syracuse University*, 164 F.3d 113 (2d Cir. 1999), discussing the second part of the three-part test.

4. Opponents of Title IX have consistently complained that women are not as interested in sports as men. This argument has been uniformly rejected by the courts. Is this a valid defense under the third prong of the three-part test?

5. There is currently a movement to add competitive cheerleading (alternatively named STUNT, or Acrobatics and Tumbling) as an emerging sport for women. Several interscholastic athletics governing bodies have already recognized cheer as a sport, offering state championships. Proponents of competitive cheer as a sport argue that females should not be limited to participating in traditional male sports and that including cheer as a sport would offer more competitive opportunities for females. Opponents emphasize that "adding" cheer would not actually increase opportunities because females currently participate in the activity even though it is not a varsity sport; it would merely allow schools to count cheerleaders as athletes for Title IX compliance purposes. They also posit that promoting cheerleading as a varsity sport promotes a stereotype of appropriate roles for females that is demeaning.

What do you perceive as the pros and cons of sanctioning competitive cheer as a varsity sport? See *Biediger v. Quinnipiac University*, 667 F.3d 910 (2d Cir. 2012), for a judicial ruling that cheerleading, at least as it was conducted at Quinnipiac University, was not a varsity sport for Title IX participation purposes.

6. Many school districts still struggle to provide equitable participation opportunities. Chicago School District 29, through a settlement agreement with OCR on July 1, 2015 (see *http://www2.ed.gov/documents/press-releases/chicago-public-schools-agreement .pdf*) is required to add teams or additional levels of competition in at least 12 high schools in the 2015–2016 school year and continue to add new opportunities annually until the district can demonstrate full compliance with at least one prong of the three-part test.

Problem 5-2

You are the athletic director at a mid-level D-I university with a very successful men's basketball team that generates net revenues of approximately $2.5 million. The basketball coach is paid $1.5 million per year — a substantial portion of which comes from privately raised funds. The men's basketball coach has also insisted that to remain competitive in recruiting athletes, he needs the use of a private jet and improved practice and training facilities for his team. With the hiring of a new coach at a nationally competitive salary ($500,000, plus some incentives), the men's football program has been improving, and that has had a positive economic impact. Three years ago, the men's football team was operating at a loss of over $1 million per year, but it is now losing only $300,000 per year. The women's basketball team produces revenue, but it operates at a net loss of over $250,000 per year. Other men's and women's athletics programs generate very little revenue. The net result is that the athletic program is being run at a deficit of approximately $1 million per year. The president of the university has been pressured by state legislators and is required by mandate from the university's board of trustees to operate the university's athletic program with a balanced budget. The president has communicated this mandate to you, as the athletics director, and has made it clear that the athletics budget needs to be balanced within two years.

Currently, 61 percent of the students at the university are women and 39 percent are men. Participation figures in intercollegiate athletics are almost reversed, with 63 percent male and 37 percent female participation in intercollegiate athletics. The football team has 110 participants, including a number of walk-ons. The school is considering adding women's swimming or women's softball, and its athletics conference recognizes both sports. The university has pool facilities that can easily be converted to use for a women's swimming team, but there is only limited interscholastic competition in swimming in the general geographical area of the university. There is interscholastic competition in softball in the area, but there are no facilities at the university. Building new facilities would involve substantial costs, and the cost of operating the softball team would be slightly higher per student-athlete than operating a swimming program. An interest survey indicates somewhat more interest in participating in softball than swimming on the part of women attending the university.

There has been some talk of dropping the men's track team, which would help some in terms of proportionality, but concerns have been raised in the community that doing so would eliminate a disproportionate number of athletes of color. Men's baseball might also be cut, but it is quite popular with the chairperson of the university's board of trustees, whose son plays on the team.

From time to time, some of the coaches of the women's teams have complained that they are paid less than their male counterparts, their teams receive less academic support (e.g., the men's basketball team takes two tutors with them on trips that exceed two days, but no other teams are permitted to bring tutors on trips), their practice and training facilities are not as good as those used by the men, and they are not given the same amount of support in terms of fund-raising and media coverage.

What steps would you take to address these problems? What additional facts would you want to know? What practical problems may arise as you deal with the gender equity and related issues raised in this problem?

B. Equal Benefits and Treatment

The majority of Title IX cases have focused on equal participation opportunities, but a significant number of cases have also examined the requirements for equal benefits and treatment of student–athletes. *McCormick v. School District of Mamoroneck*, 370 F.3d 275 (2d Cir. 2004), illustrates judicial application of OCR regulations to determine whether an educational institution has afforded female athletes equivalent treatment and benefits as compared to male athletes. The plaintiffs in *McCormick* were two girls who claimed that their school districts violated Title IX by scheduling girls' high school soccer in the spring and boys' high school soccer in the fall. Because the New York regional and state championships in soccer were scheduled at the end of the fall season, the plaintiffs claimed that the district deprived girls, but not boys, of the opportunity to compete in their sports championships. Girls' soccer was the only sport offered at the defendant school districts that was scheduled out of the state championship competition season. Because of conflicts with other opportunities to play soccer during the spring, plaintiffs decided not to play on their high school soccer teams. Plaintiffs alleged that the school districts do not provide equal opportunities to girls and boys in the scheduling of games and practice time.

The court established the following road map for compliance with Title IX:

1. Is there disparity in a program component (e.g., scheduling of games) that negatively affects one sex? "[A] disparity is a difference, on the basis of sex, in benefits, treatment, services, or opportunities that has a negative impact on athletes of one sex when compared with benefits, treatment, services, or opportunities available to athletes of the other sex." *Id.* at 293.

2. Is the disparity substantial enough to deprive members of that sex of equality of opportunity? *Id.*

3. Is the disparity disadvantaging one sex in a component of a school's athletics program offset by a comparable advantage to that sex in another component of the athletics program? Compliance is determined on a programwide rather than sport-specific basis. For example, "a school that provides better equipment to the men's basketball team than to the women's basketball team would be in compliance with Title IX if it provided comparably better equipment to the women's soccer team than to the men's soccer team. . . . " *Id.* at 293–94.

4. Can the school establish that the "differences in kind, quality, or availability were the result of nondiscriminatory factors"? *Id.* at 292.

Applying the foregoing standards, the court found that the scheduling of girls' soccer in the spring created a disparity — "boys can strive to compete in the Regional and State Championships in soccer and girls cannot." *Id.* at 294.

The court next found that (1) the disparity was significant enough to deny girls equality of athletic opportunity in that scheduling soccer out of championship season placed a ceiling on "the possible achievement of the female soccer players that they cannot break through no matter how hard they strive," and (2) the disparity sent a message that girls on the soccer teams were "not expected to succeed" and their school did not value their athletic abilities as much as those of boys. Moreover, the disadvantage in scheduling of girls' soccer had not been offset by any advantage to girls in another area.

The court also rejected defendants' alleged nondiscriminatory justifications that moving girls' soccer to the fall would be financially and administratively burdensome. It noted that the "fact that money needs to be spent to comply with Title IX is obviously not a defense to the statute." *Id.* 297. The court also stated: "There is no reason that the boys' soccer teams should be entitled to the fields, coaches, and officials in the fall simply because they were in the fall first." Noting that all students must make choices, the court rejected defendants' argument that moving soccer to the fall would hurt girls because it would require them to choose between soccer and other sports. It also suggested the defendants make adjustments such as alternating the season during which boys and girls would play soccer if field space was limited.

In another case involving equivalent benefits, *Daniels v. School Board of Brevard County, Florida (Daniels I)*, 985 F. Supp. 1458 (M.D. Fla. 1997), members of a high school girls' softball team and their parents sued a school board alleging disparities between the girls' softball team and the boys' baseball programs. Disparities in benefits identified by the court included the following: (1) the boys' baseball field had an electronic scoreboard, and the girls' field had no scoreboard (sending a message that girls' softball was not as valuable as boys' baseball); (2) the boys' baseball team had a batting cage, and the girls' softball team did not; (3) the bleachers on the girls' softball field were of lesser quality and seated fewer spectators than those on the boys' field; and (4) disparities (to the disadvantage of girls) existed with respect to signage,

bathroom facilities, concession stands, press box, announcer's booth, field maintenance, and lighting.

The court concluded:

> [T]he cumulative effect of the inequalities in the two athletic programs is so significant
> as to give Plaintiffs a substantial likelihood of success on the merits of the Title IX and
> Florida Act claims. The Defendant has chosen to favor the boys' baseball team with a
> lighted playing field, a scoreboard, a batting cage, superior bleachers, signs publicizing
> the team, bathroom facilities, and a concession stand/press box/announcer's booth, but
> has not seen fit to provide the girls softball team with any of these things. This disparity
> implicates several of the considerations listed in 34 C.F.R. §106.41. *See* §106.41(2)
> ("provision of equipment and supplies"), (3) ("[s]cheduling of games and practice
> times"), (7) ("[p]rovision of . . . practice and competitive facilities"), (8) ("[p]rovision
> of . . . training facilities"), and (10) ("[p]ublicity").
>
> The Defendant seeks to avoid liability on the basis that it provides equal funding
> for the boys' and girls' programs. According to the Defendant, each team has a separate
> booster club which engages in separate fund-raising activities. The Defendant suggests
> that it cannot be held responsible if the fund-raising activities of one booster club are
> more successful than those of another. The Court rejects this argument. It is the
> Defendant's responsibility to ensure equal athletic opportunities, in accordance with
> Title IX. This funding system is one to which Defendant has acquiesced; Defendant is
> responsible for the consequences of that approach.

Id. at 1462. The Court determined that plaintiffs were entitled to a preliminary
injunction to remedy these gender inequities. Since public funds were at stake,
however, the Court afforded defendant an opportunity to submit a plan addressing
how it proposes to remedy them.

In a subsequent case, *Daniels v. School Board of Brevard County, Florida (Daniels II)*,
995 F. Supp. 1394 (M.D. Fla. 1997), the court assessed the compliance plan submitted
by the defendant. The school board proposed not to spend any funds to remedy the
inequities identified in *Daniels I* because of "financial limitations and tight budgetary
constraints under which the School Board is forced to operate. Any monies spent on
athletics must obviously be taken from another area of operations which is already
lacking in funds." *Id.* at 1395.

The court rejected the board's proposed remedial measures, which largely
involved taking away boys' advantages rather than enhancing components of the
girls' softball program.

> In giving the School Board the opportunity to submit a plan, the Court had hoped for
> constructive input, such as a long-range fiscal plan to remedy the inequities identified in
> the Court's prior Order. Unfortunately, the Board's plan leaves much to be desired; it
> creates the impression that the Board is not as sensitive as it should be regarding the
> necessity of compliance with Title IX. The Court is inclined to agree with Plaintiffs
> that many of the Board's proposals seem more retaliatory than constructive. The
> Board's approach essentially imposes "separate disadvantage," punishing both the girls
> and the boys, rather than improving the girls' team to the level the boys' team has
> enjoyed for years. The Court is sensitive to the financial constraints imposed upon
> public educational institutions in this day and age; that is yet another reason the Court

gave the Board an opportunity to submit a remedial plan, rather than simply entering an injunction decreeing the expenditure of funds by a date certain. However, the fact remains that Plaintiffs have presented substantial evidence that the School Board has violated, and continues to violate, an Act of Congress mandating gender equality in public education.

Id. at 1397.

QUESTIONS

1. What is the specific harm that plaintiffs suffered in *McCormick* as a result of being treated unequally? In *Daniels I*?
2. Although compliance with Title IX requires a comparison of boys' and girls' sports on a programwide basis, *McCormick* and *Daniels I* demonstrate that disparate treatment of male and female teams for the same sport may be significant enough to violate this law. What constitutes an illegal disparity for purposes of Title IX? Other cases in which female athletes have prevailed in unequal treatment claims at the high school or college level include *Communities for Equity v. Michigan High School Athletic Assn.*, 178 F. Supp. 2d 805 (W.D. Mich. 2001); *Landow v. School Bd. of Brevard County*, 132 F. Supp. 2d 958 (M.D. Fla. 2000); *Ollier v. Sweetwater Union High School District*, 768 F.3d 843 (2014); and *Parker v. Franklin County Community School Corporation*, 667 F.3d 910 (2012).
3. Like effective accommodation cases, courts are reluctant to order a school to take specific action to remedy gender-based unequal treatment that violates Title IX. Rather, courts allow schools the flexibility to formulate their own compliance plan within certain parameters. In this regard, do courts afford schools too much deference? Why did the court in *Daniels II* reject the proposed remedial measures suggested by the school board? What type of changes did the court hope that the board would enact?

REVERSE DISCRIMINATION CLAIMS AND TITLE IX

Although Title IX has been instrumental in increasing opportunities for girls' sports participation, a persistent and invidious criticism of Title IX is that it hurts men's sports. Courts have uniformly held that cutting men's sports in an effort to achieve substantial proportionality in athletic participation opportunities does not violate Title IX or male athletes' equal protection rights. See, e.g., *Miami Univ. Wrestling Club v. Miami Univ.*, 302 F.3d 608 (6th Cir. 2002); *Chalenorv. University of N. D.*, 291 F.3d 1042 (8th Cir. 2002); *Kelly v. Board of Trustees*, 35 F.3d 265 (7th Cir. 1994); *Equity in Athletics, Inc. v. Dept. of Educ.*, 675 F. Supp. 2d 660 (W.D. Va. 2009). While budget reductions and limitations may challenge athletics administrators' creativity in managing a broad-based athletics program, choices must be made in a way that provides equal opportunity. Ideally, schools would remedy past discrimination by increasing opportunities for women. However, Title IX allows schools to choose the type of athletics program they offer. See Jocelyn Samuels and Kristen Galles, *In Defense of Title IX: Why Current Policies Are Required to Ensure Equality of Opportunity*, 14 Marq. Sports L. Rev. 11, 31 (2003).

The *Neal* case, which follows, involves a gender reverse-discrimination lawsuit in which male college athletes allege that the discontinuance of their sport violates Title IX and their federal equal protection rights. It illustrates the reasoning and analysis courts often employ in rejecting the claims of male student-athletes.

Neal v. Board of Trustees of the California State Universities
198 F.3d 763 (9th Cir. 1999)

HALL, Circuit Judge:

[This] suit alleged that the decision of California State University, Bakersfield ("CSUB") to reduce the number of spots on its men's wrestling team, undertaken as part of a university-wide program to achieve "substantial proportionality" between each gender's participation in varsity sports and its composition in the campus's student body, violated Title IX and the Equal Protection Clause of the United States Constitution. . . .

Defendant/Appellant CSUB is a large public university where female students outnumbered male students by roughly 64% to 36% in 1996. The composition of CSUB's varsity athletic rosters, however, was quite different. In the 1992–93 academic year, male students took 61% of the university's spots on athletic rosters and received 68% of CSUB's available athletic scholarship money.

[Editors' note: This imbalance prompted a Title IX lawsuit by the California chapter of the National Organization for Women (NOW). A consent decree arising from a settlement of the lawsuit mandated, among other things, that each California State campus have a proportion of female athletes that was within five percentage points of the proportion of female undergraduate students at that school. Because of budgetary constraints, CSUB adopted squad-size targets, which would encourage the expansion of the women's teams while limiting the size of the men's teams. To comply with the consent decree, CSUB opted for smaller men's teams across the board, rejecting the alternative of eliminating some men's teams entirely. As part of this across-the-board reduction, the size of the men's wrestling team was capped at 27. Despite protests by the wrestling coach and team captain, the smaller CSUB wrestling team performed exceptionally well, winning the Pac-10 Conference title and finishing third in the nation in 1996. In 1996–1997, the men's wrestling roster was capped at 25, and 4 of these spots went unused. Nevertheless, in response to the rumored elimination of the men's wrestling team, on January 10, 1997, the team filed this lawsuit. The district court granted a preliminary injunction to prevent CSUB from reducing the size of the wrestling team.]

Appellees . . . suggest that gender-conscious remedies are appropriate only when necessary to ensure that schools provide opportunities to males and females in proportion to their relative levels of interest in sports participation. By contrast, Appellants contend that schools may make gender-conscious decisions about sports-funding levels to correct for an imbalance between the composition of the undergraduate student body and the composition of the undergraduate student athletic participants pool. This disagreement has real significance: Men's expressed interest in participating in varsity sports is apparently higher than women's at the present time — although the "interest gap" continues to narrow — so permitting gender-conscious remedies until the proportions of students and athletes are roughly proportional gives universities more remedial freedom than permitting remedies only until expressed interest and varsity roster spots correspond. . . .

In other words, Appellees' interpretation of Title IX would have allowed universities to do little or nothing to equalize men's and women's opportunities if they could point to data showing that women were less interested in sports. But a central aspect of Title IX's purpose was to *encourage* women to participate in sports. The increased number of roster spots and scholarships reserved for women would gradually increase demand among women for those roster spots and scholarships.[4]

Title IX is a dynamic statute, not a static one. It envisions continuing progress toward the goal of equal opportunity for all athletes and recognizes that, where society has conditioned women to expect less than their fair share of the athletic opportunities, women's interest in participating in sports will not rise to a par with men's overnight. The percentage of college athletes who are women rose from 15% in 1972 to 37% in 1998, and Title IX is at least partially responsible for this trend of increased participation by women. . . . Title IX has altered women's preferences, making them more interested in sports, and more likely to become student athletes. . . .

Adopting Appellees' interest-based test for Title IX compliance would hinder, and quite possibly reverse, the steady increases in women's participation and interest in sports that have followed Title IX's enactment.

A number of courts of appeals have addressed another potentially dispositive issue in this appeal — namely, whether Title IX permits a university to diminish athletic opportunities available to men so as to bring them into line with the lower athletic opportunities available to women. Every court, in construing the Policy Interpretation and the text of Title IX, has held that a university may bring itself into Title IX compliance by increasing athletic opportunities for the underrepresented gender (women in this case) *or* by decreasing athletic opportunities for the overrepresented gender (men in this case). . . . An extensive survey of Title IX's legislative history and the regulations promulgated to apply its provisions to college athletics concluded that boosters of male sports argued vociferously before Congress that the proposed regulations would require schools to shift resources from men's programs to women's programs, but

---

[4]That is, the creation of additional athletic spots for women would prompt universities to recruit more female athletes, in the long run shifting women's demand curve for sports participation. As more women participated, social norms discouraging women's participation in sports presumably would be further eroded, prompting additional increases in women's participation levels. . . .

that Congress nevertheless sided "with women's advocates" by deciding not to repeal the HEW's athletics-related Title IX regulations. Congress thus appears to have believed that Title IX would result in funding reductions to male athletic programs. If a university wishes to comply with Title IX by leveling down programs instead of ratcheting them up, as Appellant has done here, Title IX is not offended. . . .

Finally, the district court below rejected the interpretation of Title IX advocated by the OCR and Appellants on the ground that such a reading of the statute might violate the Constitution. . . .

[T]he Seventh Circuit has held that "the remedial scheme established by Title IX and the applicable regulation and policy interpretation are clearly substantially related to" the objective of prohibiting "educational institutions from discriminating on the basis of sex. . . . " The district court's final basis for rejecting the OCR's interpretation of Title IX was therefore erroneous. . . .

We REVERSE, and VACATE the preliminary injunction.

QUESTIONS

1. In *Neal*, why does the Ninth Circuit reject plaintiffs' claim that capping rosters for men's sports or eliminating men's teams violates Title IX? Based on statistical data, it appears that most schools are adding women's sports without cutting men's sports and that men's sports participation has continued to increase (not decrease) at a slightly higher proportion as women's sports participation grows. While some men's program have been cut, women's sports have been cut from college programs as well. Limited budgets are not the reason for cutting men's teams, as the wealthiest programs are the ones that are cutting men's sports. Donna Lopiano, *It's Time for Straight Talk About Title IX*, Sports Bus. J., April 30–May 6, 2001, at 33.

2. One critic of Title IX has argued that Title IX should be eliminated and that schools would continue to equitably allocate resources for both male and female athletes because of social and economic demands. See Richard A. Epstein, *Law and Economics: Just Scrap Title IX*, Nat'l L. J., Oct. 14, 2002.

   For a contrary view, see Daniel R. Marburger and Nancy Hogshead-Makar, *Is Title IX Really to Blame for the Decline in Intercollegiate Men's Nonrevenue Sports?*, 14 Marq. Sports L. Rev. 65 (2003). Marburger and Hogshead-Makar conclude that many NCAA D-I athletics programs sacrifice both men's and women's nonrevenue sports to increase the allocation of resources to football and men's basketball programs. Do you agree that schools would offer equal athletics opportunities for males and females without Title IX? How has the D-I emphasis on marketing and promoting football and men's basketball as spectator and revenue-producing sports in a highly competitive market affected athletics administrators' decisions regarding resource allocation?

TITLE IX AND SEXUAL HARASSMENT

Title IX prohibits all forms of sex discrimination in educational programs and activities at schools that receive federal funding. Sexual harassment is a form of discrimination based on sex, and is therefore prohibited under Title IX. In 1997, the OCR issued *Sexual Harassment Guidance: Harassment of Students by School Employees, Other Students, or Third Parties*, 62 Fed. Reg. 12,034 et seq., to inform school officials of their obligations under Title IX to protect students from sexual harassment. In *Gebser v. Lago Vista Independent School District*, 524 U.S. 274 (1998), the Supreme Court established that acts of teacher-student sexual harassment were actionable under Title IX and the following year held that schools may also be liable for peer harassment. See *Davis v. Monroe County Board of Education*, 526 U.S. 629 (1999).

The OCR defines sexual harassment as:

Unwelcome sexual advances, requests for sexual favors and other verbal, nonverbal or physical conduct of a sexual nature when

1) Submission of such conduct is a term or condition of a student's participation in a program or activity
2) Submission to or rejection of unwelcome sexual advances, requests for sexual favors, or other conduct of a sexual nature is used as the basis for an educational decision
3) Such conduct has the purpose or effect of unreasonably limiting a student's ability to participate in or benefit from an educational program or activity or creates an intimidating, hostile or offensive environment.

An institution is strictly liable for the harassing acts of employees such as coaches, assistants, or adult volunteers within the scope of their responsibilities. If the institutional employee is acting outside the scope of his or her duties, the school must take prompt and effective action to stop the harassment and prevent its recurrence as soon as it becomes aware of the harassment. The institution is considered to have engaged in its own discrimination if it fails to act and allows the student to be subjected to a hostile environment that denies or limits the student's ability to participate in or benefit from the school's program once the harassing behavior became known or reasonably should have been known. The harasser can be the same sex or opposite sex of the victim.

According to the Supreme Court in *Davis*, the plaintiff must prove the following to establish a Title IX sexual harassment claim: that the plaintiff is a member of a protected group; that she/he was subjected to unwelcome sexual harassment; that the harassment was based on sex; that the conduct was severe and pervasive enough to create an abusive educational environment; and that the institution knew of the conduct and intentionally failed to take proper action. *Davis*, 526 U.S. at 634–35 (1999). In *Bostic v. Smyrna Sch. Dist.*, 418 F.3d 355 (2d Cir. 2005), the court acknowledged that a teacher's harassment of a student falls within the ambit of Title IX but ultimately refused to hold the school liable because there was no proof that the school had actual knowledge of a sexual relationship between a 15-year-old student and her track coach.

The Supreme Court in *Gebser* and *Davis* did not address the issue of whether a school could raise an affirmative defense by having an effective sexual harassment policy, but OCR regulations, 65 Fed. Reg. 66,092 (Nov. 2, 2000), require schools to adopt and publish grievance procedures to address sexual discrimination. Schools are expected to send a notice of policies and procedures to students, parents (for elementary and secondary students), and employees that includes where complaints may be filed. Once policies and procedures are established, it is expected that the school will actually adhere to the procedures when complaints are made alleging harassment. This would include an adequate, reliable, and impartial investigation of the complaint, including the opportunity to present witnesses and other evidence, conducted within a designated, prompt time frame. Notice of the outcome of the complaint must be given to the parties involved with assurances provided that the school will take corrective measures to eliminate current harassment and similar instances of harassment in the future. In *Ericson v. Syracuse Univ.*, 35 F. Supp. 2d 326 (S.D.N.Y. 1999), a complaint was filed by former members of the women's tennis team alleging that their former coach sexually harassed them. The athletes claimed that some university administrators who investigated the charges had actual knowledge of the harassment but conspired to conduct a sham investigation. The court held that there was sufficient evidence to state a claim against the university under Title IX.

A. Coach-Athlete Sexual Harassment

Although the liability of the institution is the same whether the harasser is a teacher or a coach and the victim is student or an athlete, there are unique circumstances in the athletics context that merit close attention. The number of female athletes has increased dramatically over the past 40 years, but the number of female coaches has decreased. In 1972, 90 percent of the coaches of women's teams were women, but in 2014, 57.1 percent of women's teams are coached by men. See R. Vivian Acosta and Linda Jean Carpenter. *Women in Intercollegiate Sport. A Longitudinal, National Study, Thirty-Seven-Year Update. 1977–2014, http://acostacarpenter.org/2014%20 Status%20of%20Women%20in%20Intercollegiate%20Sport%20-37%20Year%20Update %20-%201977-2014%20.pdf*). This increases the ratio of men coaching female athletes and also increases the opportunity and possibility of sexual harassment. Male coach/female athlete is not the only context in which sexual harassment occurs, but it is significantly greater than any other combination. Other factors have also been identified as creating special opportunities for sexual harassment: (1) the coach–student-athlete relationship, which is marked by the immense authority and power coaches exercise over student-athletes and the one-on-one contact coaches have with student-athletes; (2) the physical nature of sports, in which coaches often apply a hands-on approach to instructing athletes and frequent physical contact between coaches and athletes for celebratory purposes; and (3) focus on the athlete's body, around which daily discussions between coach and student-athlete revolve. Nancy Hogshead-Maker and Sheldon E. Steinbach, *Intercollegiate Athletics' Unique*

Environment for Sexual Harassment Claims: Balancing the Realities of Athletics with Preventing Potential Claims, 13 Marq. Sports L. Rev. 173 (2003).

B. Peer Sexual Harassment

Almost 85 percent of female athletes report having experienced sexually harassing behaviors, and complaints of peer harassment are increasing dramatically. At the University of Pittsburgh, a female swimmer filed a lawsuit seeking reinstatement to the university swim team. She claimed that she was discriminated against because she was released as a result of her complaints of harassment against a swimmer on the men's team. A former placekicker on the University of Colorado football team publicly alleged that she was sexually harassed by her teammates, who treated her "like a piece of meat" and called her "names that are unrepeatable." The student-athlete indicated that she reported the incidents to the coach several times during the season, but the harassment persisted. She ultimately transferred to the University of New Mexico. See *Female Place-Kicker Alleges Harassment at University of Colorado*, Aug. 22, 2003, *http://sports.espn.go.com/espn/wire?id=1601161*. A school is liable for peer or third-party harassment if an official with apparent authority knew or reasonably should have known of the harassment and failed to reasonably respond.

Accusations of sexual assault and rape involving intercollegiate student-athletes at dozens of schools have made the headlines, embarrassing the athletics departments and the institutions. Sexual assault or rape is a severe form of sexual harassment and may be sufficient to establish a hostile environment actionable under Title IX. See *Vance v. Spencer County Pub. Sch. Dist.*, 231 F.3d 253 (6th Cir. 2000); *Brzonkala v. Virginia Polytechnic Institute*, 132 F.3d 949, 959 (4th Cir. 1997). Because sexual harassment disrupts and deprives students of equal access to education, the OCR distributed a Dear Colleague Letter addressing sexual violence on April 4, 2011. The purpose of "Dear Colleague Letter: Sexual Violence" is "to provide recipients with information to assist them in meeting their obligations and to provide members of the public with information about their rights, under the civil rights laws and implementing regulations. . . . " Sexual assault is currently a hot-button topic on all college campuses, resulting in increased preventative education, more timely investigations of complaints, and hiring of dedicated Title IX coordinators and investigators.

Colleges and universities have also been named as defendants in lawsuits when student-athletes have raped other students, both on and off campus. In *Williams v. Board of Regents of the University System of Georgia*, 477 F.3d 1282 (11th Cir. 2007), a female student was allegedly gang-raped by three male student-athletes in an on-campus dormitory. The plaintiff argued that the university was liable under Title IX because the coach, athletics director, and university president were all aware that the student-athlete who attacked the plaintiff had a history of sexual assaults before he was recruited and admitted to the university. The Eleventh Circuit held that given the past history of the recruited student-athlete, the institution had "before the fact notice" and should have made efforts to prevent future harassment from occurring.

In *Simpson v. University of Colorado*, 500 F.3d 1170 (10th Cir. 2007), plaintiffs alleged they were sexually assaulted at an off-campus party by football players and recruits. According to plaintiffs, the University of Colorado (CU) had an official policy that paired recruits with "female ambassadors" to ensure that the recruits would be shown a good time. In determining the viability of plaintiffs' Title IX claim, the court framed the central issue as whether a risk existed that a sexual assault might occur during a recruiting visit. The court found evidence sufficient to establish such a risk, including the head football coach's general knowledge of the serious risk of sexual assault during recruiting visits, the coach's specific knowledge that assaults had occurred during recruiting visits at CU, the coach's maintenance of an unsupervised player-host program notwithstanding this knowledge, the inadequacy of steps taken by CU to reduce the risk of sexual assaults during recruiting visits, and conduct by the head coach in resisting recruiting reforms.

In settlement of plaintiffs' claims, CU agreed to pay the victims a total of $2.5 million. The settlement terms also required CU to hire an external Title IX monitor who will focus on the university's sexual harassment and gender discrimination issues, and to add staff to its victims' assistance center. See Allison Sherry, *$2.85 Million CU Settles Case Stemming from Recruit Scandal*, Denver Post, Dec. 6, 2007, at A01.

QUESTIONS

1. How can universities prevent student-athletes from committing sexual assault or rape? Does the revenue-producing and spectator-driven nature of D-I athletics place significant pressure on legal counsel, athletic directors, and/or coaches to cover up misconduct by student-athletes who participate in sports such as football and basketball?

   Significant media attention has focused on former Florida State quarterback Jameis Winston, who was accused of sexual assault. Winston was not criminally prosecuted, and a student conduct hearing determined there was inconclusive evidence Winston was guilty of rape or sexual misconduct, but OCR is currently investigating whether the university responded appropriately when it became aware of the allegations. The alleged victim has also filed a civil lawsuit against Winston (see *Kinsman v. Winston*, 6:15-cv-00696-ACC-GJK (Mid. Dist. Florida)). What are the difficulties in successfully prosecuting successful athletes? Are personal liability lawsuits the only way to achieve justice in these situations?

2. In the *Williams* and *Simpson* cases, none of the defendants were convicted of criminal sexual assault or rape charges, yet the universities were held liable under Title IX. Explain the legal liability standard.

3. It is important to note that individual school officials (such as coaches or athletics administrators) can also be held personally liable for acts of harassment under §1983 for violating a student's civil rights in addition to a school's liability under Title IX. Timothy Davis and Keith E. Smith, *Eradicating Student-Athlete Sexual Assault of Women: Section 1983 and Personal Liability Following Fitzgerald v. Barnstable*, 2009 Mich. St. L. Rev. 629.

GENDER-BASED EMPLOYMENT DISCRIMINATION IN ATHLETICS

A. Employment Discrimination

KEY TERMS
- Equal Pay Act
- Title VII
- Title IX

Since 1977, R. Vivien Acosta and Linda Jean Carpenter have conducted a longitudinal study, *Women in Intercollegiate Sport* (see *http://acostacarpenter.org/2014%20 Status%20of%20Women%20in%20Intercollegiate%20Sport%20-37%20Year%20Update %20-%201977-2014%20.pdf*). According to the study, there are more women currently employed in administrative and coaching positions in intercollegiate athletics than ever before. However, only 22.3 percent of athletics directors are women, which is dramatically lower than the 90 percent representation in the 1970s, when most colleges and universities had separate men's and women's athletics departments. There are no female administrators at all in 11.3 percent of college athletics programs. Less than half (43.4 percent) of women's athletics teams have a female head coach, even though the majority (56.8 percent) of paid assistant coaches of women's teams are women. The gender barrier for female coaches is also apparent, as less than 3 percent of men's teams are coached by a female head coach. Sports medicine and sports information lag woefully behind, with only 32.4 percent of women employed as head athletics trainers. Athletics communications appears to mirror the professional sports media, as only 12.1 percent of sports information directors are women.

Fuhr v. School Dist. of Hazel Park, 364 F.3d 753 (6th Cir. 2004), illustrates the sports cultural bias against hiring female coaches. Geraldine Fuhr had significant experience as the girls' varsity basketball coach at Hazel Park High School for ten years and concurrently as the assistant boys varsity basketball coach for eight years. Fuhr applied for the boys' varsity coach position, and only one other candidate, a male teacher who had been coaching the boys' freshman basketball team for the past two years, also applied. Both candidates were interviewed, and the superintendent of schools informed the search committee that several members of the school board did not want Fuhr as the boys' coach and that they had to honor their wishes. The president of the school board announced that he "was very concerned about a female being the head boys' basketball coach in Hazel Park." *Id*. at 757. Barnett, the other candidate, was hired, and Fuhr sued the school district for sex discrimination under Title VII and the Elliot-Larsen Act, a Michigan civil rights act that prohibits gender discrimination. A jury held in Fuhr's favor, awarding her $455,000 in damages. Subsequently, the district court ordered Hazel Park to hire Fuhr as the boys' varsity basketball coach. Hazel Park appealed, but the Sixth Circuit affirmed, finding that Hazel Park had intentionally discriminated against Fuhr on the basis of sex by not hiring her as the head boys' basketball coach.

In addition to barriers in employing women in college athletics programs, a gender gap also exists in salaries, with female coaches earning on average only 62 percent of what male coaches make. Barbara Osborne and Marilyn V. Yarbrough. *Pay Equity for Coaches and Athletic Administrators: An Element of Title IX?*, 34 U. Mich. J.L. Reform 231 (2001). In the mid-1990s, two cases were decided that marked important victories for plaintiffs alleging gender-based employment discrimination in intercollegiate athletics. In *Tyler v. Howard Univ.*, No. 91-CA11239 (D.C. June 28, 1993), a women's basketball coach claimed that the disparity between her salary and that of the men's basketball coach and the difference in their office facilities violated Title IX, the Equal Pay Act, and state law. The Howard men's basketball coach was paid $34,500 more annually than Tyler and had a spacious office, while Tyler's office was in a storage room. The jury awarded Tyler $2.34 million in damages, although the judge eventually reduced the award to $250,000. This case marked the first time a plaintiff had received a jury award based on such allegations. Similarly, in *Pitts v. Oklahoma State Univ.*, No. CIV-93-1341-A (W.D. Okla. 1994), another jury awarded damages of $36,000 to a women's college golf coach because her salary was $28,000 a year less than the men's golf coach. She alleged that this disparity violated Title IX and other laws.

The following case illustrates the various alleged causes of action and potential remedies for gender-based wage discrimination by educational institutions against those seeking to ensure compliance with Title IX in the context of athletics.

Deli v. University of Minnesota
863 F. Supp. 958 (D. Minn. 1994)

MAGNUSON, District Judge.

Background

Plaintiff Katalin Deli is the former head coach of the University of Minnesota (University) women's gymnastics team. In June 1992, the University terminated her employment. Ms. Deli challenged this dismissal through the University grievance procedure. After review, the University upheld the termination, finding there existed just cause for her termination. . . .

Deli filed the present action against the University, alleging the University improperly paid her less than head coaches of several men's athletic teams. Deli contends that this pay differential, allegedly based on the gender of the athletes she coached, constituted prohibited discrimination on the basis of sex, in violation of Title VII of the Civil Rights Act, 42 U.S.C. §2000e; the Equal Pay Act, 29 U.S.C. §206(d); and Title IX. . . .

Plaintiff contends the Defendant discriminated in the compensation it paid her on the basis of the gender of the athletes she coached. Significantly, Plaintiff does not claim that the University discriminated against her on the basis of Plaintiff's gender, i.e. she does not claim that the University's motivation for paying her less money than the coaches of men's sports was the fact that Plaintiff was a woman and the coaches of men's sports were men. Plaintiff also does not challenge in this action the circumstances, justification or legality of her discharge from employment by the University. . . .

I. Title VII Claim

Title VII prohibits employers from "discriminating against any individual with respect to his compensation . . . *because of such individual's* race, color, religion, sex or national origin. . . . " 42 U.S.C. §2000e-2(a)(1) (1981). [Emphasis added.] The clear terms of the statute prohibit discrimination in compensation based on the sex of the recipient. The statute does not proscribe salary discrimination based on the sex of other persons over whom the employee has supervision or oversight responsibilities. Even assuming, arguendo, that the University did discriminate in payment of salaries on the basis of the gender of the athletes the Plaintiff coached, such discrimination is not within the scope of Title VII, which prohibits discrimination based on the claimant employee's gender. . . .

II. Equal Pay Act Claims

A. *"Factor Other than Sex" Exception*

Plaintiff Deli also claims the Defendant violated the Equal Pay Act because it paid Plaintiff less than the coaches of men's athletics teams, thus discriminating against her on the basis of the gender of the athletes she supervised. Again assuming arguendo that the Defendant did discriminate in the payment of salary based on the gender of athletes supervised, such action would not support this Plaintiff's claim for violation of the Equal Pay Act.

The Equal Pay Act (EPA) prohibits an employer from discriminating between employees on the basis of sex by paying wages to employees . . . at a rate less than the rate at which [the employer] pays wages to employees of the opposite sex . . . for equal work on jobs the performance of which requires equal skill, effort, and responsibility, and which are performed under similar working conditions, except where such payment is made pursuant to . . . (iv) a differential based on any other factor other than sex. 26 U.S.C. §206(d)(1). . . . After review of the admittedly less-than-clear language of the statute and its history, this Court concurs with the reasoning of the Seventh Circuit — the EPA prohibits discrimination based on the gender of the claimant only and does not reach compensation differentials based on the gender of student athletes coached by a claimant. . . .

B. *Position Not Substantially Equal*

Even if Plaintiff had alleged discrimination in salary based on her own gender, her claim could not withstand summary judgment. . . . [T]he Ninth Circuit recently held that a women's basketball coach who was paid less than a men's basketball coach at the same university failed to show that she would likely prevail on her claims for violation of the Equal Pay Act or Title IX. *Stanley v. University of Southern California*, 13 F.3d 1313 (9th Cir. 1994). The Ninth Circuit affirmed that, consistent with the Equal Pay Act, an employer may pay different salaries to coaches of different genders if the coaching positions are not substantially equal in terms of skill, effort, responsibility, and working conditions. . . . In order to state an Equal Pay Act claim, a Plaintiff must show her position was substantially equal to that of the comparator positions with respect to each of the foregoing attributes.

The comparators Deli has chosen in this suit are the coaches of the men's football, hockey and basketball teams. Defendant has presented evidence to show that all three of those teams are larger than the women's gymnastics team. The University also proffers evidence that the head coaches in those sports supervise more employees than Deli supervised. Further, Defendant has provided evidence to show that the three teams enjoy significantly greater spectator attendance and generate substantially more revenue for the University than the women's gymnastics team. Finally, the University has alleged and provided evidence to support its contention that the coaches of the three men's athletic teams have greater responsibility for public and media relations than Deli had as the coach of the women's gymnastics team. The foregoing evidence alone, if undisputed, is enough to show the Plaintiff's job and that of the head coaches of men's basketball, football and hockey are not "substantially equal" in terms of responsibility and working conditions. . . . Deli offers no evidence to refute the foregoing. . . .

III. Title IX Claims

Plaintiff's Title IX claims fail on the merits. . . . According to the OCR Policy Interpretation, differential compensation of coaches violates Title IX "only where compensation or assignment policies or practices deny male and female athletes coaching of equivalent quality, nature or availability" 44 Fed. Reg. at 71416. . . . The Investigator's Manual confirms that the crux of the inquiry is whether differentials in coaches' compensation result in denial of equal athletic opportunity for athletes. "The intent of [the regulation implementing Title VII] is for equal athletic opportunity to be provided to participants, not coaches." OCR Title IX Investigator's Manual (1990) at 58.

Plaintiff does not assert in her Complaint or elsewhere that the athletes she supervised received lesser quality coaching as a result of the difference between Plaintiff's salary and salaries paid to coaches of the men's football, hockey and basketball teams. . . . Because Plaintiff does not claim or provide any evidence to suggest that due to her receipt of a lower salary than that received by coaches of some men's athletic teams, Plaintiff's coaching services were inferior in "quality, nature or availability" to those provided to the men's teams, she has failed to make out a prima facie claim for violation of Title IX. The Defendant is entitled to summary judgment on Plaintiff's Title IX claims. . . .

QUESTIONS

1. Why did *Deli* reject plaintiff's Equal Pay Act (EPA) and Title IX claims? What would a plaintiff have to plead and prove to establish successful claims under each of these federal statutes?

   After the *Stanley* decision relied on by the *Deli* court, the Equal Employment Opportunity Commission (EEOC) revised its guidelines to clarify how the EPA should be applied in such cases. The guidelines require that an educational institution provide a non-gender-based reason for paying a male coach more than a female coach. Men and women involved in coaching are to be evaluated based on their duties, not their sports. Should the EEOC adopt further guidelines to address what many female coaches refer to as the "chicken and egg" problem — that is, if they were paid more and given more resources to market their programs, would they be able to overcome social inequities that have developed over a long period of time and develop programs that would be as successful as men's programs? A pertinent Title IX regulation states:

   > A recipient shall not make or enforce any policy or practice which, on the basis of sex: (a) Makes distinctions in rates of pay or other compensation; (b) Results in the payment of wages to employees of one sex at a rate less than that paid to employees of the opposite sex for equal work on jobs the performance of which requires equal skill, effort, and responsibility, and which are performed under similar working conditions.

   34 C.F.R. §106.54 (2003).

2. Female athletes often state that they prefer male coaches, and most male athletes state that they prefer male coaches. Is this a justification for hiring a male coach over a female coach? Why or why not? What can or should be done to increase the number of women working in sports?

B. Retaliatory Discharge or Punitive Action

Men and women have asserted that they have been discharged in retaliation for complaining about gender disparities in institutions' athletic programs. Fresno State University has been involved in litigation related to gender discrimination for much of the past decade. First, Diane Milutinovich, an athletics administrator, was dismissed from her position after she complained about inequities in the men's and women's athletics programs. Then the women's volleyball coach, Lindy Vivas, and women's basketball coach, Stacy Johnson-Klein, were fired after questioning administrators and complaining about inequities in facilities, staffing, and employment between the men's and women's athletics programs. Fresno State settled with Milutinovich for $3.5 million. Juries in separate trials found that the university intentionally discriminated against the coaches and awarded $5.85 million to Vivas and $19.1 million to Johnson-Klein.

A threshold issue is whether there is an implied private right of action under Title IX for retaliation on behalf of employees of educational institutions who raise concerns regarding compliance with the substantive provisions of Title IX. In *Jackson v.*

Birmingham Board of Education, 125 S. Ct. 1497 (2005), in a 5–4 decision, the Supreme Court resolved a split in the circuits when it held that Title IX's private right of action encompasses retaliation against an employee who complains about gender-based discrimination. The court explained:

> Title IX prohibits sex discrimination by recipients of federal education funding. The statute provides that "[n]o person in the United States shall, on the basis of sex, be excluded from participation in, be denied the benefits of, or be subjected to discrimination under any education program or activity receiving Federal financial assistance." 20 U.S.C. §1681(a). More than 25 years ago, in *Cannon v. University of Chicago*, 441 U.S. 677, 690–693 (1979), we held that Title IX implies a private right of action to enforce its prohibition on intentional sex discrimination. In subsequent cases, we have defined the contours of that right of action. In *Franklin v. Gwinnett County Public Schools*, 503 U.S. 60 (1992), we held that it authorizes private parties to seek monetary damages for intentional violations of Title IX. We have also held that the private right of action encompasses intentional sex discrimination in the form of a recipient's deliberate indifference to a teacher's sexual harassment of a student, *Gebser v. Lago Vista Independent School Dist.*, 524 U.S. 274, 290-291 (1998), or to sexual harassment of a student by another student, *Davis v. Monroe County Bd. of Ed.*, 526 U.S. 629, 642 (1999).
>
> In all of these cases, we relied on the text of Title IX, which, subject to a list of narrow exceptions not at issue here, broadly prohibits a funding recipient from subjecting any person to "discrimination" "on the basis of sex." 20 U.S.C. §1681. Retaliation against a person because that person has complained of sex discrimination is another form of intentional sex discrimination encompassed by Title IX's private cause of action. Retaliation is, by definition, an intentional act. It is a form of "discrimination" because the complainant is being subjected to differential treatment. [Citations omitted.] Moreover, retaliation is discrimination "on the basis of sex" because it is an intentional response to the nature of the complaint: an allegation of sex discrimination. We conclude that when a funding recipient retaliates against a person *because* he complains of sex discrimination, this constitutes intentional "discrimination" "on the basis of sex," in violation of Title IX. *Jackson v. Birmingham Board of Education*, 125 S.Ct. 1497 (2005).

In *Bryant v. Gardner*, 587 F. Supp. 2d 951 (E.D. Ill. 2008), a coach brought a civil action under Title IX against his high school's principal and the Chicago Board of Education alleging his termination as head coach of the men's basketball team was a result of retaliation against him for complaining about unequal treatment of male and female athletes at his high school. He asserted that female players were allowed to participate in open gym while male players were prohibited from doing so. The defendants moved for summary judgment, which the court denied, holding that a reasonable jury might find that the board's reasons for terminating the coach were merely a pretext designed to cover a retaliatory motive.

· · · · · · · · ·

As more girls participate in sports and more women seek degrees and careers in the sports industry, gender discrimination will remain a critical legal issue. Because sports are still considered a male domain in the United States, gender equity in the sports arena has lagged behind cultural norms in education and in business. Awareness and education are key components in preventing discrimination, while enforcement and litigation serve to correct injustices and punish those who perpetuate discrimination.

Racial Equity Issues in Athletics

6

INTRODUCTION

This chapter focuses on racial inequity, an increasingly complex issue in sports. Notwithstanding its prevalence, the role of race in sports is often overlooked until a particular event brings it into focus. The event may be a derisive comment made by a radio personality in reference to an athlete of color, or an event that marks progress toward racial equity such as the hiring of an African-American NFL head coach. Events seemingly unrelated to sports may also inspire discussion of race in sport. Following the election of President Barack Obama on November 4, 2008, commentators wondered if his achievement might increase access to administrative positions in sports for people of color. They also offered their views regarding whether the presence of African Americans in leadership positions in sports might have influenced Americans to vote for President Obama.

The goal of this chapter is to introduce some of the issues that arise when examining race in the sports context. It attempts to achieve this goal through commentary and leading cases that address race-related issues. The chapter begins with historical perspectives regarding the role of race in American sport.

HISTORICAL PERSPECTIVE

During the early years of professional and collegiate sports, a period extending from after the Civil War to the late 1800s and early 1900s, African Americans participated in organized sports at the amateur and professional levels, including boxing, horse racing, baseball, and cycling. The opportunity to participate during this period was not accompanied by equality of treatment. African Americans were both exploited for their athletic ability and subjected to the indignities that flowed from racial discrimination. To illustrate, African-American athletes suffered the racial epithets of fans and opposing players and the discriminatory acts (e.g., physical attacks) of their own teammates.

The early years of inclusion in amateur and professional sports, albeit limited, were followed by a period during which formal and informal rules excluded blacks from organized professional and collegiate sports. One scholar cites two reasons for the segregation of sports:

> The most obvious [reason] was simply the desire of whites not to associate with African-Americans. . . . Associated with this desire for separation was . . . the other broad explanation: a view that African-Americans were inferior. This view, of course, finds its roots in slavery and provided a common excuse for separation of the races.

Kenneth L. Shropshire, In Black and White: Race and Sports in America 31 (1996). This period of segregation was followed by what some have coined as the reintegration of sports, which is discussed in this chapter.

The following discussion illustrates the web of formal and informal rules that historically prevented African-American athletes from playing for white southern colleges and universities and severely limited their ability to play for northern colleges and universities. In reading these materials, be mindful that similar rules were used to enforce segregation in professional sports in America.

A. Racial Segregation: Intercollegiate Athletics[1]

1. Formal Rules of Exclusion

During the late nineteenth and early twentieth centuries, legally countenanced segregation affected virtually every aspect of social behavior and interaction, including sports. In college sports, a series of rules and customs limited black participation to historically black colleges and a few predominantly white colleges located in the northern United States.

In the South, prohibitions against blacks attending white colleges and universities effectively excluded the black athlete from playing for predominantly white Southern institutions. Moreover, Jim Crow laws enacted to prohibit whites and blacks from social interaction extended to bar direct sporting competition between them. For example, a Texas Penal Code provision, enacted in 1933, prohibited any "boxing, sparring, or wrestling contest or exhibition between any person of the Caucasian or 'White' race and one of the African or 'Negro' race. . . . " Likewise, a 1932 Atlanta city ordinance prohibited amateur baseball clubs of different races from playing within two blocks of each other.

More broadly written statutes prohibited any form of athletic competition between whites and African Americans. Legislative Act 579 is illustrative. Enacted by the Louisiana legislature in 1956, the statute prohibited interracial sports

---

[1] This section is adapted from Timothy Davis, *The Myth of the Superspade: The Persistence of Racism in Intercollegiate Athletics*, 22 Fordham Urban L.J. 615 (1995).

participation. Although similar legislation was defeated in Mississippi, Mississippi state institutions adopted what has been referred to as unwritten but ironclad segregation policy. That such a policy was adopted with respect to sport may be explained by the fact that Mississippi led former states of the Confederacy in enacting laws and policies to ensure what was arguably effectively apartheid.

One commentator observed, "What was left for blacks generally was participation of black against black and the formation of Negro leagues. At a less organized level, it meant acceptance of the Jim Crow laws which called for separate (but almost never equal) playgrounds, public parks, swimming pools, and other recreational facilities." John A. Lucas and Ronald A. Smith, Saga of American Sport 275 (1978). Under such a regime, the idea of competition in the South between white and black collegians was out of the question.

2. Informal Rules of Discrimination

During the late nineteenth and early twentieth centuries, blacks played sports for a limited number of northern colleges such as Harvard, Amherst, and Oberlin. Informal rules reinforced by social strictures, however, were as effective as legislation in limiting the opportunities available to black athletes to compete at predominantly white institutions outside the South.

These informal limitations appeared in various guises. In some instances, they were manifested as a virtual prohibition of African Americans from becoming student-athletes. For instance, few black students competed in sports for Catholic universities, because most such institutions excluded African-American students during this period. Often, informal Jim Crow laws prohibited blacks from playing sports for the schools that did admit black students.

African-American students' experience at the University of Kansas is illustrative. No formal Jim Crow laws were passed in the state of Kansas. Nevertheless, the official policy of the university attempted to minimize the presence of black students in order to remove them from the mainstream of the school's social and extracurricular activities. One historian notes, "Blacks were denied practically every right except that of attending classes." Raymond Wolters, The New Negro on Campus: Black College Rebellions of the 1920s 316 (1975). The university's denial of African-American students' rights to participate in most extracurricular activities included the right to participate on the university's athletic teams. The head of athletics at Kansas in the 1930s insisted, "[N]o colored man will ever have a chance as long as [he is there]." Loren Miller, *The Unrest Among College Students*, 34 Crisis 187 (1927). The situation at University of Kansas illustrates the lack of opportunity for black students to compete for northern universities, which often paralleled those institutions' attitudes and policies toward black students in general.

The environment encountered by black students and student-athletes at the University of Kansas was not unique. Certain athletic conferences, such as the Missouri Athletic Conference (with the exception of Nebraska), systematically excluded black athletes pursuant to so-called gentlemen's agreements that prohibited blacks from participating in league contests. These gentlemen's agreements constituted a series of written rules or tacit understandings precluding black participation in organized sports.

The reach and impact of these gentlemen's agreements extended beyond the walls of the institutions that relied on them to exclude black athletes. They severely affected the few black athletes who were participating for northern universities. Prior to World War II, most northern teams with blacks on their rosters either did not schedule games against southern teams or would leave their African-American players at home when the team traveled south. It has also been suggested that a promise to withdraw voluntarily from games against southern schools was an element of the consideration that some northern institutions extracted from their black athletes.

Illustrations abound of northern schools forcing black players to sit out games against southern teams. For instance, in 1916, Paul Robeson, a member of Rutgers University's football team, was barred from the field of play when Washington and Lee College threatened not to play if he was allowed to participate. Such racially exclusionary practices resulted in black colleges providing the only significant opportunities for the black athlete to compete in college athletics prior to the 1930s.

Northern institutions adopted other informal rules. These rules carried the weight of law and, thus, restricted the ability of black athletes to compete for white colleges and universities. Informal quotas typically restricted the slots open to black athletes to no more than one or two players on a team. In addition to numerical quotas, northern colleges imposed another requirement that limited the number of black student-athletes allowed to compete on their teams. Many of these institutions imposed a "superspade" requirement. In other words, the typical African-American student-athlete playing for a predominantly white college prior to the 1930s tended to be an exceptionally talented starter.

Black student-athletes competing for the few predominantly white colleges willing to admit them were not spared the indignities of racism at their home institutions. Black athletes were excluded from the mainstream of campus social, academic, and athletic life. Black student-athletes were typically not permitted to reside in campus housing or otherwise engage in campus social life. They encountered demeaning comments from coaches, teammates, and other members of the university community, as well as the populace of the local communities in which those colleges were located. This sense of isolation was heightened by an absence of other black students, as well as black faculty, coaches, or administrators.

By the end of World War II, virtually every major collegiate program outside the South had opened its doors to permit at least one African-American player to compete for it. Southern colleges and universities resisted this fundamental change in college sports and continued after World War II to exclude African-American student-athletes. The integration of college sports at predominantly white colleges in the South did not occur until the latter part of the 1960s, during which time the numbers of African-American players competing for these institutions mushroomed. For example, whereas African Americans represented 22 percent of all collegiate basketball players in the South in 1970, by 1985 this figure had increased to 61 percent. For discussions of the integration of intercollegiate sports, see Davis, *supra*, at 633–37; Timothy Davis, *Race and Sports in America: An Historical Overview*, 7 Va. Sports & Enter. L.J. 291 (2008); and Forest J. Berghorn, *Racial Participation and Integration in Men's and Women's Intercollegiate Basketball: Continuity and Change, 1958–1985*, 5 Sociology Sport J. 107, 111 (1988).

B. Racial Segregation: Professional Sports

Prior to World War II, the experiences of racial and ethnic minorities in professional sports largely paralleled those of their amateur counterparts. Baseball provides an excellent illustration of the experiences of African Americans in professional sports prior to World War II. It is estimated that approximately 24 blacks played in organized professional baseball during the 1880s. By the 1890s, however, segregation of professional baseball emerged pursuant to a gentleman's agreement that resulted in the total exclusion of black and dark-skinned Latino players from Major League Baseball (MLB). Seeking alternative venues in which to play baseball, blacks and dark-skinned Latinos played in the Negro Leagues, and Latin America, and barnstormed against white players. (Opportunities for interracial play in a barnstorming capacity were reduced beginning in the 1920s, when MLB's first commissioner, Judge Kenesaw Landis, prohibited major league all-star teams from competing against the Negro Leagues teams.) Fair-skinned Latinos were permitted to play MLB during its segregated era. Those who played, however, were subjected to images that depicted them as "lazy, passive, and inferior" and other forms of discrimination that continued into the post–World War II era. In addition, Latinos who initially entered American professional baseball systematically received lower-paying contracts than their white counterparts.

In dealing with segregated sports leagues, black athletes acted as African Americans did with respect to other segregated institutions (e.g., cultural and educational); they found opportunity in parallel leagues. Baseball's Negro Leagues provide one of the better examples of an alternative developed to provide opportunities despite the exclusion of blacks from major sports leagues.

According to Professor Alfred Mathewson, the term "Negro Leagues" generally has been used somewhat casually to refer to teams that played in the United States between 1880 and 1995. Alfred D. Mathewson, *Major League Baseball's Monopoly Power and the Negro Leagues*, 35 Am. Bus. L.J. 291, 292 (1998). These consisted primarily of black professional baseball players and black owners. *Id.* He goes on to note that although formal leagues existed, "particularly the Negro American and National Leagues," most Negro League teams were unaffiliated with a formal league and operated independently. *Id.* Professor Mathewson adds that most of these teams traveled throughout the United States engaging in "barnstorming sport" that resulted in them playing both black and white local teams. "Frequently, the games were significant social events in Black communities. Even those teams that were members of formal leagues barnstormed before, during, and after joining leagues. The Kansas City Monarchs, who introduced night baseball in 1930, and the Indianapolis Clowns were two of the most successful barnstorming teams." *Id.* at 293.

C. The Reintegration of Professional and Amateur Sports

Baseball remained segregated until Jackie Robinson joined the Brooklyn Dodgers in 1947. The formal desegregation of baseball would not occur, however, until 1959, when the Boston Red Sox, the last major league baseball team to field an all-white team, promoted Pumpsie Green to the major leagues. The National Football League (NFL) had been integrated from the year of its founding in 1920 until 1934, when a gentlemen's agreement between NFL owners, seeking to remake the league, banned the signing of black players. Daniel Coyle, *Invisible Men*, Sports Illustrated, Dec. 15, 2003, p. 124. The NFL was reintegrated in 1946 when Kenny Washington joined the Los Angeles Rams. Similar to football, basketball had less of a history of exclusion than baseball. African Americans competed against whites in professional basketball up until World War I. In 1950, a year after the National Basketball Association (NBA) was formed, Chuck Cooper was selected in a draft by the Boston Celtics. In 1966, basketball also provided the first African-American coach in a major professional sports league when Bill Russell became coach of the Celtics. See Kenneth L. Shropshire, In Black and White: Race and Sports in America 29–31 (1996).

A confluence of social, political, and economic variables resulted in the integration of professional sports and broader American society. Significant among these variables are (1) expectations for desegregation created by the "democratic idealism spawned by World War II," (2) opportunities created by a shortage of players because of World War II's decimation of the talent pool of white athletes, (3) political activism by blacks and their white allies demanding the desegregation of professional sports, (4) Supreme Court desegregation decisions, and (5) enactment of federal civil rights legislation. Additional factors converged to provide incentives for colleges and universities to recruit African-American student-athletes, including political decisions, such as congressional passage of the G.I. Bill (which increased the presence of African Americans on college campuses) and the increased professionalism of college sports following World War II. Historian Adolph Grundman posits that colleges' recruitment of African Americans served a dual purpose: It helped these schools strengthen their athletic programs, while at the same time it promoted the advancement of race relations.

RACE AND RACIAL EQUITY IN MODERN SPORTS: AN EVOLVING DEBATE

For the past few decades, the majority of the players on the field of play in professional football and basketball have been African Americans. The disproportionate presence of African Americans in basketball and football is misleading to the extent that it suggests that race has become a nonissue in American sports. See Jeremi Duru, *Friday Night Lite: How De-Racialization in the Motion Picture* Friday Night Lights *Disserves the Movement to Eradicate Racial Discrimination from American Sport*, 25 Cardozo Arts & Ent. L.J. 485, 487 (2007) (arguing "rather than signaling an end to discrimination in sports, [b]lack visibility in collegiate and professional sports has merely served to mask the racism that pervade[s] the entire sport establishment"). To the contrary, the debate regarding race has merely shifted from the question of distributive justice (e.g., participation opportunities for African Americans in the major sports) to other matters.

These include (1) opportunities for minorities in administrative and coaching positions; (2) the underrepresentation of racial minorities in sports other than football, basketball, and to a lesser extent, baseball; and (3) the implications, for sports, when issues relating to race converge with those relating to gender, globalization, and economic exploitation. The following discussion illustrates the complex and evolving role of race in American sports. See Timothy Davis, *Race and Sports in America: An Historical Overview*, 7 Va. Sports & Ent. L.J. 291, 307–11 (2008) (identifying other present-day manifestations of the role of race in sports, including recent studies suggesting that race may influence officiating in the NBA and MLB, the convergence of race and economics to create impediments to access in certain sports such as golf, stereotype threat, the alleged economic exploitation of African-American men's basketball and football players in big-time college athletic programs, the dearth of Latino athletes in college athletics, and racial insensitivity by some members of the media in sport).

A. College Sports Coaching and Administrative Opportunities

1. Coaching

Sylvester Croom became the first African-American head football coach in the history of the Southeastern Conference (SEC) in December 2003, when he was hired to take the reins of Mississippi State University's football team. At the time of his hiring, Croom became the fifth active African-American head football coach among the then-117 schools that composed the NCAA's Division I-A (now the Football Bowl Subdivision (FBS)). Shortly after Croom was hired, the University of Georgia hired Damon Evans as its athletic director, making him the first African American to hold such a position in the SEC. The hires of Croom and Evans were particularly significant given the SEC's history of being one of the last conferences to integrate its universities' athletics programs.

Although appropriately recognized as evidence of increased racial equity in college sports, the hiring of Croom and Evans brought to the forefront the issue of whether African Americans and other racial minorities are denied equal access to coaching and administrative positions. The statistics tell a mixed story. Between 1996 and 2007, 196 head football coaching vacancies arose in FBS schools. See Black Coaches Association, Who You Know and Who Knows You: The Hiring Process and Practice of NCAA FBS and FCS Head Coaching Positions 8 (C. Keith Harrison, ed., 2007–2008). Coaches of color were selected for 6 percent of those positions. At the beginning of the 2008 college football season, African Americans held six (5 percent), a Latino held one (0.8 percent), and a Polynesian held one (0.8 percent) of the head football coaching positions at FBS institutions. See the Institute for Diversity and Ethics in Sport, The Buck Stops Here: Assessing Diversity Among Campus and Conference Leaders for Football Bowl Subdivision (FBS) Schools in the 2008–09 Academic Year 3 (Richard Lapchick, ed., Nov. 6, 2008). The number of African-American head football coaches was reduced from six to three with the firing of Ty Willingham and resignations of Croom and Ron Prince during the 2008 season. *Id.* By early 2009, the number of African-American football coaches had increased to seven, with hires at New Mexico, Miami of Ohio, and Eastern Michigan. When the 2011 season began, there were 16 African-American coaches leading FBS teams. For the most recent numbers and links to various reports addressing racial matters in sport, visit the "Racial and Gender Report Card" published periodically by DeVos Sport Business Management at *http://www.tidesport.org/racialgenderreportcard.html.*

The slow pace of hiring African-American college football coaches has prompted numerous actions. In October 2003, the Black Coaches Association (BCA) announced a framework for a report card that annually would evaluate Division I (D-I) institutions' search and hiring processes for head football coaches. The results of the BCA's first report card were released in October 2004. Institutions are evaluated based on several factors, including an institution's contact with the BCA during the hiring process, the extent to which institutions make efforts to interview candidates of color, and the diversity of the hiring process. Accompanying the release of its 2008 report card, the BCA called on the National Collegiate Athletic Association (NCAA) to initiate a college version of the NFL's Rooney Rule and threatened legal action to redress what it characterizes as the continued segregation of college football at the head coach position.

In 2005, the NCAA created the Diversity and Inclusion Department, which "is responsible for leading the Association in the development and implementation of strategies, policies, and programs that promote diversity and inclusion throughout intercollegiate athletics." A program that now falls under the umbrella of the Diversity and Inclusion Department and was launched in 2003 is the NCAA Football Coaches Academy, which seeks to enhance the skills required for advancement in football coaching. It has three components, the first of which is an advanced coaching program that consists of workshops that address skill development in areas including communications, booster/alumni relations, fiscal responsibility, moral and ethical considerations, and interview preparation. Another important component of the program is a mentoring initiative that pairs program participants with experienced head football coaches, athletic directors, and conference commissioners. Through its Diversity and Inclusion Department, the NCAA has developed other programs aimed at addressing the shortage of senior-level ethnic minorities in administrative positions at its member institutions.

2. Athletic Administration

Minorities are underrepresented in various aspects of collegiate sports including, for example, athletic directors, league commissioners, faculty athletics representatives (FARs), referees, game officials, and coaches. A detailed discussion of the extent of this underrepresentation, given the breadth of administrative opportunities within intercollegiate athletics, is beyond the scope of this book. Comprehensive information in this regard, however, may be found at the Institute for Diversity and Ethics in Sport, in the annual "Racial and Gender Report Card: College Sport" which Professor Richard Lapchick edits. The NCAA also periodically examines the racial and gender demographics of its member institutions.

B. Professional Sports

On September 20, 2003, attorneys Cyrus Mehri and Johnnie Cochran released *Black Coaches in the National Football League: Superior Performance, Inferior Opportunities,* a report concluding that African-American football coaches are victims of discrimination with respect to hiring and firing notwithstanding their superior coaching performance. Following the report's release, Cochran and Mehri suggested that the NFL would be sued if it failed to take concrete steps to increase the number of African Americans who are head coaches of the league's 32 franchises. Shortly thereafter, an NFL Committee issued guidelines as a part of its policy to foster greater opportunities for African Americans to gain head coaching positions. The guidelines, commonly known as the Rooney Rule, include provisions that require at least one person of color be interviewed as a candidate for coaching vacancies and documentation of each interview.

The 2007 Super Bowl, in which two NFL teams coached by African-American coaches met, exemplified the progress made in the hiring of black coaches. Richard Lapchick, The 2008 Racial and Gender Report Card: National Football League (hereinafter NFL Report Card) 3 (Aug. 27, 2008). Aided by the Rooney Rule, the number of black head NFL coaches increased from two in 2001 to seven in 2006. *Id.* The 2007 season also saw the number of people of color in NFL assistant coaching positions grow to 172 (38 percent). Progress also may be taking root at the general manager level. At the beginning of the 2008 season, there were four black general managers in the NFL. In winning the 2008 Super Bowl, the NFL's New York Giants became the first Super Bowl winner with an African-American general manager. The 2011 season began with eight people of color serving as head coaches. Richard Lapchick, The 2010 Racial and Gender Report Card 2 (Sept. 15, 2011).

Although the foregoing progress is to be applauded, people of color continue to be underrepresented in administrative positions (e.g., general managers, coaches, team vice presidents) and ownership in professional sports. For comprehensive information in this regard, see the racial report cards for each major professional sport league generated annually by the Institute for Diversity and Ethics in Sport at the University of Central Florida. For discussions of racial equity relating to coaching and administrative positions in sports, see N. Jeremi Duru, *The Fritz Pollard Alliance, the Rooney Rule, and the Quest to "Level the Playing Field" in the National Football League,* 7 Va. Sports & Ent. L.J. 179 (2008); Jacquelyn Bridgeman, *The Thrill of Victory and the Agony of Defeat: What Sports Tell Us About Achieving Equality in America,* 7 Va. Sports & Ent. L.J. 248 (2008); and Robert E. Thomas and Bruce L. Rich, *Under the Radar: The Resistance of Promotion Biases to Market Forces,* 55 Syracuse L. Rev. 301 (2005).

C. Intersections

1. Race and Gender

The racial demographics of women who participate in college sports exemplify the intersection of race and gender. In 2013–2014, African-American women accounted for approximately 51.1 percent of D-I women basketball players and 26.8 percent of D-I women outdoor track athletes. The profile of women of color participating in D-I athletics overall during the 2013–14 season was as follows: African-Americans women comprised approximately 15 percent, Latinas 4.5 percent, Asians 2.3 percent, and Native Americans 0.4 percent. Richard Lapchick, The 2014 Racial and Gender Report Card: College Sport 16–17 (March 3, 2015), *http://www.tidesport.org/ 2014%20College%20Sport%20Racial%20&%20Gender%20Report%20Card.pdf.*

The data suggest that minority women are not participating in the increased athletic opportunities created by sports such as rowing, golf, lacrosse, and soccer, which institutions added to comply with Title IX. Consequently, women of color appear not to be in a position to derive the same level of benefits from Title IX as white women. Addressing this issue in the context of African-American women, one scholar commented:

> African American women have encountered stereotyping and stacking within the sports world which steers them into basketball and track. The steering into basketball and track and away from other sports reduces the participation opportunities for which they may compete. . . . Training and development at the higher levels of competition in other sports depend upon access to the lower levels of organized competition in those sports. Sports such as ice hockey, field hockey, tennis, and golf have socio-economic dimensions that limit their accessibility to Black girls at the lower levels of the amateur systems.

Alfred D. Mathewson, *Black Women, Gender Equity and the Function at the Junction,* 6 Marq. Sports L.J. 239 (1996). Professor Marilyn Yarbrough identified race and gender as the dual prohibitions that confront women of color in sports. Marilyn V. Yarbrough, *If You Let Me Play Sports,* 6 Marq. Sports L.J. 229 (1996). Similarly, two scholars have written, "[F]or African-American girls, gender, race, and class converge in ways that make participation in sports a gamble." Deborah L. Brake and Verna L. Williams, *The Heart of the Game: Putting Race and Educational Equity at the Center of Title IX,* 7 Va. Sports & Enter. L.J. 199, 210-211 (2008). See also Lauren Smith, *Black Female Participation Languishes Outside Basketball and Track,* Chron. Higher Educ., June 29, 2007.

2. Race and Economic Exploitation

Professor Rodney Smith has drawn attention to one possible example of the intersection of race and economic exploitation in examining whether African-American student-athletes, who are disproportionately overrepresented in collegiate revenue-producing sports, are exploited. He questions whether a decreased likelihood that these African-American student-athletes will benefit academically from their collegiate experience combines with their revenue generation to produce economic exploitation. Professor Smith illustrates this possibility in the context of D-I college basketball.

With the clear dominance (65 percent) of African-American males in Division I basketball, for example, the current diversion of profits generated from that enterprise to other uses raises serious questions of potential exploitation. . . . Those revenues, in turn, largely fund the entire operations of the NCAA. To compound matters, Division I basketball also generates significant profits for member institutions, with profits per institution averaging $1.6 million in 1994. While other intercollegiate sports typically operate at a loss, Division I football, like basketball, tends to be profitable, generating an average profit of $3.9 million per institution. The profits generated as a result of the labors of male athletes of color, therefore, largely fund the NCAA and support other predominantly non-minority sports at the institutional level. This use of revenues largely generated by male athletes of color for purposes other than supporting the efforts of those minority athletes to obtain an education raises questions of exploitation or, perhaps even, conversion. . . .

Rodney K. Smith, *When Ignorance Is Not Bliss: In Search of Racial and Gender Equity in Intercollegiate Athletics*, 61 Mo. L. Rev. 329 (1996).

3. Race and Globalization

As is true for many industries, American sports have been affected by globalization. Illustrations include the worldwide televising of American professional sports, playing American professional sports in overseas venues, international sales of licensed merchandise, programs created to increase the popularity of American professional sports leagues, and the increasing numbers of foreign players who play in American professional sports leagues. The dramatic increase in the recruitment of Latino players by MLB raises the issue of the unsavory side of globalization. Commentators allege that MLB systematically affords Latino baseball prospects less favorable treatment than American baseball prospects. See Arturo J. Marcano and David P. Fidler, *The Globalization of Baseball: Major League Baseball and Mistreatment of Latin American Baseball Talent*, 6 Ind. J. Global Legal Stud. 511 (1999).

As described by some commentators, the inequitable treatment of Latino baseball prospects allegedly manifests in "MLB scouts getting Latino children to sign blank pieces of paper as 'contracts' to play professional baseball; MLB teams paying no or only paltry signing bonuses for Latino baseball prospects; and, MLB teams systematically discouraging Latino baseball prospects from retaining agents." Marcano and Fidler, *supra*, at 532. These and other commentators allege that such treatment would not be tolerated in the United States. They also contend that it represents a form of discrimination against Latino children.

Global soccer is another sector worthy of a brief note regarding a response to racism. While governmental and league efforts have been at times successful in countering racist behavior in global soccer, activist athletes using social media have proven powerful in their own right, at least with respect to their responses to abuse from fans. For instance, after being serenaded with monkey noises and having bananas thrown at them and other players of color in Spain's First Division during the 2013–2014 season, Barcelona players Neymar and Dani Alves planned a social media counterattack. They decided that when a banana was next thrown at one of them during a game, he would peel it and eat it on the field in view of the cameras, and Alves did just that on April 27, 2014. Immediately thereafter, Neymar posted a picture on social media sites eating a banana with the note, "We are all monkeys." Before long, other athletes, celebrities, and dignitaries around the world — including Brazil's president, Dilma Rousseff — posted similar messages in solidarity with the targeted players. Fernando Kallas, *Neymar Planned Alves' Banana Eating Anti-racist Protest*, AS, April 29, 2014, *http:// as.com/diarioas/2014/04/29/english/1398770114_882297.html.*

QUESTIONS

1. Explanations offered for the dearth of African-American head football college coaches include interference by influential white alumni and fans that hinders the hiring of African-American head football coaches, the refusal of athletic administrators to admit that a problem exists in hiring procedures, and black coaches' lack of experience because many did not play in central positions during college. Do you agree or disagree with any of the foregoing reasons? Are there other reasons for the underrepresentation of racial minorities in coaching and management positions in college and professional sports? Professor Kenneth Shropshire argues that the inability of African Americans to break into leadership is attributable in large part to negative stereotypes. These stereotypes, in conjunction with the "good old boy" system of hiring, result in lower numbers of blacks in authority positions in sports. Shropshire, *supra*, at 83–85.

2. Stacking involves the assignment of certain individuals to specific athletic positions based on race or ethnicity rather than ability. The following account describes the history of stacking in the NFL. Rather than having the opportunity to compete at the "thinking" positions of quarterback, linebacker, and safety, black players were "stacked" at running back and wide receiver. Fortunately, in recent years, the competition on the field for positions is more reliant on talent than color. See David Meggyesy, *Let Players Decide Who Coaches Will Be*, Sports Bus. J., Oct. 21–27, 2002. Does stacking continue to exist in professional and amateur sports? If so, in which sports and for which positions?

3. The disproportionate number of African-American men in basketball and football gives a false impression that they dominate the world of professional sports. With a couple of exceptions (e.g., baseball and soccer for Latino men), African American and other racial minorities are underrepresented in most other sports. What reasons exist for the absence of racial minorities in most sports other than basketball, football, baseball, and to some extent soccer?

• • • • • • • • •

Another matter that has been the subject of intense debate is whether sports are overemphasized in the African-American community. (Interestingly, the same issue has been raised with respect to young prospective baseball players who live in Latin American countries.) Some commentators argue that far too many young African-American males consider sports their "ticket to upward mobility." The statistics paint a clear picture that very few athletes who compete in high school sports will play at the professional level. The NCAA estimates that the percentage of high school athletes who will play professional basketball is 0.03 percent. The figure for professional football is 0.08 percent.

Some argue, however, that the emphasis that young African-American males place on athletics is understandable given the historically high profile of and reverence paid to black athletes. Notes one author, given how media — for better or worse — pay more attention to singers and football players, it's no surprise that people who excel in such pursuits get more attention than teachers or accountants. Lori Shontz, *Focus on Sports Hurts Blacks, Some Say*, St. Louis Post-Dispatch, Feb. 22, 2004, at A1. Reasons offered to explain the focus by young African Americans on sports include the devaluation of African-American males' academic achievement and negative perceptions concerning the likelihood that African-American males will succeed in enterprises outside sports. *Id.* Whatever reasons may underlie this untoward emphasis on sports, many commentators argue the situation must be turned around.

CASE LAW

KEY TERMS
- Disparate impact
- Disparate treatment
- Initial eligibility rules
- Prima facie

The cases and summaries that follow address four (among many) contexts in which race has emerged as an issue in sports: (1) the development and promulgation of NCAA initial eligibility rules; (2) employment discrimination claims asserted by minority coaches; (3) the use by American sports teams of Native American mascots, names, and symbols; and (4) racially hostile environments. Collectively, these cases provide a glimpse of the complexity of the race-related legal issues that arise in sports.

A. Academic Racism and Marginalization: NCAA Initial Eligibility Rules

The topic of manipulating eligibility rules to bring about higher-level academic performance can cause stakeholders a great deal of trepidation. Initial eligibility rules are designed to improve the academic level of achievement of those playing intercollegiate sports. This is done by setting eligibility rules with ever-increasing grade point averages (GPAs) and standardized test scores. This ever-changing landscape is illustrated by the debate surrounding the eligibility standards that incoming college student-athletes must meet to be eligible to receive scholarships and to participate in intercollegiate competition.

In 2003, the NCAA reported that graduation rates of student-athletes who matriculated in 1996 rose to 61 percent, an all-time high. This was the first group of student-athletes who entered college subject to Proposition 16, a regulation that mandated that students were ineligible to participate in intercollegiate athletics because they had not achieved a minimum standardized test score. Graduation rates for black male basketball players and football players increased. The rate for black male basketball players increased to 41 percent, compared to 35 percent for black male basketball players who entered in 1995. For black football players, the increase was from 46 percent to 49 percent. The graduation rate for all D-I football players was 54 percent. The rate for all D-I basketball players was 44 percent. The rate for women basketball players was 66 percent, a 1 percent increase over the 65 percent graduation rate for women basketball players who matriculated in 1995. The NCAA also reported that 3 percent fewer African-American athletes entered colleges in 1996 than in 1995. NCAA graduation data released in 2008 showed that graduation rates for black football and basketball players remained much higher than pre-Proposition 16 rates. According to federal graduation data, 50 percent of FBS black football players who entered college in 2001–2002 graduated (the Graduation Success Rate (GSR) compiled by the NCAA, which includes transfer students, was 54 percent). The federal rate for black male basketball players was 44 percent (the GSR was 54 percent). The continued improvement in athlete graduation rates has been attributed to an increased emphasis on academics, the Academic Progress Rate (APR), and heightened initial eligibility requirements. See Chapter 3 for a discussion of the APR.

Proposition 16 was not the first major NCAA reform related to its initial eligibility requirements. In 1983, NCAA initial eligibility rules known as Proposition 48 were enacted to take effect in 1986. Proposition 48's minimum standards required that a student-athlete achieve a minimum of 2.00 GPA in at least 11 designated high school courses (core courses). In addition, it required a minimum combined score of 700 on the SAT or 15 on the ACT. As was true of Proposition 16, critics assailed Proposition 48's requirement as racially biased. They argued that heightened standards would reduce many black student-athletes' access to college; standardized tests are culturally biased against African Americans; and standardized tests fail to take into account the unique circumstances of student-athletes. Proponents of stricter initial eligibility rules argued that such requirements would help to restore academic integrity to colleges and universities that had been undermined by scandals arising within intercollegiate athletics and represented a means of ensuring that student-athletes have a reasonable chance of obtaining a meaningful degree. Informative discussions of the debate surrounding the enactment of NCAA initial eligibility rules can be found in Davis, *supra*, at 664–67; and Kenneth L. Shropshire, *Colorblind Propositions: Race, the SAT, and the NCAA*, 8 Stan. L. & Pol'y Rev. 141 (1997).

Not surprisingly, courts have been called on to enter the debate. In 1997, minority student-athletes sued the NCAA, claiming that Proposition 16 violated regulations promulgated under Title VI of the 1964 Civil Rights Act because of its disparate impact on African-American athletes. The district court concluded that Proposition 16 had a disparate impact on African-American athletes in violation of the regulations and permanently enjoined the enforcement of Proposition 16. It did so even though it accepted the NCAA's stated justification that Proposition 16 was a way to raise all student-athletes' graduation rates. *Cureton v. NCAA*, 37 F. Supp. 2d 687 (E.D. Pa. 1999).

On appeal, however, the Third Circuit reversed that decision. *Cureton v. NCAA*, 198 F.3d 107 (3d Cir. 1999). The appellate court concluded that the regulations in question applied only to specific programs or activities using federal funds, not to the whole entity. Because the NCAA program allegedly receiving direct funding was not at issue, the regulations could become applicable only if the NCAA had controlling authority over some relevant program receiving federal funding, such as a member school's athletic scholarship program. The court concluded that the NCAA did not exercise controlling authority over member institutions' ultimate decisions about student-athletes' eligibility to participate in athletics, and thus it was not subject to the regulations. For discussions of *Cureton v. NCAA* and the controversy surrounding the standardized test component of the NCAA's initial eligibility rules, see Diane Heckman, *Tracking Challenges to NCAA's Academic Eligibility Requirements Based on Race and Disability*, 222 Ed. L. Rep. 1 (2007); Kenneth L. Shropshire, *Colorblind Propositions: Race, the SAT, and the NCAA*, 8 Stan. L. & Pol'y Rev. 141 (1997).

Another example is *Pryor v. NCAA*, 288 F.3d 548 (3d Cir. 2002). In that case, the plaintiffs, black student athletes, alleged that "[t]he NCAA purportedly tried to improve graduation rates among black student athletes by adopting Proposition 16, a facially neutral rule that establishes scholarship and athletic eligibility criteria for incoming student athletes. As a result of these criteria, Plaintiffs allege, Proposition 16 has caused increased numbers of black student athletes to lose eligibility for receiving athletic scholarships and for participating in intercollegiate athletics during their freshmen year. Plaintiffs further alleged that defendant knew of these effects and intended them. And thus, Plaintiffs suggest that the NCAA actually adopted Proposition 16 to 'screen out' more black student athletes from ever receiving athletic scholarships in the first place, with the asserted goal of increased graduation rates serving as a mere 'pretext.' . . ." The *Pryor* court ruled that the issue of purposeful discrimination under Title VI of the Civil Rights Act of 1964, 42 U.S.C. §2000d *et seq.* (1994) and 42 U.S.C. §1981 (1994), should be explored further and remanded the case to the lower court.

What are your thoughts? Is there any reason that the NCAA would seek to reduce the number of black student athletes eligible to compete?

In November 2002, the NCAA passed legislation that radically changed its initial eligibility rules. This legislation became effective with the class of student-athletes who matriculated in 2005. The revised initial eligibility standards eliminate the cutoff score for the standardized test component of the initial eligibility requirements. For example, a student with a 3.0, or solid B, average needs to score 620 on the SAT to be eligible for competition and financial aid during his or her first year. The minimum SAT score ranges from 400 (for students with a GPA of 3.550 or more) to 1010 (for students with a 2.0 GPA). The scoring range on the SAT is 400 to 1600. The number of core courses increased from 13 to 14 for student-athletes who matriculated in 2005. This number increased to 16 for students who entered college in 2008. The NCAA's initial eligibility index can be found at *http://fs.ncaa.org/Docs/eligibility_center/*

Quick_Reference_Sheet.pdf. Late NCAA president Myles Brand articulated the following rationale for the revised standard:

> The goal in developing the most recent eligibility models was to maximize graduation rates while minimizing disparate impact. . . . We believe that eliminating the test-score cut will increase access and that the new progress-toward-degree benchmarks — particularly in the student-athlete's first two years — will put athletes on track to graduate at even higher rates than they already do.

Athlete Graduation Rates Continue to Climb, NCAA News, Sept. 1, 2003, at 1, 11.

QUESTIONS

What are the implications of the NCAA change in its initial eligibility rules? What impact will it have on the ability of colleges and universities to enroll student-athletes and provide them with scholarships? Do the revised standards enhance the importance of the academic standards adopted by each institution for the admission of student-athletes?

Problem 6-1

The NCAA is considering a number of proposals designed ostensibly to increase graduation rates of basketball players at D-I level. The BCA has asked for your advice regarding a couple of the proposals. One proposal is designed to improve graduation rates by creating disincentives for programs with lower graduation rates. The proposal in question would provide for a reduction of two scholarships for programs with graduation rates that fall below 50 percent, and four scholarships for programs with graduation rates below 25 percent. A number of coaches fear that the proposals will harm their programs because they take players from weaker high schools, many of which are poorly funded inner-city schools in which a large percentage of the students are racial minorities. The coaches believe that it is more difficult to maintain the higher graduation standards with student-athletes from these poorer schools. As such, they believe that the proposal is questionable on racial equity grounds. A second proposal calls for incentives in the form of additional scholarships for schools with graduation rates above 60 percent (one new scholarship at 60 percent, two at 70 percent, and three at 80 percent or higher). Once again, many of the coaches believe that this requirement may benefit universities that recruit heavily from wealthier school districts, which include fewer minority students. A few coaches in the association disagree and argue that the graduation incentives and disincentives programs will ultimately increase the number of minority athletes graduating from universities. Are there legal or ethical problems with the proposals as outlined? What response should the BCA offer to such proposals at the legislative level within the NCAA?

B. Employment Discrimination

As discussed previously, race has been identified as a factor that limits access to coaching and administrative positions and promotion opportunities for African-Americans in college and professional sports. In the few instances in which minority coaches have alleged racial discrimination in hiring and promotion in sports, they have resorted to Title VII and Section 1981 of the Civil Rights Act. Title VII prohibits discrimination in employment. Under Title VII, a plaintiff is likely to assert claims premised on disparate treatment (which focuses on intentional racial discrimination) or disparate impact (which focuses on the use of facially neutral employment practices) that unjustifiably discriminate against members of a protected group. Section 1981 is broader in scope in that it applies to the making, performance, and enforcement of all contracts, not just employment contracts. Section 1981 proscribes intentional discrimination.

Jackson v. University of New Haven provides a detailed examination of the proof that plaintiffs must establish in order to prevail in Title VII and Section 1981 actions. *Jackson* also reveals, however, that the proof required to establish a cognizable Title VII or Section 1981 claim limits the effectiveness of these traditional antidiscrimination norms for those seeking redress for alleged racial discrimination. See Neil Forester, Comment, *The Elephant in the Locker Room: Does the National Football League Discriminate in the Hiring of Head Coaches?*, 34 McGeorge L. Rev. 877 (2003) (outlining the elements of Title VII and Section 1981 claims). Before reading *Jackson*, review the following comment, which sheds light on the reality of hiring in professional sports:

> The statistical composition of sports management's upper echelon would seem to implicate at least one of [the antidiscrimination norms]. A key problem, however, lies in the informal nature of hiring practices in the sports industry. . . .
>
> According to a study conducted by the NAACP in 1994, the majority of the professional sports associations or teams do not have specifically identified hiring or promotion practices that can be pointed to as either intentionally discriminatory or resulting in disparate treatment of or impact on minority candidates. Employers in sports tend to use a series of subjective criteria that vary among employment decisions, with no elements necessarily being weighed more heavily than others. With no unique employment practice to target as discriminatory, it is difficult to bring an action under Title VII, no matter what the statistics show regarding the under-representation of any group at any job level.
>
> The nature of the law indicates that the most viable suit for individuals is one brought by a party denied a job opportunity on the basis of race or a discriminatory selection device or hiring practice. Thus if there is no party wronged, no person denied employment based on discriminatory criteria, then no viable cause of action exists. . . . When those in power tap a friend or family member for a job opening, it is difficult to prove that a particular African-American candidate has been denied an opportunity for employment; in an industry run through contacts and word of mouth, it is likely that there were no other applicants. So, very often, no individual is harmed when a management position goes to yet another white male, because there were no other applicants who could prove that they were denied the job on the basis of race. And in many instances, race was not a factor. The *McDonnell Douglas* formula is wholly inapplicable because the African-American candidate rarely even gets into the pipeline. The positions also do not remain "unfilled," as required under the *McDonnell* test. . . .

Complicating the difficulty in forming a successful discrimination lawsuit against the hiring practices in professional sports is the fact that at the management level, particularly in sports, many employment decisions rest significantly on factors not objectively quantifiable. Judges typically are reluctant to override an employer's decision and impose their own judgments of a candidate's qualifications, especially when the criteria are highly subjective. The instances of judges professing a lack of expertise or refusing to step in and overrule hiring decisions for high-level employment positions are legion in case law.

The sports industry has the added patina of unique talent-identification criteria, particularly for coaching and general manager positions. Courts have been particularly reluctant to interfere with purely sports-related decisions of private sporting enterprises. . . . Whether a specific African-American would be a better coach than the white applicant hired is not an issue in which a court is likely to become involved.

Kenneth L. Shropshire, *The Front Office and Antidiscrimination Law*, in Black and White: Race and Sports in America65-68 (1996).

Jackson v. University of New Haven
228 F. Supp. 2d 156 (D. Conn. 2002)

DRONEY, District Judge.

I. Introduction

[Editors' note: James C. Jackson (Jackson) brought a lawsuit alleging that the University of New Haven (UNH) and its athletic director, Deborah Chin, discriminated against him in hiring in violation of federal antidiscrimination laws. The court granted defendants' motion for summary judgment.]

II. Facts

In February 1999 the head football coach at the University of New Haven ("UNH") left to take a position with the Cleveland Browns of the National Football League. This dispute arises out of the ensuing search for a new head coach at UNH.

Beginning in early February of 1999, UNH posted the head coach position both internally and with the "NCAA market," an online professional publication for university and college athletics. The postings for the head coaching position listed the following requirements:

A bachelors degree is required, master's degree preferred. *Successful collegiate coaching experience required.* Experience in recruiting, game coaching and knowledge of NCAA rules and regulations is essential.

Further, the duties were listed as follows:

> Implement and manage all aspects of a national caliber Division II football program in accordance with NCAA and university regulations. Areas of responsibility include, but are not limited to coaching, recruiting qualified student athletes, budget management, scheduling, hiring and supervising coaching staff, academically monitoring student-athletes, and promotions and fund-raising.

After receiving 36 applications, UNH's Search Committee, which had been established to select a new head coach, decided to interview six applicants — all of whom had college coaching experience and are Caucasian. Jackson, an African-American, was not among the six applicants interviewed. Jackson had no college experience, but had been a professional minor league football coach, earned several "coach of the year" honors as such a coach, and was inducted into the minor league football hall of fame. The defendants assert that they decided not to interview Jackson because he lacked the requisite collegiate coaching experience. From the six applicants interviewed, the Search Committee ultimately selected Darren Rizzi, who had been an assistant coach at UNH for four years, to fill the position of head coach.

At the heart of this dispute lies the "collegiate coaching experience" requirement. The parties are in agreement that the posted job qualifications included that requirement and that all of the applicants selected for interviews possessed such experience. However, the parties differ markedly in their characterizations of that prior experience requirement. The defendants maintain that prior NCAA coaching experience was essential to ensure the selection of a candidate sufficiently well-versed in NCAA rules and regulations to both pass the NCAA's annual tests on such regulations and manage the UNH football team successfully. Jackson, however, asserts that the requirement of previous collegiate coaching experience was not necessary to ensure familiarity with NCAA rules and regulations and that it served to exclude otherwise qualified minority applicants, such as himself.

Jackson asserts that the requirement that applicants have prior college coaching experience amounts to discrimination in violation of 42 U.S.C. §1981, 42 U.S.C. §2000d (Title VI), and 42 U.S.C. §2000e-5 (Title VII). Jackson asserts all three of these statutory causes of action against defendant UNH. However, only the §1981 claim is asserted against defendant Chin.

Jackson appears to base his complaint on both the "disparate treatment" and "disparate impact" theories of recovery in that he alleges both that the challenged qualification had a discriminatory effect upon African Americans (disparate impact) and that the defendants intentionally discriminated against him based on his race (disparate treatment). . . .

IV. Analysis

A. Disparate Treatment Claim

As mentioned, Jackson alleges that he has been discriminated against in violation of 42 U.S.C. §§1981, 2000d (Title VI), and 2000e-5 (Title VII). To the extent that he claims that he has been discriminated against intentionally, the U.S. Supreme Court has developed a "burden shifting framework" for claims brought under Title VII alleging "disparate treatment." *McDonnell Douglas Corp. v. Green*, 411 U.S. 792, 802, 93 S.Ct. 1817, 36L.Ed.2d 668 (1973). Courts have subsequently applied the same burden-shifting framework articulated in *McDonnell Douglas* to disparate treatment claims arising under 42 U.S.C. §§1981 and 2000d (Title VI). . . . Thus, because the test is the same under each of the three statutes, this Court will apply the same *McDonnell Douglas* burden-shifting framework to the plaintiff's disparate treatment claim.

Under the burden-shifting framework of *McDonnell Douglas*, a plaintiff alleging disparate treatment based on race and national origin must first establish a prima facie case of discrimination. 411 U.S. at 802, 93 S.Ct. 1817.5 The burden then shifts to the defendant to offer a legitimate, nondiscriminatory rationale for its actions. *See James v. New York Racing Ass'n*, 233 F.3d 149, 154 (2d Cir.2000). Finally, if the defendant does offer a non-discriminatory reason for its decision, the burden again shifts to the plaintiff to show that the defendant's stated reason is a mere pretext for discrimination. *See Id.* (citing *St. Mary's Honor Ctr. v. Hicks*, 509 U.S. 502, 506–10, 113 S.Ct. 2742, 125 L.Ed.2d 407 (1993)). In some circumstances, . . . after the plaintiff offers evidence to show that the defendant's asserted non-discriminatory reason for the hiring is pretextual, the evidence that established the prima facie case will be sufficient to survive a summary judgment motion. . . . Here, the burden-shifting framework does not reach this stage because Jackson has failed to establish a prima facie case.

To establish a prima facie case of discrimination, a plaintiff must show (1) membership in a protected class, (2) qualification for the employment, (3) an adverse employment decision, and (4) circumstances that give rise to an inference of discrimination. *McDonnell Douglas*, 411 U.S. at 802, 93 S.Ct. 1817. . . . Courts have acknowledged this framework is "not inflexible," but that "in establishing a prima facie case the plaintiff must show that [he] applied for an available position for which [he] was qualified, but was rejected under circumstances that give rise to an inference of discrimination." *Brown v. Coach Stores, Inc.*, 163 F.3d 706, 710 (2d Cir.1998) (citing *Texas Dep't of Cmty. Affairs v. Burdine*, 450 U.S. 248, 253, 101 S.Ct. 1089, 67 L.Ed.2d 207 (1981)) (internal quotation marks omitted).

The parties do not dispute that Jackson is a member of a protected class. Nor do they dispute that the defendants' decision to hire Rizzi instead of Jackson was adverse to him. However, the parties disagree as to whether Jackson meets the second prong of *McDonnell Douglas:* qualification for the position. In their Motion for Summary Judgment, the defendants assert that Jackson was not qualified because he failed to meet an express condition of the employment, that he did not have prior NCAA coaching experience. Although he maintains that he is qualified, Jackson does not dispute that prior collegiate coaching was an expressly listed qualification for the UNH head coach position, nor does he contend that he had any prior experience coaching in college. However, Jackson's subjective determination that he is qualified for the position is not enough to carry his burden of making out a prima facie case.

Consistent with this understanding, courts have afforded employers considerable latitude in selecting employment qualifications. For example, in *Schaffner v. Glencoe Park Dist.*, 256 F.3d 616 (7th Cir.2001) the Seventh Circuit considered the "qualification prong" of the *McDonnell Douglas* burden-shifting framework in the context of an

ADEA claim. 256 F.3d at 620. There the plaintiff was denied a promotion to the position of "program manager" for park recreational programs—a position that listed as one of its requirements one of several types of bachelor's degrees. The court held that the plaintiff failed to meet the qualification prong of the *McDonnell Douglas* test because she did not possess any of the specified degrees, and was therefore not qualified for the position. . . .

[D]eference must be given the defendants in selecting college coaching experience as a qualification for the position of head coach. Nor is it appropriate for this Court to mandate that the defendants equate Jackson's experience in coaching minor league football with college coaching experience. . . .

There are, however, limits to an employer's latitude in selecting hiring criteria. For example, in *Howley v. Town of Stratford*, 217 F.3d 141 (2d Cir.2000) the Second Circuit rejected the defendant's argument that the plaintiff, a female firefighter, was "ineligible" for a promotion to assistant-chief because she did not have the required four years of line-officer experience. 217 F.3d at 151. The Court acknowledged that the town was "entitled to set its own criteria" for the position, but held that because the Town had "relaxed" that standard for two male firefighters, the plaintiff's lack of experience should not have resulted in summary judgment for the defendant. *Id.* at 151–52.

Here there is no claim, and Jackson has put forth no evidence, that the defendants failed to apply the prior college coaching experience requirement uniformly to African-Americans and others. Absent any such showing, the defendants are entitled to the deference in selecting hiring criteria recognized in *Thornley*. Moreover, the prior college coaching experience requirement at issue here appears reasonable on its face. There is an obvious and significant nexus between the defendants' need to select a head coach well-versed in NCAA regulations and the requirement that candidates have actual experience in college coaching. Thus, Jackson has failed to make out a prima facie case of disparate treatment in that he has failed to demonstrate that he was qualified for the position of head coach. As Jackson has failed to meet his burden, this Court grants summary judgment as to his disparate treatment claim brought pursuant to 42 U.S.C. §§1981, 2000d (Title VI), and 2000e-5 (Title VII).

B. Disparate Impact

Unlike disparate treatment, in asserting a claim of disparate impact under Title VII a plaintiff need not allege that the discrimination was intentional. *Griggs v. Duke Power Co.*, 401 U.S. 424, 430-32, 91 S.Ct. 849, 28 L.Ed.2d 158 (1971) ("'[G]ood intent or absence of discriminatory intent does not redeem employment procedures or testing mechanisms that operate as 'built in head winds'"). It is enough that a facially-neutral policy, such as the prior college coaching experience requirement at issue here, be shown to have an adverse impact on a protected group. . . .

However, unlike disparate treatment, the disparate impact theory of recovery is available only for claims brought pursuant to Title VII, and not for claims under 42 U.S.C. §1981 or §2000(d) (Title VI). The U.S. Supreme Court has held that these latter provisions can only be violated by intentional discrimination and that they therefore cannot support a "disparate impact" claim. *See Alexander v. Sandoval*, 532 U.S. 275, 280-85, 121 S.Ct. 1511, 149 L.Ed.2d 517 (2001) (holding that §2000d

(Title VI) proscribes only intentional discrimination and therefore does not support a disparate impact theory of recovery) (citing *Regents of Univ. of Cal. v. Bakke*, 438 U.S. 265, 98 S.Ct. 2733, 57 L.Ed.2d 750 (1978)). . . . Thus, to the extent that Jackson alleges a disparate impact theory of recovery, his claim is cognizable only under Title VII.

Disparate impact cases, like disparate treatment cases, are governed by a "burden-shifting" framework. The Second Circuit reviewed the disparate impact burden-shifting framework in *NAACP, Inc. v. Town of East Haven*, 70 F.3d 219, 225 (2d Cir.1995):

> "[A] plaintiff may establish a prima facie case of disparate impact by showing that use of the test causes the selection of applicants . . . in a racial pattern that significantly differs from that of the pool of applicants." Such a showing can be established through the use of statistical evidence which discloses a disparity so great that it cannot reasonably be attributed to chance. To establish a prima facie case, the statistical disparity must be sufficiently substantial to raise an inference of causation. After a prima facie case is established, the employer has the burden of coming forward with evidence to show that the test has "'a manifest relationship to the employment in question.'" If the employer can make such a showing, the plaintiff may nonetheless prevail if he can suggest alternative tests or selection methods that would meet the employer's legitimate needs while reducing the racially disparate impact of the employer's practices. [Citations omitted.]

Id. at 225. . . . As the Court noted in *East Haven*, this framework was statutorily enacted by the Civil Rights Act of 1991. *Id.* at 225 fn. 6. *See also* 42 U.S.C. §2000e-2(k).

Here, as in the disparate treatment context, Jackson has failed to meet his burden of setting forth a prima facie case of disparate treatment. In making out a prima facie case for disparate impact under Title VII, the plaintiff bears the burden of demonstrating that a specific policy or practice of the defendant has had a disproportionately negative impact on the plaintiff's protected class. 42 U.S.C. Section 2000e-2(k)(1)(A) . . . ; *Griggs*, 401 U.S. at 432, 91 S.Ct. 849. "To make this showing, a plaintiff must (1) identify a policy or practice, (2) demonstrate that a disparity exists, and (3) establish a causal relationship between the two." *Robinson*, 267 F.3d at 160 (citing 42 U.S.C. §2000e-2(k)(1)(A)(I)). Here, Jackson alleges that the defendants' facially neutral hiring criteria (requiring prior college coaching experience), had a discriminatory impact on African-Americans. Specifically, Jackson asserts that because African-Americans have historically been under-represented in the ranks of NCAA coaches this requirement disproportionately excludes African-Americans from consideration.

Statistics are often an important component of a disparate impact claim. *See Robinson*, 267 F.3d at 160 ("[S]tatistical proof almost always occupies center stage in a prima facie showing of a disparate impact claim"). . . .

The defendants here attack the sufficiency of the plaintiff's statistics. They argue that the plaintiff has not offered any statistical evidence to indicate a causal link between UNH's prior college coaching experience requirement and its negative impact on African-Americans. However, Jackson does offer statistics suggesting a causal link between the prior experience requirement and its impact on African-Americans, by comparing the pool of applicants to those who were ultimately selected for interviews. Jackson notes that, of the 14 applicants whose race was identified, only 10% of the Caucasians (1 out of 10) did not have college coaching experience, but 50% of the African-American candidates (2 out of 4) did not have college coaching experience. Further, Jackson noted that all six of the applicants selected for interviews were Caucasian. However, this statistical evidence fails to establish a sufficient causal link between the defendants' employment criterion and its impact on African-Americans. The Second Circuit has recognized that exceedingly small sample sizes often result in statistically unreliable evidence. *Lowe v. Commack Union Free Sch. Dist.*, 886 F.2d 1364, 1371–72 (2d Cir.1989) (holding that the fact that two out of three candidates under age 40 received favorable ratings while only 16 out of 34 candidates over age 40 received such ratings did not support a disparate impact claim in part because of "the unreliability of such a small statistical sample") (superseded by statute on other grounds). The Second Circuit has also indicated that a plaintiff's statistics must meet a certain threshold level of substantiality. . . . Here, the relevant sample size is only 14 (of the 36 applicants, the race of only 14 has been identified), which is too small to yield a statistically significant result. . . . In this case, the plaintiff has failed to provide a sufficiently substantial disparity to survive summary judgment, because the sample is too small.

In addition to the statistics discussed above, the plaintiff has presented an article from the *Sports Business Journal*, which purportedly demonstrates the disparity of college football coaches that are African-American. However, this article—without more—does not present the type of substantial statistical evidence contemplated by the Second Circuit in *Smith*. It is only two pages long, and most of it is an opinion piece rather than a scientific statistical analysis. . . . [T]he essence of a disparate impact analysis is a *comparison*. In *Carter v. Ball*, 33 F.3d 450 (4th Cir.1994) . . . , the court emphasized that "[i]n a case of discrimination in hiring or promoting, the relevant comparison is between the percentage of minority employees and the percentage of potential minority applicants in the qualified labor pool. . . . The mere absence of minority employees in upper-level positions does not suffice to prove a *prima facie* case of discrimination without a comparison to the relevant labor pool." *Id*. . . .

Finally, also in support of his disparate impact claim, the plaintiff asserts that the use of the prior college coaching experience requirement has yielded discriminatory results when applied to other athletic programs at UNH. The plaintiff contends that only one out of 23 coaches hired since 1993, when the plaintiff asserts the prior college coaching experience requirement was adopted for most head coaching positions at UNH, has been African-American. However, even if true, the Supreme Court held in *Wards Cove* that "[t]he percentage of nonwhite workers found in other positions in the employer's labor force is irrelevant to the question of a prima facie statistical case of disparate impact." 490 U.S. at 653, 109 S.Ct. 2115. Thus, the plaintiff has failed to meet his burden of establishing a prima facie case of disparate impact, and this Court also grants summary judgment as to that claim.

For the forgoing reasons, the defendant's Motion for Summary Judgment . . . is GRANTED and the case is DISMISSED.

QUESTIONS

1. The plaintiff based his complaint on "disparate treatment" and "disparate impact" grounds. What is the difference between these arguments as a factual and a legal matter? How much latitude should a university be given in setting coaching experience and related requirements as a prerequisite for consideration in the hiring process? If you were representing a university involved in such a search, what would you recommend as a legal and practical matter?

2. Are African-American athletes and coaches expected to behave in a way that dilutes their racial identity? For example, African Americans have complained that white coaches and players are afforded much greater latitude to express themselves than their African-American counterparts. According to this view, the African-American athlete and coach runs the risk of incurring costly sanctions if they speak out on racially or politically sensitive issues. See Alfred D. Mathewson, *Grooming Crossovers*, 4 J. Gender Race & Just. 225 (2001) (discussing the role of black athletes in struggling for political, racial, and economic equity in sports). Such allegations lie at the core of two notable lawsuits that have been filed by an African-American coach and player.

Nolan Richardson, an African American, was head coach of the University of Arkansas at Fayetteville's (UAF) men's basketball team from 1985 until he was fired in March 2002. *Richardson, Jr. v. Sugg*, 325 F. Supp. 2d 919 (E.D. Ark. 2004). Richardson alleged that "he was fired because of his race and because he spoke out on matters of public concern (race)." *Id.* at 922. Richardson asserted employment and racial discrimination claims that were rejected by the court based on its conclusion that Richardson failed to produce evidence in support of his claims.

As it relates to the intersection of race and the First Amendment, Richardson alleged that his termination was in retaliation for his making comments regarding (1) the difficulties of recruiting African Americans to UAF given Fayetteville's small black population and the social adjustment issues confronting African-American athletes in the Fayetteville community, and (2) the low graduation rates of UAF's men's basketball team.

In assessing Richardson's First Amendment claim, the court articulated the following standard:

> Courts generally use a three-step analysis when evaluating First Amendment retaliation claims. First, to prove a violation of her or his First Amendment rights, a public employee must demonstrate that the speech in which he is engaged is protected speech. To establish this, he must show that the speech can be "fairly characterized as constituting a matter of public concern," and not a matter of private interest. Speech is a "matter of public interest or concern" when it touches upon "any matter of political, social or other concern to the community." Opposition to racial discrimination *is* a "matter of inherently public concern." (internal footnotes omitted).

Id. at 941–42.

Applying the foregoing standard, the court found that Richardson's comments regarding the social environment at Fayetteville could not be regarded as attempts to raise the social consciousness of the public, or to challenge UAF for anything that it had either done or not done regarding the issue of race as it related to student athletes. The district court opinion was affirmed in *Richardson v. Sugg*, 448 F.3d 1046 (8th Cir. 2006).

3. Free speech considerations lie at the core of the issues raised in *Hodges v. National Basketball Association*, 1998 WL 26183 (N.D. Ill.). There, basketball player and coach Craig Hodges alleged that the NBA conspired to keep him out of basketball because he was "an outspoken African-American activist" who commented on political issues, particularly those involving the African-American community. *Id.* at *1. As framed by the court, Hodges asserted that "racial discrimination is at the root of the conspiracy, a conclusion supported by the fact that white players with backgrounds similar to his are free to express themselves politically without suffering any retaliation." *Id.* The court did not have an opportunity to address the merits of Hodges's claims. His suit was dismissed because it was not filed within the applicable two-year statute of limitations.

Do African-American participants in sports become the subject of criticism or retaliation if their behavior fails to conform to standards deemed acceptable by the majority? Can you define any such standards? If so, what are the parameters of those standards?

Problem 6-2

Midwestern State University, a Division I-A football power that had fallen on hard times, advertised for a new head football coach. The ad indicated that previous football coaching experience was required. Several applicants applied, including Coach Ross, the head football coach at another college, who was also a friend and former colleague of Midwestern's athletic director, Shoemaker. Ross, who had over 15 years of collegiate coaching experience, including 8 years as a head coach, applied after being persuaded by Shoemaker to do so. Ross and Shoemaker are both white.

A search committee, chaired by Shoemaker, reviewed numerous applications and invited two applicants for on-campus interviews. One applicant was Ross. The other was an African American, Coach Pegues, who had played college and professional football. Pegues coached at a D-I institution for four years, where he served first as running back and then as wide receiver coach. From there, Pegues moved to the NFL, where he coached for seven years for two teams. He served as quarterback coach for the first team for two years. For the past five years, Pegues has served as offensive coordinator of a highly regarded NFL team.

During the on-campus interviews, Ross and Pegues met with various constituencies, including football players, the search committee, a faculty committee, and athletic department personnel. Both received favorable responses from the groups with whom they met. However, the faculty, athletes, and athletic personnel stated that they preferred Pegues. During the deliberations of the search committee, Shoemaker stated, "Perhaps I shouldn't say this, but I have to be honest. I feel uneasy with Pegues. How do we know if he'll be outspoken like that Nolan Richardson? I'm also concerned with how the major donors to our football program will react to him. We wouldn't want to lose a major source of financial support by hiring this guy. It wouldn't be worth it." After vigorous debate, the search committee concluded that both candidates were qualified to serve as head football coach. The committee understood, however, that it served in an advisory capacity and the final decision rested with the athletic director, Shoemaker.

Shoemaker extended an offer to Ross, who declined. Shoemaker decided not to extend an offer to Pegues. In explaining why he did not, Shoemaker stated, "Pegues is highly qualified, and I wish him well. I simply don't think he is a good fit for our program."

Pegues has come to your office seeking advice on whether he should pursue an action for employment discrimination on account of race. How would you advise him?

C. Stereotypes: Racially Stereotyped Mascots—Racism or Pride?

Similar issues have also emerged related to team logos, mascots, and nicknames that negatively stereotype Native Americans. A leading case in this area is *Pro-Football, Inc. v. Harjo*, 284 F. Supp. 2d 96 (D.D.C. 2003). In that case, *Pro-Football, Inc.* (Pro-Football), which owned the NFL's Washington Redskins football team, holds six trademarks containing the word "redskin(s)," or a derivative of it, that are registered with the Patent and Trademark Office (PTO). The oldest of the six trademarks involved in the litigation was issued in 1967, and the newest was issued in 1990.

In 1992, the plaintiff and six other Native Americans petitioned the U.S. Patent and Trademark Office's Trademark Trial and Appeal Board (TTAB) to cancel the six federal trademark registrations held by Pro Football. Plaintiffs argued that use of the word "redskin(s)" is "scandalous," "may . . . disparage" Native Americans, and may cast Native Americans into "contempt, or disrepute" in violation of section 2(a) of the Lanham Trademark Act of 1946. In 1999, the board canceled the registrations, finding that the marks "may disparage" Native Americans or "bring them into contempt or disrepute." *Harjo v. Pro-Football, Inc.*, 50 U.S.P.Q.2d 1705, 1749 (Trademark Tr. & App. Bd. 1999). Among the issues before the court was whether the board's finding of disparagement was supported by substantial evidence.

Apart from the issue examined, the case provides a vivid picture of the difficulty involved in bringing about change regarding a matter that many feel to be clearly derogatory. Ultimately, the plaintiffs were unsuccessful in this case.

QUESTIONS

1. Opponents of the use of Native American names and mascots argue that these symbols are disparaging to American Indians. Proponents argue that such symbols honor Native Americans. Should it matter that an entity that uses a Native American name or symbol does so with dignity? For instance, in *Pro-Football*, the district court ruled that plaintiffs were required to show that the use of the term "redskins" is offensive when used in the context of the services offered by Pro-Football. Do you agree or disagree?

2. Does Notre Dame's use of the "Fighting Irish" and Leprechaun mascots raise the same issues as a school's use of Native Americans as mascots? Why? Why not?

3. Should it matter if members of the general population or Native Americans find the use of such names and symbols offensive?

· · · · · · · · · ·

In *Pro-Football*, the district court found that whether "redskins" is disparaging should be based not on whether the general population considers the term disparaging, but whether Native Americans consider "redskins" disparaging. The court also found that the survey results failed to demonstrate that a "substantial composite" of Native Americans found "redskins" offensive as a reference for Native Americans. These results were consistent with a poll taken by *Sports Illustrated* in 2002, which revealed the following:

> Asked if high school and college teams should stop using Indian nicknames, 81% of Native American respondents said no. As for pro sports, 83% of Native American respondents said teams should not stop using Indian nicknames, mascots, characters and symbols. Opinion is far more divided on reservations, yet a majority (67%) there said the usage by pro teams should not cease, while 32% said it should.

S.L. Price, *The Indian Wars*, Sports Illustrated, March 4, 2002, at 67, 69. Contrasting scholarly views on the use of Native American mascots can be found in Symposium, *Braves or Cowards? Use of Native American Images and Symbols as Sports Nicknames*, 1 Va. Sports & Ent. L.J. 257 (2002). Despite contrasting views, efforts to end the use of Native American names and mascots have been successful. One report revealed that between 1969 and 2001, more than 1,200 schools had discontinued the use of Indian mascots. Jeff Dolley, *The Four R's: Use of Indian Mascots in Educational Facilities*, 32 J.L. & Educ. 21, 24 n. 12 (2003).

In the wake of the *Harjo* plaintiffs' defeat, a younger group of petitioners led by Amanda Blackhorse — against whom the laches argument (that they had delayed too long in bringing the action) would be inapplicable — essentially reinitiated the *Harjo* plaintiffs' effort, asking the TTAB to cancel Pro-Football's federal trademark registrations. On June 18, 2014, the U.S. Patent and Trademark Office (USPTO) ordered the cancellation of the trademark registrations of the NFL's Washington Redskins team, holding that the evidence supported the petitioners' claim that the term "Redskins" was potentially disparaging to Native Americans at the time the trademarks were registered. For further discussion, see Rodney K. Smith, *The Washington*

Redskins Must Deal with the Reality of a Racist Brand, USA Today, June 21, 2014, *http://www.deseretnews.com/article/865605572/The-Washington-Redskins-must-deal -with-the-reality-of-a-racist-brand.html?pg=all.* The TTAB held that the trademark was granted in error and must be cancelled to correct the mistake. *Blackhorse v. Pro-Football, Inc.,* Cancellation No. 92046185, United States Patent and Trademark Office (June 18, 2014). As in the *Harjo* case, the club then sought to overrule the TTAB decision by suing the petitioners in federal district court, but this time, the district court hearing the case sided with the petitioners, reaffirming the TTAB's determination as to the disparaging effect of the club's name. *Pro-Football, Inc. v. Blackhorse,* 2015 WL 4096277 (E.D. Va.). The club immediately announced that it would appeal the district court's decision. *Id.*

In late 2003, the Executive Committee of the NCAA declined to pass a recommendation of its Subcommittee on Gender and Diversity that would have required the elimination of all Native American nicknames, mascot names, and logos in NCAA publications and announcements. The committee approved, however, recommendations requesting that member institutions using Native American mascots, nicknames, or logos undertake a self-analysis to determine if the use might be deemed offensive.

In August 2005, however, the NCAA Executive Committee approved a policy that "prohibits NCAA colleges and universities from displaying hostile and abusive racial/ethnic/national origin mascots, nicknames or imagery at any of the 88 NCAA championships" unless the schools identified made changes prior to February 1, 2006. Gary T. Brown, *Policy Applies Core Principles to Mascot Issue,* 42 NCAA News, Aug. 15, 2005, at 1, 19. This restriction has three components. First, any institution that hosts a NCAA championship competition must cover up any and all offensive references at the site of the competition. Second, institutions can no longer have offensive references on "team mascots, cheerleaders, dance teams, [or] band uniforms" that travel to NCAA championships beginning August 1, 2008. Effective February 1, institutions with offensive references on their competitive uniforms were prohibited from wearing or displaying them at NCAA-sponsored championships.

The policy allowed institutions to appeal the categorization of their school as one "whose mascots are considered hostile or abusive." *Id.* at 19. The NCAA stated that it would find any evidence that a namesake tribe had "formally approved of the use of the mascot, name, and imagery by the institution" to be compelling evidence. *NCAA Executive Committee Approves Native American Mascot Appeals Process, http://fs.ncaa.org/ Docs/PressArchive/2005/Announcements/NCAA%2BExecutive%2BCommittee%2B Approves%2BNative%2BAmerican%2BMascot%2BAppeals%2BProcess.html.* Several institutions, including Florida State University, Central Michigan University, and the University of Utah, established to the satisfaction of the NCAA's Executive Committee that their use of a Native American name, mascot, or symbol was inoffensive. Others, such as the University of North Dakota, had their appeals rejected. Rebecca Aronauer, *Tribes' Views on Mascot Names Hold Sway with NCAA,* Chron. Higher Educ., Oct. 15, 2005. In each instance in which the NCAA accepted an appeal, the institution had support from a Native American tribe or tribes, such as the Seminole Tribe of Florida and the Seminole Nation of Oklahoma, which both supported Florida State's appeal. In contrast, two Sioux tribes expressed opposition to the University of North Dakota's use of the "Fighting Sioux." *Id.*

In contrast to Florida State, the NCAA denied an appeal by the University of North Dakota (UND). After the NCAA denied its appeal, UND sued the NCAA. In late 2007, the parties agreed to a settlement under which UND would have three years within which to obtain namesake tribe approval of its nickname and related imagery. If such approval was not granted after three years, UND agreed to transition to a new nickname and logo.

In April 2010, the North Dakota Supreme Court ruled that the North Dakota Board of Higher Education had valid authority to choose to discontinue using UND's "Fighting Sioux" nickname prior to the expiration of this three-year deadline, which the board had voted to do. The university's action to discontinue use of the mascot appeared to resolve the issue. In 2011, however, the North Dakota legislature passed a law, which was signed by the governor, that banned higher education and university officials from taking action to discontinue use of the name. Emma G. Fitsimmons, *North Dakota and N.C.A.A. Are at Odds Again over University's Sioux Mascot*, NY Times, July 12, 2011. However, the Board of Higher Education announced that it would not comply with this law and would require UND to discontinue usage of the "Fighting Sioux" nickname and imagery by August 2011, and UND's president, Robert Kelley, stated that the university would comply with the board's instructions. In February 2012, President Kelley publicly stated that the university would continue to use the "Fighting Sioux" while the issue was put to a state vote. The NCAA responded by indicating that they intend to continue to punish UND for using the nickname. In June 2012, the citizens of North Dakota voted overwhelmingly to abolish the "Fighting Sioux" mascot. See Levi Rickert, *North Dakotans Vote to Get Rid of "Fighting Sioux" Mascot by a 2 to 1 Margin*, June 13, 2012, *http://www .nativenewsnetwork.com/north-dakotans-vote-to-get-rid-of-fighting-sioux-mascot-by-2-to-1-margin.html*.

In what may be the last major case surrounding the University of North Dakota mascot issue, *Spirit Lake Tribe of Indians v. NCAA*, 75 F.3d 1089 (2013), the Eighth Circuit addressed claims asserted by the Spirit Lake Tribe and a member of another tribe, the Standing Rock Sioux, seeking to enjoin the NCAA from sanctioning the university for the use of the "Fighting Sioux" name. Plaintiffs alleged that discontinuing use of the name would dishonor the sacred ceremony during which permission was granted for the university to use the name. (In 1969, elders of the Standing Rock Sioux and one elder of the Spirit Lake Tribe ceremonially approved of the university's use of the "Fighting Sioux" name.) Plaintiffs asserted, *inter alia*, that the NCAA's actions leading to the discontinuance by the university's use of the Fighting Sioux name gave rise to a 42 U.S.C. §1981 claim. The court found that the plaintiffs failed to establish the intentional discrimination element of a §1981 action, in that there was no showing that the "NCAA enacted the policy in order to eradicate Sioux culture, as the [plaintiffs] allege." *Id.* at 1093. The court also rejected plaintiffs' claim that the NCAA's policy tortiously interfered with a contract that arose from the 1969 ceremony. The court found that the ceremony did not create a contract, given an absence of the mutual intent required to create a contractual obligation and because any such obligation that might have arisen would have lacked sufficient certainty. *Id.*

Problem 6-3

In 1995, Donor gave $500,000 to University. In 2000, Donor pledged another $100 million to University to construct a new state-of-the-art hockey facility for the school and possibly fund another program. Well into the construction of the facility, controversy erupted concerning whether University should change its nickname, the "Fighting Sioux," and its logo, a majestic Indian head that was designed three years ago by a highly regarded Native American artist. University is one of the country's leading schools in Native American studies and graduates an estimated 25 percent of the Native American doctors in the United States. The controversy arose when a group of white and Native American students and nonstudents protested the nickname and logo. The controversy was only heightened after Donor entered the fray. Donor threatened to halt construction if the school did not retain the name and logo. As legal counsel for University, how would you advise University to proceed? Are there ethical issues to consider?

D. Racially Hostile Environments and Conduct

The history of sports is replete with examples of racially hostile environments emanating from acts perpetrated by teammates, coaches, and opposing players toward minority athletes. Problem 6-4 illustrates what Professor Phoebe Williams characterizes as the overlooked issue of racially hostile environments created by fans. Phoebe Williams, *Racially Hostile Environments*, 6 Marq. Sports L.J. 287, 289 (1996). Several issues emerge when examining fan-based racial animus against athletes, including the following: In the professional sports setting, to what extent do leagues and teams owe a responsibility to athletes to address racial harassment? How pervasive is racially motivated fan conduct against athletes of color? With respect to Problem 6-4, assume that the fans' conduct toward Crawford did not include overtly racist statements or conduct. Also assume that Crawford was not outspoken, but rather was having a season in which he had severely underperformed. To what extent is fan criticism of athletes race-based even though it is not accompanied by obviously racist conduct? Are black athletes, particularly those who are highly paid, subjected to a double standard as it relates to their on-the-field performance? On the other hand, are athletes of color overly sensitive to harsh criticism of fans? Are athletes of color too quick to assume that criticism of them is motivated in part by racial attitudes?

Professor Williams notes the difficulty in determining when harassment of players is racially motivated. "Where the taunts are not obviously racial but disparately based on race, the motivation of the parties will be difficult to establish." She also asks how can the sports industry determine when or if harassment is motivated by racial animus, behavior on the part of the athlete, or simply fan displeasure with the athlete or the team with which he or she is associated? *Id.* at 312. Is racial harassment one of the tools that fans use in an effort to assist their team in winning? Is racial harassment simply a part of the game?

What reasonable reaction should the leagues and teams expect of athletes who are on the receiving end of overtly racial statements and conduct? When confronted with racial hostility, should minority athletes be expected to behave as "model citizens"? Professor Phoebe Williams argues that when confronted with racial hostility, "African-American athletes are expected to endure and defer to racially hostile environments without protest." *Id.* at 308. Professor Williams adds that "standards of professionalism become a metaphor for condoning unlawful racist activity. . . . " *Id.* According to Williams, the prevailing attitude is that it becomes the obligation of the athlete as a professional not to lose control. Consequently, professionalism shifts responsibility "for providing an environment free of racial harassment from the employer to the athlete player." *Id.* at 311.

Similar issues emerge when the racially hostile sports environment emanates not from fans, but from teammates, management, opposing players, or some combination thereof. One example of such hostility is set forth in *Priester v. Lowndes County*, 354 F.2d 414 (5th Cir. 2004). In *Priester*, a teammate was the source of the racial hostility. The alleged hostility was by a white football player at practice and was related to another player's race and weight. Where these and similar issues emerge, the focus is on the legal duty of institutions to stymie racially motivated conduct against athletes of color and the adequacy of the law to address racial hostility in sport. This area highlights, as does the Native American mascot issue, the difficulty the law has in eliminating socially problematic racial matters.

Problem 6-4

A highly paid and very talented African-American NFL running back, Jerome Crawford, had a reputation for being outspoken on what he believed were racial inequities within American society. This resulted in conflicts between Crawford and his teammates and management. During an away game, Crawford was subjected to verbal abuse from fans. Although most of the fans' statements were not racially based, a few were. The latter included threats, such as "we will kill you," and a dummy in blackface with Crawford's number on it. The player reacted by directing an obscene gesture toward the fans. Because of his response, the player was fined $10,000 by the NFL for a lack of professionalism. The player refused to play until the league and individual teams implemented measures to protect African-American and other minority football players from racially motivated abuse by fans.

You are general counsel for the team on which Crawford plays. What advice should you give to team management as to how it should respond to Crawford's refusal to perform?

Health, Safety, and Risk Management Issues in Sports

7

INTRODUCTION

This chapter illustrates the wide range of health and safety issues, and the corresponding need for careful risk management, that arise in a variety of sports-related contexts. Initially, we will explore how common law tort principles are used to allocate the risks of injury and establish liability rules for injuries occurring while observing or participating in sporting events. The materials demonstrate judicial recognition that the unique characteristics and features of athletic competition may require modification of general tort principles to further various policy objectives. Also, courts have uniquely applied criminal law principles to determine what injury-causing conduct constitutes criminally culpable behavior between participants in sporting events. The chapter also examines the liability of high schools and colleges to athletes participating in sports activities. It concludes with a discussion of sovereign and qualified immunity defenses that may shield public schools and colleges from liability for injuries incurred by their athletes. We begin, however, with an overview of basic tort principles.

A *tort* is a wrong, a careless or intentional act, that causes harm to another. It is a private, civil law concept that comes from societal expectations of appropriate inter-personal actions and behavior. Negligence is an unintentional tort that occurs when a person fails to behave in a way that protects others from reasonable harm. This is determined by examining four elements: duty, breach, causation, and damage. *Duty* is established by the relationship between the parties, which indicates the obligatory conduct owed by one party to the other. *Breach* is the failure to act as a reasonable person would in the same or similar circumstance. *Causation* occurs when the natural and unbroken sequence of events foreseeably produces an event without which the harm would not have occurred. Finally, *damage* is the actual harm or injury directly related to the breach or act that was sustained and should be compensated for in order to make things right. *Intentional torts* are those civil wrongs that result in harm to another by an act knowingly committed. Intent does not have to be malicious but merely indicates that the tortfeasor wanted to commit an act with an understanding of the consequences that would likely result from it. *Reckless behavior* falls somewhere between the carelessness of negligence and the deliberateness of an intentional act. Note the way each of the courts in the following cases identifies and defines these tort principles.

LIABILITY FOR ATHLETICS-RELATED INJURIES

A. Injury to Athletes

1. Co-Participant Tort Liability

KEY TERMS
- Assumption of risk
- Inherent risk
- Intentional tort
- Negligence: duty, breach, causation, damage
- Reckless conduct

Injuries frequently occur during all levels of athletic competition and are an inherent risk of participating in sports, which participants generally assume and must bear the resulting costs. Inherent risk would include all of the ordinary harms that one would reasonably expect to occur while engaged in a particular activity. In some instances, a fellow participant or another party may be liable for an injury caused by tortious conduct during a sports event. The following case considers the appropriate legal standard for co-participant tort liability.

Shin v. Ahn
165 P.3d 581 (Cal. 2007)

CORRIGAN, J.

In *Knight v. Jewett* (1992) 3 Cal.4th 296, 11 Cal.Rptr.2d 2, 834 P.2d 696 (*Knight*), we considered the duty of care that should govern the liability of sports participants. We recognized that careless conduct by co-participants is an inherent risk in many sports, and that holding participants liable for resulting injuries would discourage vigorous competition. Accordingly, those involved in a sporting activity do not have a duty to reduce the risk of harm that is inherent in the sport itself. They do, however, have a duty not to increase that inherent risk. Thus, sports participants have a limited duty of care to their co-participants, breached only if they intentionally injure them or "engage[] in conduct that is so reckless as to be totally outside the range of the ordinary activity involved in the sport." This application of the *primary assumption of risk doctrine* recognizes that by choosing to participate, individuals assume that level of risk inherent in the sport.

This case represents the next generation of our *Knight* jurisprudence. *Knight* involved touch football. We expressly left open the question whether the primary assumption of risk doctrine should apply to noncontact sports, such as golf. We address that question here. We hold that the primary assumption of risk doctrine does apply to golf and that being struck by a carelessly hit ball is an inherent risk of the sport. As we explain, whether defendant breached the limited duty of care he owed other golfers by engaging in conduct that was "so reckless as to be totally outside the range of the ordinary activity involved in [golf]" depends on resolution of disputed material facts. Thus, defendant's summary judgment motion was properly denied. . . .

Plaintiff and defendant were playing golf with Jeffrey Frost at the Rancho Park Golf Course in Los Angeles. Defendant, the first of the threesome to complete the 12th hole, went to the 13th tee box. Plaintiff and Frost then finished putting and followed him. Frost took the cart path to the 13th tee box, which placed him perpendicular to, or slightly behind, defendant and to his right. Plaintiff took a shortcut, which placed him in front of defendant and to his left. Plaintiff stopped there to get a bottle of water out of his golf bag and to check his cell phone for messages. He did so even though he knew (1) that he was in front of the tee box, (2) that defendant was preparing to tee off, and (3) that he should stand behind a player who was teeing off. Defendant inadvertently "pulled" his tee shot to the left, hitting plaintiff in the temple. When struck, plaintiff was 25 to 35 feet from defendant, at a 40- to 45-degree angle from the intended path of the ball. Plaintiff claims his injuries were "disabling, serious, and permanent. . . . "

A majority of this court has since extended *Knight's* application of the primary assumption of risk doctrine to other sports. . . .

[*Cheong v. Antablin*, 946 P.2d 817 (1997),] involved skiing. One skier sued another for injuries he suffered when the other skier turned and unintentionally ran into him. We concluded that, "under the applicable common law principles, a skier owes a duty to fellow skiers not to injure them intentionally or to act recklessly, but a skier may not sue another for simple negligence. . . . " Because there was no evidence that the defendant acted recklessly or intentionally injured the plaintiff, we concluded that the defendant's motion for summary judgment was properly granted. . . .

[*Avila v. Citrus Community College Dist.*, 131 P.3d 383 (2006)] involved intercollegiate baseball. A pitcher on the Rio Hondo Community College team (Rio Hondo) hit a batter on the Citrus Community College team (Citrus). The next inning the Citrus pitcher allegedly retaliated by hitting a Rio Hondo batter with a "beanball." The Rio Hondo player sued the Citrus Community College District for negligence. We held the suit was barred by the primary assumption of risk doctrine. It is against the rules of baseball to intentionally throw at a batter. Nevertheless, "being intentionally thrown at is a fundamental part and inherent risk of the sport of baseball. It is not the function of tort law to police such conduct."

The lesson to be drawn from *Knight* and its progeny, as well as the weight of authority in sister states, is that the primary assumption of risk doctrine should be applied to golf. Thus, we hold that golfers have a limited duty of care to other players, breached only if they intentionally injure them or engage in conduct that is "so reckless as to be totally outside the range of the ordinary activity involved in the sport."

The Court of Appeal relied too heavily on one of golf's rules of etiquette involving safety. Golf's first rule of etiquette provides that "[p]layers should ensure that no one is standing close by or in a position to be hit by the club, the ball or any stones, pebbles, twigs or the like when they make a *stroke* or practice swing." (USGA, The Rules of Golf, *supra*, §1, Etiquette, p. 1.) The Court of concluded that "[t]his duty included the duty to ascertain Shin's whereabouts before hitting the ball."

Rules of etiquette govern socially acceptable behavior. The sanction for a violation of a rule of etiquette is social disapproval, not legal liability. This is true, generally, of the violation of the rules of a game. "The cases have recognized that, [in sports like football or baseball], even when a participant's conduct violates a rule of the game and may subject the violator to internal sanctions prescribed by the sport itself, imposition of legal liability for such conduct might well alter fundamentally the nature of the sport by deterring participants from vigorously engaging in activity that falls close to, but on the permissible side of, a prescribed rule." . . .

Here, summary judgment was properly denied because there are material questions of fact to be adjudicated.

In determining whether defendant acted recklessly, the trier of fact will have to consider both the nature of the game and the totality of circumstances surrounding the shot. In making a golf shot, the player focuses on the ball, unlike other sports in which a player's focus is divided between the ball and other players. That is not to say that a golfer may ignore other players before making a shot. Ordinarily, a golfer should not make a shot without checking to see whether others are reasonably likely to be struck. Once having addressed the ball, a golfer is not required to break his or her concentration by checking the field again. Nor must a golfer conduct a headcount of the other players in the group before making a shot.

Many factors will bear on whether a golfer's conduct was reasonable, negligent, or reckless. Relevant circumstances may include the golfer's skill level; whether topographical undulations, trees, or other impediments obscure his view; what steps he took to determine whether anyone was within range; and the distance and angle between a plaintiff and defendant.

Here plaintiff testified at his deposition that he and defendant made eye contact "as I was cutting up the hill." He did not make clear, however, how far he had proceeded up the hill, how far away he was from the defendant, or whether he was stationary when the eye contact occurred. At his deposition, defendant said he looked to see if the area "directly ahead" of him was clear. It is not apparent just how broad or limited that area was. This record is simply too sparse to support a finding, as a matter of law, that defendant did, or did not, act recklessly. This will be a question the jury will ultimately resolve based on a more complete examination of the facts. We do not suggest that cases like this can never be resolved on summary judgment, only that this record is insufficient to do so.

The judgment of the Court of Appeal is affirmed. The case is remanded with directions that litigation should continue under the primary assumption of risk doctrine.

QUESTIONS

As a matter of policy, should the liability standard for co-participant injuries occurring in amateur sports be the same as for professional sports? In determining the appropriate standard, should any distinction be drawn among adult recreational or intramural sports, intercollegiate athletics, high school sports, and youth sandlot games? Why or why not?

NOTE

The prevailing standard for co-participant liability. Most jurisdictions permit recovery in sports injury cases between co-participants only for intentional or reckless conduct, regardless of the level of competition, age, or experience of the participants or the organizational structure of the sport. A minority of courts apply a negligence standard that is premised on the duty of reasonable care that one person owes to guard against foreseeable injuries to others. One of the significant differences between the application of the intentional/recklessness and negligence standards is that mere careless or rough play does not establish liability under the former standard. After the Wisconsin Supreme Court held that negligence "is suitable for cases involving recreational team contact sports," the state legislature enacted a statute establishing liability "only if the participant who caused the injury acted recklessly or with intent to cause injury" in a "recreational activity that includes physical contact between persons in a sport involving amateur teams" or "professional teams in a professional league." Compare *Lestina v. West Bend Mutual Insurance Co.*, 501 N.W.2d 28 (Wis. 1993), with Wis. Stat. Ann. §895.525(4m)(a) and (b).

In determining the legal standard for co-participant liability, some courts draw a distinction between different sports based on the inherent risks of physical contact among participants or with the sport's playing equipment or other instrumentalities. However, as illustrated by *Shin*, the trend is toward the abandonment of the contact versus noncontact sport distinction and toward a focus on whether the risk of injury is inherent to the sporting activity.

Public policy dictates that people should be careful not to harm others; thus liability attaches to the careless, who are negligent. Damages are awarded to compensate the injured party. Similarly, people should not intentionally harm one another, so those who intentionally act are responsible for not only the harm that they cause, but also punitive damages to discourage bad behavior. Consider whether the possibility of tort liability actually deters socially undesirable conduct in a game or changes how a particular sport is played.

An overwhelming majority of courts hold that whether a co-participant is liable to another for an injury during athletic competition is assessed according to an intentional or reckless conduct standard. The majority of courts also generally find that injuries resulting from a co-participant's violation of the rules of a sport typically will not alone result in the breach of one's legal duty owed to fellow participants because rules violations are inherent and anticipated aspects of sports contests. The intentional/reckless standard of care is premised on the recognition that injuries are an inherent part of sports participation and a desire to avoid chilling vigorous competition in sporting events. Courts have expressed concern that imposing legal liability based on a mere failure to use reasonable care (i.e., negligent conduct) while participating in a sport will lead to a flood of litigation. In *Pfenning v. Lineman*, 947 N.E.2d 392 (Ind. 2011), however, the court adopted a variation of the limited duty rule (discussed in detail later in this chapter). The court stated that rather than focusing on the existence or nonexistence of a duty, emphasis should be placed on whether the duty was breached. It held that negligence claims against a co-participant will not result in liability if the conduct is within the ordinary range of that of participants in the sport. Having adopted this standard, the court stated that "as to the golfer's hitting an errant drive which resulted in plaintiff's injury, such conduct is clearly within the range of ordinary behavior of golfers and thus is reasonable as a matter of law and does not establish the element of breach required for a negligence action." *Id.* at 404.

Problem 7-1

Consider whether any of the following conduct should give rise to tort liability:

(a) During his warm-up between innings, a high school pitcher deliberately throws at an opposing team's player and hits him in the ribs while the batter is in the batter's circle attempting to time the pitcher's pitches.
(b) A professional boxer throws a third below-the-belt punch in a match, is disqualified by the referee, and seriously injures his opponent.
(c) A National Hockey League (NHL) player strikes an opposing player in the head with his fist during a fight and renders him unconscious.
(d) A college hockey player breaks an opponent's nose during a fight and is given a three-game suspension for violating league rules prohibiting any fighting.

2. Co-Participant Criminal Liability

 **KEY TERMS**
- Assault
- Assumption of risk
- Felony reckless manslaughter
- Manslaughter

As was discussed in the tort cases involving co-participant liability, American society values free and vigorous participation in athletics activities. Some people lament that competitive contact sports are becoming too violent, while others believe that high levels of aggression enhance the entertainment value of sports. Still others believe that severe acts of violence in the athletics arena should be punished in the same way that those acts would be treated in society — using the criminal law system.

Criminal law protects the health, safety, and welfare of society. All crimes have two components, a voluntary, conscious act, known as *actus reas*, and an evil intention, known as *mens rea*. The criminal code defines what action and corresponding mentality constitute a crime in that jurisdiction. A relatively minor affront to society is generally a misdemeanor, and the guilty party may be assessed a fine or a jail sentence of less than one year. More serious offenses are known as felonies and may result in larger fines and longer periods of incarceration. A prosecutor represents the people/society in the case and has the burden of proving that the defendant is guilty beyond a reasonable doubt.

In an early case, *People v. Fitzsimmons*, 34 N.Y.S. 1102, 1109 (1895), the court instructed the jury as follows in a case involving the prosecution of a professional boxer for a blow that killed his opponent during a sparring exhibition:

> The public has an interest in the personal safety of its citizens, and is injured where the safety of any individual is threatened, whether by himself or another. A game which involves a physical struggle may be a commendable and manly sport, or it may be an illegal contest. This depends upon whether it is a game which endangers life. . . .
>
> [I]f the rules of the game and the practices of the game are reasonable, are consented to by all engaged, are not likely to induce serious injury, or to end life, if then, as a result of the game, an accident happens, it is excusable homicide.
>
> No rules or practice of any game whatever can make that lawful which is unlawful by the law of the land, and the law of the land says you shall not do that which is likely to cause the death of another.

The jury acquitted the defendant of manslaughter.

The following cases provide a modern view of criminal liability for injuries that occur during competitive or recreational sports. Note how each court defines both the action of the defendant, as well as the accompanying mental state.

People v. Schacker
670 N.Y.S.2d 308 (N.Y. Dist. Ct. 1998)

DONOHUE, Judge.

[Editors' note: During a hockey game, a player, Robert Schacker, struck another player in the back of his neck after a play was over and the whistle had been blown. The struck player's head hit the crossbar of the net, and he suffered a concussion. A brain scan and other testing revealed that the struck player's injuries were minor.

The defendant, Schacker, who was charged with assault, pled not guilty. The court stated that for the defendant to be convicted, the prosecution had to prove that "the defendant possessed the conscious intent to cause physical injury to the complainant."

The court added, "The fact that the act occurred in the course of a sporting event is a defense that tends to deny that the requisite intent was present."]

Persons engaged in athletic competition are generally held to have legally assumed the risk of injuries which are known, apparent, and reasonably foreseeable consequences of participation. Hockey players assume the risk of injury by voluntarily participating in a hockey game at an ice rink.

This tort rule states a policy "intended to facilitate free and vigorous participation in athletic activities." *Benitez v. New York City Board of Education*, 73 N.Y.S.2d 650, 657, 543 N.Y.S.2d 29, 541 N.E.2d 29. This policy would be severely undermined if the usual criminal standards were applied to athletic competition, especially ice hockey. If cross checking, tripping, and punching were criminal acts, the game of hockey could not continue in its present form.

The complainant does not assume the risk of reckless or intentional conduct. However, it must be recognized that athletic competition includes intentional conduct that has the appearance of criminal acts. In fact, in many sporting events, physical injuries are caused by contact with other players. However, the players are "legally deemed to have accepted personal responsibility for" the risks inherent in the nature of sport. This includes intentional acts which result in personal injury. Thus, in order to allege a criminal act which occurred in a hockey game, the factual portion of the information must allege acts that show that the intent was to inflict physical injury which was unrelated to the athletic competition. Although play may have terminated, the information herein does not show that the physical contact had no connection with the competition. Furthermore, the injuries must be so severe as to be unacceptable in normal competition, requiring a change in the nature of the game. That type of injury is not present in this case. Firstly, the physical injury resulted from hitting the net, not from direct contact with the defendant. Secondly, the hospital records do not indicate severe trauma to the complainant.

The idea that a hockey player should be prosecuted runs afoul of the policy to encourage free and fierce competition in athletic events. The People argued at the hearing that this was a non-checking hockey league. While the rules of the league may prohibit certain conduct, thereby reducing the potential injuries, nevertheless, the participant continues to assume the risk of a strenuous and competitive athletic endeavor. The normal conduct in a hockey game cannot be the standard for criminal activity under the Penal Law, nor can the Penal Law be imposed on a hockey game without running afoul of the policy of encouraging athletic competition.

For the foregoing reasons, the interest of justice requires a dismissal of this charge pursuant to CPL 170.40.

Regina v. McSorley
2000 B.C. Prov. Ct. 0116 (Crim. Div. 2000)

KITCHEN, Judge.

[Editors' note: The Vancouver Canucks and the Boston Bruins were both struggling to make the playoffs. Early during the game's first period, Marty McSorley and Donald Brashear engaged in a fight, consisting mainly of clutching and grappling while blows were exchanged. Brashear was much more successful at this than McSorley, delivering several heavy lefts to the side and top of McSorley's head, but with surprisingly little effect. The fight ended with Brashear apparently delivering a heavy body blow and wrenching McSorley to the ice surface. McSorley did react to this; it is clear he was in considerable pain at this time. He promptly came to his feet after the linesmen intervened and skated off to the penalty box, showing no adverse effects from the encounter. Brashear, for his part, skated past the Boston bench "dusting off" his hands, suggesting he had made short work of McSorley. This was obviously intended to upset the Boston players.

At the midpoint of the first period, McSorley again attempted to fight with Brashear. McSorley approached Brashear from behind and cross-checked him to the ice. As Brashear was coming to his feet, helmet off, McSorley used his glove to swat Brashear about the head several times. Brashear failed to respond to this and attempted to skate away. The referee gave McSorley three penalties for this—back-to-back two-minute minors for cross-checking and roughing and a ten-minute major for inciting. Shortly afterward, Brashear himself was penalized for interfering with the Boston goalie during play.

From the Brashear penalty in the middle of the first period until the middle of the third period, the game had settled down, and play between the two teams had evened out. During the third period, Brashear was making a play to come from the corner to the front of the Boston net. A Bruin slashed Brashear to prevent this and was given a penalty. During the stoppage in play, Brashear returned to the Vancouver bench, performing what witnesses described as a Hulk Hogan pose for the benefit of the Boston bench. Once again this was an obvious attempt to antagonize the opposing players, and it was effective. Boston complained to the referee, but no action was taken; it was determined that the Boston players had been mocking him at the same time.

With 20 seconds left in the game, which the Canucks were certain to win, McSorley was sent on to the ice by the Bruins coach to regain Boston pride by challenging Brashear to fight again. McSorley unsuccessfully tried to do so. With only 3 seconds left to play, McSorley, while skating up from behind him, struck Brashear in the head with his stick, bringing it around with his hands together on a horizontal plane like a baseball bat swing. As he was struck on the side of the head, Brashear's helmet was lifted out of position and his shoulder shrugged upward, an apparent reflex reaction to the blow of the stick. The blow was of significant force and caused Brashear to fall to the ice and strike his head. As he collapsed to the ice, he had a grand mal seizure before recovering consciousness. Brashear suffered a grade three concussion and could not take part in physical activity for another month. See https://www.youtube.com/watch?v=eTOfso JAij4 to view the incident giving rise to Marty McSorley's prosecution.]

[T]here is an unwritten code of conduct agreed to by the players and the officials. This amalgam of written rules and the unwritten code leads to composite rules, such as the following. It is a legitimate game strategy to slash another player, but if done with sufficient force, and if the referee sees it, then the offender's team plays one player short for two minutes. It is a legitimate game strategy to fight another consenting player, but the offenders are kept off the ice for a period of time determined by the referee. . . .

So the rules of the NHL game of hockey consist of the written rules in the rulebook, a co-existing unwritten code of conduct impliedly agreed to by the players and officials, and guidelines laid down by the officials from game to game. It is within this somewhat indefinite framework that players must play the game. . . .

It is the position of the Crown that this body of evidence permits only two possibilities—that McSorley deliberately struck Brashear to the head without Brashear's consent, or that he recklessly struck him to the head, not necessarily aiming for the head directly. Recklessness in this case may be likened to willful blindness—ignoring a known risk. . . .

If the blow to the head was intentional, it is common ground that it was an assault. Brashear himself said in evidence that he did not consent to being struck in that manner. The other witnesses agreed that stick blows to the head were not permitted in either the written rules, or the unwritten code . . . players in the NHL would not accept a blow such as that as part of the game. . . .

If the slash was intended for the shoulder, delivered with the intention of starting a fight, my conclusion would be that it was within the common practices and norms of the game. . . .

I conclude that the following occurred.

McSorley had fought Brashear and he had been briefly hurt. He was nevertheless prepared to fight him again, but Brashear frustrated his attempts to do so. Brashear taunted the Boston players and was seen to be responsible for taking the Boston goalie out of the game. This was all fairly routine for McSorley. He was credible when he said he was prepared to let things wind down at the end of the game.

Then Laperriere effectively directed him to get Brashear with about twenty seconds left. This was really too little time to fight but he felt himself pressured to do something. He found himself gliding in from centre ice toward Brashear, sizing him up for possible ways to confront him. Brashear crossed directly in front of him, presenting an easy target. Brashear was the focus of all of McSorley's and Boston's frustrations. McSorley had to do something; he might still be able to start a fight. In the words of McSorley, "It has to be an instantaneous reaction." He had an impulse to strike him in the head. His mindset, always tuned to aggression, permitted that. He slashed for the head. A child, swinging as at a Tee ball, would not miss. A housekeeper swinging a carpetbeater would not miss. An NHL player would never, ever miss. Brashear was struck as intended.

Mr. McSorley, I must find you guilty as charged.

People v. Hall
999 P.2d 207 (Col. 2000)

BENDER, Justice.

We hold that Nathan Hall must stand trial for the crime of reckless manslaughter. While skiing on Vail mountain, Hall flew off of a knoll and collided with Allen Cobb, who was traversing the slope below Hall. Cobb sustained traumatic brain injuries and died as a result of the collision. The People charged Hall with felony reckless manslaughter. . . .

The charge of reckless manslaughter requires that a person "recklessly cause the death of another person." For his conduct to be reckless, the actor must have consciously disregarded a substantial and unjustifiable risk that death could result from his actions. We hold that, for the purpose of determining whether a person acted recklessly, a particular result does not have to be more likely than not to occur for the risk to be substantial and unjustifiable. A risk must be assessed by reviewing the particular facts of the individual case and weighing the likelihood of harm and the degree of harm that would result if it occurs. Whether an actor consciously disregarded such a risk may be inferred from circumstances such as the actor's knowledge and experience, or from what a similarly situated reasonable person would have understood about the risk under the particular circumstances.

We hold that under the particular circumstances of this case, whether Hall committed the crime of reckless manslaughter must be determined by the trier of fact. Viewed in the light most favorable to the prosecution, Hall's conduct—skiing straight down a steep and bumpy slope, back on his skis, arms out to his sides, off-balance, being thrown from mogul to mogul, out of control for a considerable distance and period of time, and at such a high speed that the force of the impact between his ski and the victim's head fractured the thickest part of the victim's skull—created a substantial and unjustifiable risk of death to another person. A reasonable person could infer that the defendant, a former ski racer trained in skier safety, consciously disregarded that risk. For the limited purposes of a preliminary hearing, the prosecution provided sufficient evidence to show probable cause that the defendant recklessly caused the victim's death . . .

Like other activities that generally do not involve a substantial risk of death, such as driving a car or installing a heater, "skiing too fast for the conditions" is not widely considered behavior that constitutes a high degree of risk. However, we hold that the specific facts in this case support a reasonable inference that Hall created a substantial and unjustifiable risk that he would cause another's death. . . .

QUESTIONS

1. When, if ever, is it appropriate to criminally prosecute for player conduct that occurs during competitive or recreational sporting events? What other factors should be considered?

2. Will the possibility of criminal liability have the detrimental effect of chilling vigorous participation and competition in athletic activities? *Hall* illustrates the possibility of criminal liability for engaging in dangerous conduct during recreational sports. In *People v. Hall*, 59 P.3d 298 (Colo. Ct. App. 2002), the court upheld a jury verdict finding defendant guilty of criminally negligent homicide.

   After finding Marty McSorley guilty of assaulting Donald Brashear with a weapon (a hockey stick), Judge Kitchen provided the following explanation for the sentence he imposed:

   > The finding of guilt is the real consequence here; the further step of entering a conviction is not necessary. I have concluded that specific deterrence and rehabilitation are served by this. I have concluded that protection of the public is a lesser consideration here. The real concern is that such a sentence may not send the correct message to the community. It must be kept in mind that the consequences to Mr. McSorley are already considerable. He has been without income since the incident, and he has had significant expense in preparing his defence. He has had to endure embarrassing publicity, much more than would be the situation in other assault matters. He will carry the stigma of this with him for the rest of his career; even the rest of his life. If that is not enough to convince anyone that such an offence is to be avoided, there is nothing more a court can do to persuade such a person otherwise. . . .
   >
   > I grant you a conditional discharge for 18 months. You must keep the peace and be of good behaviour. You are bound by a condition that you will not engage in any sporting event where Donald Brashear is on the opposition.

   Regina v. McSorley, 2000 B.C.P.C. 0117 (Oct. 6, 2000).

3. By comparison, consider the following sentences for criminal convictions resulting from on-field conduct (i.e., does the punishment fit the crime?):

   a. In 1988 Minnesota North Star player Dino Ciccarelli was sentenced to one day in jail and fined $1,000 for striking an opposing player several times in the head with his stick during an NHL game.

   b. In February 2001, after being convicted of criminally negligent homicide, Nathan Hall was sentenced to 90 days in jail, was ordered to perform 240 hours of community service, and was barred from drinking alcohol and recreational skiing during a probationary term.

   c. In February 2000, Tony Limon, a Texas high school basketball player, was sentenced to five years in the state penitentiary for deliberately elbowing an opponent in the face (who suffered a concussion and fractured nose) during a game. This conduct was unrelated to any ongoing play, but no foul was called. Limon had previously pled guilty to burglary and was given four years' probation, but he had no prior history of violent behavior.

d. In September 2000, a 16-year-old Illinois high school hockey player was sentenced to two years' probation, ordered not to participate in any contact sports during that time, and required to perform 120 hours of community service after entering an Alford plea (no admission of guilt, but acknowledgment that sufficient evidence to convict exists) to a misdemeanor battery charge. As a high school hockey game was ending, he cross-checked an opponent from behind, causing him to crash headfirst into the boards and permanently paralyzing him from the chest down.

e. In 2009, a Canadian high school rugby player was found guilty of manslaughter for an opponent's death, which was caused by fatal injuries resulting from the player's lifting his opponent into the air with his feet facing upward and driving him head first into the ground. The trial judge found that the "defendant intentionally applied force that was outside the rules of the game or any standard by which the game is played." See *Canadian Player Guilty of Manslaughter over Spear Tackle*, New Zealand Herald (May 29, 2009).

NOTE

Similar to tort law, physical contact resulting in even severe injury is not criminal if it is "part of the game." Consent is a defense to alleged criminal assault, and it is necessary to determine "whether the conduct of defendant constituted foreseeable behavior in the play of the game" and whether a plaintiff's injury "occurred as a by-product of the game itself." *State v. Shelley*, 929 P.2d 489, 493 (Wash. Ct. App. 1997). Courts have affirmed criminal convictions for injuries caused by intentionally thrown punches during basketball and football games. See, e.g., *Shelley*, 929 P.2d at 493 ("There is nothing in the game of basketball, or even rugby or hockey, that would permit consent as a defense to such conduct"). See generally Jeff Yates and William Gillespie, *The Problem of Sports Violence and the Criminal Prosecution Solution*, 12 Cornell J.L. & Pub. Pol'y 145, 168 (2002) ("Criminal prosecutions can be an effective means by which to send the message that society will not tolerate acts of unnecessary violence by sports participants").

Problem 7-2

During his warm-up between innings, a college pitcher deliberately throws at an opposing team player standing in the on-deck circle 24 feet away from the batter's box. The player was attempting to gauge the speed and time of the pitches, but he did not see the thrown ball in time to avoid it. A high-speed fastball hit him in the face, causing a broken cheekbone and orbital fracture. He now has two permanent blind spots in his left eye. The pitcher's coach told his pitchers to "brush back" any opponents attempting to time their pitches. Although admitting an effort to intimidate his opponent, the pitcher denied that he was trying to hit him with the thrown ball. Should the pitcher be criminally prosecuted?

LIABILITY OF EDUCATIONAL INSTITUTIONS (AND ORGANIZATIONS)

A high school, college, or university acts through the conduct of its employees and generally is responsible for harm caused by their tortious conduct that injures student-athletes. Absent applicable tort immunity or a valid contractual waiver of tort liability (see *infra*), an educational institution may be liable for the tortious conduct of employees such as coaches, athletic trainers, and administrative personnel.

A. High School

KEY TERMS	• Assumption of risk
	• Duty of care
	• Proper supervision

Negligence is the theory traditionally relied on by student-athletes who sue their high schools for sports-related injuries. A high school is not an insurer of a student-athlete's safety and is not strictly liable for his or her injuries. To recover for an injury, a high school athlete is required to prove tortious conduct on the part of a school district or its employees. For example, in *Beckett v. Clinton Prairie Sch. Corp.*, 504 N.E.2d 552, 553 (Ind. 1987), the court recognized that high school personnel have a duty to exercise ordinary and reasonable care for safety of student athletes under their authority. See also *Benitez v. New York City Bd. of Educ.*, 541 N.E.2d 29, 32, 543 N.Y.S.2d 29 (1989) (high school owed student athlete voluntarily competing in interscholastic football game a duty to protect against injuries arising from unassumed, concealed, or unreasonably increased risks).

Increasingly, courts have limited the range of risks for which high schools will incur tort liability to their student-athletes. This is in part because of judicial extension of the reckless and intentional conduct standard adopted in co-participant injury cases (see *supra*) to limit the liability of coaches and trainers for certain forms of conduct that result in injury to high school student-athletes. Similarly, courts' increased willingness to enforce liability waivers against high school student-athletes has limited institutions' tort liability.

In determining the appropriate liability standard for injuries suffered while participating in interscholastic athletics, the following case illustrates that courts must strike a balance between the responsibility that arises out of the custodial relationship between schools and their student-athletes (most of whom are minors) and the participants' assumption of the risk of injury inherent in athletic participation. Other relevant policy considerations include the age, skill, and experience levels of those involved in the activity and the extent to which imposing liability may fundamentally alter the nature of the sport. Timothy Davis, *Avila v. Citrus Community College District: Shaping the Contours of Immunity and Primary Assumption of the Risk*, 17 Marq. Sports L. Rev. 259 (2006).

Kahn v. East Side Union High School District
75 P.3d 30, 4 Cal. Rptr. 3d 103 (Cal. 2003)

GEORGE, C.J.

This case presents a question concerning the proper application of the doctrine of primary assumption of risk. At the time of her injury, plaintiff was a 14-year-old novice member of defendant school district's junior varsity swim team. She was participating in a competitive swim meet when she executed a practice dive into a shallow racing pool that was located on defendant school district's property and broke her neck. She alleged that the injury was caused in part by the failure of her coach, a district employee, to provide her with any instruction in how to safely dive into a shallow racing pool. She also alleged lack of adequate supervision and further that the coach breached the duty of care owed to her by insisting that she dive at the swim meet despite her objections, her lack of expertise, her fear of diving, and the coach's previous promise to exempt her from diving.

In *Knight v. Jewett* (1992) 3 Cal.4th 296, 11 Cal.Rptr.2d 2, 834 P.2d 696 (*Knight*), we considered the proper duty of care that should govern the liability of a sports participant for an injury to a co-participant. We concluded that, in recognition of the circumstance that some risk of injury is inherent in most sports, . . . it is appropriate to hold that a participant breaches a duty of care to a co-participant only if he or she "intentionally injures another player or engages in conduct that is so reckless as to be totally outside the range of the ordinary activity involved in the sport." In the present case, we recognize that the relationship of a sports instructor or coach to a student or athlete is different from the relationship between co-participants in a sport. But because a significant part of an instructor's or coach's role is to challenge or "push" a student or athlete to advance in his or her skill level and to undertake more difficult tasks, and because the fulfillment of such a role could be improperly chilled by too stringent a standard of potential legal liability, we conclude that the same general standard should apply in cases in which an instructor's alleged liability rests primarily on a claim that he or she challenged the player to perform beyond his or her capacity or failed to provide adequate instruction or supervision before directing or permitting a student to perform a particular maneuver that has resulted in injury to the student. A sports instructor may be found to have breached a duty of care to a student or athlete only if the instructor intentionally injures the student or engages in conduct that is reckless in the sense that it is "totally outside the range of the ordinary activity" involved in teaching or coaching the sport.

The general proposition that a sports instructor or coach owes a duty of due care not to increase the risk of harm inherent in learning an active sport is consistent with a growing line of Court of Appeal opinions that have applied the *Knight* analysis to claims against such defendants. In these cases, . . . the Courts of Appeal have agreed that although the coach or athletic instructor did not have a duty to eliminate the risks presented by a sport, he or she did have a duty to the student not to increase the risk inherent in learning, practicing, or performing in the sport.

Subsequent decisions have clarified that the risks associated with *learning* a sport may themselves be inherent risks of the sport, and that an instructor or coach generally does not increase the risk of harm inherent in learning the sport simply by urging the student to strive to excel or to reach a new level of competence. . . . The cases point out that instruction in a sport frequently entails challenging or "pushing" a student to attempt new or more difficult feats, and that "liability should not be imposed simply because an instructor asked the student to take action beyond what, with hindsight, is found to have been the student's abilities." (*Bushnell v. Japanese-American Religious & Cultural Center, supra*, 43 Cal.App.4th at p. 532, 50 Cal.Rptr.2d 671). As a general matter, although the nature of the sport and the relationship of the parties to it and to each other remain relevant, a student's inability to meet an instructor's legitimate challenge is a risk that is inherent in learning a sport. To impose a duty to mitigate the inherent risks of learning a sport by refraining from challenging a student, as these cases explain, could have a chilling effect on the enterprise of teaching and learning skills that are necessary to the sport. At a competitive level, especially, this chilling effect is undesirable. . . .

We agree that the object to be served by the doctrine of primary assumption of risk in the sports setting is to avoid recognizing a duty of care when to do so would tend to alter the nature of an active sport or chill vigorous participation in the activity. This concern applies to the process of learning to become competent or competitive in such a sport. Novices and children need instruction if they are to participate and compete, and we agree with the many Court of Appeal decisions that have refused to define a duty of care in terms that would inhibit adequate instruction and learning or eventually alter the nature of the sport. Accordingly, we believe that the standard set forth in *Knight* as it applies to co-participants, generally should apply to sports instructors, keeping in mind, of course, that different facts are of significance in each setting. In order to support a cause of action in cases in which it is alleged that a sports instructor has required a student to perform beyond the student's capacity or without providing adequate instruction, it must be alleged and proved that the instructor acted with intent to cause a student's injury or that the instructor acted recklessly in the sense that the instructor's conduct was "totally outside the range of the ordinary activity" involved in teaching or coaching the sport.

[W]e believe that triable issues of material fact exist regarding the question whether coach McKay breached a duty of care owed to plaintiff, thereby causing her injury, by engaging in conduct that was reckless in that it was totally outside the range of ordinary activity involved in teaching or coaching the sport of competitive swimming. . . .

Concurring and Dissenting Opinion by KENNARD, J.

Persons participating in active sports have to expect that a co-participant may play too roughly and thus cause injury. By contrast, coaches of student athletes teach them the skills necessary to perform their sport of choice safely and effectively. Because student athletes, particularly minors, often consider their coach a mentor or role model, they trust the coach not to carelessly and needlessly expose them to injury. The majority's decision puts an end to that trust: Coaches are under no legal obligation to use reasonable care in training their students how best to perform a sport without incurring personal injury. . . .

Because participation in active sports always entails some risk of harm, the traditional negligence standard imposes liability on an athletic coach only for conduct that exposes players to an *"unreasonable* risk" of such harm. . . . Thus, contrary to the majority's view, applying the negligence standard here would leave coaches free to challenge or push their students to advance their skills level as long as they do so without exposing the student athletes to an unreasonable risk of harm. . . .

Although coaches generally have a legal duty to use reasonable care and not to increase the risks of injury inherent in a sport, some courts recently have ruled that a coach is liable only for intentionally injuring a student or engaging in reckless conduct that is "totally outside the range of the ordinary activity" involved in teaching or coaching the sport. *Kahn*, 75 P.3d at 32–33. These courts have reasoned that applying an intentional/reckless standard is appropriate because a significant aspect of a coach's job is to push students to advance their skills, which requires encouraging them to attempt more difficult tasks. Coaches may, however, be held liable under a negligence theory for not adequately informing students of the need to wear protective equipment, requiring a high school athlete to continue play notwithstanding the coach's knowledge of an existing injury, and not providing prompt medical treatment to a high school athlete.

QUESTIONS

Does *Kahn* strike the appropriate balance between enabling coaches to promote athletic performance and protecting young athletes from increased risks of injury? Considering the objectives of competitive interscholastic athletics, what policy considerations should be given paramount weight? Should injury resulting from negligent coaching be an inherent risk of playing a sport that is assumed by a young athlete?

NOTES

1. Determining inherent risks. A school is not liable for a player's injury resulting from the inherent risks of a sport if it has used reasonable care in conducting the activity. Determining the inherent risks of a sport requires a fact-specific analysis of what activities are "part of the game" and which risks of injury are assumed by all participants. An inherent risk is one that is indivisible from the sport. In other words, the inherent risk inquiry focuses on whether the activity at issue constitutes a risk that is among the consequences attendant to normal competition in a sport. For instance, the risk of being hit by a ball is a consequence of playing baseball. However, there are some risks that are not inherent to the sport, including injuries from safety equipment not required to be worn or defective equipment that was not properly inspected. *Henney v. Shelby City Sch. Dist.*, 2006 WL 747475, at *3 (Ohio Ct. App. March 23, 2006) (coach can be held negligent for failing to supply proper athletic equipment); *Baker v. Briarcliff Sch. Dist.*, 613 N.Y.S.2d 660, 663 (N.Y. App. Div. 1994) (coach inadequately warned players about the "risks involved in not wearing a mouthpiece . . . thereby exposing [plaintiff] to unreasonably increased risks of injury"). But see *Bukowski v. Clarkson Univ.*, 19 N.Y.3d 353, 357 (N.Y. June 5, 2012) (in refusing to impose liability, the court draws a distinction between accidents resulting from defective equipment and those resulting from suboptimal playing conditions).

2. Failure to provide proper emergency medical care. High school coaches have a duty to promptly obtain emergency medical care for an injured athlete. *Mogabgab v. Orleans Parish Sch. Bd.*, 239 So. 2d 456, 460–61 (La. Ct. App. 1970) (noting that when coaches did not seek medical attention for an injured athlete until two hours after his symptoms appeared, they were negligent in causing his death). Although lay athletic personnel are not charged with the knowledge of medical experts, they must recognize a medical emergency and act reasonably under the circumstances. *Pirkle v. Oakdale Union Grammar Sch. Dist.*, 253 P.2d 1, 4 (Cal. 1953); *Kersey v. Harbin*, 531 S.W.2d 76, 80–81 (Mo. Ct. App. 1975).

3. Liability for aggravation of existing injury. Requiring a high school athlete to continue playing with a known injury may create tort liability for aggravation of the injury. In *Morris v. Union High School District A*, 294 P. 998 (Wash. 1931), the Washington Supreme Court held that a school district was liable for a coach's negligence in inducing a student to continue playing football with a back injury. The court ruled, "[If] the coach knew that a student in the school was physically unable to play football, or in the exercise of reasonable care should have known it, but nevertheless permitted, persuaded, and coerced such student to play, with the result that he sustained injuries, the district would be liable." *Id.* at 999. Permitting an injured athlete to return to play without using reasonable care to determine his or her medical condition also may result in institutional liability. *Jarreau v. Orleans Parish Sch. Bd.*, 600 So. 2d 1389 (La. Ct. App. 1992). However, in *Cerny v. Cedar Bluffs Junior/Senior Pub. Sch.*, 679 N.W.2d 198 (Neb. 2004), the Nebraska Supreme Court affirmed the lower court's finding that a coach exercised reasonable care by properly evaluating a high school football player for symptoms of a concussion and allowing him to reenter a game. See also *Mercier v. Greenwich Academy, Inc.*, 2013 WL 3874511 (D. Conn., July 25, 2013) (following *Kahn*, the court extends the reckless and intentional standard in rejecting plaintiff's claim that a coach negligently failed to remove her from competition after she exhibited concussion symptoms; the court concluded, however, that the allegations stated a claim for recklessness); but see *Dugan v. Thayer Acad.*, 2015 WL 3500385, *3 (Mass. Super. May 27, 2015) (holding that a player's own coach must exercise that degree of care of a reasonably prudent coach (i.e., the negligence standard) and may face liability "without proof of recklessness" where plaintiff claimed coach allowed her to play without first evaluating the athlete's injuries").

4. Duty of state high school athletic association to protect athlete's health and safety. State high school athletic associations often promulgate competition and equipment rules for interscholastic sports played within their respective jurisdictions.

Courts have held that these governing bodies have a legal duty to exercise reasonable care when formulating safety rules governing high school athletic competition. See, e.g., *Mohr v. St. Paul Fire & Marine Ins. Co.*, 674 N.W.2d 576 (Wis. App. 2003); *Wissel v. Ohio High Sch. Athletic Assn.*, 605 N.E.2d 458 (Ohio App. 1992).

B. Colleges and Universities

KEY TERMS	• Foreseeability
	• Special relationship

Like the body of law defining a high school's legal duty to protect its students' health and safety, the nature and scope of a university's corresponding legal duty also is rapidly developing. As you read the following cases, consider how the differences between intercollegiate and interscholastic athletics, as well as the nature of the relationship between a university and its student-athletes, influence judicial definition of the parameters of this duty.

In *Kleinknecht v. Gettysburg College*, 989 F.2d 1360 (3d Cir. 1993), the Third Circuit ruled that a university has a legal duty to use reasonable care to provide prompt and adequate emergency medical care to student-athletes injured while participating in intercollegiate athletics. Drew Kleinknecht was a 20-year-old sophomore student at Gettysburg College, which had recruited him for its Division III intercollegiate lacrosse team. During practice, Drew, who had no history of heart problems, collapsed and suffered cardiac arrest. At the time Drew was stricken, there was no athletic trainer or other person qualified to perform cardiopulmonary resuscitation or provide emergency medical care present. No telephone was readily available to call for help; rather, coaches and other student-athletes had to run to an off-field site on campus to summon help. Despite resuscitation efforts, which allegedly were delayed by the college's failure to have an appropriate emergency medical plan, Drew died of cardiac arrest. No athlete at the college had experienced cardiac arrest while playing lacrosse or any other sport.

The Third Circuit held that "a special relationship existed between the College and Drew that was sufficient to impose a duty of reasonable care on the College" for the following reasons:

> Drew chose to attend Gettysburg College because he was persuaded it had a good lacrosse program, a sport in which he wanted to participate at the intercollegiate level. Head Trainer Donolli actively recruited Drew to play lacrosse at the College. At the time he was stricken, Drew was not engaged in his own private affairs as a student at Gettysburg College. Instead, he was participating in a scheduled athletic practice for an intercollegiate team sponsored by the College under the supervision of College employees. . . .
>
> Drew was not acting in his capacity as a private student when he collapsed. Indeed, the Kleinknechts concede that if he had been, they would have no recourse against the College. There is a distinction between a student injured while participating as an intercollegiate athlete in a sport for which he was recruited and a student injured at a

college while pursuing his private interests, scholastic or otherwise. This distinction serves to limit the class of students to whom a college owes the duty of care that arises here. [T]he fact that Drew's cardiac arrest occurred during an athletic event involving an intercollegiate team of which he was a member does impose a duty of due care on a college that actively sought his participation in that sport. We cannot help but think that the College recruited Drew for its own benefit, probably thinking that his skill at lacrosse would bring favorable attention and so aid the College in attracting other students. . . .

Id. at 1368. The court ruled that, although no other athlete at the college had experienced cardiac arrest while playing lacrosse or any other sport, the risk of death or serious injury to an intercollegiate athlete is sufficiently foreseeable to impose a legal duty of reasonable care:

> [T]he Kleinknechts produced ample evidence that a life-threatening injury occurring during participation in an athletic event like lacrosse was reasonably foreseeable. . . . The foreseeability of a life-threatening injury to Drew was not hidden from the College's view. Therefore, the College did owe Drew a duty to take reasonable precautions against the risk of death while Drew was taking part in the College's intercollegiate lacrosse program.
>
> Having determined that it is foreseeable that a member of the College's inter-scholastic lacrosse team could suffer a serious injury during an athletic event, it becomes evident that the College's failure to protect against such a risk is not reasonable. The magnitude of the foreseeable harm — irreparable injury or death to one of its student athletes as a result of inadequate preventive emergency measures — is indisputable.

Id. at 1370.

In the following case, another court refused to extend the duty of care that universities owe to their student-athletes beyond the context of emergency medical care under the factual circumstances in *Kleinknecht*.

Orr v. Brigham Young University
960 F. Supp. 1522 (D. Utah 1994), *aff'd*, 108 F.3d 1388 (10th Cir. 1997)

SAM, District Judge.

[Editors' note: Plaintiff Vernon Peter Orr attended Brigham Young University (BYU) from the fall of 1988 until April 1990 and played on the varsity football team for two football seasons. Orr denied having any lower back pain or injury prior to attending BYU. He asserted that he experienced back pain resulting from participating in football practice and intercollegiate competition. Following postseason bowl practice at the conclusion of the 1989 playing season, Orr experienced back pain and a medical examination revealed three herniated disks. Orr left BYU to play professional football in Finland. Orr did not return to BYU to complete his education.

Orr asserted a litany of conduct that represented BYU's negligent breach of its duty of care owed to him, including (1) engendering a win-at-all-cost mentality, (2) using psychological pressure to increase performance at the sacrifice of his health, (3) employing unqualified persons to diagnose and treat football-related injuries, (4) misdiagnosing his injuries, (5) approving him for and encouraging him to play after being injured, (6) placing greater emphasis on winning football games than on his physical and mental health, and (7) losing interest in him and failing to assist him further in his education.]

BYU argues that "[e]xcept for those duties relating to claims of medical negligence or violations of medical standards of care, the long list of alleged duties owed to Orr and breached by BYU are ones that have never been identified or recognized as duties owed as a matter of law."

Much of Orr's claim of negligence is based upon the breach of purported duties of care created by the special relationship between a university and its student athletes. . . . Orr, in essence, urges that BYU, having recruited him to play football, assumed the responsibility for his safety and deprived him of the normal opportunity for self-protection. . . .

Arguably, Orr, as a collegiate football player, had both demands and advantages distinct from those of the average college student. However, in the court's view, any distinctions are more of a contractual nature than a custodial nature mandating special duties of care and protection beyond those traditionally recognized under a simple negligence theory of liability. BYU, in exchange for a student's promise to play football, agrees to provide the student with such benefits as special consideration in meeting entrance requirements, financial assistance, training table meals, training equipment, medical services, and academic support. Certainly when training and medical services are provided and then negligently performed, liability could result under existing theories of negligence. However, nothing in the facts supports Orr's contentions that, by playing football for BYU, he became in essence a ward of the university without any vestige of free will or independence. At the time Orr began attending BYU, he was twenty-two years old, married with one child. The court finds no facts which suggest that Orr's relationship with BYU was custodial in nature. . . .

An athlete's choice to participate in a sport is not coerced. Voluntary association with a collegiate athletic team does not make the student less of "an autonomous adult or the institution more a caretaker." *Beach [v. University of Utah]*, 726 P.2d [413], at 419. n. 5. As noted earlier, the court views any distinctions between a regular student and a student athlete as more contractual in nature than custodial. In short, the court finds no compelling reasons to impose upon colleges and universities additional duties beyond those owed to other students or those presently recognized and available to collegiate athletes under acknowledged legal theories. . . . [T]he court concludes that the supreme court of Utah would reject Orr's claim that duties are owed to him on the basis of a special relationship with the university by virtue of his football player status. . . .

[Editors' note: The court granted BYU's motion for summary judgment on all of Orr's claims except any arising out of the alleged negligent provision of medical care.]

QUESTION

Should a university owe a duty of care to student-athletes that is different than the duty of care for all students? The courts have been fairly consistent in recognizing that colleges and universities have a duty of reasonable care for the health and safety of athletics participants. In *Searles v. Trustees of St. Joseph's College*, 695 A.2d 1206 (Me. 1997), the Maine Supreme Court held "that a college has a legal duty to exercise reasonable care towards its students," which encompasses the duty of college coaches and athletic trainers to exercise reasonable care for the health and safety of student athletes." A scholarship basketball player sued his coach, alleging that, notwithstanding medical advice that he should not continue to play basketball with a knee injury, the coach required him to continue playing, thereby causing an aggravated and permanent knee injury. The court concluded there was sufficient evidence to raise an issue of material fact regarding the coach's breach of his duty to exercise reasonable care for the plaintiff's health and safety. See also *Lamorie v. Warner Pacific College*, 850 P.2d 401 (Or. Ct. App. 1993) (appellate court ruled that a jury could reasonably find that the player's re-injury of his eye was a foreseeable risk of being directed to resume playing basketball, for which the university could be held liable). Similarly, in *Davidson v. University of North Carolina at Chapel Hill*, 543 S.E.2d 920 (N.C. App. 2001), *cert. denied*, 550 S.E.2d 771 (N.C. 2001), a North Carolina appellate court held that a university has a duty to use reasonable care to protect members of school-sponsored intercollegiate cheerleading team from injury. But see *Bukowski v. Clarkson Univ.*, 2012 WL 1986521, *3 (N.Y. June 5, 2012) (ruling that the coach and university were not liable for injuries sustained by a pitcher who was hit by a line drive during indoor practice because the player, who was a knowledgeable and experienced baseball player, assumed the inherent risk of being hit by a line drive); *Sandford v. Long*, 2012 WL 874678 (Cal Ct. App. March 15, 2012) (rejecting student-athlete's argument that special relationship between university and student-athlete imposed duty of coach to protect an athlete against the intentional conduct of a teammate).

NOTES

1. Medical treatment. In *Stineman v. Fontbonne College*, 664 F.2d 1082 (8th Cir. 1981), the Eighth Circuit held that a university has a duty to refer an injured intercollegiate athlete to a physician for medical treatment. The plaintiff was struck in the eye by a ball thrown during softball practice. The team's coaches did not recommend that plaintiff see a physician for treatment of her injury. Because of a delay in obtaining medical treatment, the plaintiff lost the vision in her eye. Without considering the plaintiff's potential contributory negligence, the court awarded her damages of $600,000.

The National Collegiate Athletic Association (NCAA) publishes a sports medicine handbook on its website that provides guidelines for protecting the health and safety of student-athletes and for minimizing the risk of significant injury for participants in intercollegiate athletics. These guidelines may be relevant in determining the nature and scope of a university's duty to use reasonable care in connection with sports medicine issues affecting its athletics program. See *Wallace v. Broyles*, 961 S.W.2d 712, 713-16 (Ark. 1998) (asserting that a university may be liable for negligently permitting student-athletes, in violation of NCAA guidelines, to have access to controlled substances in athletic department facilities without prescriptions, labels, instructions, or warnings regarding the dangers or side effects of usage).

2. University duty to protect opponents' health and safety. The law continues to develop regarding the scope of a university's legal duty to prevent one of its athletes from injuring an opposing player. Courts have refused to recognize that a special relationship exists between a university and student-athletes at another school. *Avila v. Citrus Community College Dist.*, 38 Cal. 4th 148, 131 P.3d 383, 41 Cal. Rptr. 3d 299 (Cal. 2006) (although university has a legal duty not to increase the risks inherent in an intercollegiate sport, it has no legal duty to prevent its pitcher from intentionally throwing at an opposing team's batter because "being intentionally thrown at is a fundamental part and inherent risk" of baseball); *Kavanagh v. Trustees of Boston Univ.*, 795 N.E.2d 1170, 1178 (Mass. 2003) (university "would have to have specific information about a player suggesting a propensity to engage in violent conduct" to be held directly liable for player's tortious conduct).

3. Association liability for safety rules. Like state high school athletics governing bodies, the NCAA has a legal duty to use reasonable care when promulgating rules to protect athletes' safety. *Sanchez v. Hillerich & Bradsby Co.*, 128 Cal. Rptr. 2d 529 (Cal. App. 2002) (NCAA may be liable for approving baseball bat if its performance capabilities are proved to increase unreasonably a pitcher's inherent risk of being hit by batted ball). An Indiana court recently came to a different conclusion. In *Lanni v. NCAA*, 2015 WL 5037294 (Ind. Ct. App. Aug. 26, 2005), a student-athlete who was struck in the face with a sabre while observing a fencing competition asserted a negligence claim against the NCAA. The plaintiff claimed that by virtue of its role in regulating the field of play and adopting rules and policies regarding safety issues, the NCAA possessed a general duty of care and assumed a duty of care to protect spectators from the risks that resulted in her injury.

In upholding the trial court's motion for summary judgment in favor of the NCAA, the appellate court turned to Indiana Supreme Court precedent that refused to hold national fraternities liable for the conduct of local chapters. As to a general duty of care, the court cited to *Yost v. Wabash College*, 3 N.E.3d 509 (Ind. 2014), in which the court emphasized the absence of day-to-day management by the national fraternity over a local fraternity's affairs. The *Yost* court also reasoned that imposing liability would discourage national fraternal organizations from adopting programs to promote safety. Finding that the NCAA's relationship with student-athletes mirrored that between a national fraternity and its chapters, the *Lanni* court concluded that it would not impose a general duty of care on the NCAA.

Holding also that the NCAA did not assume a duty of care, the *Lanni* court also relied on decisions involving fraternities.

Just as in *Yost* and *Smith* [*v. Delta Tau Delta*, 9 N.E.3d 154 (Ind. 2014)], the specific duties taken by the NCAA with respect to the safety of student-athletes was simply to provide information and guidance to the NCAA's member institutions and student-athletes. . . . Actual oversight and control cannot be imputed from the fact that the NCAA has promulgated rules and regulations and required compliance with those rules and regulations. The NCAA's conduct does not demonstrate that it undertook or assumed a duty to actually oversee or directly supervise the actions of the member institutions and the NCAA's student-athletes.

Lanni, 2015 WL 5037294, ★10.

Problem 7-3

Amos is a scholarship athlete who is the star wide receiver at Big U, a private university with an outstanding football program team. The week before the game with Large U, Big U's hated rival, Amos suffered a very painful neck injury that prevented him from practicing. Although Big U's team physician recommended that Amos not play, Big U's coach pressured Amos to play because the Large U game would decide the conference championship. Amos suffered a broken neck, causing permanent paralysis, when he was injured during the game in a vicious helmet-to-helmet tackle by Brutus, a Large U defensive back, who was penalized 15 yards for "spearing." Is Big U liable for Amos's permanent neck injury and paralysis? Is Large U liable?

C. Injury to Spectators

 **KEY TERMS**
- Invitee
- Licensee
- Limited duty rule
- Premises liability
- Trespasser

The previous section focused on the duties of participants and sport managers for the safety and welfare of those playing the game. The focus now shifts to the safety and welfare of those who come to watch those participating. *Premises liability* is the responsibility of a landowner for injuries that happen to others on the landowner's property. The status or reason that the person is on the property is an important consideration in determining the liability of the landowner. An *invitee* is someone who comes onto the property by either an express or implied invitation. A *licensee* is a person whose presence on the property is known and tolerated by the landowner but is on the land for his or her own interest or convenience. A *trespasser* does not have the permission of the landowner to be on the property. Landowners must take reasonable care to keep the premises in safe condition for invitees, but they are required to keep licensees safe only from known dangers that may be concealed. The landowner owes no duty to keep trespassers safe unless the landowner creates an unjustified risk of injury, such as setting traps or spring guns.

Sports event spectators generally are characterized as invitees, meaning they are invited to enter a venue to view a game or event (usually as a paying customer). Thus, "the owner of a [sports] facility has a duty of reasonable care under the circumstances to invitees." *Allred v. Capital Area Soccer League, Inc.*, 669 S.E.2d 777 (N.C. App. 2008). This duty requires a facility owner or operator to maintain the premises and equipment therein in a reasonably safe condition to prevent spectator injury from normal use of the facility. If this duty is breached and causes harm to a spectator, there is potential liability for negligence.

The duty of a facility owner or operator to exercise reasonable care to protect invitees does not extend to protect spectators attending sporting events against risks inherent to a particular sport. As it relates to the liability of a stadium owner, player, or team to an injured spectator, the majority of courts have adopted what is frequently referred to as the *limited duty rule*. Pursuant to this rule, "there is no legal duty to protect or warn spectators about the 'common, frequent, and expected' inherent risks of observing a sporting event such as being struck by flying objects that go into the stands." *Jones v. Three Rivers Mgmt. Corp.*, 394 A.2d 546, 551 (Pa. 1978). As the Allred court explained:

> When an operator of a baseball facility provides some seating which has a screen to protect patrons from errant baseballs, they "are held to have discharged their full duty to spectators in safeguarding them from the danger of being struck by thrown or batted balls[.]" This rule applies even if there is an unusually large crowd, and patrons desiring screened seating are unable to obtain it.

Allred, supra at 780–81. One commentator has succinctly explained that "[g]iven the plaintiff's awareness of danger and choice of seat, the sports operator's only duty is to provide some reasonably safe accommodations." See generally Dan B. Dobbs, The Law of Torts §215 at 547 (West 2000).

A rationale frequently articulated in support of the limited duty rule is that spectators assume injury-causing risks that are an inherent part of the activity in question. Another rationale rests on the protection of consumer preference. Proponents of this view argue that not imposing a duty on facility owners for risks inherent in the game promotes allowing owners to construct facilities that enhance consumer choice. Consumers may elect to sit in protected seats or find seats in unprotected areas where their view may be unobstructed and they can become more intimately involved in the particular game.

Notwithstanding their limited duty, facility operators and teams possess a legal duty not to increase the inherent risks of injury from watching a game or athletic event. This exception to the limited duty rule was addressed in *Lowe v. California League of Professional Baseball*, 65 Cal. Rptr. 2d 105 (Cal. App. 1997). The plaintiff was facing forward and watching a baseball game when the team mascot, a seven-foot-tall caricature of a dinosaur, suddenly and without warning, began touching him from behind with a tail protruding from his costume. As plaintiff turned to see what was touching him, he was struck in the face by a foul ball and suffered serious injury.

The court found that the presence of a team mascot is not an integral part of the game of baseball. It held that the mascot's antics in hitting plaintiff with his tail, while the game was being played, created a triable issue of fact as to whether the club increased the inherent risks of watching a baseball game by distracting plaintiff and preventing him from seeing and protecting himself from injury by a batted ball. Similarly, in *Gil de Rebollo v. Miami Heat Assns., Inc.*, 137 F.3d 56 (1st Cir. 1998), a club was held liable for mascot's negligent antics during timeout entertainment routine that caused injury to spectator. Yet not all courts agree with this rule. In *Harting v. Dayton Dragons Prof. B'ball Club*, 870 N.E.2d 766 (Ohio App. 2007), the court held that a spectator assumed the risk of injury from a foul ball by watching the mascot perform rather than the game.

What if the flying object that hits a spectator is a piece of food rather than a piece of game equipment? Robert Coomer was sitting in the stands watching a Kansas City Royals baseball game when he was struck in the eye by a hot dog that the Royals' mascot, Sluggerrr, threw into the stands as part of a product promotion. Sluggerrr took no care with the throw, tossing it behind his back, and the damage to Coomer's eye required surgery. Coomer sued, and the Royals defended based on the "baseball rule," arguing that they were no more liable to Coomer than they would have been if he were hit by a foul ball. On appeal, the Missouri Supreme Court concluded as a matter of law that:

> [T]he risk of injury from Sluggerrr's hotdog toss is not one of the risks inherent in watching the Royals play baseball that Coomer assumed merely by attending a game at Kauffman Stadium. This risk can be increased, decreased or eliminated altogether with no impact on the game or the spectators' enjoyment of it. As a result, Sluggerrr (and, therefore, the Royals) owe the fans a duty to use reasonable care in conducting the Hotdog Launch and can be held liable for damages caused by a breach of that duty.

Coomer v Kansas City Royals, 437 S.W. 3d 184, 203 (Mo. 2014).

A facility operator also may be liable for failing to use reasonable care in regulating crowd control and fan conduct during sporting events. Some courts have held that injury caused by fellow spectators while pursuing a ball that goes into the stands as a souvenir is not an inherent risk of attending and observing a game. Ruling that a university has a legal duty to protect spectators against a foreseeable risk of such harm, the court in *Hayden v. Univ. of Notre Dame*, 716 N.E.2d 603, 606 (Ind. App. 1999), explained:

> [W]e find that the totality of the circumstances establishes that Notre Dame should have foreseen that injury would likely result from the actions of a third party in lunging for the football after it landed in the seating area. As a result, it owed a duty to Letitia Hayden to protect her from such injury. . . . Notre Dame well understands and benefits from the enthusiasm of the fans of its football team. It is just such enthusiasm that drives some spectators to attempt to retrieve a football to keep as a souvenir. There was evidence that there were many prior incidents of people being jostled or injured by efforts of fans to retrieve the ball.

716 N.E.2d at 606.

The application of the limited duty rule owed to a spectator attending a sporting event is illustrated in the following case.

Thurmond v. Prince William Professional Baseball Club, Inc.
574 S.E.2d 246 (Va. 2003)

KEENAN, Justice.

In August 1997, Thurmond attended a night baseball game conducted by the Prince William Professional Baseball Club, Inc. . . . In the stadium, spectators were warned of the risk of being struck by objects batted or thrown from the field. Warning signs, measuring three feet by three feet, were posted at entrances to the seating areas. These signs stated: "Be Alert! Objects batted or thrown into the stands may be dangerous." All persons entering the stadium walked past one of these entrances, regardless of the location of their seats.

In addition, the back of each admission ticket contained a printed warning that stated, in relevant part:

The holder of this ticket assumes all risk and danger incidental to the game of baseball . . . including specifically (but not exclusively) the danger of being injured by thrown bats, thrown or batted balls, . . . and agrees that the participating clubs or their officials, agents and players are not liable for injury related from such causes.

Twenty to thirty seats were reserved for each game in the screened area behind home plate for those spectators who requested to be reseated because they were not comfortable sitting in the unscreened areas of the stadium.

Thurmond sat with her family and friends "high in the bleachers" on the third base side of the stadium. This was Thurmond's first visit to the stadium, and she did not know that she could have requested a seat in the screened area behind home plate. She also did not read the warning printed on the back of the admission ticket because she never had possession of her ticket, which her friends had given to her husband. However, Thurmond remained alert at all times during the game, watching the hitters and batted baseballs.

During the eighth inning, a "line drive foul" ball was batted toward Thurmond. Although Thurmond saw the baseball approaching in her direction, the ball was moving too rapidly to allow her to take any evasive action. The ball struck Thurmond directly on the right side of her face, and she sustained various injuries, including fractures of her facial bones, damage to her right eye socket, and extensive nerve damage.

Thurmond . . . alleged that she was injured as a result of the defendants' negligence in failing to provide adequate warnings at the stadium and to operate and maintain the stadium in a safe condition to prevent injuries to invitees.

In response, the defendants [argued] that Thurmond assumed the risk of injury as a matter of law when she chose to sit in an unscreened area of the stadium. . . .

In deciding this issue, we first state the general principles that govern our inquiry. In this Commonwealth, a person's voluntary assumption of the risk of injury from a known danger operates as a complete bar to recovery for a defendant's alleged negligence in causing that injury. Application of the defense of assumption of risk requires use of a subjective standard, which addresses whether a particular plaintiff fully understood the nature and extent of a known danger and voluntarily exposed herself to that danger. Thus, the defense of assumption of risk ordinarily presents a jury question, unless reasonable minds could not differ on the issue. . . .

[The assumption of the risk] doctrine requires us to consider whether a particular plaintiff fully understood the nature and extent of a known danger and voluntarily exposed herself to that danger. Thus, we hold that when a particular adult spectator of ordinary intelligence is familiar with the game of baseball, that spectator assumes the normal risks of watching a baseball game, including the danger of being hit by a ball batted into an unscreened seating area of a stadium.

We conclude that reasonable persons could not disagree that Thurmond, who conceded that she remained alert throughout the game and observed hitters and batted balls for more than seven innings before being injured, was familiar with the game of baseball, knew the risk of being injured by a batted ball, and voluntarily exposed herself to that risk by remaining seated in an unscreened area.

Accordingly, we hold that the trial court did not err in awarding summary judgment to the defendants, because Thurmond's assumption of the risk was a complete bar to her recovery in this negligence action.

The prevailing principle is that there is no legal duty to protect or warn spectators about the "common, frequent, and expected inherent risks of observing a sporting event such as being struck by flying objects that go into the stands." *Jones v. Three Rivers Mgmt. Corp.*, 394 A.2d 546, 551 (Pa. 1978). Although an owner may not owe a duty of care to spectators for inherent risks, the owner or facility operator must not enhance the risks that are inherent to a particular sport. *Edward C. v. City of Albuquerque*, 241 P.3d 1086, 1088 (N.M. 2010) ("spectator must exercise ordinary care to protect himself or herself from the inherent risk of being hit by a projectile that leaves the field of play and the owner/occupant must exercise ordinary care not to increase that inherent risk"). See generally Timothy Davis, *Avila v. Citrus Community College District: Shaping the Contours of Immunity and Primary Assumption of the Risk*, 17 Marq. Sports L. Rev. 259 (2006).

QUESTIONS

Why did the *Thurmond* court reject the plaintiff's negligence claim? Are there sound public policy reasons for doing so?

NOTES

1. The scope of the limited duty rule. In *Thurmond*, the court rejected the negligence claim of a spectator who was injured while seated as a game was being played. Courts have also rejected the negligence claims of spectators who were injured before a game had officially begun. In *Allred v. Capital Area Soccer League, Inc.*, 669 S.E.2d 777, 781 (N.C. App. 2008), the court stated, "principles of assumption of the risk apply not only to being struck during the course of a game, but also to preliminary and warm-up activities."

2. Application to minors. Should the limited duty rule apply to minors? As it relates to a spectator's knowledge, generally "adult spectators of ordinary intelligence" who are familiar with the sport at issue will be presumed to possess an awareness of the normal risk of watching a sport. On March 16, 2002, a 13-year-old girl was struck in the head by a deflected hockey puck while watching an NHL game between the Columbus Blue Jackets and the Calgary Flames in Columbus, Ohio. Two days later, she died from a blood clot caused when her head violently snapped back when hit by the puck, the first spectator to be fatally injured in the NHL's 85-year history. Phil Taylor, *Death of a Fan*, Sports Illustrated, April 1, 2002 at 58. Her parents received a $1.2 million settlement from the NHL and the arena in which the game was played. Following a common practice in European hockey rinks, the NHL subsequently required its member clubs to install protective netting approximately 30 feet in height and 120 feet in width behind the goals in their playing facilities.

Problem 7-4

A spectator, an avid hockey fan, attended a professional ice hockey game. The spectator, who was seated in an unscreened area, was struck during pregame warm-ups when a player took a shot at the goal. The shot misfired, and the puck hit the spectator. The hockey club, which owned the arena, communicated no warnings to spectators of the risk of being struck by an errant puck.

Is the club liable in tort to the spectator? See *Hurst v. East Coast Hockey League, Inc.*, 2005 WL 6218747 (S.C. Com. Pl.).

TORT IMMUNITIES

KEY TERMS
- Charitable immunity
- Discretionary function
- Ministerial function
- Qualified immunity
- Sovereign immunity

There are times when a defendant is granted an exemption, or immunity, from a duty or penalty contrary to the general rule of law. Under the doctrine of *sovereign immunity*, a public educational institution, as a subsidiary agency of the state, may be immune from tort liability for negligent acts of its employees, such as coaches, athletic trainers, and administrative personnel, that cause injury to a high school athlete. See also *Evans v. Oaks Mission Pub. Sch.*, 945 P.2d 492 (Okla. 1997); *Grandalski v. Lyons Township High Sch. Dist. 204*, 711 N.E.2d 372 (Ill. App. Ct. 1999). The scope of sovereign immunity, which may be statutory or common law, varies on a state-by-state basis.

An exception to sovereign immunity occurs when the injury was caused by a state actor engaged in commercial activity rather than its usual role in governing. Courts generally hold that the operation of an interscholastic athletics program is a governmental function that is covered by the immunity defense rather than a proprietary function, which is not. *Fowler v. Tyler Indep. Sch. Dist.*, 232 S.W.3d 335 (Tex. Ct. App. 2007). In *Lovitt v. Concord Sch. Dist.*, 228 N.W.2d 479 (Mich. Ct. App. 1975), a Michigan appellate court held that a public high school football program was a physical education activity encompassed within the governmental function of providing education. Finding that the district's athletics program had been operating at a deficit for five years, the court rejected plaintiff's claim that the football program was a proprietary function because an admission fee was charged to games.

Like a public high school system, a public university may have sovereign immunity from liability for negligence in connection with the operation of its athletic program, although this immunity may be considered to be waived to the extent that negligent conduct arising out of a public university's sports program is covered by insurance. *Shriver v. Athletic Council of Kan. State Univ.*, 564 P.2d 451, 455 (Kan. 1977). Some courts have held that sponsoring revenue-generating sports such as intercollegiate football is a proprietary function of a public university that is not protected by sovereign immunity. *Brown v. Wichita State Univ.*, 540 P.2d 66, 86–89 (Kan. 1975). Thus, sovereign immunity would not bar negligence suits by athletes injured while participating in these sports. Other courts have reached the opposite conclusion, ruling that university sponsorship of intercollegiate athletics is a governmental function of a public university that confers sovereign immunity, even if some sports generate revenue. *Harris v. Univ. of Mich. Bd. of Regents*, 558 N.W.2d 225, 228 (Mich. Ct. App. 1996)). See also *Ward v. Michigan State Univ.*, 782 N.W.2d 514 (Mich. App. 2010) (university's operation of hockey rink constituted a governmental function since it did not operate the rink primarily to generate a profit); *University of Texas at El Paso v. Moreno*, 172 S.W.3d 281 (Tex. Ct. App. 2005) (university entitled to immunity from liability for claims filed by fan who asserted he was injured by conduct of other fans after he streamed onto football field and hung from goal post following postgame celebration).

Some athletes have attempted to circumvent the application of sovereign immunity by seeking recovery for negligent injury treatment rendered by public school personnel under the guise of federal constitutional rights violations. In *Burden v. Wilkes-Barre Area School District*, 16 F. Supp. 2d 569 (M.D. Pa. 1998), a federal district court rejected plaintiff's contention that an educational institution's decision not to hire a certified athletic trainer to protect the health and safety of students participating in competitive sports violated an athlete's constitutional right to life and liberty. See also *Davis v. Carter*, 555 F.3d 979 (5th Cir. 2009) (rejecting parents' constitutional claims as means of circumventing immunity defense because evidence failed to establish coaches acted willfully or maliciously in case in which minor football player died during intense voluntary workout); *Livingston v. Desoto Indep. School Dist.*, 391 F. Supp. 2d 463 (N.D. Tex. 2005) (despite the egregious facts in this case, a public high school, coach, and athletic trainer did not violate federally protected constitutional rights because their allegedly improper first aid did not establish deliberate indifference to student's constitutionally protected liberty interest in health and bodily integrity).

Other athletes attempt to avoid the qualified immunity defense by arguing that a coach's conduct was grossly negligent, and therefore the defense was unavailable because of the gross negligence exception to the qualified immunity defense. In *Smith v. Kroesen*, 9 F.Supp.3d 439 (D. N.J. 2014), a plaintiff injured by a co-participant alleged the other player's coach was liable for negligent coaching. Attempting to avoid the coach's qualified immunity defense, the plaintiff argued that the coach's gross negligence brought him within the gross negligence exception to the qualified immunity afforded volunteer coaches. Defining gross negligence as referring to "behavior which constitutes indifference to consequences," the court found that the plaintiff failed to present evidence that the coach was grossly negligent in performing his coaching duties. *Id.* at 443.

Private universities may be protected from negligence suits by intercollegiate athletes by the doctrine of *charitable immunity*. Charitable immunity exempts an organization from legal liability based on its charitable purpose. Application of this doctrine varies by jurisdiction. See *Gilbert v. Seton Hall Univ.*, 332 F.3d 105 (2d Cir. 2003) (applying conflict of law principles to determine applicability of charitable immunity doctrine in suit by injured club team player against private university).

The doctrine of *qualified immunity* may protect public school employees (e.g., coaches and athletic trainers) from negligence liability when they are exercising a discretionary act, but not a ministerial act. A discretionary act involves exercising personal deliberation or judgment, such as examining facts, weighing options, and reaching an independently reasoned conclusion that is not specifically directed. Conversely, the execution of a specific action given a specific situation is a ministerial act. In *Prince v. Louisville Municipal School Dist.*, 741 So. 2d 207 (Miss. 1999), the Mississippi Supreme Court distinguished between a coach's discretionary and ministerial function when exploring the parameters of this defense. A high school football player alleged that he suffered a heat stroke during practice as a result of his coaches' negligent failure to properly monitor his health and condition, to provide necessary liquids, and to provide necessary medical care in a timely manner. The court ruled that the qualified immunity doctrine immunized the coaches from negligence liability because they were engaged in a discretionary function while conducting practice:

> In a typical practice there are strains, sprains, and complaints from a coach's players. A coach must consider the good order and discipline of the team when confronted with

situational complaints by the players. A coach must use his discretion in judging whether or not an individual player is injured and then, whether the player should report to a trainer or seek other medical aid. There was no evidence presented in the lower court to show that either Bowman or Chambliss did anything beyond exercising ordinary discretion in supervising the Nanih Waiya football practice on August 29, 1991. Prince produced no facts that evidenced any disregard for his health or any other outrageous action on the part of Bowman or Chambliss that might have warranted a departure from our previous holdings. The trial court correctly found the coaches were protected by qualified immunity. . . .

Id. at 212.

Dissenting from the majority's conclusion, another judge asserted:

[T]he coaches were acting in their ministerial capacities, not with discretion. Qualified immunity is not warranted. . . . Coaches Chambliss and Bowman maintained duties to manage their players. Randall Prince suffered harm because his coaches failed to perform their duties such that he suffered heatstroke, and because those same coaches failed to take proper actions afterwards. As coaches directly responsible for serving the general needs of Prince while he is under their power as a football player, the coaches should have more closely monitored Prince's condition. When it became possible that Prince was a candidate for heatstroke, the coaches should have given him rest out of the sun, provided him additional liquids, or simply excused him from practice. There are no means by which to grant qualified immunity. The instant case deals with an extracurricular activity internal to the school, not a promotion of government policy and public good. Accordingly, I dissent. . . .

Id. at 215–16. For informative discussions of the sovereign and qualified immunity defenses, see David Feingold, *Who Takes the Heat? Criminal Liability for Heat-Related Deaths in High School Athletics*, 17 Cardozo J.L. & Gender 359 (2011); David Marck, *Necessary Roughness? An Argument for the Assignment of Criminal Liability in Cases of Student-Athlete Sustained Heat-Related Deaths*, 21 Seton Hall J. Sports & Ent. L. 177, 187–92 (2011); Ryan Mulkins, *High-School Football Injuries: Who Besides the Players May Take A Hit?*, 2 Willamette Sports L.J. 1, 16–21 (2006); Thomas R. Hurst and James N. Knight, *Coaches' Liability for Athletes' Injuries and Deaths*, 13 Seton Hall J. Sport L. 27, 44–47 (2003).

QUESTION

Is it fair that an individual who is injured as a result of the negligence of a coach at a public school would not be compensated for his or her injuries, even when compensation would have been granted if the coach were at a private athletics club?

Problem 7-5

Consider whether a coach at a public educational institution would be entitled to qualified immunity in the following scenarios.

(a) An instructor accidentally hits a college student-athlete with a baseball bat during a hitting demonstration at a baseball camp. See *Quinn v. Mississippi State Univ.*, 720 So. 2d 843, 849 (Miss. 1998) (overruled on other grounds, *City of Jackson v. Estate of Stewart ex rel. Womack*, 908 So. 2d 702. 709 (Miss. 2005)).

(b) A high school baseball player, who was not wearing a batting helmet, was injured by a ball thrown by one of his teammates during batting practice. Prior to his injury, the player's coach failed to enforce a rule requiring all student-athletes to wear batting helmets while taking batting practice. See *Yanero v. Davis*, 65 S.W.3d 510, 529 (2002).

VALIDITY OF LIABILITY WAIVERS

KEY TERMS
- Adhesion contract
- Exculpatory agreement

The following materials explore the enforceability of pre-injury contracts pursuant to which a person agrees to release a school district or its employees from liability for negligent failure to use reasonable care to protect the health and safety of students during athletic activities. These contracts may be referred to by many names, including exculpatory clauses, releases, covenants not to sue, and hold harmless agreements. Although technical differences exist in specific types of such contracts, what lies at their core is an agreement by one party to accept the risk of harm resulting from another's conduct. If enforceable under applicable state law, these waivers of liability bar a plaintiff's ability to seek recovery from the defendant for harm caused by certain tortious conduct.

Some courts have refused to enforce pre-injury waivers on the grounds that they violate public policy. In one group of cases, which probably represents the majority view, courts rely on public policy grounds to refuse to permit a high school to enforce waivers against a student-athlete or his or her parents or guardian who signed it. In what can be characterized as an intermediate approach, other jurisdictions allow high schools to enforce such waivers against a parent or guardian who signs it, but not against a minor. A minority of jurisdictions have adopted a position that permits parents to sign a release that binds both the parent and minor. The cases that follow, *Wagenblast* and *Sharon*, represent contrasting perspectives on the validity of liability waivers.

Wagenblast v. Odessa School District No. 105-157-166J

110 Wash. 2d 845, 758 P.2d 968 (Wash. 1988)

ANDERSEN, Justice.

Can school districts require public school students and their parents to sign written releases which release the districts from the consequences of all future school district negligence, before the students will be allowed to engage in certain recognized school related activities, here interscholastic athletics?

We hold that the exculpatory releases from any future school district negligence are invalid because they violate public policy.

Probably the best exposition of the test to be applied in determining whether exculpatory agreements violate public policy is that stated by the California Supreme Court. In writing for a unanimous court, the late Justice Tobriner outlined the factors in *Tunkl v. Regents of Univ. of Cal.*, 60 Cal.2d 92, 383 P.2d 441, 32 Cal.Rptr. 33, 6 A.L.R.3d 693 (1963):

1. *The agreement concerns an endeavor of a type generally thought suitable for public regulation.*

Regulation of governmental entities usually means self-regulation. Thus, the Legislature has by statute granted to each school board the authority to control, supervise, and regulate the conduct of interscholastic athletics. In some situations, a school board is permitted, in turn, to delegate this authority to the Washington Interscholastic Activities Association (WIAA) or to another voluntary nonprofit entity. In the cases before us, both school boards look to the WIAA for regulation of interscholastic sports. The WIAA handbook contains an extensive constitution with rules for such athletic endeavors. . . .

Clearly then, interscholastic sports in Washington are extensively regulated, and are a fit subject for such regulation.

2. *The party seeking exculpation is engaged in performing a service of great importance to the public, which is often a matter of practical necessity for some members of the public.*

This court has held that public school students have no fundamental right to participate in interscholastic athletics. Nonetheless, the court also has observed that the justification advanced for interscholastic athletics is their educational and cultural value. As the testimony of then Seattle School Superintendent Robert Nelson and others amply demonstrate, interscholastic athletics is part and parcel of the overall educational scheme in Washington. The total expenditure of time, effort and money on these endeavors makes this clear. The importance of these programs to the public is substantive; they represent a significant tie of the public at large to our system of public education. Nor can the importance of these programs to certain students be denied; as Superintendent Nelson agreed, some students undoubtedly remain in school and maintain their academic standing only because they can participate in these programs. Given this emphasis on sports by the public and the school system, it would be unrealistic to expect students to view athletics as an activity entirely separate and apart from the remainder of their schooling. . . .

In sum, under any rational view of the subject, interscholastic sports in public schools are a matter of public importance in this jurisdiction.

3. *Such party holds itself out as willing to perform this service for any member of the public who seeks it, or at least for any member coming within certain established standards.*

Implicit in the nature of interscholastic sports is the notion that such programs are open to all students who meet certain skill and eligibility standards. This conclusion finds direct support in the testimony of former Superintendent Nelson and the WIAA eligibility and nondiscrimination policies set forth in the WIAA handbook.

4. *Because of the essential nature of the service, in the economic setting of the transaction, the party invoking exculpation possesses a decisive advantage of bargaining strength against any member of the public who seeks the services.*

Not only have interscholastic sports become of considerable importance to students and the general public alike, but in most instances there exists no alternative program of organized competition. For instance, former Superintendent Nelson knew of no alternative to the Seattle School District's wrestling program. While outside alternatives exist for some activities, they possess little of the inherent allure of interscholastic competition. Many students cannot afford private programs or the private schools where such releases might not be employed. In this regard, school districts have near-monopoly power. And, because such programs have become important to student participants, school districts possess a clear and disparate bargaining strength when they insist that students and their parents sign these releases.

5. *In exercising a superior bargaining power, the party confronts the public with a standardized adhesion contract of exculpation, and makes no provision whereby a purchaser may pay additional reasonable fees and obtain protection against negligence.*

Both school districts admit to an unwavering policy regarding these releases; no student athlete will be allowed to participate in any program without first signing the release form as written by the school district. In both of these cases, students and their parents unsuccessfully attempted to modify the forms by deleting the release language. In both cases, the school district rejected the attempted modifications. Student athletes and their parents or guardians have no alternative but to sign the standard release forms provided to them or have the student barred from the program.

6. *The person or property of members of the public seeking such services must be placed under the control of the furnisher of the services, subject to the risk of carelessness on the part of the furnisher, its employees or agents.*

A school district owes a duty to its students to employ ordinary care and to anticipate reasonably foreseeable dangers so as to take precautions for protecting the children in its custody from such dangers. This duty extends to students engaged in interscholastic sports. As a natural incident to the relationship of a student athlete and his or her coach, the student athlete is usually placed under the coach's considerable degree of control. The student is thus subject to the risk that the school district or its agent will breach this duty of care.

In sum, the attempted releases in the cases before us exhibit all six of the characteristics denominated in [*Tunkl*]. Because of this, and for the aforesaid reasons, we hold that the releases in these consolidated cases are invalid as against public policy. . . .

Sharon v. City of Newton
437 Mass. 99, 769 N.E.2d 738 (2002)

CORDY, Judge.

[Editors' note: A 16-year-old student was injured while participating in cheerleading practice at her high school. The injured cheerleader sued, and the defendant asserted as a defense a waiver of liability that she and her father had signed.]

2. Summary Judgment

We conclude that enforcement of the release is consistent with our law and public policy, and Newton is entitled to judgment as a matter of law. . . .

b. Public Policy

Merav . . . contends that enforcement of the release against her claims would constitute a gross violation of public policy. This argument encompasses at least three separate public policy contentions: first, that it is contrary to public policy to permit schools to require students to sign exculpatory agreements as a prerequisite to participation in extracurricular school sports; second, that public policy prohibits a parent from contracting away a minor child's right to sue for a future harm; and third, that the enforcement of this release would undermine the duty of care that public schools owe their students. . . .

(1) Releases. Massachusetts law favors the enforcement of releases. . . . "There can be no doubt . . . that under the law of Massachusetts . . . in the absence of fraud a person may make a valid contract exempting himself from any liability to another which he may in the future incur as a result of his negligence or that of his agents or employees acting on his behalf." *Schell v. Ford*, 270 F.2d 384, 386 (1st Cir. 1959).

Although Merav has suggested that, if the release at issue here is valid, there is nothing to prevent cities or towns from requiring releases for "simply allowing a child to attend school," such a conclusion does not necessarily follow. We have not had occasion to rule on the validity of releases required in the context of a compelled activity or as a condition for the receipt of essential services (e.g., public education, medical attention, housing, public utilities), and the enforceability of mandatory releases in such circumstances might well offend public policy. . . . In this case, Merav's participation in the city's extracurricular activity of cheerleading was neither compelled nor essential, and we conclude that the public policy of the Commonwealth is not offended by requiring a release as a prerequisite to that participation.

(2) Parent's waiver of a minor's claim. Merav contends that a parent cannot waive, compromise, or release a minor child's cause of action, and that enforcement of such a release against the child would violate public policy.

The purpose of the policy permitting minors to void their contracts is "to afford protection to minors from their own improvidence and want of sound judgment." *Frye v. Yasi*, 327 Mass. 724, 728, 101 N.E.2d 128 (1951). . . . Moreover, our law presumes that fit parents act in furtherance of the welfare and best interests of their children, . . . and with respect to matters relating to their care, custody, and upbringing have a fundamental right to make those decisions for them.

In the instant case, Merav's father signed the release in his capacity as parent because he wanted his child to benefit from participating in cheerleading, as she had done for four previous seasons. He made an important family decision cognizant of the risk of physical injury to his child and the financial risk to the family as a whole. In the circumstance of a voluntary, nonessential activity, we will not disturb this parental judgment. This comports with the fundamental liberty interest of parents in the rearing of their children, and is not inconsistent with the purpose behind our public policy permitting minors to void their contracts.

c. The Encouragement of Athletic Activities for Minors

To hold that releases of the type in question here are unenforceable would expose public schools, who offer many of the extracurricular sports opportunities available to children, to financial costs and risks that will inevitably lead to the reduction of those programs. It would also create the anomaly of a minor who participates in a program sponsored and managed by a nonprofit organization not having a cause of action for negligence that she would have had had she participated in the same program sponsored as an extracurricular activity by the local public school. This distinction seems unwarranted, inevitably destructive to school-sponsored programs, and contrary to public interest.

Merav contends that to enforce the release would convey the message that public school programs can be run negligently, in contravention of the well-established responsibility of schools to protect their students. We disagree. There are many reasons aside from potential tort liability why public schools will continue to take steps to ensure well-run and safe extracurricular programs—not the least of which is their ownership by, and accountability to, the citizens of the cities and towns they serve. Moreover, the Legislature has already made the judgment that the elimination of liability for negligence in nonprofit sports programs is necessary to the encouragement and survival of such programs. . . . The enforcement of the release is consistent with the Commonwealth's policy of encouraging athletic programs for youth and does not contravene the responsibility that schools have to protect their students. . . .

C. Conclusion

For the reasons set forth above, we conclude that Merav's father had the authority to bind his minor child to an exculpatory release that was a proper condition of her voluntary participation in extracurricular sports activities offered by the city. Summary judgment for the city that was entered on the basis of the validity of that release is therefore affirmed. . . .

Consistent with *Sharon*, other courts have exhibited a willingness to enforce liability waivers for negligent injury to minors participating in competitive or recreational sports. *Mohney v. USA Hockey, Inc.*, 5 Fed. Appx. 450 (6th Cir. 2001) (release signed by minor hockey player and his father was valid and applied to injuries sustained by the player); *Zivich v. Mentor Soccer Club, Inc.*, 696 N.E.2d 201 (Ohio 1998) (release signed by mother of injured child barred child's claim for negligence against volunteers and sponsors of nonprofit sport activities). In *Platzer v. Mammoth Mountain Ski Area*, 128 Cal. Rptr. 2d 885 (Cal. App. 2002), a mother who enrolled her eight-year-old son in a ski resort's sports school signed a form assuming the risk of injury associated, among other things, with use of the chairlifts. Her son fell from a lift during a lesson. In upholding the validity of the exculpatory clause, the court rejected plaintiff's argument that public policy precluded enforcement of the release. It noted that California courts have consistently refused to invalidate exculpatory agreements in the recreational sports context. See also *Pollock v. Highlands Ranch Community Assn., Inc.*, 140 P.3d 351 (Colo. App. 2006) (discussing statute superseding case that had invalidated a release waiving minor child's negligence claim).

However, it would be premature to conclude at this point in time that *Sharon* and these cases represent an emerging trend of greater enforcement of exculpatory clauses signed by parents on behalf of their minor children. Although these judicial decisions represent an erosion of the majority rule illustrated by *Wagenblast*, other cases demonstrate that many jurisdictions remain reluctant to enforce waiver clauses. See, e.g., *Galloway v. State*, 790 N.W.2d 252, 258 (Iowa 2010) (holding that public policy precludes the enforceability of pre-injury waiver a parent signs on behalf of child and characterizing *Sharon* as reflective of the minority rule); *J.T. ex rel. Thode v. Monster Mountain, LLC*, 754 F. Supp. 2d 1323, 1327 (M.D. Ala. 2010) (refusing to enforce liability waiver where court approval had not been obtained); *Hawkins v. Blair Peart*, 37 P.3d 1062, 1066 (Utah 2001) (invalidating on public policy grounds a waiver of liability and indemnity agreement signed by parent on behalf of minor child); *Hojnowski v. Vans Skate Park*, 868 A.2d 1087, 1096 (N.J. Super. Ct. App. Div. 2005) ("without statutory authority or judicial authorization, a parent has no ability to release a claim properly belonging to a child; therefore liability waiver signed by parent of minor is unenforceable"). In *Eriksson v. Nunnink*, 183 Cal. Rptr. 3d 234 (Cal. Ct. App. 2015), the court held that a release signed by a minor absolved a coach from liability to a student injured in equestrian competition unless the coach engaged in willful and wanton negligence. It also held, however, that the release would not necessarily bar a mother's wrongful death claim, which was a cause of action distinct from the deceased child's.

QUESTIONS

1. In *Wagenblast*, the Washington Supreme Court held that requiring a student and his parent or guardian to sign a standard form releasing the school district from liability for negligence in connection with the student's participation in interscholastic athletics violated public policy. What factors did the court rely on to reach its decision? Although *Sharon* recognized the ability of a minor (i.e., person under the age of 18) to void a contract, the court upheld a waiver signed by the minor's parent. Which factors most influenced the court's decision?
2. Which court, *Wagenblast* or *Sharon*, most effectively reconciles the competing public policies regarding whether pre-injury liability waivers should be enforced?

Although the law is still developing, courts are more likely to uphold waivers executed by adult intercollegiate athletes than minor interscholastic athletes:

> In recent years, some college athletes have chosen to play a sport in spite of a known medical condition, although doing so exposes them to an enhanced risk of injury. For example, Monte Williams played basketball at Notre Dame University, and Stephen Larkin played baseball at the University of Texas — both with known heart conditions that may have increased their risk of sudden death during competition. Both athletes signed waivers releasing their universities from liability for any harm that might result from playing with their medical condition. Fortunately, neither of them experienced any adverse health effects while playing their respective intercollegiate sports.
>
> Courts generally uphold pre-injury waivers of liability for negligent acts by sponsors of recreational athletic events executed by competent adult athletes. Relying on this authority, a court might enforce a university's pre-injury liability waiver against an intercollegiate athlete for harm arising out of that athlete's informed and voluntary decision to play a sport with a known medical condition. On the other hand, a court may find that such a waiver violates public policy and is unenforceable.

Matthew J. Mitten, *Emerging Legal Issues in Sports Medicine: A Synthesis, Summary, and Analysis*, 76 St. John's L. Rev. 5, 65 (2002); also see George L. Blum, *Release or Compromise or Waiver by Parent of Cause of Action for Injuries to Child as Affecting Right of Child*, 75 A.L.R. 6th 1, §§12 & 13 (2012).

Sports Medicine, Concussions, Compensation, and Impairment in Sports

8

INTRODUCTION

This chapter further illustrates the wide range of health and safety issues in the sports context set forth in the previous chapter. Here, the discussion continues with a focus on sports medicine, concussions, compensation, and impairment issues. In addition to tort and criminal law principles, state and federal statutes (e.g., workers' compensation and disability antidiscrimination statutes) are increasingly being used to regulate relationships among sports industry members and participants that present health and safety issues. Examples include the participation rights of athletes who potentially pose a health risk to themselves and others, and various policy issues that arise as leagues and governing bodies grapple with the drug problem in both amateur and professional sports. We begin with sports medicine.

SPORTS MEDICINE MALPRACTICE LIABILITY

KEY TERMS
- Contributory negligence
- Informed consent
- Malpractice

A. Team Physicians

Professional teams and collegiate educational institutions generally hire a physician or group of physicians to provide medical care to their athletes. Many high schools also select a physician to provide pre-participation physical examinations and emergency medical care to athletes participating in interscholastic athletics.

A "team physician" provides medical services to athletes that are arranged for, or paid for, at least in part, by an institution or entity other than the patient or his parent or guardian. Joseph H. King, Jr., *The Duty and Standard of Care for Team Physicians*, 18 Hous. L. Rev. 657, 658 (1981). The team physician's primary responsibility is to provide for the physical well-being of athletes. The team physician must provide medical treatment and advice consistent with an individual athlete's best health interests because there is a physician-patient relationship between them. Although one of the team physician's objectives is to avoid the unnecessary restriction of athletic activity, his paramount responsibility should be to protect the competitive athlete's health. See generally Matthew J. Mitten, *Team Physicians and Competitive Athletes: Allocating Legal Responsibility for Athletic Injuries*, 55 U. Pitt L. Rev. 129, 140–41 (1993). Team physicians may face extreme pressure from coaches, team management, fans, or the athlete to provide medical clearance to participate or treatment enabling immediate return to play.

There are few reported cases discussing the appropriate standard of care for physician malpractice in the sports medicine setting. In malpractice suits involving a medical specialist, the trend is to apply a national standard of care because national specialty certification boards exist to ensure standardized training and certification procedures. Team physicians generally are internists, family practitioners, or orthopedic surgeons. Other specialists such as cardiologists and pediatricians also provide sports medicine care to athletes. Team physicians have a legal duty to conform to the standard of care corresponding to their individualized specialty training. Historically, courts ruled that sports medicine is not a separate medical specialty, because no national medical specialty board certification or standardized training previously existed. See, e.g., *Fleischmann v. Hanover Ins. Co.*, 470 So. 2d 216, 217 (La. Ct. App. 1985) (refusing to recognize subspecialty in sports medicine). This judicial view is likely to change as sports medicine continues to become a recognized and accepted area of specialization within the medical profession. The American Osteopathic Association has a certification board for sports medicine, and the specialty boards for family practice, internal medicine, emergency medicine, and pediatrics within the American Board of Medical Specialties now recognize sports medicine as a subspecialty. See generally Matthew J. Mitten, *Emerging Legal Issues in Sports Medicine: A Synthesis, Summary, and Analysis*, 76 St. John's L. Rev. 5 (2002).

Recent sports medicine malpractice cases adopt an "accepted practice" standard of care in determining physician liability. In other words, a physician who treats an athlete must "practice in accordance with good and accepted standards of medical care." *Classen v. Izquierdo*, 520 N.Y.S.2d 999, 1002 (N.Y. Sup. Ct. 1987). For example, in *Mikkelsen v. Haslam*, 764 P.2d 1384, 1386 (Utah Ct. App. 1988), a Utah appellate court upheld a jury verdict imposing liability on an orthopedist who advised a patient with a total hip replacement that snow skiing was permissible because it "is a departure from orthopedic medical profession standards." Under this standard, acceptable or reasonable medical practices (rather than what has been customary) define the boundaries of a physician's legal duty of care in treating athletes. In a malpractice action, expert testimony regarding the appropriate standard of physician sports medicine care generally is required to prove liability. In *Gibson v. Digiglia*, 980 So. 2d 739 (La. App. 2008), the court affirmed the dismissal of an athlete's malpractice claim because there was "no evidence to establish the standard of care required of a 'team medical director/coordinator' nor have they presented any evidence to support a claim that [the physician's] actions fell below the standard of care for that alleged sub-specialty of physicians."

The team physician must have an athlete's informed consent before providing any medical treatment. Informed consent occurs when a participant has a clear understanding of the facts, risks, and potential consequences of voluntarily choosing to engage in an activity. This doctrine is based on the principle of individual autonomy — namely, that a competent adult has the legal right to determine what to do with his or her body, including accepting or refusing medical treatment. A competent adult athlete can provide consent to medical care, but consent for treatment of athletes who are minors generally must be obtained from a parent or guardian. Consent may be implied under the circumstances, such as when an athlete has been rendered unconscious during play and needs emergency medical treatment. In these cases, the law generally assumes that if the injured athlete had been aware of his condition and was competent mentally, then he or she would have authorized appropriate treatment.

In addition to following accepted or reasonable sports medicine practices in providing diagnosis and treatment of athletic injuries and in making medical eligibility recommendations, the team physician must fully inform an athlete of any material risks of playing a sport in light of his physical condition. Failure to do so may expose the team physician to liability based on intentional tort or negligence principles.

Courts have held that a team physician's intentional or negligent failure to provide an athlete with full disclosure of material information about playing with his medical condition or the potential consequences of proposed treatment is actionable. In *Krueger v. San Francisco Forty Niners*, 234 Cal. Rptr. 579 (Cal. Ct. App. 1987), a California appellate court held that a professional football team's conscious failure to inform a player that he risked a permanent knee injury by continuing to play was fraudulent concealment. The court found that the plaintiff was not informed by team physicians of the true nature and extent of his knee injuries, the consequences of steroid injection treatment, or the long-term dangers associated with playing professional football with his medical condition. The court found that the purpose of this nondisclosure was to induce plaintiff to continue playing football despite his injuries, thereby constituting fraud. The jury awarded Krueger $2.36 million in damages, and he ultimately settled his claim for between $1 million and $1.5 million.

B. Athletic Trainers

Athletic trainers typically provide a variety of sports medicine services to athletes, such as physical conditioning, injury prevention, emergency medical care, and injury rehabilitation, which may give rise to legal liability if rendered improperly. In *Searles v. Trustees of St. Joseph's College*, 695 A.2d 1206, 1210 (Me. 1997), the Maine Supreme Court held that an athletic trainer "has the duty to conform to the standard of care required of an ordinary careful trainer" when providing care and treatment to athletes. The court ruled that an athletic trainer may incur negligence liability for failing to communicate the severity of a player's injuries to the team's coach, or for failing to advise an athlete that he should not continue playing with his medical condition. In *Jarreau v. Orleans Parish School Board*, 600 So. 2d 1389 (La. Ct. App. 1992), a Louisiana appellate court upheld a jury finding that a high school football team's trainer negligently failed to refer a player with a wrist injury to an orthopedist until after the season ended. The athletic trainer's delay in referring the player for treatment of his fracture necessitated an extended period of treatment and caused a permanent disability.

An athletic trainer, like any other provider of sports medicine care, is not negligent merely because the treatment provided exacerbates an athlete's injury. In *Gillespie v. Southern Utah State College*, 669 P.2d 861 (Utah 1983), the Utah Supreme Court held that a student athletic trainer was not liable for treating a basketball player's ankle injury that ultimately would have healed by itself without medical treatment. The court ruled that the athletic trainer's liability depended on proof of negligent treatment contributing to the athlete's enhanced injury.

C. Athlete's Contributory Negligence

An athlete has a legal duty to use reasonable care to protect his own health and safety. The doctrine of contributory negligence prohibits a plaintiff from recovering damages if the plaintiff contributed in any way to his or her own harm. For example, an athlete must truthfully disclose his medical history and physical symptoms to the team physician. In *Jarreau v. Orleans Parish School Board*, 600 So. 2d 1389 (La. Ct. App. 1992), the court, applying contributory negligence principles, found an injured high school football player to be one-third at fault for failing to consult his own physician or requesting that he be referred to a school physician. See also *McGee v. Covington County Sch. Dist.*, 2012 WL 48026 (Miss. App.) (absolving nurse practitioner, who conducted pre-participation physical examination of high school student-athlete who later died during practice, from liability where the athlete and his mother failed to truthfully disclose the athlete's medical history).

An athlete generally may rely on the recommendations of the team physician or his designated consulting specialists regarding when it is appropriate to return to play after an injury without seeking a second medical opinion. Both *Mikkelsen* and *Krueger*, *supra*, held that reliance on the team physician's recommendations ordinarily is considered reasonable because of the doctor's sports medicine expertise and that the athlete is not required to obtain a confirming medical opinion.

On the other hand, an athlete's failure to follow his physician's instructions constitutes contributory negligence that may reduce or bar his recovery. In *Gillespie v. Southern Utah State College*, 669 P.2d 861 (Utah 1983), a college basketball player was found to be solely responsible for aggravating an ankle injury by not following physician instructions concerning proper treatment and rehabilitation. See also *Holtman v. Reese*, 460 S.E.2d 338 (N.C. Ct. App. 1995) (engaging in high-impact aerobics, snow skiing, and waterskiing contrary to chiropractor's advice; *Starnes v. Caddo Parish Sch. Bd.*, 598 So. 2d 472 (La. Ct. App. 1992) (playing volleyball without wearing knee brace against doctor's advice).

D. Concussion

Research conducted over the past two decades has increased awareness of the medical severity of head injuries contracted during sports participation. All 50 states now have some type of concussion legislation, primarily modeled after the Zackery Lystedt Law enacted by the Washington state legislature in 2009 (2009 Wa. HB 1824). Because of the concern for children's safety and public school liability, this legislation typically requires schools to provide education about head injuries to sports participants and their parents, and develop concussion identification and treatment protocols. Additionally, if an athlete is suspected of having sustained a concussion in practice or competition, he or she is required to be removed from participation immediately and evaluated by an appropriate health care professional, and cannot return to play until receiving written clearance from the health care professional. In many states, schools that comply with the legislation have immunity from head injury-related lawsuits. (See Chapter 2 for more information about head injury and youth sports.)

The National Collegiate Athletic Association (NCAA) and all the professional sports leagues have also developed concussion safety policies, prompted in part by hundreds of lawsuits filed against the National Football League (NFL). Typically, a medical malpractice lawsuit is filed against the medical professional that caused the harm. However, in 2011, the first lawsuits were filed by former players alleging that the NFL knowingly exposed them to debilitating brain trauma and failed to disclose the risk. The lawsuit asserted that the NFL knew or should have known since 1928 that football caused brain damage. Instead of warning the players of these dangers and enacting rules to protect player safety and long-term welfare, the NFL allegedly engaged in a campaign to deny the risks and deliberately deceived players with faulty research that refuted the link between concussion and neurodegenerative disease. Hundreds of lawsuits were filed, and the cases were consolidated, with more than 4,500 players represented in the class. The case was finally settled in 2015, requiring the NFL to pay for medical exams for retired players, no cap on the amount paid to former players who suffer cognitive injury, and additional funding for head trauma research and education (*In re Nat'l Football League Players' Concussion Injury Litig.*, 2015 WL 1822254 (E.D.Pa.) (April 22, 2015) (final order approving settlement).

Currently, the NFL concussion protocol begins with a complete medical history, physical examination, and baseline neuropsychological testing. This includes tests that assess memory, reaction time, attention span, problem-solving abilities, and other cognitive skills. On the field, a certified athletic trainer watches play for conditions that would indicate potential head trauma; players with symptoms are removed immediately and assessed by a physician on the sideline. Additionally, a neurotrauma expert physician unaffiliated with an NFL team will be available on the sideline as a consultant for the medical team or NFL player. Players diagnosed will be monitored and slowly reintroduced to activity as symptoms abate (*http://www.nfl.com/news/story/0ap2000000253716/article/nfls-2013-protocol-for-players-with-concussions*).

The NFL concussion lawsuit has inspired similar concussion-related lawsuits against the NCAA and National Hockey League (NHL). Former NHL players allege that the NHL intentionally concealed and negligently failed to inform them of the long-term serious neurological risks associated with head injuries while playing hockey (see *In re National Hockey League Players' Concussion Injury Litigation,* 2015 WL 1334027 (D. Minn.)). At the college level, Adrian Arrington suffered multiple concussions while playing football at Eastern Illinois University. In 2011, he filed a class action lawsuit against the NCAA for his injuries and the lingering pain and suffering related to the concussions (*Arrington et al. v. Nat'l Collegiate Athletic Ass'n,* No. 11-cv-06356 (N.D. Ill.)). Other lawsuits were subsequently consolidated with *Arrington* (see *In re NCAA Student-Athlete Concussion Injury Litig.,* 988 F. Supp. 2d 1373 (J.P.M.L. 2013)). The NCAA reached a proposed settlement that would have provided $70 million for a Medical Monitoring Fund and an additional $5 million for concussion research. The settlement was rejected without prejudice by the district court (see 2014 U.S. Dist. LEXIS 174334), the parties resumed negotiations, and another proposed settlement is awaiting review. The NCAA recently enacted a concussion policy requiring member institutions to (1) educate student-athletes about the signs and symptoms of concussion, (2) have a process to remove student-athletes exhibiting signs of head injury from sports activities and be evaluated by a medical staff member, (3) keep those diagnosed with concussion from returning to play the same day, and (4) require medical clearance before the student-athlete is allowed to return to play (*http://www.ncaa.org/sites/default/files/3.2.4.17-ConcussionManagement.pdf*).

It will be interesting to see how litigation and legislation affect the way that professional and amateur sports leagues treat concussion, as well as how players evaluate and respond to the risks and potential long-term effects of brain trauma. For example, Chris Borland, a former San Francisco 49ers linebacker, retired after his rookie season because of concerns about the effects that his prior concussions while playing football will have on his future health. Pop Warner football reported a decrease in participation of more than 23,000 players (almost 10 percent) between 2010 and 2012, but high school participation rebounded in 2015 after five years of steady decline. Perceptions about the safety of participation in football were cited in both studies.

INJURY COMPENSATION FOR PROFESSIONAL ATHLETES

 **KEY TERMS**
- Compensable event
- Injury by accident
- Intentional injury exception
- Voluntary participation
- Workers' compensation

Like other athletes, professional athletes generally assume the inherent risks of injury while participating in their respective sports. However, league collective bargaining agreements and standard player contracts generally establish a contractual right of professional athletes to receive team-provided or paid medical care and rehabilitation for injuries suffered during training and games. Major league professional athletes also have contractual injury protection guarantees and benefits for career-ending injuries and sport-related disabilities. Disputes between a player and team concerning the parties' respective rights and responsibilities under these agreements generally must be submitted to binding arbitration. *Sherwin v. Indianapolis Colts, Inc.*, 752 F. Supp. 1172 (N.D.N.Y. 1990). But see *Bentley v. Cleveland Browns Football Co.*, 2011 WL 2652343 (Ohio App. July 7, 2011) (club's alleged fraudulent and negligent misrepresentations regarding its postoperative rehabilitation facility for players do not require interpretation of NFL CBA and are not required to be submitted to arbitration).

As employees, professional team sport athletes also may be eligible to recover state workers' compensation benefits for injuries or diseases arising from playing a sport. See, e.g., *Norfolk Admirals v. Jones*, 2005 WL 2847392 (Va. App. 2005) (professional hockey player entitled to receive workers' compensation benefits for injuries suffered in a fight with an opposing player during a game, which was ordered by his coach). Workers' compensation laws provide a simple and inexpensive method for employees to obtain compensation and medical expenses for work-related injuries and illnesses. The theory underlying these laws is that industries should bear the burden of industrial accidents as a component of the cost of production. Thus, workers' compensation is premised on the idea that workplace accidents are a cost of doing business and therefore should be borne by the enterprise that engendered them. In this sense, workers' compensation is a transfer of economic losses from injured workers to industry and, ultimately, to the public.

Under workers' compensation legislation, benefits are available to injured workers without having to prove breach of an employer's common law tort or other statutory liability. Defenses available in common law tort actions, such as contributory negligence and assumption of risk are unavailable to employers in workers' compensation actions. The removal of such requirements enables injured employees to avoid the impediments that left many workers uncompensated under the common law.

Employees obtain the security of workers' compensation benefits on a no-fault basis in exchange for relinquishing rights to pursue tort actions against their employers. A worker who accepts workers' compensation benefits or has successfully prosecuted a workers' compensation claim is barred from bringing a common law tort action. Limitations are also imposed on the amount of damages that workers can recover. For example, workers' compensation statutes generally preclude employees from recovering for pain and suffering or punitive damages. Available remedies are typically limited to compensation for disability, medical, death, and burial expenses. Thus, employees waive tort claims against their employers in exchange for a simplified but limited recovery under workers' compensation laws.

State statutes are generally the source of employee rights to workers' compensation benefits. Therefore, absent a specific exclusion under a particular state's law, injured professional athletes normally are eligible to receive workers' compensation benefits. A few states exclude professional athletes from the definition of employee for workers' compensation purposes or otherwise severely limit the extent to which workers' compensation benefits are available to professional athletes. See, e.g., Fla. Stat. Ann. §440.02(17)(c)(3) (West 2006); Mass. Gen. Laws Ann. Ch. 152, §1(4)(b) (West 2008); and 2003 Wyo. Sess. Laws, §27-14-102(vii)(F) (2007). The Florida and Wyoming statutes provide coverage for professional athletes when their team purchases insurance for the specific purpose of providing workers' compensation benefits for its athletes.

Typically, the right of an employee to receive benefits under workers' compensation laws is dependent on two important criteria: (1) Is the person seeking benefits an "employee," as defined by the relevant state statute? (2) Is the injury for which compensation is sought work-related, or, as is commonly stated, did the injury "arise out of" and "in the course of" the claimant's employment? A helpful review and analysis of general workers' compensation principles is provided in Arthur Larson, Larson's Workers' Compensation Law (LEXIS 2008). For discussion of various issues relating to professional athletes and workers' compensation see the following: Timothy Davis, *Tort Liability of Coaches for Injuries to Professional Athletes: Overcoming Policy and Doctrinal Barriers*, 76 UMKC L. Rev. 571, 587–90 (2008) (discussing the intentional conduct exception to the exclusivity of workers' compensation remedies); Matthew J. Mitten, *Team Physicians as Co-Employees: A Prescription That Deprives Professional Athletes of an Adequate Remedy for Sports Medicine Malpractice*, 50 St. LouisU. L.J. 211 (2006); and Matthew J. Mitten, *Emerging Legal Issues in Sports Medicine: A Synthesis, Summary, and Analysis*, 76 St. John L. Rev. 5, 44–49, 57–59 (2002).

To be in a position to claim benefits, an injured employee must provide timely notice to his or her employer and file a claim within the time frame established by the relevant workers' compensation statute. According to a prominent commentator, "The purpose is dual: First, to enable the employer to provide immediate medical diagnosis and treatment with a view to minimizing the seriousness of the injury; and second, to facilitate the earliest possible investigation of the facts surrounding the injury." Arthur Larson, Larson's Workers' Compensation Law (2002) at §126.01.

Although professional athletes most often can readily establish the existence of an employee/employer relationship, this characterization sets the stage for the introduction of a myriad of other legal issues that potentially affect injured athletes' entitlement to workers' compensation benefits against their teams. The following material provides two illustrations of contemporary issues involving workers' compensation and professional athletics: (1) what injuries are compensable under workers' compensation statutes, and (2) exceptions to the exclusivity of workers' compensation benefits system as the sole state law remedy for player injuries.

Pro-Football, Inc. v. Uhlenhake
558 S.E. 2d 571 (Va. App. 2002)

BENTON, Judge.

The Workers' Compensation Commission entered an award of permanent partial disability benefits in favor of Jeffrey A. Uhlenhake, a professional football player, for injury to his left foot and denied him an award of benefits for injury to his left knee. Pro-Football, Inc., trading as the Washington Redskins, contends that injuries to a professional football player are not covered by the Act and, alternatively, that the evidence does not support the award of benefits for injury to Uhlenhake's left foot.

Uhlenhake contends the evidence proved a compensable injury to his left knee. For the reasons that follow, we affirm the commission's award.

Pro-Football contends that "injuries resulting from voluntary participation in activities where injuries are customary, foreseeable, and expected are not accidental within the meaning of the Virginia Workers' Compensation Act." It argues that "in determining whether an injury is accidental, the relevant focus is upon the predictability of the injury based upon the activity performed."

As a guiding principle, the Workers' Compensation Act provides that "'injury' means only injury by accident arising out of and in the course of employment." Code §65.2-101. The Act does not . . . specifically define the term "injury by accident." Consequently, the phrase has been the subject of judicial interpretation. . . .

To establish an "injury by accident," a claimant must prove (1) that the injury appeared suddenly at a particular time and place and upon a particular occasion, (2) that it was caused by an identifiable incident or sudden precipitating event, and (3) that it resulted in an obvious mechanical or structural change in the human body. . . .

Pro-Football initially posits that Uhlenhake seeks to recover for "injuries resulting from *voluntary* participation in activities." (Emphasis added.) The evidence proved, however, that Uhlenhake was engaged in an activity required by his employment. He was employed by Pro-Football to train, practice, and play in football games, which is the business of Pro-Football. No evidence proved Uhlenhake undertook a voluntary task when he engaged in the activity, which he alleges caused his injury. This is not a case of an injury "resulting from an employee's voluntary participation in employer-sponsored off-duty recreational activities which are not part of the employee's duties." Code §65.2-101 (specifying an exclusion from injury by accident). Likewise, this is not a case in which the "injury was the direct result of [an employee] taking a risk of his own choosing, independent of any employment requirements, and one that was not an accepted and normal activity at the place of employment." *Mullins v. Westmoreland Coal Co.*, 10 Va. App. 304, 308, 391 S.E.2d 609, 611 (1990). Uhlenhake was at all relevant times engaged in an activity within the scope of his employment contract.

Pro-Football argues that by engaging in conduct which is physically dangerous and which has a high likelihood of injury, Uhlenhake must "automatically expect to be injured. . . . Pro-Football . . . asserts that "professional football players must accept the risk of injury if they wish to play the game" and argues that "the commission's broadened definition will extend compensability to . . . others who voluntarily participate in employment where injury is either highly probable or certain." It has long been understood, however, that the legislature abolished various common law doctrines, including assumption of the risk, when it adopted the Workers' Compensation Act. . . . In effect, Pro-Football's argument, if accepted, would introduce into the workers' compensation law the concept of assumption of the risk for a hazard that is undisputedly an incident of a worker's occupation.

"To say that football injuries are not accidental because of the probability of injury is, if one looks at it more closely, no more than to say that any activity with a high risk factor should be ruled noncompensable." 2 Larson at §22.04[1][b]. The commission properly rejected this misguided notion and ruled that "the nature of the employment and the foreseeability of a potential injury does not determine whether an injury sustained in the ordinary course of an employee's duties is an accident." The business of Pro-Football is to engage in the activity of professional football. It employs individuals to constantly perform in a strenuous activity that has risks and hazards. As with coal miners, steel workers, firefighters, and police officers, who are covered by the Act, other classes of employees are regularly exposed to known, actual risks of hazards because "the employment subjects the employee to the particular danger." *Olsten v. Leftwich*, 230 Va. 317, 319, 336 S.E.2d 893, 894 (1985). The commission correctly ruled that professional football players are not exempt from the coverage of the Act when they suffer injuries in the game they are employed to perform.

[Editors' note: Based on the foregoing standard of review, the court found that credible evidence supported the commission's finding awarding Uhlenhake permanent partial disability benefits for loss of use of his left foot. The court next considered Uhlenhake's challenge of the sufficiency of the evidence to support the commission's finding that his left knee injury resulted from cumulative trauma and, therefore, is not compensable. Noting that the employee bears the burden of proving by a preponderance of the evidence that an injury by accident occurred, the court concluded that credible evidence supported the commission's finding that the "that the [knee] injury was the result of cumulative events" and consequently was not compensable.]

For these reasons, we affirm all aspects of the commission's decision.

QUESTION

Finding that Uhlenhake failed to establish a connection between the knee injury and a compensable event, the court upheld the denial of workers' compensation for injury to his left knee. Uhlenhake's ability to recover would have been enhanced if he had provided timely notice of the injury. Generally, an injured employee must provide timely notice to his or her employer and file a claim within the time frame established by the relevant workers' compensation statute. See *Pittsburgh Steelers Sports, Inc. v. Workers' Comp. Appeal Bd.*, 814 A.2d 788 (Pa. Commw. Ct. 2002) (notification of injury given to team trainer is sufficient to meet statutory notice requirements for workers' compensation). What is the purpose of the notice requirement?

NOTE

Off-season injuries. The time of the occurrence of an injury may affect a player's right to workers' compensation benefits. See, e.g., *Dandenault v. Workers' Compensation Appeals Bd.*, 728 A.2d 1001 (Pa. Commw. Ct. 1999) (professional ice hockey player's participation in a summer hockey league to get into shape for the upcoming season was not within the scope of employment when there was no evidence that the player's team either required or encouraged him to engage in that activity); but see *Farren v. Baltimore Ravens*, 720 N.E.2d 590 (Ohio Ct. App. 1998) (summary judgment inappropriate where player, who was injured during the off-season while between contracts, received ambiguous communications and instructions from the team concerning his employment status, thereby creating a question of fact as to his employment status).

Rather than seeking the no-fault fixed benefits provided by workers' compensation, an injured player instead may prefer trying to obtain an uncertain, but potentially much larger, judgment in tort litigation. In some jurisdictions (for example, California), a professional sports club may be subject to tort liability for fraudulent concealment of material medical information concerning a player's fitness to play. In *Krueger v. San Francisco Forty Niners*, 234 Cal. Rptr. 579 (Cal. Ct. App. 1987), the court held that a professional football team fraudulently failed to disclose that a player risked permanent disability by continuing to play with a chronic knee condition. Evidence established that the team "consciously failed" to disclose that the player's knee lacked the anterior cruciate ligament, that steroid injection treatments might have adverse effects, and that he risked permanent injury by continuing to play without surgery. The exclusivity provisions of the California workers' compensation statute were inapplicable because they expressly permitted the recovery of tort damages if the employee's injury was aggravated by the employer's fraudulent concealment of the existence of the injury. However, absent such a statutory exception, courts generally have refused to allow a player to bring a fraud action against a team for misrepresenting or failing to disclose material information about his physical condition, thereby limiting recovery for aggravated injuries to workers' compensation benefits.

Similarly, the exclusive remedy provisions of workers' compensation laws will not bar a tort action against an employer for harm caused by conduct that is intended to injure an employee. If the requisite intent is established, an employee may elect to either receive workers' compensation benefits or bring a tort claim. As the following case illustrates, courts generally are not receptive to a professional athlete's claim that his team "intended" his injury.

DePiano v. Montreal Baseball Club, Ltd.
663 F. Supp. 116 (W.D. Pa. 1987)

WEBER, District Judge.

[Editors' note: Jeffrey DePiano, a minor league baseball player, suffered a career-ending shoulder injury during a game. DePiano sued his minor league team and its major league parent, the Montreal Expos, alleging "negligence in their failure to provide timely and adequate medical care for his injury, and for requiring him to continue playing despite his injury. Plaintiff alleges that continued play aggravated his injury and ended his career."]

The intentional injury exception to the exclusivity of New York's Workers' Compensation Act is very narrow. In *Finch v. Swingly*, 42 A.D.2d 1035, 348 N.Y.S.2d 266 (1973), the New York Supreme Court recited the rule:

> Where injury is sustained to an employee due to an intentional tort perpetrated by the employer or at the employer's direction, the Workmen's Compensation Law is not a bar to a common law action for damages. A valid complaint under this theory of recovery must allege an intentional or deliberate act by the employer causing harm to the employee. In order to constitute an intentional tort, the conduct must be engaged in with the desire to bring about the consequences of the act. A mere knowledge and appreciation of a risk is not the same as the intent to cause injury. . . .
>
> In the present case, the only evidence advanced by plaintiff in response to the summary judgment motion goes to the employers' negligence in failing to provide medical treatment and in leaving that decision to an allegedly unqualified person, the team trainer. However, there is nothing in the evidence to indicate that the defendants' intention was to injure plaintiff. Negligence alone, no matter the degree, does not satisfy the intentional injury exception to the compensation bar. Despite full opportunity to advance evidence of intentional injury, plaintiff has succeeded only in establishing a prima facie case of negligence.
>
> Plaintiff insists that defendants knew of the risk of further injury or even that injury was "substantially certain" to occur. As we noted above, such evidence is insufficient. . . . Plaintiff also argues that defendants insisted on keeping plaintiff in the lineup despite his injury because the Jamestown team was short of outfielders. If indeed this is true, it disproves rather than supports plaintiff's case because it establishes a motive for defendants' conduct other than an intention to injure plaintiff. . . .
>
> Summary judgment will be granted in favor of defendants. . . .

In jurisdictions that recognize the intentional injury exception to the exclusivity effect of workers' compensation laws, courts are rather exacting with regard to the burden imposed on the employee. As *DePiano* illustrates, the employee must prove that the employer intended to injure or aggravate an injury when requiring a player to continue playing. See *Brocail v. Detroit Tigers, Inc.*, 268 S.W.3d 90, 108 (Tex. App. 2008) (discussing standard for determining when a tort is deemed intentional in the workers' compensation context).

In an effort to assert claims for sports medicine malpractice, players have attempted to characterize the team physician as an independent contractor rather than a team employee to avoid the workers' compensation bar to tort against co-employees. Despite earlier authority adopting such a characterization, see *Bryant v. Fox*, 515 N.E.2d 775 (Ill. App. Ct. 1987), recent case law has rejected it. *Lotysz v. Montgomery*, 766 N.Y.S.2d 28 (N.Y. App. Div. 2003); *Daniels v. Seattle Seahawks*, 968 P.2d 883 (Wash. App. Ct. 1998). In *Hendy v. Losse*, 819 P.2d 1 (Cal. 1991), a professional football player sued team physicians for negligently diagnosing and treating a knee injury suffered during a game and for advising him to continue playing football. In dismissing these claims, the California Supreme Court held that California's workers' compensation law bars tort suits between co-employees for injuries caused within the scope of employment. The court found that the plaintiff and defendant were both employed by the San Diego Chargers and that the defendant acted within the scope of his employment in treating the plaintiff. Thus, the plaintiff's exclusive remedy for his harm was workers' compensation. See also *Stringer v. Minnesota Vikings Football Club, LLC*, 705 N.W.2d 746 (Minn. 2005) (workers' compensation co-employee doctrine bars tort claim against NFL club's athletic trainers for alleged improper treatment of player who died from heat stroke during preseason practice).

PARTICIPATION RIGHTS OF ATHLETES WITH PHYSICAL OR MENTAL IMPAIRMENTS

 **KEY TERMS**
- Disability
- Major life activity
- Reasonable accommodation

Health and safety issues in sports are generally a matter of tort law. However, constitutional law principles have been invoked when athletes with physical or mental medical conditions seek the opportunity to play. The U.S. Supreme Court has ruled that persons with a physical disability are not a suspect or quasi-suspect class justifying a heightened scrutiny of alleged discrimination in violation of the equal protection clause of the U.S. Constitution. *City of Cleburne v. Cleburne Living Center, Inc.*, 473 U.S. 432 (1985). Because a professional league is not a state actor whose rules and conduct is subject to federal constitutional scrutiny, courts have rejected claims by physically impaired professional athletes (e.g., an athlete with blindness in one eye) that their exclusion from athletics violates the federal constitution. *Neeld v. American Hockey League*, 439 F. Supp. 459 (W.D.N.Y. 1977). In *Grube v. Bethlehem Area School District*, 550 F. Supp. 418, 423 (E.D. Pa. 1982), the court expressed doubt that a public high school's exclusion of a student with one kidney from contact sports denies equal protection of the law. Such exclusion is constitutionally justifiable if the school's reliance on its team physician's medical recommendation that an athlete not play rationally furthers its permissible objective of ensuring students' health and safety.

However, in *Neeld v. American Hockey League*, 439 F. Supp. 459 (W.D.N.Y. 1977), the court enjoined enforcement of a professional league bylaw prohibiting one-eyed athletes from playing hockey. The court ruled that this bylaw violated New York's Human Rights Law, which protected employees from discrimination based on disability unless the characteristic is a bona fide occupational qualification. There was no evidence that blindness in one eye substantially detracted from the plaintiff's ability to play hockey.

Today, disability discrimination claims by athletes against professional sports leagues or clubs, sports governing bodies, or educational institutions are most likely to be brought under the federal Rehabilitation Act of 1973 or the Americans with Disabilities Act of 1990.

A. Rehabilitation Act of 1973

The Rehabilitation Act, 29 U.S.C.A. §§701 et seq., is primarily intended to provide persons with physical or mental impairments with an opportunity to participate fully in activities in which they have the physical capabilities and skills to perform. Qualified handicapped athletes must be given an "equal opportunity for participation" in interscholastic and intercollegiate athletics.

To prevail in a claim alleging violation of the Rehabilitation Act, an athlete with a physical impairment must establish that he or she is (1) an "individual with handicaps," (2) "otherwise qualified" to participate, (3) being excluded or discriminated against solely by reason of the handicap, and (4) excluded from a program or activity receiving federal funds.

The athletics programs of most colleges and high schools generally do not receive direct federal funding, but they nevertheless are subject to the Rehabilitation Act if any part of its educational institution receives federal financial assistance, which generally is the case. Professional sports leagues and governing bodies generally are not subject to the Rehabilitation Act because they do not receive federal funding.

An athlete is an "individual with handicaps" entitled to the act's protection if he or she has a physical impairment that substantially limits a major life activity. It is relatively easy for an athlete to establish the existence of a permanent physical impairment such as a heart condition, congenital back or spine abnormality, or loss of a paired organ (e.g., eye or kidney) — all of which are covered under the act. It is more difficult to satisfy the requirement that the athlete's physical impairment substantially limits a major life activity. Some courts have held that exclusion of an impaired athlete from intercollegiate or interscholastic sports does not constitute a substantial limitation on a major life activity. In *Knapp v. Northwestern University*, 101 F.3d 473 (7th Cir. 1996), *cert. denied*, 520 U.S. 1274 (1997), the Seventh Circuit held that a college basketball player was not protected by the act because "[p]laying intercollegiate basketball obviously is not in and of itself a major life activity." Finding that learning was the player's affected major life activity, the court concluded that his "inability to play intercollegiate basketball at Northwestern foreclose[d] only a small portion of his collegiate [learning] opportunities" and did not substantially limit his college education, because his athletic scholarship continued in effect.

Even if participation in athletics were deemed to impair a major life activity, the athlete must be "otherwise qualified" (i.e., has the requisite physical ability and skills to play the sport in spite of his physical impairment) and excluded "solely by reason of handicap" (i.e., his or her ineligibility to participate in a sport is based entirely on consideration of his physical impairment or medical condition) to have a valid disability discrimination claim under the act. Failure to select an otherwise qualified disabled athlete for a position on a competitive sports team is not necessarily a violation of the act. In *Doe v. Eagle-Union Community School Corp.*, 101 F. Supp. 2d 707 (S.D. Ind. 2000), *vacated on other grounds*, 248 F.3d 1157 (7th Cir. 2001), a federal district court held that a coach's decision not to select a disabled student for the varsity basketball team after a tryout did not violate the act. The court found that the disabled student was given the same opportunity to try out for the team as students without disabilities, and was graded in a nondiscriminatory manner based on the coach's same subjective and objective criteria. The court explained that "the term 'otherwise qualified' did not mean that the student must be selected for the basketball team despite his handicap; it prohibited the non-selection of the student when the student had the skills to make the team but was not selected."

An educational institution must make reasonable accommodations to enable physically impaired athletes to participate in its athletic programs. An impaired athlete is "otherwise qualified" if able to meet a school's physical and medical requirements with reasonable accommodations, such as medication, monitoring, or protective padding or braces, that effectively reduce the risk of injury to himself or others. For example, in *Grube v. Bethlehem Area School District*, 550 F. Supp. 418, 424 (E.D. Pa. 1982), the court ruled that the act required a high school to permit a student-athlete with one kidney to play football if he wore a protective flak jacket, which it found to be a reasonable accommodation.

Courts have ruled that preventing a significant risk of harm to the health and safety of other participants is a valid ground for refusing to permit an athlete covered by the act to play a particular sport if supported by valid medical evidence. In *Doe v. Woodford County Board of Education*, 213 F.3d 921 (6th Cir. 2000), the Sixth Circuit held that a public high school district's decision to place a member of its junior varsity basketball team, who suffered from hepatitis B, on "hold" status pending receipt of medical clearance from his physician, did not violate the Rehabilitation Act. Observing that one could be excluded from athletics if one's participation posed a direct threat to the health and safety of others, the court found that the school district was attempting to determine whether there was a significant risk of transmission of hepatitis B to other athletes. The student's membership on the team was never terminated, and the school district ultimately allowed him to participate fully on the team with no medical restrictions.

The Rehabilitation Act permits the exclusion of a physically impaired athlete from a sport if necessary to prevent a significant risk of substantial harm to the athlete. In *Pahulu v. University of Kansas*, 897 F. Supp. 1387 (D. Kan. 1995), a federal district court upheld the team physician's "conservative" medical disqualification of a college football player with an abnormally narrow cervical canal after an episode of transient quadriplegia during a scrimmage. After consulting with a neurosurgeon, the team physician concluded that the athlete was at extremely high risk for sustaining permanent, severe neurologic injury, including permanent quadriplegia, if he continued playing football. The athlete wanted to resume playing because three other medical specialists concluded that he was at no greater risk of permanent paralysis than any other player. The university agreed to honor the athlete's scholarship, although he was not allowed to play football despite his willingness to sign a waiver absolving the university of legal liability if he were injured. The court held that university officials' adherence to the team physician's recommendation against playing does not violate the Rehabilitation Act, concluding that the university's medical disqualification decision "has a rational and reasonable basis and is supported by substantial competent evidence for which the court is unwilling to substitute its judgment."

Similarly, in *Knapp v. Northwestern University*, 101 F.3d 473 (7th Cir. 1996), *cert. denied*, 520 U.S. 1274 (1997), the Seventh Circuit held that Northwestern University did not violate the Rehabilitation Act by accepting its team physician's recommendation that an athlete with idiopathic ventricular fibrillation not play intercollegiate basketball because doing so would expose him to a significant risk of cardiac arrest during competitive athletics. The team physician's recommendation was based on Knapp's medical records and history, the 26th Bethesda Conference guidelines for athletic participation with cardiovascular abnormalities, and opinions of two consulting cardiologists.

As a high school senior, Nicholas Knapp suffered sudden cardiac arrest while playing recreational basketball, which required cardiopulmonary resuscitation and defibrillation to restart his heart. Thereafter, he had an internal cardioverter-defibrillator implanted in his abdomen. He subsequently played competitive recreational basketball without any incidents of cardiac arrest and received medical clearance to play college basketball from three cardiologists who examined him. Northwestern agreed to honor its commitment to provide Knapp with an athletic scholarship, although he was medically disqualified from playing intercollegiate basketball.

At the time, no person had ever played college or professional basketball after suffering sudden cardiac arrest or after having a defibrillator implanted. Taking into account his internal defibrillator, Knapp's experts testified that playing intercollegiate basketball would expose him to a risk of death between 1 in 34 and 1 in 100; although this risk is higher than that for the average male collegiate basketball player, they believed it to be an acceptable level of risk. Northwestern's experts agreed with the school's team doctor that, although the precise risk cannot be quantified, Knapp's participation in intercollegiate basketball significantly increased his risk of death to an unacceptable degree.

Observing that "legitimate physical qualifications may in fact be essential to participation in particular programs," the Seventh Circuit ruled that Knapp's exclusion from the Northwestern University basketball team did not violate the Rehabilitation Act:

> A significant risk of personal physical injury can disqualify a person from a position if the risk cannot be eliminated. But more than merely an elevated risk of injury is required before disqualification is appropriate. Any physical qualification based on risk of future injury must be examined with special care if the Rehabilitation Act is not to be circumvented, since almost all disabled individuals are at a greater risk of injury. . . .
>
> We do not believe that, in cases where medical experts disagree in their assessment of the extent of a real risk of serious harm or death, Congress intended that the courts—neutral arbiters but generally less skilled in medicine than the experts involved—should make the final medical decision. Instead, in the midst of conflicting expert testimony regarding the degree of serious risk of harm or death, the court's place is to ensure that the exclusion or disqualification of an individual was individualized, reasonably made, and based upon competent medical evidence. So long as these factors exist, it will be the rare case regarding participation in athletics where a court may substitute its judgment for that of the school's team physicians.
>
> In closing, we wish to make clear that we are *not* saying Northwestern's decision necessarily is the right decision. We say only that it is not an illegal one under the Rehabilitation Act. On the same facts, another team physician at another university, reviewing the same medical history, physical evaluation, and medical recommendations,

might reasonably decide that Knapp met the physical qualifications for playing on an intercollegiate basketball team. Simply put, all universities need not evaluate risk the same way. What we say in this case is that if substantial evidence supports the decision-maker — here Northwestern — that decision must be respected.

Section 794 prohibits authorities from deciding without significant medical support that certain activities are too risky for a disabled person. Decisions of this sort cannot rest on paternalistic concerns. Knapp, who is an adult, is not in need of paternalistic decisions regarding his health, and his parents — more entitled to be paternalistic toward him than Northwestern — approve of his decision. . . . But here, where Northwestern acted rationally and reasonably rather than paternalistically, no Rehabilitation Act violation has occurred. The Rehabilitation Act "is carefully structured to replace . . . reflexive actions to actual or perceived handicaps with actions based on reasoned and medically sound judgments. . . . "

101 F.3d, at 485–86.

B. Americans with Disabilities Act of 1990

The Americans with Disabilities Act (ADA), 42 U.S.C. §§12101 et seq., is patterned after the Rehabilitation Act and has similar policy objectives. The ADA's scope, however, is broader than that of the Rehabilitation Act because it covers entities that do not receive federal funding, such as professional sports leagues and their member teams. Depending on the particular sport, the ADA's provisions covering employers, public entities, and places of public accommodation may apply. The ADA applies to public entities such as public high schools, universities, and colleges; employers, such as professional leagues and clubs, with 15 or more employees; and private persons or entities that own, lease, or operate a place of public accommodation, such as the Professional Golfers Association Tour, NCAA, youth sports leagues, and sports instructional schools.

Courts generally construe the ADA in a manner consistent with judicial interpretations of the Rehabilitation Act. The factors governing the legality of excluding a physically disabled athlete from a sport under the ADA are essentially the same as those relevant under the Rehabilitation Act.

Like the Rehabilitation Act, the ADA requires a valid medical basis for excluding an athlete from competition on the ground that his physical condition exposes other participants to an increased risk of serious harm. In *Anderson v. Little League Baseball, Inc.*, 794 F. Supp. 342 (D. Ariz. 1992), a federal district court held that a youth baseball league policy prohibiting coaches in wheelchairs from being on the field violated the ADA because the plaintiff's on-field coaching in a wheelchair did not pose a direct threat to the health and safety of others. It enjoined enforcement of the baseball league's policy because it illegally discriminated against the plaintiff.

Courts have held it is legally permissible to exclude an athlete from participating in competitive sports with an infectious disease if no reasonable accommodation will prevent a direct threat to the health and safety of other participants. In *Montalvo v. Radcliffe*, 167 F.3d 873 (4th Cir.), *cert. denied*, 528 U.S. 813 (1999), the Fourth Circuit ruled that a karate studio was permitted to exclude an HIV-positive 12-year-old boy from full contact karate classes, which involved frequent physical contact among students and instructors that resulted in bloody injuries. Relying on medical expert testimony that the human immunodeficiency virus (HIV) can be transmitted through blood-to-blood contact and evidence that this type of contact frequently occurred in these karate classes, the court concluded that the plaintiff's participation would pose a direct threat to the health and safety of others by exposing them to the risk of HIV transmission. The court further found that there were no possible modifications that could effectively reduce the significance of this risk, while also maintaining the fundamental nature of the studio's "hard-style" Japanese karate. The studio's offer to give the plaintiff private karate lessons, which was rejected by him and his parents, was found to be a reasonable accommodation of the plaintiff's disability. See generally John T. Wolohan, *An Ethical and Legal Dilemma: Participation in Sports by HIV Infected Athletes*, 7 Marq. Sports L.J. 373 (1997).

Unlike the well-established judicial precedent recognizing harm to one's self as a valid justification for exclusion from athletics under the Rehabilitation Act, there is little precedent regarding whether exclusion of a disabled athlete from a sport solely because of a potentially enhanced risk of injury is a legally valid justification under the ADA. To date, there have not been any ADA cases in which a professional athlete with a physical abnormality has challenged his or her medical disqualification from a sport to prevent exposure to an enhanced risk of significant harm. Although the underlying medical issues may be the same, courts may develop a different legal framework for resolving participation disputes involving professional athletes than the one for college athletes established by the *Pahulu* and *Knapp* cases, *supra*, under the Rehabilitation Act. An important distinction is that sports are a professional athlete's livelihood, rather than an extracurricular activity that is merely one component of one's education. See Matthew J. Mitten, *Enhanced Risk of Harm to One's Self As a Justification for Exclusion from Athletics*, 8 Marq. Sports L.J. 189 (1998).

In *PGA Tour, Inc. v. Martin*, 532 U.S. 661 (2001), the U.S. Supreme Court ruled that, although the essence of sports is that everyone plays by the same rules, a sports governing body (including those that regulate professional sports at the highest level of competition) must make reasonable accommodations to provide a physically impaired athlete with an opportunity to compete in the subject sport. The PGA Tour had refused to provide Casey Martin, a professional golfer with a circulatory disorder that inhibits his ability to walk, with an exception to its rule that all golfers must walk the course during tournament play because of its position that walking injected an element of fatigue into championship golf. This decision effectively precluded him from playing in PGA tournaments, although his demonstrated golf skills qualified him to participate.

The Court ruled that waiver of the PGA Tour's walking rule to allow Martin to use a cart was a reasonable accommodation that did not fundamentally alter the nature of professional championship golf. The "essence of the game has been shot-making," according to the Court, and the "walking rule . . . is not an essential attribute of the game itself." The Court recognized that "waiver of an essential rule of competition for anyone would fundamentally alter" the PGA's tournaments, but concluded that "the walking rule is at best peripheral to the nature of petitioner's athletic events, and thus it might be waived in individual cases without working a fundamental alteration." *Id.* at 689.

Relying on undisputed trial testimony that "Martin easily endures greater fatigue even with a cart than his able-bodied competitors do by walking," the Court held:

> Under the ADA's basic requirement that the need of a disabled person be evaluated on an individual basis, we have no doubt that allowing Martin to use a golf cart would not fundamentally alter the nature of petitioner's tournaments. As we have discussed, the purpose of the walking rule is to subject players to fatigue, which in turn may influence the outcome of tournaments. Even if the rule does serve that purpose, it is an uncontested finding of the District Court that Martin "easily endures greater fatigue even with a cart than his able-bodied competitors do by walking." The purpose of the walking rule is therefore not compromised in the slightest by allowing Martin to use a cart. A modification that provides an exception to a peripheral tournament rule without impairing its purpose cannot be said to "fundamentally alter" the tournament. What it can be said to do, on the other hand, is to allow Martin the chance to qualify for and compete in the athletic events petitioner offers to those members of the public who have the skill and desire to enter. That is exactly what the ADA requires. As a result, Martin's request for a waiver of the walking rule should have been granted.
>
> The ADA admittedly imposes some administrative burdens on the operators of places of public accommodation that could be avoided by strictly adhering to general rules and policies that are entirely fair with respect to the able-bodied but that may indiscriminately preclude access by qualified persons with disabilities. But surely, in a case of this kind, Congress intended that an entity like the PGA not only give individualized attention to the handful of requests that it might receive from talented but disabled athletes for a modification or waiver of a rule to allow them access to the competition, but also carefully weigh the purpose, as well as the letter, of the rule before determining that no accommodation would be tolerable.

Id. at 690–91. In a vigorous dissent, Justice Scalia asserted:

> Nowhere is it writ that PGA TOUR golf must be classic "essential" golf. Why cannot the PGA TOUR, if it wishes, promote a new game, with distinctive rules (much as the American League promotes a game of baseball in which the pitcher's turn at the plate can be taken by a "designated hitter")? If members of the public do not like the new rules — if they feel that these rules do not truly test the individual's skill at "real golf" (or the team's skill at "real baseball") they can withdraw their patronage. But the rules are the rules. They are (as in all games) entirely arbitrary, and there is no basis on which anyone — not even the Supreme Court of the United States — can pronounce one or another of them to be "nonessential" if the rulemaker (here the PGA TOUR) deems it to be essential. . . .

Id. at 699–700.

Justice Scalia expressed concern with a legal standard establishing "one set of rules that is 'fair with respect to the able-bodied' but 'individualized' rules, mandated by the ADA, for 'talented but disabled athletes.'" *Id.* at 703. He cautioned "it should not be assumed that today's decent, tolerant, and progressive judgment will, in the long run, accrue to the benefit of sports competitors with disabilities." *Id.* at 704. In his view, because the *Martin* majority's legal standard requires courts to determine which rules of a sport are "essential," sports governing bodies that "value their autonomy have every incentive to defend vigorously the necessity of every regulation" and "to make sure the same written rules are set forth for all levels of play and to never voluntarily grant any exceptions." *Id.* at 704–05.

QUESTIONS

1. Should the federal disability discrimination laws be construed to permit judicial modification of uniform and neutral playing rules on a case-by-case basis? If not, what is an effective alternative means of ensuring that impaired persons have an equal opportunity to participate in athletics commensurate with their interests, skills, and abilities?
2. Is there a principled judicial basis for distinguishing between "an essential rule of competition" and a nonessential rule that has a peripheral impact on the game?

NOTES

1. Post-*Martin* cases: Reasonable accommodations versus fundamental alterations. In May 2007, the Ladies Professional Golfers Association (LPGA) allowed MacKinzie Kline, a 15-year-old golfer with a congenital heart condition that prevented her from walking long distances without becoming fatigued, to ride in a cart and use an oxygen delivery system when necessary during an LPGA Tour event. LPGA commissioner Carolyn Bivens determined that these accommodations would not provide her with an unfair competitive advantage.

In *Kuketz v. Petronelli*, 821 N.E. 2d 473 (2005), the Massachusetts Supreme Judicial Court ruled that the ADA does not require that a wheelchair-bound paraplegic, who is a nationally ranked player in wheelchair racquetball competitions, be permitted to play in a health club's men's A-level league with footed players and be given two bounces to hit the ball. He was permitted in play in nonleague matches with footed racquetball players, but wanted to compete against the best footed players in league competition to prepare for an upcoming international wheelchair racquetball tournament. The official rules of racquetball require the ball to be returned on one bounce in a game between footed players, but allow for two bounces if both participants are playing in wheelchairs.

The court explained:

> Unlike the use of carts in golf, the allowance for more than one bounce in racquetball is "inconsistent with the fundamental character of the game." The essence of the game of racquetball, as expressly articulated in the rules, is the hitting of a moving ball with a racquet before the second bounce. Giving a wheelchair player two bounces and a footed player one bounce in head-to-head competition is a variation of the official rules that would "alter such as essential aspect of the game . . . that it would be unacceptable even if it affected all competitors equally." The modifications sought by [plaintiff] create a new game, with new strategies and new rules. The club certainly is free to establish or

enter into a league that plays this variation of racquetball, but it is not required by the ADA to do so.

Id. at 479–80. See generally Paul M. Anderson, *A Cart That Accommodates: Using Case Law to Understand the ADA, Sports, and Casey Martin*, 1 Va. Sports & Ent. L.J. 211 (2002).

2. Learning disabilities. Ironically, judicial decisions illustrate that high school student-athletes with the same disability (e.g., a learning disability) may not have the same athletic participation rights under the ADA. For example, in determining whether granting a waiver of a state high school athletic association eligibility rule (e.g., 19-year-old maximum age rule) would fundamentally alter the nature of a sport by providing a competitive advantage or would adversely affect other participants' safety, the student-athlete's individual size, skills, and athletic prowess are the dispositive factors. This is a fact-specific inquiry; whether the ADA requires that a disabled student-athlete be given an opportunity to participate depends on the individual's physical characteristics and athletic abilities as well as the subject sport.

In *Cruz v. Pennsylvania Interscholastic Athletic Assn.*, 157 F. Supp. 2d 485 (E.D. Pa. 2001), a federal district court ruled that a 19-year-old public school special education student who was classified as "educable mentally retarded" could not be excluded from participation in any high school sports without an individualized evaluation of whether doing so was necessary to prevent a threat to the health and safety of other participants or to prevent competitive unfairness. The court noted that he is five foot three inches tall and weighs 130 pounds and is not a "star" player in any of his interscholastic sports. Observing that there is a no "cut" policy for both teams, the court suggested he should be permitted to continue playing football because there he is only "a marginal player" and participating in track because he "is not a fast runner." However, it implied that he could be excluded from wrestling because "he may have a competitive advantage based on his outstanding dual meet record."

Similarly, in *Baisden v. West Virginia Secondary Schools Activities Commission*, 568 S.E.2d 32 (W. Va. 2002), the West Virginia Supreme Court stated:

> While we decide, through this opinion, that individualized assessments are required in cases of this nature and that reasonable accommodations may be made through waiver of the age nineteen rule under certain circumstances, we do not believe that the facts of this case justify waiver as an accommodation. Mr. Baisden turned nineteen on July 27, 2001. He is six feet four inches tall and weighs 280 pounds. He runs the forty-yard-dash in 5.3 seconds. His participation in high school football would permit him to compete in this contact sport against students approximately five years younger. The safety of younger, smaller, more inexperienced students would be unreasonably compromised. In our view, this would fundamentally alter the structure of the interscholastic athletic program, a result which is not required by reasonable accommodation standards in anti-discrimination law.

Although courts have ruled that the ADA applies to the National Collegiate Athletic Association, there are relatively few reported cases applying *Martin*'s reasonable accommodation/fundamental alteration legal framework to intercollegiate athletics. In *Matthews v. NCAA*, 179 F. Supp. 2d 1209 (E.D. Wash. 2001), a Washington federal district court held that a request by a student-athlete with a learning disability for a waiver of an NCAA rule requiring student-athletes to earn at least 75 percent of their annual required credit hours during the regular academic year would not fundamentally alter its academic eligibility requirements. See generally Maureen A. Weston, *Academic Standards or Discriminatory Hoops? Learning-Disabled Student-Athletes and the NCAA Initial Academic Eligibility Requirements*, 66 Tenn. L. Rev. 1049 (1999).

3. Competition between able-bodied and disabled athletes. In *Badgett v. Alabama High School Athletic Assn.*, 2007 WL 2461928 (N.D. Ala.), an Alabama federal district court refused to order a state high school athletics association to allow the state's only track and field wheelchair division athlete, who suffered from cerebral palsy, to compete against able-bodied runners in the state track and field championship based on its conclusion that her doing so "would raise legitimate competitive, fairness and administrative concerns" and fundamentally alter the sports of track and field. It also determined that her participation "would raise legitimate safety concerns that are inherent in having able-bodied athletes and wheelchair athletes compete in mixed heats." The court concluded that the establishment of a separate wheelchair division for track and field, whose competing athletes earned equivalent recognition and medals for state championship results, was a reasonable accommodation, which satisfied the requirements of the ADA.

South African athlete Oscar Pistorius had both legs amputated below the knee when he was 11 months old, because he was born without the fibula in his lower legs and had other defects in his feet. Running with "Cheetah" prosthetic legs — a pair of J-shaped carbon fiber blades that touch only a few inches of ground and that attach to his knees — he easily won the 100- and 200-meter sprints at the 2007 Paralympic World Cup. He has had world-record performances for disabled athletes in the 100-, 200-, and 400-meter races, all of which would have won him gold medals in equivalent women's events at the 2004 Olympics. Currently, there are limited biomechanical studies of amputee runners, and his speed on prosthetic legs cannot be precisely compared with what his speed would be on natural legs.

In 2008, the Court of Arbitration for Sport (CAS) ruled that Pistorius was eligible to run in track events sanctioned by the International Association of Athletics Federations (IAAF) with his prosthetic legs. *Pistorius v. IAAF*, CAS 2008/A/1480, award of May 16, 2008. An IAAF rule prohibited the use of "any technical device that incorporates springs, wheels or any other element that provides the user with an advantage over another athlete not using such a device." However, the CAS panel rejected the IAAF's argument that the use of a technical device providing an athlete "with any *advantage*, however small, in any part of a competition . . . must render that athlete ineligible to compete regardless of any compensating disadvantages." It concluded that the use of a passive device such as the "Cheetah" prosthetic legs does not violate this rule "without convincing scientific proof that it provides him with *an overall net advantage* over other athletes." The panel concluded that because scientific evidence did not prove that Pistorius obtained a metabolic or biomechanical advantage from using the "Cheetah" prosthetic legs, his exclusion would not further the rule's purpose of ensuring fair competition among athletes. Pistorius was unable to qualify for the 2008 Beijing Olympics, but four years later, he qualified for the 2012 London Olympics, representing South Africa in both the 400-meter individual race and the 4 × 400-meter relay.

4. Disabled spectators and fans. In some instances, disabled spectators have successfully brought disability discrimination claims against professional leagues or operators of sports venues. See, e.g., *Paralyzed Veterans of America v. D.C. Arena L.P.*, 117 F.3d 579 (D.C. Cir. 1997) (violation not to provide line of sight over standing spectators for those in wheelchairs); *Feldman v. Pro Football, Inc.*, 2008 U.S. Dist. Lexis 85149 (D. Md.) at *31 (ADA requires NFL club and stadium operator to provide equal access to aural information broadcast over the FedExField public address system, including "music with lyrics, play information, advertisements, referee calls, safety/emergency information, and other announcements"). See also *Celano v. Marriott Int'l, Inc.*, 2008 WL 239306 (N.D. Cal. 2008) (failure to provide "accessible" or "single-rider" carts to enable disabled persons to play golf at defendant's courses violates ADA).

Problem 8-1

A local public school board voted to bar a parent from continuing to coach his son's high school football team. The parent is a former paramedic who apparently contracted HIV infection several years ago while treating an automobile accident victim subsequently discovered to be HIV positive. School board members are concerned that the parent could transmit HIV to players while coaching or rendering first aid to injured players. One board member who is a physician does not think it is a good idea for the parent to continue coaching. Does the school board's action violate the ADA or Rehabilitation Act?

Intellectual Property Issues in Sports

9

INTRODUCTION

Sports-related intellectual property rights such as trademarks, service marks, and copyrights generate billions of dollars in annual revenue for sports entities such as professional leagues and clubs, the U.S. Olympic Committee, and the National Collegiate Athletic Association (NCAA), and university and high school athletics programs. These revenues are derived from various sources, such as the sale of television, radio, and Internet broadcasting rights for sports events; trademark and official team logo licensing agreements; and league, team, or event sponsorship deals with advertisers. In addition, popular athletes and coaches license various aspects of their identity, such as their names or photographs, to others for commercial purposes, thereby earning a substantial amount of money for endorsing various products and services.

Sports event broadcasting rights are the largest source of revenue for professional sports leagues and organizations, as well as the NCAA and its member universities; sports events are one of the few things people watch live, which maximizes the viewing audience and attracts the substantial advertising dollars necessary for broadcasters to pay multibillion-dollar rights fees to these entities. For example, the television contracts that the National Football League (NFL) has with Fox, CBS, DirecTV, ESPN, and NBC will pay the NFL an average of $5.9 billion a year in rights fees through 2022. The television contracts of Major League Baseball (MLB) with media entities will generate approximately $1.6 billion annually through 2021. The Los Angeles Dodgers will receive $8.35 billion from Time Warner Cable to televise its games for 25 years beginning in 2014, and a 30-year television deal between the New York Yankees and the YES Network paid $95 million in its first year (2012) and increases 5 percent annually each year thereafter. In April 2010, the NCAA entered into an agreement with CBS and Turner Sports pursuant to which they will pay almost $11 billion for the television rights to the "Final Four" men's basketball tournament for 14 years.

The licensing and merchandising of sports brands (i.e., trademarks and logos) also generate billions of dollars in aggregate revenues for professional and amateur sports leagues and other entities. The estimated value of collegiate sports licensing revenues alone is more than $3 billion. Plunkett Research estimates that companies and businesses spend approximately $32 billion annually for sports-related advertising in the United States, which includes naming rights and sponsorship of professional, Olympic, and intercollegiate sports events and organizations, professional leagues and their member clubs, colleges and universities, and others.

Well-known athletes and coaches have entered into lucrative deals to promote and endorse a wide variety of products and services. In some instances, income earned from the licensing of a player's identity to sell products and services may be greater than that derived from his or her athletic ability or success. For example, Michael Jordan signed his first Nike endorsement contract in 1985 for $2.5 million, and he has earned more money from endorsement deals than from playing basketball in the National Basketball Association (NBA). Before ever playing in a NBA game, LeBron James signed a five-year, $5 million endorsement deal with Upper Deck trading cards and a seven-year shoe endorsement deal with Nike that was worth more than $90 million. In 2011, Tiger Woods earned approximately $55 million in endorsement income, Roger Federer earned $45 million, David Beckham earned $37 million, Maria Sharapova earned $23.5 million from endorsements, and Danica Patrick earned $12.5 million.

This chapter initially considers how trademark and unfair competition law protects the owners of sports-related trademarks, logos, and other identifying insignia from infringement and economic harm to their rights. Next, the nature and scope of legal protection for real-time game accounts and broadcasting of sporting events under federal copyright law, as well as state misappropriation and unfair competition laws, is addressed. Finally, an athlete's protected interest in his or her privacy, reputation, and identity is considered.

TRADEMARKS, LOGOS, AND OTHER IDENTIFYING SPORTS INSIGNIA

KEY TERMS
- Anticybersquatting Consumer Protection Act of 1999 (ACPA)
- Inherently distinctive mark
- Lanham Act
- Likelihood of confusion
- Secondary meaning
- Ted Stevens Olympic and Amateur Sports Act (ASA)
- Trademark Counterfeiting
- Trademark Dilution Revision Act of 2006 (TDRA)
- Trademark/service mark
- Trademark/service mark infringement
- Unfair competition
- Uniform Domain Name Dispute Resolution Policy (UDRP)

A. Trademark Infringement and Unfair Competition

Common law trademark and service mark rights are acquired by first usage of a name, logo, or other symbol to identify one's products or services and to distinguish them from those of others. In *White v. Board of Regents of Univ. of Nebraska*, 614 N.W.2d 330 (Neb. 2000), the court determined that a university acquired rights in "Husker Authentics" by virtue of its first use of this mark in connection with the advertising and sale of products to season ticket holders, alumni, and boosters. Professor Thomas McCarthy observes that "the exclusive 'property' right of a trademark is defined by consumer perception." 1 J.T. McCarthy, McCarthy on Trademarks and Unfair Competition, §2:14 (4th ed., West 2012). In other words, the nature and scope of one's property interest in a trademark generally stem from the right to prevent consumer confusion. As the Seventh Circuit explained, "[T]he trademark laws exist not to 'protect' trademarks, but . . . to protect the consuming public from confusion, concomitantly protecting the trademark owner's right to a non-confused public." *James Burrough, Ltd. v. Sign of the Beefeater, Inc.*, 540 F.2d 266, 276 (7th Cir. 1976).

A sports team's name functions as a trademark or a service mark by virtue of public association of that name with a particular team. Sports team names generally are either inherently distinctive or have acquired "secondary meaning," therefore entitling them to trademark protection. An inherently distinctive mark is one that is coined or arbitrary in relation to the goods or services it identifies, such as "Miami Dolphins" for an NFL club, or is suggestive of the club's desired characteristics, such as "Tennessee Titans." See *In re WNBA Enterprises LLC*, 70 U.S.P.Q.2d 1153 (TTAB 2003) (finding "Orlando Miracle" to be an inherently distinctive mark for a Women's National Basketball Association (WNBA) club in Orlando). As one court explained, "Secondary meaning is the consuming public's understanding that the mark, when used in context, refers, not to what the descriptive word ordinarily describes, but to the particular business that the mark is meant to identify." *Maryland Stadium Authority v. Becker*, 806 F. Supp. 1236, 1241 (D. Md. 1992) (finding that public identifies "Camden Yards" with a Baltimore baseball stadium).

Courts have recognized that the popularity of NFL football, combined with its extensive media coverage and advertising, creates a public association of its team names with its member clubs (*NFL Properties, Inc. v. N.J. Giants, Inc.*, 637 F. Supp. 507 (D. N. J. 1986)), which also is true of the other U.S. major professional leagues. Sports team logos such as the Oakland Raiders' pirate and the Ohio State University's "Brutus Buckeye" function as trademarks that identify particular teams. Distinctive helmet and uniform designs and colors also can function as trademarks. See, e.g., *Board of Supervisors of the La. State Univ. v. Smack Apparel Co.*, 550 F.3d 465 (5th Cir. 2008) (finding that well-known and long-used color schemes, logos, and designs identify university's sports teams); *Dallas Cowboys Cheerleaders, Inc. v. Pussycat Cinema, Ltd.*, 604 F.2d 200, 204 n.5 (2d Cir. 1979) (finding trademark rights in uniform "universally recognized as the symbol of the Dallas Cowboys Cheerleaders"). In addition, a term or phrase may become associated with a sports team (e.g., "Evil Empire" for the New York Yankees baseball club) through public usage or fan recognition, thereby conferring trademark rights on the team. *New York Yankees Partnership v. Evil Enterprises, Inc.*, 2013 WL 1305332 (T.T.A.B.).

Trademark rights exist indefinitely so long as the mark continues to be used and serves as an indication of the source of the seller's goods or services. *Boston Prof'l Hockey Assn. v. Dallas Cap & Emblem Mfg., Inc.*, 510 F.2d 1004, 1011 (5th Cir. 1975) ("[T]here is no reason why trademarks should ever pass into the public domain by the mere passage of time."). However, such rights are lost if usage of the mark to identify, advertise, or promote the seller's goods or services is discontinued.

The Lanham Act, 15 U.S.C. §1051, et seq., provides nationwide legal protection for federally registered trademarks. Federal registration provides prima facie evidence of the registrant's ownership and exclusive right to use of the mark for the subject goods or services as well as the validity of the registration. Legal proceedings to prevent and remedy infringement of federally registered marks may be brought in federal courts.

1. Name of Sports Team or Event

Courts have held that a professional sports club retains the right to continue using its name with a different geographical identifier if it relocates to another city. In *Johnny Blastoff, Inc. v. L.A. Rams Football, Co.*, 188 F.3d 427 (7th Cir. 1999), the Seventh Circuit held that the NFL's Los Angeles Rams club retained its rights to continue using "Rams" to identify the team name even though it was relocating to St. Louis. Observing that the franchise was founded in 1937 as the Cleveland Rams, it moved to become the Los Angeles Rams in 1946, and was again moving to become the St. Louis Rams in 1995, the court concluded, "[T]he Rams organization and the NFL had a long-established priority over the use of the 'Rams' name in connection with the same professional football team, regardless of urban affiliation." See also *Indianapolis Colts, Inc. v. Metropolitan Baltimore Football Club Ltd. P'ship*, 34 F.3d 410 (7th Cir. 1994) ("A professional sports team is like Heraclitus's river: always changing, yet always the same . . . [T]he record discloses there is as much institutional continuity between the Baltimore Colts of 1984 and the Indianapolis Colts of 1994 as there was between the Baltimore Colts of 1974 and the Baltimore Colts of 1984.").

Legal considerations aside, business reasons may justify treating the favorable goodwill developed by a popular local sports franchise over the years as "a non-transportable cultural institution." For example, the NFL decided to leave the "Browns" identity in Cleveland when the franchise relocated to Baltimore in 1996. The franchise formerly named the "Cleveland Browns" established a new identity as the "Baltimore Ravens." The NFL expansion club that began playing in Cleveland in 1999 is named the "Cleveland Browns."

Infringement of the prior user's rights occurs if another's use of the same or similar mark creates a likelihood of consumer confusion regarding the source, affiliation, endorsement, or sponsorship of sports-related products or services. For example, in *Champions Golf Club, Inc. v. Champions Golf Club, Inc.*, 78 F.3d 1111 (6th Cir. 1996), the court found a likelihood of consumer confusion regarding the (nonexistent) affiliation between two independently owned and operated golf courses located in Nicholasville, Kentucky, and Houston, Texas, that were concurrently using the "Champions" mark.

However, the use of the same mark by different teams, even if playing the same sport, does not inevitably create a likelihood of consumer confusion. Rather, a fact-specific inquiry must be made on a case-by-case basis. In *Harlem Wizards Entertainment Basketball, Inc. v. NBA Properties, Inc.*, 952 F. Supp. 1084 (D. N.J. 1997), the court held that a NBA club's proposed name change to the "Washington Wizards" would not infringe a "show basketball" team's prior use of "Harlem Wizards." Unlike the Washington NBA club, the Harlem club was not a competitive sports team that played in a professional league. The Harlem Wizards combined trick basketball and comedic basketball in a form of entertainment similar to that of the world-famous Harlem Globetrotters. Although the Harlem club had the right to use "Wizards" for its entertainment services, the court concluded that the NBA club's concurrent use of the same mark would not create a likelihood of confusion among basketball fans. The teams did not compete with each other for fan patronage. The Harlem club marketed its games to event organizers at high schools, colleges, and charitable organizations through direct mail, trade shows, and trade magazines; the NBA club advertised its games directly to fans. According to the court, survey results evidenced that consumer familiarity with the Harlem Wizards team "is almost nonexistent." There was a significant disparity between the parties' respective ticket prices, and the court found it "unlikely that consumers will attend a Harlem Wizards' game expecting to see NBA basketball or purchase NBA tickets expecting to see the Harlem Wizards perform show basketball."

2. Unauthorized Affixation of Sports Team Mark to Merchandise

American consumers annually purchase several hundred million dollars' worth of merchandise bearing the names and logos of their favorite teams. In *National Football League Properties, Inc. v. Consumer Enterprises, Inc.*, 327 N.E.2d 242, 246 (Ill. App. 1975), the court observed that the NFL's "trademarks are associated with highly successful football teams that enjoy tremendous notoriety. Through the extensive licensing arrangements developed and perpetuated by [the NFL] and its licensees, the buying public has come to associate the trademark with the sponsorship of the NFL or the particular member team involved." It concluded "that the trademarks of the teams copied by defendant indicate sponsorship or origin in addition to their ornamental value." See also *University Bookstore v. Board of Regents of the Univ. of Wis. Sys.*, 33 U.S.P.Q.2d 1385, 1405 (TTAB 1994) ("[T]he mark of a university on clothing can signify that the university endorses and licenses the sale of such wearing apparel by the manufacturer . . . . It is a question of fact as to whether consumers view such indicia as 'merely ornamental' or as symbols that identify a secondary source of sponsorship.").

Major professional sports leagues such as the NFL, NBA, MLB, and the National Hockey League (NHL) currently market, license, and enforce their clubs' trademark rights collectively through a central league-operated entity.[1] The NCAA and many of

---

[1] To maximize the revenues from its national sponsorship agreements, which generally are distributed pro rata to its member clubs, a sports league may have exclusive agreements with its official sponsors and corresponding limits on its member clubs' individual sponsorships with other companies. A club that violates league restrictions on its local sponsorship agreements may be liable for breach of contract and fiduciary duty, tortious interference with contractual relationships, and trademark infringement. See *NFL Properties, Inc. v. Dallas Cowboys Football Club, Ltd.*, 922 F. Supp. 849 (S.D.N.Y. 1996). See Chapter 11, section C.5, for a discussion of antitrust law challenges to a professional league's exclusive control and licensing of its member clubs' trademarks.

its member universities now utilize Collegiate Licensing Company, a private company, to individually market and license their respective marks for use by third parties.

To avoid weakening valuable trademark rights that may be licensed and generate substantial revenues, professional teams and educational institutions (or an entity that they have authorized to act on their behalf) must carefully monitor unauthorized third-party usage of their trademarks and take timely, necessary steps to prevent infringement of its marks. Under the Lanham Act or similar state trademark infringement laws, a "likelihood of confusion" must be shown to prove trademark infringement. The existence of actual confusion of consumers is a factor to be considered, but is not a required element. In *Board of Governors of the Univ. of North Carolina v. Helpingstine*, 714 F. Supp. 167, 172 (M.D. N.C. 1989), the court observed:

> While cases have indicated at one extreme that an alleged infringer's use of a mark with the knowledge that the public will be aware of the mark's origin is enough to establish likelihood of confusion, . . . and at the other that likelihood of confusion occurs only where there would be confusion as to the origin of the goods themselves, . . . the majority of courts have taken the middle ground on this issue. This middle position, which both parties recognize in this case, is that the requisite likelihood of confusion will exist where there is likelihood of confusion as to source, sponsorship or endorsement of the goods.

The following case illustrates how courts apply a multifactor test to determine whether the unauthorized usage of a sports team mark creates a likelihood of consumer confusion.

National Football League Properties, Inc. v. New Jersey Giants, Inc.
637 F. Supp. 507 (D.N.J. 1986)

BARRY, District Judge.

[Editors' note: Plaintiff, the New York Football Giants, Inc., owned and operated the New York Giants, an NFL team that had played all of its home games at Giants' Stadium in East Rutherford, New Jersey, since 1976. In what was then the New York Football Giants' 60-year history, the team's home games had been played at several locations in the New York metropolitan area, including Connecticut and New Jersey. To maintain continuity of tradition, the club always had used the name "New York Giants," which along with "Giants" is a federally registered trademark under the Lanham Act and under New Jersey and New York state law.

Plaintiff National Football League Properties, Inc. (NFLP), is the marketing arm of the NFL's member clubs and is licensed by the clubs to use their trademarks and is authorized to protect them from infringement. NFLP had licensed selected companies to use the "Giants" and "New York Giants" marks on a wide variety of merchandise, including T-shirts, sweatshirts, caps, jackets, and other wearing apparel. NFLP had a quality control program in which it supervised and approved the conception, design, color combinations, production, and distribution of all merchandise licensed to bear the marks of the Giants and other NFL clubs.

Defendant, the New Jersey Giants, Inc., in an effort to exploit the anomaly of a team bearing the name of one state while playing in another, began to sell various items of inferior-quality sports-related apparel bearing the words "New Jersey GIANTS" without authorization from NFLP or the New York Giants club.]

Defendant's "New Jersey GIANTS" merchandise competes directly with licensed NFL merchandise bearing the New York Football Giants' marks, because NFLP has licensed the same types of merchandise sold by defendant. Moreover, defendant's "New Jersey GIANTS" merchandise is likely to confuse consumers into believing that it is part of the wide array of licensed merchandise sponsored and approved by the New York Football Giants and available to the public through NFLP's licensing program.

The Giants and NFLP have no control over defendant's business activities or over the nature and clearly inferior quality of the merchandise sold by defendant and, indeed, the quality of that merchandise does not satisfy the quality control standards imposed by NFLP on its licensees. The sale of inferior quality merchandise bearing the NFL marks, or colorable imitations thereof, will adversely affect NFLP's business including the poor impression of the NFL and its Member Clubs that will be held by the consumer. . . .

Defendant's use of its trade name and the solicitation and sale of "New Jersey GIANTS" merchandise is also likely to confuse the public into believing that the New York Football Giants has changed the team's name to the New Jersey Giants or does not object to being referred to by that name. Neither is true, of course, and while one may wonder why the New York Giants resist a new name and may wish, perhaps, that it were otherwise, the fact remains that the Giants have the right to retain the long-standing goodwill and reputation they have developed in the name "New York Giants" and efforts in that regard will be undermined were defendant's conduct permitted to continue. . . .

In a case for service mark or trademark infringement and unfair competition, a plaintiff is entitled to a permanent injunction against a defendant by showing that that defendant's activities are likely to confuse consumers as to the source or sponsorship of the goods. In order to be confused, a consumer need not believe that a plaintiff actually produced a defendant's merchandise and placed it on the market. Rather, a consumer's belief that a plaintiff sponsored or otherwise approved the use of the mark satisfies the confusion requirement.

In a suit, as here, involving competing goods, the relevant factors to be considered in a determination as to whether a likelihood of confusion exists are:

(1) The degree of similarity between the owner's mark and the alleged infringing mark;
(2) The strength of the owner's mark;

(3) The price of the goods and other factors indicative of the care and attention expected of consumers when making a purchase;
(4) The length of time the defendant has used the mark without evidence of actual confusion;
(5) The intent of the defendant in adopting the mark;
(6) The evidence of actual confusion.

Defendant's mark "New Jersey GIANTS" is similar to the Giants' registered marks "New York Giants" and "Giants" and the dominant element of the mark—"Giants"—is identical, rendering those marks particularly confusing. . . .

The second . . . factor is similarly satisfied. Through extensive media coverage and commercial use, the NFL marks, including those of the Giants, are extremely strong, and, accordingly, are entitled to a wide range of protection.

With reference to the third . . . factor, the likelihood of confusion in this case is enhanced because both NFLP's licensed apparel bearing the Giants' marks and defendant's apparel, which is the same type of apparel, are low to moderately priced and purchasers will not exercise a high degree of care in determining whether the merchandise has been sponsored or approved by the NFL and the Giants.

Defendant, which only began selling its merchandise in 1982 and had total sales of less than $5000.00 at the time its activities were halted by the restraining order, used the mark without evidence of actual confusion. In establishing the existence of a likelihood of confusion in actions such as this, however, there is no requirement that incidents of actual confusion be shown and such evidence is unnecessary where other factors so strongly suggest the likelihood of confusion.

[T]he consumer survey conducted by Dr. Jacoby and Guideline Research demonstrated substantial actual confusion and a substantial potential for further actual confusion. The results of the survey, which found that over 57% of respondents were actually and likely confused and that football fans were confused in even higher percentages (67%), is extremely strong evidence of likely confusion, and far in excess of the evidence relied upon by courts for this purpose . . . .

Defendant's intentional, willful, and admitted adoption of a mark closely similar to the existing marks "Giants" and "New York Giants" manifested . . . an intent to confuse. . . .

Defendant's use of the Giants' marks is likely to cause confusion or mistake or deceive purchasers of such merchandise as to the source, sponsorship or approval by the NFL and the Giants. . . .

QUESTION

Why was defendant's use of "New Jersey Giants" on apparel found to infringe the New York Giants marks for "entertainment services in the form of professional football games and exhibitions"?

NOTES

1. Application of likelihood of confusion standard. Whether the requisite likelihood of confusion exists is a question of fact decided on a case-by-case basis. Examples of infringement cases include *Johnny Blastoff, Inc. v. L.A. Rams Football Co.*, 188 F.3d 427 (7th Cir. 1999) (use of "St. Louis Rams" for a fictional, cartoon sport team); *NFL v. Coors Brewing Co.*, 205 F.3d 1324 (2d Cir. 1999) (advertising Coors beer as "Official Beer of the NFL Players" without NFL's permission); *Boston Athletic Assn. v. Sullivan*, 867 F.2d 22 (1st Cir. 1989) (unauthorized use of "Boston Marathon" to sell T-shirts); *University of Ga. Athletic Assn. v. Laite*, 756 F.2d 1535 (11th Cir. 1985) (use of University of Georgia bulldog mark and logo portraying an English bulldog for "Battlin' Bulldog Beer"); *Auburn Univ. v. Moody*, 2008 WL 4877542 (M.D. Ala.) (enjoining unauthorized use of Auburn's trademarks on six-finger foam hands).

The intentional and unauthorized use of a mark on a product that is known to be "identical with, or substantially indistinguishable from" a federally registered mark (15 U.S.C. §1127) and creates a likelihood of confusion also constitutes trademark counterfeiting (15 U.S.C. §1114), which may enable the mark owner to recover statutory damages and attorneys' fees under the Lanham Act. See, e.g., *Ohio State University v. Skreened, Ltd.*, 16 F. Supp.3d 905 (S.D. Ohio 2014) (defendant's unauthorized sale of shirts bearing marks identical to or substantially indistinguishable from a university's federally registered marks on shirts sold by its licensees constitutes counterfeiting, as well as trademark infringement and unfair competition).

2. Non-infringing fair use or parody of a trademark. In *WCVB-TV v. Boston Athletic Association*, 926 F.2d 42, 46 (1st Cir. 1991), the First Circuit explained, "In technical trademark jargon, the use of words for descriptive purposes is called a 'fair use,' and the law usually permits it even if the words themselves also constitute a trademark." The court held that a television station's use of "Boston Marathon" to describe its unlicensed broadcast of the event is not trademark infringement, although another local television station was exclusively authorized to broadcast this event. This was judicially characterized as fair use of the Boston Marathon mark merely to describe the event the defendant was broadcasting that did not create any viewer confusion.

For the same reason that underlies the fair use defense, the parody of a trademark is not infringing. In *Cardtoons, L.C. v. Major League Baseball Players Assn.*, 95 F.3d 959 (10th Cir. 1996), the Tenth Circuit held that parody trading cards with caricatures of baseball players and critical commentary does not create public confusion regarding the source of the cards. The court explained that "as with all successful parodies, the effect of the cards is to amuse rather than confuse." *Id.* at 967.

B. Trademark Dilution

The Trademark Dilution Revision Act of 2006 (TDRA), which is part of the Lanham Act, protects the owner of a "famous mark" from unauthorized use of its mark or similar mark that is likely to cause dilution of the mark's distinctiveness. 15 U.S.C. §1125(c). Proof that the defendant's unauthorized usage creates an actual or likelihood of confusion or actual economic injury is not required. The statute provides a remedy for tarnishing the goodwill associated with a famous mark by using it in a disparaging manner outside the context of permissible parody, or a blurring of the mark's distinctiveness because it is used to identify a wide range of unrelated goods and services.

To be "famous," the mark must be "widely recognized by the general consuming public of the United States as a designation of source of the goods or services of the mark's owner." 15 U.S.C. §1125(c)(2)(A). The trademarks and logos of major U.S. sports events, such as the Indianapolis 500 auto race, Kentucky Derby horse race, and Masters golf tournament, as well as those of major league professional teams; sports governing bodies such as the United States Olympic Committee (USOC), the NCAA, and the National Association of Stock Car Auto Racing (NASCAR); and many universities with successful football and basketball teams are well known among sports fans and may be considered "famous" marks. In *New York City Triathlon LLC v. NYC Triathlon Club Inc.*, 95 U.S.P.Q.2d 1451 (S.D.N.Y. 2010), the court ruled that the "New York City Triathlon," "NYC Triathlon," and "NYC Tri" marks are famous because of their extensive national and international promotion and recognition. See also *Dallas Cowboys Football Club, Ltd. v. America's Team Properties*, 616 F. Supp. 2d 622 (N.D. Tex. 2009) (the Dallas Cowboys' "long duration and geographic reach" of the "America's Team" mark in connection with various products advertised and sold to public, combined with survey evidence showing recognition of the mark among a relevant consumer base, establishes that the mark is "famous" under federal dilution statute).

In *Dallas Cowboys Football Club, Ltd. v. America's Team Properties*, the court ruled that the unauthorized use of "America's Team" on apparel "blurs the uniqueness" of the mark and tarnishes it because it is used in connection with the defendant's inferior goods. Similarly, in *New York City Triathlon LLC v. NYC Triathlon Club Inc.*, another court held that defendant's unauthorized usage of the "New York City Triathlon" marks as the name of its athletic club blurred and tarnished their distinctiveness in violation of the dilution statute by creating a negative association because of defendant's reputation for poor customer service.

The following cases, which were decided prior to the enactment of the TDRA, provide graphic examples of usages that tarnish sports marks. In *NBA Properties v. Untertainment Records LLC*, 1999 WL 335147 (S.D.N.Y. 1999), a federal district court held that the unauthorized use of an altered NBA logo showing a silhouetted basketball player dribbling a basketball with a handgun in his other hand to advertise a rap album violates the federal dilution statute. Because "linking the NBA Logo with violence and drugs will adversely color the public's impressions of the NBA," the court concluded that "[a]ny suggestion that the NBAP or the NBA endorses violence, gunplay, or drug use, or that they have chosen to associate themselves with those who do, will likely tarnish their reputation with their corporate customers and partners, as well as the public at large." Similarly, in *Dallas Cowboys Cheerleaders, Inc. v. Pussycat Cinema, Ltd.*, 604 F.2d 200, 205 (2d Cir. 1979), the Second Circuit ruled that the unauthorized use of female actors wearing well-known Dallas Cowboys Cheerleaders uniforms in a "sexually depraved film . . . has 'tendency to impugn (plaintiff's services) and injure plaintiff's business reputation.'" See also *Boston Red Sox Baseball Club LP v. Sherman*, 88 U.S.P.Q.2d 1581 (affirming refusal to register "Sex Rod" for clothing because it would disparage MLB club's well-known "Red Sox" mark).

C. Anticybersquatting Consumer Protection Act of 1999

The significant expansion and use of the Internet in recent years has given rise to "cyber-squatting," which is the registration of well-known trademarks (including those of sports teams and events) as domain names (i.e., website addresses) by non–trademark holders. Their objective is to try to sell rights to the domain names back to the trademark owners at a profit or to attract Internet users to their websites, such as online sports gambling. Cybersquatting that creates a likelihood of consumer confusion constitutes trademark infringement and unfair competition. See, e.g., *March Madness Athletic Assn. v. Netfire, Inc.*, 2003 WL 22047375 (N.D. Tex. 2003) (www.marchmadness.com infringes NCAA's federally registered "March Madness" mark for basketball tournament); *Quokka Sports, Inc. v. Cup Int'l Internet Ventures*, 99 F. Supp. 2d 1105 (N.D. Cal. 1999) (defendants' website, www.americascup.com, "masquerad[es] as an official site associated with the America's Cup event," located at *www.americascup.org*, and infringes registered mark "America's Cup"). It also may constitute trademark dilution and violate the Anti-cybersquatting Consumer Protection Act (ACPA) of 1999, 15 U.S.C. §1129.

The ACPA provides a trademark owner with a cause of action against a defendant for bad-faith registration or use of a domain name that is (1) identical to or confusingly similar to a distinctive mark; or (2) identical to or confusingly similar to, or dilutes, a famous mark. 15 U.S.C. §1125 (d)(1). See *March Madness Athletic Assn. v. Netfire, Inc.*, 2003 WL 22047375 (N.D. Tex.) (finding that defendants' registration and use of www.march-madness.com violates ACPA, entitling NCAA to injunctive relief). In addition to available remedies under the Lanham Act, the ACPA provides for statutory damages for bad-faith registration of domain names after the November 29, 1999, effective date of the statute. 15 U.S.C. §1117(d). The ACPA also authorizes an action against the domain name itself for forfeiture or transfer to the trademark owner if the domain name registrant cannot be located or is not subject to personal jurisdiction by an American court. 15 U.S.C. §1125(d)(2)(A).

As a faster and less expensive alternative to litigation against a cybersquatter under the Lanham Act or ASCP, a mark owner may choose to instead utilize arbitration procedures under the Uniform Domain Name Dispute Resolution Policy (UDRP). The domain name registration agreement incorporates the terms of the UDRP, which governs disputes between the domain name registrant and others concerning the registration and use of a domain name. Several sports-related domain name disputes have been resolved by UDRP proceedings, including the first decided case under this procedure. See *World Wrestling Fed'n Entm't, Inc. v. Bosman*, WIPO, Case No. D99-0001, January 14, 2000, available at *http://pub.bna.com/ptcj/d990001.htm* (finding bad faith registration and use of www.worldwrestlingfederation.com domain name, which is identical or confusingly similar to federally registered World Wrestling Federation trademark and service mark, and ordering transfer of domain name registration to owner of marks).

D. Olympic Marks

The USOC owns the exclusive right to use and license the Olympic marks within the United States. *United States Olympic Comm. v. Intelicense Corp., S.A.*, 737 F.2d 263 (2d

Cir. 1984), *cert. denied*, 469 U.S. 982 (1984). The Ted Stevens Olympic and Amateur Sports Act (ASA) prohibits the unauthorized usage of the Olympic name and marks, including the five-ring Olympic symbol, "for the purpose of trade, to induce the sale of any goods or services, or to promote any theatrical exhibition, athletic performance, or competition." 36 U.S.C. §220506(c). The ASA extended the USOC's exclusive property rights to include the "Pan-American" and "Paralympiad" marks, which are now protected to the same extent as the Olympic marks. *United States Olympic Comm. v. Toy Truck Lines, Inc.*, 237 F.3d 1331 (Fed. Cir. 2001).

The Olympic marks have a broader scope of protection under federal law beyond that generally provided to other trademarks and service marks. In *San Francisco Arts & Athletics, Inc. v. United States Olympic Committee*, 483 U.S. 522 (1987), the Supreme Court held that the ASA's language and legislative intent evidenced Congress's intent to grant the USOC exclusive rights to control use of the Olympic marks regardless of whether their unauthorized usage creates a likelihood of confusion. The Court explained:

> One reason for Congress to grant the USOC exclusive control of the word "Olympic," as with other trademarks, is to ensure that the USOC receives the benefit of its own efforts so that the USOC will have an incentive to continue to produce a "quality product," that, in turn, benefits the public. See 1 J. McCarthy, Trademarks and Unfair Competition §2:1, pp. 44–47 (1984). But in the special circumstance of the USOC, Congress has a broader public interest in promoting, through the activities of the USOC, the participation of amateur athletes from the United States in "the great four-yearly sport festival, the Olympic Games." . . . The USOC's goal under the Olympic Charter, Rule 24(B), is to further the Olympic movement, that has as its aims: "to promote the development of those physical and moral qualities which are the basis of sport"; "to educate young people through sport in a spirit of better understanding between each other and of friendship, thereby helping to build a better and more peaceful world"; and "to spread the Olympic principles throughout the world, thereby creating international goodwill." Congress' interests in promoting the USOC's activities include these purposes as well as those specifically enumerated in the USOC's charter. Section 110 directly advances these governmental interests by supplying the USOC with the means to raise money to support the Olympics and encourages the USOC's activities by ensuring that it will receive the benefits of its efforts.

Id. at 537–38. Defendant's unauthorized use of "Gay Olympic Games" for an athletics competition in San Francisco was found to be infringing regardless of whether it tends to cause any confusion. See also *USOC v. Xclusive Leisure & Hospitality Ltd.*, 2008 WL 3971120 (N.D. Cal.) (enjoining unauthorized usage of Olympic marks in United States to advertise and sell tickets and hospitality packages to the Beijing Olympics).

The ASA "grandfathers" the rights of those who lawfully used the Olympic marks prior to 1950 (the date that the ASA's predecessor statute was enacted) to advertise and sell their goods or services. However, such users may not expand the scope of their goods or services sold under the Olympic mark, or adopt new marks with the word "Olympic" therein. In *O-M Bread, Inc. v. United States Olympic Committee*, 65 F.3d 933 (Fed. Cir. 1995), the Federal Circuit held that the proposed use of "Olympic Kids" for bakery products is not a permitted extension of a prior user's grandfathered right to use the Olympic mark for bakery products. The court found these "different marks present a different commercial impression and are not legal equivalents." *Id.* at 938. It concluded that "commercial growth into new 'Olympic'-based marks is outside the letter of the statute, as well as outside its spirit."

The ASA does not prohibit all unauthorized uses of the Olympic marks. As one court observed, "[B]ecause the [ASA] grants the USOC rights over and above both the common law and [the Lanham Act], the language and scope of the Act must be strictly construed." *United States Olympic Committee v. American Media, Inc.*, 156 F. Supp. 2d 1200, 1209 (D. Colo. 2001). For example, the media may report about Olympic sports competitions, which would include use of the word "Olympic" and competition photographs containing Olympic marks in news reporting. In *American Media*, the court ruled that the mere publication of an Olympic preview magazine titled "Olympics USA" is noncommercial speech that does not infringe the USOC's rights under the ASA. However, the publisher's usage of the Olympic marks in a manner falsely suggesting that the USOC officially endorses or authorizes its magazine would violate the Lanham Act.

Problem 9-1

(a) Can the NFL prevent a women's professional football league from identifying itself as the "National Women's Football League" and calling its championship game the SupHer Bowl?

(b) Consider whether any of the following unauthorized usages violates the USOC's rights in the Olympic marks:

(i) An Iowa farmer prunes his cornfield into the shape of the interlocking Olympic rings during the summer before the 2002 Salt Lake City Winter Olympics. Does the question of violation depend on whether he charges a fee to enter his cornfield and view the Olympic rings?

(ii) A group holds the "Redneck Olympics," featuring the cigarette flip, bobbing for pigs' feet, mud pit belly flop, toilet seat throwing, big hair contest, and seed spitting.

AMBUSH MARKETING

Ambush marketing is a creative advertising practice by a business other than an official sponsor that seeks to create an association with a sports event without using the event's name, trademarks, or logos. It encompasses "intentional efforts to weaken [a] competitor's official association with a sport organization, which has been acquired through the payment of sponsorship fees," as well as seeking "to capitalize on the goodwill, reputation, and popularity of a particular sport or event by creating an association without the authorization or consent of the necessary parties." Steve

McKelvey and John Grady, *Ambush Marketing: The Legal Battleground for Sports Marketers*, 21 Ent. & Sports L. 8, 9 (2004).

Official event sponsors claim that ambush marketing dilutes the value of their sponsorships. Ambush marketing may harm event organizers, which need sponsorship money to fund production of a sporting event. When ambush marketers receive commercial benefits by free-riding on an event's popularity or goodwill, the value of an official sponsorship may be significantly reduced. This creates an economic disincentive to be an official event sponsor, with a corresponding incentive to engage in ambush marketing instead. This in turn reduces the value of official sponsorships and causes sports event organizers to lose sponsorship revenues. See *United States Olympic Comm. v. American Media, Inc.*, 156 F. Supp. 2d 1200, 1204 (D. Colo. 2001) (alleging that defendant's ambush marketing will encourage other companies to do so, which will adversely affect USOC's ability to fund U.S. participation in the Olympic Games). Successful ambush marketing campaigns also may harm consumers of sporting events. A decrease in sponsorship revenues could force event organizers to find new revenue sources (e.g., cable or pay-per-view television broadcasts rather than free-to-air telecasts), or possibly result in the discontinuance of sports events that lack adequate commercial sponsorship support.

Under current U.S. law, ambush marketing is illegal only if it creates a likelihood of consumer confusion. In *Federation Internationale de Football v. Nike, Inc.*, 285 F. Supp. 2d 64 (D.D.C. 2003), the court refused to preliminarily enjoin Nike's use of "USA 03" to advertise and sell various products in connection with its sponsorship of the U.S. Women's National Soccer Team. Plaintiff Fédération Internationale de Football (FIFA) used "USA 2003" in connection with its 2003 women's soccer World Cup held in the United States. Nike was not a World Cup sponsor and was not authorized to use FIFA's marks. Although Nike did not use FIFA's name or refer to the World Cup, FIFA alleged that Nike's usage of "USA 03" was infringing and illegally interfered with its official sponsorship contracts.

Holding that FIFA has not shown a substantial likelihood of success on the merits of its claims, the court observed:

> Nike argues that its use of "USA 03" (or "United States 2003") is innocent, given the company's sponsorship of the Women's National Team. After all, the team that Nike is backing is the United States team for the year 2003, and therefore, "USA 03" is an appropriate and understandable way for Nike to associate itself with that group of players. The Court agrees that Nike's preexisting and entirely legitimate relationship with the Women's World Cup provides an important context for its use of the disputed marks. For there can be little doubt, in light of the success that the U.S. women enjoyed in the 1999 World Cup, that the team and the event are already linked in the public mind. As such, Nike's careful use of a mark that might be affiliated with both is not necessarily an indication of bad faith, but instead of savvy marketing. Whenever that team plays in this country, it is to be expected that the sponsors of both the team and the event would want to use trademarks that reflect the United States and that emphasize this year's date. Nike's doing so here thus may not indicate a deliberate attempt to deceive the buying public.

Id. at 73–74.

Even if there currently are only limited legal remedies for combating ambush marketing, a sports event organizer can minimize its successful use and resulting detrimental effects by developing a comprehensive anti–ambush marketing plan. For example, it can contractually prohibit broadcasters from selling commercial time to the competitors of official sponsors. Nonsponsor advertisements and signage in connection with a sporting event should be carefully monitored to ensure that the event's name, marks, and logos are not included therein.

Courts will enforce contract rights to prevent unfair competition that causes a likelihood of consumer confusion. In *Mastercard International, Inc. v. Sprint Communications Co.*, 1994 WL 97097 (S.D.N.Y.), *aff'd*, 23 F.2d 397 (2d Cir. 1994), an international soccer federation granted exclusive rights to Mastercard to use the 1994 World Cup Soccer Tournament trademarks on "all card-based payment and account access devices." The court held that Mastercard's contract rights precluded the U.S. Local Organizing Committee from authorizing Sprint Communications to use and imprint those marks on phone cards. Finding that Sprint's conduct violated the Lanham Act, the court concluded: "Sprint wishes to use the World Cup marks to convey to the world the false impression that its use of the marks on calling cards is officially sanctioned by the World Cup organization. Clearly, that is not the case, and Mastercard, which has the exclusive right to use the mark for such purposes, is entitled to enjoin this deceptive use."

Problem 9-2

Zeebok paid a $25 million sponsorship fee to the USOC to be designated as the official sneaker of the 2012 Olympic Games. One week before the Games begin, Badidas, a rival athletic footwear company, begins airing a series of commercials with scenes from past Olympic Games showing medal-winning track athletes wearing its sneakers. Consider whether Badidas's ambush marketing campaign is illegal and what additional information might be needed to make this determination.

REAL-TIME GAME ACCOUNTS AND BROADCASTING RIGHTS

KEY TERMS
- Athletic events not copyrightable
- Copyright Act of 1976
- Copyright infringement
- Misappropriation
- Patent law
- Unauthorized public performance of copyrighted work

A. Historical Background

Historically, producers of sporting events sought to protect live game broadcasts and play-by-play descriptions from unauthorized viewer usage under state misappropriation, unfair competition, and contract laws. The then-current federal copyright laws did not provide any legal protection for sports events or their broadcasts. Relying primarily on the misappropriation doctrine established by the Supreme Court in *International News Service v. Associated Press*, 248 U.S. 215 (1918), courts broadly held that the creator of a game or athletic event has an exclusive property right in its commercial value under state law. Recognizing that the production of athletic events requires the expenditure of substantial time, effort, and money, these courts prohibited observers and listeners—whether inside or outside the facility in which the event occurred—from unauthorized transmission of live game broadcasts and descriptions to the public for commercial benefit.

For example, in *Pittsburgh Athletic Co. v. KQV Broadcasting Co.*, 24 F. Supp. 490 (W.D. Pa. 1938), the court held: "the Pittsburgh Athletic Company [owner of the Pittsburgh Pirates professional baseball club], by reason of its creation of the game, its control of the park, and its restriction of the dissemination of news therefrom, has a property right in such news, and the right to control the use thereof for a reasonable time following the games." The Pittsburgh Athletic Company sold the exclusive rights to broadcast Pirates games played at Forbes Field to General Mills, Inc. The defendant broadcast play-by-play accounts of Pirates games as described by observers stationed outside Forbes Field who were able to see them being played. Finding that the defendant's conduct violated the baseball club's property rights, the court ruled that its unauthorized broadcast of Pirates games constitutes misappropriation, unfair competition, and unlawful interference with the parties' contract rights.

B. Nature and Scope of Copyright Law Protection

To encourage creative expression such as books, movies, music, and other works, the federal Copyright Act of 1976 protects only "original works of authorship fixed in any tangible medium of expression." 17 U.S.C. §102(a). It does not protect ideas, procedures, systems, or methods of operation "regardless of the form in which it is described, explained, illustrated, or embodied." 17 U.S.C. §102(b). Therefore, neither the underlying idea for a type of athletic event nor a system or method of playing a sport is copyrightable.

In *Hoopla Sports and Entertainment, Inc. v. Nike, Inc.*, 947 F. Supp. 347 (N.D. Ill. 1996), the court held that the concept of an international high school all-star basketball game is not copyrightable and plaintiff cannot prevent defendant from using its idea to conduct a similar event. The court observed that "the methods or rules of playing basketball games are not generally copyrightable."

Similarly, in *Seltzer v. Sunbrock*, 22 F. Supp. 621, 639 (S.D. Cal. 1938), the court rejected the plaintiff's claim that his idea of staging a transcontinental roller-skating race is protected by copyright law. It held: "What [plaintiff] really composed was a description of a system for conducting races on roller skates. A system, as such, can never be copyrighted. If it finds any protection, it must come from the patent laws."[2]

In *NBA v. Motorola, Inc.*, 105 F.3d 841 (2d Cir. 1997), the Second Circuit ruled that athletic events are not copyrightable. It concluded:

> In our view, the underlying basketball games do not fall within the subject matter of federal copyright protection because they do not constitute "original works of authorship" under 17 U.S.C. §102(a). Section 102(a) lists eight categories of "works of authorship" covered by the act, including such categories as "literary works," "musical works," and "dramatic works." The list does not include athletic events, and, although the list is concededly non-exclusive, such events are neither similar nor analogous to any of the listed categories.
>
> Sports events are not "authored" in any common sense of the word. There is, of course, at least at the professional level, considerable preparation for a game. However, the preparation is as much an expression of hope or faith as a determination of what will actually happen. Unlike movies, plays, television programs, or operas, athletic events are competitive and have no underlying script. Preparation may even cause mistakes to succeed, like the broken play in football that gains yardage because the opposition could not expect it. Athletic events may also result in wholly unanticipated occurrences, the most notable recent event being in a championship baseball game in which interference with a fly ball caused an umpire to signal erroneously a home run.
>
> What "authorship" there is in a sports event, moreover, must be open to copying by competitors if fans are to be attracted. If the inventor of the T-formation in football had been able to copyright it, the sport might have come to an end instead of prospering. Even where athletic preparation most resembles authorship — figure skating, gymnastics, and, some would uncharitably say, professional wrestling — a performer who conceives and executes a particularly graceful and difficult — or, in the case of wrestling, seemingly painful — acrobatic feat cannot copyright it without impairing the underlying competition in the future. A claim of being the only athlete to perform a feat doesn't mean much if no one else is allowed to try.

Id. at 846.

Although the underlying sports event is not copyrightable, the broadcast of a sports event is subject to copyright protection under the Copyright Act of 1976. The *Motorola* court explained:

> [R]ecorded broadcasts of NBA games — as opposed to the games themselves — are now entitled to copyright protection. The Copyright Act was amended in 1976 specifically to insure that simultaneously-recorded transmissions of live performances and sporting events would meet the Act's requirement that the original work of authorship be "fixed in any tangible medium of expression." 17 U.S.C. §102(a). . . . Congress specifically had sporting events in mind: "[T]he bill seeks to resolve, through the definition of 'fixation' in section 101, the status of live broadcasts — sports, news

---

[2] To be patentable under federal law, a sport or game must be useful, nonobvious, and novel and satisfy other requirements established by the Patent Act. For example, the Arena Football League (AFL) obtained U.S. Patent No. 4,911,433, which was issued on March 27, 1990, for its unique system for playing indoor professional football. The Patent Office also issued U.S. Patent No. 5,616,089 for a particular method of golf putting.

coverage, live performances of music, etc.—that are reaching the public in unfixed form but that are simultaneously being recorded." H.R. No. 94-1476 at 52, *reprinted in* 1976 U.S.C.C.A.N. at 5665. The House Report also makes clear that it is the broadcast, not the underlying game, that is the subject of copyright protection. . . .

Id. at 847.

The Copyright Act of 1976 grants a copyright owner several exclusive rights, including, as most relevant for purposes of this discussion, the right to copy or duplicate a copyrighted broadcast of a sports event and to "publicly perform" it. 17 U.S.C. §106. The act provides that anyone who violates any of these exclusive rights engages in copyright infringement. 17 U.S.C. §501(a). The owner of a copyright has a variety of available remedies for infringement, including injunctive relief and the recovery of actual or statutory damages, the infringer's profits, and attorney fees. 17 U.S.C. §§502–505.

A threshold issue is who owns the copyright to the broadcast of a sports event—the clubs playing the particular game, the league, the broadcaster of the game, or the players participating in the game? In general, ownership of a copyright initially vests in the "author(s)" of the work. 17 U.S.C. §201(a). The Copyright Act recognizes that a work may be jointly authored and its copyright co-owned. 17 U.S.C. §201(a). Within a sports league, broadcasting rights and copyright ownership of broadcast games generally are determined by contract. A broadcaster's camera angles, types of shots, use of instant replays, split screens, special effects, and commentary supplies the creativity necessary for "authorship" of a broadcast sports event. *Baltimore Orioles, Inc. v. Major League Baseball Players Assn.*, 805 F.2d 663, 668-69 (7th Cir. 1986); *National Assn. of Broadcasters v. Copyright Royalty Tribunal*, 675 F.2d 367, 377–79 (D.C. Cir. 1982). Ownership of the copyright for a sports broadcast vis-à-vis the league/clubs and the broadcaster generally is contractually determined. See, e.g., *NFL v. Insight Telecomm. Corp.*, 158 F. Supp. 2d 124, 128 (D. Mass. 2001) ("The NFL owns the copyright in all regular season and post-season NFL game telecasts, as confirmed by the League's contracts with the networks").

In *Baltimore Orioles, Inc. v. Major League Baseball Players Association*, 805 F.2d 663, 670 (7th Cir. 1986), the Seventh Circuit held:

> Because the Players are employees and their performances before broadcast audiences are within the scope of their employment, the telecasts of major league baseball games, which consist of the Players' performances, are works made for hire within the meaning of §201(b). . . . Thus, in the absence of an agreement to the contrary, the Clubs are presumed to own all of the rights encompassed in the telecasts of the games. The district court found that there was no written agreement that the Clubs would not own the copyright to the telecasts, and, therefore, that the copyright was owned by the Clubs.

See also *Big Fights Inc. v. Ficara*, 40 U.S.P.Q.2d 1377, 1378 (S.D.N.Y. 1996) (the promoter of a professional boxing match, not the boxers, owns copyright in the film of the match).

C. Copyright Infringement of a Sports Broadcast

In *NFL v. McBee & Bruno's, Inc.*, 792 F.2d 726 (8th Cir. 1986), the court ruled that the unauthorized interception of the broadcast of a sports event through the use of satellite dish antennae by a commercial establishment, which occurred in the mid-1980s, constitutes copyright infringement. It explained, "The Copyright Act protects 'original works of authorship fixed in any tangible medium,' 17 U.S.C. §102(a), including 'motion pictures and other audiovisual works,' 17 U.S.C. §102(a)(6). As for live broadcasts, such as the football games at issue here, the Act states that '[a] work consisting of sounds, images, or both, that are being transmitted, is "fixed" . . . if a fixation of the work is being made simultaneously with its transmission,' 17 U.S.C. §101; '[t]o "transmit" is defined as "to communicate . . . by any device or process whereby images or sounds are received beyond the place from which they are sent." *Id.* at 731–32. This was an unauthorized public performance of a copyrighted sports broadcast, which violates federal copyright law.

The following case illustrates that the Internet provides a modern means for infringing copyrighted sports event broadcasts, including by transmissions originating outside the United States, and enables unauthorized webcasts to occur throughout the world—conduct that violates U.S. law, but possibly not foreign laws.

NFL v. TVRadioNow Corp.
53 U.S.P.Q.2d 1831 (W.D. Pa. 2000)

ZIEGLER, J.

This is a civil action for money damages and equitable relief, filed by the National Football League ("NFL"), National Basketball Association ("NBA"), and NBA Properties, Inc. ("NBA Properties") (collectively "the Sports Leagues") . . . contending that defendants violated the Copyright Act, 17 U.S.C. Section 106. . . .

The gravamen of this dispute concerns the public performance of plaintiffs' copyrighted programming from Toronto, Canada, to computer users in the United States since November 30, 1999, over the Internet. Specifically, defendants have streamed copyrighted professional football and basketball games as well as copyrighted programs such as "60 Minutes," "Ally McBeal," and "Star Trek Voyager," framed with advertisements obtained by defendants. Plaintiffs allege that defendants have captured United States programming from television stations in Buffalo, New York and elsewhere, converted these television signals into computerized data and streamed them over the Internet from a website called iCraveTV.com. According to plaintiffs, any Internet user may access iCraveTV.com by simply entering three digits of any Canadian area code, one of which is provided to the user on the site itself, and by clicking two other buttons. Further, Internet users from the United States and elsewhere easily may revisit the site because iCraveTV causes a small file, or cookie, to be deposited in a user's computer during his or her initial visit so that the user can automatically bypass defendants' screening process. . . . [T]he Court is mindful of the long-standing precept that the United States copyright laws do not have extraterritorial operation. *See Allarcom Pay Television, Ltd. v. General Instrument Corp.*, 69 F.3d 381 [36 USPQ2d 1654] (9th Cir.1995).

Defendants argue that their website is for Canadian viewers only and it is not intended for citizens of the United States and elsewhere. Thus, the argument continues, the alleged improper acts are limited to Canada.

Plaintiffs have presented testimony, sworn affidavits and declarations establishing that Pennsylvania residents have accessed defendants' website and viewed the programs which were streamed thereon. Further, defendants posted an article on the Website by a United States citizen noting that access to defendants' website could be obtained by any United States citizen with little or no difficulty.

Accordingly, when an allegedly infringing act occurring without the United States is publicly performed within the United States, the Copyright Act is implicated and a district court possesses jurisdiction. Subject matter jurisdiction exists because, although the streaming of the plaintiffs' programming originated in Canada, acts of infringement were committed within the United States when United States citizens received and viewed defendants' streaming of the copyrighted materials. These constitute, at a minimum, public performances in the United States . . . .

The plaintiffs have established without rejoinder from the defendants that they have copyright . . . ownership of several items, including, among others, the Super Bowl, the NBA Finals, and the NFL playoff games and regular League games. . . .

Defendants do not deny that they have copied these items, represented themselves as the authors and that they have publicly performed them over the Internet. Rather, defendants argue that there is no desire on the part of defendants for any United States residents to access iCraveTV. Notwithstanding defendants' intentions, the Court finds that plaintiffs have presented sufficient facts to establish their claims of copyright . . . infringement. . . .

A January 25, 2000 breakdown of "impressions" and "clicks" onto the iCraveTV website, generated by a private ad serving system (DART) utilized by Cox, reported 1.6 million impressions (page views) from United States visitors on the iCraveTV website. This figure was second only to the figure for Canada, which was 2.0 million.

Defendants also use a "Real Video" server to stream video programming through their website. This server maintains "logs" of the Internet Protocol addresses of computers that contact defendants' server to obtain access to video programming. An analysis of the Real Video server logs shows that substantial numbers of persons in the United States received the streaming of programming, including programming in which plaintiffs own copyrights. . . . [E]vidence in the record shows that plaintiffs are likely to succeed in showing that defendants are unlawfully publicly performing plaintiffs' copyrighted works in the United States. Defendants do so by transmitting (through use of "streaming" technology) performances of the works to the public by means of the telephone lines and computers that make up the Internet. 17 U.S.C. Section 101. This activity violates plaintiffs' rights to perform their works publicly and to authorize others to do so. 17 U.S.C. Sections 106, 501(a). . . .

Defendants have submitted a declaration of a Canadian law professor, Michael Geist, which argues that defendants' activities are permissible under Canadian law.

However, because plaintiffs seek relief under U.S. law for infringements of the U.S. Copyright Act, there is no need for this Court to address any issue of Canadian law. . . .

[Editors' note: The court preliminarily and permanently enjoined defendants from infringing plaintiffs' copyrighted works through streaming or other means into the United States via the iCraveTV.com site or any other Internet site or online facility without plaintiffs' prior consent.]

QUESTION

Why does the defendants' conduct constitute copyright infringement?

NOTE

What is infringing conduct? Tape-recording televised sports broadcasts for solely in-home, personal use is not copyright infringement. *Sony Corp. of Am. v. Universal City Studios, Inc.*, 464 U.S. 417, 449 (1984) (characterizing this activity as "time-shifting for private home use" that is noninfringing fair use of copyrighted broadcast pursuant to §107 of Copyright Act).

However, the unauthorized public performance of taped broadcasts of sports events (which would include posting on YouTube) constitutes copyright infringement. In *New Boston Television, Inc. v. Entertainment Sports Programming Network, Inc.*, 215 U.S.P.Q. 755 (D. Mass. 1981), ESPN contended that its rebroadcast of taped sports event highlights is permissible fair use. Rejecting this alleged defense and finding copyright infringement, the court stated:

> While protection of the public right of access to [newsworthy] information is a primary justification for the fair use defense, this right is sufficiently protected merely by enabling defendants to report the underlying facts which the plaintiff's videotapes record. It does not however permit defendants to appropriate the plaintiff's expression of that information by copying the plaintiff's films themselves.

Id. at 756.

In *NBA v. Motorola, Inc.*, 105 F.3d 841 (2d Cir. 1997), the Second Circuit held that the defendants' reproduction of real-time NBA basketball game statistics (e.g., teams playing, score, time in possession of the ball, time remaining in game) which information was obtained from games broadcast on television and radio does not constitute copyright infringement. Defendants hired persons to gather this real-time game information from NBA games broadcast on television, which was keyed into a computer and then compiled and formatted for retransmission via satellite and FN radio networks to purchasers of its SportTrax paging devices that displayed this information. The court explained:

> Although the broadcasts are protected under copyright law, the district court correctly held that Motorola and STATS did not infringe NBA's copyright because they

reproduced only facts from the broadcasts, not the expression or description of the game that constitutes the broadcast. The "fact/expression dichotomy" is a bedrock principle of copyright law that "limits severely the scope of protection in fact-based works." *Feist Publications, Inc. v. Rural Tel. Service Co.*, 499 U.S. 340, 350, 111 S.Ct. 1282, 1290, 113 L.Ed.2d 358 (1991). "'No author may copyright facts or ideas. The copyright is limited to those aspects of the work — termed 'expression' — that display the stamp of the author's originality.'" *Id.* (quoting *Harper & Row, Publishers, Inc. v. Nation Enter.*, 471 U.S. 539, 547, 105 S.Ct. 2218, 2224, 85 L.Ed.2d 588 (1985)).

> We agree with the district court that the "[d]efendants provide purely factual information which any patron of an NBA game could acquire from the arena without any involvement from the director, cameramen, or others who contribute to the originality of a broadcast."

Id. at 847.

D. Misappropriation of Real-Time Game Accounts and Scores

In *Motorola*, the Second Circuit ruled that federal copyright law preempted (i.e., barred or precluded) the NBA's state law commercial misappropriation claim because the defendants' collection and dissemination of "strictly factual information about the games," which was obtained from NBA games broadcast on television and radio and already in the public domain, did not have an adverse economic effect on the production or broadcasting of NBA games.

In *Morris Communications Corp. v. PGA Tour, Inc.*, 235 F. Supp. 2d 1269 (M.D. Fla. 2002), *aff'd*, 364 F.3d 1288 (11th Cir. 2004), *cert. denied*, 543 U.S. 919 (2004), a federal district court held that the producer of a sports event may limit access to real-time scores and game information by contract (for example, by allowing admission only if ticket holders or members of the media agree to comply with certain conditions), which would give rise to a misappropriation claim if violated. The court stated:

> The PGA Tour's property right does not come from copyright law, as copyright law does not protect factual information, like golf scores. *See Feist Publications v. Rural Tel. Serv. Co.*, 499 U.S. 340, 348, 111 S.Ct. 1282, 113 L.Ed.2d 358 (1991). However, the PGA Tour controls the right of access to that information and can place restrictions on those attending the private event, giving the PGA Tour a property right that the Court will protect. . . . [T]he instant case deals with facts that are not subject to copyright protection. The compiler of the information . . . collects information, which it created, at a cost. Also the events occur on private property to which the general public does not have unfettered access, and the creator of the event can place restrictions upon those who enter the private property. The vastly increased speed that the Internet makes available does not change the calculus or the underlying property right. Accordingly, the PGA Tour . . . has a property right in the compilation of scores, but that property right disappears when the underlying information is in the public domain.

Id. at 1281–82.

In *National Football League v. Governor of the State of Delaware*, 435 F. Supp. 1372 (D. Del. 1977), the court reached a similar result. The NFL sought to enjoin the unauthorized use of its game schedules and scores as the basis for a Delaware state football lottery. Although defendants profited from public popularity generated by NFL games, the court found no misappropriation of the league's property because this information was "obtained from public sources and are utilized only after plaintiffs have disseminated them at large and no longer have any expectation of generating revenue from further dissemination." However, it cautioned that defendants could not use NFL game scores in a manner that creates a likelihood of consumer confusion regarding the NFL's authorization or sponsorship of its lottery.

In *Wisconsin Interscholastic Athletic Assn. v. Gannett Co., Inc.*, 658 F.3d 614 (7th Cir. 2011), the Seventh Circuit held that a high school athletic association, which the parties stipulated is a state actor, has a property right in its tournament games and that its exclusive contract to stream games over the Internet does not violate the First Amendment. Relying on *Zacchini v. Scripps-Howard Broadcasting Co.*, the court ruled that the "WIAA has the right to package and distribute its performance; nothing in the First Amendment confers on the media an affirmative right to broadcast entire performances." *Id.* at 622.

Problem 9-3

MLB Advanced Media, MLB's Internet subsidiary, claims ownership of all real-time data used by sports websites to provide live graphic simulations of baseball games over the Internet. However, some webcasters operate sites providing very detailed game accounts, including the location of each pitch, that are updated every 30 to 90 seconds. Some webcasters obtain this information from employees who are present at MLB games, whereas others get their data from employees who are watching televised games or listening to radio broadcasts. One webcaster is licensed to use the real-time data from MLB games, but no others are willing to pay the fee for obtaining licensing rights. Evaluate whether the unauthorized description of a baseball game infringes MLB's intellectual property rights.

ATHLETES' LANHAM ACT AND STATE LAW PRIVACY, REPUTATION, AND PUBLICITY RIGHTS

Today's professional athlete is a celebrity and probably attains that status, at least locally, much earlier than the onset of his or her professional career. However, it has been only in relatively recent years that astounding amounts of money are made from the utilization of the celebrity athlete's name and likeness. The best-known athletes have entered into lucrative deals to promote and endorse a wide variety of products and services. Income earned from the licensing of a player's identity to sell products and services may be greater than that derived from his or her athletic earnings. For example, the most elite and widely recognized male and female athletes, such as LeBron James, Tiger Woods, and Maria Sharapova, earn millions annually, far surpassing their income from purely athletic accomplishments. All of them have multiple endorsement deals carefully crafted by their representatives. In 2014–2015, James's salary was $20.8 million and his endorsement income was $44 million; Woods's earnings were $600,000 and his endorsement income was $50 million; and Sharapova's earnings were $6.7 million and her endorsement income was $23 million (see *http://www.forbes.com/athletes/list/#tab:overall*, which also includes lots of information on other athletes). However, others may attempt to capitalize on an athlete's name, likeness, or identity without authorization, which may violate the federal Lanham Act or various state laws.

A. Lanham Act

The unauthorized misappropriation of an athlete's name, likeness, or other aspects of his or her identity violates §43(a) of the Lanham Act, 15 U.S.C. §1125(a), if it causes consumer confusion regarding whether he or she has endorsed or sponsored particular products and services. This federal statutory claim provides a consumer protection–based cause of action. Various state laws establish a similar standard as well. As the Ninth Circuit has observed: "Many people may assume that when a celebrity's name is used in a television commercial, the celebrity endorses the product advertised." *Abdul-Jabbar v. General Motors Corp.*, 85 F.3d 407, 413 (9th Cir. 1996).

In *Hillerich & Bradsby v. Christian Brothers*, 943 F. Supp. 1136 (D. Minn. 1996), the defendant was selling its Pro-Rite hockey blades with the name "Messier" clearly affixed on the blade and product label, without the permission of Mark Messier, one of professional hockey's most recognized players, who led the Edmonton Oilers and the New York Rangers to a total of six Stanley Cup championships and was twice voted the most valuable player in the NHL. The court ruled that this unauthorized commercial use of Messier's name created the false impression that he endorsed the defendant's hockey blades and enjoined the defendant from using Messier's name on its products or in connection with their advertising and sale without his express permission.

An athlete may use his or her name as a trademark or service mark, and it may be federally registered under the Lanham Act after acquiring secondary meaning as the source or origin of goods or services (i.e., it is a brand name the public associates with an identifiable athlete). For example, the name "Tiger Woods" has been federally registered as a trademark for art prints, calendars, mounted photographs, notebooks, pencils, pens, posters, trading cards, and unmounted photographs. Unauthorized usage of an athlete's federally registered name that creates a likelihood of consumer confusion regarding the source or sponsorship of goods or services constitutes trademark infringement and unfair competition in violation of the Lanham Act and various state laws.

Courts require that a person's photo, image, or likeness actually function as a trademark to be protected by the Lanham Act's provisions prohibiting trademark infringement. In *ETW Corp. v. Jireh Publishing, Inc.*, 332 F.3d 915, 922 (6th Cir. 2003), the Sixth Circuit observed:

> Here, ETW claims protection under the Lanham Act for any and all images of Tiger Woods. This is an untenable claim. ETW asks us, in effect, to constitute Woods himself as a walking, talking trademark. Images and likenesses of Woods are not protectable as a trademark because they do not perform the trademark function of designation. They do not distinguish and identify the source of goods. They cannot function as a trademark because there are undoubtedly thousands of images and likenesses of Woods taken by countless photographers, and drawn, sketched, or painted by numerous artists, which have been published in many forms of media, and sold and distributed throughout the world. No reasonable person could believe . . . they all originated with Woods.

However, in *Pirone v. Macmillan, Inc.*, 894 F.2d 579, 583 (2d Cir. 1990), the Second Circuit acknowledged that "[u]nder some circumstances, a photograph of a person may be a valid trademark — if, for example, a particular photograph was consistently used on specific goods."

B. State Laws

 • Defamation
• First Amendment
• Right of publicity

In the United States, state laws protecting the reputation, privacy, and publicity rights of celebrities, including athletes, are still developing and vary by jurisdiction. The First Amendment of the U.S. Constitution, which protects freedom of speech and expression, provides a significant limit on the ability of state laws to recognize and protect reputation, privacy, and publicity rights and must always be considered.

1. Defamation

The tort of defamation includes both oral (slander) and written (libel) statements. The scope of its legal protection is not limited to celebrities, but defamation assumes special significance in this context. Professional athletes are a constant source of media and other commentary. The celebrity athlete's life, both professionally and personally, is scrutinized, at times to excruciating degrees, and statements made may be false and harm an athlete's reputation.

Although there are variations in state law definitions, a general definition of defamation is set forth in the Restatement (Second) Torts, §558, which provides, "To create liability for defamation, there must be: (a) a false and defamatory statement concerning another; (b) an unprivileged communication to a third party; (c) fault amounting at least to negligence on the part of the publisher; and (d) either actionability of the statement irrespective of special harm or the existence of special harm caused by the publication."

Statements must be both false and defamatory, meaning that they tend to damage the reputation of the person identified by the statement in the minds of others. Not included in the definition but generally accepted as a part thereof is that the false statement must be one of fact, not merely opinion. Most of what is written about the professional performance of athletes is opinion, which is not legally actionable even if it harms his or her reputation. For example, a statement in a newspaper article that a coach "usually finds a way to screw things up" and "[t]his season will be no different" is nonactionable opinion regarding a team's potential for the upcoming season and the coach's ability. *Washington v. Smith,* 893 F. Supp. 60 (D.D.C. 1995), 80 F.3d 555 (D.C. Cir. 1996). On the other hand, asserting that an athlete "fixed" a boxing match and used cocaine with his opponent thereafter, *Cobb v. Time, Inc.,* 278 F.3d 629 (6th Cir. 2002), or knowingly used "loaded" gloves, *Dempsey v. Time, Inc.,* 252 N.Y.S.2d 186 (N.Y. Sup. Ct. 1964), are statements of fact that harm one's professional reputation and may cause resulting economic loss. Making false factual statements about an athlete's personal life, such as criminal conduct, also is defamatory.

During the past 50 years, the traditional state law elements of defamation have been modified by federal constitutional law; therefore, First Amendment free speech issues must also be considered. A prominent athlete is considered to be a "public figure" who must prove by clear and convincing evidence that a defamatory statement was made with "actual malice," meaning the defendant had knowledge of its falsity or a reckless disregard regarding whether or not it was true. Thus, although athletes receive some protection through the laws of defamation, it is not the primary legal theory used to protect most invasions of an athlete's dignity rights.

2. Right of Privacy

The right of privacy, as a distinct concept of legal protection, was first enunciated in a famous law review article by Samuel Warren and Louis Brandeis that was published in the *Harvard Law Review* in 1890, in which they argued that a distinct tort protecting a person's right to privacy existed at common law and should be recognized. Samuel D. Warren and Louis D. Brandeis, *The Right to Privacy,* 4 Harv. L. Rev. 193 (1890). A further impetus to the development of the right of privacy occurred some years later through the various writings of Professor William Prosser. His last formulations set forth four separate categories that he advocated should be subsumed under a general concept of privacy: (1) protection against intrusion into one's private affairs; (2) avoidance of disclosure of one's embarrassing private fact; (3) protection against publicity placing one in a false light in the public eye; and (4) remedies for appropriation, usually for commercial advantage, of one's name or likeness. William Prosser, *Privacy,* 49 Cal. L. Rev. 383 (1960). All or some of these four categories of torts have largely been adopted in all states, though there is no unanimity as to the nature and scope of their common law development by courts. In some states, statutes have codified these torts.

The first three torts provide legal remedies for intrusions into one's private life and affairs, and athletes have relied on one or more of these legal theories in asserting various invasion of privacy claims. In some early cases, athletes asserted that the unauthorized use of their name or likeness in connection with the advertising or sale of products violated their common law privacy rights. *O'Brien v. Pabst Sales Co.,* 124 F.2d 167 (5th Cir. 1941), illustrates that courts generally were not receptive to these claims. In *O'Brien,* a famous professional football player alleged that the unauthorized use of his photograph in a calendar advertising defendant's beer invaded his right of privacy. Because he was not a private person and "the publicity he got was only that which he had been constantly seeking and receiving," the Fifth Circuit adopted the reasoning of the district court in holding: "Considered from the stand-point merely of an invasion of plaintiff's right of privacy, no case was made out, because plaintiff was an outstanding national football figure and had completely publicized his name and his pictures." *Id.* at 169.

However, courts have recognized claims for statements placing an athlete in a false light in the public eye. In *Spahn v. Julian Messner, Inc.,* 286 N.Y.S.2d 832 (N.Y. 1967), the court held that publication of an unauthorized fictionalized biography of a well-known baseball player violates New York statutory privacy law. In *Chuy v. Philadelphia Eagles Football Club,* 595 F.2d 1265 (3d Cir. 1979), an NFL club was found liable for its team physician's known false published statement that a player had a fatal blood disease, which caused him severe emotional distress.

3. Right of Publicity

The unauthorized commercial appropriation of an individual's identity is distinguishable from the other four privacy torts because of its recognition of the commercial value in one's name or likeness. Today, most states recognize a separate right of publicity, either as a common law or statutory right. Unlike the rights of reputation and privacy, the right of publicity is a property right that may be transferred and is descendible to the celebrity's surviving heirs in many states (if the jurisdiction recognized such right at the time of the person's death).

Courts initially refused to characterize celebrity names and likenesses as protectable property rights. In *Hanna Mfg. Co. v. Hillerich & Bradsby Co.,* 78 F.2d 763, 766 (5th Cir. 1935), the Fifth Circuit held that "fame is not merchandise." It concluded that an athlete has a valid claim for unauthorized commercial use of his name only if such usage falsely suggests that he uses or endorses the product, thereby constituting unfair competition.

In 1953, a U.S. court recognized the right of publicity for the first time. *Haelan Laboratories, Inc. v. Topps Chewing Gum, Inc.,* 202 F.2d 866 (2d Cir. 1953), *cert. denied,* 346 U.S. 816 (1953). The case involved a dispute over the rights to use baseball players' images on bubble gum trading cards. One company had been assigned these rights by the players; however, the defendant produced its own cards without the players' permission. One of the central issues was whether the players' rights, if any, were assignable, or were they strictly personal to the player. The Second Circuit held that New York law recognized a common law right of publicity, which is a freely transferable property right, not just a personal right. The court explained "in addition to and independent of the right of privacy . . . a man has a right in the publicity value of his photograph, i.e., the right to grant the exclusive privilege of publishing his picture." *Id.* at 868.

Since the *Haelan* decision over 50 years ago, there has been a lot of litigation to determine if a common law right of publicity exists in a particular jurisdiction. The common law development of the right of publicity certainly has not been uniform nationwide. In many states, the right of publicity has been created and defined by statute. See 1 J. Thomas McCarthy, Rights of Publicity and Privacy §§6.1–6.9 (2d ed., West 2012).

By common law or statute, a majority of states (but not all) now recognize a right of publicity property-based claim for unauthorized commercial use of an athlete's identity. As one court observed, "a celebrity has a legitimate proprietary interest in his public personality. A celebrity must be considered to have invested his years of practice and competition in a public personality which eventually may reach marketable status. . . . A name is commercially valuable as an endorsement of a product or for use for financial gain only because the public recognizes it and attributes good will and feats of skill or accomplishments of one sort or another to that personality." *Uhlaender v. Henricksen,* 316 F. Supp. 1277, 1282–1283 (D. Minn. 1970).

a. Nature and Scope of the Right of Publicity

In *Newcombe v. Adolph Coors Co.,* 157 F.3d 686 (9th Cir. 1998), the Ninth Circuit held that Don Newcombe, a well-known former MLB pitcher, had California common law and statutory right of publicity claims against a brewery for using an identifiable likeness of his distinctive pitching style without his permission in a magazine advertisement for one of its products. The court observed:

> Having viewed the advertisement, we hold that a triable issue of fact has been raised as to whether Newcombe is readily identifiable as the pitcher in the advertisement. Initially, we note that the drawing in the advertisement and the newspaper photograph of Newcombe upon which the drawing was based are virtually identical. The pitcher's stance, proportions, and shape are identical to the newspaper photograph of Newcombe; even the styling of the uniform is identical, right down to the wrinkles in the pants. . . . It may be the case that Newcombe's stance is essentially generic, but based on the record before us, Newcombe is the only one who has such a stance. The record contains pictures of other pitchers in the windup position but none of these pitchers has a stance similar to Newcombe's, thus giving us no basis to reach the conclusion proposed by the defendants that the pitcher in the advertisement is 'generic.' . . . [T]here is a genuine issue of material fact as to whether Newcombe's stance was so distinctive that the defendants used his likeness by using a picture of Newcombe's stance.

Id. at 692–693.

Consistent with *Newcombe,* courts have broadly defined the protected aspects of an athlete's identity to encompass more than merely his or her name or photo, including an athlete's birth name (even after it was changed, such as after conversion to Islam or as a personal choice), nickname, or voice, a robotic caricature of an athlete, a distinctive car driven by a professional racer, an athlete's facial features, and athletes' monikers such as "The Greatest" and "Crazy Legs." In a case involving the famous entertainer Johnny Carson, a court even extended publicity rights to the phrase "Here's Johnny!" *Carson v. Here's Johnny Portable Toilets, Inc.*, 698 F.2d 831 (6th Cir. 1983). A state statutory or common law right of publicity may even protect an athletic performance — for example, a human cannonball act. Athletes earn royalties for licensing the use of their individual publicity rights in commercials, print ads, and in-person appearances, as well as by exploiting their fame online via Twitter (e.g., by including @SPONSOR/COMPANY in a tweet) or Instagram (e.g., showing their use of a product or including it in photos of them).

Infringement of an athlete's right of publicity occurs if an aspect of his or her identity was used without permission to advertise and sell a product or service. Other examples of infringing commercial usage include incorporating an athlete's photo into a product such as sports trading cards, drinking glasses, or clothing. Courts generally refuse to characterize the use of a famous athlete's name or identity in connection with the sale of a product as legally permissible incidental or informational use. Rather, such usage is unauthorized commercial appropriation of the athlete's persona that violates one's right of publicity. In *Abdul-Jabbar v. General Motors Corp.*, 85 F.3d 407 (9th Cir. 1996), the Ninth Circuit held that, although such information is newsworthy, an auto manufacturer's use of the name and college basketball records of Kareem Abdul-Jabbar (formerly Lew Alcindor) in a television advertisement is commercial usage. The auto manufacturer gained a commercial advantage from the advertisement, which attracted the attention of television viewers of the 1993 NCAA men's basketball tournament. See also *Jordan v. Jewel Food Stores, Inc.*, 2015 WL 1204282 (N.D. Ill.) (a Chicago grocery store ad in magazine's commemorative issue congratulating former Chicago Bulls player Michael Jordan on his induction into the Basketball Hall of Fame violates his right of publicity under Illinois law if "purposes of advertising or promoting [its] products" is proved to be its objective).

Unauthorized usage of an athlete's identity is a necessary element of a claim for misappropriation or infringement of publicity rights. An athlete's consent to the use of his or her identity for commercial purposes may be either express or implied under the circumstances. The nature and scope of such consent is necessarily determined on a case-by-case basis and requires careful review of a contract delineating which rights are conferred.

Although college and high school athletes have the same legally protectable publicity rights under state laws as professional athletes, the NCAA and state high school athletics governing bodies historically have prohibited their exercise in order to be eligible to participate in intercollegiate or interscholastic sports competition as an "amateur" athlete. For example, to retain his eligibility to play college football for the University of Colorado, the NCAA prohibited U.S. Olympic moguls skier Jeremy Bloom from commercially exploiting his right of publicity to earn future endorsement and modeling contract income needed to finance his training as a skier. *Bloom v. NCAA*, 93 P.3d 621 (Colo. App. 2004). In 2003, the Ohio High School Athletic Association (OHSAA) declared LeBron James ineligible to continue playing high school basketball for violating its rule prohibiting "capitalizing on athletic fame by receiving money or gifts of monetary value." James had accepted two "throwback" jerseys (worth a combined $845) from an Akron, Ohio, sporting goods store for posing for photos to be displayed on its walls. Although an Ohio trial court ultimately enjoined the OHSAA from enforcing its rule, James was required to serve a two-game suspension for his conduct. As discussed below, a group of former and current college athletes recently prevailed in litigation asserting that the unauthorized use of their identities in video games violates their publicity rights.

b. First Amendment Limitations

The First Amendment of the U.S. Constitution limits the protection of publicity rights under state law. In *Titan Sports, Inc. v. Comics World Corp.*, 870 F.2d 85, 88 (1989), the Second Circuit explained there is an "inherent tension between the protection of an individual's right to control the use of his likeness and the constitutional guarantee of free dissemination of ideas, images, and newsworthy matter in whatever form it takes." Courts have struggled to draw the line between unauthorized commercial use of one's identity that may be prohibited by state law and communicative or expressive use protected by the First Amendment.

In *Zacchini v. Scripps-Howard Broadcasting, Inc.*, 433 U.S. 562 (1977), the U.S. Supreme Court held that the media's right to report newsworthy events does not permit the unauthorized broadcast of a performer's entire act, which threatens harm to its economic value. A local Ohio television station sent a news crew to film the act of Hugo Zacchini, the "human cannonball," who was performing at a county fair. This was done despite Zacchini's request that his performance not be filmed. His entire 15-second performance was shown on the evening news. Rejecting Zacchini's misappropriation claim, the Ohio Supreme Court held in favor of the television station, citing its right to report newsworthy events under the First Amendment. However, in a 5–4 decision, the Supreme Court reversed and ruled that showing his entire act is not permitted by the First Amendment's protection of news reporting. Under the majority's view, the television station's broadcast is not protected by the U.S. Constitution because it reduces the commercial value of Zacchini's entertainment product and corresponding economic incentive to produce his performance.

The *Zacchini* case is notable not for the clarity of its line-drawing, but for its clear demonstration that such line-drawing regarding the scope of First Amendment protections is one that is often difficult and likely to be criticized, whatever the result reached. When the usage of an athlete's identity moves from the purely commercial, as is clearly the case in the advertising or sale of a product, to a more-mixed medium — such as films, television, radio, newspapers, and other literary works — the more likely it becomes that First Amendment issues will arise.

The media may use a celebrity's name, photograph, and other aspects of his or her identity in connection with truthful news reporting. The First Amendment broadly immunizes the media from state law liability for infringement of publicity rights, even though media publications and broadcasts usually are for-profit commercial activity. Courts generally extend constitutional protection to media republications of news coverage of sporting events and athletic accomplishments even if used for advertising purposes. For example, in *Montana v. San Jose Mercury News, Inc.*, 34 Cal. App. 4th 790 (Cal. Ct. App. 1995), the court held that a newspaper may contemporaneously reproduce a full-page account of the San Francisco 49ers' four Super Bowl victories in the 1990s in poster form for public sale without violating the publicity rights of Joe Montana, the team's quarterback. Even though his name and likeness appeared on the posters, they were depictions of newsworthy events in which Montana had played a prominent role.

On the other hand, the use of news coverage of an athletic event incorporating an athlete's name or likeness to advertise or sell unrelated products is not constitutionally protected. In *Pooley v. National Hole-in-One Association*, 89 F. Supp.2d 1108 (D. Ariz. 2000), the defendant made a videotape of a professional golfer's hole-in-one and used his name to promote its hole-in-one fund-raising competitions. Denying the defendant's motion to dismiss the plaintiff's right of publicity claim, the court ruled:

> [W]hile Plaintiff's hole-in-one at the Bay Hill Classic was open to national observation and public videotaping, its *subsequent* unauthorized reproduction was not automatically privileged simply because the hole-in-one continued to be a "newsworthy" event. Defendant did not create the videotape in connection with a news account. Defendant did not include Plaintiff's name and videotape footage simply to communicate an idea. It capitalized on Plaintiff's name, reputation, and prestige in the context of an advertisement. The promotional videotape went one step further and implied a false connection between the Plaintiff and its business. The Court finds that the use of Plaintiff's identity was strictly commercial and not protected by the First Amendment.

Id. at 1114.

The First Amendment has been judicially construed to permit the limited usage of historical accounts of player records and accomplishments as well as video depictions of their athletic performances. In *Gionfriddo v. Major League Baseball*, 94 Cal. App. 4th 400 (Cal. Ct. App. 2001), a group of retired professional baseball players claimed the unauthorized use of their names and likenesses in for-profit print and video publications providing historical information about MLB players violated their right of publicity. The court found that "[t]he public has an enduring fascination in the records set by former players and in memorable moments from previous games, . . . [which] are the standards by which the public measures the performance of today's players." Affirming summary judgment for defendants, it concluded: "Balancing plaintiffs' negligible economic interests against the public's enduring fascination with baseball's past, we conclude that the public interest favoring the free dissemination of information regarding baseball's history far outweighs any proprietary interests at stake." *Id.* at 415.

Similarly, in *C.B.C. Distribution and Marketing, Inc. v. Major League Baseball Advanced Media*, 505 F.3d 818 (8th Cir. 2007), the Eighth Circuit ruled that the unauthorized use of MLB players' names and statistics in online fantasy baseball games is protected by the First Amendment. The court explained that "the information used in CBC's fantasy baseball games is all readily available in the public domain, and it would be strange law that a person would not have a first amendment right to use information that is available to everyone." The court found the *Gionfriddo* court's views "persuasive:" "recitation and discussion of factual data concerning the athletic performance of [players on MLB's website] command a substantial public interest, and, therefore, is a form of public expression due substantial constitutional protection." *Id.* at 823–24.

In *Cardtoons, L.C. v. Major League Baseball Players Assn.*, 95 F.3d 915, 969 (10th Cir. 1996), the Tenth Circuit recognized a First Amendment parody defense to a right of publicity claim challenging Cardtoons' production of a series of baseball cards lampooning readily identifiable individual MLB players. The court explained:

> Cardtoons' parody trading cards receive full protection under the First Amendment. The cards provide social commentary on public figures, major league baseball players, who are involved in a significant commercial enterprise, major league baseball. While not core political speech (the cards do not, for example, adopt a position on the Ken Griffey, Jr., for President campaign), this type of commentary on an important social institution constitutes protected expression.

In *ETW v. Jireh Publishing, Inc.*, 332 F.3d 915 (6th Cir. 2003), the Sixth Circuit held that the First Amendment protects a sports artist's freedom of expression to include the likenesses of famous professional athletes (e.g., Tiger Woods and other legendary professional golfers) in a painting commemorating Woods's historic victory in the 1997 Masters tournament, reprints of which were sold to the public. The court explained that the First Amendment protects expressive materials "including music, pictures, films, photographs, paintings, drawings, engravings, prints, and sculptures," which is not limited even if it is sold. Observing that famous athletes, "through their pervasive presence in the media . . . have come to symbolize certain ideas and values in our society and have become a valuable means of expression in our culture," the court concluded, "While the right of publicity allows celebrities like Woods to enjoy the fruits of their labors, here Rush has added a significant creative component of his own to Woods's identity. Permitting Woods's right of publicity to trump Rush's right of freedom of expression would extinguish Rush's right to profit from his creative enterprise." *Id.* at 938.

Courts have ruled that the unauthorized use of identifiable traits and characteristics of college athletes in videogames are not protected by the First Amendment. In *In re NCAA Student-Athlete Name and Licensing Litigation*, 724 F.3d 1268 (9th Cir. 2013), the Ninth Circuit held that an NCAA college football video game produced by Electronic Arts (EA) violated former Arizona State and Nebraska quarterback Sam Keller's right of publicity. It ruled that EA's depiction of him in its *NCAA Football* videogame is not sufficiently transformative for the First Amendment to bar his California right of publicity claims. In the game, the virtual quarterback for Arizona State and Nebraska shares many of his characteristics. For example, the virtual player wears his same jersey number, is the same height and weight, and is from the same home state. Although Keller's name is omitted from the virtual player's jersey, a videogame user can upload rosters of college football team names obtained from third parties so that their names appear on the virtual players' jerseys.

The Ninth Circuit concluded EA's use of Keller's likeness does not have sufficient transformative elements that add "significant creative elements so as to be transformed into something more than a mere celebrity likeness or imitation." *Id*. at 1273. Rather, EA replicated his physical characteristics, and users of its game manipulated the virtual player incorporating these traits while performing his same real-life activity—namely, college football. In other words, "Keller is represented as 'what he was: the starting quarterback for Arizona State and Nebraska,' and 'the game's setting is identical to where the public found [Keller] during his intercollegiate career: on the football field.'" *Id*. at 1275. The court rejected EA's contention that "focusing primarily on Keller's likeness and ignoring the transformative elements of the game as a whole" improperly applies the transformative use defense, explaining "[the fact] that the avatars appear in the context of a videogame that contains many other creative elements does not transform the avatars into anything other than exact depictions of [college football players] doing exactly what they do as celebrities." *Id*. at 1276.

Thereafter, the NCAA paid $20 million to settle plaintiffs' right of publicity claims, which alleged that the NCAA had sanctioned EA's use of college football and basketball players' likenesses in video games without authorization. EA, which subsequently discontinued producing NCAA videogames, and Collegiate Licensing Company paid $40 million to settle plaintiffs' claims against them. This $60 million fund will be distributed to college basketball and football players whose identities were used in EA's videogames according to a court-approved formula based on the number of times that this infringing conduct occurred. This illustrates that the unauthorized use of sports-related intellectual property rights should be avoided to prevent substantial damages.

Currently, there is a split of authority among courts regarding whether the producer's copyrighted broadcast of a game or sports event violates participating athletes' right of publicity. In *Dryer v. NFL*, 55 F.Supp.3d 1181 (D. Minn. 2014), a Minnesota federal district court ruled that the NFL's use of former players' names and images in "compilations of clips of game footage into theme-based programs describing a football game or series of games and the players on the field" is protected by the First Amendment as non-commercial expressive work. It characterized these productions as "a history lesson of NFL football," observing that the "only way for NFL Films to tell such stories is by showing footage of the game—the plays, the players, the coaches, the referees, and even the fans." Concluding that "the challenged uses of Plaintiffs' likenesses in game footage are akin to the use of game footage in sports news broadcasts, newspapers, and magazines," it ruled that plaintiffs "failed to establish that the uses of which they complain are truly different from the uses found permissible in *C.B.C*, *CBS*, and *Gionfriddo*." Observing that plaintiffs do not challenge the NFL's right to "exploit the original game broadcast by showing that full broadcast on the NFL Network or ESPN Classic," the court also held that these productions incorporated copyrighted game footage; therefore, federal copyright law preempted plaintiff's right of publicity claims because they were not used to advertise a separate, unrelated product. See also *Marshall v. ESPN, Inc.*, 2015 WL 3606645 (M.D. Tenn.) (intercollegiate athletes do not have a right of publicity in televised sports events in which they participate that are produced by others under Tennessee law). In *In re NCAA Student–Athlete Name & Likeness Licensing Litigation*, 2013 WL 5778233 (N.D. Cal.), a California federal district court ruled that college football and basketball players' right of publicity claims arising out of alleged unauthorized usage of their images in televised game footage are not preempted by the First Amendment or Copyright Act.

Problem 9-4

Consider whether the following use of player names or identities without authorization from the player or players union violates any legally protected rights.

(a) A company makes and sells bobblehead dolls depicting famous professional athletes and identifies them by name in the product's packaging.

(b) A minor league baseball league affixes the names and photos of members of its All-Star team to merchandise such as T-shirts, mugs, and other souvenirs that are sold in the venue hosting its All-Star Game.

Coaches' Contracts and Related Issues

10

INTRODUCTION

It was once common for coaches to negotiate contracts with professional teams or educational institutions without the assistance of lawyers or agents. In fact, more than a few coaching contracts were sealed with a handshake. Although many coaches (particularly those outside the sports of football, basketball, and baseball) continue to be employed without a written contract, it is no longer uncommon for coaches to have written contracts with their institutions. The changing landscape of sports and the coaching profession has transformed the manner in which coaching contracts are consummated. The past several years have been marked by escalating salaries paid to football and men's basketball coaches. Increased compensation has been accompanied, however, by expanded duties and increased pressure on these coaches to win. The end result is a profession notable for high visibility and job stress, but low job security. Consequently, the terms that regulate the rights and duties of parties to coaching contracts take on more significance than perhaps in the past. Coaching contracts are "sophisticated endeavors—no standard forms, no two that look the same, no union protecting their interests, and no data bank that correctly reports the intricacies of their packages." Martin J. Greenberg, *College Coaching Contracts Revisited: A Practical Perspective*, 12 Marq. Sports L. Rev. 127 (2001). Given these and other dynamics, coaches require the assistance of agents or lawyers in drafting and negotiating contracts that adequately protect the interests of both parties.

Those who represent coaches in contract negotiations must be prepared to address many issues, including the scope of a coach's responsibilities, the duration of a contract, reassignment to noncoaching positions, termination of the relationship for cause and without cause, entitlement to perquisites and fringe benefits, and buyout provisions. The materials that follow are intended to provide a glimpse at clauses that increasingly find their way into coaching contracts and provide the source of disputes. The following discussion also briefly examines other issues that confront those who enter into the coaching profession. (Issues involving coaches are also discussed in other chapters, including Chapters 5, 6, 7, and 8, which examine gender equity, racial equity, health and safety issues, and impairment and concussion issues, respectively.)

The relationships between coaches and their colleges or professional teams are governed largely by the general principles of contract law to which you are introduced in Chapter 3. As discussed in this chapter, however, specific contract law principles (e.g., employment at will) take on particular significance in the coaching context. In addition, constitutional law (e.g., property and liberty interest and due process), to which you are introduced in Chapters 1 and 3, plays a limited role in determining the nature of the relationships between coaches and their employers.

IS THERE A PROPERTY INTEREST IN ATHLETIC EMPLOYMENT?

 **KEY TERMS**
- Employment at will/at-will employment
- Implied-in-fact promise
- Indefinite duration
- Just cause termination
- Liberty interest
- Property interest

A frequently litigated issue is what procedures, if any, an employer must follow before terminating a coach. Because professional coaches are typically hired for a specified number of years, most of the litigation regarding this issue involves high school or college coaches hired under contracts of indefinite duration (i.e., contracts without a set time period). These contracts are often referred to as establishing *at-will employment,* which generally permits a high school or college to terminate a coach without the institution having to establish just cause (i.e., conduct by an employee that gives an employer a legally justifiable reason to fire the employee). Another important aspect of the at-will concept is the right of a college or high school to terminate a coach without allowing the coach to present evidence at a hearing challenging the termination.

Kish v. Iowa Central Community College, 142 F. Supp. 2d 1084 (N.D. Iowa 2001), provides a good illustration of the factual circumstances in which these issues arise. There, a coach who was fired alleged that the mere existence of a contract between him and his employer gave rise to a property interest that required that he be afforded due process (a hearing) before being relieved from his coaching responsibilities. Rejecting the coach's claim, the court stated "Kish had no cognizable property interest in his coaching contract." *Id.* at 1097. The court further stated that "Kish has not demonstrated any contractual or statutory limitations on Iowa Central's ability to terminate his coaching contract, nor has he demonstrated that a protectable property interest arose from any implied contract arising out of customs, practices, or de facto policies. . . . Instead, Kish's coaching contract expressly provided to the contrary, by stating, 'This contract is not continuing in nature and may be terminated at the pleasure of the Board [of Iowa Central]."' *Id.* at 1098. See *Jones v. Washington Interscholastic Athletic Assn.,* 2008 WL 351013 (W.D. Wash. 2008) (there is no fundamental right to coach an interscholastic or high school football team); *Price v. Univ. of Alabama,* 318 F. Supp. 2d 1084 (N.D. Ala. 2003) (university was entitled to fire a coach without allowing him to permit evidence at a hearing where the coach and university had reached a written contract).

There are exceptions to the general rule articulated in *Kish.* One such instance arises where a terminated coach proves the existence of an implied-in-fact promise that "he would not be terminated as football coach except for cause." *Kingsford v. Salt Lake City School District,* 247 F.3d 1123, 1132 (10th Cir. 2001). The *Kingsford* court noted, "An implied-in-fact promise to terminate only for cause can be demonstrated by 'conduct of the parties, announced personnel policies, practices of that particular trade or industry, or other circumstances which show the existence of such a promise.'" *Id.*

QUESTIONS

1. In *Kish,* why was the coach not entitled to a hearing that would have permitted him to challenge the college's decision to terminate his employment? Do you think all coaches should receive a hearing when terminated?
2. What responsibilities do you feel should be covered in a head coach's contract? List them. After completing your list, rank the responsibilities in order of importance.

Problem 10-1

William Barr was the head coach of the Richmond football team on a yearly basis for ten years. His current contract term was from 2015 to 2018. During a football game, a local sports reporter informed Mr. Reynolds, Richmond's principal, that Barr had shouted a racial epithet at a player on the opposing team. At some point after this game, the principal met with the school district's superintendent and discussed the renewal of Barr's coaching contract. In January 2016, at the conclusion of the football season, Reynolds informed Barr that he would be fully compensated for the entire term of his coaching contract, but that all of Barr's duties as coach would cease immediately. (Barr received the total amount due under his coaching contract.) Reynolds provided no reasons for terminating Barr and did not afford Barr a hearing to contest his termination. The school denied Barr's request that he be permitted to present evidence at a hearing as to why his contract should be renewed. Mr. Reynolds announced to the local newspaper that "Coach Barr's contract will not be renewed." He made no comments as to the reasons why the contract would not be renewed. Following his termination, Barr sent out applications for several head football coaching positions but received no job offers.

> Barr has filed suit alleging breach of contract and that he has been deprived of his fundamental rights to continued employment and to his reputation. Consider the preceding materials in determining whether Barr is likely to prevail on his claims. Also see *Puchalski v. School Dist. of Springfield*, 161 F. Supp. 2d 395 (E.D. Penn. 2001); *Ridpath v. Board of Governors Marshall Univ.*, 447 F.3d 292 (4th Cir. 2006) (university's labeling as "corrective action" its reassignment of athletic director to a position outside of athletic department created a charge of a serious character defect, which in turn gave rise to a liberty interest and entitled plaintiff to a hearing that allowed him to contest the reassignment).

A. Termination

The following materials initially discuss conduct (e.g., violation of National Collegiate Athletic Association (NCAA) rules and engaging in personal indiscretions) that may constitute grounds for an educational institution or a professional team to justifiably terminate a coach. The discussion then addresses the compensation issues that may arise when an institution's termination of a coach is unjustified and therefore constitutes a breach of contract. The materials conclude with a discussion of payment issues that emerge when a coach leaves one institution, prior to the expiration of his or her contract term, to coach a team at another institution.

1. Constitutes Termination for "Cause"?

A wide array of events may give an institution or team a right to terminate a coach for cause. At the collegiate level, contracts typically contain provisions allowing an institution the right to terminate a coach if the coach has committed serious violations of NCAA rules and regulations. Similarly, a contract may include a provision that grants the institution the discretion to terminate a coach if a member of his or her coaching staff committed an NCAA rules violation if such violation was under the control or direction of the head coach. Among the more common provisions in coaching contracts at both the collegiate and professional levels are those that permit termination for cause if a coach (1) refuses or is unable (e.g., because of death or incapacity) to perform duties either stipulated in the contract or reasonably associated with the position of coach, (2) is convicted of a serious criminal offense, (3) engages in fraud or dishonesty in the performance of his or her duties, or (4) participates or encourages participation in gambling or betting involving sports. Finally, coaching contracts typically give colleges and professional clubs the right to terminate a coach if he or she engages in conduct that is detrimental to the best interests of the institution or club.

An issue that may arise at both the collegiate and professional levels is whether a team's poor winning percentage gives a team or institution grounds to terminate a coach for cause. At the professional level, this issue arose when Larry Brown was terminated from his position as head coach of the National Basketball Association's (NBA's) New York Knicks. Brown was fired in the first year of a five-year contract after posting a franchise low record of 23–59. The Knicks withheld payment of the remaining amount due under the contract, $41 million, claiming that Brown was fired for cause. Brown sued to recover the contract amount, as well as $12 million in damages. In a settlement, the Knicks agreed to pay Brown $18.5 million. See ESPN, *Knicks, Brown Reach Undisclosed Contract Settlement*, Oct. 30, 2006, *http://sports.espn.go.com/espn/print?id=2644227&type=HeadlineNews&imagesPrint=off*; and Phil Sheridan, *Leave Larry Brown Behind Forever*, Philadelphia Inquirer, April 29, 2010, at D01.

This issue was also addressed by the Montana Supreme Court in *Cole v. Valley Ice Garden, L.L.C.*, 113 P.3d 275 (Mont. 2005). A five-year employment contract between a coach and a professional hockey team provided the coach could be terminated for cause. The agreement failed to define cause. After the team terminated the coach because of his team's poor performance, he filed suit for breach of contract alleging that he was wrongfully terminated. The coach argued that because the contract failed to expressly require that he maintain a specific win/loss ratio, the court could not imply such a term into the agreement. He did not contest the right of the team to terminate him. Rather, he argued that termination would not end the team's obligation to pay off the remainder of the compensation due to him under the contract. Relying on definitions from other contexts to lend meaning to the term "cause," the court ruled in favor of the team, finding that "[d]ischarging the coach of a professional sports team which is performing poorly, despite management's good faith efforts, is a discretionary decision related to the legitimate needs of the business and constitutes 'cause.'" *Id.* at 280. See Robert H. Lattinville and Robert A. Boland, *Coaching in the National Football League: A Market Survey and Legal Review*, 17 Marq. Sports L. Rev. 109 (2006) (discussing termination provisions included in National Football League (NFL) coaching contracts).

QUESTIONS

If a professional coach leads a team to a poor record, should the organization be able to terminate his/her contract for cause? What about a collegiate coach? What about a high school coach?

2. Termination for Rules Violations and Non-Sports-Related Indiscretions

Institutions and teams have terminated coaches for exercising poor judgment that ranges from abusive conduct toward players (discussed below) to violating NCAA rules to off-the-field indiscretions. In 2003, the number and severity of incidents involving alleged and established improper conduct by coaches in intercollegiate basketball reached such a level that, in a move characterized as unprecedented, the

National Association of Basketball Coaches convened a mandatory ethics summit for all NCAA Division I (D-I) men's head coaches. One of the more notorious incidents, which also provided a major catalyst for the coaching summit, involved Dave Bliss, former head men's basketball coach at Baylor University. Bliss was forced to resign following an investigation that revealed that Bliss lied to school officials who were investigating the death of Baylor basketball player Patrick Dennehy, that Bliss instructed coaches and players to lie to those investigators and to portray Dennehy as a drug dealer, and that Bliss improperly paid the tuition for players on the basketball team. See Jeff Caplan, *Baylor's Situation Catalyst for Summit*, Star-Telegram, Sept. 5, 2003.

Other incidents involving poor judgment and indiscretions by coaches occurring in 2003 alone included the following:

- Mike Price's termination as the University of Alabama's head coach for conduct that included a visit to a topless bar and reports that a young woman charged $1,000 for room service at a hotel at which Price stayed (in December 2003, the University of Texas–El Paso hired Price as its head football coach);
- University of Washington's firing of head football coach Rick Neuheisel after he admitted that he bet more than $6,000 on the NCAA D-I men's basketball tournament (in December 2007, Neuheisel was named head football coach of the UCLA Bruins and coached the team until he was fired in November 2011);
- Alabama State University's firing of head football coach L.C. Cole in the aftermath of allegations of improper academic support for players and players being entertained by strippers;
- Larry Eustachy's resignation as Iowa State University's head men's basketball coach after the release of a photograph showing him surrounded by and kissing younger women and drinking a beer at a college party following a basketball game (in March 2004, Eustachy was named head basketball coach at the University of Southern Mississippi; in 2011, he was named head coach at Colorado State University);
- The now-deceased Nolan Richardson III's termination as head men's basketball coach at Tennessee State University after he pulled a gun on an assistant coach.

Craig Bennett et al., *One Year Later: A Look Back at College Scandals, the People Involved and Where They Stand*, USA Today, June 15, 2004, at C3; Welch Suggs, *A Hard Year in College Sports*, Chron. Higher Educ., Dec. 19, 2003, at A37; John L. Pulley and Welch Suggs, *Coaches Will Be Coaches?*, Chron. Higher Educ., May 16, 2003, at A40. See also Martin J. Greenberg, *Termination of College Coaching Contracts: When Does Adequate Cause to Terminate Exist and Who Determines Its Existence?*, 17 Marq. Sports L. Rev. 197 (2006).

In 2012, the highly successful head coach of the University of Arkansas's football team, Bobby Petrino, was terminated for cause. Relying in part on the morals clause contained in Petrino's contract, the university based the termination on the coach's alleged failure to be forthcoming with university officials regarding a motorcycle accident that involved a 25-year-old football staff member with whom Petrino allegedly had an inappropriate relationship. See Jack Carey, *Other Fallen Coaches Returned to Sideline*, USA Today, April, 12, 2012, at 8C. In January 2014, the University of Louisville entered into a $24.5 million, seven-year contract with Petrino to become head coach of the university's football team. Petrino's contract with Louisville includes a morals clause allowing the school to terminate his contract or to take corrective action if he violates it.

A 2007 case addresses whether NCAA rules violations constitute grounds for a good-cause termination and the significance of contract provisions granting colleges such discretion. In *O'Brien v. The Ohio State Univ.*, 2007 WL 2729077 (Ohio App. 10 Dist. 2007), the former head coach of Ohio State's men's basketball team was terminated for violating NCAA rules prohibiting institutional representatives from providing extra benefits to players (namely, giving a loan to a student-athlete). Plaintiff filed a breach of contract action alleging wrongful termination. The critical issue before the court was whether the coach's violations of NCAA rules constituted a breach of contract sufficient to permit a discharge of the university's obligations and allow it to terminate O'Brien without having to pay him. In concluding that O'Brien's failure to comply with NCAA rules did not constitute such a breach, the court found that compliance with NCAA rules represented only one of the coach's duties stipulated in the contract. In addition, the court pointed to contract language providing that the parties' failure to perform in each instance would not necessarily justify termination for cause. Since O'Brien's violation of NCAA rules and his failure to promptly report his violations were not so fundamental that they defeated "the essential purpose of the contract" and "thus rendered performance by defendant impossible," the court held that plaintiff's breach was not material and defendant did not have cause to terminate his employment. The court also upheld the trial court's damages award of approximately $2.49 million. See also *Harrick v. NCAA*, 454 F. Supp. 2d 1255 (N.D. Ga. 2006) (former head and assistant coaches who were subject of investigation involving NCAA rules violations were unable to establish that NCAA wrongfully interfered with their contracts with the University of Georgia).

QUESTIONS

1. The termination or forced resignations of coaches raises questions of whether coaches are being held to standards that are too high, particularly if the indiscretion does not involve rules violations or matters related to the athletics program. What interest does a university have in regulating the personal behavior of coaches? Which clause or clauses within a coach's contract is an institution likely to contend justify its termination of a coach for cause for non-athletic-related behavior? How does the situation involving the legendary Joe Paterno of Penn State fit into this discussion?

2. How could Ohio State have avoided the result reached in its dispute with former basketball coach O'Brien?

> ## Problem 10-2
>
> You are a coach of a D-I men's basketball team. You violate an NCAA rule by sending a prospective student-athlete two more text messages than NCAA rules permit. Should such a violation give your school grounds for just cause termination? Should the school have grounds to terminate you if the violation was committed by one of your assistants? What factors will determine if the school can terminate you under either scenario?

3. Termination for Abusive Conduct

When a coach crosses the thin line that separates appropriate tough discipline from abuse, institutions are justified in terminating a coach for cause. Throughout his coaching career, former Texas Tech and Indiana University (IU) men's basketball coach Bobby Knight fended off criticism that he verbally and physically abused his players. In 2002, Knight sued IU for breach of contract and defamation following his termination for violating a "zero tolerance" behavior policy when he grabbed a student by the arm. He alleged the termination caused him to lose more than $2 million in media and clothing contracts, endorsements, and camp fees. In October 2003, a judge dismissed Knight's lawsuit. The state judge noted that Knight's contract contained a provision that allowed IU to terminate him at will and that IU was not required to give Knight another chance.

In *Campanelli v. Bockrath*, 100 F.3d 1476 (9th Cir. 1996), Louis Campanelli was fired as head coach of the men's basketball team at the University of California at Berkeley. Newspaper accounts attributed Campanelli's firing to his conduct toward players. A *Washington Post* article described Campanelli as "an abusive bully" who "perpetuate[d] a cycle of abuse" and psychologically attacked his players. Tony Kornheiser, *When the Boot Fits*, Washington Post, Feb. 17, 1993, at C1. In another matter, Winston Bennett pled guilty to fourth-degree assault. Bennett was suspended and later fired from his position as head men's basketball coach at Kentucky State University after he struck a player in the face. The player later filed assault charges that ended in a plea bargain. Bennett was ordered to complete 200 hours of community service and to obtain anger management counseling or serve 90 days in jail. *Finish Line*, Rocky Mountain News, Feb. 27, 2004, at 22C. See *Board of Directors of Ames Cmty. Sch. Dist. v. Cullinan*, 745 N.W. 2d 487 (2008 Iowa) (evidence establishing that a coach engaged in threatening and intimidating treatment of student-athletes is sufficient to support a good-cause termination).

Allegations of coach abuse of players more recently led to two high-profile terminations. Mike Leach, the highly successful football coach at Texas Tech University who compiled a ten-season record of 84–43, was fired for cause on December 30, 2009, based on allegations that the coach had improperly treated a player who had suffered a concussion. On January 10, 2010, Leach, who had signed a five-year contract extension on January 1, 2009, filed a lawsuit against Texas Tech alleging wrongful termination and defamation. Leach alleged that the university fired him to avoid making an $800,000 bonus payment due to Leach on December 31, 2009. In 2010, a judge rejected Texas Tech's sovereign immunity defense and allowed Leach's breach of contract claim to move forward. The university appealed the ruling. On January 20, 2011, a state appellate court reversed the trial court ruling and found that Texas Tech is immune from Leach's breach of contract claim. *Leach v. Texas Tech*, 335 S.W.3d 386 (Tex. Ct. App. 2011). Leach asked the Texas Supreme Court to review his case. Without explanation, the Texas Supreme Court issued an order denying Leach's request for review on February 17, 2012. See *Leach v. Texas Tech*, 335 S.W.3d 386 (Tex. Ct. App. 2011); review denied Feb. 17, 2012.

On March 15, 2010, former University of South Florida head football coach Jim Leavitt sued the university alleging wrongful termination of his contract. The university terminated Leavitt for cause following allegations that Leavitt had mistreated a walk-on running back. The coach disputed allegations that he had grabbed the player by his throat and struck him during halftime of a game and filed a wrongful termination suit against the university. On January 11, 2011, the University of South Florida and Leavitt reached a settlement that paid Leavitt $2.75 million. Specifically the settlement included $2 million for "salary and benefits" and also $750,000 for Leavitt's contributions to building USF's "nationally respected" football program. See Associated Press, *Jim Leavitt Gets $2.75M in Settlement*, Jan. 11, 2011, *http://sports .espn.go.com/ncf/news/story?id=6013605*.

In April 2013, video emerged of former Rutgers University head men's basketball coach, Mike Rice, physically assaulting his players. Brittany Brady, *Rutgers Coach Fired After Abusive Video Broadcast*, CNN.com, Apr. 4, 2013, *http://www.cnn.com/2013/04/ 03/sport/rutgers-video-attack/*. The video showed Rice throwing basketballs at his players and forcefully pushing them while verbally insulting them. *Id*. Although such coaching tactics are certainly not novel and are viewed by some as appropriate, hard-nosed coaching, others find them appalling. Rutgers initially punished Rice with a three-game suspension and a $75,000 fine, but after being pressured by state officials, the university terminated him. *Id*. Still, Rice received $475,000 in severance pay. Angela Delli Santi, *Rutgers, Mike Rice Settlement: Fired Basketball Coach to Receive $475,000 Under Agreement*, Huffington Post, Apr. 18, 2013, *http://www .huffingtonpost.com/2013/04/18/rutgers-mike-rice-settlement-coach-paid_n_3113310.html*. On April 5, 2013, Rutgers fired its athletic director, Tim Pernetti. See Jerry Carino and Keith Sargeant, *Rutgers AD Tim Pernetti Out After Mike Rice Firing*, USA Today (Apr. 5, 2013). For a detailed discussion of abusive coaching conduct see Alexander *Wolff, Abuse of Power,* Sports Illus. 51(Sept. 28, 2015).

QUESTION

In the absence of contract language specifying behavior that is cause for termination, what types of conduct should always be unacceptable?

Problem 10-3

Coach entered into a five-year contract with University at an annual base salary of $250,000, not including perquisites, which contained the following provision:

> NOTICE OF APPOINTMENT AND CONTRACT: During the term of Coach's contract, Coach shall hold the appointment, title, and duties of Head Coach in the University's men's basketball program, except that at any time during the Appointment Term with 30 days' notice, the appointment, title, and duties of Head Coach may be terminated and another title and duties assigned. The University's termination of Coach's appointment, title, and duties as Head Coach of the men's basketball program, and its reassignment of Coach to other appointment, title, and duties within the University shall be within the discretion of University and may be exercised with or without cause.

During the first two years of his contract, the basketball team had a losing record of 8–45. University, which previously had a highly regarded men's basketball program, lost money on its men's basketball program and attendance was down during these two years. In a letter to Coach dated March 15 of his third year, University's athletic director stated:

> University hereby notifies you that your appointment as Head Coach of University's men's basketball team, and all duties associated with your title as Head Coach, will terminate as of April 16. University hereby offers to reassign you to the position of compliance coordinator for NCAA rules and regulations. A change in leadership of the basketball team is required and this reassignment is for the good of the athletic department. If you accept University's offer of reassignment, it will take effect April 16, 2016. You will continue to receive your annual base salary of $250,000 for each of the remaining three years of your contract, except you will not be entitled to receive perquisites that are normally associated with the position of head basketball coach.

Coach is very upset and believes University's reassignment of him constitutes an effort to get him to resign. He is also concerned that accepting a noncoaching position will detrimentally affect his ability to secure another coaching position. Coach would like nothing better than to sue University and comes to you for advice. What advice would you offer to Coach? What are the legal and professional consequences of Coach accepting the reassignment, and of Coach rejecting the reassignment? What type of compromise might Coach consider? In advising Coach, consider the following materials: *Monson v. Oregon*, 901 P.2d 904 (Or. Ct. App. 1995); and Martin J. Greenberg and James T. Gray, *Sports Law Practice*, vol. 1, pp. 585–87

(2d ed. 1998). See also *Dennison v. Murray State Univ.*, 465 F. Supp. 2d 733 (W.D. Ky. 2006) (even though athletic director's contract stated that the university could only reassign him to job with responsibilities consistent with the duties of an athletic director, university acted properly in reassigning plaintiff to position of director of corporate giving since contract also included a provision providing that it was subject to all university policies, which included its transfer/reassignment policy).

4. Free Speech and Retaliation Issues

In *Ridpath v. Board of Governors Marshall University*, 447 F.3d 291 (4th Cir. 2006), a compliance officer at Marshall University became aware of a number of violations of NCAA rules, including the school's practice of providing student-athletes with jobs at "above-market" wages. After bringing this information to the attention of university officials, the compliance officer alleged he was prevented from assisting in the investigation, blamed for the violations, and subjected to "corrective action" and transferred to another position on campus that significantly diminished his ability to obtain future employment in his chosen occupation of athletic compliance. The court denied the university's immunity defense and found that the compliance officer had a liberty interest in his reputation or choice of occupation for due process purposes. The court held, in this regard, that the transfer was in fact a demotion and was only labeled as a transfer as a way of avoiding potential liability for demoting the compliance officer.

The court next examined the First Amendment issue and confirmed that a public employer "contravenes a public employee's First Amendment rights when it discharges or refuses to rehire the employee or when it makes decisions relating to the promotion, transfer, recall, and hiring in the exercise of that employee's free speech rights." The court held that the plaintiff had sufficiently alleged that he was speaking as a private citizen and not as a public employee, and that his interest in exercising his First Amendment rights was not outweighed by the university's interest in his speech because the school was unable to show how the plaintiff's remarks had interfered with its legitimate operations. On the other hand, in *Richardson v. Sugg*, 448 F.3d 1046 (8th Cir. 2006) (discussed in Chapter 6), the court held that the firing of an African-American head basketball coach was not an abridgment of his First Amendment rights and was not racially motivated. As to the First Amendment claim, the court held that the detrimental impact of Richardson's comments regarding the university outweighed any free speech right he may have asserted. The *Richardson* and *Ridpath* cases illustrate the nature of proof that must be proffered to prevail on free speech and retaliation grounds and how public universities must respond to such allegations.

B. Compensation and Other Financial Matters

KEY TERMS
- Performance incentive
- Perquisites

In the event that a coach is justifiably terminated pursuant to one of the circumstances set forth in his or her contract, the institution is not liable to the coach for any damages other than those that may be specified in the contract between the parties. Coaches, however, often are terminated prior to the lapse of the contract term because of the poor performance of the team or other matters, such as conflicts between a coach and a team owner or university administrators. Assuming that the termination is unjustified (i.e., without cause), the coach is entitled to compensation for the duration of the contract term of employment. Therefore, if a coach with a three-year contract is unjustifiably terminated after the second year of his or her contract with a team, the coach generally would be entitled to compensation for the third year of the three-year contract term.

In these circumstances, it is not unusual for the coach and institution to disagree over what compensation the coach is owed. These issues are addressed in *Rodgers v. Georgia Tech Athletic Assn.*, 303 S.E.2d 467 (Ga. App. 1983). In this case, Franklin C. "Pepper" Rodgers was relieved from his duties as head football coach at Georgia Tech approximately two years before his contract term was to end. He remained employed by the university. The court held that the "disassociation of Rodgers from his position and duties was not 'for cause' pursuant to the terms of the contract. Therefore, the Association was obligated to pay Rodgers that part of the amount set forth in the contract 'which he himself was entitled to receive as compensation for his services.'" *Id.* at 470–471. In addition to his salary, Rodgers's contract provided that he was entitled "'to various insurance and pension benefits and perquisites' as he became eligible therefore." *Id.* at 471. Rodgers brought a breach of contract action against the Georgia Tech Athletic Association to recover the value of certain perquisites to which he was entitled under his employment contract.

As noted above, the court stated that Rodgers was entitled to recover his base salary for the remainder of his contract term. In addition to a salary, health insurance, and pension benefits, the contract provided that Rodgers, as an employee of the association, was entitled to "perquisites" as he became eligible therefore. The dispute between Rodgers and Georgia Tech involved his entitlement to "recover the value of certain perquisites or 'fringe benefits' of his position as head coach of football under the terms of his contract of employment with the Association." *Id.* at 469.

The court defined "perquisites" as "'[e]moluments or incidental profits attaching to an office or official position, beyond the salary or regular fees.' Black's Law Dictionary 1299 (4th ed. 1968)." *Id.* Alternatively, the court defined perquisites as "'a privilege, gain, or profit incidental to an employment in addition to regular salary or wages; *esp*: one expected or promised [e.g.,] the [perquisites] of the college president include a home and car . . . .' Webster's Third New International Dictionary 1685 (1981)." *Id.* It stated as a general guideline that Rodgers was entitled to the perquisites (or their value) for which he was eligible during the duration of his contract.

Rodgers listed 29 separate items as perquisites for which he claimed he should be compensated. They were divided into two categories. One category consisted of items provided directly to him by the association but discontinued when Rodgers was relieved of his duties. Items in this category included season tickets to Georgia Tech home football and basketball games, automobile expenses, parking privileges at Georgia Tech sporting events, meals available at the Georgia Tech training table, and expenses related to joining certain country clubs.

The other grouping consisted of items provided by sources other than the association by virtue of Rodgers's position as head coach of football and included profits from Rodgers's radio and television football shows, use of an automobile, and profits from Rodgers's summer football camps.

In resolving the dispute, the court first found that Rodgers's entitlement to receive perquisites must turn on whether the parties intended that Rodgers would receive perquisites, as he became eligible for them, based on his position as head coach of football and not merely as an employee of the association.

Examining the items in the first grouping, Georgia Tech argued that "Rodgers was not entitled to any of the items . . . because they were expense account items — 'tools' to enable him to more effectively execute his duties as head coach of football. Rodgers counter[ed] that those items were an integral part of the total compensation package that he received as head coach of football and constituted consideration for his contract of employment." *Id.* at 471–472. The court concluded that "with three exceptions, we cannot say as a matter of law either that Rodgers was entitled to the items listed in Section A as perquisites of his employment, or that he was not." *Id.* at 472. The three items disallowed "the services of a secretary, the services of an administrative assistant, and the cost of trips to football conventions [and] clinics" related to aiding Rodgers in fulfilling his duties as a head coach. *Id.*

With respect to perquisites Rodgers received from sources other than the association by virtue of his position as head coach of football, the court adopted the following principles to guide its analysis: "[T]he consideration of a contract need not flow directly from the promise [or] [here, the Association], but may be the promise or undertaking of one or more third persons.'" *Bing v. Bank of Kingston*, 5 Ga. App. 578, 580, 63 S.E. 652 (1908)." *Id.* at 473. "'Damages growing out of a breach of contract, in order to form the basis of a recovery, must be such as can be traced solely to the breach, must be capable of exact computation, must have arisen naturally and according to the usual course of things from such breach, and must be such as the parties contemplated as a probable result of the breach.' *Sanford-Brown Co. v. Patent Scaffolding Co.*, 199 Ga. 41, 33 S.E.2d 422 (1945)." *Id.*

Applying these principles, the court disallowed recovery for items relating to housing and the cost of premiums on a life insurance policy because they were discontinued several years prior to the association's breach of contract and were, in fact, not related to the breach. It also disallowed voluntary gifts which he had on occasion received from third parties in the past because "such voluntary contributions to his financial well-being are totally incapable of exact computation, for a gift made in one year is no assurance of a similar gift in the next. In fact, Rodgers concedes that he did not receive these gifts each year. Thus, the item which listed various financial gifts was properly excluded from recovery." *Id*. Finally, the court concluded that Rodgers was not entitled to compensation for several items including free lodging at certain hotels and certain club membership because there was no evidence "showing that the Association had any knowledge" of them. *Id*. Therefore, the "loss of these items could not be such as was contemplated as a probable result of a breach of the contract." *Id*. Items identified as commonly falling within perquisites coaches received included "profits from his television and radio shows and from his summer football camp plus the loss of use of a new automobile and tickets to professional sporting events." *Id*. at 473–474. These items would be recoverable if Rodgers established that "such items were contemplated by the parties at the time the contract was executed as perquisites or fringe benefits to which Rodgers would be entitled as the result of his position as head coach of football at Georgia Tech." *Id*. at 474. If the evidence so established, Rodgers's "removal from that position would result in the loss of these benefits." *Id*.

QUESTION

In the *Rodgers* case, the court identified three perquisites in category 1 that, under his contract, Rodgers was not entitled to: (1) the services of a secretary, (2) the services of an administrative assistant, and (3) the cost of trips to football conventions and clinics. Why did the court deem these perquisites nonrecoverable?

· · · · · · · · ·

A major component of what has been characterized as the athletics arms race in big-time intercollegiate athletics is escalating salaries paid to coaches. For example, as of January 2006, 42 college football bowl subdivision head coaches earned at least $1 million per year. By 2010, that number had risen to 59. In 2011, 64 football bowl subdivision head coaches earned at least $1 million, 32 made at least $2 million, and 4 head football coaches made over $4 million per year. See Erick Brady, Jodi Upton, and Steve Berkowitz, *Coaches Pay Soars Again*, USA Today, Nov. 12, 2011, at A1–2. Moreover, the average pay for major-college football head coaches increased by 55 percent, from $950,000 per year in 2006 to $1.47 million in 2011. *Id*. See also Steve Wieberg and Jodi Upton, *College Football Coaches Calling Lucrative Plays*, USA Today, Dec. 5, 2007, *http://www.usatoday.com/sports/college/football/2007-12-04-coaches-pay_N.htm*. By 2015, 72 college football head coaches earned at least $1 million per year, 51 made at least $2 million, and 11 made at least $4 million. See *http://sports.usatoday.com/ncaa/salaries/*. Factors that have fueled the dramatic rise in the salaries of college football coaches are the proliferation of money from football bowl games and television contracts. Another factor has been the substantial rise since the mid-1990s in agents representing coaches in their contract negotiations. Increased competition for coaches fueled by the willingness of NFL teams to hire college coaches, and colleges to hire NFL coaches, has also contributed to rising salaries. Even coaches at institutions that do not have powerhouse football or basketball teams are often the highest-paid personnel at a college or university. One commentator argues that the escalation in coaches' salaries is also attributable to the failure of institutions to compensate football student-athletes. See Richard T. Karcher, *The Coaching Carousel in Big-Time Intercollegiate Athletics: Economic Implications and Legal Considerations*, 20 Fordham Intell. Prop. Media & Ent. L.J. 1 (2009).

Examples of the approximate annual compensation (which includes university- and nonuniversity-based compensation, excluding bonuses) earned by coaches include the following:

- Nick Saban (head football coach at University of Alabama): $7.1 million
- Bob Stoops (head football coach at University of Oklahoma): $5.06 million
- John Calipari (head men's basketball coach at University of Kentucky): $6.4 million
- Tom Izzo (head men's basketball coach at Michigan State University): $4 million
- Mike Krzyzewski (head men's basketball coach at Duke University): $6 million

See Steve Berkowitz & Judi Upton, *2014 NCAAF Coaches Salaries*, USA Today, http://sports.usatoday.com/ncaa/salaries/ (Nov. 19, 2014); Steve Berkowitz & Judi Upton, *2014 NCAAB Tournament Coaches Pay*, USA Today, *http://sports .usatoday.com/ncaa/salaries/mens-basketball/coach*.

Perquisites and various performance incentives continue to represent significant components of college coaches' salaries. When Bobby Knight became head men's basketball coach at Texas Tech University, he refused a base salary of $250,000 but still received $650,000 in the form of perquisites and bonuses from the university. See Rion A. Scott, *Competing at the Division I Level*, Press & Sun-Bulletin, Feb. 29, 2004, at 1A.

After a sex and recruiting scandal concerning the University of Colorado's football team erupted in 2003, the spotlight was directed toward the compensation paid to its head football coach, Gary Barnett. Barnett's annual base salary was $180,350. His total compensation, however, included the following: $63,235 annual incentive from athletic department funds, which included money from concession and ticket sales; "$510,000 for radio and television appearances; $125,000 through CU's sponsorship contract with Nike; $5,000 worth of Nike gear; $100,000 deferred compensation; about $18,000 in interest on [a $2 million incentive if he renews a five-year contract that was to end in July 31, 2007]"; a car; membership in the Boulder Country Club; and tickets to football and basketball games. See Kelly Pate Dwyer, *Even If Fired, Coach May Still Get Paid Threshold High to End $1 Million-a-Year Deal*, Denver Post, Feb. 20, 2004, at A8.

QUESTIONS

1. Is the compensation paid to D-I coaches justified? See Karcher, *supra*; and Martin J. Greenberg and Jay S. Smith, *A Study of Division I Assistant Football and Men's Basketball Coaches' Contracts*, 18 Marq. Sports L. Rev. 25 (2007).

2. Should the contracts of college coaches include financial incentives and disincentives related to the academic performance and off-campus conduct of student–athletes? Professor Linda Greene's analysis of the contracts of head football coaches revealed a trend in which a coach's responsibility for student–athlete academic performance was explicitly articulated in contractual provisions. In contrast, fewer coaches' contracts included provisions penalizing coaches for student–athlete misbehavior. According to Professor Greene, "The . . . trend of contracts without explicit coach responsibility for athlete misconduct seems counterintuitive." Linda S. Greene, *Football Coach Contracts: What Does the Student-Athlete Have to Do with It?*, 76 UMKC L. Rev. 665, 688–89 (2008).

3. In 2010, it was reported that institutions are beginning to insert clauses into contracts with coaches that are tied to teams' Academic Progress Rates (APR). For example, the Connecticut head men's basketball coach reportedly will lose $100,000 of annual salary if his team loses scholarships based on APR penalties. Do you agree with the approach adopted by the University of Connecticut?

TERMINATION, BREACH, AND LIQUIDATED DAMAGES

 **KEY TERMS**
- Buyout
- Liquidated damages provision
- Negative injunctive relief

It is common for coaches to attempt to move up to a more prestigious college or university. For this reason, institutions increasingly seek some form of compensation when a coach leaves an institution prior to the expiration of the term of his or her contract. When the coach quits before his or her contract has expired, that coach has committed a breach of contract. The options theoretically available to an institution are to seek negative injunctive relief (i.e., a court order that would prevent the coach from coaching for another institution), to sue for damages, or simply to cancel the contract and allow the coach to leave. Institutions will most likely resort to an increasingly popular additional option: seek compensation under a buyout or liquidated damages provision. Liquidated damages are the amount specified in a contract that the parties have agreed is a reasonable estimation of the costs to the parties in the event of a breach. This amount must be a good faith estimate of actual damages and not merely a deterrence for breach or a penalty for the party that breaches. The amounts due to institutions under such provisions are often paid by the breaching coaches' new institutions.

The *DiNardo* case discusses the standards that courts apply in determining the validity of these contractual provisions, which are commonly referred to a liquidated damages clauses or provisions in coaching contracts.

Vanderbilt University v. DiNardo
174 F.3d 751 (6th Cir. 1999)

GIBSON, Circuit Judge.

[Editors' note: In November 1994, Louisiana State University (LSU) contacted Vanderbilt in hopes of speaking with Gerry DiNardo about becoming the head football coach for LSU. Paul Hoolahan, Vanderbilt's athletic director, gave DiNardo permission to speak to LSU about the position. On December 12, 1994, DiNardo announced that he was accepting the LSU position. Vanderbilt demanded that DiNardo pay liquidated damages under section 8 of the contract. Vanderbilt believed that DiNardo was liable for three years of his net salary: one year under the original contract and two years under the addendum. DiNardo did not respond to Vanderbilt's demand for payment.

The contract contained reciprocal liquidated damage provisions. Vanderbilt agreed to pay DiNardo his remaining salary should Vanderbilt replace him as football coach, and DiNardo agreed to reimburse Vanderbilt should he leave before his contract expired. Section 8 of the contract stated:]

> Mr. DiNardo recognizes that his promise to work for the University for the entire term of this 5-year Contract is of the essence of this Contract to the University. Mr. DiNardo also recognizes that the University is making a highly valuable investment in his continued employment by entering into this Contract and its investment would be lost were he to resign or otherwise terminate his employment as Head Football Coach with the University prior to the expiration of this Contract. Accordingly, Mr. DiNardo agrees that in the event he resigns or otherwise terminates his employment as Head Football Coach (as opposed to his resignation or termination from another position at the University to which he may have been reassigned), prior to the expiration of this Contract, and is employed or performing services for a person or institution other than the University, he will pay to the University as liquidated damages an amount equal to his Base Salary, less amounts that would otherwise be deducted or withheld from his Base Salary for income and social security tax purposes, multiplied by the number of years (or portion(s) thereof) remaining on the Contract.

[Vanderbilt sued DiNardo for breach of contract. The district court entered summary judgment for Vanderbilt, awarding $281,886.43 pursuant to section 8 of the employment contract. On appeal, DiNardo argued that the district court erred in concluding "that the contract provision was an enforceable liquidated damage provision and not an unlawful penalty under Tennessee law."]

We affirm the district court's ruling that the employment contract contained an enforceable liquidated damage provision and the award of liquidated damages under the original contract. . . .

I

DiNardo first claims that section eight of the contract is an unenforceable penalty under Tennessee law. DiNardo argues that the provision is not a liquidated damage provision but a "thinly disguised, overly broad non-compete provision," unenforceable under Tennessee law. . . .

Contracting parties may agree to the payment of liquidated damages in the event of a breach. . . . The term "liquidated damages" refers to an amount determined by the parties to be just compensation for damages should a breach occur. . . . Courts will not enforce such a provision, however, if the stipulated amount constitutes a penalty. . . . A penalty is designed to coerce performance by punishing default. . . . In Tennessee, a provision will be considered one for liquidated damages, rather than a penalty, if it is reasonable in relation to the anticipated damages for breach, measured prospectively at the time the contract was entered into, and not grossly disproportionate to the actual damages. . . . When these conditions are met, particularly the first, the parties probably intended the provision to be for liquidated damages. However, any doubt as to the character of the contract provision will be resolved in favor of finding it a penalty. . . .

The district court held that the use of a formula based on DiNardo's salary to calculate liquidated damages was reasonable "given the nature of the unquantifiable damages in the case." The court explained:

> The potential damage to [Vanderbilt] extends far beyond the cost of merely hiring a new head football coach. It is this uncertain potentiality that the parties sought to address by providing for a sum certain to apply towards anticipated expenses and losses. It is impossible to estimate how the loss of a head football coach will affect alumni relations, public support, football ticket sales, contributions, etc. . . . As such, to require a precise formula for calculating damages resulting from the breach of contract by a college head football coach would be tantamount to barring the parties from stipulating to liquidated damages evidence in advance.

Id. at 642.

DiNardo contends that there is no evidence that the parties contemplated that the potential damage from DiNardo's resignation would go beyond the cost of hiring a replacement coach. He argues that his salary has no relationship to Vanderbilt's damages and that the liquidated damage amount is unreasonable and shows that the parties did not intend the provision to be for liquidated damages.

DiNardo's theory of the parties' intent, however, does not square with the record. The contract language establishes that Vanderbilt wanted the five-year contract because "a long-term commitment" by DiNardo was "important to the University's desire for a stable intercollegiate football program," and that this commitment was of "essence" to the contract. Vanderbilt offered the two-year contract extension to DiNardo well over a year before his original contract expired. Both parties understood that the extension was to provide stability to the program, which helped in recruiting players and retaining assistant coaches. Thus, undisputed evidence, and reasonable inferences therefrom, establish that both parties understood and agreed that DiNardo's resignation would result in Vanderbilt suffering damage beyond the cost of hiring a replacement coach.

This evidence also refutes DiNardo's argument that the district court erred in presuming that DiNardo's resignation would necessarily cause damage to the

University. That the University may actually benefit from a coaching change (as DiNardo suggests) matters little, as we measure the reasonableness of the liquidated damage provision at the time the parties entered the contract, not when the breach occurred, *Kimbrough & Co.*, 939 S.W.2d at 108, and we hardly think the parties entered the contract anticipating that DiNardo's resignation would benefit Vanderbilt.

The stipulated damage amount is reasonable in relation to the amount of damages that could be expected to result from the breach. As we stated, the parties understood that Vanderbilt would suffer damage should DiNardo prematurely terminate his contract, and that these actual damages would be difficult to measure. *See Kimbrough & Co.*, 939 S.W.2d at 108. . . .

Vanderbilt hired DiNardo for a unique and specialized position, and the parties understood that the amount of damages could not be easily ascertained should a breach occur. Contrary to DiNardo's suggestion, Vanderbilt did not need to undertake an analysis to determine actual damages, and using the number of years left on the contract multiplied by the salary per year was a reasonable way to calculate damages considering the difficulty of ascertaining damages with certainty. *See Kimbrough & Co.*, 939 S.W.2d at 108. The fact that liquidated damages declined each year DiNardo remained under contract, is directly tied to the parties' express understanding of the importance of a long-term commitment from DiNardo. Furthermore, the liquidated damages provision was reciprocal and the result of negotiations between two parties, each of whom was represented by counsel.

We also reject DiNardo's argument that a question of fact remains as to whether the parties intended section eight to be a "reasonable estimate" of damages. The liquidated damages are in line with Vanderbilt's estimate of its actual damages. . . . Vanderbilt presented evidence that it incurred expenses associated with recruiting a new head coach of $27,000.00; moving expenses for the new coaching staff of $86,840; and a compensation difference between the coaching staffs of $184,311. The stipulated damages clause is reasonable under the circumstances, and we affirm the district court's conclusion that the liquidated damages clause is enforceable under Tennessee law.

Accordingly, we affirm the district court's judgment that the contract contained an enforceable liquidated damage provision, and we affirm the portion of the judgment reflecting damages calculated under the original five-year contract. . . .

DAVID A. NELSON, Circuit Judge, concurring in part and dissenting in part.

It seems to me that [section 8 of the contract] was designed to function as a penalty, not as a liquidation of the university's damages.

My principal reasons for viewing section eight as a penalty are these: (1) although the damages flowing from a premature resignation would normally be the same whether or not Coach DiNardo took a job elsewhere, section eight does not purport to impose liability for liquidated damages unless the coach accepts another job; (2) the section eight formula incorporates other variables that bear little or no relation to any reasonable approximation of anticipated damages; and (3) there is no evidence that the parties were attempting, in section eight, to come up with a reasonable estimate of the university's probable loss if the coach left. . . .

QUESTIONS

Do you agree with the majority or the dissent? What is the likely practical effect of buyout clauses such as that in *DiNardo*? Are liquidated damages clauses such as in *DiNardo* intended primarily to deter a coach from leaving an institution or to compensate an institution for the damages attributable to the loss of a coach's services? Shortly after the trial began, DiNardo settled the dispute by agreeing to pay Vanderbilt an undisclosed sum.

NOTE

University of West Virginia v. Rodriguez. The validity of a $4 million liquidated damages provision was at issue in a lawsuit filed by the University of West Virginia against its former head football coach Rich Rodriguez, who left the school in 2007 to assume the same position at the University of Michigan. The disputed $4 million liquidated damages provision was included in the Rodriguez–West Virginia contract after the coach had received an offer from another school. Rodriguez argued that he was induced by fraud and improper pressure to sign the agreement, that the disputed clause was an unenforceable penalty provision, and that West Virginia breached the contract by failing to abide by an oral commitment to reduce the agreed-on damage amount in the event that he resigned before the end of his contract term. The university argued the clause was valid and entered into in good faith. In July 2008, Rodriguez agreed to a $4 million settlement, pursuant to which Rodriguez and Michigan would pay $1.5 million and $2.5 million, respectively, to West Virginia. Rodriguez's new employer would also pay his attorney fees incurred in the litigation. Rodriguez's new contract with Michigan included a $4 million liquidated damages provision. See Vicki Smith, *Rodriguez, Michigan to Pay WVU $4 Million*, Pittsburgh Tribune, July 10, 2008. In November 2011, Rodriguez assumed the head coaching position at the University of Arizona. For a discussion of the factors that courts consider in determining the validity of a liquidated damages provision, see *Fleming v. Kent State Univ.*, 17 N.E. 3d 620 (Ohio. Ct. App. 2014).

EXPLORING OTHER CONTRACTUAL RELATIONSHIPS

As alluded to in Chapter 1's discussion of the role of contract law in sports, and as demonstrated in the foregoing discussion, contract is the predominant body of law in regulating many relationships in sports. The following discussion provides two illustrations of how contract law defines the rights and obligations of parties in two relationships: sport sponsorships and venue agreements.

A. *Sponsorship Agreements*

A *sponsorship agreement* is a contractual relationship whereby a company or organization sponsors (i.e., compensates) a sports league, team, athlete, or event in exchange for brand recognition. For example, in the National Association of Stock Car Auto Racing (NASCAR), a corporation may be a sponsor of NASCAR, an event, a team, or a driver. To enhance its brand recognition, a corporation may purchase the naming rights to a stadium at which a college or professional sports team plays its games. Similarly, a beer manufacturer will pay hundreds of millions of dollars to become the official beer sponsor of a sports league. A shoe manufacturer will enter into a sponsorship agreement with an athlete to wear and promote the manufacturer's athletic shoes, or a headphone company will enter into such an agreement with an athlete to advertise the company's headphones.

The increase in sports sponsorships and the evolution of sports sponsorship from traditional forms of advertising have increased the range of relevant legal and business issues that implicate substantive legal doctrine, including the law of agency, intellectual property, tax, and torts, which ultimately affect whether parties involved in sponsorship relationships achieve their business objectives.

Contract law, however, lies at the core of determining the contours of sports sponsorship relationships. Contract determines the scope of the sponsorship relationship, including whether it is an exclusive relationship; the outlines of the product categories to which the sponsorship relates; its duration, renewal, and termination of the relationship; and the parties' rights upon breach by one party or the other. In its endorsement contract with a coach or player, a company will include a "morals clause" in an effort to allow it to terminate the agreement if an athlete engages in behaviors that the company believes may damage its brand. See *Mendenhall v. HanesBrand, Inc.,* 856 F.Supp.2d 717 (M.D. N.C. 2012). Contract law will also serve as the source of law if a conflict should arise between a team and league regarding whether a team can enter into a sponsorship arrangement with a beer or apparel company other than the company with which the league has entered into an exclusive sponsorship arrangement. See *NFL Properties v. Dallas Cowboys,* 922 F.Supp. 49 (S.D. N.Y. 1996). Finally, a party's right to renew a sponsorship agreement will be largely governed by the law of contract. For a detailed discussion of sports sponsorship, see John A. Fortunato, Sports Sponsorship: Principles and Practices (2013).

B. Venue Agreements

Another type of agreement in which contract law plays a prominent role are *venue agreements,* which typically mean the lease agreements that teams enter into so that their teams can have a stadium at which to play. These agreements are complicated for many reasons, including that the team leases the stadium or facility from a city or other governmental entity. Contract law principles are critically relevant to matters relating to venue agreements, including the duration of the lease agreement; the purposes for which a team can use a stadium; a team's rental payment for use of the stadium; the allocation of responsibility for maintaining the stadium; the division of revenue generated by the facility; and the manner in which the lease agreement can be terminated. The venue agreement also intersects with other types of agreements, such as sponsorships and insurance, which also implicate contract law. For a detailed discussion of venue agreements, see Peter A. Carfagna, Negotiating and Drafting Sports Venue Agreements (2011).

Professional Sports League Governance and Legal Regulation

INTRODUCTION

This chapter focuses primarily on the governance and legal regulation of professional sports leagues, although it is important to recognize that other types of professional sports associations have similar characteristics and encounter similar legal problems. The greatest emphasis is on major league sports, particularly the National Football League (NFL), the National Basketball Association (NBA), Major League Baseball (MLB), and the National Hockey League (NHL). Other leagues (e.g., Major League Soccer (MLS)) and individual-performer sports (e.g., golf, tennis, and auto racing) also are considered. The professional sports leagues and other individual sport governing bodies are overwhelmingly driven by economics, which drives most internal decision making and creates most of the legal issues. Although there are substantial similarities in their internal regulatory regimes, each sport, whether it is a team or individual-performer sport, faces unique challenges. Consequently, generalization is hazardous, but certain common characteristics can be identified and analyzed.

We begin by describing the development of the North American professional sports industries (particularly team sports), their unique features, and their primary components. Next, internal league governance and a league commissioner's "best interests" of the sport authority are discussed. An introduction to federal antitrust law (specifically §1 of the Sherman Act), baseball's broad antitrust exemption, and antitrust law limits on other professional sports league rules and internal governance are considered. Finally, the historical responses of established leagues to the formation of rival leagues and resulting antitrust litigation under §2 of the Sherman Act is briefly reviewed.

ORIGIN AND EVOLUTION OF MODERN NORTH AMERICAN PROFESSIONAL SPORTS INDUSTRIES

The origins of today's most popular North American individual and team professional sports are to a large degree shrouded in mystery. The so-called Great American Pastime of baseball may not be American in origin at all. Some claim that it is a derivative of the English game of rounders. Of course, the well-known and honorable American claim for decades was that baseball started with Abner Doubleday in Cooperstown, New York. We even had a major league commission that investigated the matter over 100 years ago and verified that Doubleday was indeed the creator. That finding has been debunked and a better estimate is that baseball, at least as we know it, may have started on the Elysian Fields in New Jersey in 1848.

Football, the American version, has equally obscure beginnings. Most would attribute its modern origin to games at Harvard in 1871, when the rules were altered to allow players to scoop up the round ball and run with it. From that point forward, football would be played with more than feet. We do know that in the early 1900s, football had reached sufficient levels of mayhem to be condemned by the old Rough Rider himself, Theodore Roosevelt.

We are not at all certain of even the origin of the word *hockey*. Some of the theories are certainly amusing. It may have come from the French word *hoquet*, meaning "shepherd's crook." A more fanciful theory is that French explorers in North America observed Iroquois Indians playing a version of the game, striking a hard ball with sticks, and yelling, "Hogee!" ("It hurts!"). What is known is that something resembling the modern version was played in Canada as early as the 1830s.

The one sport that seems uncontroversial concerning its origins is basketball. Dr. James Naismith did nail a peach basket to a wall in the YMCA in Springfield, Massachusetts, on a cold, wintry day in 1891. He did this to provide something to keep the young men in his charge occupied. The appeal and potential for the sport for both men and women were established almost from the date of its founding. The first collegiate game between women was played at Smith College in 1893, and women at Stanford and the University of California at Berkeley introduced a female-rules version of the game in 1895.

As popular as these sports are in their present form, none can equal the foundations of golf and its journey to the modern day. Golf was so popular that in 1457, King James II of Scotland had his parliament ban it, lest it detract from more serious pursuits such as archery. But this ban was largely ignored and was completely overturned when King James IV of Scotland took up the game in the early sixteenth century. His granddaughter Mary, Queen of Scots, was a great devotee of the sport and took the game with her to France. She was attended by a host of young male admirers, known as *cadets*, who followed her over the meadows. They eventually were called *caddies*. Most caddies today probably are unaware of their noble lineage.

This brief history simply underscores the unique appeal that sports have always had, and these are but summary examinations of only a few of the sports that might be explored. From their humble origins, it is small wonder that sports have evolved in our modern age into overriding obsessions and commercial successes.

A. Evolution of Sports into a Business and Profession

Sports as activities, diversions, and cohesive societal events have been with us for centuries, but sports as professions, businesses, and industries are of more recent vintage. Along with the Industrial Revolution in the 1800s, a sports revolution occurred as well. This was no coincidence. Activity became a business, and business evolved into industry. For sports, the roots were perhaps not as obvious as the invention of steam locomotion or electricity harnessed into light, but sports took advantage of emerging industrial technologies just as surely as the wings of birds inspired the flight of man.

Each new step in the advancement of technology led to increased opportunities for sports exposure and thus expansion. Transportation was the first crucial ingredient. Communications was the second. The two have been powerful concomitants — necessary elements to allow sports to transcend the confines of the ballpark or arena and to enter the homes of millions of sports fans. Although the movers and shakers in early professional sports ventures could not have recognized fully the enormous commercial potential within their grasp, such is not true today. The preeminent sports business entrepreneurs are those with the greatest vision and ability to exploit this vast potential. Sports as commercial successes owe much to technological advances and to greater understanding of business and marketing techniques. There is still the game itself, with winners and losers, but there is a driving force — economic success — that is equally influential in just how, when, and where a game is played and who ultimately plays it.

In the United States, the sport of baseball was the pioneer for professional players, teams, and leagues. The Cincinnati Red Stockings are generally acknowledged as the first truly professional team, touring the country in 1869 and taking on all challengers. The National League, which still exists today, was founded in 1876, although some may take issue with it being designated as the first professional sports league. Though it bears perhaps small resemblance to its current structure within MLB, it was a significant start on the road to professionalization.

As baseball wended its uncertain way in developing the professional sports model, the sports of football, hockey, and basketball proceeded along even more tenuous paths. Their efforts were often greeted by apathy or even antipathy. The NFL's predecessor initially struggled and almost folded in 1920. Today, however, the NFL's ultimate astounding success and popularity are beyond dispute.

The NHL actually predated the NFL by two years, starting in 1918 in the aftermath of a one-year wonder, the National Hockey Association. However, the "national" designation signified Canada, not the United States. The first U.S. team, the Boston Bruins, did not join the league until 1924. Today, the number of American clubs significantly exceeds that of Canadian clubs. When the league took a more permanent form, four of the six clubs were located in the United States, with this trend continuing as the NHL expanded. Historically, NHL players were almost exclusively Canadian; this changed as hockey developed in the United States, leading to more U.S.-born NHL players. Additionally, the NHL increasingly looks to Europe for an infusion of talent. This grand mixture, with global implications, is in full force today.

The history of professional basketball has been circuitous. Players used to be called *cagers* because of the wire netting surrounding the court to keep the players from hurtling into the stands near the sidelines. The makeshift, precarious nature of the court was a fitting description for the business of basketball as well. There were teams who played for money, and there were leagues here and there. Through the 1920s and 1930s, the sport gained popularity but headed in directions both unknown and uncharted. The end of World War II caused a new beginning for sports in the United States, enabling the American public to seek new diversions. Professional basketball rode this wave. The NBA owes its foundations to the Basketball Association of America (BAA) in 1946.

Soccer, known to the rest of the world as *football,* is truly global in its nature and fan appeal, more so than any other American team sport. Its World Cup is the premier worldwide team sports event. Although MLS has not yet generated the economic revenues of the other leagues, it currently outdraws both the NBA and NHL in per-game attendance, securing a position now in the "Big Five."

Two individual-performer sports, among many, deserve mention. Tennis and golf have carved out special niches both in the United States and globally. But their movements from merely recreational activities to businesses have also been slow and often tested. Tennis and golf are more truly global than team sports because the top players in both sports come from all parts of the globe. American players currently do not dominate competition in these sports, and at times take a distinct backseat to foreign players. The star players attract fans, but there is the lack of local or regional identification because there is no "home team" to cheer or to jeer. Despite loyal and avid followings, the overall depth of support for these individual-performer sports pales in comparison to team sports, at least in the United States.

Professional tennis has existed since at least the 1920s, but the main action was in amateur tournaments. The pros were reduced to barnstorming, with the prevailing champion taking on the latest challenger from the amateur ranks. The big tournaments were closed to professionals. Only with the arrival of the open tennis era in 1968 did professional tennis truly emerge.

Golf also had its share of early professionals, with the U.S. Open dating from 1895 and later with Walter Hagen's winning the first Professional Golfers' Association (PGA) Championship in 1921. However, it was not until after World War II that professionals came to dominate the sport of golf.

Auto racing currently is one of the country's most popular professional spectator sports. The first Indianapolis 500 Mile Race was held in 1911. The National Association of Stock Car Auto Racing (NASCAR) has been in existence since 1951. NASCAR and the Indy Racing League each sponsors an annual series of popular auto races at tracks throughout the nation.

B. Unique Features of Professional Team Sports

Professional sports can be divided, in many respects, into two different categories: team sports and individual-performer sports. There is, at times, a confluence of the two, such as when golfers come together as a team for the Ryder or Walker Cup or tennis players do battle in the Davis Cup competitions. Individual performers, of course, also participate to a limited degree as teams in the Olympics and other international competitions. One might expand these types of sports to the team efforts leading to individual accomplishments in such sports as NASCAR or Indy auto racing. Even so, the heart of these athletic exploits is of an individual nature.

Team sports, which garner the major attention and dollars in the United States (except for perhaps the popular sports of auto racing and golf), have unique features that permeate their foundations and influence greatly how they operate. In turn, the legal consequences of these unique qualities raise ever-changing and complex challenges.

In team sports, a team must have other teams to play, of course. It is best if this is done on a continuing basis from one year to the next. Thus, there has to be competition in the playing of the games. But to sustain interest, at least theoretically, the competition cannot be too one-sided in favor of any single team from year to year. Team owners, players, and ultimately consumers tire of being perennial losers (although a few teams have a knack for doing so).

Without any agreed-on limitations, there is nothing to prevent teams from being economic competitors. Meaningful on-field competition economically benefits all league teams, but too much off-field economic competition can be harmful. The league's viability and the economic health of all teams necessitate some reasonable limits on economic competition among its member clubs.

Economic competition does exist among various sports leagues, either those who offer games in the same sport or those who offer different sports. Again, in the case of different sports, there are certain mutual advantages in not having too much economic competition. Teams in different sports located in the same city may peacefully coexist. On the other hand, each team needs a fan base for its sport and must appeal to a group of potential consumers who may transfer their interest from one sport to another as the fortunes of the various local teams ebb and flow. For example, professional hockey and basketball franchises in the same city, whose playing seasons largely overlap, often experience the whims of fair-weather fans.

Add to this mix the fact that professional sports leagues, while in existence in some form for well over a century, are relatively new as multibillion-dollar national and even international business operations. Even in the twenty-first century, teams and their owners, as well as their respective leagues, are still to a degree in an embryonic phase. Part of this results from the unique nature of professional team sports. There are no analogous models in other industries. The strong desire to compete successfully on the playing field versus the simultaneous need to limit economic competition among league clubs to some degree presents significant challenges to businesspeople accustomed to ruthless competition in other industries. To work both competitively and cooperatively can be very difficult.

If one adds players to this mix, business and legal issues multiply in their complexity. Highly skilled players are essential to the game's economic success and attractiveness to consumers. Sports, as commercial vehicles, thrive on the special talents of players, their celebrity status, and their resulting marketability. Major league professional athletes have unique talents and playing abilities, but they also must fit into the business and legal structures of the various sports.

The following section explores in greater depth how the respective roles of teams, leagues, players, and other important components of the sports industries interact and often conflict. This interplay illustrates the need for legal regulation of this complex web of relationships.

C. The Principal "Players" in the Professional Sports Industries

The old cliché "you can't tell the players without a scorecard" aptly describes why we cannot appreciate the dimensions of sports business and legal problems unless we understand what interests are involved and how these interests both intersect and conflict. The following discussion concerning the principal players uses the team-sports model; with only minor adjustments, it might also apply to individual-performer sports.

In general, the league, its commissioner, and the teams are aligned on one side; the players, their union, and player agents are on the other. However, a host of related entities play integral roles in a sports league's operations. For example, television and other media, as well as advertisers and corporate sponsors, significantly influence the business aspects of the professional team sports and individual-performer sports industries. Each of these components adds a layer of complexity and raises corresponding legal issues.

1. Leagues

North American professional sports leagues have existed since baseball's National League was founded in 1876. In essence, a sports league is a group of club owners that join together in a formal association to produce, market, and sell their product — organized athletic competition among their member teams. The formation of a league raises questions as to the legal nature of its relationship to its member clubs, as well as that among themselves and with a multitude of other entities.

2. Clubs or Teams

The terms *club* and *team* are used interchangeably in the professional sports context. Each major professional league (e.g., NFL, MLB, NBA, NHL, and MLS) has several member clubs located in cities throughout the United States or Canada, which may be expanded or contracted from time to time. Indeed, the growth in the popularity of professional sports is often tracked by the expansion in a league's number of teams. By the same token, a decline in interest is often marked by a reduction in teams and perhaps the demise of an entire league.

The legal nature and character of the interrelationship between a league and its member clubs are important from a legal standpoint, particularly for purposes of the antitrust laws. Even within a particular league, all clubs are not on equal footing. There is substantial variation in their approaches to the business in which they are engaged. A club's geographical location usually determines its potential consumer (i.e., fan) and economic base. Another important factor is the club's ownership, which in turn determines who operates and manages the club, thereby undoubtedly influencing who plays for the team and its performance level.

3. Commissioners

The concept of a league commissioner with broad governing authority came to fruition when MLB club owners appointed their first commissioner, Judge Kenesaw Mountain Landis, to his throne in 1921. This bold act was done to ensure that baseball would not witness another scandal such as befell the Chicago White Sox in the 1919 World Series. Commissioner Landis was given sweeping powers to act "in the best interests of baseball." He and his successors generally have not been hesitant to use those powers. The other North American major professional team sports have followed baseball's example by adopting a league commissioner model of governance. The existence of a commissioner with broad powers is an invitation to legal conflict. In this regard, there has been no shortage of disputes regarding a league commissioner's exercise of his plenary authority in a wide variety of situations.

4. Players

For professional athletes, sports are his or her livelihood, with many major league professional athletes earning multimillion-dollar annual salaries. However, most professional athletes have relatively short careers in their respective sports, which constitute a business that is part of the broader entertainment industry. He or she must be cognizant of the cold realities of this frequently harsh business, which may implicate his or her legal rights. The multitude of legal issues (primarily labor and antitrust law) involving professional athletes is fully explored in Chapter 12.

5. Players Associations

In most team sports, players associations today are usually certified labor unions. Players are employees of the club who have the right to organize as a union under federal labor law, which frequently gives rise to some unique legal issues; these issues are examined in Chapter 12.

6. Player Agents

Player agents, sometimes referred to as sports agents, most of whom are lawyers and trained professionals, represent professional team sport athletes in contract negotiations with their respective clubs. They also represent individual performer sport athletes. Player agents frequently handle or participate in the management of most aspects of their players' business affairs. As discussed in Chapter 13, agents who represent athletes in major league team sports are regulated by the players' union for the subject sport, and they also are subject to various federal and state laws.

7. Other Industries Integral to Modern Professional Sports

Several industries have both contributed to and benefited from the operation of professional sports leagues and associations. A prime example is the media, particularly television. Society today is much more pervasively connected to sports because professional sports events and news can be accessed throughout North America and many parts of the world through television, radio, print media, the Internet, and various handheld devices. Pervasive media coverage of sports has injected billions of dollars into the professional sports industries. Corporations provide huge sums to professional sports leagues, associations, and athletes for advertising and sponsorships. This produces a complex set of often conflicting interests and aspirations with corresponding legal problems.

INTERNAL LEAGUE GOVERNANCE AND COMMISSIONER AUTHORITY

Leagues and associations generally have a constitution and bylaws, which create a contractual relationship among the parties (e.g., clubs or individual members) that defines their respective legal rights and obligations. A central system of governance is identified, and there is a strong likelihood that one particular individual is given substantial authority to oversee the general operation of the organization. This individual is often designated as the commissioner of that particular league or association. The constitution and bylaws are considered to be the primary authority for the governance of the league or association. Because it is a private contract between the parties, only rarely can its terms and provisions be legally challenged in a successful manner—a circumstance more fully detailed in the paragraphs that follow. The following material focuses on relations and disputes between the league and its member clubs and their owners. To a limited extent, it also considers the nature and scope of regulatory authority of associations formed to govern individual-performer sports.

A. Legal Limits on Internal League Governance

 • Contract law
• De novo judicial review
• Fiduciary duty
• Law of private associations

American professional sports leagues and associations are private entities and are therefore not required to respect the federal constitutional rights of their members and players including First Amendment rights of free speech and freedom of association. *Long v. National Football League*, 870 F. Supp. 101 (W.D. Pa. 1994), *aff'd*, 66 F.3d 311 (3d Cir. 1994). The league or association constitution, bylaws, and rules create binding contractual rights and responsibilities if they are reasonable and do not infringe on other parties' rights. Thus, the legal relationships among member clubs or individuals of professional sports leagues are primarily governed by contract law and the law of private associations. The federal antitrust laws also play a significant role in circumscribing the governing activities of professional leagues and associations.

Courts recognize that private associations must be accorded considerable latitude in rule making and enforcement in order to accomplish their legitimate objectives. They generally permit professional sports leagues and associations to establish their respective systems of self-governance and are reluctant to interfere with or second-guess their internal decision making. Contract law generally binds their members to the terms of the sports league or association's constitution, bylaws, and other governing documents unless there is a breach of fiduciary duty, a conflict of interest, bad faith, or violation of applicable laws such as, for example, federal antitrust law. But otherwise there is broad discretion accorded to a sports league or association to interpret its own rules without judicial intervention, as illustrated by the following cases.

In *Koszela v. National Association of Stock Car Auto Racing, Inc.*, 646 F.2d 749 (2d Cir. 1981), the Second Circuit rejected the claims of a stock car owner and driver that NASCAR misapplied its rules in determining that another car and driver were the winners of two races. The court found that the plaintiffs' membership contract with NASCAR did not provide for an administrative appeal or judicial review of official decisions regarding race procedures or determination of car positions. The court concluded that the plaintiffs had been given an opportunity to be heard by NASCAR officials and had exhausted all available rights. The court affirmed the dismissal of the plaintiffs' claims and held that NASCAR was not in violation of any contractual duties owed to the plaintiffs.

A similar result was reached in *Crouch v. National Association of Stock Car Auto Racing, Inc.*, 845 F.2d 397 (2d Cir. 1988). At issue was whether NASCAR violated its own procedures in determining the winner of a stock car race. The court initially drew a distinction between reviewing the decisions made by private organizations and reviewing the procedures used in reaching those decisions. The court recognized the appropriateness of intervening if there were inadequate procedures to safeguard a member's rights, but the plaintiffs did not make any such assertions. Nor was there any allegation that NASCAR violated its own rules or that NASCAR officials acted in bad faith in reviewing the plaintiffs' challenge to the race results. The Second Circuit held that the lower court erred in delving into NASCAR's rulebook and providing de novo judicial review (i.e., substituting its judgment for that of the governing body and deciding the merits of the dispute, rather than simply determining whether it complied with its own rules and rendered a reasonable decision). Instead, the proper approach was to defer to an association's interpretation of its own rules absent a showing of bad faith or violation of any state or federal laws.

Despite a general judicial reluctance to oversee a professional sports organization's affairs to avoid becoming mired down in areas outside their expertise, courts will nevertheless provide a forum for resolution of internal governance disputes. At least at the major league level, a professional sports league is often without direct competition from another league. Because of the for-profit and monopolistic nature of major professional sports leagues and associations, there is a recognized need for some limited judicial oversight to prevent exploitation and blatant unfairness toward any of the organization's members or participants. As the *Koszela* court observed, when a sports organization has such a "'strangle-hold'" that all teams or individuals desiring to participate in a sport must join it, "rigid adherence to a 'hands off' policy is inappropriate." 646 F.2d at 754.

A sport governing body has a legal obligation to follow its own rules and bylaws; its failure to do so may give rise to a breach of contract claim by an aggrieved member whose interests are harmed. Courts will intervene and grant appropriate legal relief "(1) where the rules, regulations or judgments of the association are in contravention to the laws of the land or in disregard of the charter or bylaws of the association and (2) where the association has failed to follow the basic rudiments of due process of law." *Charles O. Finley & Co. v. Kuhn*, 569 F.2d 527, 544 (7th Cir. 1978). In addition, courts will intervene if an association's decision-making process is arbitrary or capricious, or is tainted by malice or bad faith.

Gilder v. PGA Tour, Inc., 727 F. Supp. 1333 (D. Ariz. 1989), *aff'd*, 936 F.2d 417 (9th Cir. 1991), illustrates the potential for conflicts of interest that may require judicial intervention when individuals with vested interests make rules and policy for the association as a whole. Nine members of the PGA Tour sued the PGA for amending its tournament regulations to prohibit the use of golf clubs with U-shaped grooves. The PGA's then-existing bylaws permitted these rules to be amended only by an affirmative vote of a majority of its ten-member board (including at least three of the four directors who were professional golfers playing on the PGA Tour) at a regular meeting attended by a quorum. At a meeting of the board attended by all ten members, the ban on U-shaped grooved irons was passed when three members who were not touring professionals voted in favor of the amendment and the other seven board members abstained because of possible conflicts of interest because each of them had endorsement deals with manufacturers of U-shaped grooved irons. Four of the abstaining members were touring professionals in competition with those using the U-shaped grooved clubs, and three others were officers of the PGA.

After the plaintiffs, a group of professional golfers who wanted to use clubs with U-shaped grooves, complained about this voting procedure, the board unanimously voted to permit amendments to the PGA's tournament regulations by a majority vote of present board members who actually voted. The same three PGA board members again voted to ban the U-shaped irons, and the other seven members once again abstained from voting.

Observing that the effect of the PGA board's amended voting requirement and the abstentions by seven directors was to ban U-shaped irons, the district court issued a preliminary injunction against this prohibition based on the board's failure to follow its own rules. The Ninth Circuit affirmed and held that the touring professional golfers serving on the PGA's board owe a fiduciary duty to act in the best interests of the association as a whole and are prohibited from using their position for potential personal gain. Their vote to amend the bylaws' voting procedures, which resulted in U-shaped irons being banned, breached their fiduciary duty.

Courts have also imposed implied covenants of good faith and fair dealing in contracts governing the internal affairs of professional sports leagues; an example is a case arising out of the Oakland Raiders' initial move to Los Angeles in the early 1980s. The Ninth Circuit applied California law in ruling that league teams owed each other a reciprocal duty "to refrain from doing anything to injure the right of the other to receive the benefits of the agreement . . . [and] the duty to do everything that the contract presupposes that he will do to accomplish the purpose." *Los Angeles Memorial Coliseum Commission v. National Football League*, 791 F.2d 1356, 1361 (9th Cir. 1986). Concerning franchise relocation, the court held that each league member must exercise its contractual right of approval or disapproval or its discretionary power over the interests of others in good faith.

Similarly, in *Professional Hockey Corp. v. World Hockey Assn.*, 191 Cal. Rptr. 773, 777 (Cal. Ct. App. 1983), the court ruled that each club's representative on the board of directors of a professional sports league structured as a corporation "owes the league as a whole the traditional fiduciary duties in this commonly shared corporate purpose." It explained: "The law requires, irrespective of the competitive personal feelings the various owners of teams may have towards each other, when they or their representatives sit on the board of directors of [the World Hockey Association (WHA)] to the extent they have common corporate goals, they have a duty to make decisions for the benefit of the corporation, the hockey league as a whole."

In summary, these cases illustrate that courts generally are reluctant to interfere with the internal affairs of a professional sports league or association unless there are specific breaches of its rules or contracts with its member clubs or individuals, evidence of bad faith dealing, or violations of state or federal law.

B. League Commissioner's "Best Interests of the Game" Authority and Legal Limits

KEY TERMS
- Commissioner "best interests of the game" authority
- Procedural due process

The major professional sports leagues in the United States have all adopted a model of organization and governance that places an independent commissioner in control of internal affairs. This official is certainly more powerful than a chairperson of the board of a corporation, and he or she probably wields more power than a typical president of a company. Although selected by and answerable to the league owners and their governing body, a sports league commissioner traditionally has been accorded certain powers and attendant enforcement rights that create a special role.

The first commissioner in any U.S. professional sport was Judge Kenesaw Mountain Landis, who assumed that position in baseball in 1920 to ensure that the infamous Black Sox scandal involving the "fixing" of games by Chicago White Sox players during the 1919 World Series would not recur. Reportedly, at his insistence, Judge Landis was accorded the authority to do whatever was necessary to protect the "best interests" of baseball. That same sweeping power — to act in the best interests of the sport — is found in similar phraseology in the description of powers and duties vested in all commissioners of the American major professional sports leagues. To that end, the commissioner is delegated disciplinary powers, dispute resolution authority, and decision-making responsibility. Although an employee of the league, the commissioner is granted virtual autonomous authority to govern a great extent of a league's affairs without direct supervision or control by the member clubs. The commissioner is hired by the owners and can be fired; however, while in office, the commissioner cannot easily be challenged successfully.

A league's commissioner is an integral part of the league's governance structure, whose role often consists of the following functions:

1. To create a fair and impartial internal authority to resolve disputes within the league and to enforce independently a disciplinary process — these being essential to maintain the game's integrity and provide rudimentary due process protections necessary to avoid judicial oversight of league affairs.
2. To take action when needed to restrain the unwarranted exercise of power by the league's owners to the detriment of fans and others, again to avoid judicial intervention.
3. To serve as a centralized administrative authority to facilitate efficient decision making and league governance.
4. To be a skillful mediator when owners cannot agree.
5. To be the lead negotiator for leaguewide contracts, such as the all-important television deals.
6. At times, to become involved in labor disputes between the owners and the players — in fact, in some leagues, the commissioner is the lead negotiator on behalf of the owners. (Such is the case today in the NBA and the NHL.)

Despite having the above powers, it must be emphasized that a league commissioner does not have unfettered independence or authority. At times, he or she must walk a tightrope to avoid undermining or losing his or her authority. The commissioner, for example, has certain disciplinary authority over the league's club owners and can make decisions adverse to some or even all of them and their interests. Even so, the commissioner's job security is subject to the will of these owners, and a commissioner may be put in the middle of disputes that pose threats to his position. A commissioner may feel compelled to compromise to avoid alienating owners, which could possibly reduce his or her authority or possibly jeopardize his or her continued employment. For example, MLB commissioner Fay Vincent resigned in August 1992 under pressure from MLB club owners after making a series of controversial decisions.

A sports league commissioner's authority is contractual in nature and derived from the league's constitution, bylaws, and operating rules. The most sweeping power that a league commissioner is typically granted is the ability to take action deemed necessary to further the best interests of the sport. As illustrated by the following case, interpretation of the nature and scope of the commissioner's contractual authority ultimately is a question for judicial resolution. Courts usually provide substantial deference to the commissioner's exercise of judgment and carefully consider the customs and usages under which the current commissioner and predecessors have operated. However, a court will require a league commissioner to have valid authority to act, to comply with basic notions of due process, to not act in bad faith, and to not contravene any state or federal laws.

Charles O. Finley & Co., Inc. v. Kuhn
569 F.2d 527 (7th Cir. 1978), *cert. denied*, 439 U.S. 876 (1978)

SPRECHER, Circuit Judge.

The defendant Bowie K. Kuhn is the Commissioner of baseball (Commissioner), having held that position since 1969. On June 18, 1976, the Commissioner disapproved the assignments of the contracts of [Joe] Rudi, [Rollie] Fingers and [Vida] Blue [by the Oakland Athletics MLB club] to the Red Sox and Yankees "as inconsistent with the best interests of baseball, the integrity of the game and the maintenance of public confidence in it." The Commissioner expressed his concern for (1) the debilitation of the Oakland club, (2) the lessening of the competitive balance of professional baseball through the buying of success by the more affluent clubs, and (3) "the present unsettled circumstances of baseball's reserve system." . . .

II

Basic to the underlying suit brought by Oakland and to this appeal is whether the Commissioner of baseball is vested by contract with the authority to disapprove player assignments which he finds to be "not in the best interests of baseball." In assessing the measure and extent of the Commissioner's power and authority, consideration must be given to the circumstances attending the creation of the office of Commissioner, the language employed by the parties in drafting their contractual understanding, changes and amendments adopted from time to time, and the interpretation given by the parties to their contractual language throughout the period of its existence. . . .

In November, 1920, the major league club owners unanimously elected federal Judge Kenesaw Mountain Landis as the sole Commissioner of baseball and appointed a committee of owners to draft a charter setting forth the Commissioner's authority. In one of the drafting sessions an attempt was made to place limitations on the Commissioner's authority. Judge Landis responded by refusing to accept the office of Commissioner.

On January 12, 1921, Landis told a meeting of club owners that he had agreed to accept the position upon the clear understanding that the owners had sought "an authority . . . outside of your own business, and that a part of that authority would be a control over whatever and whoever had to do with baseball." Thereupon, the owners voted unanimously to reject the proposed limitation upon the Commissioner's authority, they all signed what they called the Major League Agreement, and Judge Landis assumed the position of Commissioner. Oakland has been a signatory to the Major League Agreement continuously since 1960. The agreement, a contract between the constituent clubs of the National and American Leagues, is the basic charter under which major league baseball operates.

The Major League Agreement provides that "[t]he functions of the Commissioner shall be . . . to investigate . . . any act, transaction or practice . . . not in the best interests of the national game of Baseball" and "to determine . . . what preventive, remedial or punitive action is appropriate in the premises, and to take such action. . . ." Art. I, Sec. 2(a) and (b).

The Major League Rules, which govern many aspects of the game of baseball, are promulgated by vote of major league club owners. Major League Rule 12(a) provides that "no . . . (assignment of players) shall be recognized as valid unless . . . approved by the Commissioner."

The Major Leagues and their constituent clubs severally agreed to be bound by the decisions of the Commissioner and by the discipline imposed by him. They further agreed to "waive such right of recourse to the courts as would otherwise have existed in their favor." Major League Agreement, Art. VII, Sec. 2. . . .

The Commissioner has been given broad power in unambiguous language to investigate any act, transaction or practice not in the best interests of baseball, to determine what preventive, remedial or punitive action is appropriate in the premises, and to take that action. He has also been given the express power to approve or disapprove the assignments of players. In regard to nonparties to the agreement, he may take such other steps as he deems necessary and proper in the interests of the morale of the players and the honor of the game. Further, indicative of the nature of the Commissioner's authority is the provision whereby the parties agree to be bound by his decisions and discipline imposed and to waive recourse to the courts. . . .

In view of the broad authority expressly given by the Major League Agreement to the Commissioner, particularly in Section 2 of Article I, we agree with the district court that Section 3 does not purport to limit that authority.

III

Despite the Commissioner's broad authority to prevent any act, transaction or practice not in the best interests of baseball, Oakland has attacked the Commissioner's disapproval of the Rudi-Fingers-Blue transactions on a variety of theories which seem to express a similar thrust in differing language.

The complaint alleged that the "action of Kuhn was arbitrary, capricious, unreasonable, discriminatory, directly contrary to historical precedent, baseball tradition, and prior rulings and actions of the Commissioner." In pre-trial answers to interrogatories, Oakland acknowledged that the Commissioner could set aside a proposed assignment of a player's contract "in an appropriate case of violation of (Major League) Rules or immoral or unethical conduct." . . .

The plaintiff has argued that it is a fundamental rule of law that the decisions of the head of a private association must be procedurally fair. Plaintiff then argued that it was "procedurally unfair" for the Commissioner to fail to warn the plaintiff that he would "disapprove large cash assignments of star players even if they complied with the Major League Rules."

It must be recalled that prior to the assignments involved here drastic changes had commenced to occur in the reserve system and in the creation of free agents. In his opinion disapproving the Rudi, Fingers, and Blue assignments, the Commissioner said that "while I am of course aware that there have been cash sales of player contracts in the past, there has been no instance in my judgment which had the potential for harm to our game as do these assignments, particularly in the present unsettled circumstances of baseball's reserve system and in the highly competitive circumstances we find in today's sports and entertainment world."

Absent the radical changes in the reserve system, the Commissioner's action would have postponed Oakland's realization of value for these players. Given those changes, the relative fortunes of all major league clubs became subject to a host of intangible speculations. No one could predict then or now with certainty that Oakland would fare better or worse relative to other clubs through the vagaries of the revised reserve system occurring entirely apart from any action by the Commissioner. . . .

[T]he Commissioner was vested with broad authority and that authority was not to be limited in its exercise to situations where Major League Rules or moral turpitude was involved. When professional baseball intended to place limitations upon the Commissioner's powers, it knew how to do so. In fact, it did so during the 20-year period from 1944 to 1964.

The district court found and concluded that the Rudi-Fingers-Blue transactions were not, as Oakland had alleged in its complaint, "directly contrary to historical precedent, baseball tradition, and prior rulings." During his almost 25 years as Commissioner, Judge Landis found many acts, transactions, and practices to be detrimental to the best interests of baseball in situations where neither moral turpitude nor a Major League Rule violation was involved, and he disapproved several player assignments.

On numerous occasions since he became Commissioner of baseball in February 1969, Kuhn has exercised broad authority under the best interests clause of the Major League Agreement. Many of the actions taken by him have been in response to acts, transactions or practices that involved neither the violation of a Major League Rule nor any gambling, game-throwing or other conduct associated with moral turpitude. Moreover, on several occasions Commissioner Kuhn has taken broad preventive or remedial action with respect to assignments of player contracts. . . .

We conclude that the evidence fully supports, and we agree with, the district court's finding and conclusion that the Commissioner "acted in good faith, after investigation, consultation and deliberation, in a manner which he determined to be in the best interests of baseball" and that "(w)hether he was right or wrong is beyond the competence and the jurisdiction of this court to decide." . . .

We affirm the district court's judgment. . . .

> NOTE

Judicial interpretation of "best interests" power. As in *Finley*, in *Oakland Raiders v. National Football League*, 131 Cal. App. 4th 621, 32 Cal. Rptr. 3d 266 (Cal. App. 2005), a California state appellate court rejected the Oakland Raiders club's claim that the NFL and Commissioner Paul Tagliabue took various actions that were discriminatory toward the Raiders and placed it at a competitive disadvantage vis-à-vis other member clubs. Finding that "the Raiders had not shown any evidence of a violation of a clear and unambiguous provision of the NFL constitution," the court explained, "We observe that the rationale of [judicial] abstention from intra-association disputes applies with particular force in this instance. Given the unique and specialized nature of this association's business — the operation of a professional football league — there is significant danger that judicial intervention in such disputes will have the undesired and unintended effect of interfering with the League's autonomy in matters where the NFL and its commissioner have much greater competence and understanding than the courts." *Id.* at 284.

Although a court generally will not second-guess a league commissioner's exercise of discretionary judgment, it will require that the commissioner have valid authority to take the challenged action. In *Chicago National League Ball Club, Inc. v. Vincent*, 1992 WL 179208 (N.D. Ill. 1992), a federal district court held that the MLB commissioner could not order involuntary realignment of the teams in the National League pursuant to his "best interests of the game" authority. The Chicago Cubs successfully challenged Commissioner Vincent's authority to transfer the club to the Western Division of the National League. In 1992, ten National League clubs voted to realign their two divisions so that the Cubs and St. Louis Cardinals would move to the Western Division, and the Atlanta Braves and Cincinnati Reds would move to the Eastern Division. The Cubs and New York Mets voted against the proposed realignment. The National League Constitution required approval by three-fourths of the league's clubs for divisional realignment but provided that no club could be transferred to a different division without its consent. Nevertheless, acting on the request of several National League clubs to intervene, Commissioner Vincent ordered the proposed realignment in accordance with his "best interests" power. The court preliminarily enjoined the commissioner's order from taking effect based on its finding that he exceeded his authority and impaired the Cubs' contract rights under the National League Constitution. Although the Major League Agreement empowered the commissioner to resolve disputes among member clubs and conferred broad "best interests" power, this authority did not extend to disputes whose resolution is otherwise expressly provided for in the constitution of either Major League.

When exercising disciplinary authority, courts require a league commissioner to provide due process to the party subject to sanctions. A party is entitled to notice of the alleged misconduct and a fair opportunity to be heard before any discipline is imposed or its rights are adversely affected. The league's constitution generally establishes contractual procedural safeguards or enables the commissioner to formulate rules necessary to satisfy the minimum requirements of due process in connection with a disciplinary proceeding.

A league commissioner must follow established procedural rules when exercising disciplinary authority and act in an impartial and fair manner without prejudging the merits of the matter before him. In *Rose v. Giamatti*, No. A8905178, 1989 WL 111447 (Ct. Com. Pl. Ohio, Hamilton Co. June 26, 1989), a state trial judge temporarily enjoined MLB commissioner Bart Giamatti from holding a disciplinary hearing to determine whether Pete Rose placed bets on MLB games. The court relied on affidavit testimony alleging that Rose was being denied his right to a fair hearing before the commissioner. After reviewing a report prepared by his special investigator, the commissioner wrote a letter to a federal judge on behalf of Ron Peters, a convicted drug dealer who was awaiting sentencing. The letter stated that Peters had provided sworn testimony concerning allegations that Rose had bet on MLB, and that the commissioner was satisfied that Peters had told the truth to his special investigator. Commissioner Giamatti and Rose ultimately entered into a settlement agreement pursuant to which Rose accepted a lifetime suspension from baseball, which has prevented Rose from being eligible for induction into baseball's Hall of Fame.

Problem 11-1

Soon after an audio recording became public in which Los Angeles Clippers owner Donald Sterling made racist comments indicating that he did not welcome African Americans at Clippers games, NBA Commissioner Adam Silver fined him $2.5 million and indefinitely banned him from having any involvement in the management or operation of the club. Sterling's comments promptly attracted substantial outrage: Clippers team members protested by tossing their warm-up jackets on the floor at midcourt and wearing their team jerseys inside out before a game, several companies terminated their sponsorship agreements with the Clippers, and a number of NBA players publicly condemned his remarks and suggested the possibility of boycotting Clippers games. Consider whether this disciplinary action against Sterling was a valid exercise of Commissioner's Silver's "best interests" authority, and whether a court would uphold it if challenged by Sterling.

FEDERAL ANTITRUST LAW LIMITS ON LEAGUE RULES AND GOVERNANCE

A. Overview

The federal antitrust laws, specifically §1 of the Sherman Act (15 U.S.C. §1), prohibit agreements and collective action that unreasonably restrain "interstate trade or commerce" in order to preserve a competitive marketplace that provides consumers with a variety of desired and affordable products and services. In other words, businesses that produce the same product should compete with each other on price, product quality, and other characteristics rather than agree to eliminate economic competition among themselves. Because of the unique nature of professional sports (particularly team sports), it is very difficult for courts to apply the antitrust laws in a principled and consistent fashion. In order to produce professional sports competition in a form attractive to consumers (e.g., close and exciting games), numerous agreements (including rules) between and among a league, its member clubs, and its players are necessarily required—all of which are potentially subject to antitrust challenge under §1. Traditional antitrust law jurisprudence does not provide a simple means of accurately measuring whether a professional sports league's governing rules, agreements, and conduct enhance or harm consumer welfare as represented by the interests of sports fans. As a result, courts have found it difficult to apply federal antitrust law to professional sports.

B. Baseball's Antitrust Exemption

In 1922, the Supreme Court decided its first antitrust case involving professional sports, deciding specifically the issue of whether organized professional baseball is subject to the Sherman Act while demonstrating its reluctance to apply the federal antitrust laws to professional sports. In *Federal Baseball Club of Baltimore, Inc. v. National League of Professional Baseball Clubs*, 259 U.S. 200 (1922), the Court ruled that professional baseball is a business (i.e., it constitutes "trade or commerce"), but that it is not interstate in nature, as required to be regulated by the Sherman Act:

> The business is giving exhibitions of baseball, which are purely state affairs. It is true that, in order to attain for these exhibitions the great popularity that they have achieved, competitions must be arranged between clubs from different cities and States. But the fact that in order to give the exhibitions the Leagues must induce free persons to cross state lines and must arrange and pay for their doing so is not enough to change the character of the business. According to the distinction insisted upon in *Hooper v. California*, 155 U.S. 648, 655 . . . the transport is a mere incident, not the essential thing. That to which it is incident, the exhibition, although made for money would not be called trade or commerce in the commonly accepted use of those words. As it is put by the defendants, personal effort, not related to production, is not a subject of commerce. That which in its consummation is not commerce does not become commerce among the States because the transportation . . . takes place. To repeat the illustrations given by the Court below, a firm of lawyers sending out a member to argue a case . . . does not engage in such commerce because the lawyer . . . goes to another State.

In a 1953 case, *Toolson v. New York Yankees*, 346 U.S. 356 (1953), the Supreme Court reaffirmed *Federal Baseball Club*, observing that baseball had been allowed to develop for more than 30 years without being subject to the antitrust laws. The Court also observed that Congress did not eliminate baseball's antitrust exemption, thereby evidencing its intention that organized baseball not be covered by the antitrust laws.

Two dissenting justices vigorously argued that professional baseball is interstate in nature and that Congress had not expressly exempted baseball from the Sherman Act.

On the other hand, after *Toolson*, the Supreme Court held that other professional sports such as football (*Radovich v. National Football League*, 352 U.S. 445 (1957)), basketball (*Haywood v. NBA*, 401 U.S. 1204 (1971)), and boxing (*United States v. Int'l Boxing Club of N.Y., Inc.*, 348 U.S. 236 (1955)) are subject to antitrust laws because their respective business activities occur in interstate commerce. Regarding baseball, however, court decisions continued to follow *Toolson*, holding that professional baseball retained its immunity from federal antitrust laws. See, e.g., *Salerno v. American League of Prof'l Baseball Clubs*, 429 F.2d 1003 (2d Cir. 1970); *Portland Baseball Club, Inc. v. Baltimore Baseball Club, Inc.*, 282 F.2d 680 (9th Cir. 1960).

This background set the stage for the Supreme Court's 1972 reconsideration of whether professional baseball is subject to federal antitrust law.

Flood v. Kuhn
407 U.S. 258 (1972)

Mr. Justice BLACKMUN delivered the opinion of the Court.

For the third time in 50 years the Court is asked specifically to rule that professional baseball's reserve system is within the reach of the federal antitrust laws. . . .

[Editors' note: Curt Flood rose to fame as a center fielder with the St. Louis Cardinals during the years 1958–1969 and distinguished himself as a star player. But at the age of 31, in October 1969, Flood was traded to the Philadelphia Phillies of the National League in a multiplayer transaction. He was not consulted about the trade. He was informed by telephone and received formal notice only after the deal had been consummated. In December, he complained to the baseball commissioner and asked that he be made a free agent and be placed at liberty to strike his own bargain with any other major league team. His request was denied. Thereafter, he filed an antitrust challenge to baseball's reserve system, which effectively precluded him from contracting with the major league baseball club of his choice. Flood declined to play for Philadelphia in 1970, despite a $100,000 salary offer, and he sat out the year. After the season was concluded, Philadelphia sold its rights to Flood to the Washington Senators. Washington and the petitioner were able to come to terms for 1971 at a salary of $110,000. Flood started the season, but apparently because he was dissatisfied with his performance, he left the Washington club on April 27, early in the campaign. From this time until he filed suit, Flood had not played baseball. Relying on *Federal Baseball Club* and *Toolson*, the U.S. Court of Appeals for the Second Circuit affirmed the district court's dismissal of Flood's suit.]

It seems appropriate now to say that:

1. Professional baseball is a business and it is engaged in interstate commerce.
2. With its reserve system enjoying exemption from the federal antitrust laws, baseball is, in a very distinct sense, an exception and an anomaly. *Federal Baseball* and *Toolson* have become an aberration confined to baseball.

3. Even though others might regard this as "unrealistic, inconsistent, or illogical," the aberration is an established one, and one that has been recognized not only in Federal Baseball and *Toolson*, but in *Shubert, International Boxing*, and *Radovich*, as well, a total of five consecutive cases in this Court. . . . It is an aberration that has been with us now for half a century, one heretofore deemed fully entitled to the benefit of stare decisis, and one that has survived the Court's expanding concept of interstate commerce. It rests on a recognition and an acceptance of baseball's unique characteristics and needs.

4. Other professional sports operating interstate—football, boxing, basketball, and, presumably, hockey and golf—are not so exempt.

5. The advent of radio and television, with their consequent increased coverage and additional revenues, has not occasioned an overruling of *Federal Baseball* and *Toolson*.

6. The Court has emphasized that since 1922, baseball, with full and continuing congressional awareness, has been allowed to develop and to expand unhindered by federal legislative action. Remedial legislation has been introduced repeatedly in Congress but none has ever been enacted. The Court, accordingly, has concluded that Congress as yet has had no intention to subject baseball's reserve system to the reach of the antitrust statutes. This, obviously, has been deemed to be something other than mere congressional silence and passivity.

7. The Court has expressed concern about the confusion and the retroactivity problems that inevitably would result with a judicial overturning of *Federal Baseball*. It has voiced a preference that if any change is to be made, it come by legislative action that, by its nature, is only prospective in operation.

8. The Court noted in *Radovich*, 352 U.S., at 452, 77 S.Ct., at 394, that the slate with respect to baseball is not clean. Indeed, it has not been clean for half a century.

This emphasis and this concern are still with us. We continue to be loath, 50 years after *Federal Baseball* and almost two decades after *Toolson*, to overturn those cases judicially when Congress, by its positive inaction, has allowed those decisions to stand for so long and, far beyond mere inference and implication, has clearly evinced a desire not to disapprove them legislatively.

Accordingly, we adhere once again to *Federal Baseball* and *Toolson* and to their application to professional baseball. We adhere also to *International Boxing* and *Radovich* and to their respective applications to professional boxing and professional football. If there is any inconsistency or illogic in all this, it is an inconsistency and illogic of long standing that is to be remedied by the Congress and not by this Court. If we were to act otherwise, we would be withdrawing from the conclusion as to congressional intent made in *Toolson* and from the concerns as to retrospectivity therein expressed. Under these circumstances, there is merit in consistency even though some might claim that beneath that consistency is a layer of inconsistency. . . .

The judgment of the Court of Appeals is affirmed. . . .

If all other professional sports leagues, organizations, and governing bodies are subject to the federal antitrust laws, why should baseball continue to have a broad common law antitrust immunity?

NOTE

Lower courts' interpretation of *Flood*. Most courts have broadly construed *Flood* to exempt all aspects of the "business of baseball" from federal antitrust laws, including the following: disputes concerning compensation of minor league clubs for harm to their assigned territories (*Portland Baseball Club, Inc. v. Kuhn*, 491 F. Supp. 1101 (9th Cir. 1974)); exercise of the commissioner's "best interests of baseball authority" (*Charles O. Finley & Co., Inc. v. Kuhn*, 569 F.2d 527 (7th Cir. 1978)); the minor league player assignment system, club location system, and scheduling rules (*Professional Baseball Schools and Clubs, Inc. v. Kuhn*, 693 F.2d 1085 (11th Cir. 1982)); major league club owners' alleged unfair labor practices during a players' strike (*McCoy v. Major League Baseball*, 911 F. Supp. 454 (W.D. Wash. 1995)); major league club location issues (*City of San Jose v. MLB*, 766 F.3d 686 (9th Cir. 2015)); and a state attorney general's investigation of a proposed sale and relocation of a baseball club (*Major League Baseball v. Christ*, 331 F.3d 1177 (11th Cir. 2003), and *Minnesota Twins Partnership v. Hatch*, 592 N.W.2d 847 (Minn. 1999)). However, in *Laumann v. NHL* 56 F.3d 280, 297 (S.D.N.Y. 2014), a consumer antitrust suit challenging the territorial broadcasting rights systems established by MLB and the NHL, a federal district court ruled that baseball's antitrust exemption was inapplicable: "Exceptions to the antitrust laws are to be construed narrowly. Moreover, the Supreme Court has expressly questioned the validity and logic of the baseball exemption and declined to extend it to other sports. I therefore decline to apply the exemption to a subject that is not central to the business of baseball, and that Congress did not intend to exempt — namely baseball's contracts for television broadcasting rights."

C. Application of Sherman Act §1

1. Concerted Action Requirement

KEY TERM • Single economic entity defense

Professional leagues and their member clubs are economically interdependent. One team cannot survive without other league teams as on-field competitors. To offer an attractive product desirable to consumers, a professional sports league must maintain on-field competitive balance among its member teams and preserve the long-term financial viability of each club. In an effort to achieve these objectives, league rules may either prohibit certain conduct by an individual club owner or require its approval by a majority of other member clubs to avoid harming the league's collective economic interests. League rules or its member clubs' collective decisions may limit an individual club owner's ability to sell or relocate the club, contract with third parties in an effort to maximize the team's revenues, or take other desired action.

As a defense to Sherman Act §1 claims, professional sports leagues (particularly the NFL) have argued that the league and its member clubs collectively produce a single product (e.g., NFL football) that no individual club is capable of producing. Therefore, unlike competing producers of other products that do not require cooperation to produce (e.g., McDonald's, Burger King, and Wendy's hamburgers), a professional sports league's rules and member clubs' collective decisions should not be subject to §1.

Most lower federal courts historically rejected the "single economic entity" defense. For example, in *Los Angeles Memorial Coliseum Comm'n v. NFL*, 726 F.2d 1381 (9th Cir.), *cert. denied*, 469 U.S. 990 (1984), the Ninth Circuit rejected the NFL's claim that the league is in essence a single economic entity, like a partnership that shares profits and losses, precluding application of §1, which prohibits only agreements among business entities with economically separate interests that restrain trade:

> Our inquiry discloses an association of teams sufficiently independent and competitive with one another to warrant rule of reason scrutiny under §1 of the Sherman Act. The NFL clubs are, in the words of the district court, "separate business entities whose products have an independent value." The member clubs are all independently owned. Most are corporations, some are partnerships, and apparently a few are sole proprietorships. Although a large portion of League revenue, approximately 90%, is divided equally among the teams, profits and losses are not shared, a feature common to partnerships or other "single entities." In fact, profits vary widely despite the sharing of revenue. The disparity in profits can be attributed to independent management policies regarding coaches, players, management personnel, ticket prices, concessions, luxury box seats, as well as franchise location, all of which contribute to fan support and other income sources.
>
> In addition to being independent business entities, the NFL clubs do compete with one another off the field as well as on to acquire players, coaches, and management personnel. In certain areas of the country where two teams operate in close proximity, there is also competition for fan support, local television and local radio revenues, and media space.

Subsequently, in *American Needle, Inc. v. NFL*, 130 S. Ct. 2201 (2010), the Supreme Court unanimously ruled that a professional sports league comprising separate, independently owned and operated, and for-profit member clubs is not a single economic entity immune from §1 as a matter of law when engaged in joint marketing and licensing of its member clubs' trademarks (e.g., Chicago Bears). The Court explained that the key inquiry is whether there is an agreement "amongst 'separate economic actors pursuing separate economic interests.'" In other words, "[t]he question is whether the agreement joins together 'independent centers of decisionmaking.'" It concluded that "[a]lthough NFL teams have common interests such as promoting the NFL brand, they are still separate, profit-maximizing entities, and their interests in licensing team trademarks are not necessarily aligned. Common interests in the NFL brand '*partially* unit[e] the economic interests of the parent firms,' but the teams still have distinct, potentially competing interests." The Court's ruling suggests that other aspects of a professional sports league's cooperative operations and internal governance decisions also are subject to §1. See, e.g., *Laumann v. NHL*, 907 F.Supp.2d 465 (S.D.N.Y. 2012) (alleged agreements among MLB and NHL clubs to create exclusive local television territories and broadcasting rights for each club and to grant their respective leagues the exclusive right to sell television and Internet broadcasting rights to those games outside these local territories are subject to §1 scrutiny).

On the other hand, if a professional sports league or association is governed by an entity that wholly owns and controls all of its member clubs, or by an independent company with separate ownership and control from its clubs (similar to NASCAR's business model), it appears that there would be the requisite complete unity of economic interest under *American Needle* to justify characterizing it as a single economic entity.

Construing *American Needle* soon after it was decided by the Supreme Court, in *Deutscher Tennis Bund v. ATP Tour, Inc.*, 610 F.3d 820, 835-836 (3d Cir. 2010), the Third Circuit suggested that an agreement among Association of Tennis Professionals (ATP) member tournaments regarding the stratification of ATP tennis tournaments is subject to antitrust scrutiny under §1:

> At trial, ATP contended it constitutes a single enterprise, and . . . its internal decisions cannot violate §1 of the Sherman Act. It asserted each of its tournament members is dependent on the others to produce a common product — a marketable annual professional tennis tour that competes with other forms of entertainment, within and without the sports arena. ATP maintained its members do not compete but instead cooperate to produce the Tour, and its adoption of the Brave New World plan was the core activity of producing this product. . . . The District Court concluded "there [were] at least underlying facts that [were] critical to" a determination of "whether the ATP and its members function as a single business entity," and that these facts are "beyond [the] Court's purview and in need of attention by a jury." . . . [T]he agreement among the ATP's tournament members in the Brave New World Plan might have deprived the marketplace of potential competition. Professional sports teams or tournaments always have an interest in obtaining the best players possible. *Brown v. Pro Football, Inc.,* 518 U.S. 231, 116 S.Ct. 2116, 135 L.Ed.2d 521 (1996). The record in this case indicates that the individual tennis tournaments traditionally compete for player talent. An agreement restricting this competition should not necessarily be immune from §1 scrutiny merely because the tournaments cooperate in various aspects of producing the ATP Tour.

2. Unreasonable Restraint of Trade

KEY TERMS
- Anticompetitive effects
- Procompetitive effects
- Rule of reason

The production of professional sports athletic competition requires many aspects of cooperation and some limits on economic competition among league teams in order for exciting and appealing games and events to exist. Thus, league rules and internal agreements precluding or limiting economic competition among league clubs are not irrefutably presumed to be anticompetitive and per se illegal. It is well-settled law that the rule of reason, which involves a complicated case-by-case analysis, is the applicable standard for evaluating the competitive effects of collective action by professional sports league members or organizations under §1 of the Sherman Act. *National Collegiate Athletic Association v. Board of Regents of the Univ. of Oklahoma*, 468 U.S. 85 (1984). Virtually all professional sports industry restraints that allegedly violate §1 require detailed consideration of both their anticompetitive effects and procompetitive benefits to determine their net competitive consequences and effect on consumer welfare. If the restraint has predominately anticompetitive effects, it is unreasonable and illegal. Conversely, if it has predominately procompetitive effects, it is reasonable and legal.

Regarding application of the rule of reason to restraints in the sports industry, in *Law v. NCAA*, 134 F.3d 1010, 1019 (10th Cir. 1998), the Tenth Circuit explained:

> [T]he plaintiff bears the initial burden of showing that an agreement had a substantially adverse effect on competition. . . . If the plaintiff meets this burden, the burden shifts to the defendant to come forward with evidence of the pro-competitive virtues of the alleged wrongful conduct. . . . If the defendant is able to demonstrate procompetitive effects, the plaintiff then must prove that the challenged conduct is not reasonably necessary to achieve the legitimate objectives or that those objectives can be achieved in a substantially less restrictive manner. . . . Ultimately, if these steps are met, the harms and benefits must be weighed against each other in order to judge whether the challenged behavior is, on balance, reasonable.

a. Acquisition, Ownership, and Sale of a Franchise

The following case considers an antitrust suit by a prospective club owner denied entry into a league. As you read this case, consider why the court rejected his claim that the league's refusal to approve the proposed sale of the club was an antitrust violation.

Levin v. NBA
385 F. Supp. 149 (S.D.N.Y. 1974)

OWEN, District Judge.

The plaintiffs, two businessmen, in 1972 had an agreement to buy the Boston Celtics basketball team, one of the 17-member National Basketball Association.

The N.B.A., as its constitution recites, is a joint venture "organized to operate a league consisting of professional basketball teams, each of which shall be operated by a member of the Association." It has been in existence since 1946. Each of its joint venturers holds a franchise to operate a team. While the teams compete vigorously on the basketball court, the joint venturers are dependent upon one another as partners in the league format to make it possible. N.B.A. operates through its Board of Governors which consists of one governor designated by each member. Action by the Board on a transfer of membership requires the affirmative vote of three-quarters of the members of the Board. [Editors' note: When the plaintiffs applied to become owners of the Celtics franchise, only 2 votes were cast favorable to their application, 13 were opposed, and 1 club owner was not present.]

Plaintiffs immediately demanded and were granted a personal hearing before the Board. Following the presentation of their case a second vote was taken. It was, however, to identical effect.

There is a sharp dispute on the reason for the rejection. Plaintiffs contend that they were rejected because of their friendship and business associations with one Sam Schulman, owner of the Seattle SuperSonics, who was an anathema to the other members of the league. . . .

On the other hand, the reason given by the N.B.A. for the rejection was that the business association between the plaintiffs and Schulman violated the "conflict of interest" provision of the N.B.A. constitution. That provision reads: A member shall not exercise control, directly or indirectly, over any other member of the Association. . . . This provision is necessary, N.B.A. claims, in order that the league may enjoy public support because there is in fact, and the public believes there is, intense competition in the league framework between the teams operated by the N.B.A. members. . . .

In order to survive defendants' motion for summary judgment, plaintiffs must demonstrate that the conduct complained of is a violation of the antitrust laws. While it is true that the antitrust laws apply to a professional athletic league, and that joint action by members of a league can have antitrust implications, this is not such a case. Here the plaintiffs wanted to join with those unwilling to accept them, not to compete with them, but to be partners in the operation of a sports league for plaintiffs' profit. Further, no matter which reason one credits for the rejection, it was not an anti-competitive reason. Finally, regardless of the financial impact of this rejection upon the plaintiffs, if any, the exclusion of the plaintiffs from membership in the league did not have an anticompetitive effect nor an effect upon the public interest. The Celtics continue as an operating club, and indeed are this year's champion. . . .

Since there was no exclusion of plaintiffs from competition with the alleged excluders, nor anti-competitive acts by them and no public injury occasioned thereby, the defendants' acts did not constitute a violation of the antitrust laws and defendants' motion for summary judgment is granted.

NOTE

Judicial reluctance to invalidate league rules and votes regarding sale of clubs. As illustrated by *Levin*, it is difficult for a prospective purchaser of a professional sports club (even one who has reached an agreement with the current owner to buy the team) to prove that the league's refusal to approve the sale has anticompetitive effects. This rejection does not reduce the number of league clubs, which remains the same as before the denial of the proposed transfer of club ownership. As the *Levin* court observed, all it does is preclude a particular party from owning a league franchise. Even if the requisite anticompetitive effects can be proved, rejection of a prospective owner based on adequate evidence that the purchaser lacks the minimally necessary financial capital, character and fitness, or business skills to successfully operate a league club may have the procompetitive effect of preventing the league from being weakened with a corresponding reduction in its ability to compete successfully against other forms of entertainment for consumer patronage. See *Nat'l Basketball Assn. v. Minnesota Professional Basketball Limited Partnership*, 56 F.3d 866 (8th Cir. 1995).

b. Franchise Relocation

In recent years, local communities, including mid-major cities such as Nashville, Memphis, Charlotte, and Oklahoma City, have provided multimillion-dollar public subsidies for playing facilities to attract major league professional sports franchises. Many other communities have made similar investments of public funds to keep their local sports franchises and prevent them from relocating. Courts generally rule that these arrangements are a legitimate use of state and local tax dollars to promote the public good, although these significant public expenditures combined with favorable lease terms provide substantial economic benefits to privately owned professional sports clubs.

Depending on the specific circumstances, a sports league's refusal to permit one of its clubs to relocate to another city may violate the antitrust laws. Former Oakland Raiders owner Al Davis's antitrust litigation against the NFL provides an example of a successful case arising out of the league's initial rejection of his 1980 request to move the Raiders from Oakland to Los Angeles.

In 1978, the owner of the Los Angeles Rams, Carroll Rosenbloom, decided to locate his team in a new stadium, the "Big A," in Anaheim, California, which left the Los Angeles Coliseum without a major tenant. Coliseum officials then began searching for a new NFL team occupant. After NFL Commissioner Pete Rozelle informed them it was not possible to place an expansion franchise there at the time, they negotiated with existing NFL teams in the hope that one might leave its home and move to Los Angeles.

The L.A. Coliseum ran into a major obstacle in its attempts to convince a team to move because it was located in the home territory of the Rams franchise. Rule 4.3 of Article IV of the NFL Constitution stated: "The League shall have exclusive control of the exhibition of football games by member clubs within the home territory of each member. No member club shall have the right to transfer its franchise or playing site to a different city, either within or outside its home territory, without prior approval by the affirmative vote of three-fourths of the existing member clubs of the League."

After the Oakland Raiders' lease with the Oakland Coliseum expired in 1978, Davis, the club's majority owner, and L.A. Coliseum officials signed a March 1, 1980, "memorandum of agreement" outlining the terms of the Raiders' proposed relocation to Los Angeles. However, on March 10, 1980, the NFL clubs voted 22–0 against the Raiders' proposed move (with 5 teams abstaining), which did not meet Rule 4.3's three-quarters approval requirement.

In response, the Raiders brought a claim in Los Angeles federal court under §1 of the Sherman Act alleging that the refusal of the NFL and its member clubs to permit the club to relocate to Los Angeles was an unreasonable restraint of trade. This action resulted in a jury verdict in favor of the Raiders awarding $11.55 million in damages, which was automatically trebled (i.e., tripled) as a prevailing party in an antitrust suit. The trial court enjoined the NFL from preventing the Raiders from moving to Los Angeles.

In *Los Angeles Memorial Coliseum Comm'n v. NFL*, 726 F.2d 1381 (9th Cir. 1984), *cert. denied*, 469 U.S. 990 (1984), the Ninth Circuit affirmed the jury's finding that the NFL's refusal to approve the Raiders club's relocation to Los Angeles violated the rule of reason. It concluded that Rule 4.3 has the anticompetitive effect of dividing geographical markets among the NFL clubs, precluding the Raiders from engaging in economic competition with the Rams in the Los Angeles NFL market. These exclusive territories insulated each NFL team from economic competition with other clubs, enabling them to set monopoly prices for tickets to the detriment of consumers.

Regarding the NFL's claim that Rule 4.3 has procompetitive effects because it helps the league maintain its overall geographical scope, regional balance, and coverage of both major and minor markets, the court acknowledged:

> Exclusive territories aid new franchises in achieving financial stability, which protects the large initial investment an owner must make to start up a football team. Stability arguably helps ensure no one team has an undue advantage on the field. Territories foster fan loyalty, which in turn promotes traditional rivalries between teams, each contributing to attendance at games and television viewing.

However, the court determined that the NFL's denial of the Raiders' proposed move did not actually further any of these objectives:

> [T]he NFL made no showing that the transfer of the Raiders to Los Angeles would have any harmful effect on the League. Los Angeles is a market large enough for the successful operation of two teams, there would be no scheduling difficulties, facilities at the L.A. Coliseum are more than adequate, and no loss of future television revenue was foreseen. Also, the NFL offered no evidence that its interest in maintaining regional balance would be adversely affected by a move of a northern California team to southern California.

Subsequently, in *Nat'l Basketball Assn. v. SDC Basketball Club, Inc.*, 815 F.2d 562, 567 (9th Cir. 1987), the Ninth Circuit reiterated that league rules regarding franchise relocation, including requiring a club to seek league approval before moving, are not per se illegal; rather, "rule of reason analysis governed a professional sports league's efforts to restrict franchise movement." Thus, a professional sports league can avoid antitrust liability if its franchise relocation rules are carefully tailored and properly applied to achieve legitimate procompetitive objectives, such as franchise financial stability, competitive balance among its member clubs, and an appropriate geographical distribution of its teams. Alternatively, rather than prohibiting a club from moving, a league may permit it to do so upon payment of a relocation fee that is divided pro rata (i.e., equally) among its clubs.

The relocation of professional sports franchises causes great upset among the local populace and has spawned both breach of contract and antitrust litigation against club owners by their respective host cities, states, or local governing bodies. Such litigation is motivated by the potential loss of economic benefits to a city and its local businesses, outstanding bond indebtedness to finance the departing club's playing facility, and wounded community pride resulting from the loss of a major league professional sports franchise. These lawsuits seek to prevent loss of the franchise, to keep the local team from moving before its stadium lease expires and without an opportunity to retain the franchise, or to require the league to provide a replacement franchise.

A well-drafted stadium lease is the most effective means of protecting a host community's public investment in the playing facility that houses a local team and ensuring that the local populace receives the full benefit of its contractual bargain. For example, expressly authorizing a court to enjoin a club from relocating prior to the expiration of its lease or requiring a relocating club to pay agreed liquidated damages (i.e., an agreed predetermined amount) of several million dollars for breach of a playing facility lease may be an effective means of protecting a host community's interests. In *Metropolitan Sports Facilities Comm'n v. Minnesota Twins Partnership*, 638 N.W.2d 214, 225 (Minn. Ct. App. 2002), the court rejected the contention that money damages are adequate to compensate a public stadium authority for the breach of a playing facility lease if MLB contracted by eliminating the Minnesota Twins franchise prior to the 2002 season. Finding that the Twins club does not pay rent for using the Metrodome to play its home games, the court observed "that the use agreement at issue here is not a typical commercial lease." The court explained, "[T]he benefit of the bargain that the commission received was the Twins' promise to play their home games at the Metrodome for the duration of their lease. Indeed, the stated purpose for building and operating the stadium was to attract major league sport franchises to play at the stadium for the enjoyment of fans." The trial court's injunction requiring the Twins club to play its 2002 home games in the Metrodome and prohibiting MLB from interfering with this contractual obligation was affirmed.

c. Restrictions on Intellectual Property Rights Licensing and Sales

The NFL, MLB, NBA, and NHL are geographically dispersed throughout the United States and Canada. Their respective clubs are located in cities with vastly different populations and economic bases — for example, large-market metropolitan areas such as New York City, Los Angeles, and Chicago, as well as much smaller markets like Kansas City, Milwaukee, and Pittsburgh. Thus, league clubs' respective revenue-generating potential from ticket sales (including personal seat licenses), concessions, parking fees, sponsorships, merchandising rights, and game broadcasts within differing local markets varies considerably.

As a means of preventing significant disparities in local revenue streams from inhibiting or destroying on-field competitive balance and fan interest in league games, the NFL, MLB, NBA, and NHL have implemented varying degrees of revenue sharing among their member clubs. In each league, national television and broadcasting rights revenues are shared equally among league clubs. Individual clubs' trademarks and logos are collectively licensed by a central league authority, with revenues equally distributed to league clubs. A recent trend is for leagues to require their clubs' Internet rights to be consolidated and centrally licensed (while prohibiting or limiting each club's ability to do so), with revenues shared equally among league clubs. Gate receipts from individual ticket sales frequently are also shared between the home and visiting teams in an agreed percentage.

The NFL currently has the most significant degree of revenue sharing among its member clubs, which provides the Green Bay Packers, located in a metropolitan area of approximately 100,000 people, with the financial resources to compete effectively on the field with large market clubs such as the Chicago Bears. Except for designated local advertising and facility-related revenues, NFL clubs share virtually all other revenues in an effort to jointly produce exciting games between closely matched teams that attracts fan interest.

In testimony before Congress, former NFL commissioner Pete Rozelle stated that "revenue sharing is the key to maintaining geographic and competitive balance in professional football . . . and ensure[s] that each club, irrespective of the size of its community, stadium, or television market, has a comparable opportunity to field a championship team." See William J. Hoffman, Comment, *Dallas' Head Cowboy Emerges Victorious in a Licensing Showdown with the NFL*: National Football League Properties v. Dallas Cowboys Football Club, 7 Seton Hall J. Sport L. 255, 262 (1997).

The exclusive licensing or sale of pooled intellectual property rights by a central league marketing arm (e.g., NFL Properties), along with corresponding restrictions on individual clubs, is designed to (and often does) maximize their aggregate economic value and total revenues generated by the league. However, the revenue received by the most popular individual league clubs or those in the largest markets may be significantly less than the percentage of total revenues generated by the intellectual property associated with those clubs. In an effort to enhance its individual revenues, a club may attempt to circumvent league intellectual property licensing restrictions. Such conduct may force the league to bring breach of contract and trademark infringement litigation to protect its clubs' collective economic interests and exclusive sponsorship agreements with third parties from being harmed. *NFL Properties, Inc. v. Dallas Cowboys Football Club, Ltd.*, 922 F. Supp. 849 (S.D.N.Y. 1996) (holding that Dallas Cowboys used NFL and club marks without authorization to solicit sponsorship agreements with Dr. Pepper, Pepsi, and Nike, which were competitors of official NFL sponsors, in violation of federal and state laws).

Third parties seeking trademark licensing rights from individual clubs have asserted that leaguewide exclusive trademark licensing violates the antitrust laws. In *American Needle, Inc. v. NFL*, 130 S. Ct. 2201 (2010), a hat manufacturer alleged that the NFL's exclusive trademark licensing program, which resulted in the termination of its trademark license, and corresponding restrictions on its member clubs' ability to license their respective trademarks violate §1 of the Sherman Act. Although the Court rejected the NFL's argument that NFL Properties' trademark licensing decisions are unilateral conduct not subject to §1, the Court recognized that a professional sports league has a "legitimate and important interest" in maintaining competitive balance among its clubs and that it is "unquestionably an interest that may well justify a variety of collective decisions made by the teams." See *American Needle, Inc. v. New Orleans Louisiana Saints*, 2014 WL 1364022 (N.D. Ill.) (observing that "exclusive license arrangement encouraged additional licensee commitment and had numerous procompetitive effects, including improvements in product design, quality, distribution, and coordination of styles with other apparel items"). The parties subsequently reached a settlement, pursuant to which the NFL paid an undisclosed sum to American Needle, and NFL Properties' exclusive product licensing regime remained intact.

In *Major League Baseball Properties, Inc. v. Salvino, Inc.*, 542 F.3d 290 (2d. Cir. 2008), the Second Circuit rejected a §1 antitrust claim challenging the centralized trademark licensing program of Major League Baseball Properties (MLBP). The court ruled that MLBP's refusal to grant a trademark license to plaintiff, a manufacturer of plush filled bears called "Bammers," was not clearly anticompetitive. The agreement among MLB clubs establishing MLBP as the exclusive licensor of their trademark rights did not expressly limit or necessarily reduce the number of licenses issued to third parties. In fact, the total number of licensees increased substantially after the formation of MLBP by facilitating "one stop shopping" for the right to use MLB clubs' trademarks, thereby having the procompetitive effect of increasing the quantity of trademarked MLB merchandise available to consumers.

Similarly, in *Madison Square Garden, L.P. v. NHL*, 270 Fed. Appx. 56, 2008 WL 746524 (2d Cir.), the Second Circuit ruled that requiring the New York Rangers NHL club to migrate its website to a common technology platform managed by the NHL, rather than allowing its independent operation, is not clearly anticompetitive conduct that violates §1. It affirmed the lower court's finding that the NHL's challenged conduct has several plausible procompetitive effects, including a standardized website layout to attract national sponsors and advertisers interested in uniform exposure across the NHL.com network, which is a key element of the NHL's strategy to enhance its national brand to better compete against other sports and entertainment products.

On the other hand, in *Laumann v. NHL*, 907 F.Supp.2d 465, 491 (S.D.N.Y. 2012), the court refused to dismiss consumers' §1 claims alleging that agreements among MLB and NHL clubs limiting the telecasting of league games outside of assigned geographical territories violate antitrust law, and explained: "Plaintiffs have adequately alleged harm to competition with respect to the horizontal agreements among individual hockey and baseball clubs, as part of the NHL and MLB, to divide the television market. Making all games available as part of a package, while it may increase output overall, does not, as a matter of law, eliminate the harm to competition wrought by preventing the individual teams from competing to sell their games outside their home territories in the first place. And plaintiffs in this case — the consumers — have plausibly alleged that they are the direct victims of this harm to competition."

D. Application of Sherman Act §2

KEY TERMS	• Attempted monopolization • Illegal exclusionary conduct with anticompetitive market effects • Legal, fair competition on the merits • Monopolization • Monopoly power • Sherman Act §2

There has been a historical tendency toward a single major professional league for the most popular North American team sports of baseball, football, basketball, and hockey. Throughout the twentieth century, competition among rival leagues in the same sport has never continued for any appreciable period of time. Most recently, two competing women's professional basketball leagues, the American Basketball League (ABL) and the Women's National Basketball Association (WNBA), began play in the late 1990s. The ABL, despite having some of the best women's basketball players on its clubs' rosters, ceased operations after only a few years of existence because of its inability to market its product and finance its operations as well as did the WNBA, many of whose clubs are owned and operated by the NBA teams in their respective locations. Unlike most industries in which there are multiple producers of similar products, there is currently only one North American professional league that produces baseball (MLB), basketball (the NBA), football (the NFL), hockey (the NHL), and soccer (MLS) at the major league level.

To be economically viable, a major professional sports league needs several resources, including (1) franchise owners with the financing and business acumen to successfully operate its member clubs, (2) teams in several large cities throughout the country with the population and economic base to support them, (3) access to adequate playing facilities, (4) major league–quality players, and (5) a national television broadcasting contract. Even if a new league is able to satisfy these minimum requirements, its long-term survival as a profitable independent entity is not ensured. Upstart leagues often fold after a relatively short period of existence because of financial problems or improper management and strategic business decisions, or fans may choose to support an established league rather than a new league.

The formation of a new league challenges an established league's dominance of a major professional league sport and threatens its popularity and profitability. Whether the threat is actual or simply potential, the established league may be tempted to react in ways that are anticompetitive and raise antitrust concerns. On several occasions during the twentieth century and with mixed results, a new league has brought antitrust litigation against the preexisting dominant league for allegedly restricting access to one or more of the essential inputs necessary to produce competing professional team sports in a national or local market in the United States.

Most antitrust challenges have been brought under §2 of the Sherman Act, 15 U.S.C. §2, which prohibits monopolization or attempted monopolization. Unlike §1 that governs only concerted action, §2 applies to unilateral conduct such as a professional sports league's conduct in response to the formation of a rival league.

Monopolization requires proof that (1) the defendant possesses monopoly power in the relevant market; and (2) the defendant has wilfully acquired or maintained that power rather than having grown or developed power as a consequence of a superior product, business acumen, or historic accident. *United States v. Grinnell Corp.*, 384 U.S. 563, 570-71 (1966). Attempted monopolization requires proof "(1) that the defendant has engaged in predatory or anticompetitive conduct with (2) a specific intent to monopolize and (3) a dangerous probability of achieving monopoly power." *Spectrum Sports, Inc. v. McQuillan*, 506 U.S. 447, 456 (1993). Although the elements of monopolization and attempted monopolization are different, both require analysis of the defendant's degree of control over the relevant market and a determination of whether its conduct is legal, fair competition on the merits, or is illegal exclusionary conduct with anticompetitive market effects.

The mere fact that there is only a single major league for a particular sport does not violate §2 of the Sherman Act because there may be certain inherent conditions in the professional sports industries that predispose each sport to dominance by one league at the major league level. One potential reason for this phenomenon is that fans may prefer a single champion for the highest level of competition within the sport. If so, over time, fans will prefer the product of one league over that of another, thereby leading to the demise of the disfavored league. There is no §2 violation if a league's market dominance results from winning the off-field competitive economic struggle by providing a superior entertainment product that is most desirable to sports fans. On the other hand, this phenomenon may be the result of an established league's efforts to illegally prevent a rival league from competing with it in violation of §2.

Determining whether a professional sports league has monopoly power for Sherman Act §2 purposes requires definition of both the relevant product and geographical markets and calculation of the defendants' market share in order to evaluate the actual or potential anticompetitive effects of the challenged league rules or conduct. Although courts generally require at least a 70 percent market share to justify a finding of monopoly power, no rigid mathematical approach is used in §2 sports antitrust cases. Rather, the dispositive issue is whether the relevant market is appropriately defined, which determines whether the league has monopoly power and the corresponding ability to exclude rivals and prevent economic competition.

For example, in *American Football League v. National Football League*, 323 F.2d 124, 130 (4th Cir. 1963), the Fourth Circuit ruled that the NFL did not have sufficient control of the market to prevent a newly formed rival from competing with it:

> The relevant market is nationwide, though the fact that there are a limited number of desirable sites for team locations bears upon the question of [the NFL]'s power to monopolize the national market. The District Court's finding that [the NFL] did not have the power to monopolize the relevant market appears plainly correct. In 1959, it occupied eleven of the thirty-one apparently desirable sites for team locations, but its occupancy of some of them as New York and San Francisco-Oakland was not exclusive, for those metropolitan areas were capable of supporting more than one team. Twenty of the thirty-one potentially desirable sites were entirely open to American. Indeed, the fact that the American League was successfully launched, could stage a full schedule of games in 1960, has competed very successfully for outstanding players, and has obtained advantageous

contracts for national television coverage strongly supports the District Court's finding that [the NFL] did not have the power to prevent, or impede, the formation of the new league. Indeed, at the close of the 1960 season, representatives of the American League declared that the League's success was unprecedented.

A large market share or monopoly power does not violate §2 by itself. Even a monopolist is not prohibited from fairly competing on the merits for fan support. The antitrust laws do not prohibit the dominant professional sports league from winning a competitive marketplace struggle by producing a product that is highly desirable to consumers (e.g., NFL football). In *American Football League*, the court held that the NFL could expand its business operations in response to increasing consumer demand for its product and compete with the AFL for the best available remaining geographical areas in which to place a professional football franchise, which is legal, fair competition on the merits.

The essence of illegal monopolization is conduct that excludes actual or potential rivals from the market by unfair or predatory means. To draw the line between lawful competition on the merits and unlawful exclusion or predation, it is important to consider the effects of a monopolist's challenged conduct on consumers. For example, a dominant league's clubs are permitted to compete fairly with an upstart rival league's clubs for the services of the best available players and to enforce valid, existing player contracts, thereby preventing their players from switching leagues before their respective contracts expire. As one court explained, "[n]obody has ever thought, so far as we can find, that in the absence of some monopolistic purpose everyone had not the right to offer better terms to another's employee so long as the latter is free to leave." *Washington Capitols Basketball Club, Inc. v. Barry*, 419 F.2d 472, 478 (9th Cir. 1969). On the other hand, in *Philadelphia World Hockey Club, Inc. v. Philadelphia Hockey Club, Inc.*, 351 F. Supp. 462 (E.D. Pa. 1972), the court ruled that the NHL's efforts to control the supply of major league professional hockey players through a series of agreements with Canadian and U.S. amateur and minor professional leagues was illegal monopolistic conduct designed to prevent the WHA from competing in the North American major league professional hockey market.

If a new league successfully proves the dominant league has engaged in monopolization or attempted monopolization in violation of §2 of the Sherman Act, the typical remedies are an injunction against the illegal practices and damages. In *Philadelphia World Hockey Club*, the court enjoined the NHL from attempting to prevent players from signing new contracts with WHA clubs after their NHL contacts expired. In *United States Football League v. NFL*, 842 F.2d 1335 (2d Cir. 1988), the Second Circuit affirmed the jury's award of only nominal damages (i.e., $1.00, which is automatically trebled under the antitrust laws) to the United States Football League (USFL). Although the jury found that the NFL had monopolized the U.S. major professional football market, it determined that the USFL's bad, self-destructive business decisions were the primary cause of its inability to compete successfully against the NFL.

In *United States Football League*, the court rejected the USFL's proposed judicial restructuring of major league professional football as a remedy for the NFL's antitrust violation, which included its request that all USFL clubs be granted membership in the NFL; separation of the NFL into two leagues, with each league being limited to one network television contract; or a prohibition on the NFL from broadcasting its games in more than one afternoon time slot on Sunday. The court explained:

> Absent a showing of an unlawful barrier to entry, however, new sports leagues must be prepared to make the investment of time, effort, and money that develops interest and fan loyalty and results in an attractive product for the media. The jury in the present case obviously found that patient development of a loyal following among fans and an adherence to an original plan that offered long-run gains were lacking in the USFL.

842 F.2d at 1380.

Problem 11-2

After the ABL ceased operations a few years ago, the WNBA has been the only women's professional basketball league in the United States. It currently has 12 teams, primarily in cities in which NBA teams play. It is a summer league that plays its games from May through September (when the NBA is not playing). Each WNBA team has a roster of 11 players and plays 32 regular-season games. ESPN2 nationally televises a regular season "game of the week" and all of the league's playoff games. The WNBA currently is negotiating with both ESPN and ESPN2 to televise more games in the future.

Because of the increasing popularity of women's professional basketball, a group of wealthy investors is seeking to resurrect the ABL as an 8-team league with franchises in different American cities than the WNBA's clubs. They plan to play a 24-game regular season, with each club having a roster of ten players. The ABL's season will run from October through December.

The WNBA's commissioner is considering whether the league should increase its regular season to 36 games and allow 6 teams (rather than the current 4 teams) to participate in the WNBA playoffs. This would extend the WNBA's season into late October. She also is pondering whether to recommend that the league go forward with its plan to expand into Boston and Dallas, two cities in which ABL franchises will be located. She also is concerned about the enforceability of a provision in the WNBA standard player contract that prohibits a player from playing professional basketball for anyone other than her current team while the contract is in effect. Advise the WNBA commissioner whether any of these proposed actions and the WNBA standard player contract provision violates §2 of the Sherman Act.

Professional Sports Labor Law and Labor Relations

12

INTRODUCTION

Contract, labor, and antitrust fields of law historically have been the most important areas of law regulating labor relations between professional athletes and either professional sports clubs and leagues or the organizers of individual performer sports events. From the 1970s to the present, the combination of these three areas of law has significantly influenced the development of professional sports leagues in the United States. It is important to understand the basics and interrelated nature of contract, labor, and antitrust law as applied to labor relations.

CONTRACT LAW

KEY TERM • Negative injunction

Owners of the first professional sports teams encountered player contract problems almost from the outset of their business operations. When an outstanding player was contractually bound to play for a particular club, but another club desired his services, legal problems ensued.

A leading early case, *Philadelphia Ball Club, Ltd. v. Lajoie*, 51 A. 973 (Pa. 1902), emanated from conflicts associated with the formation of the American League in 1900. National League star Napoleon Lajoie attempted to leave the league's Philadelphia club before his player contract expired and join its crosstown rival in the new American League. Lajoie's club sought a court order preventing him from playing for another club during the period covered by his contract. Although it could not compel Lajoie to play for his current club, the court granted this request and explained:

> Where one person agrees to render personal services to another, which require and presuppose a special knowledge, skill, and ability in the employee, so that in case of a default the same service could not easily be obtained from others, although the affirmative specific performance of the contract is beyond the power of the court, its performance will be negatively enforced by enjoining its breach. . . . The damages for breach of such contract cannot be estimated with any certainty, and the employer cannot, by means of any damages, purchase the same service in the labor market.

Id. at 973. Finding that Lajoie was an outstanding baseball player, the court concluded:

> He has been for several years in the service of the plaintiff club, and has been re-engaged from season to season at a constantly increasing salary. He has become thoroughly familiar with the action and methods of the other players in the club, and his own work is peculiarly meritorious as an integral part of the team work which is so essential. In addition to these features which render his services of peculiar and special value to the plaintiff, and not easily replaced, Lajoie is well known, and has great reputation among the patrons of the sport, for ability in the position which he filled, and was thus a most attractive drawing card for the public. He may not be the sun in the baseball firmament, but he is certainly a bright particular star. We feel, therefore, that the evidence in this case justifies the conclusion that the services of the defendant are of such a unique character, and display such a special knowledge, skill, and ability, as renders them of peculiar value to the plaintiff, and so difficult of substitution that their loss will produce "irreparable injury," in the legal significance of that term, to the plaintiff. . . .

Id. at 974.

For more than a century, *Lajoie* has represented the prevailing judicial view regarding the availability of equitable relief to remedy a professional athlete's breach of contract. Pursuant to a "negative injunction," a player is not ordered to perform for his former club but is instead ordered not to perform for his new club or elsewhere. A negative injunction may be granted if the court concludes that damages alone (which may be uncertain and very difficult to ascertain) are not an adequate legal remedy for the loss of a player's services. The *Lajoie* court concluded that a professional player of Lajoie's status was sufficiently special to merit injunctive relief to prevent his breach of contract. The court focused on the irreparable harm to Lajoie's club if it lost a player of his ability prior to the expiration of his contract, observing that "[h]e may not be the sun in the baseball firmament, but he is certainly a bright particular star."

In evaluating whether a professional athlete has "unique" skills, courts have reached different conclusions using various measures. In *Winnipeg Rugby Football Club v. Freeman,* 140 F. Supp. 365 (N.D. Ohio 1955), a federal court opined that even if the player was not unique by simply being a "good" National Football League (NFL) player, he might be unique in the Canadian Football League, where the quality of play might be lower. Thus, the player, who was in breach, was enjoined from playing for an NFL club. In *Dallas Cowboys Football Club, Inc. v. Harris,* 348 S.W.2d 37 (Tex. Civ. App. 1961), the court ruled that a player who played only for one year, with minimal success, could be found not "unique," but the subject player had not proved his "nonunique" status. Based on these cases and others, even if a court considers evidence that a player is not unique, the player has a substantial burden to prove this factually. Today, it is probably a safe assumption that those who make the major leagues in any sport are almost certain to be characterized as "unique."

The UPCs in North American major leagues typically have a provision stating that the player acknowledges he is unique and that a negative injunction can be obtained against him if he refuses to perform. Although this is not necessarily conclusive and a court might refuse to enforce this provision, this is highly unlikely. The greatest hurdle to obtaining a negative injunction relates to its scope and duration. If a court finds the requested injunction will create an unreasonable hardship to the party sought to be restrained, the injunction will be denied or its scope may be limited. What constitutes unreasonableness, or undue harshness, varies with the particular circumstances. Factors considered by a court may include the length of the requested injunction, its geographical reach, the types of employment or activities prohibited under the injunction, and its potential effects in preventing employment or other opportunities for the restrained party. However, these factors are balanced against the resulting damage to the plaintiff if an injunction is not granted.

In the absence of an express agreement, an injunction normally will not be imposed beyond the time period specified in the contract. For example, when basketball star Rick Barry decided to abandon the National Basketball Association (NBA) for the American Basketball Association (ABA) in the late 1960s, he had an option year remaining on his NBA contract. Faced with an injunction barring his immediate move to the ABA, Barry simply sat out his option year and did not play for anyone. After that year, when he joined the ABA, his old NBA club sought a further injunction preventing him from playing in the ABA until he fulfilled his option year obligation. However, the court ruled that the duration of his contract had lapsed and that an injunction would not be granted for any additional length of time. See *Lemat Corporation v. Barry*, 275 Cal. App. 2d 671 (1969).

Today, there are professional leagues for many sports (e.g., soccer, basketball, baseball, and hockey) in several countries throughout the world. If a player breaches his contract with a club in one country by choosing to play with a club in another country, breach of contract litigation may have global implications. In *Boston Celtics v. Shaw,* 908 F.2d 1041 (1st Cir. 1990), a U.S. court ordered Brian Shaw to honor a valid contract with the Boston Celtics and not to breach this contract by playing basketball for an Italian professional team. Although the court could not require Shaw to play for the Celtics, it had the power to hold Shaw in contempt of court if he failed to honor his Celtics contract. Shaw ultimately complied with the court's negative injunction by playing for the Celtics rather than risking contempt sanctions by playing for the Italian club.

The duration and scope of an injunction may present complex issues when the activity contemplated in the contract is a single event, such as a tennis or golf tournament or exhibition, or a boxing match. For example, in *Lewis v. Rahman,* 147 F. Supp. 2d 225 (S.D.N.Y. 2001), Lennox Lewis, the former heavyweight champion of the world, claimed a contractual right to fight a rematch against Hasim Rahman, the heavyweight champion of the world at the time, within 150 days of an April 21, 2001, match in which Rahman defeated Lewis, and Lewis sought to enjoin Rahman from fighting another opponent before the rematch occurred. Granting the requested injunctive relief, the court stated:

> I find that Lewis would suffer irreparable harm were he denied the opportunity to regain his championship title. It is undisputed that the heavyweight championship is the most prestigious title in professional boxing. The opportunity to fight for the heavyweight championship, and especially the opportunity to regain the championship, cannot be measured in money. Because of his age, Lewis has only a limited time to regain his title and restore his reputation. Rahman, in contrast, is only 28 years old. Even if he chose not to box for 18 months, he would still have several productive years left in his career. Rahman concedes that he has a contractual obligation to fight Lewis in a rematch eventually, although he prefers to fight an interim bout. When asked if he wished to fight Lewis immediately, he said, "I don't have a problem with it." . . .
>
> A preponderance of the credible evidence shows that Lewis will not be able to fight for more than the next two years. Even during the next two years, his boxing abilities may diminish. An injunction for 18 months provides an effective remedy for Lewis' irreparable harm and does not unfairly impede Rahman. Cf. *Machen*, 174 F. Supp. at 529–531 (denying injunctive relief based on the finding that a limited injunction would be ineffective and an indefinite injunction would unduly burden the defendant). If I were to limit the injunction to 150 days, as Rahman urges, I would be permitting Rahman to escape his obligation by letting a short period of time elapse. As soon as Rahman complies with his obligation, he will be free to fight other bouts. The power to end the restriction is in his hands.

Id. at 232–37.

QUESTIONS

1. Why won't a court order a player under contract to play for his current club?
2. How would a club's damages for a player's breach of his contract be calculated? (Hint: The standard measure of damages for breach of contract is to award the nonbreaching party the "benefit of the bargain" expected to be gained if the contract had been fully performed by the breaching party.)

Problem 12-1

Driver Johnny Joe Milton has compiled an enviable record on the National Association of Stock Car Auto Racing (NASCAR) circuit since joining the Il Penseroso racing team two years ago. In fact, he has been so successful that he has attracted the attention of other race team owners, including Claude Forsooth. Despite the fact that Johnny has a year remaining on his three-year contract with Il Penseroso, not to mention two one-year options exercisable by Il Penseroso, Johnny agrees to leave that team and join For-sooth and his Formula One racing team. Though Johnny regrets leaving the NASCAR circuit, he looks forward to the new challenges of Formula One. He will race mainly in Europe in Grand Prix events, but will also be in the United States for such races as the Indianapolis 500 and two or three other similar events.

Il Penseroso's owner, Alfonse Allegro, is not about to allow Johnny to leave his team that easily. He points to wording in his written contract with Johnny whereby Johnny promises to render "his race driving services *exclusively*" to Il Penseroso for the term of the contract. Allegro files suit against Johnny for breach of contract and seeks a worldwide injunction to restrain him from racing for Forsooth for the three-year remaining duration of his contract.

Considering the governing law and practical realities, what would be the best-case resolution of this matter from the perspective of each of the parties?

LABOR LAW

KEY TERMS
- Mandatory subjects of bargaining
- National Labor Relations Act (NLRA)
- National Labor Relations Board (NLRB)
- Fair Labor Standards Act (FLSA)

Our nation's labor laws have become predominant influences in the structure and operations of professional sports leagues in the United States. If sports leagues engage in interstate commerce, which almost all do, they come under the aegis of our national labor laws. Players are employees of teams; when players organize into groups to voice and advance their interests collectively, they become labor unions. The federal labor laws have had a profound impact on the development of professional sports leagues, particularly those at the major league level, for the past 40 years. To understand these effects more fully, we need to first consider the general role of the National Labor Relations Act (NLRA) and then analyze its application to the professional sports industries.

The NLRA, 29 U.S.C. §§151 et seq., was enacted by Congress in 1935. The NLRA, which is known as the Wagner Act, and its numerous amendments (in particular, the Taft-Hartley Act of 1947 and the Landrum-Griffin Act of 1959) provide the basic legal structure governing management-workers relations in the United States. Section 7 of the NLRA provides three basic rights for workers: (1) the right to form, join, and assist labor organizations; (2) the right to bargain collectively through representatives chosen by the workers; and (3) the right to engage in "concerted activities" such as picketing and strikes to advance and protect their interests. 29 U.S.C. §157.

Section 8(a) of the NLRA sets forth prohibited employer conduct, including interference with employees' rights to organize and bargain collectively, domination or interference with the formation or administration of a labor union, discrimination against employees to discourage union membership, retaliation against employees for exercising their rights, and refusing to bargain in good faith. 29 U.S.C. §158(a). All these prohibited employer actions may constitute unfair labor practices. The NLRA also prohibits unfair labor practices by a labor union; for example, a refusal to bargain collectively in good faith. 29 U.S.C. §158(b).

The oversight and enforcement of these rights comes under the jurisdiction of the National Labor Relations Board (NLRB) and the federal courts. The NLRB enforces the federal labor laws by adjudicating claims of "unfair labor practices" allegedly committed by either management or the union. The NLRB also administers the process that determines appropriate units or groups of employees qualified to vote in a union representation election. It also conducts such elections to determine which, if any, union will represent all employees who are part of that unit.

The NLRB also determines which issues are subject to negotiation under the labor laws, delving into questions concerning the required scope of bargaining. Under the NLRA, scope of bargaining includes all issues relating to wages, hours, and terms and conditions of employment. 29 U.S.C. §158(d). Wages include pay, fringe benefits, and bonus payments; hours encompass time spent on the job; and working conditions cover factors influencing the work environment, such as work rules, seniority, and safety. Most importantly, these three areas—wages, hours, and working conditions—are considered mandatory subjects of bargaining. If either labor or management requests bargaining on issues that are mandatory under the labor laws, the other side must bargain over these issues in good faith. A failure to do so is an unfair labor practice that violates §8 of the NLRA. However, what actually constitutes wages, hours, or conditions of employment is not always crystal clear. In particular, it is not uncommon for labor and management to disagree regarding what is a condition of employment. Such disputes must be resolved by the NLRB.

If an issue is not a mandatory subject of bargaining, it is either a permissive or illegal subject. See *NLRB v. Wooster Div. of Borg-Warner Corp.*, 356 U.S. 342 (1958). It is permissive if it is a nonmandatory lawful subject of bargaining, for example, a ballot or recognition clause included in the collective bargaining agreement (CBA). If a subject is permissive, management may choose to negotiate with the union on that issue, but it is not required to do so and may unilaterally include or impose terms and conditions regarding these subjects. It is an illegal subject of bargaining if one or more federal or state laws prohibit it from being implemented, even if it were successfully negotiated, for example, if the union and league agreed to pay some players less than the legally required minimum wage. If the subject is illegal, neither side has the freedom to bargain about such issues.

For purposes of the NLRA, there are two additional important factors to consider. First, a union that is duly certified by the NLRB pursuant to the prescribed procedures becomes the exclusive bargaining agent for all employees within the unit. As a practical matter, all active players in a professional sports league with clubs in the United States come under the aegis of the union that has been chosen to represent them. Although a player is not required to become a member of the union that the

NLRB recognizes for his or her league, the player is bound by (and benefits from) the union's actions and the terms of any CBA it negotiates with the league and its member clubs.

Second, those who are not currently active players for clubs in the league (as defined by the bargaining unit) are *not* members of the union and, as such, have no vote and little voice in union affairs. Even so, to a large extent, the actions of the union may determine or otherwise affect their rights. For example, college players who want to play professionally usually find that their eligibility to do so is determined by the CBA between the league and the players' union. (See the discussion of Maurice Clarett's unsuccessful litigation challenging the rule that three years must have elapsed since a player graduated from high school before being eligible for the NFL draft, *infra*.) The same may be true for foreign players and others, such as high school graduates seeking the opportunity to play in a unionized professional league. It is important to understand that the union does not represent former or retired players in collective bargaining negotiations or disputes with the league or its clubs because they are not members of the bargaining unit.

Until 1969, the NLRB was reluctant to assert jurisdiction over labor relations in the context of professional sports. For example, it had declined to do so for the thoroughbred horse-racing industry, which was deemed to be merely a local activity. *Walter A. Kelley*, 139 N.L.R.B. 744 (1962); *Los Angeles Turf Club, Inc.*, 90 N.L.R.B. 20 (1950). However, in *American League of Professional Baseball Clubs and Association of National Baseball League Umpires*, 180 N.L.R.B. 190 (1969), the NLRB ruled that professional baseball is an industry affecting interstate commerce and, as such, was within the board's jurisdiction. This case, which involved the efforts of umpires to unionize, enabled professional athletes to form unions and avail themselves of the protections of the NLRA. Thus, the stage was set for the federal labor laws to govern labor relations in the professional sports industries.

Shortly thereafter, the first CBAs were entered in the major professional sports leagues. Labor and management reached rudimentary (by today's standards), but significant, agreements. Within months of each other, the National Basketball Association (NBA), National Football League (NFL), and Major League Baseball (MLB) all reached formal agreements with the players' unions in their respective leagues. The National Hockey League (NHL) also reached a series of less formal agreements with the National Hockey League Players' Association.

The benefits of unionization and collective bargaining to professional athletes are illustrated by the substantial salary differences between minor and MLB players' salaries. Since MLB players formed the Major League Baseball Players Association (MLBPA), MLB minimum annual salaries have increased by 2,500 percent, to $507,500 for the 2015 season. By comparison, over the same time period, the salaries of minor league players, who have not unionized, have increased by only 70 percent, and some minor league players are paid only $1,100 per month. In *Senne v. Kansas City Royals Baseball*, 2015 WL 2412245 (N.D. Cal.), a group of minor league baseball players alleged that their effective hourly compensation violates the Fair Labor Standards Act (FLSA), which requires employers to pay nonexempt employees at least the federal minimum wage and overtime pay. The suit is currently pending against MLB and the 22 of its clubs, and its outcome will be determined by the court's determination of whether playing minor league baseball is "a career . . . a good time, or something in between," and, if it is considered employment, whether it is appropriately categorized as "seasonal" employment exempt from the FLSA's requirements. Tony Dokoupil, *Major League Baseball's 'Working Poor': Minor Leaguers Sue over Pay*, NBCSports.com, July 15, 2014, *http://www.nbcnews.com/news/sports/ major-league-baseballs-working-poor-minor-leaguers-sue-over-pay-n156051*.

These brief descriptions of the rights and duties of labor and management under the NLRA and its administration by the NLRB are simplifications of a complex matrix of rules that govern labor relations in the professional sports industries. The national labor laws are intended to guide relations between management and labor, but it is questionable whether the NLRA and its administrative enforcement arm, the NLRB, have effectively achieved this objective. Even so, the impact of national labor policy and regulation has been crucial in shaping and defining much of professional sports in the United States.

The rest of this section explores how labor law has influenced the development of North American major professional sports leagues and examines their application to the professional sports industries. Five important, interrelated areas are explored and analyzed: (1) the collective bargaining process; (2) professional team sports drug-testing programs; (3) the activities of either a league and its clubs or the players' union that constitute unfair labor practices under the NLRA; (4) the duty of a players' union to represent all of its members fairly; and (5) the labor arbitration process, which is established pursuant to the CBA to resolve disputes between players and the league or a club. Careful consideration of these topics provides a sense of the pivotal role that labor law and relations have played in the context of professional sports over the past approximately 50 years, as well as forecasts their future effects.

A. Collective Bargaining in the Professional Sports Industries

KEY TERMS
- Collective bargaining agreement (CBA)
- Competitive balance or luxury tax
- Free agency restrictions
- Reserve clause
- Salary cap
- Uniform player contract (UPC)

The primary basis for determining the legal relationships between owners and players in professional sports is the collective bargaining agreement (CBA) reached between the players' union and the owners' multiemployer bargaining unit, which prevails over a league's rules and the individual player-club agreements. Multiemployer collective bargaining is the prevailing norm in professional team sports because the league is an integrated group of clubs with common labor issues, which exercises a high degree of centralized control over labor relations. As a result, the terms of the CBA are collectively bargained on behalf of, and are binding on, all league clubs and players.

The focus of collective bargaining between players and owners has shifted since the first CBAs in the late 1960s, which largely concentrated on player job security issues such as minimum salaries, fringe benefits such as health and life insurance, and pension plans. These are still important considerations, but three main issues driven by the changing economics of sports have dictated a shifting focus in collective bargaining negotiations. The first issue is the allocation of rights to a player to a particular club through a draft of new or rookie players initially eligible to play in the league. The second issue involves free agency restrictions (i.e., limitations on a player's ability to play for another league club after his contract expires). Leagues contend that both a player draft and free agency restrictions are necessary to maintain competitive balance among their member clubs. Third, leagues have sought restrictions on aggregate player salaries by clubs through constraints such as team salary caps, competitive balance or luxury taxes, and other devices aimed to discourage excessive spending. All of the foregoing restrictions directly affect players' wages and conditions of employment and thus are mandatory subjects of bargaining, which raise contentious issues in CBA negotiations and have triggered strikes or lockouts in all of the major professional leagues at one time or another. A fourth issue, which has become increasingly important in recent years, is the nature and scope of a league commissioner's authority to discipline players for off-field misconduct.

The NBA was the first league to institute a salary cap on the maximum amount that each club could annually pay in player salaries. This occurred in 1983, at a time when the NBA was clearly struggling financially. In an unprecedented move, the league opened its books for inspection by the players' union, which reluctantly agreed to a salary cap. The cap was fraught with vagueness, and the parties had contemplated the many ways in which its provisions could be circumvented. The NBA has a "soft cap" because there are many ways by which a team could exceed the cap and still be within its provisions. The chief exception, often used, was to pay salaries to a team's own veteran players that sent the overall team salary far beyond the official league team limit. Since its inception, the NBA salary cap has undergone several collectively bargained revisions, including more explicit limits on both veteran and rookie salaries, but it still remains, in most respects, a "soft" cap, which a club may exceed at the cost of paying a competitive balance or luxury tax to the league.

Approximately ten years later, the NFL instituted a "hard cap." Each year, a team maximum salary is determined based on prior and projected league revenues. Each team's total aggregate player salaries cannot exceed a maximum amount, without exception. It has led to clubs' restructuring of its players' contracts to attract or retain desired players while complying with the cap. For example, players enter into new contracts wherein their immediate salary is low, but a new signing bonus provides most of the money that they would have received under their old contract. The signing bonus, however, is then allocated equally over the years of the new contract, thus reducing the club's immediate cap obligations. Another device to change a club's cap obligations is to have the player sacrifice immediate income provided in the old contract for even greater future rewards in a new contract.

MLB does not have a salary cap but has attempted to curtail some teams' spending by requiring a club to pay a tax if its spending on aggregate player salaries exceeds a certain maximum. In an effort to maintain competitive balance among league clubs, the MLB CBA requires clubs above a certain level ($178 million for the 2012 and 2013 seasons and $189 million for the 2014, 2015, and 2016 seasons) to pay a competitive balance tax to the league for distribution to lower-income clubs.

Until 2005, the NHL had no salary cap or luxury tax, which led to sharply escalating salaries (with the club owners' cooperation, of course). After the NHL CBA expired at the conclusion of the 2004 season, Commissioner Gary Bettman declared that some type of salary cap was necessary. The players' union announced its unequivocal opposition. In response, the NHL instituted a player lockout that caused the 2004–2005 season not to be played. The parties reached agreement on a new CBA in mid-July 2005, which included a hard salary cap.

Beginning in the 1890s with the National League in baseball, major professional leagues and their clubs unilaterally established rules tying players to a particular team through a draft of players initially entering the league, a "reserve clause" that purportedly gave a club perpetual rights to a player even after his contract expired, and other restrictions on player movement to other teams. In some instances, as discussed *infra*, NFL, NBA, and NHL players successfully challenged free agency restrictions on antitrust grounds, a means of legal recourse not available to MLB players because of baseball's broad common law antitrust immunity. However, MLB players gained free agency through a 1976 landmark labor arbitration decision, *National & American League Professional Baseball Clubs v. Major League Baseball Players Association*, 66 Labor Arbitration 101 (1976), discussed *infra*. In modern times, the nature and scope of restrictions on player mobility usually are a contentious part of collective bargaining negotiations in all of the major professional leagues that are unionized.

Each league has a uniform player contract (UPC; also called a *standard player contract*) incorporated into its CBA, which is an integral part of it. Although each league's UPC is different, they are quite similar. As a collectively bargained agreement, the terms of the UPC (which frequently incorporate specific CBA terms) take precedence over the league's constitution, bylaws, and rules, as well as the provisions of individually negotiated contracts between clubs and players.

Unless prohibited or otherwise limited by the CBA or UPC, the following terms in individual player contracts generally are negotiable: (1) basic salary above the collectively bargained league minimum amount; (2) individual and team signing, roster, and performance bonuses; (3) guaranteed income clauses; (4) limitations on the assignment of a player's contract rights to other clubs; (5) additional economic protections in case of injury; and (6) length of contract.

Because player disciplinary sanctions for misconduct are mandatory subjects of collective bargaining, the players' union is empowered to protect the players' interests by negotiating with a sports league the conduct subject to discipline, sanctions for violations, and grievance or appeal mechanisms. In most instances, the union is able to limit the otherwise broad authority of a club or league commissioner to discipline players through effective use of the collective bargaining process. There generally is a collectively bargained range of disciplinary sanctions for on-field or off-field player misconduct that violates league or club rules promulgated to (1) maintain competitive balance (e.g., doping, use of impermissible equipment, etc.); (2) preserve the sport's integrity (e.g., gambling, doping); (3) maintain the sport's public image (e.g., criminal conduct, domestic violence, doping); (4) protect player health and safety (e.g., violence injuring opposing player, doping); and (5) maintain team unity and appropriate decorum. Absent limits imposed by the CBA, courts generally provide a professional sports league and its clubs with substantial discretion to impose player discipline and are very deferential to their decisions. See, e.g., *Molinas v. NBA*, 190 F. Supp. 241 (S.D.N.Y. 1961) (upholding league commissioner's indefinite suspension of player for admittedly gambling on his team's games in violation of his contract and league rules). On the other hand, as discussed *infra*, an arbitrator may be more willing to reduce the severity of discipline imposed on a player by the league commissioner.

B. Professional Team Sports Drug-Testing Programs

Two types of drug problems have plagued professional sports in recent years. One is "performance-enhancing drugs" such as anabolic steroids, which are taken to help the athlete perform better despite their associated health risks. The use of these banned drugs constitutes a form of cheating that provides an unfair competitive advantage over clean athletes not using these substances. The other is the widespread use of recreational or "street" drugs such as marijuana and cocaine. Various questions are posed by the regulation of either type of drug by a professional sports league. One is whether sports club owners and leagues have any legitimate reason to interfere with the private decisions made by individual adult athletes, at least in instances when their on-field athletic performances are not impaired and no threat is posed to the safety of others. Second, because the usage and possession of these drugs for other than legitimate medical reasons are illegal in most U.S. jurisdictions, does the damage done to the image of sports outweigh an individual's freedom to choose?

Three major issues differentiate the legal framework governing drug testing in professional sports as contrasted with interscholastic, intercollegiate, and Olympic sports, which is discussed in other chapters. First, professional sports leagues are private in nature. There are no public professional sports leagues, in contrast to the thousands of public universities and public high school systems. Thus, the U.S. Constitution does not provide the basis for any legal challenge to drug-testing programs in the professional ranks because no governmental or "state" action, which is required to assert federal constitutional law claims, is involved. Thus, players such as Terry Long of the Pittsburgh Steelers, who tested positive for anabolic steroids, have been unable to show a sufficient nexus between a professional sports league's drug policies and the actions of government officials or state actors to assert any federal constitutional claims such as violation of their privacy rights. *Long v. National Football League*, 66 F.3d 311 (3d Cir. 1994).

Second, despite the lack of federal constitutional law oversight, professional sports leagues are in many respects more constrained in their ability to implement drug testing programs than are universities or other educational institutions. Professional team sport athletes are usually employees either of a club, the league, or both. When athletes agree to have a union represent them, they gain the protections of the NLRA, pursuant to which drug testing programs are mandatory subjects of collective bargaining. Consequently, in unionized professional team sports, leagues and teams cannot unilaterally institute drug programs, which must be implemented through collective bargaining with the agreement of the players' union. Although one would expect a players' union to consent to a drug-testing program because drug usage has adverse health effects on players, its nature and scope, as well as sanctions for violations, often are the subject of considerable debate and negotiation. Individual athlete privacy concerns, the validity of testing measures for specific substances, and the consequences of proven drug usage have caused players' unions to have significant trepidation about wide-ranging testing procedures and the penalties for impermissible drug use. As new drugs enter the scene, and new pressures arise, problems multiply.

Third, a strong reason for union hesitancy to agree to stringent drug-testing programs is pressure from athletes and their agents. A great deal is at stake for professional athletes, arguably more so than for amateur athletes at the interscholastic and intercollegiate levels or even Olympic athletes. Professional careers may end prematurely through noncompliance with league drug-testing and treatment programs. Salaries, bonuses, and endorsement opportunities may be lost, often costing a professional athlete hundreds of thousands, even millions, of dollars. Economically, the stakes are high. Consequently, both the players' union and clubs' multiemployer bargaining unit must scramble to reach reasonable solutions, with common ground and compromise frequently difficult to achieve.

In general, two overriding concerns need to be addressed and resolved if adequate drug-testing programs are implemented. One is protection of privacy of the individual athlete, to the greatest extent possible. In addition, there must be a clear and definite articulation of the purposes, procedures, and sanctions for the particular drug-testing program.

In 2005, several members of the U.S. Congress raised questions about performance-enhancing drug use by professional athletes, and various congressional committees held hearings. Subsequently, without any legislative action by Congress, the major professional sports leagues and their respective unions agreed to more extensive and stringent drug-testing measures, which are set forth in league CBAs. For example, MLB, NBA, and NFL players now are subject to testing for human growth hormone. Current suspensions for a first drug testing violation (e.g., anabolic steroids) are 4 games for NFL players, 10 games for NBA players, 20 games for NHL players, and 80 games for MLB players. Sanctions increase significantly for subsequent offenses. For example, for MLB players, the sanction for use of a performance-enhancing drug increases to 162 games (i.e., a full season) for a second offense and a lifetime ban for a third offense.

The league CBA generally provides a player who has been disciplined for a doping offense to appeal to an independent arbitrator. For example, New York Yankees player Alex Rodriguez successfully challenged his 211-game suspension imposed by MLB Commissioner Bud Selig for his use of performance-enhancing substances and obstruction of MLB's investigation before an arbitrator, who reduced its length to 162 games plus any postseason games for which his team qualified. As a result, Rodriguez did not play during the 2014 season, but he resumed playing for the Yankees in 2015.

QUESTIONS

1. Why should professional athletes be prohibited from using certain performance-enhancing substances (e.g., anabolic steroids) if they are willing to subject themselves to the associated health risks?

2. Do you believe the current professional sports league drug-testing programs adequately deter the use of banned substances by professional athletes? If not, what changes would you propose?

Problem 12-2

You are the commissioner of the indoor professional lacrosse league for which the current CBA expires at the end of this year. Recently, several high-profile lacrosse players have been arrested for possession or use of illegal recreational drugs. Consistent with the World Anti-doping Code, the international lacrosse federation has banned several athletes for two years for using performance-enhancing substances. What recommendations would you make to club owners regarding a drug-testing program for the league?

To address adequately the concerns of the players and their union regarding mandatory drug testing, note that a wide range of issues will have to be agreed on through collective bargaining with the lacrosse players' union, including the following:

1. Which players would be subject to testing? Would random testing be instituted, or would players be tested only if there was reasonable cause that they were using performance-enhancing substances?

2. How would the tests be conducted, and how often? Who would conduct tests, and with what safeguards? Would there be an opportunity to appeal a positive test result?

3. Which drugs are prohibited? How is this determined? What is the basis for initial selection? Can the list of prohibited drugs be expanded (or reduced), and by what procedure?

4. What are the sanctions for a positive test result? Mandatory treatment? Suspension? Loss of salary and other benefits?

5. What appeal procedures are available?

C. Unfair Labor Practices

KEY TERMS
- Exclusive bargaining representative
- Failure to bargain in good faith
- Impasse

- Lockout
- Multiemployer collective bargaining unit
- Strike
- Unfair labor practice

Section 8(d) of the NLRA imposes a mutual obligation on representatives of both management and labor "to meet at reasonable times and confer in good faith with respect to wages, hours, and other terms and conditions of employment," so-called mandatory subjects of collective bargaining. 29 U.S.C. §158(d). Either side's failure to bargain in good faith constitutes an unfair labor practice. However, this obligation "does not compel either party to agree to a proposal or require the making of a concession." *Id.* Labor disputes are to be resolved by collective bargaining or resort to economic coercion in the form of a strike by players or a lockout by league clubs.

The NLRB enforces the requirements of the NLRA and polices the unionization and collective bargaining processes. After issuance of an administrative complaint alleging that a party has committed an unfair labor practice, the NLRB may petition a federal district court for an injunction prohibiting a party from engaging in the alleged unfair labor practice pending its final resolution. 29 U.S.C. §160(j). After an administrative hearing, the NLRB is empowered to order either labor or management to cease and desist from engaging in any unfair labor practice. 29 U.S.C. §160(a). The NLRB may petition the appropriate federal circuit court for judicial enforcement of its order if either side refuses to comply with it. 29 U.S.C. §160(e).

In the context of professional sports, allegations of unfair labor practices have arisen in a variety of circumstances. A refusal by the league's multiemployer bargaining unit to bargain in good faith over a mandatory subject of collective bargaining is a relatively common allegation. Other illustrative examples of alleged unfair labor practices arising in the professional sports industries are as follows.

1. League Interference with Players' Rights to Unionize

Section 8(a) prohibits an employer from attempting to interfere with the rights of employees to choose freely which union represents them, or from discriminating against any employee to encourage or discourage union membership. 29 U.S.C. §158(a)(1) and (2). In September 2000, the NLRB filed unfair labor practice charges against the Arena Football League (AFL), alleging that its club owners both threatened players and illegally promised them benefits to coerce them to accept the Arena Football League Players Organizing Committee (AFLPOC) as their union. Two AFL players alleged that players had been illegally pressured to select AFLPOC as their union, which was unduly sympathetic to league management and had been formed primarily at the club owners' behest to immunize them from antitrust liability. The NLRB found evidence that an uncoerced majority of players did not support AFLPOC. After the NLRB's complaint was filed, the AFL reached a settlement that resolved both the unfair labor practice claims and pending antitrust litigation, and the AFL players regained the right to choose which union was to represent them.

2. League Refusal to Recognize Union as Exclusive Bargaining Representative

Player associations in professional sports date as far back as the 1880s, but effective associations were not formed until the 1950s and 1960s. It was several years before these associations, functioning as unions, were able to obtain the first CBAs with the various major professional sports leagues. A difficult threshold task was to obtain full recognition as the players' exclusive bargaining representative, especially by a newly formed league. This was particularly true in the case of the now-defunct North American Soccer League (NASL). Two cases underscore the obstinacy that a nascent union faced in its initial efforts to collectively bargain with NASL club owners. The legal principles developed in these cases have general application to labor relations involving professional team sports.

In *North American Soccer League v. National Labor Relations Bd.*, 613 F.2d 1379 (5th Cir. 1980), the NASL disputed the NLRB's certification of "all NASL players of clubs based in the United States" as the appropriate collective bargaining unit, which was requested by the players' union. The Fifth Circuit upheld the NLRB's determination that there is a "joint employer relationship" among the NASL and its member clubs:

> [T]he League exercises a significant degree of control over essential aspects of the clubs' labor relations, including but not limited to the selection, retention, and termination of the players, the terms of individual player contracts, dispute resolution and player discipline. Furthermore, each club granted the NASL authority over not only its own labor relations but also, on its behalf, authority over the labor relations of the other member clubs.

Id. at 1382.

The court concluded that a "leaguewide unit of players" for purposes of collective bargaining is appropriate:

> Notwithstanding the substantial financial autonomy of the clubs, the Board found they form, through the League, an integrated group with common labor problems and a high degree of centralized control over labor relations. In these circumstances the Board's designation of a leaguewide bargaining unit as appropriate is reasonable, not arbitrary or capricious.

Id. at 1383. This effectively required the NASL's member clubs to function as a multi-employer collective bargaining unit in labor relations issues with the players, which means that all clubs are represented by the same negotiator and are bound by the terms of the CBA.

Once certified, the union is the exclusive bargaining representative of the league's players. 29 U.S.C. §159(a). In *Morio v. North American Soccer League*, 501 F. Supp. 633 (S.D.N.Y. 1980), the court enjoined the NASL from refusing to collectively bargain with the players' union and continuing to negotiate contracts with individual players. To avoid undermining the union's authority, the league's "duty to bargain with the exclusive representative carries with it the negative duty not to bargain with individual employees." *Id.* at 639.

3. Retaliation Against Union Activists

Section 8(a)(3) prohibits an employer from discriminating against any employee to encourage or discourage union membership. 29 U.S.C. §158(a)(3). A club's release of a player or termination of his contract because of his union activities, if proved, is an unfair labor practice. The following case illustrates the difficulty of determining why a player active in union activities was cut by a team and raises the question of whether federal labor law potentially interferes with a club's efforts to field its best possible team.

In *Nordstrom d/b/a Seattle Seahawks*, 292 NLRB 899 (1989), Sam McCullum asserted that the Seattle Seahawks NFL club cut him from the team's final roster in violation of §8(a)(3). McCullum started as a wide receiver for the Seahawks during the 1976–1981 seasons. In 1981, his teammates selected him to be their union player representative. McCullum's union activities incurred head coach Jack Patera's ire, particularly for his orchestration of a "solidarity handshake" between his teammates and players on the opposing team prior to the first 1982 preseason game. Despite starting all of the Seahawks' 1982 preseason games, McCullum was cut shortly after the club acquired Roger Carr, another wide receiver.

McCullum and the National Football League Players Association claimed that his union activities were a "motivating factor" in the termination of his employment with the Seahawks. The club asserted that he would have been cut even without his participation in union activities based on his relative skills in comparison to the team's other wide receivers. The Seahawks claimed a stronger team need for Carr's services and the inability to keep McCullum as a fifth wide receiver without harming the need for players at other positions.

In a divided opinion, the NLRB affirmed the administrative law judge's ruling that McCullum's termination was illegal discrimination based on his role "as a fairly aggressive union spokesman." Patera's attempted heavy fines for team players' participation in the solidarity handshake evidenced his animus toward union activity, for which McCullum was the focal point. Patera also had the final authority regarding player cuts, and there was some evidence that Carr was acquired to enable McCullum's release because of his union activities. A dissenting NLRB member concluded that McCullum's release was a valid exercise of team management's business judgment regarding its personnel needs, which decision would have been made absent any antiunion motivation. See *Nordstrom v. NLRB*, 984 F.2d 479 (D.C. Cir. 1993) (affirming $301,000 award of back pay to McCullum for the period that he would have been employed by the Seahawks but for his unlawful termination, 11 years after his 1982 release).

4. Breach of Duty to Bargain in Good Faith or Provide Relevant Information Concerning Mandatory Subjects of Collective Bargaining

Both the league's multiemployer bargaining unit and the players' union have a duty to collectively bargain over wages, hours, and other terms and conditions of employment. The players' union generally wants to bargain over a wide range of issues, but league clubs may be reluctant to do so. The following material considers what constitutes mandatory subjects of collective bargaining in the context of professional sports labor relations as well as the parties' mutual obligation to provide relevant information concerning these subjects to the other side.

Silverman v. Major League Baseball Player Relations Committee, Inc. (Silverman I)
516 F. Supp. 588 (S.D.N.Y. 1981)

Believing that [the] bargaining position [of Major League Baseball's Players Relations Committee (PRC)] on the issue of player "compensation" was based at least in part on the financial difficulties of certain member clubs, on May 7, 1981, the Players Association filed an unfair labor practice charge with the Board alleging respondents' failure to bargain in good faith by refusing to comply with the Players Association's request for financial disclosure in violation of Sections 8(a)(1) and (5) of the Act, 29 U.S.C. §§158(a)(1) and (5).

Following investigation and pursuant to Section 10(b) of the Act, 29 U.S.C. §160(b), the Board filed a complaint charging respondents with violating Sections 8(a)(1) and (5) of the Act [and sought a court order requiring the PRC to provide the requested financial information] . . . .

The Board alleges in its petition that the public statements by club owners regarding claims of financial difficulties created a reasonable belief on the part of the Players Association that respondents' bargaining position during this second round of negotiations was based, "at least in part, on the present or prospective financial difficulties of certain of Respondents' member clubs." Although Marvin Miller has expressed some doubt as to club owners' inability to pay rising player salaries, he nevertheless takes the position that the Players Association must have the financial information it requests if it is to fulfill its duty of fair representation. If deprived of that information, the Association claims that it must blindly decide whether to press its demands and risk the loss of jobs for its members if the clubs cannot survive under the "compensation" terms proposed by the Association, or to recede from its position and accept the PRC's proposal without verifying owners' claims of financial distress caused by "free agency." Thus, the Association brought an unfair labor practice charge against the PRC for its failure to disclose the requested financial data after the clubs allegedly put into issue their inability to pay. . . .

Petitioner admits that at no time during bargaining sessions have respondents made a claim of inability to pay. Nevertheless, petitioner urges the Court to find that public statements made by several club owners as well as the Commissioner of Baseball about the financial condition of the industry are sufficient to support a finding of reasonable cause to believe that respondents have injected the inability to pay into the negotiations.

The cases cited by petitioner in support of its position are simply inapposite. In each case, inability to pay was put in issue at the bargaining table. . . .

Thus, Petitioner concedes, as it must, that the Board and courts have never found that an employer has injected financial condition into negotiations, absent statements or conduct by the employer at the bargaining table. Nevertheless, it urges this Court to find, on the basis of statements by Commissioner Kuhn and various owners, that the financial issue has become relevant to the negotiations regarding "compensation" because of the unique nature of collective bargaining in baseball. . . .

It is the PRC Board of Directors which is charged with the exclusive authority to formulate the collective bargaining position of the clubs and to negotiate agreements with the Players Association. Indeed, Grebey, the official spokesman for the PRC in collective bargaining matters, has consistently denied that the clubs' financial status is at issue in the current negotiations. . . .

In a multi-employer bargaining unit as large and publicly visible as the Major League Baseball Clubs, it is inevitable that extraneous statements will be made by individuals affiliated in some way with the group which are inconsistent with the official position of the unit. This only underscores the necessity, recognized by the PRC, for centralized bargaining responsibility and authority. Clearly, individual expressions of opinion cannot serve to bind the entire bargaining unit in the absence of authority to speak for the group. . . .

The Act has provided for collective bargaining between the parties through their authorized representatives. If this Court were to find that the several public statements by club officials and the Commissioner were sufficient to support a finding that the PRC and its negotiating team view the respondents' "compensation" proposal as related to the financial condition of the clubs, it would do violence to the intent and purpose of the Act which limits the jurisdiction of this Court. . . .

NOTE

Labor dispute legal requirements and options. The *Silverman I* judge was following well-established legal precedent in finding that the PRC's refusal to provide the MLB Player Association with the requested financial information does not constitute an unfair labor practice and refusing to grant an injunction. It generally takes more than a few outsider comments, even by owners, about potential economic hardship to require the clubs to open their books. In general, league clubs prefer not to disclose information about their finances. However, there have been some instances in which disclosure of league financial information has occurred. In 1982, the NFLPA filed a successful unfair labor practices claim, pursuant to which the NFL was required to divulge the terms of its television contracts to allow the players association to evaluate its fair share of such proceeds. In 1982–1983, the NBA voluntarily opened its books to demonstrate to players the tenuous state of its finances, thus leading to the first professional sports CBA with an aggregate player salary cap.

In *Silverman v. Major League Baseball Player Relations Committee, Inc.*, 880 F. Supp. 246 (S.D.N.Y. 1995) (*Silverman II*), the court distinguished between mandatory and permissive subjects of collective bargaining. The case provides guidance on the role that labor law plays in regulating unilateral action by a league's multiemployer bargaining unit in a labor dispute. It ruled:

> Having freely entered into the free agency and reserve systems in their Basic Agreement, the Owners are bound to that system until they bargain in good faith to an impasse.
>
> In view of the abundant case law in the professional sports context that has found that constituent parts of the reserve/free agency system are mandatory subjects of collective bargaining, I find that the Board had substantial reasonable cause to conclude, and a substantial likelihood of success ultimately in establishing, that the unilateral changes made by the Owners to the free agency system before impasse violated the rule against changes to mandatory subjects of bargaining. In summary, the Board has clearly met its injunctive remedy standard in demonstrating that the Owners committed an unfair labor practice by their unilateral abrogation of Article XX(F) and the free agency system. . . .

Id. at 257.

In an effort to ensure stable, peaceful labor relations, the federal labor laws require the league and its member clubs to maintain the status quo when the CBA expires. The expired CBA's terms must remain in effect until the parties reach a new agreement, bargaining negotiations reach an impasse, or the collective bargaining process ends by the players' decertification of their union or an extremely long impasse accompanied by the defunctness of the league's multiemployer bargaining unit. An "impasse" is "a recurring feature in the bargaining process, . . . a temporary deadlock or hiatus in negotiations which in almost all cases is eventually broken, through either a change of mind or the application of economic force." *Charles D. Bonanno Linen Service, Inc. v. NLRB*, 454 U.S. 404, 412 (1982). If there is an impasse in collective bargaining negotiations, which is frequently a recurring part of this process, the league may (but is not required to) unilaterally implement new terms and conditions of player employment "'reasonably comprehended' within [its] preimpasse proposals (typically the last rejected proposals)" if it has bargained in good faith and has not otherwise committed any unfair labor practices. *Brown v. Pro Football, Inc.*, 518 U.S. 231, 238 (1996). However, if a league does so, it invites a strike by the union or its filing of unfair practice charges with the NLRB alleging that there is no impasse or that the league failed to bargain in good faith. Alternatively, the players may terminate the union's status as their collective bargaining representative and bring an antitrust suit claiming that the unilaterally imposed new terms and conditions of employment are an unreasonable restraint of trade.

5. Discrimination Against Striking Players

Players have a statutory right to strike, which is an important aspect of U.S. labor laws and is designed to facilitate peaceful and productive collective bargaining relations. If the players strike, league clubs may hire replacement players for the duration of the strike, as the NFL did during the 1987 three-week strike by its players. A professional sports league may cease operations and lock out its players, as the National Hockey

Association did (which resulted in the loss of its 2004–2005 season) and both the NFL and NBA did in 2011 when their respective CBAs expired. See *Brady v. NFL*, 644 F.3d 661 (8th Cir. 2011) (court cannot enjoin NFL lockout during ongoing labor dispute). However, the league and its member clubs are prohibited from retaliating against striking players.

In *NFL Management Council*, 309 N.L.R.B. 78 (1992), the NFL sought to punish striking players, which the NLRB ruled is illegal:

> In sum, the Respondents' Wednesday deadline prohibited employees who returned from the strike on October 15 from playing in the following weekend's games and prohibited their Club from paying them for that game on the basis of their absence from the Club during the strike. The only players subject to such restrictions were those who chose to participate in the strike, a concerted activity protected by the Act. Players absent from their Club for other reasons were not subject to any similar restriction on their eligibility to participate in games; players ineligible to play for other reasons were nevertheless still entitled to be paid. Accordingly, for the reasons stated above, we find that the Respondents' maintenance and enforcement of its Wednesday deadline rule violated Section 8(a)(1) and (3) of the Act. . . .
>
> To remedy the unfair labor practices which we have found, we shall order the Respondents to cease and desist, and to take certain affirmative action necessary to effectuate the purposes of the Act. Specifically, we shall order the Respondents to make whole all employees who were denied wages and declared ineligible for the games played on October 18 and 19, 1987, on the basis of the Respondents' Wednesday eligibility rule for strikers, with interest computed in the manner set forth in the judge's decision. The Respondents shall also make whole those injured players denied compensation on account of their participation in the strike in the manner set forth in the judge's decision. . . .

Id. at 83–87.

QUESTIONS

1. Why doesn't the NLRB or court review the reasonableness of the parties' respective collective bargaining positions on the merits?
2. In each of the major professional sports leagues (e.g., NFL, NBA, MLB, NHL, MLS), do club owners or players have greater economic leverage to exercise in a labor dispute?
3. Section 8(d) of the NLRA defines mandatory subjects of bargaining as "wages, hours, and other terms and conditions of employment." Consider which of the following examples are mandatory subjects of bargaining:
   a. Whether players can be fined for leaving the bench and going onto the field when there is an altercation among other players
   b. The dimensions of a hockey rink or baseball field
   c. The addition (in the National League) or elimination (in the American League) of baseball's designated hitter rule
   d. The expansion or contraction of the number of teams in a league, including which teams and locations will be affected

D. Union's Duty of Fair Representation

Unlike most other unions, a labor union representing professional athletes faces unique challenges. It must represent the diverse interests of a few thousand extremely talented athletes who have overcome difficult odds to rise to the top of a very elite profession. The small number of athletes who ever get the chance to play their sport at a major league level for even a brief period is far outnumbered by those who seek to do so. Even within the membership ranks of players, there are significant divisions, with a spectrum that includes relatively few superstars, several very good players, numerous marginal players, and some perennial benchwarmers.

The career of a major league professional athlete is, on average, very short in relation to most other professional careers. Thus, the substantial economic rewards that may be gained in the brief time allotted to a professional athlete must be maximized. That is why professional athletes have turned to agents, attorneys, accountants, marketing specialists, and others in an effort to maximize their earning potential. It is also why the task of the labor union representing them is difficult.

The NLRA grants a union exclusive negotiating and other rights to act on behalf of all members of the collective bargaining unit. As a result, the union has the ability and authority to sacrifice or compromise particular players' rights to further the collective good of all players. In 1944, the Supreme Court held that the NLRA implicitly requires a union to fairly represent all members of the collective bargaining unit, *Steele v. Louisville & Nashville Railroads*, 323 U.S. 192 (1944), which includes incoming rookie players and those currently ineligible to play in the league (e.g., Maurice Clarett). The NLRB has determined that a union's breach of its duty of fair representation is an unfair labor practice. *Miranda Fuel Co.*, 140 N.L.R.B. 181 (1962).

Because the nonstatutory labor exemption, which is discussed *infra*, precludes any antitrust challenge to the terms of the CBA, the union's duty to fairly represent all current and prospective players' interests is particularly important. However, breach of this duty has seldom been proved in the sports context. In *Peterson v. Kennedy*, 771 F.2d 1244, 1253 (9th Cir. 1985), the Ninth Circuit explained:

> A union breaches its duty of fair representation only when its conduct toward a member of the collective bargaining unit is "arbitrary, discriminatory, or in bad faith." The duty is designed to ensure that unions represent fairly the interests of all of their members without exercising hostility or bad faith toward any. It stands "as a bulwark to prevent arbitrary union conduct against individuals stripped of traditional forms of redress by the provisions of federal labor law." . . .
>
> The Supreme Court has long recognized that unions must retain wide discretion to act in what they perceive to be their members' best interests . . . . To that end, we have "stressed the importance of preserving union discretion by narrowly construing the unfair representation doctrine." . . . We have emphasized that, because a union balances many collective and individual interests in deciding whether and to what extent it will pursue a particular grievance, courts should "accord substantial deference" to a union's decisions regarding such matters.
>
> A union's representation of its members "need not be error free." . . . We have concluded repeatedly that mere negligent conduct on the part of a union does not constitute a breach of the union's duty of fair representation. . . .

E. Labor Arbitration

 **KEY TERM**   • Law of the shop

Most disputes between a league and the players' union (or a player and his or her club) regarding the meaning of terms in the CBA, UPC, or individual player contract are resolved by an independent arbitrator mutually selected by the league and players' union for each sport. Although arbitration decisions do not have the same precedential effect as court decisions, arbitrators usually consider previous arbitration awards resolving similar issues, particularly those in the same league.

In contract dispute arbitration, the arbitrator usually is given broad authority to construe the meaning of the parties' contract(s) and to grant appropriate relief to the nonbreaching party, including damages and ordering an action that is necessary to remedy a breach of contract. For example, an arbitrator ordered basketball player Brian Shaw to comply with the terms of his new contract with the Boston Celtics by rescinding the second year of his contract with an Italian club (which he had a contractual right to do) and not playing for any other club for the duration of his Celtics' contract. *Boston Celtics Ltd. Partnership v. Shaw*, 908 F.2d 1041 (1st Cir. 1990) (judicially confirming labor arbitration award).

Arbitration by an independent arbitrator also is generally used to resolve player legal challenges to discipline imposed by the club or league for on- or off-field misconduct. The union typically files a grievance on the player's behalf and represents him in the arbitration proceeding. The arbitrator determines whether the league or club had "just cause" to impose the challenged disciplinary sanction, which is upheld if this standard has been met, or nullified or reduced if it has not. See, e.g., *NBA Players Association on Behalf of Player Latrell Sprewell and Warriors Basketball Club and NBA* (Feerick, Arbitrator; May 4, 1998) (reducing NBA's one-year suspension of Latrell Sprewell to 68 games with $6.4 million loss of salary for attacking Golden State Warriors coach P.J. Carlesimo twice during a team practice). However, the NFL CBA provides that Commissioner Roger Goodell or his designee is the "arbitrator" for the purposes of reviewing league discipline imposed on a player, which has led to litigation in which the NFL players' union and individual players (e.g., Adrian Peterson, Tom Brady) have asked a court to vacate the disciplinary sanction on the grounds that it is unauthorized by the CBA or the product of partial decision making.

Both MLB and the NHL use a collectively bargained arbitration process to resolve salary disputes between teams and individual players, which is available only in limited situations but has far-reaching effects on player salaries within the league. The MLB CBA's salary arbitration provisions generally apply only to players who have between three and six years of credited major league service. One of the most notable aspects of baseball salary arbitration is that it utilizes "final offer arbitration." This means that, without knowing what the other side will submit as a salary figure, the team and the player each submit an amount for a one-year contract. This requires substantial thought by both parties, because the arbitration panel must select one figure or the other. There can be no compromise. Thus, if the matter is decided by arbitration, the end result will be a one-year, nonguaranteed contract (with no bonuses) at a salary submitted by the club or the player. See generally William B. Gould, *Labor Issues in Professional Sports: Reflections on Baseball, Labor and Antitrust Law*, 15 Stan. L. & Pol'y Rev. 61 (2004) (addressing development of salary arbitration); Brien M. Wassner, *Major League Baseball's Answer to Salary Disputes and the Strike Final Offer Arbitration: A Negotiation Tool Facilitating Adversary Agreement*, 6 Vand. J. Ent. L. & Prac. 5 (2003).

Unlike MLB's final offer arbitration, the NHL's salary arbitration system is premised on a conventional arbitration model. Like MLB's system, the NHL's salary arbitration system contains eligibility requirements that must be met in order for players to seek salary arbitration. Procedures are in place for selecting arbitrators, and limitations are imposed on the factors that the arbitrator can consider in determining a player's compensation. Because it is based on a conventional arbitration model, the salary determined by the arbitrator can be the offer of either the player or the club, or any amount ranging between the two offers. Another notable difference is the binding effect of the arbitrator's award. Generally, the arbitrator's decision is final and binding on both the player and club. However, clubs have a limited right to reject a salary award (a walk-away right), which may be exercised no more than three times in two continuous years and not more than twice in the same year. If this right is exercised, the player becomes a free agent. If he does not receive a better offer from another team, he may accept his prior team's last offer prior to becoming a free agent. See generally Melanie Aubut, *When Negotiations Fail: An Analysis of Salary Arbitration and Salary Cap Systems*, 10 Sports Law. J. 189, 205 (2003); Stephen J. Barlett, *Contract Negotiations and Salary Arbitration in the NHL: An Agent's View*, 4 Marq. Sports L.J. 1 (1993).

Although an arbitration award generally binds only the parties thereto, some awards have broader implications and have significantly altered the way that a league conducts its business with players. For example, the following 1976 arbitration involving baseball players Dave McNally and Andy Messersmith invalidated MLB's nearly 100-year-old reserve clause, which had been unilaterally imposed by the clubs and unsuccessfully challenged in the *Flood v. Kuhn* antitrust litigation. This arbitration award effectively laid the groundwork for a collectively bargained system of free agency for MLB players.

National & American League Professional Baseball Clubs v. Major League Baseball Players Association
66 Labor Arbitration 101 (1976)

SEITZ, Arbitrator.

The Chairman understands the dispute in arbitration to be as follows: The Association claims that the terms of the Uniform Player Contracts of [Andy] Messersmith and [Dave] McNally, respectively, having expired, the two players are at liberty to negotiate contract relationships with any of the other clubs in the leagues and that they are not to be regarded as having been "reserved" by the Los Angeles and Montreal clubs, respectively, in such manner as to inhibit clubs from dealing with them.

The leagues and the clubs assert that the terms of the contracts of these players have not expired; that they are still under contract; and that, in any event, the grievants have been duly "reserved" by their respective clubs; and, accordingly, they are not free to deal with other clubs for the performance of services for the 1976 season; nor are such other clubs free to deal with them for that season excepting under circumstances and conditions not here obtaining. . . .

The league's argument is based on the language in §10(a) of the Player's Contract that the Club "may renew this contract for the period of one year *on the same terms*" (emphasis supplied); and that among those "terms" is the right to further contract renewal.

In the law of contract construction, as I know it, there is nothing to prevent parties from agreeing to successive renewals of the terms of their bargain (even to what has been described as "perpetuity"), provided the contract expresses that intention with explicit clarity and the right of subsequent renewals does not have to be implied. . . .

There is nothing in Section 10(a) which, explicitly, expresses agreement that the Players Contract can be renewed for any period beyond the first renewal year. The point the leagues present must be based upon the implication or assumption, that if the renewed contract is "on the same terms" as the contract for the preceding year (with the exception of the amount of compensation) the right to additional renewals must have been an integral part of the renewed contract. I find great difficulties, in so implying or assuming, in respect of a contract providing for the rendition of personal services in which one would expect a more explicit expression of intention. . . .

Traditionally, the leagues have regarded the existence of a contract as a basis for the reservation of players. In Club's Exhibit No. 15 there is set forth the Cincinnati Peace Compact of the National and American Leagues, signed January 10, 1903—probably the most important step in the evolution and development of the present Reserve System. In that document it provided:

Second—A *reserve rule* shall be recognized, by which each and every club may reserve *players under contract*, and that a uniform contract for the use of each league shall be adopted. (Emphasis supplied.)

This emphasis on the existence of a contract for reservation of a player to be effective was perpetuated in the Major League Rules. . . .

Thus, I reach the conclusion that, absent a contractual connection between Messersmith and the Los Angeles Club after September 28, 1975, the Club's action in reserving his services for the ensuing year by placing him on its reserve list was unavailing and ineffectual in prohibiting him from dealing with other clubs in the league and to prohibit such clubs from dealing with him.

In the case of McNally whom the Montreal Club had placed on its disqualified list, a similar conclusion has been reached. . . .

I am not unmindful of the testimony of the Commissioner of Baseball and the Presidents of the National and American League given at the hearings as to the importance of maintaining the integrity of the Reserve System. It was represented to me that any decision of the Arbitration Panel sustaining the Messersmith and McNally grievances would have dire results, wreak great harm to the Reserve System and do serious damage to the sport of baseball.

Thus, for example, it was stated that a decision favoring these grievants would encourage many other players to elect to become free agents at the end of the renewal years; that this would encourage clubs with the largest monetary resources to engage free agents, thus unsettling the competitive balance between clubs, so essential to the sport; that it would increase enormously the already high costs of training and seasoning young players to achieve the level of skills required in professional baseball and such investments would be sacrificed if they became free agents at the end of a renewal year; that driven by the compulsion to win, owners of franchises would over-extend themselves financially and improvident bidding for players in an economic climate in which, today, some clubs are strained, financially; that investors will be discouraged from putting money in franchises in which several of the star players on the club team will become free agents at the end of a renewal year and no continuing control over the players' services can be exercised; and that even the integrity of the sport may be placed in hazard under certain circumstances.

I do not purport to appraise these apprehensions. They are all based on speculations as to what may ensue. Some of the fears may be imaginary or exaggerated; but some may be reasonable, realistic, and sound. After all, they were voiced by distinguished baseball officials with long experience in the sport and a background for judgment in such matters much superior to my own. However, as stated above, at length, it is not for the Panel (and especially the writer) to determine what, if anything, is good or bad about the reserve system. The Panel's sole duty is to interpret and apply the agreements and undertakings of the parties. If any of the expressed apprehensions and fears are soundly based, I am confident that the dislocations and damage to the reserve system can be avoided or minimized through good faith collective bargaining between the parties. There are numerous expedients available and arrangements that can be made that will soften the blow—if this decision, indeed, should be regarded as a blow. This decision is not the end of the line by any means. The parties, jointly, are free to agree to disregard it and compose their differences as to the reserve system in any way they see fit. . . .

However strong my conviction that the basic dispute should be determined by the parties, in collective bargaining rather than by an Arbitration Panel, that Panel could not justify any further delay, and the accompanying Award, accordingly, is being rendered. The parties are still in negotiation, however, and continue to have an opportunity to reach agreement on measures that will give assurance of a reserve system that will meet the needs of the clubs and protect them from the damage they fear this decision will cause, and, at the same time, meet the needs of the players. . . .

Grievance upheld.

NOTES

1. Aftermath. The MLB club owners were given advance notice of the arbitrator's probable resolution of the Messersmith and McNally grievances. Rather than attempting to reach a new agreement with the players regarding free agency restrictions, the club owners appealed the arbitrator's decision to the federal courts. In *Kansas*

City Royals v. Major League Baseball Players Association, 532 F.2d 615, 632 (8th Cir. 1976), the Eighth Circuit upheld the *Messersmith-McNally* arbitration decision:

> The arbitration panel had jurisdiction to hear and decide the Messersmith-McNally grievances, that the panel's award drew its essence from the collective bargaining agreement, and that the relief fashioned by the District Court was appropriate. Accordingly, the award of the arbitration panel must be sustained, and the District Court's judgment affirmed. In so holding, we intimate no views on the merits of the reserve system. We note, however, that Club Owners and the Players Association's representatives agree that some form of a reserve system is needed if the integrity of the game is to be preserved and if public confidence in baseball is to be maintained. The disagreement lies over the degree of control necessary if these goals are to be achieved. Certainly, the parties are in a better position to negotiate their differences than to have them decided in a series of arbitrations and court decisions. We commend them to that process and suggest that the time for obfuscation has passed and that the time for plain talk and clear language has arrived. Baseball fans everywhere expect nothing less.

After going through an initial period of readjustment, in which every MLB player then in the American League or National League was given one opportunity to be a free agent and to sign a contract with the club of his choosing, the owners and players entered into a new CBA providing that a player can earn free agent status after six years of credited major league service, which remains the standard today.

2. Judicial review of arbitration awards. An arbitration award is final and binding on the parties, but it is subject to judicial review by a federal court under the Labor Management Relations Act. Although an arbitrator's "evident partiality" is a ground for vacating an arbitration award, the party challenging the award has the "heavy burden" of proving that the parties' agreed arbitrator had "improper motives." See, e.g., *Williams v. NFL*, 582 F.3d 863, 885-886 (8th Cir. 2009) (rejecting NFLPA's claim that an arbitration award by Jeffrey Pash, the NFL's general counsel, is inherently partial because the NFL CBA provided that "the Commissioner or his designee will preside as Hearing Officer" and resolve the subject dispute). A court's review of the merits of an arbitration award is very limited, and the award will be vacated only on very narrow grounds. In *Major League Baseball Players Association v. Garvey*, 532 U.S. 504, 509 (2001), the Supreme Court explained:

> Courts are not authorized to review the arbitrator's decision on the merits despite allegations that the decision rests on factual errors or misinterprets the parties' agreement. We recently reiterated that if an "arbitrator is even arguably construing or applying the contract and acting within the scope of his authority," the fact that "a court is convinced he committed serious error does not suffice to overturn his decision." It is only when the arbitrator strays from interpretation and application of the agreement and effectively "dispenses his own brand of industrial justice" that his decision may be unenforceable. When an arbitrator resolves disputes regarding the application of a contract, and no dishonesty is alleged, the arbitrator's "improvident, even silly, factfinding" does not provide a basis for a reviewing court to refuse to enforce the award.

In *National Football League Management Council v. National Football League Players Association*, 2015 U.S. Dist. LEXIS (S.D. N.Y., September 3, 2015), a New York federal district court vacated Commissioner Goodell's arbitration award, which had upheld the NFL's imposition of a four-game suspension on quarterback Tom Brady for having knowing involvement in the deflation of game balls by New England Patriots equipment personnel during the 2015 AFC Championship game, as well as the willful destruction of potentially relevant evidence (i.e., his cell phone). The court determined that Goodell "failed to draw [his] award from the essence of the collective bargaining agreement" because Brady had no notice that a player's involvement in deflating footballs during a game and his failure to cooperate in an ensuing league investigation would result in the same discipline (i.e., a four-game suspension) that applied to a player who violated the NFL Policy on Anabolic Steroids and Related Substances for the first time. *Id.* at ★40. The court reasoned: "It is the 'law of the shop' to provide professional football players with (advance) notice of prohibited conduct and of potential discipline. . . . Because there was no notice of a four-game suspension in the circumstances presented here, Commissioner Goodell may be said to have "dispense[d] his own brand of industrial justice." *Id.* at ★42.

THE INTERSECTION OF ANTITRUST AND LABOR LAW

KEY TERMS
- Anticompetitive effect
- Curt Flood Act of 1998
- Decertification
- Nonstatutory labor exemption
- Procompetitive effect
- Rule of reason
- Statutory labor exemption

One of the more perplexing aspects of labor relations in professional team sports is the inherent tension between, and intersection of, federal antitrust and labor law.

The objective of antitrust law is to promote competition among buyers and sellers of goods and services. Section 1 of the Sherman Act prohibits agreements that unreasonably restrain interstate trade or commerce. 15 U.S.C. §1. Applied literally, §1 prohibits both employees and employers from engaging in joint activity or making agreements that unreasonably restrain the labor market. Section 1 requires employers in an industry (e.g., league clubs) to compete independently for employee (e.g., player) services. Similarly, employees must individually compete for employment. Theoretically, consumers will benefit because the operation of free market forces in the labor market will result in the most efficient allocation of human resources.

In the 1970s, players sought to use antitrust law to advance their economic interests by challenging league unilaterally imposed labor market restraints such as player drafts and free agency restrictions. NFL players successfully challenged the then-existing 16-round draft and certain free agency restrictions on antitrust grounds. See, e.g., *Smith v. Pro Football, Inc.*, 593 F.2d 1173 (D.C. Cir. 1978); *Kapp v. National Football League*, 586 F.2d 644 (9th Cir. 1978); *Mackey v. National Football League*, 543 F.2d 606 (8th Cir. 1976). Antitrust litigation challenging similar restraints that had been unilaterally implemented by the NBA and NHL also was successful. *Robertson v. Nat'l Basketball Assn.*, 389 F. Supp. 867 (D.D.N.Y. 1975); *Philadelphia World Hockey Club, Inc. v. Philadelphia Hockey Club, Inc.*, 351 F. Supp. 462 (E.D. Pa. 1972). From the players' perspective, the antitrust laws became powerful weapons for effectuating changes in how sports leagues conduct business vis-à-vis the players. However, MLB's unique antitrust exemption barred professional baseball players' antitrust claims. *Flood v. Kuhn*, 407 U.S. 258 (1972).

On the other hand, labor law permits employees to unionize and collectively bargain, which is an allowable form of anticompetitive behavior that reduces economic competition among them regarding employment opportunities. Multiemployer bargaining within an industry pursuant to which one entity represents all employers, which is similarly anticompetitive, is legal under labor law. Such concerted action among otherwise competing groups of employees (e.g., players) and employers (e.g., league clubs) squarely conflicts with §1 of the Sherman Act.

To resolve this conflict, Congress enacted two statutes (§6 of the Clayton Act and the Norris-LaGuardia Act), the combined effect of which is to create a *statutory labor exemption*, which provides a labor union with immunity from antitrust liability for its unilateral efforts to further its members' economic interests. Thus, in general, union collective bargaining activities over issues of wages, hours, and conditions of employment, as well as strikes, picketing, and boycotts of employers, do not violate the antitrust laws. *United States v. Hutcheson*, 312 U.S. 219 (1941). To facilitate the collective bargaining process, courts have held that the activities of multiemployer bargaining units to further their members' common interests, such as collective strike insurance and lockouts, also are protected by the statutory exemption. *Kennedy v. Long Island Rail Road Co.*, 319 F.2d 366 (2d Cir. 1963), *cert. denied*, 375 U.S. 830 (1963).

However, the statutory labor exemption, which applies only to unilateral union conduct such as collective bargaining and strikes, does not immunize the terms of CBAs with employers from antitrust challenge on the ground that they are anticompetitive terms and conditions of employment. In *Connell Construction Co. v. Plumbers, Local 100*, 421 U.S. 616, 622 (1975), the Supreme Court recognized the need for a nonstatutory labor exemption to further "the strong labor policy favoring the association of employees to eliminate competition over wages and working conditions" through collective bargaining.

Courts have created a broad nonstatutory labor exemption, which not only precludes the parties from challenging the terms of an existing CBA on antitrust grounds, but also precludes any antitrust litigation even after it expires, so long as there is an ongoing collective bargaining relationship between the league and its players. This furthers the strong U.S. labor policy that permits employees, including professional athletes, to unionize and engage in collective bargaining concerning their wages and working conditions.

In a series of cases, federal appellate courts held that the nonstatutory labor exemption immunized the terms of existing CBAs from antitrust attack by any of the parties subject to its terms, thereby permitting league clubs and the players' union to agree to contract terms such as a player draft, salary cap, or free agency restrictions that otherwise may violate antitrust laws. *Wood v. Nat'l Basketball Assn.*, 809 F.2d 954 (2d Cir. 1987); *McCourt v. California Sports, Inc.*, 600 F.2d 1193 (6th Cir. 1979); *Reynolds v. National Football League*, 584 F.2d 280 (8th Cir. 1978). In *Clarett v. National Football League*, 369 F.3d 124 (2d Cir. 2004), *cert. denied*, 544 U.S. 961 (2005), the Second Circuit held that the nonstatutory labor exemption precludes a prospective player from bringing an antitrust challenge to eligibility requirements in a CBA that prevented him from playing NFL football for a particular period of time. The court ruled that the union has the exclusive authority to negotiate the terms and conditions of prospective NFL players' employment (e.g., requiring that at least three full college seasons have elapsed since their high school graduation before they are eligible to be drafted or signed as free agents). Eligibility rules are a mandatory subject of collective bargaining between the league and the players' union because they pertain to players' wages, hours, and other terms and conditions of employment. As part of its efforts to obtain a CBA providing the best overall deal for all NFL players, federal labor law gives the union the ability to disadvantage one category of prospective players vis-a-vis others (e.g., those who met the eligibility requirement) so long as it does not breach its federal labor law duty of fair representation or violate federal laws prohibiting unfair labor practices or employment discrimination.

The Eighth Circuit extended the scope of the nonstatutory labor exemption by ruling that terms of an expired CBA (which labor law generally requires the league to maintain in effect until a new CBA is reached) do not lose their antitrust immunity even if the players' union and league multiemployer collective bargaining unit reach an impasse (i.e., a temporary deadlock) in their efforts to negotiate a new agreement. *Powell v. NFL*, 930 F.2d 1293 (8th Cir. 1989), *cert. denied*, 498 U.S. 1040 (1991).

In 1996, the Supreme Court significantly expanded the scope of the nonstatutory labor exemption even further by holding that it bars antitrust litigation challenging new terms and conditions of employment unilaterally imposed by the league so long as there is an ongoing collective bargaining relationship with the players. In *Brown v. Pro Football, Inc.*, 518 U.S. 231 (1996), the Court held that the exemption shields all restraints on the labor market for players' services (e.g., player drafts, team salary caps, and player free agency restrictions) from antitrust challenge so long as there is an ongoing collective bargaining process between the league and the players' union. If there is, federal labor law, which permits employers to unilaterally impose terms and conditions of employment if certain conditions are satisfied, exclusively governs labor relations between the parties.

In *Brown*, the NFL unilaterally established a maximum weekly salary of $1,000 for all developmental squad players (i.e., nonroster players) after collectively bargaining to impasse on this important issue (historically, all major professional sports league salaries have been individually negotiated between a player and his club). The players claimed that this conduct was illegal wage fixing in violation of §1 of the Sherman Act, but the Court ruled that they could not bring their antitrust claim:

[T]he [nonstatutory] antitrust exemption applies to the employer conduct at issue here. That conduct took place during and immediately after a collective-bargaining negotiation. It grew out of, and was directly related to, the lawful operation of the bargaining process. It involved a matter that the parties were required to negotiate collectively. And it concerned only the parties to the collective-bargaining relationship.

518 U.S. at 250.

The Court, however, explained that its holding "is not intended to insulate from antitrust review every joint imposition of terms by employers, for an agreement among employers could be sufficiently distant in time and in circumstances from the collective bargaining process that a rule permitting antitrust intervention would not significantly interfere with that process." 518 U.S. at 250. It suggested that the nonstatutory labor exemption would end if the players terminated the collective bargaining process with the league by decertification of their union, which would then permit them to bring an antitrust suit challenging any agreements among league clubs that restrained the market for their services. *Decertification* is a formal process requiring at least 50 percent of the players to vote to decertify the union in an NLRB-supervised election. If this occurs, they cannot vote to reunionize (and thereby engage in collective bargaining with the league) before the lapse of a 12-month period.

Because of the broad scope of the nonstatutory labor exemption, it generally precludes professional athletes from using antitrust law to resolve labor relations disputes. However, there are three general situations in which it is inapplicable, and courts will consider the merits of antitrust challenges to anticompetitive restraints on the terms and conditions of professional athletes' employment.

One, players in team sports can choose not to unionize (in the case of a newly formed professional league) or they (including MLB players) may decertify their union, thereby preventing or discontinuing the collective bargaining process and negating the applicability of the nonstatutory labor exemption as *Brown* suggests. A federal statute, the *Curt Flood Act of 1998*, 15 U.S.C. §26b, limits the otherwise broad scope of baseball's common law antitrust immunity (see Chapter 11) by providing MLB players with the same antitrust remedies as other professional athletes such as football, basketball, hockey, and soccer players. Because the Act is not intended to affect judicial construction and application of the nonstatutory labor exemption, unionized MLB players do not have any antitrust remedies. 15 U.S.C. §26b(d)(4). Like players in other professional leagues, MLB players could decertify their union to challenge any unilaterally imposed terms and conditions of their employment on antitrust grounds. If they do so, the act expressly permits antitrust challenges only to conduct or agreements "directly relating to or affecting employment of MLB players to play baseball at the major league level." 15 U.S.C. §26b(a). It does not provide a basis for challenging conduct or agreements relating to employment as a minor league baseball player, the amateur or first-year player draft, or any reserve clause applied to minor league players. 15 U.S.C. §26b(b)(1).

Two, courts generally hold that the nonstatutory labor exemption does not bar an antitrust challenge by nonparties to CBA terms that have anticompetitive effects outside the internal league labor market for players' services. In *Philadelphia World Hockey Club, Inc. v. Philadelphia Hockey Club, Inc.*, 351 F. Supp. 462 (E.D. Pa. 1972), the court ruled that this exemption does not preclude a rival league's claim that the NHL's reserve clause violates the antitrust laws. The World Hockey Association (WHA) prevailed on its antitrust claim by proving that the reserve clause in the NHL's CBA, which provided an NHL club with rights to a player's services for three years after his contract expired, deprived the WHA from competing for the services of players with the ability to play major league professional hockey. The WHA needed access to such players in order to produce major league professional ice hockey in competition with the NHL.

Third, the nonstatutory labor exemption has not been applied to individual-performer sports, such as tennis, golf, and boxing. See, e.g., *Blalock v. Ladies Prof'l Golfers Assn.*, 359 F. Supp. 1260 (N.D. Ga. 1973) (finding that golfer's one-year suspension imposed by LPGA with "completely unfettered, subjective discretion" by a group of her competitors violates the antitrust laws). Professional players in individual-performer sports generally are not unionized employees who engage in collective bargaining activities. Even if athletes in the sport form a players' association and enter into agreements with event promoters or organizers, this generally does not constitute collective bargaining under the federal labor laws or make the nonstatutory labor exemption applicable.

Because there are several instances where antitrust litigation is not barred by the nonstatutory labor exemption, we must examine briefly the developing framework of antitrust analysis applicable to challenged labor market restraints. Most litigation seeking to invalidate player labor market restraints involves claimed violations of §1 of the Sherman Act, which requires concerted conduct that unreasonably restrains trade. In *McNeil v. NFL*, 790 F. Supp. 871 (D. Minn. 1992), the court held that agreements among league clubs to reduce competition for player services are subject to §1. However, courts recognize that some agreement among league clubs regarding the permissible scope of competition for player services is necessary to jointly produce competitive games attractive to fans; therefore, a league's need for competitive balance among its clubs is an important factor to be considered when assessing the reasonableness of the challenged player restraints. *McNeil v. NFL*, 1992 WL 315292 at *4 (D. Minn. 1992).

Because the unique features of the sports industry require some uniform rules and agreements among competing teams in order to produce on-field competition that is appealing to consumers, *National Collegiate Athletic Association v. Board of Regents of the University of Oklahoma*, 468 U.S. 85, 101 (1984), courts generally apply the flexible *rule of reason* on a case-by-case basis to determine whether particular restraints affecting the market for player services violate the antitrust laws rather than automatically invalidating them. See, e.g., *National Hockey League Players' Assn. v. Plymouth Whalers Hockey Club*, 325 F.3d 712 (6th Cir. 2003); *McNeil v. NFL*, 790 F. Supp. 871 (D. Minn. 1992).

Applying the rule of reason to player restraints requires complicated analysis and balancing of several different factors and their economic effects. Considering the validity of the NBA's then-current draft eligibility rules, one court observed:

The primary disadvantages of the "rule of reason" are that it requires difficult and lengthy factual inquiries and very subjective policy decisions which are in many ways essentially legislative and ill-suited to the judicial process. For instance, in the present case, a complex economic inquiry would be required to determine the economic necessity of action of this type. In addition, the court would be required to determine a standard which could be used to weigh the various public policy goals which might be alleged as justification by the NBA. The court would further be forced to determine whether the [player restraint] was genuinely motivated by the purposes given or by other reasons. Frequently, these motives are closely intertwined.

See *Denver Rockets v. All-Pro Management*, 325 F. Supp. 1049, 1063 (C.D. Cal. 1971).

Under the rule of reason, a player must prove that the challenged restraint has the anticompetitive effect of reducing economic competition among league clubs for player services. For example, agreements among league clubs to fix players' wages, which thereby eliminate individual salary negotiations, have clear anticompetitive effects. *McNeil v. NFL*, 790 F. Supp. 871, 877 (D. Minn. 1992). Because their adverse economic effects are not as direct and less clear, other labor market restraints such as player drafts, free agency restrictions, and related forms of allocating players among league clubs may require detailed market analysis to determine their effects on economic competition. In such cases, the plaintiff must prove the relevant market for the services of players and that the defendant league and its clubs have a sufficiently large market share to adversely affect competition. The relevant market has both a product and geographical component. The product market includes all prospective purchasers of player services that are reasonable substitutes from the players' perspective in terms of earning potential, prestige, and other economic factors. *Smith v. Pro Football, Inc.*, 593 F.2d 1173, 1185 n.48 (D.C. Cir. 1979) (finding that employment in the Canadian Football League is not reasonable substitute for employment with an NFL team). The geographical market is the geographical area "to which players can turn, as a practical matter, for alternate opportunities for employment" as professional athletes. *Fraser v. Major League Soccer, LLC*, 284 F.3d 47, 63 (1st Cir. 2002), *cert. denied*, 537 U.S. 885 (2002) (upholding jury finding of an international market for the services of professional soccer players).

If the player proves the requisite anticompetitive effects, the league (and clubs) must prove the challenged restraint is necessary to achieve the procompetitive effect of enhancing a professional sports league's ability to more effectively compete with other forms of entertainment. *Sullivan v. NFL*, 34 F.3d 1091, 1111–13 (1st Cir. 1994). Even if it does, a labor market restraint may be invalidated if there is a less restrictive means of achieving the league's procompetitive objective. *Smith v. Pro Football, Inc.*, 593 F.2d 1173, 118 (D.C. Cir. 1979) (holding that the NFL's 16-round draft violated §1 because "significantly less anticompetitive alternatives" exist).

As an illustration of how courts have applied the rule of reason to labor market restraints, see *Mackey v. NFL*, 543 F.2d 606, 620-22 (8th Cir. 1976):

The focus of an inquiry under the Rule of Reason is whether the restraint imposed is justified by legitimate business purposes, and is no more restrictive than necessary. . . .

In defining the restraint on competition for players' services, the district court found that the Rozelle Rule [which required NFL Commissioner Pete Rozelle to award compensation in the form of players, draft choices, or both from the club that contracted with a free agent player to his former club if they could not agree on compensation for the player] significantly deters clubs from negotiating with and signing free agents; that it acts as a substantial deterrent to players playing out their options and becoming free agents; that it significantly decreases players' bargaining power in contract negotiations; that players are thus denied the right to sell their services in a free and open market; that as a result, the salaries paid by each club are lower than if competitive bidding were allowed to prevail; and that absent the Rozelle Rule, there would be increased movement in interstate commerce of players from one club to another.

We find substantial evidence in the record to support these findings. Witnesses for both sides testified that there would be increased player movement absent the Rozelle Rule. . . .

In support of their contention that the restraints effected by the Rozelle Rule are not unreasonable, the defendants asserted a number of justifications. First, they argued that without the Rozelle Rule, star players would flock to cities having natural advantages such as larger economic bases, winning teams, warmer climates, and greater media opportunities; that competitive balance throughout the League would thus be destroyed; and that the destruction of competitive balance would ultimately lead to diminished spectator interest, franchise failures, and perhaps the demise of the NFL, at least as it operates today. Second, the defendants contended that the Rozelle Rule is necessary to protect the clubs' investment in scouting expenses and player development costs. Third, they asserted that players must work together for a substantial period of time in order to function effectively as a team; that elimination of the Rozelle Rule would lead to increased player movement and a concomitant reduction in player continuity; and that the quality of play in the NFL would thus suffer, leading to reduced spectator interest, and financial detriment both to the clubs and the players. Conflicting evidence was adduced at trial by both sides with respect to the validity of these asserted justifications.

The district court held the defendants' asserted justifications unavailing. . . . The court further concluded that elimination of the Rozelle Rule would have no significant disruptive effects, either immediate or long term, on professional football. In conclusion the court held that the Rozelle Rule was unreasonable in that it was overly broad, unlimited in duration, unaccompanied by procedural safeguards, and employed in conjunction with other anticompetitive practices such as the draft, Standard Player Contract, option clause, and the no-tampering rules.

We agree that the asserted need to recoup player development costs cannot justify the restraints of the Rozelle Rule. That expense is an ordinary cost of doing business and is not peculiar to professional football. Moreover, because of its unlimited duration, the Rozelle Rule is far more restrictive than necessary to fulfill that need.

We agree, in view of the evidence adduced at trial with respect to existing players' turnover by way of trades, retirements and new players entering the League, that the club owners' arguments respecting player continuity cannot justify the Rozelle Rule. . . .

In sum, we hold that the Rozelle Rule, as enforced, unreasonably restrains trade in violation of §1 of the Sherman Act. . . .

QUESTIONS

1. What is the statutory labor exemption, and what conduct does it preclude from being challenged on antitrust law grounds?
2. What is the nonstatutory labor exemption, and according to *Brown*, why does it bar any antitrust claims so long as there is an ongoing collective bargaining process between a league's clubs and players?
3. What are MLB players' options under the labor and antitrust laws if MLB and its clubs unilaterally impose a team salary cap after the current CBA expires?

Representing Players and Teams: The Athlete-Agent Industry

13

The use of agents by professional athletes can be traced back to as early as the mid-1920s, when Charles Pyle negotiated a football contract and endorsement and movie deals for National Football Player (NFL) player Harold "Red" Grange. The increase in the number and use of agents by athletes did not occur until the 1960s and 1970s, as a result of the demise of reserve and option clauses in standard-form contracts between players and clubs, competition for players between rival leagues (e.g., the NFL and the American Football League (AFL)), the growing strength of labor unions and their positive impact on players' salaries, the increased income of athletes that necessitated advice on matters ranging from taxes to estates, and the increase in players' opportunities to generate outside income through endorsement contracts.

The proliferation in the use of agents has been accompanied by an expansion in the range of services that they perform. The role of agents extends beyond the commonly held belief that their job is to negotiate a player's contract with his or her club. The functions performed by agents include contract negotiation; endorsement advice and solicitation; tax, estate, and financial planning; and career, personal development, legal, insurance, and sports medicine consultation. Walter T. Champion, Jr., *Attorneys Qua Sports Agents: An Ethical Conundrum,* 7 Marq. Sports L.J. 349, 351–52 (1997).

The range of services that athletes' agents perform is indicative of the breadth of substantive expertise required in order for agents to effectively represent athletes. The problem is that few people, even the best, have either the ability or expertise to perform all the tasks listed above. All too often, perhaps out of ignorance or perhaps out of greed, agents take on more than they can competently handle. Unless they are part of a company, with individuals of diverse professional expertise ready to assist, agents may well overreach and perform at levels approaching negligence. Despite the useful functions provided by agents, other inappropriate agent conduct that is detrimental to athletes is also a pervasive part of the relationship. This chapter examines various legal mechanisms that regulate the agent-athlete relationship and seek to enhance the likelihood that agents and athletes will fulfill their respective obligations. This matrix consists of a web of common law rules, state and federal legislation, and regulations promulgated by players' associations.

An important change that could dramatically affect the athlete-agent industry is worth noting. As this book went to press, the National Football League Players Association was reportedly examining the development of a structure that would result in the union, rather than agents, negotiating contracts on behalf of players and providing information that would enable players to negotiate their own contracts. This is a possible development that bears watching. Tom Pelissero, *NFL Players Mull Freeing Agents from Future Contract Negotiations*, USA Today, July 21, 2015 *http:// www.usatoday.com/story/sports/nfl/2015/07/21/nflpa-union-contracts-no-agents-russell-okung-rashad-jennings-eric-winston/30490459/*. Our examination begins, however, with an analysis of common law principles, derived principally from the law of agency and contract, which are instrumental in regulating the agent-athlete relationship.

THE NATURE OF THE ATHLETE-AGENT RELATIONSHIP

A. The Agent's Basic Duties

 KEY TERMS

- Agent
- Fiduciary
- Principal

This section examines the legal duties that agents owe to their athlete clients and the standard of care adopted by courts to determine if those duties are competently performed. The agent's relationship with athletes is governed by many of the basic contract principles introduced in Chapter 3. Agency law principles also play a major role in governing the agent-client relationship. The following excerpt[1] introduces basic agency law principles and provides the legal framework within which to consider the materials in this chapter:

> The agency relationship is defined as "the fiduciary relationship which results from the manifestation of consent by one person to another that the other shall act in his behalf and subject to his contract, and consent by the other so to act." The principal is "the one for whom action is to be taken." In the sports context, the athlete is the principal. The agent is the one who is to act" for the principal. The essential nature and character of the agency relationship is that the principal authorizes his agent to contract on his behalf with one or more third parties." [Restatement (Second) of Agency, §1(1) (1958).]
>
> These definitions tell us that the agency relationship is consensual — typically expressed in a contract. This is certainly the case in the sports context in which the major sports leagues have developed model contracts for the agent/principal

---

[1] Originally published in Kenneth L. Shropshire, Timothy Davis, and N. Jeremi Duru, The Business of Sports Agents (3d ed. 2015). Reprinted with permission of the University of Pennsylvania Press.

relationship. For example, the National Football League Players Association (NFLPA) has developed a "Standard Representation Agreement" for mandatory use by agents and their football-player clients. [T]he NFLPA agreement sets forth general principles including the concept that the "Contract Advisor" acts "in a fiduciary capacity." . . .

The above definitions relating to agency also inform us that the most basic obligations that agents owe to their principals are defined not only by contract, but by the fiduciary characteristics of the relationship. A fiduciary is defined as "one who acts primarily for the benefit of another." [Restatement (Third) of Agency § 1.01 (2006).] Consequently, the essence of the principal/agent relationship spawns a fundamental obligation that the "agent owes his principal the fiduciary duty of undivided loyalty and the duty to act in good faith at all times. This fiduciary relationship is imposed by law upon the agent because the very nature of the agency relationship involves the principal entrusting his fortune, reputation, and legal rights and responsibilities to his agent whose actions, for better or worse, vitally affect the economic well-being and reputation of the principal." Leonard Lakin and Martin Schiff, The Law of Agency 2 (Kendall/Hunt 2d ed. 1996), at 97.

[I]t is an agent's duty to carry out the desires of its principal. This certainly makes sense, as the agent acts not to carry on its own business affairs, but those of the principal. Thus it is the agent's duty to act in accordance with his or her principal's instructions even if the agent believes they are unwise. As stated by two commentators, "[a]n agent has the duty to obey all of his principal's lawful instructions no matter how arbitrary or capricious any of those instructions seem to the agent or anyone else. . . . By contrast, if the principal's instructions are illegal, immoral, unethical, or opposed to public policy, as where the principal instructs his agent to bribe another to obtain business for his principal, the agent has no duty to obey." Id. at 97-98. Moreover, by acting on its principal's behalf, the agent assumes a duty that it "possesses a degree of skill commensurate with the job to be done and that he will use such skill with diligence." Id. at 124. In exercising this duty of reasonable care and skill, it is important to emphasize that the agent does not guarantee or ensure that he or she will achieve the result desired by the client unless the agent has expressly agreed to do so. Rather the agent has fulfilled his or her duty by acting with the care and skill employed by a reasonable person under the same circumstances. . . .

Another basic duty of the agent to the principal seems particularly relevant in the sports context. The agent must account to its principal for all of the principal's funds that come into the agent's possession as a part of the agency relationship. Id. at 100. Other basic duties that the agent owes to the principal include the duty to comply with the law, the duty to notify the principal of all matters that may affect the principal's interests, and the duty not to delegate their performance to another without the consent of the principal. Id.

Finally, the agent owes a duty of loyalty and good faith to its principal. This duty precludes an agent from acting on behalf of parties adverse to his or her principal. Courts have attempted to incorporate these core concepts into rulings addressing matters ranging from agent malpractice to conflict of interest. . . .

The agent-athlete relationship is governed primarily by contract law principles. In addition, the agent is viewed as having a fiduciary relationship with the athlete. A fiduciary is defined as "one who acts primarily for the benefit of another." Duties that flow from the fiduciary character of the relationship between athletes and agents include the duties of loyalty and good faith.

B. The Agent's Standard of Care

As noted above, agents agree to perform certain services and athletes agree to pay for those services. Athletes sometimes assert that they have been relieved of their payment obligation because an agent failed to provide competent services. In addition to arguing that agents have provided substandard service, athletes assert that agents breached other basic obligations owed to them or engaged in some form of illegal conduct. The *Zinn* case, which follows, examines the legal principles that courts use in assessing whether an agent performed his or her services sufficiently so as to require an athlete to pay for those services.

Zinn v. Parrish
644 F.2d 360 (7th Cir. 1981)

BARTELS, Judge.

[Editors' note: Leo Zinn, an experienced agent, negotiated Lamar Parrish's first NFL contract with the Cincinnati Bengals. Zinn received a commission of 10 percent of Parrish's $16,500 salary. Thereafter, on April 10, 1971, Zinn and Parrish signed a one-year renewable representation agreement, under which Zinn agreed to "use 'reasonable efforts' to procure pro-football employment for Parrish." Under the agreement, Zinn also agreed, at Parrish's request, to (1) negotiate job contracts, (2) furnish advice on business investments, (3) secure professional tax advice, (4) obtain endorsement contracts, and (5) attempt to secure for Parrish "gainful off-season employment."

Between 1971 and 1973, Zinn negotiated base salaries and bonuses for Parrish. In 1974, Zinn negotiated a three-year contract for Parrish that saw Parrish's yearly base salary increase from $35,000 to $250,000 (the salary increase was a result of competition between the NFL and the rival World Football League (WFL) for players' services). Zinn performed a number of other services at Parrish's request, including assisting Parrish in purchasing a residence and an apartment building to be used for rental income, assisting in managing the apartment building, forwarding to Parrish the stock purchase recommendations of other individuals, negotiating an endorsement contract, unsuccessfully attempting to obtain off-season employment for Parrish, and arranging for Parrish's taxes to be prepared each year by H&R Block.

Shortly after he signed the 1974 series of contracts with the Bengals, Parrish informed Zinn (orally, and later in writing) that he "no longer needed his services." He also stated he would not pay Zinn a 10 percent commission on those contracts. Zinn sued Parrish for breach of contract, alleging he was entitled to receive commissions totaling $304,500 plus interest.]

We consider next the district court's judgment that Zinn failed to perform the terms and conditions of his contract. . . . [T]he court concluded that Zinn "was unable to and did not provide the services which he was obligated to provide by the contract under which he sues."

Employment Procurement

Zinn's obligation under the 1971 Management Contract to procure employment for Parrish as a pro football player was limited to the use of "reasonable efforts."

Parrish had no objection to Zinn's performance under the professional management contract for the first three years up to 1973, during which time Zinn negotiated football contracts for Parrish. A drastic change, however, took place in 1974 when a four-season contract was negotiated with the Bengals for a total of $250,000 plus a substantial signing bonus. At that time, the new World Football League came into existence and its teams, as well as the teams of the Canadian Football League, were offering good terms to professional football players as an inducement to jump over to their leagues from the NFL. In order to persuade Parrish to remain with the team, the Bengals club itself first initiated the renegotiation of Parrish's contract with an offer of substantially increased compensation. This was not surprising.

Parrish claims, however, that Zinn should have obtained offers from the World Football League that would have placed him in a stronger negotiating position with the Bengals. . . . Given what Zinn accurately perceived as the unreliability of any offers he might have obtained from the WFL, his representation of Parrish during this period was more than reasonable. . . . We conclude that up to that point, it is impossible to fault Zinn in the performance of his contract, nor can we find any basis for Parrish to complain of Zinn's efforts in 1974 with respect to procuring employment for him as a pro-football player.

Other Obligations

Zinn was further obligated to act in Parrish's professional interest by providing [other services]. Each of these obligations was subject to an implied promise to make "good faith" efforts to obtain what he sought. . . . Under Illinois law, such efforts constitute full performance of the obligations. . . . Until Parrish terminated the contract, the evidence was clear that Zinn made consistent, good faith efforts to obtain off-season employment and endorsement contracts. Indeed the district court found that Zinn at all times acted in good faith, with a willingness "to provide assistance within his ability." The district court confused success with good faith efforts in concluding that Zinn's failure to obtain in many cases jobs or contracts for Parrish was a failure to perform. Moreover, Zinn did give business advice to Parrish on his real estate purchases, and he did secure tax advice for him.

[Editors' note: The court ruled that Zinn had the right to recover a 10 percent commission on all amounts earned by Parrish under the 1974, 1975, 1976, and 1977 Bengals contracts.]

QUESTIONS

1. The athlete–agency relationship is defined as a "fiduciary relationship." What are the special characteristics of a fiduciary, and how do they differ from those present in other types of contractual relationships, such as an athlete–team relationship?

2. In *Zinn*, the court adopted two standards in rejecting Parrish's defense. What was the first standard adopted by the court and its source? The court also adopted a standard of good faith as a basis for determining whether an agent has competently performed his or her duties.

C. Agent Financial Improprieties

A serious issue confronting the athlete-agent industry is agent conduct that has a negative impact on an athlete's financial well-being. Inappropriate conduct ranges from agents and financial advisors misappropriating for their own use funds that athletes have entrusted with them, to their persuading athletes to enter into poor investment schemes. One of the more notorious cases of financial mismanagement and illegal conduct involved William "Tank" Black, who rose to fame as a successful agent of clients including Sterling Sharpe, Vince Carter, Fred Taylor, and Ike Hilliard. An investigation resulted in allegations that Black not only made under-the-table payments to players; he also fraudulently involved athletes in a pyramid scheme and laundered money. Black and his company's general counsel eventually pled guilty to federal charges that they laundered the money of drug traffickers. In June 2001, Black received a federal sentence of six years and ten months, followed by three years of supervised probation. In a separate lawsuit, a Florida jury convicted Black of conspiring to commit mail and wire fraud.

In asserting claims against agents and financial advisors for alleged mismanagement of their financial affairs, athletes have resorted to several legal theories. Prominent theories on which athletes seek to recover include breach of contract, fraud, breach of fiduciary duty, and negligence. Athletes include tort-based claims such as fraud in order to increase the possibility of recovering punitive damages, which cannot be recovered in a breach of contract claim.

An illustrative case is *Williams v. CWI, Inc.*, 777 F. Supp. 1006 (D.D.C. 1991). Reginald Williams, a young basketball player, signed a contract worth $1 million per year to play for the NBA's Los Angeles Clippers. Looking for investment opportunities, Williams and his wife met with a financial advisor who agreed to provide financial and tax advice for the couple. Claiming a high investment return and tax benefits, the advisor persuaded the couple to invest in a venture involving the purchase of a device known as an atmospheric reverse refrigeration heating unit. The Williamses agreed to purchase $1 million worth of the devices at $10,000 each. They forwarded $50,000 to the advisor, who appropriated the money for his own use. The Williamses sued the advisor alleging breach of contract and fraud. The court entered a judgment for the Williamses on both their breach of contract and fraud theories in the amount of $137,300, which included $50,000 in punitive damages.

The court made the following observations concerning the predicament of many young athletes such as Williams:

Like many young professional athletes, Mr. Williams was earning a considerable salary but had no experience in making investments or managing his money. He needed reliable expert advice and did not find any readily available. Because Mr. Williams' predicament appears to be a recurring problem for basketball players and other athletes who suddenly receive large disposable incomes, it seems that it would be appropriate for either the NBA, or the players' team, or the players' organization to develop a three-pronged program to assist these young people. First, they could offer at least some rudimentary education in business and finance. Second, they could assemble a package of low-risk blue chip investments for young players that will provide for their futures, as well as a system for referring them to wise and ethical professionals who can advise them on managing money. Third, they might offer a financial incentive for players to place a portion of their funds in a deferred investment program.

Id. at 1007.

A Securities and Exchange Commission (SEC) lawyer involved in the Tank Black matter offered similar observations: "Professional athletes are prime candidates for financial fraud. Many are unsophisticated in financial matters and suddenly find themselves with a six- or seven-figure salary. They're young, they're trusting, and they've been taken care of most of their lives." L. Jon Wertheim, *Web of Deceit*, Sports Illustrated, May 29, 2000, at 80.

It is important to note that players will not always prevail in lawsuits against their agents. Agents have argued successfully that they properly performed the services rendered. Moreover, an agent will argue that an athlete's financial plight is the result of the athlete's poor handling of his financial resources rather than the agent's mishandling. In one case, an agent successfully argued that the athlete's assets had been depleted because the athlete "wasted his assets by making exorbitant purchases, transferring large sums of money to his family members and friends, and refusing to save for the future or consider the consequences if he were injured or unable to continue playing football. . . . " *Clark v. Weisberg*, 1999 WL 543191, at *2 (N.D. Ill).

A similar occurrence came to a head on July 16, 2009, when Nevada deputies arrested former National Basketball Association (NBA) star Antoine Walker after Walker wrote a series of ten bad checks totaling $1 million in Las Vegas. After the arrest, it was revealed that Walker owed over $4 million to various creditors but was broke despite earning over $110 million as an NBA player. The squandering of Walker's fortune was based on several factors. Walker traveled with a massive entourage. Walker's mother estimates that during his playing days, Walker was supporting 70 different friends and family members in one way or another. Walker also had a mansion built for his mother, which included an indoor pool, ten bathrooms, and a full-size basketball court. Walker was also a top-line watch collector and had a fleet of cars, including two Bentleys, two Mercedes, a Range Rover, a Cadillac Escalade, and a bright red Hummer. Those close to Walker also described him as a notoriously large gambler. Shira Springer, *For Walker, Financial Fouls Mount*, Boston Globe, Oct. 25, 2009.

Unfortunately, Walker's situation is not unique. Data show that 60 percent of NBA players are broke within five years of being retired; and in the NFL, 78 percent of retired players reportedly are bankrupt or are under serious financial stress within two years after their playing careers end. Some of the most frequent contributors to players' financial problems are their dealings with financial advisers, extravagant living, and family issues such as divorce and child support. Because most professional athletes have large bank accounts but minimum knowledge in managing financial matters, they are often targets for con artists and shady financial advisers. An NFLPA report stated that from 1999 to 2002, at least 78 players lost more than $42 million combined to their financial advisers.

Unofficial estimates by sports agents and athletes put the divorce rate for professional athletes between 60 and 80 percent. What often makes divorces particularly damaging for professional athletes is that the majority of them occur in retirement, when a player's peak earning period is over and making a comparable living is virtually impossible. Further exacerbating the problem is that, according to celebrity divorce lawyer Raoul Felder, "[t]he percentage of prenups amongst athletes is appreciably lower compared with nonathletes at the same economic level." Another frequent issue is that of child support. For example, former NFL running back Travis Henry was ordered to pay $170,000 each year to support his nine kids. Pablo S. Torre, *How (and Why) Athletes Go Broke*, Sports Illustrated, March 23, 2009, *http://www.si.com/vault/2009/03/23/105789480/how-and-why-athletes-go-broke*.

QUESTIONS

1. The *Williams* court identified several factors that render athletes particularly vulnerable to unscrupulous agents and financial managers. Do you agree with the court? The court also suggested the development of a three-pronged program to assist young athletes with money management. What were the three parts of the proposed system, and what practical approaches would you recommend be included in such a program? Who do you think should be responsible for the creation of such a system?

2. As an agent, what is your duty if one of your clients asks you to procure a deal that you are sure is financially irresponsible? What is your duty if one of your clients asks you to procure a deal that you feel is unethical?

· · · · · · · · ·

In 2002, the NFLPA became the first professional sports union to attempt to curb the abuse of financial advisors with its promulgation of the NFLPA Regulations and Code of Conduct Governing Registered Player Financial Advisors. The regulations represent the NFLPA's response to incidents involving mismanagement of players' financial affairs. Those financial advisors who agree to participate, by applying to become registered in the voluntary program, are given "unique information on NFL players, their benefits, and compensation structure." *Introduction*, NFLPA Regulations and Code of Conduct Governing Registered Player Financial Advisors 3 (as amended March 2012. For a discussion of the NFLPA's Financial Advisor Regulations, see Shropshire, Davis, and Duru, *supra* note 1, at 140–143.

In *Atwater v. National Football League Players Assn.*, 626 F.3d 1170 (11th Cir. 2010), former NFL players sued the NFLPA alleging that it had negligently performed background checks on Kirk Wright, a financial advisor, who defrauded the athletes and other investors out of more than $100 million. Although the NFLPA prevailed in the lawsuit, it suspended its financial advisor program, only to reinstate it in 2012 after making changes (e.g., requiring applicants to have eight rather than the previously required five years of licensed experience).

A major problem confronting the agent-athlete industry is agent and financial advisor misappropriation of athletes' money. Agents and financial advisors will often place athletes' monies in risky investments or simply use it to cover agents' and advisors' personal and business expenses. Several legal theories, including breach of contract, negligence, and fraud have been employed by athletes in their efforts to recover misappropriated money.

Problem 13-1

William Wills, a professional football player, hired Terry Davis as his sports agent. Davis, an attorney, is registered as a player representative with the NFLPA. Wills and Davis entered into the NFLPA's standard representation agreement between a player and contract advisor. From 2007 to 2011, with Wills's authorization, Davis received most of Wills's income. He gave Wills an allowance for living expenses and occasionally gave Wills advances against his salary when Wills asked for them. In addition to his salary, Wills was paid $20,000 a year to be invested in an annuity on his behalf. Davis was supposed to invest these amounts each year in an annuity for Wills but did not do so. Between 2007 and 2011, Davis used much of Wills's income to cover Davis's business and personal expenses. In 2010, Wills began to suspect that Davis was misappropriating his income and requested an accounting, which Davis said was forthcoming but never provided. Wills became certain that something was wrong when in early 2011, he was informed by the Internal Revenue Service (IRS) that he had not paid his tax deficiencies for the years 2007 to 2010. Davis had told Wills that he was paying his taxes at the time he filed Wills's tax returns. The tax returns, which were signed by Wills, were filed by Davis, who had not paid the tax deficiencies. Wills has a tax liability of over $240,000 as a result of the actions taken by Davis. What causes of action may Wills assert in a lawsuit against Davis? See *Willoughby v. Commissioner of Internal Revenue*, 1994 WL 444427 (Tax Ct. 1994).

D. Agent Conflicts of Interest with Athletes

KEY TERMS
- Conflict of interest
- Nondisclosure

One of an agent's fundamental obligations is not to compromise the interests of his or her principal. The requirement that an agent avoid conflicts of interest is derived from the duties of undivided loyalty and good faith that agents owe to their principals. In the sports context, numerous factual scenarios present real or potential conflicts of interest. Historically, the classic conflict of interest scenario has involved "nondisclosure by an agent of a financial interest that conflicts with that of the athlete client." Shropshire, Davis, and Duru, *supra* note 1, at 88. See also Melissa Neiman, *Fair Game: Ethical Considerations in Negotiation by Sports Agents*, 9 Tex. Rev. Ent. & Sports L. 123 (2007); Jamie E. Brown, *The Battle the Fans Never See: Conflicts of Interest for Sports Lawyers*, 7 Geo. J. Legal Ethics 813, 816 (1994).

As the following discussion reveals, however, nondisclosure represents only one of the factual scenarios where conflicts arise in the sports representation business. Nevertheless, we begin our discussion with a case that presents the paradigmatic conflict of interest.

The Detroit Lions, Inc. v. Argovitz
580 F. Supp. 542 (D. Mich. 1984)

DeMascio, District Judge.

[Editors' note: On July 1, 1983, Billy Sims, a former college football Heisman Trophy winner, signed a contract with the Houston Gamblers of the fledgling United States Football League (USFL). Later that year, Sims and the team for which he had been under contract, the NFL's Detroit Lions, requested that a court invalidate the contract between Sims and the Gamblers because Sims's agent breached fiduciary duties when he negotiated Sims's contract with the Gamblers. Sims and the Lions also alleged the Sims-Gamblers contract was otherwise tainted by fraud and misrepresentation.

In February or March 1983, Sims's agent, Jerry Argovitz, told Sims that he had applied for a Houston franchise in the newly formed USFL, but Argovitz failed to disclose to Sims the extent of the agent's interest in the Gamblers Argovitz was obligated for 29 percent of a 1.5 million letter of credit and, if his application was approved, would receive from the Gamblers an annual salary of $275,000 and 5 percent of the yearly cash flow. While his application for the franchise was pending, Argovitz continued his negotiations with the Lions on behalf of Sims.

Following the approval of his application, Argovitz sought an offer for Sims from the Gamblers. Later, one of Argovitz's partners in the Gamblers, Bernard Lerner, agreed to negotiate a contract with Sims. At a point in negotiations where the Lions were very close to reaching an agreement on the value of Sims's services, at Lerner's behest, Sims and his wife went to Houston to negotiate with the Gamblers, with Simms believing that the Lions organization was not negotiating in good faith based on information supplied by Argovitz. On June 30, 1983, the Gamblers offered Sims a "$3.5 million five-year contract, which included three years of skill and injury guarantees. The offer included a $500,000 loan at an interest rate of 1 percent over prime. It was from this loan that Argovitz planned to receive the $100,000 balance of his fee for acting as an agent in negotiating a contract with his own team. The offer received the guarantee that Sims wanted from the Lions, guarantees that Argovitz dropped without too much quarrel." Argovitz failed to inform Sims that he thought the Lions would match the Gamblers' financial package or ask Sims whether he (Argovitz) should telephone the Lions. During the negotiations at the Gamblers' office, Argovitz declined to accept a telephone call from the Lions' representative, even though Argovitz was at his office. Sims agreed to become a Gambler on the terms offered.]

Conclusions of Law . . .

3. An agent's duty of loyalty requires that he not have a personal stake that conflicts with the principal's interest in a transaction in which he represents his principal. . . .

4. A fiduciary violates the prohibition against self-dealing not only by dealing with himself on his principal's behalf, but also by dealing on his principal's behalf with a third party in which he has an interest, such as a partnership in which he is a member. . . .

5. Where an agent has an interest adverse to that of his principal in a transaction in which he purports to act on behalf of his principal, the transaction is voidable by the principal unless the agent disclosed all material facts within the agent's knowledge that might affect the principal's judgment.

6. The mere fact that the contract is fair to the principal does not deny the principal the right to rescind the contract when it was negotiated by an agent in violation of the prohibition against self-dealing. . . .

7. Once it has been shown that an agent had an interest in a transaction involving his principal antagonistic to the principal's interest, fraud on the part of the agent is presumed. The burden of proof then rests upon the agent to show that: his principal had full knowledge, not only of the fact that the agent was interested, but also of every material fact known to the agent that might affect the principal and that, having such knowledge, the principal freely consented to the transaction.

8. It is not sufficient for the agent merely to inform the principal that he has an interest that conflicts with the principal's interest. Rather, he must inform the principal "of all facts that come to his knowledge that are or may be material or which might affect his principal's rights or interests or influence the action he takes." *Anderson v. Griffith*, 501 S.W.2d 695, 700 (Tex. Civ. App. 1973).

9. Argovitz clearly had a personal interest in signing Sims with the Gamblers that was adverse to Sims' interest—he had an ownership interest in the Gamblers and thus would profit if the Gamblers were profitable, and would incur substantial personal liabilities should the Gamblers not be financially successful. Since this showing has been made, fraud on Argovitz's part is presumed, and the Gamblers' contract must be rescinded unless Argovitz has shown by a preponderance of the evidence that he informed Sims of every material fact that might have influenced Sims' decision whether or not to sign the Gamblers' contract.

10. We conclude that Argovitz has failed to show by a preponderance of the evidence either: (1) that he informed Sims of the following facts, or (2) that these facts would not have influenced Sims' decision whether to sign the Gamblers' contract.

    a. The relative values of the Gamblers' contract and the Lions' offer that Argovitz knew could be obtained.

b. That there was significant financial differences between the USFL and the NFL not only in terms of the relative financial stability of the Leagues, but also in terms of the fringe benefits available to Sims.

c. Argovitz's 29 percent ownership in the Gamblers; Argovitz's $275,000 annual salary with the Gamblers; Argovitz's five percent interest in the cash flow of the Gamblers.

d. That both Argovitz and Burrough failed to even attempt to obtain for Sims valuable contract clauses which they had given to [another player Jim] Kelly on behalf of the Gamblers.

e. That Sims had great leverage, and Argovitz was not encouraging a bidding war that could have advantageous results for Sims. . . .

11. The careless fashion in which Argovitz went about ascertaining the highest price for Sims' service convinces us of the wisdom of the maxim: no man can faithfully serve two masters whose interests are in conflict.

Judgment will be entered for the plaintiffs rescinding the Gamblers' contract with Sims.

QUESTIONS

Describe how Argovitz violated his duties of undivided loyalty, good faith, and fair dealing. Will an athlete's knowledge of a conflict or a potential conflict necessarily absolve an agent of liability for a conflict of interest? In *Argovitz,* the court concluded that knowledge by Sims of Argovitz's ownership of the Gamblers franchise or approval of the application failed to absolve the agent of responsibility. Why?

Problem 13-2

Agent represents basketball players Williams and Smith, who play for different teams in the same NBA conference. Williams, who is considered by many to be the greatest basketball player of all time, is also the highest-paid athlete (salary and endorsements) in the world. One of Williams's teammates complains about the aggressive play of Smith, who is a solid player but not a superstar. Williams takes these complaints to Agent, who is currently in the midst of negotiating Smith's contract with his current team, Team A. Team B has also expressed an interest in Smith. Agent rejects Team A's offer of $8.1 million for three years and secures for Smith a $9.6 million deal with Team B, which plays in another NBA conference. Under his contract with Team B, Smith will receive only $6.4 million in his first three years. Agent says that the deal with Team B is better because it will pay Smith $3.2 million ($1.5 million of which is guaranteed) in his fourth year and has less deferred money. Team A's president says that Team A was willing to compromise on the issue of deferred money. What, if any, conflicts or potential conflicts are present here?

COMPETITION FOR CLIENTS: CONFLICTS BETWEEN AGENTS

A. Introduction

The underlying source of conflicts between agents is the fierce competition for clients. Factors that contribute to the intense competition that breeds conflict among agents include the significant fees that are potentially available if an agent signs an athlete, the substantial increase in the number of agents between the 1960s and the present, the relatively small pool of potential athlete clients, industry consolidation, and the ease with which provisions in standard agent representation agreements allow athletes to terminate their contracts with agents. As of January 2006, fewer than 100 of the 350 registered agents in the NBA had athlete clients. Fewer than 50 percent of the estimated 800 to 1,000 certified NFL agents had clients. An NFLPA commissioned study reported that in 2003, "a small percentage of agents represent the majority of players; just over 100 agents — barely more than 10 percent of all agents — represent three of every four players on an active roster. And nearly 90 percent of agent fees are at the 3 percent maximum." National Football League Players Association, *Agents: Research Documents.*

B. Consolidation

The wave of consolidations that proliferated during the 1990s and resulted in what were then the four major sports representation firms — IMG, SFX, Octagon, and Assante — intensified the competition for clients. Consolidation increased the competition for clients among smaller firms and individual agents who often lack the resources to compete effectively against larger firms. In addition, agents within larger sports representation firms often employ aggressive tactics in recruiting athletes; some of these tactics are products of resources that give larger athlete representation firms a competitive edge. For a discussion of industry consolidation and the demise of large representation firms such as SFX and Assante and the emergence of new firms such as Creative Artists Agency (CAA), the Wasserman Group (WMG), Stealth Sports, and Relativity Sports, see Shropshire, Davis, and Duru, *supra* note 1 at 36–50.

The consolidations of the 1990s eventually showed fault lines. Many agents who helped to create larger firms during the 1990s later departed to create smaller representation firms or become associated with more recent industry giants such as CAA. Unfortunately, departures are often accompanied by allegations of client stealing. An example is the dispute between David Dunn and Leigh Steinberg. Dunn, a partner in what was then Steinberg, Moorad, & Dunn (a division of Assante), departed to start his own firm. His new firm represented several clients of his previous firm. This led to a lawsuit in which the Steinberg firm alleged that Dunn's new firm conspired to lure clients away from it and that Dunn violated a noncompete covenant. A Los Angeles jury awarded Steinberg $44.66 million in damages after it decided that Dunn had breached his contract, engaged in unfair competition, and had acted with fraud and malice. In 2005, a California appellate court vacated the $44.66 million jury award. *Steinberg Moorad & Dunn Inc. v. Dunn*, 136 Fed. Appx. 6 (9th Cir. 2005). A more recent case demonstrating conflict between agents is *Miller v. Walters*, 2014 WL 5333473 (Supreme Ct. N.Y., Oct. 9, 2014), where the focus was on the ever present problem of one agent being accused of poaching a client from the other.

C. Termination

Competition in the athlete-agent industry is also intensified by the ease at which agent representation agreements can be terminated. A representative example of a termination provision in a standard player-agent contract follows.

NFLPA STANDARD REPRESENTATION AGREEMENT

(as amended through March 2012)

12. Term

The term of this Agreement shall begin on the date hereof and shall remain in effect until such time that it is terminated by either party in which case termination of this Agreement shall be effective five (5) days after written notice of termination is given to the other party. Notice shall be effective for purposes of this paragraph if sent by confirmed facsimile or overnight delivery to the appropriate address contained in this Agreement. . . .

If the Contract Advisor's Certification is suspended or revoked by the NFLPA or the Contract Advisor is otherwise prohibited by the NFLPA from performing the services he/she has agreed to perform herein, this Agreement shall automatically terminate, effective as of the date of such suspension or termination.

D. Disparagement

In the fierce competition for clients, agents try to convince athletes to sign with them both by expressing the virtues of their organization and by disparaging the competition. All sorts of negative information may be communicated regarding a competing agent. Experienced agents believe that the corruption in the industry has reached an all-time high. This has resulted in agents filing "an unprecedented number of lawsuits, charging one another with stealing clients, fraud, extortion, and slander." Liz Mullen, *Sleaze Factor off the Charts, Agents Allege*, Sports Bus. J., June 24–30, 2002, at 1, 30. A recent trend that may have contributed to the increase in suits alleging tampering was described as follows: "In the past, while agents competed against each other as aggressively as anyone could imagine, once the client came to an agreement with an agent, everybody in essence backed off. . . . That was the end of the game. What is going on now is once an agent signs a client, the second game begins." *Id.*

Bauer v. The Interpublic Group of Companies, Inc., 255 F. Supp. 2d 1086 (N.D. Cal. 2003) represents a fairly realistic depiction of the recruiting techniques employed by agents. Asserting an intentional interference with contract claim, an agent, Frank Bauer, contended that rival agents acted improperly in persuading an NFL rookie quarterback, David Carr, to terminate his representation agreement with him and to sign with them. Bauer alleged that Carr's decision to terminate their contractual relationship was a consequence of negative information concerning Bauer that was disseminated by the defendants. The court rejected Bauer's claim for lack of evidence to support the allegations. In the aftermath of *Bauer*, the NFLPA changed the termination provisions of its Standard Representation Agreement. Generally, either the agent or athlete may terminate the relationship effective five days after written notice is given to the other party. However, an agreement between an agent and a rookie (a player who has never signed an NFL player contract) cannot be terminated by the rookie until 30 days after the player signed the representation agreement. A recent case involving issues of disparagement is *Champion Pro Consulting Group, Inc. v. Impact Sports Football, LLC*, 2013 WL 5461829, ★17–18 (M.D. N.C., Sept. 30, 2013).

E. What Is Permissible Competition?

KEY TERM   • Competitor's privilege

Agents are permitted considerable leeway in attempting to recruit the business of athletes from rival agents. However, their competitive activities are not unlimited. This was illustrated in *Speakers of Sport, Inc. v. ProServe, Inc.*, 178 F.3d 862 (7th Cir. 1999). Speakers of Sport, a sports representation agency, filed a lawsuit asserting that another athlete-agent firm, ProServ, had wrongfully interfered in Speaker's contractual relationship with baseball player Ivan Rodriguez. In 1991, Rodriguez had signed the first of several one-year contracts making Speakers his agent. ProServ promised Rodriguez that it would get him between $2 million and $4 million in endorsements if he signed with it. Thereafter, Rodriguez terminated his at-will contract with Speakers and signed a representation agreement with ProServ. ProServ's failure to obtain significant endorsements for Rodriguez subsequently led to his decision to switch to another firm.

After ruling that Rodriguez had not breached its contract with Speakers because their relationship was terminable at will, the court considered whether ProServ had exceeded the bounds of permissible competition. The court articulated the principle that there is nothing wrong with one sports agent trying to take a client from another, so long as it can be done without precipitating a breach of contract. According to the court, competition "which though painful, fierce, frequently ruthless, sometimes Darwinian in its pitilessness, is the cornerstone of our highly successful economic system." *Id.* at 865. Calling this the "competitor's privilege," the court concluded that although competition that induces a breach of contract is improper, the competitor's privilege permits conduct that induces the lawful termination of a contractual relationship.

The court stated that the competitor's privilege does not permit an agent to engage in unlawful means such as fraud in attempting to get business from a competitor. The court concluded that under Illinois law, however, ProServ had not committed fraud in stating that it could get a certain amount of endorsement income for Rodriguez:

> The promise of endorsements was puffing not in the most common sense of a cascade of extravagant adjectives but in the equally valid sense of a sales pitch that is intended, and that a reasonable person in the position of the "promisee" would understand, to be aspirational rather than enforceable — an expression of hope rather than a commitment. It is not as if ProServ proposed to employ Rodriguez and pay him $2 million a year. That would be the kind of promise that could found an enforceable obligation. ProServ proposed merely to get him endorsements of at least that amount. They would of course be paid by the companies whose products Rodriguez endorsed, rather than by ProServ.

Id. at 866. See also *Wright v. Bonds*, 117 F.3d 1427 (9th Cir. 1999) (finding agent had not improperly interfered with an athlete's former agent).

QUESTIONS

The *Speakers* court adopted the concept of the competitor's privilege, which validates a broad range of activities in which an agent can engage in attempting to lure clients away from a competitor. What limitation did the court impose on an agent's permissible conduct in attempting to recruit clients in an established relationship with an agent?

One critic of the *Speakers* case argues that although it and other cases "appear legally accurate, they provide a broad spectrum of competition that borders on interference thereby tolerating unfair and corrupt dealing." Bryan Couch, Comment, *How Agent Competition and Corruption Affects Sports and the Athlete-Agent Relationship and What Can Be Done to Control It*, 10 Seton Hall J. Sport L. 111, 119 (2000). Is the range of permissible competitive behavior validated in *Speakers* too broad? For discussions of competition and its implications for the athlete-agent industry, see Timothy Davis, *Regulating the Athlete-Agent Industry: Intended and Unintended Consequences*, 42 Willamette L. Rev. 781 (2006); Lloyd Z. Remick and Christopher J. Cabott, *Keeping out the Little Guy: An Older Contract Advisor's Concern, A Younger Contract Advisor's Lament*, 12 Vill. Sports & Ent. L.J. 1 (2005); and Couch, *supra*.

F. The Issue of Race

Although the majority of NFL and NBA players are African American, most are not represented by African-American agents. Some assert that this reality suggests the existence of underlying racial tensions within the athlete-agent industry. Such tensions arose in a lawsuit that C. Lamont Smith, an African-American NFL sports agent, filed against another agent, Tom Condon. Smith's suit alleged that Condon, who is white, "may have told other current or perspective NFL players . . . that they should not become clients of plaintiff Smith because Smith had alienated general managers of NFL clubs by 'playing the race card.'" Liz Mullen, *Lawsuit Targets IMG Football Chief Condon*, Sports Bus. J., Sept. 8-14, 2003. According to Smith, Condon made his statements when they competed to sign clients during the 2001–2003 NFL drafts with the alleged intent of blackballing him. Smith also stated, "It leads a player to think you are not accepted in NFL circles, which could not be further from the truth." *Id.*

Much like other positions in the sports business world, African Americans have faced numerous obstacles in the athlete-agent industry. For example, in the 2007 NFL draft, 14 of the first 15 players selected were African American, and only one of those players chose an African-American agent to represent him. Different theories are offered regarding the reasons that underlie impediments to the success of African-American agents. Bill Strickland, an African-American sports agent, suggests that the problem is the scarcity of black owners. Strickland believes that players often pick white agents because they seem better equipped to deal with white owners. Lamont Smith, an African-American agent, believes the problem is a lack of black authority figures in these athletes' lives. Smith points to college football, where the vast majority of coaches are white, as an example. Andre Farr, the chairmen and CEO of the Black Sports Agents Association (BSAA), lists self-discrimination based on past prejudices as the biggest obstacle facing African-American agents trying to sign African-American clients. "For years, not only in sports, but every area of professional management and business, [blacks] would not do business with African Americans," Farr says. "They felt like they might be locked out of the process, or that they wouldn't be able to negotiate a fair and equitable deal. That attitude hasn't vanished. Yet, it's not true. It could not be further from the truth."

QUESTION

Assuming that an agent made the comments asserted in Smith's complaint, would they exceed the bounds of what is considered permissible competition?

For discussions of race and the athlete-agent industry, see Shropshire, Davis, and Duru, *supra* note 1, at 55–58; and James G. Sammataro, *Business and Brotherhood, Can They Coincide? A Search into Why Black Athletes Do Not Hire Black Agents*, 42 Howard L.J. 535 (1999).

AN INTERNATIONAL PERSPECTIVE

Similar to the conceptualization of agents in the United States, from an international perspective, the term *agent* refers to a person who acts as "an intermediary between a sports man or woman and other parties, for example between a football player (employee or potential employee) and a club (employer or potential employer)."

Robert Parrish, *Regulating Players' Agents: A Global Perspective*, in Players' Agents Worldwide: Legal Aspects (Robert C.R. Siekmann et al., eds., 2007).

> Not surprisingly, the problems that have beset the athlete agent industry in the United States arise internationally. Noting the high number of licensed agents in countries such as Spain, Italy and England, one commentator articulates that regulation of agents is necessary "'to introduce professionalism and morality to the occupation of players' agent in order to protect players whose careers are short.' Rephrased, the absence of player agent regulation will result in a lack of professionalism, immorality and a lack of protection for players."

Id. at 4. This author goes on to describe *bungs, tapping-up,* and dual representation as examples of improper agent conduct that demonstrate the need for agent regulation.

> Bungs refer to illegal payments paid by and to agents (and others) in order to facilitate the transfer of a player. . . .
>
> Another [Fédération Internationale de Football (FIFA)] and association rule . . . was the common practice of "tapping-up," which refers to a process, often facilitated by agents, whereby players are offered for sale to other clubs without the knowledge and consent of the club with whom the player is registered. . . . FIFA Players' Agents Regulations state that a licensed players' agent must never "approach a player who is under contract with a club with the aim of persuading him to terminate his contract prematurely or to flout the rights and duties stipulated in the contract. . . . "
>
> The third issue reaching prominence in the UK in the summer of 2006, . . . was the issue of dual representation. This refers to an agent who represents both a club and a player in negotiations. This is prohibited by . . . FIFA Players' Agents Regulations which state that a licensed players' agent is required "to represent only one party when negotiating a transfer."

Id. at 6. For a discussion of the legal issues involved in the representation industry, see Kenneth L. Shropshire, Davis, and Duru, *supra* note 1, at 19–21.

As to the representation of a U.S. athlete wishing to play abroad, the agent faces a series of challenges. In all likelihood, the client is not at a skill level to play in the major league of his sport in the United States. The options are narrow concerning where he can play abroad. The number of foreign (including U.S.) players per team may well be limited by league rules. Although agents are not bound by union regulations, such as those in the United States, they may find other strictures in effect that vary among foreign leagues. Thus, obtaining the basic knowledge of business practices in other countries can be much more difficult than in the United States. Even whether there is something approaching a standard-form player contract may not be clear. The drafting and negotiation of contract provisions to protect the athlete if things go awry in a foreign country are no simple matter. For example, does an agent really want to have to seek enforcement of contractual obligations in the courts of a foreign country? If not, what are the alternatives? Added to this mix is the need to understand the complexities of the U.S. tax laws and foreign immigration laws. As to immigration, the foreign club may be of assistance. As to tax, the agent advising the athlete is probably on his or her own. See Carole C. Berry, *Taxation of U.S. Athletes Playing in Foreign Countries*, 13 Marq. Sports L. Rev. 1 (2002).

EXTERNAL REGULATION AND LEGISLATION

The problems within the agent industry that we have thus far examined in this chapter have hastened the call for better solutions. Incidents occurring in 2009 and 2010 underscored the need to regulate the industry but also revealed that athlete litigation against agents will not completely solve problems within the industry.

On June 10, 2010, a National Collegiate Athletic Association (NCAA) investigation and subsequent report revealed that former University of Southern California (USC) running back, Reggie Bush, had received impermissible benefits from two men attempting to form a sports agency in conjunction with Bush and his family. According to the NCAA, the improper benefits included cash, merchandise, an automobile, housing, hotel lodging, and airline transportation. That same NCAA investigative report revealed that former USC guard O. J. Mayo had also received impermissible benefits from a representative of a sports agency while playing at the school. The violations caused both Bush and Mayo to be permanently disassociated with USC and resulted in Bush voluntarily relinquishing his Heisman Trophy. (See *https://www.washingtonpost.com/blogs/early-lead/post/reggie-bush-finally-returns-heisman-trophy/2012/08/16/3a8a0aee-e7b3-11e1-a3d2-2a05679928ef_blog.html*.) Also in 2010, it was found that during the recruitment of eventual Heisman Trophy-winning Auburn quarterback Cam Newton, a man said to be representing Newton attempted to secure a six-figure sum in exchange for Newton signing a National Letter of Intent (NLI) to attend Mississippi State University. The investigation resulted in findings of improper dealings on the part of Kenny Rodgers and Cecil Newton, Cam Newton's father. See Erick Smith, *NCAA Rules Auburn's Newton Eligible for Now After Rules Violation*, Dec. 1, 2010, *http://content.usatoday.com/communities/campusrivalry/post/2010/12/auburn-cam-newton-ncaa-eligible/1*.

On October 11, 2010, the NCAA ruled two University of North Carolina (UNC) football players permanently ineligible for taking improper benefits from agents. The two players, Greg Little and Robert Quinn, were found to have accepted benefits totaling $4,952 and $5,642, respectively. The gifts provided by the agents included travel accommodations to various locations, diamond earrings, and black diamond watches. See *Agent Scandal Costs UNC Three Players*, Associated Press, Oct. 11, 2010, *http://sports.espn.go.com/ncf/news/story?id=5673405*. A third UNC football player, Marvin Austin, was dismissed from the team after it was revealed that he had accepted over $10,000 in improper benefits. The fallout from the UNC scandal lead to longtime NFL agent Gary Wichard receiving a nine-month suspension from the NFLPA for having impermissible contact with Austin. See *Gary Wichard Suspended 9 Months*, ESPN, Dec. 3, 2010, *http://sports.espn.go.com/nfl/news/story?id=5880708*.

The NCAA possesses no authority to regulate sports agents. The NCAA attempts, however, to prevent what it considers inappropriate agent conduct through a set of rules intended to regulate the interaction between student-athletes and agents. For example, NCAA rules prohibit student-athletes from receiving benefits from agents. Therefore, a student-athlete who receives money or other benefits from an agent risks losing his or her amateur status and being deemed by the NCAA to be ineligible to participate in intercollegiate competition. See 2011–12 NCAA Division I Manual, Bylaw 12.3, *infra*.

The materials in this section explore the various efforts that have been and are being undertaken to sanction inappropriate conduct by sports agents.

A. Federal Legislation

1. SPARTA

In September 2004, President George W. Bush signed into law the Sports Agent Responsibility Trust Act (SPARTA), the first federal legislation that specifically regulates sports agents. P.L. (Public Law) 108-304. SPARTA is modeled after key provisions of the Uniform Athlete Agents Act (UAAA), which more than 40 states have adopted. SPARTA does not preempt but rather supplements state requirements imposed by the UAAA. Indeed, SPARTA states that it is the "sense of Congress that States should enact the Uniform Athletes Agents Act . . . to protect student athletes and the integrity of amateur sports from unscrupulous sports agents. . . . " *Id.*

Like the UAAA, SPARTA prohibits agents from using improper inducements (e.g., cash payments and gifts) and misleading information to recruit student-athletes, predating or postdating agency contracts, and not providing certain disclosures. *Id.* at 2. The disclosure document must conspicuously notify student-athletes, as well as parents or guardians of athletes under the age of 18, of the potential loss of eligibility to compete as an amateur if he or she signs an agency agreement. Within 72 hours of signing an agency contract, or before the next athletic event in which the athlete is eligible to participate, both the student-athlete and agent must inform the athletic director of the educational institution at which the athlete is enrolled of the agency agreement. *Id.* at 2, 3. Violations of SPARTA can result in fines and civil actions seeking damages.

2. General Federal Laws

Prior to the enactment of SPARTA, and despite calls for it, no federal legislation existed that specifically regulated sports agents. Nevertheless, federal criminal laws have been used to address improper conduct by agents. For example, prosecutors employed the Racketeer Influenced and Corrupt Organizations Act (RICO) and mail fraud statutes in *United States v. Bloom*, 997 F.2d 1219 (7th Cir. 1993); 913 F.2d 388 (7th Cir. 1990). Norby Walters, a former nightclub owner, and Lloyd Bloom, who served as his "runner," enticed 58 student-athletes to sign exclusive representation agreements with them while they had remaining collegiate eligibility. The secret agreements were postdated to be effective after the expiration of the athletes' collegiate athletic eligibility. The athletes submitted false information to their universities regarding any restrictions on their eligibility. Facts providing the predicate for the alleged RICO violation included alleged extortion, mail fraud, and wire fraud. The mail fraud allegedly was committed against the NCAA and occurred when the athletes had their institutions send written documents to the NCAA indicating that the athletes were eligible for intercollegiate competition. The matter became a mail fraud case after prosecutors agreed to dismiss the RICO violations as a part of a plea bargain. A failure of the prosecutors to prove the elements of mail fraud resulted in the Seventh Circuit's dismissal of the claim against Walters.

Aside from relying on mail fraud, federal prosecutors have used violations of SEC regulations and federal laws prohibiting money laundering as grounds for asserting federal criminal charges against agents who have inappropriately handled their athlete-clients' assets. On occasion, the SEC has taken an aggressive stance toward agents. For example, it filed a complaint alleging that financial adviser Donald Lukens "violated federal securities laws by systematically defrauding at least 100 (and perhaps more than 200) clients and brokerage customers collectively of tens of millions of dollars in a series of investment schemes during at least the mid-to-late 1990s." Lukens is said to have represented over 40 athletes at various times. Darryl Kelley, *SEC Probe Accuses Financial Advisor*, Los Angeles Times, Nov. 3, 2001, *http://articles.latimes.com/2001/nov/03/local/me-65237*.

The use of non-agent-specific statutes and the implications of improper payments to student-athletes are demonstrated in *United States v. Piggie*, 303 F.3d 923 (8th Cir. 2002). Myron Piggie developed a scheme whereby he paid elite high school players to compete for his Amateur Athletic Union (AAU) summer basketball team. Between 1995 and 1998, Piggie realized at least $677,760 in income from his scheme. He also anticipated receiving a percentage of the compensation that his players would earn after they signed contracts with NBA teams. Piggie pled guilty to conspiracy to commit mail and wire fraud in violation of 18 U.S.C. §371 and failure to file an income tax return in violation of 26 U.S.C. §7203. He received a 37-month prison term and was ordered to pay $324,279.87 in restitution. The court described the consequences of Piggie's scheme as follows:

> NCAA regulations permit universities to award only thirteen basketball scholarships per year. When Piggie's payments to these players were discovered, the Universities became subject to NCAA penalties. Each school lost the use of one of the thirteen scholarships and lost the value of each player's participation due to the player's NCAA-required suspension. The scholarships were forfeited, and the Universities lost the opportunity to award the scholarships to other top amateur athletes, who had actual eligibility to play intercollegiate basketball. In 1999 and 2000, UCLA lost the benefit of playing Jaron Rush, the $44,862.88 scholarship awarded to him, and also forfeited $42,339 in tournament revenue; Missouri lost the benefit of playing Kareem Rush, and the $9,388.92 scholarship awarded to him; and OSU lost the benefit of playing Williams and the $12,180 scholarship awarded to him. Duke provided Maggette with a $32,696 scholarship for the 1998–1999 season based upon the false assertion that he was an eligible amateur. As a result of the ineligible athlete's participation, the validity of Duke's entire 1998-1999 season was called into question.[4]

---

[4] Maggette played the full 1998-1999 season for Duke before Piggie's scheme was uncovered. . . .

NCAA regulations also required each of the four Universities involved to conduct costly internal investigations after Piggie's scheme was discovered. UCLA spent $59,225.36 on the NCAA-mandated investigation of Jaron Rush, Duke spent $12,704.39 on the NCAA-mandated investigation of Maggette, Missouri spent $10,609 on the NCAA-mandated investigation of Kareem Rush, and OSU spent $21,877.24 on the NCAA-mandated investigation of Williams. The total monetary loss to the Universities was $245,882.79. The scandal following the disclosure of Piggie's scheme caused further intangible harms to the Universities including adverse publicity, diminished alumni support, merchandise sales losses, and other revenue losses.

Id. at 925–26.

QUESTIONS

In *United States v. Piggie*, the court articulated several detailed direct damages caused by Piggie's scheme. Can you think of other specific intangible harms? In light of this, do you believe the award of $324,279.87 in restitution was warranted, or did Piggie's actions call for a greater or lesser fine?

B. State Regulation: The UAAA

Two bodies of state law may be available to regulate the agent profession. One level consists of non-agent-specific civil and criminal laws that might be invoked to penalize agents for improprieties. The other level consists of agent-specific legislation. Prior to the year 2000, agent-specific legislation was in effect in 28 states (the state of Washington had adopted such legislation, but repealed it in 1999). States achieved a modicum of success in prosecuting agents under these statutes. For example, in 1994, agent Nate Cebrun received 30 days in jail and was fined $2,255 for conduct related to making improper payments to a Florida State football player and for failing to register in the state as a sports agent. See Shropshire and Davis, *supra* note 1, at 142–143 (discussing the Cebrun matter and other instances in which states have sanctioned athletes pursuant to agent-specific statutes).

In 2000, the National Conference of Commissioners on Uniform State Laws (now known as the Uniform Law Commission (ULC)) finished drafting the UAAA and presented it to the states for adoption. From a regulatory perspective, the primary goal of the UAAA is to protect the interests of student-athletes and academic institutions by regulating the activities of sports agents. The UAAA's other critical goal is to achieve uniformity. As of June 2012, UAAA had been adopted in over 40 states and two territories. For a listing of states, see *http://uniformlaws.org/ LegislativeFactSheet.aspx?title=Athlete%20Agents%20Act*. For discussions of the UAAA, see Shropshire, Davis and Duru, *supra* note 1, at 151–174__; Diane Sudia and Rob Remis, *Athlete Agent Legislation in the New Millennium: State Statutes and the Uniform Athlete Agents Act*, 11 Seton Hall J. Sport L. 263 (2001).

The UAAA can be found in its entirety at *http://www.uniformlaws.org/Shared/Docs/ Finals_NC/UAAA_Final_NC.wpd,* but pertinent sections of it are excerpted here.

UNIFORM ATHLETE AGENTS ACT (2000)

SECTION 2. DEFINITIONS. In this [Act]:

(1) "Agency contract" means an agreement in which a student-athlete authorizes a person to negotiate or solicit on behalf of the student-athlete a professional-sports-services contract or an endorsement contract.

(2) "Athlete agent" means an individual who enters into an agency contract with a student-athlete or, directly or indirectly, recruits or solicits a student-athlete to enter into an agency contract. The term includes an individual who represents to the public that the individual is an athlete agent. The term does not include a spouse, parent, sibling, [or] grandparent, [or] guardian of the student-athlete or an individual acting solely on behalf of a professional sports team or professional sports organization. . . .

(3) "Contact" means a communication, direct or indirect, between an athlete agent and a student-athlete, to recruit or solicit the student-athlete to enter into an agency contract.

(4) "Endorsement contract" means an agreement under which a student-athlete is employed or receives consideration to use on behalf of the other party any value that the student-athlete may have because of publicity, reputation, following, or fame obtained because of athletic ability or performance. . . .

(8) "Professional-sports-services contract" means an agreement under which an individual is employed, or agrees to render services, as a player on a professional sports team, with a professional sports organization, or as a professional athlete. . . .

(12) "Student-athlete" means an individual who engages in, is eligible to engage in, or may be eligible in the future to engage in, any intercollegiate sport. If an individual is permanently ineligible to participate in a particular intercollegiate sport, the individual is not a student-athlete for purposes of that sport. . . .

SECTION 4. ATHLETE AGENTS: REGISTRATION REQUIRED; VOID CONTRACTS.

(a) Except as otherwise provided in subsection (b), an individual may not act as an athlete agent in this State without holding a certificate of registration under Section 6 or 8. . . .

(c) An agency contract resulting from conduct in violation of this section is void and the athlete agent shall return any consideration received under the contract. . . .

SECTION 6. CERTIFICATE OF REGISTRATION; ISSUANCE OR DENIAL; RENEWAL.

(b) The [Secretary of State] may refuse to issue a certificate of registration if the [Secretary of State] determines that the applicant has engaged in conduct that has a significant adverse effect on the applicant's fitness to act as an athlete agent. . . .

SECTION 10. REQUIRED FORM OF CONTRACT. . . .

(c) An agency contract must contain, in close proximity to the signature of the student-athlete, a conspicuous notice in boldface type in capital letters stating:

WARNING TO STUDENT-ATHLETE
IF YOU SIGN THIS CONTRACT:

(1) YOU MAY LOSE YOUR ELIGIBILITY TO COMPETE AS A STUDENT-ATHLETE IN YOUR SPORT;

(2) IF YOU HAVE AN ATHLETIC DIRECTOR, WITHIN 72 HOURS AFTER ENTERING INTO THIS CONTRACT, BOTH YOU AND YOUR ATHLETE AGENT MUST NOTIFY YOUR ATHLETIC DIRECTOR; AND

(3) YOU MAY CANCEL THIS CONTRACT WITHIN 14 DAYS AFTER SIGNING IT. CANCELLATION OF THIS CONTRACT MAY NOT REINSTATE YOUR ELIGIBILITY.

(d) An agency contract that does not conform to this section is voidable by the student-athlete. If a student-athlete voids an agency contract, the student-athlete is not required to pay any consideration under the contract or to return any consideration received from the athlete agent to induce the student-athlete to enter into the contract. . . .

SECTION 11. NOTICE TO EDUCATIONAL INSTITUTION.

(a) Within 72 hours after entering into an agency contract or before the next scheduled athletic event in which the student-athlete may participate, whichever occurs first, the athlete agent shall give notice in a record of the existence of the contract to the athletic director of the educational institution at which the student-athlete is enrolled or the athlete agent has reasonable grounds to believe the student-athlete intends to enroll.

(b) [Editor's note: A student-athlete is required to provide the same notice as described in (a) above.]

SECTION 12. STUDENT-ATHLETE'S RIGHT TO CANCEL.

(a) A student-athlete may cancel an agency contract by giving notice of the cancellation to the athlete agent in a record within 14 days after the contract is signed. . . .

(c) If a student-athlete cancels an agency contract, the student-athlete is not required to pay any consideration under the contract or to return any consideration received from the athlete agent to induce the student-athlete to enter into the contract. . . .

SECTION 14. PROHIBITED CONDUCT.

(a) An athlete agent, with the intent to induce a student-athlete to enter into an agency contract, may not [(1) give any materially false or misleading information or make a materially false promise or representation; (2) furnish anything of value to a student-athlete before the student-athlete enters into the agency contract; or (3) furnish anything of value to any individual other than the student-athlete or another registered athlete agent].

(b) An athlete agent may not intentionally [(1) initiate contact with a student-athlete unless registered; (2) fail to register; (3) provide false information in the application for registration; (4) predate or postdate an agency contract; and (5) fail to inform a student-athlete of the eligibility implications of signing an agency agreement].

SECTION 15. CRIMINAL PENALTIES.

[Editors' note: The UAAA directs each state to determine the criminal sanctions that will result from its violation.]

SECTION 16. CIVIL REMEDIES.

(a) An educational institution has a right of action against an athlete agent or a former student-athlete for damages caused by a violation of this [Act]. In an action under this section, the court may award to the prevailing party costs and reasonable attorney's fees.

(b) Damages of an educational institution under subsection (a) include losses and expenses incurred because, as a result of the conduct of an athlete agent or former student-athlete, the educational institution was injured by a violation of this [Act] or was penalized, disqualified, or suspended from participation in athletics by a national association for the promotion and regulation of athletics, by an athletic conference, or by reasonable self-imposed disciplinary action taken to mitigate sanctions likely to be imposed by such an organization. . . .

SECTION 17. ADMINISTRATIVE PENALTY.

The [Secretary of State] may assess a civil penalty against an athlete agent not to exceed [$25,000] for a violation of this [Act].

• • • • • • • • •

In one of the first indictments brought pursuant to the UAAA, on October 13, 2006, a grand jury in Baton Rouge, Louisiana, charged Charles Taplin with two counts of violating Louisiana's athlete-agent statute, based on the UAAA. Taplin allegedly violated the UAAA's registration and notification provisions when he sent text messages to two Louisiana State University (LSU) football players on behalf of an agent. Taplin was not a registered agent and allegedly failed to notify LSU within seven days of contacting the players. *Man Charged with Texting LSU Players for Agent*, USA Today, April 13, 2007, *http://www.usatoday.com/sports/college/football/sec/2007-04-13-lsu-agent-texts_N.htm.* While investigating Taplin, information was allegedly uncovered that led to the arrest of Travelle Gaines, a former assistant strength coach at LSU. Gaines was booked on a felony count of engaging in activities prohibited by Louisiana's UAAA namely, allegedly inviting players to his home, where they came into contact with a California-based agent, C. J. Laboy. Adrian Angelette, *La. Law Allows Agent-Athlete Contact Within Rules*, Baton Rouge Advocate, Oct. 26, 2006, at A1. Gaines's attorney denied that his client had done anything illegal.

In October 2008, a Virginia-based and NFLPA-certified contract advisor, Raymond L. Savage, Jr., was indicted for allegedly failing to register under Alabama's UAAA and for initiating contact with a student-athlete. One of Savage's former employee's, Jason Goggins, allegedly contacted Tyrone Prothro, a University of Alabama wide receiver, while the athlete was in the hospital recovering from a broken leg. Goggins's alleged conduct led to his indictment in 2006 for alleged violations of Alabama's UAAA. Liz Mullen, *State of Alabama Say Agent Ran Afoul of Tough Recruiting Laws*, Sports Business J. 13, Nov. 10, 2008; Peter Dujardin, *Sports Agent Denies He Violated Alabama Law*, Daily Press (Newport News, VA), Oct. 15, 2008, at A11. In 2006, the state of Florida exacted a $2,500 fine against agent Jason Paul Wood for failing to notify the University of Miami after meeting with two of its baseball players, and for not registering as an agent in the state. Alan S. Zagler, *US Sports Agents*, Associated Press, Aug. 17, 2010.

Notwithstanding the foregoing prosecutions, a 2010 study conducted by the Associated Press revealed that over half of the 42 states that have enacted the UAAA had "yet to revoke or suspend a single license, or invoke penalties of any sort." Zagler, *supra.* According to the Associated Press review, "Twenty-four states reported taking no disciplinary or criminal actions against sports agents, and were unable to determine if state or local prosecutors had pursued such cases. Others described the laws as being enforced a few times, or rarely, an indication of what a low priority they are." *Id.* Texas was reportedly one of the few states that have consistently enforced the UAAA. The review found over the past two years, Texas had disciplined 31 agents and levied fines totaling $17,500. *Id.*

In a sign that it may aggressively enforce the UAAA, the North Carolina Secretary of State's office indicted several individuals who allegedly engaged in conduct that resulted in the imposition of NCAA sanctions against the University of North Carolina at Chapel Hill (UNC). (For background information discussing the conduct that violated NCAA rules, see University of North Carolina at Chapter Hill, NCAA Public Infractions Report, March 12, 2012) *http://www.unc.edu/sacs/Jan2015/Document%20Repository/CS%203.2.11%20Control%20of%20Intercollegiate%20Athletics/3.2.11%20NCAA%20Public%20Infractions%20Report%20Mar%2012%202012.pdf.* An agent was indicted for allegedly providing impermissible benefits to induce athletes to sign an agency contract. Brooke Pryor, *Sports Agent Terry Watson Indicted Related to UNC Athlete-Agent Case*, DailyTarHeel.com, Oct. 10, 2013, *http://www.dailytarheel.com/article/2013/10/second-indictment-in-related-to-unc-athlete-agent-case.*

Critics have identified concerns regarding the overall effectiveness of the UAAA. These include an increasing lack of uniformity as states adopt variations to the Act, the

UAAA's lack of effective deterrence effect arising from underenforcement and weak penalties, and the belief that the UAAA fails to adequately protect the interests of student-athletes. Responding to such concerns, the ULC formed a committee to expand the UAAA's scope and improve its effectiveness. Rich Cassidy, *Proposed Amendments to Uniform Athlete Agents Act Attract Attention in Chicago*, On Lawyering. com (Oct. 29, 2013). In January 2015, the committee submitted a draft of its proposed amendments to ULC for comment and eventual adoption. ULC, January 2015 Draft for ULC Committee on Style Review (Nov. 7-8, 2014). Changes proposed in the draft include: (1) expanding the definition of who is an agent, NCCUSL, *Memorandum: Background on the UAAA and Issues to Be Considered at the March Drafting Committee Meeting* 2–3 (March 2014); (2) defining athlete agents to include entities (and not solely individuals) (e.g., sports representation firms), *Id.*; (3) amending the definition of *student-athlete* to encompass elementary and secondary schools and to encompass professional athletes and student-athletes, *Id.* at 3; (4) revising the UAAA's reciprocity provisions to facilitate agents registering in multiple states, *Id.* at 4; (5) exploring the creation of a centralized registry and delegating the agent registration function to entities such as professional players' associations, *Id.* at 4; (6) requiring agents to secure surety bonds, *Id.* at 5; and (7) expanding the civil enforcement of the UAAA beyond student-athletes and educational institutions to include entities (e.g., collegiate conferences) that could be injured as a result of agent violations of the UAAA, *Id.* at 6–7. In July 2015, the ULC voted to adopt the revised UAAA, and it will now submit it to states for their adoption. Julie Steinberg, *Law Commission Votes to Revise Sports-Agent Act to Cover Financial Advisors*, WSJ.com, July 15, 20152015, *http://www.wsj.com/articles/law-commission-votes-to-revise-sports-agent-act-to-cover-financial-advisers-1437011042*.

What reasons may underlie the underenforcement of the UAAA?

Problem 13-3

Bruce Reynolds, a football player, met Mr. Fritz of Complete Sports Management, Inc., when Reynolds was a football player at Allstate University. Fritz is an NFLPA-certified contract advisor. On January 3, 2009, Reynolds met Fritz at the latter's car dealership. To enable Reynolds to purchase a car without paying anything, Fritz advanced Reynolds credit on a "house note." On January 18, 2009, Reynolds signed an undated, standard-form NFLPA representation agreement with Complete. Fritz told Reynolds not to send the agreement to the NFLPA, as provided for in the union's regulations. Some time thereafter, a coach advised Reynolds to sign with another agent, which the athlete did. Reynolds informed Fritz that he had signed with another agent and that he would return the automobile to Fritz. Reynolds also informed Fritz that he would reimburse him for the more than $2,900 in checks and goods that Fritz had extended to Reynolds since January 18. Reynolds was drafted by the Atlanta Falcons and signed contracts for the years 2009–2012 that provided a total compensation of $4,100,000 and other incentive bonuses.

> Did Fritz violate any rules, regulations, or laws? If so, what are the consequences of such a rules violation? Consider the UAAA, Section 1 of NFLPA Regulations Governing Contract Advisors, infra, and Article 12 of the NCAA Manual (2011-2012), infra. See *Walters v. Fullwood*, 675 F. Supp. 155 (S.D.N.Y. 1987) (dismissing agent's claims against athlete where agent paid athlete $4,000 to enter into postdated agency contract in violation of NCAA and NFLPA rules); *Chiappeparelli v. Henderson*, 2005 WL 1847221 (Cal. Ct. App.) (unpublished) (the court found that a plaintiff agent, who failed to obtain a license as required by the applicable state agent regulations, could not collect a percentage of the compensation that the defendant had earned from martial arts contests since the representation contract between the agent and defendant was illegal and unenforceable).

C. Players Associations

1. Authority to Regulate

As noted in Chapters 8 and 9, in team sports, players' associations are usually unions. These unions represent a principal component of the web of regulation that affects the athlete-agent relationship. In *Collins v. National Basketball Players Association*, the court described the abuses that prompted players' unions to legislate the agent-athlete relationship as follows:

> Specifically, players complained that the agents imposed high and non-uniform fees for negotiation services, insisted on execution of open-ended powers of attorney giving the agents broad powers over players' professional and financial decisions, failed to keep players apprised of the status of negotiations with NBA teams, failed to submit itemized bills for fees and services, and, in some cases had conflicts of interest arising out of representing coaches and/or general managers of NBA teams as well as players. Many players believed that they were bound by contract not to dismiss their agents regardless of dissatisfaction with their services and fees, because the agents had insisted on the execution of long-term agreements. Some agents offered money and other inducements to players, their families, and coaches to obtain player clients.

Collins v. National Basketball Players Association, 850 F. Supp. 1468, 1471 (D. Colo. 1991).

The following excerpt describes the genesis of players' associations and how these entities fit into the larger scheme of labor relations law that regulates the representation of employees once they have entered into a collective bargaining agreement with employers:

> The sports unions' power to regulate and certify agents represents a departure from the ways in which employees' unions typically operate. In most industries, unions (pursuant to collective bargaining agreements with employers) negotiate terms and conditions of

employment as well as all union member salaries. Professional sports unions, also pursuant to collective bargaining agreements, possess the exclusive authority to negotiate individual player salaries and other terms and conditions of employment such as minimum salaries, pension benefits, health insurance, playing conditions, travel accommodations, the ability of a player to move from one team to another, medical treatment, and grievance and arbitration procedures. However, unlike other unions, sports unions have delegated their exclusive authority to negotiate individual player salaries. Thus, players are free to select representatives to negotiate the individual terms of their contract compensation packages within the framework established by the collective bargaining agreements.

In 1983, the NFLPA asserted that it possessed the inherent authority to regulate agents who represented football players in contract negotiations with teams. Pursuant to its asserted authority, the NFLPA mandated that those agents who desired to represent its members be certified by the union. Similarly, in 1986, in response to complaints by players of abuse by agents, the NBPA established a comprehensive system of agent certification. . . .

The MLBPA asserts its authority in the MLBPA regulations by citing the NLRA and emphasizing that it is "the exclusive representative for all the employees in such unit." It then cites its collective bargaining agreement with management, noting that players may negotiate contracts with teams "in accordance with the provisions set forth in this Agreement.

Shropshire, Davis, and Duru, *supra* note 1 at 140__.

In *Collins v. National Basketball Players Association*, 976 F.2d 740 (10th Cir. 1992), a federal appellate court upheld the authority of a players' union to refuse to recertify an agent. Former NBA basketball superstar Kareem Abdul-Jabbar filed a lawsuit accusing his agent of financial improprieties. Prior to a settlement of Abdul-Jabbar's lawsuit against Collins, the agent had been decertified by the National Basketball Players Association (NBPA). After his application for recertification was denied, Collins sued the NBPA. The court rejected Collins's claim, stating as follows:

[Collins] maintains his attack on the Committee's decision to deny his certification because it was based in part on its finding that he had breached his fiduciary duty as an investment agent and money manager. He argues that his conduct outside of negotiations between players and their teams is not a legitimate interest of the union because it has no bearing on the union's interest in the wage scale and working conditions of its members. . . . The NBPA established the Regulations to deal with agent abuses, including agents' violations of their fiduciary duties as labor negotiators. It was entirely fair for the Committee to conclude that a man who had neglected his fiduciary duties as an investment agent and money manager could not be trusted to fulfill his fiduciary duties as a negotiator. The integrity of a prospective negotiating agent is well within the NBPA's legitimate interest in maintaining the wage scale and working conditions of its members.

Collins, 976 F.2d at 740. The court affirmed the district court's grant of summary judgment in favor of the NBPA.

QUESTION

U.S. professional sports unions have the unique power to regulate and certify agents in the world of employee unions. What is the rationale behind granting such authority?

2. Regulating the Athlete-Agent Relationship

a. Sanctions: Suspensions and Decertification

The most severe sanctions that a players' association can impose on an agent are suspension and decertification. Section 6 of the *NFLPA Regulations Governing Contract Advisors* provides that discipline for violation of its regulations may include suspension, revocation of an advisor's certification (decertification), and the imposition of a fine not to exceed $25,000.

Instances in which an agent's conduct was deemed sufficiently egregious to warrant suspension or decertification include the following: (1) NFLPA's 2003 decertification of Sean Jones, the agent for former NFL player Cris Dishman, for alleged financial irregularities, including Jones's failure to disclose the high level of risk associated with investments he made on behalf of the athlete (the arbitrator later reduced decertification to two-year suspension); (2) NFLPA's 2003 decertification of Ajili Hodari, "finding that the agent took his entire fee out of a signing bonus paid to a former client, Carolina Panthers wide receiver Mushin Muhammad, and also finding that Hodari offered an Ohio State football player a payment to sign with him;" (3) NFPLA's 2006 suspension (upheld by an arbitrator) of Carl Poston for conduct relating to omission of a signing bonus from a contract between his client LaVar Arrington and his team; (4) NBPA's 2008 suspension of Calvin Andrew for unspecified improprieties involving O. J. Mayo, who played college basketball for USC and went on to sign a professional contract with the NBA's Memphis Grizzlies; (5) the revocation of Josh Luch's certification in 2010; and (6) the three-month suspension of John Rickert for failing to make a number of payments, on required dates, to another certified contract advisor in accordance with a settlement agreement. See NFLPA, *NFLPA Committee Suspends Agent Rickert's Certification*, NFLPA.com (June 28, 2013), *https://www.nflpa.com/news/all-news/nflpa-committee-suspends-agent-rickerts-certification*. See Richard T. Karcher, *Fundamental Fairness in Union Regulation of Sports Agents*, 640 Conn. L. Rev. 355 (2007) (discussing the fairness of player association disciplinary processes).

b. Fees/Agent Compensation

Players' associations regulate varying aspects of the payment by athletes of fees for agent services. For example, the NFLPA agent regulations restrict the maximum amount of fees that an agent can charge for negotiating a player contract with a team. An agent can receive a maximum fee of 3 percent of the compensation that a player receives during the playing season covered by the contract that the agent negotiates. Note that agents are allowed to charge less than the maximum. The NBPA allows fees of up to 4 percent. MLB allows the market to control and sets no maximum on the size of fee an agent can earn for negotiating a player/team contract. Larger representation firms will often waive the fee the NBPA regulations allow in negotiating the first contract between an NBA team and draft picks. Such a firm is willing to forgo the fee as an incentive for the player to sign a representation agreement with it, and with the hope that it will collect a larger fee when the player signs a more lucrative contract three or four years later.

c. NFLPA Amendments

Over the past several years, attempting to confront problems aggressively in the agent industry, the NFLPA enacted several amendments to its agent regulations. In 2002, the NFLPA adopted the one-in-three rule. NFLPA-certified agents are required to negotiate at least one contract during a three-year period in order to retain their certification. In 2004, the NFLPA amended its regulations to require agents to disclose, in writing, payments they make to runners. In May 2005, the NFLPA amended its regulations to impose a heightened educational requirement. In order to be eligible for certification, prospective agents must have received a post-graduate degree from a college or university or demonstrate sufficient negotiation experience. In 2005, the NLFPA amended its regulations to require agents to obtain malpractice insurance. As with the NFLPA's one-in-three rule, a consequence of this amendment is likely to be a decrease in the number of certified NFL agents. In 2007, the NFLPA adopted a new regulation that prohibits suspended agents from directly or indirectly recruiting players during the period of his or her suspension. In 2007, the NFLPA adopted a regulation requiring an agent to disclose to player clients the identity of the coaches, including college coaches, that the agent represents. *Id.*

Amendments to the NFLPA's regulations, adopted in 2012 and 2013, include a provision requiring mandatory arbitration for disputes between agents. That revision reads: "two or more Contract Advisors with respect to their individual entitlement to fees owed, whether paid or unpaid, by a player-client who was jointly represented by such agents, or represented by a firm with which the agents in question were associated," NFLPA Legal Dept., *Memorandum from Legal Dep't, Nat'l Football League Players Ass'n, to Contract Advisors* 2 (April 10, 2012), NFLPA Regulations § 5(A)(6) and requiring additional disclosures as a part of the application process (i.e., applicants must list unsatisfied liens), NFLPA Legal Dept., *Memorandum from NFLPA Legal Dep't, to Contract Advisors* 1, (May 8, 2013). The amendment also address allowing applicants who fail the contract advisor exam 30 days within which to notify the NFLPA of their intention dispute their failing score. *Id.* In 2014, the NFLPA's Committee on Agent Regulation and Discipline announced that it would review its regulations governing contract advisors. Liz Mullen, *A Lot of Agent Missteps Prompt Wholesale NFLPA Review,* Sports Business Journal (April 21–27, 2014). Among the matters the committee will address are the agent exam, the standards for becoming certified, and the numbers of years that an agent can retain his or her certification without having a client. *Id.*

d. MLBPA Amendments

In 2010, the Major League Baseball Players Association (MLBPA) adopted the first major substantive overall of its agent regulations since they were initially adopted in 1988. The 2010 regulations include provisions relating to client poaching, solicitation and inducements, runners, and arbitration. For an overview of MLBPA's revised regulations, see Shropshire, Davis, and Duru, *supra* note 1, at __ (3d ed. 2015). In 2013, MLBPA amended its agent regulations to prohibit agents from lending money to players without first obtaining written approval from the MLBPA. MLBPA, 2013 Amendments to the MLBPA Regulations Governing Player Agents (May 3, 2013). Its regulations were further amended in 2015 to require that agent applicants take a written exam and submit to a background check. MLBPA. Liz Mullen, *MLBPA Announces Agent Certification Now Includes Background Check, Written Exam*, Sports Business Journal (Jan 13, 2015).

e. Excerpts of Players Association and NCAA Regulations

NFLPA REGULATIONS GOVERNING CONTRACT ADVISORS[3]

(as amended through June 2012)

Section 1 — Scope of Regulations
A. Persons Subject to Regulations

No person (other than a player representing himself) shall be permitted to conduct individual contract negotiations on behalf of a player and/or assist in or advise with respect to such negotiations with NFL Clubs after the effective date of these Regulations unless he/she is (1) currently certified as a Contract Advisor pursuant to these Regulations; (2) signs a Standard Representation Agreement with the player (See Section 4; Appendix D); and (3) files a fully executed copy of the Standard Representation Agreement with the NFLPA, along with any contract(s) between the player and the Contract Advisor for other services to be provided.

B. Activities Covered

The activities of Contract Advisors which are governed by these Regulations include: the providing of advice, counsel, information or assistance to players with respect to negotiating their individual contracts with Clubs and/or thereafter in enforcing those contracts; the conduct of individual compensation negotiations with the Clubs on behalf of players; and any other activity or conduct which directly bears upon the Contract Advisor's integrity, competence or ability to properly represent individual NFL players and the NFLPA in individual contract negotiations, including the handling of player funds, providing tax counseling and preparation services, and providing financial advice and investment services to individual players. . . .

Section 2 — Certification

After the effective date of these Regulations, any person who wishes to perform the functions of a Contract Advisor as described in Section 1 above must be certified by the NFLPA. . . .

C. Grounds for Denial for Certification

Grounds for denial of Certification shall include, but not be limited to, the following:

- The applicant has made false or misleading statements of a material nature in his/her application;
- The applicant has misappropriated funds, or engaged in other specific acts such as embezzlement, theft or fraud, which would render him/her unfit to serve in a fiduciary capacity on behalf of players;
- The applicant has engaged in any other conduct that significantly impacts adversely on his/her credibility, integrity or competence to serve in a fiduciary capacity on behalf of players . . . ;
- The applicant has been denied certification by another professional sports players association;
- The applicant directly or indirectly solicited a player for representation as a Contract Advisor during the period of time between the filing of his/her Application for Certification and Certification by the NFLPA;
- The applicant has not received a degree from an accredited four year college/university and a postgraduate degree from an accredited college/university, unless excepted from this requirement pursuant to Section 2(A). . . .

Section 3 — Standard of Conduct For Contract Advisors . . .
A. General Requirements

[A] Contract Advisor shall be required to:

(1) Disclose on his/her Application and thereafter upon request of the NFLPA all information relevant to his/her qualifications to serve as a Contract Advisor . . . ;

(5) Comply with the maximum fee schedule and all other provisions of these Regulations and any amendments thereto;

(6) Execute and abide by the printed Standard Representation Agreement with all players represented . . . ;

(9) Provide on or before May 1 each year, to every player who he/she represents, with a copy to the NFLPA, an itemized statement covering the period beginning March 1 of the prior year through February 28 or 29 of that year, which separately sets forth both the fee charged to the player for, and any expenses incurred in connection with, the performance of the following services: [(a) individual player salary negotiations; (b) management of the player's assets; (c) financial, investment, legal, tax and/or other advice to the player; and, (d) any other miscellaneous services].

(17) Act at all times in a fiduciary capacity on behalf of players. . . .

B. Prohibited Conduct

Contract Advisors are prohibited from:

(1) Representing any player in individual contract negotiations with any Club unless he/she (i) is an NFLPA Certified Contract Advisor; (ii) has signed the Standard Representation Agreement with such player; and (iii) has filed a copy of the Standard Representation Agreement with the NFLPA along with any other contract(s) or agreement(s) between the player and the Contract Advisor;

(2) Providing or offering money or any other thing of value to any player or prospective player to induce or encourage that player to utilize his/her services;

(3) Providing or offering money or any other thing of value to a member of the player's or prospective player's family or any other person for the purpose of inducing or encouraging that person to recommend the services of the Contract Advisor;

(4) Providing materially false or misleading information to any player or prospective player in the context of recruiting the player as a client or in the course of representing that player as his Contract Advisor . . . ;

(7) Holding or seeking to hold, either directly or indirectly, a financial interest in any professional football club or in any other business entity when such investment could create an actual conflict of interest or the appearance of a conflict of interest in the representation of NFL players . . . ;

(14) Engaging in unlawful conduct and/or conduct involving dishonesty, fraud, deceit, misrepresentation, or other activity which reflects adversely on his/her fitness as a Contract Advisor or jeopardizes his/her effective representation of NFL players;

(15) Failure to comply with the maximum fee provisions contained in Section 4 of these Regulations . . . ;

(21) (a) Initiating any communication, directly or indirectly, with a player who has entered into a Standard Representation Agreement with another Contract Advisor and such Standard Representation Agreement is on file with the NFLPA if the communication concerns a matter relating to [(1) a player's current Contract Advisor; (2) a player's current Standard Representation Agreement; (3) a player's contract status with any NFL Club(s); or (4) services to be provided by prospective Contract Advisor either through a Standard Representation Agreement or otherwise].

(b) If a player, already a party to a Standard Representation Agreement, initiates communication with a Contract Advisor relating to any of the subject matters listed in Section 3(B)(21)(a) the Contract Advisor may continue communications with the Player regarding any of those matters.

(26) Directly or indirectly soliciting a prospective rookie player for representation as a Contract Advisor . . . if that player has signed a Standard Representation Agreement prior to a date which is thirty (30) days before the NFL Draft and if thirty (30) days have not elapsed since the Agreement was signed and filed with the NFLPA. . . .

A Contract Advisor who engages in any prohibited conduct as defined above shall be subject to discipline in accordance with the procedures of Section 6 of these

Regulations. . . . [Editors' note: The sanctions listed in Section 6 include the payment of fines, suspension of certification, and decertification.]

Section 4 — Agreements Between Contract Advisors and Players; Maximum Fees . . .

B. Contract Advisor's Compensation

(1) The maximum fee which may be charged or collected by a Contract Advisor shall be three percent (3%) of the "compensation" (as defined within this Section) received by the player in each playing season covered by the contract negotiated by the Contract Advisor, except as follows: [Editors' note: The Regulations stipulate lower maximum fees for certain players such as franchise and transition players.]

(2) The Contract Advisor and player may agree to any fee which is less than the maximum fee set forth in (1) above.

(3) As used in this Section 4(B), the term "compensation" shall be deemed to include only salaries, signing bonuses, reporting bonuses, roster bonuses, Practice Squad salary in excess of the minimum Practice Squad salary specified in Article 33 of the Collective Bargaining Agreement, and any performance incentives earned by the player during the term of the contract (including any option year) negotiated by the Contract Advisor. . . .

QUESTIONS

1. May a player's parent, who is not certified by the NFLPA, represent the player in the player's contract negotiations with a team?
2. Do NFLPA regulations prohibit an agent from representing both an athlete and an NFL coach?
3. Are endorsement deals that an agent negotiates for an NFL player subject to the 3 percent maximum?
4. May an agent initiate contact with a player who is engaged in an agency agreement with another agent?
5. What types of earnings constitute compensation for purposes of an agent determining the amount of his or her fee?

NCAA BYLAW, ARTICLE 12

12.3.1 General Rule.

An individual shall be ineligible for participation in an intercollegiate sport if he or she ever has agreed (orally or in writing) to be represented by an agent for the purpose of marketing his or her athletics ability or reputation in that sport. Further, an agency contract not specifically limited in writing to a sport or particular sports shall be deemed applicable to all sports, and the individual shall be ineligible to participate in any sport. . . .

12.3.1.2 Benefits from Prospective Agents. An individual shall be ineligible per Bylaw 12.3.1 if he or she (or his or her relatives or friends) accepts transportation or other benefits from [(a) any person who represents any individual in the marketing of his or her athletics ability, or (b) an agent].

Problem 13-4

For the purposes of this question, assume that the state of Wisconsin adopted the UAAA in its entirety without any modifications and that it was in effect during Will Cheatham's dealings with Bill Jammer.

Will Cheatham was licensed to practice law in both Wisconsin and Illinois and maintained his business office in Chicago. He was not registered as an athlete agent with the Wisconsin Secretary of State's office. Through a mutual acquaintance, Cheatham induced Bill Jammer, University of Wisconsin-Madison's star basketball player, to secretly sign an agent representation agreement with him on December 1 of Jammer's senior year. This agreement was postdated to April 15 of the following year, which was after the college basketball season ended.

The day after UW was selected for the NCAA basketball tournament, the NCAA declared Jammer ineligible for NCAA tournament competition after discovering that he had entered into the agent representation agreement with Cheatham the previous December. The NCAA required UW to forfeit 20 games that Jammer played in after signing this agreement, and the university's resulting losing record caused it to be dropped from the NCAA tournament. UW lost $100,000 in revenues it would have received for participating in a first-round NCAA tournament game, and potentially more revenue that it could have earned by advancing to subsequent rounds of the tournament.

Although he was a projected second-round pick in this year's NBA draft if he performed well in the NCAA tournament, Jammer was not drafted by any NBA team. Jammer signed as a free agent with the Orlando Magic but did not receive a signing bonus. The last player selected in this year's draft received a $350,000 signing bonus. Jammer signed a contract for the upcoming NBA season but received only the minimum annual player salary of $250,000. Cheatham negotiated Jammer's contract but did not request that the Magic pay him a bonus or a higher salary than the NBA minimum. Cheatham was concerned that the Magic's payment of more money to Jammer would leave the club with less available money under the NBA salary cap to pay Michael Swisher, Cheatham's prized client (a client he represents where he is properly certified under Florida law), who was seeking a lucrative free agent deal with the Magic.

(a) Discuss Jammer's potential claims against Cheatham.
(b) Discuss UW's potential claims against Cheatham.
(c) Discuss whether Cheatham has violated the UAAA and any potential consequences.

Olympic and International Sports Issues

14

INTRODUCTION

Olympic and international sports competition demonstrates that sport is a universal cultural phenomenon, which is tremendously popular and a significant part of the world's twenty-first-century global economy. It also gives rise to several important current and future potential legal issues. Professional sports also generate legal issues with global implications. For example, the labor market for players' services in some sports (e.g., soccer, basketball, baseball, and hockey) extends beyond national borders. Some North American major professional sports leagues (e.g., the National Basketball Association (NBA)) have expressed an interest in expanding to or placing clubs in European countries.

This chapter initially provides an overview of the Olympic Games and describes how Olympic sports are structured and governed pursuant to an international hierarchy. It then discusses how Olympic sports are internally governed within the United States and regulated by a federal statute, the Ted Stevens Olympic and Amateur Sports Act (ASA). After considering the general reluctance of courts to use U.S. law to regulate Olympic and international sports competitions, this chapter describes the jurisdiction and role of the Court of Arbitration for Sport (CAS) in resolving Olympic and international sports disputes (e.g., challenged competition results, doping violations, and sanctions). It concludes by identifying and briefly discussing some developing non-Olympic international sports legal issues.

A. Origin, History, and Objectives of the Olympic Games

The Olympic Games have been held during two distinct historical time periods. The ancient Olympics began in 776 B.C. in Elis, Greece, in the valley of Olympia, to honor the mythical Greek god Zeus. The Olympics likely were not the first athletic competitions in Greece, but they represented the dawn of organized athletic activity for the Western world.

The first Games consisted of one event — a 200-meter footrace — and were subsequently expanded to include boxing, wrestling, chariot racing, and the pentathlon. Competitors included local residents in addition to those who lived outside the Greek city-states. Because of the highly competitive nature of the ancient Greeks, a victory at the Games was considered one of the greatest athletic accomplishments. The prize for winning was a simple olive tree branch, which the Greeks believed would transfer its sacred vitality to the recipient. This simple prize demonstrated the magnitude of the honor of an Olympic victory and emphasized the importance of athletics and competition in Greek life. As the Olympics grew in importance, athletes evolved from amateurs to professionals and began to train for their sports year-round and to receive substantial gifts and money from their home cities and others. The purpose of the ancient Olympics, which is the same for the modern Olympics (if not as easily recognizable today), was to promote goodwill and unity among competing nations. To facilitate this objective, a peace agreement, called *ekecheiria,* or "sacred truce," was established, providing for a three-month truce on fighting surrounding the time of the Games, which were held every four years. From their inception, the ancient Olympics continued for almost 1,200 years without interruption. They embodied the Greek ideal of transforming violent urges into playful athletic competition and provided a forum for Greeks from all city-states to gather for attempted unification through athletic competition and religious ceremonies. However, in A.D.393, the Olympics were abolished by the Christian Byzantine emperor Theodosius I because they were perceived to be a pagan festival. *Ancient Olympic Games,* in Brief History of the Olympic Games, *http://www.nostos.com/olympics.*

The Olympic Games were not held again until Baron Pierre de Courbetin of France announced their reestablishment in 1892. At the Congress of Paris in 1894, 13 nations met to create the modern Olympics . The International Olympic Committee (IOC) was created, and the modern Olympics (initially consisting of only traditional Summer Olympic events) were scheduled to be held every fourth year. Returning to their country of origin, the first modern Olympics were held in Athens, Greece, in 1896 and consisted of 300 athletes from 13 countries participating in events in ten sports.

Courbetin chose the Latin words "Citius, altius, fortius" as the motto of the modern Olympic Movement. This motto connotes not only athletic achievement, but also moral and educational development — "Citius: fast not only in the race, but with a quick and vibrant mind as well. Altius: higher, not only toward a coveted goal, but also toward the uplifting of an individual. Fortius: not only more courageous in the struggles on the field of play, but in life, also." Pierre de Courbetin, Olympism — Selected Writings at 585 (International Olympic Committee 2000).

In 1914, Courbetin designed the now widely recognized Olympic rings, consisting of five interlocking rings of blue, yellow, black, green, and red with a white background. He explained that they "represent the five parts of the world now won over to Olympism, ready to accept its fruitful rivalries. In addition, the six colors combined in this way reproduce the colors of every country without exception." *Id.* at 594.

The Winter Olympic Games began in 1924 and were held in the same years as the Summer Games until 1986, when the IOC decided to schedule the Summer and

Winter Olympic competitions in different years two years apart. The Olympic Games were canceled in 1916, 1940, and 1944 because of World Wars I and II. In modern times, the ancient Olympic truce has been renewed by the IOC with the "view to protecting, as far as possible, the interests of the athletes and sport in general, and to encourage searching for peaceful and diplomatic solutions to the conflicts around the world." *Olympic Truce, http://www.olympic.org/content/the-ioc/commissions/public-affairs-and-social-development-through-sport/olympic-truce/.*

B. Organization, Governance, and Structure of the Olympic Movement

KEY TERMS
- International Federation (IF)
- International Olympic Committee (IOC)
- National Governing Body (NGB)
- National Olympic Committee (NOC)
- Olympic Charter
- Organizing Committee for the Olympic Games (OCOG)

The modern Olympic Movement "is the concerted, organised, universal, and permanent action, carried out under the supreme authority of the IOC, of all individuals and entities who are inspired by the values of Olympism." Furthermore, "Olympism is a philosophy of life, exalting and combining in a balanced whole the qualities of body, will, and mind. Blending sport with culture and education, Olympism seeks to create a way of life based on the joy of effort, the educational value of good example, social responsibility and respect for universal fundamental ethical principles." *Fundamental Principles of Olympism*, in the Olympic Charter (in force as from August 2, 2015), *http://www.olympic.org/Documents/olympic_charter_en.pdf.* There are numerous organizations and persons that are part of the Olympic Movement, including the IOC; international federations (IFs), the international governing bodies for each Olympic sport; National Olympic Committees (NOCs), such as the U.S. Olympic Committee (USOC); national governing bodies (NGBs) for each Olympic sport in each NOC; the World Anti-Doping Agency (WADA); the Court of Arbitration for Sport (CAS); and the Olympic Museum, as well as thousands of individual athletes, judges, and coaches.

The Olympic Charter governs the Olympic Movement, which codifies the fundamental principles, rules, and bylaws adopted by the IOC, and establishes rules for the production and operation of the Olympic Games. The goal of Olympism "is to place sport at the service of the harmonious development of man with a view to promoting the preservation of human dignity." *Fundamental Principles of Olympism, supra.* The goal of the Olympic Movement itself is to "contribute to building a peaceful and better world by educating youth through sport practised in accordance with Olympism and its values." Olympic Charter, *supra*, Chap. 1, Rule 1(1). The IOC "opposes any political or commercial abuse of sport and athletes." Olympic Charter, *supra*, Chap. 2, Rule 10.

The Olympic Charter states that the IOC is the "supreme authority" of the Olympic Movement, and all members are bound by its provisions and the IOC's decisions regarding its application or interpretation. Olympic Charter, *supra*, Chap. 1, Rule 1(1). The IOC is an "international non-governmental not-for-profit organization" domiciled in Lausanne, Switzerland, and recognized by the Swiss Federal Council. Olympic Charter, *supra*, Chap. 2, Rule 15(1). Emblematic of its international authority, the IOC has 100 elected individuals who serve as its representatives in their respective home countries (see *http://www.olympic.org/ioc-members-list*); however, these individuals are not representatives of their respective countries of residence or their country's delegates to the IOC. These persons are chosen and elected by the IOC's nominations committee, and they serve for renewable eight-year terms. See generally James A.R. Nafziger, International Sports Law 17–26 (2d ed., Transnational 2004).

The IOC's organizational structure consists of an executive board, its individual members, and an administrative staff. The executive board comprises the IOC president, four vice-presidents, and ten other members, all of whom are elected by secret ballot for an eight-year term. The current IOC president is Thomas Bach of Germany, who began his term in September 2013.

Like the IOC, the IFs are private, nongovernmental organizations (NGOs). Each IF is recognized by the IOC as the worldwide governing body for a particular sport or group of sports and encompasses the NGBs that serve as affiliates for the particular sport(s) in each country. Its statutes, practices, and activities must conform to the Olympic Charter and be approved by the IOC Executive Board. The IFs establish and enforce the rules for their respective sports; establish eligibility criteria for Olympic sports competition (subject to IOC approval); select referees, judges, and umpires for competitions; establish and provide an internal dispute resolution process; and are responsible for the technical control and direction of their sports during the Olympic Games. There are 64 recognized IFs, including members of the Association of Summer Olympic International Federations (ASOIF), the Association of International Olympic Winter Sports Federations (AIOWF), the Association of the IOC Recognised International Sports Federations (ARISF), and the General Association of International Sports Federations (GAISF), ranging from the well-known International Amateur Athletic Federation (IAAF) for track and field to the lesser-known IFs such as the International Canoe Federation (ICF).

There are more than 200 NOCs, which develop and protect the Olympic Movement within their respective countries. Most of them are from nations, although the IOC does recognize independent territories, commonwealths, protectorates, and geographical areas as NGBs for Olympic sports. The NOCs are responsible for encouraging the development of high-performance sport and sports opportunities for all their citizens; recognizing NGBs for Olympic sports; taking action against discrimination and violence in sports; and fighting against the use of substances and doping procedures banned by the IOC or IFs. Each NOC has exclusive authority regarding the representation of its country at the Olympic Games and selects its Olympic teams and athletes, usually based on the recommendations of the NGB for the particular sport. The NOCs also have the authority to designate which cities may apply to host the Olympics within their respective countries.

In carrying out their responsibilities, NOCs frequently cooperate with government agencies and other nongovernmental bodies to promote sports. However, they must preserve their autonomy and resist all pressures, including those of a political, religious, or economic nature, to do anything contrary to the Olympic Charter. The NOCs are subject to the laws of their respective nations as well as the provisions of the Olympic Charter and the governing authority of the IOC. For example, the USOC must comply with the Ted Stevens Olympic and Amateur Sports Act, 36 U.S.C. §§220501 et seq., and other applicable federal and state laws.

An NGB is the national governing authority for a particular sport that is affiliated with the appropriate IF and is recognized by the country's NOC. Athletes are members of their respective NGBs, which must comply with the Olympic Charter and IF rules. The NGBs serve a function at the national level similar to that of the IFs at the international level of athletic competition. Each NGB recognized by the USOC (e.g., USA Track & Field) serves as the United States' member representative in the IF for its particular sport (e.g., IAAF) and must comply with its rules as well as the Olympic Charter. Like NOCs, NGBs also are subject to applicable domestic laws within their respective countries.

The following diagram illustrates that a series of hierarchical contractual relationships defines the Olympic Movement's governing structure:

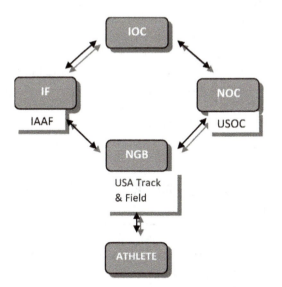

The IOC is responsible for ensuring the regular celebration of the Summer and Winter Olympic Games and exclusively owns all rights relating thereto. It selects a host city for each Olympic Games, which is entrusted with responsibility for organizing the Games along with the country's NOC, which forms an Organizing Committee for the Olympic Games (OCOG) to fulfill all responsibilities connected with the organization and hosting of the Olympic Games. The OCOG must fully comply with its contract with the IOC, NOC, and host city, as well as the Olympic Charter and the IOC Executive Board's instructions. All financial responsibility for staging the

Olympic Games is assumed jointly and severally by the OCOG and the host city. OCOGs have evolved into huge administrative entities, which are seemingly necessary to carry out the significant multiyear commitments necessary to successfully host the Olympic Games. An OCOG's governing body includes the IOC member(s) of the host country, the president and secretary general of the NOC, at least one representative of the host city, and various public authorities. In organizing the Olympic Games, an OCOG must treat every sport equally; abide by the IFs' rules of competition; ensure that no political demonstrations disrupt the Games; construct the necessary venues, stadiums, and other facilities; provide food and lodging for all athletes and officials; provide medical services; and accommodate the media. In addition, in light of recent world events, OCOGs now face the daunting task of ensuring the security of those competing in and attending the Games.

To participate in the Olympic Games, a competing athlete must satisfy several conditions, including being a national of the country of the IOC-recognized NOC that is entering him or her and complying with the Olympic Charter and applicable IF rules for the subject sport. All athletes must "respect the spirit of fair play and nonviolence and behave accordingly" on the sports field and fully comply with the World Anti-Doping Code. Olympic Charter, *supra*, Chap. 5, Rule 40. The charter states that "The Olympic Games are competitions between athletes in individual or team events, and not between countries. They bring together the athletes selected by their respective NOCs, whose entries have been accepted by the IOC. They compete under the technical direction of the IFs concerned." Olympic Charter, *supra*, Chap. 1, Rule 6(1). The IOC is the "authority of last resort on any question concerning the Olympic Games" (Olympic Charter, *supra*, Chap. 5, Rule 58), although those adversely affected by its decision may submit the dispute to final and binding arbitration before the CAS. Despite its plenary governing authority, the IOC must rely on the agreement of the IFs and NOCs — and the willingness of national governments — to enforce its decisions and those of the CAS.

REGULATION OF OLYMPIC SPORTS WITHIN THE UNITED STATES

Participation in the Olympics, the Paralympic Games, and other international athletic competitions is an important part of U.S. culture. Since the modern Olympic Games began in 1896, the United States has hosted the Games of the Olympiad in 1904 (St. Louis), 1932 (Los Angeles), 1984 (Los Angeles), and 1996 (Atlanta); and the Winter Olympic Games in 1932 (Lake Placid), 1960 (Squaw Valley), 1980 (Lake Placid), and 2002 (Salt Lake City). The United States has entered teams each year that the Olympic Games have been held with the exception of 1980, when it boycotted the Moscow Games to protest the Soviet Union's military invasion of Afghanistan. Since 1896, U.S. athletes and teams have won 2,400 medals in the Summer Games (976 gold, 758 silver, and 666 bronze) and 281 medals in the Winter Games (96 gold, 102 silver, and 83 bronze).

- De novo arbitral review
- Ted Stevens Olympic and Amateur Sports Act (ASA)
- United States Olympic Committee (USOC)
- State action

The USOC is authorized by the IOC to represent the United States in all matters relating to its participation in the Olympic Games. It is a federally chartered corporation created by Congress that must comply with the Ted Stevens Olympic and Amateur Sports Act (ASA), 36 U.S.C. §220501 et seq., a federal law that provides a framework for governing Olympic sports in the U.S. It has a statutory obligation to ensure "the most competent representation possible" for the U.S. in each event of the Olympic, Paralympic, and Pan-American Games. 36 U.S.C. §220503(4). Its mission is "[t]o support United States Olympic and Paralympic athletes in achieving sustained competitive excellence while demonstrating the values of the Olympic Movement, thereby inspiring all Americans." United States Olympic Committee, Bylaws of the United States Olympic Committee, §2.1 (effective April 8, 2014), available at *http:// www.teamusa.org/Footer/Legal/Governance-Documents*.

Athletes have no federal constitutional right to participate in the Olympic Games (or any other international sports competitions). In *DeFrantz v. United States Olympic Committee*, 492 F. Supp. 1181 (D.D.C. 1980), a group of athletes selected to be members of the U.S. Olympic team sought injunctive relief enabling them to compete in the 1980 Moscow Olympic Games. The Jimmy Carter administration urged a boycott of the Moscow Games to protest the Soviet Union's 1979 invasion of Afghanistan. Faced with political pressure from the federal government, threatened legal action by President Carter, and the possible loss of its federal funding and federal tax exemption, the USOC decided not to enter a U.S. team in the Moscow Games. The court found that under IOC rules, the USOC has the exclusive and discretionary authority to decide whether to enter a U.S. team in Olympic competition. The court held that, despite being federally chartered, the USOC is a private organization; therefore, its conduct is not "state action" subject to the constraints of the U.S. Constitution. Even if the USOC's decision constituted state action, the court ruled that athletes have no federal constitutional right to participate in the Olympic Games. The court also held that the USOC's decision does not violate the ASA, which gave it the exclusive authority to determine whether the United States would participate in the Olympic Games.

The ASA authorizes the USOC to select the NGB for each Olympic sport within the United States. The USOC typically grants the recognized NGB for each sport the exclusive right to select athletes to participate in the Olympic Games and other international athletic competitions, and its eligibility and participation criteria for U.S. athletes must be consistent with those of the IF for its sport. An NGB must provide all athletes with an equal opportunity to participate in competitions "without discrimination on the basis of race, color, religion, sex, age, or national origin" (36 U.S.C. §220522(a)(8)). Each NGB has an affirmative duty to encourage and support athletic participation opportunities for women and those with disabilities. 36 U.S.C. §220524(6)-(7). An NGB has plenary domestic authority to regulate Olympic and other international athletic competition in a sport, but it has no authority to regulate high school or college athletic competition (36 U.S.C. §220526(a)) or professional sports in the United States.

The NGBs have wide latitude to select athletes for their teams, as well as to discipline athletes for misconduct (which may give rise to disputes if an athlete is precluded from participation in an Olympic or international sport event) pursuant to their respective internal team selection and disciplinary procedures. However, NGBs must follow and apply their own rules consistently and provide athletes with a fair opportunity to be heard if disputes arise. *Harding v. U.S. Figure Skating Assn.*, 851 F. Supp. 1476 (D. Or. 1994), *vacated on other grounds*, 879 F. Supp. 1053 (D. Or. 1995). As a condition of being recognized as an NGB, it must agree to submit to final and binding arbitration to resolve athlete eligibility disputes as required by the ASA.

The ASA states that the USOC "shall establish and maintain provisions in its constitution and bylaws for the swift and equitable resolution of disputes involving any of its members and relating to the opportunity of an amateur athlete, coach, trainer, manager, administrator, or official to participate in the Olympic Games, the Paralympic Games, the Pan-American Games, world championship competition, or other protected competition. . . . " 36 U.S.C. §220509(a). It also requires the USOC to hire an ombudsman to provide independent advice to athletes at no cost in connection with disputes regarding their eligibility to participate in Olympic and international athletic competition. The ombudsman also provides advice and guidance to attorneys representing Olympic sport athletes in eligibility disputes.

The ASA does not create any substantive participation rights that athletes can enforce in a private litigation against the USOC or an NGB. Courts have ruled that athletes have no private right of action under the ASA and will not order the USOC or an NGB to compete in the Olympic Games or other international sports events. See, e.g., *Martinez v. USOC*, 802 F2d 1275 (10th Cir. 1986); *Oldfield v. Athletic Congress*, 779 F.2d 505 (9th Cir. 1985). As Judge Richard Posner remarked, "there can be few less suitable bodies than the federal courts for determining the eligibility, or the procedures for determining the eligibility, of athletes to participate in the Olympic Games." *Michels v. USOC*, 741 F.2d 155, 159 (7th Cir. 1984).

Consistent with this view, federal courts have held that the ASA immunizes an NGB from antitrust liability for rules and decisions that adversely affect an athlete's eligibility to participate in a protected competition. In *Behagen v. Amateur Basketball Ass'n of United States*, 884 F.2d 524, 529 (10th Cir. 1989), the Tenth Circuit noted that the statute expressly authorizes only one NGB to represent the United States within each IF and to recommend to the USOC individual athletes and teams in the sports that it governs. It ruled that implied antitrust immunity is necessary because "[t]he Act makes clear that Congress intended an NGB to exercise monolithic control over its particular amateur sport, including coordinating with the appropriate international sports federation and controlling amateur eligibility for Americans that participate in sport."

Section 9 of the USOC's Bylaws creates some important procedural and substantive rights for an "amateur athlete," (i.e., any athlete who meets the eligibility standards established by an NGB or Paralympic Sports Organization for the sport in which the athlete competes), which includes professional athletes who now are eligible to participate in the Olympic Games and other international sports competitions. No

NGB may deny any amateur athlete the opportunity to participate in the Olympic Games, the Pan-American Games, Paralympic Games, a world championship competition, or other protected competitions without appropriate justification. The USOC is required to "by all reasonable means, protect the opportunity of an amateur athlete to participate if selected (or to attempt to qualify for selection to participate) as an athlete representing the United States in any of the aforesaid competitions." The USOC must "seek information from the parties as to the merits of the complaint, and determine whether the complaint can be resolved to the satisfaction of the parties."

The ASA gives an amateur athlete the right to submit an eligibility dispute to final and binding arbitration in accordance with the Commercial Rules of the American Arbitration Association (AAA) if it is not resolved by the USOC to his or her satisfaction, with an expedited procedure available if necessary. The athlete must submit a list of persons that he or she believes may be adversely affected by the arbitration (e.g., other athletes). The dispute, which is an arbitration proceeding between the athlete and the NGB, is resolved by a single impartial arbitrator (usually an attorney, retired judge, sports law professor, or other individual familiar with the particular sport). The AAA arbitrator renders a reasoned award in writing, which is published on the USOC website after the parties are informed of the decision.

A court will provide only limited scrutiny of an AAA arbitration award affecting an amateur athlete's eligibility to participate in a sport, which is subject to review and enforcement under the Federal Arbitration Act, 9 U.S.C. §1 et seq. In *Gault v. United States Bobsled and Skeleton Federation*, 578 N.Y.S.2d 683, 685 (N.Y. App. Div. 1992), a New York appellate court explained: "[a]lthough we also may disagree with the arbitrator's award and find most unfortunate the increasing frequency with which sporting events are resolved in the courtroom, we have no authority to upset it when the arbitrator did not exceed his authority." However, a court will vacate or refuse to confirm an arbitration award that is "the result of 'corruption,' 'fraud,' 'evident partiality,' or any similar bar to confirmation." *Lindland v. U.S. Wrestling Ass'n, Inc.*, 227 F.3d 1000, 1003 (7th Cir. 2000).

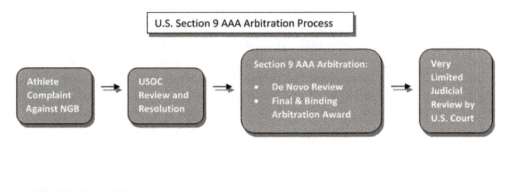

QUESTION

Why does the ASA require that athlete eligibility disputes be resolved by arbitration rather than litigation in court?

LIMITS ON THE USE OF NATIONAL LAW TO REGULATE OLYMPIC AND INTERNATIONAL ATHLETIC COMPETITION

KEY TERM
• United Nations Convention on the Recognition and Enforcement of Foreign Arbitral Awards, 9 U.S.C. §201 (New York Convention)

A U.S. court has no personal jurisdiction (i.e., valid authority to render a legally binding judgment against the defendant) over a nonresident international athletics governing body such as the IOC or an IF, unless the claims against it arise out of its activities within both the United States and the forum state. For example, in *Reynolds v. Int'l Amateur Athletic Federation,* 23 F.3d 1110 (6th Cir. 1994), the Sixth Circuit held that an Ohio court had no jurisdiction to hear American world-class sprinter Butch Reynolds's state law claims against the IAAF (then based in London), which alleged his positive drug test was erroneous (his urine sample was collected at an event in Monaco and tested in Paris). The merits of Reynolds's legal claims were resolved adversely to him in an IAAF arbitration proceeding that was held in London.

Even if there is personal jurisdiction over an international athletics governing body, American courts are very reluctant to apply the constraints of U.S. federal or state law to IOC or IF rules, which are the product of a private international agreement intended to provide for uniform, worldwide governance of sports.

For example, in *Martin v. IOC,* 740 F.2d 670 (9th Cir. 1984), the Ninth Circuit affirmed the denial of a preliminary injunction to require the organizers of the 1984 Los Angeles Summer Olympic Games to include 5,000- and 10,000-meter track events for women as already existed for men. The court rejected plaintiffs' claims that the failure to include these events constituted illegal gender discrimination, even though "the women runners made a strong showing that the early history of the modern Olympic Games was marred by blatant discrimination against women." *Id.* at 673. The majority explained, "[W]e find persuasive the argument that a court should be wary of applying a state statute to alter the content of the Olympic Games. The Olympic Games are organized and conducted under the terms of an international agreement—the Olympic Charter. We are extremely hesitant to undertake the application of one state's statute to alter an event that is staged with competitors from the entire world under the terms of that agreement." *Id.* at 677.

The dissenting judge argued:

The IOC made concessions to the widespread popularity of women's track and field by adding two distance races this year. The IOC refused, however, to grant women athletes equal status by including all events in which women compete internationally. In so doing, the IOC postpones indefinitely the equality of athletic opportunity that it could easily achieve this year in Los Angeles. When the Olympics move to other countries, some without America's commitment to human rights, the opportunity to tip the scales of justice in favor of equality may slip away. Meanwhile, the Olympic flame — which should be a symbol of harmony, equality, and justice — will burn less brightly over the Los Angeles Olympic Games.

Id. at 683.

American courts also have rejected state discrimination law claims by foreign athletes seeking to march in opening ceremonies in Olympic Games held in the United States under flags of countries not recognized by the IOC. See, e.g., *Spindulys v. Los Angeles Olympic Organizing Comm.*, 175 Cal. App. 3d 206, 220 Cal. Rptr. 565 (Cal. App. 1985).

QUESTION

Is it appropriate for courts to refuse to apply laws prohibiting discrimination to Olympic and other international sports events held in the United States?

· · · · · · · · ·

As previously discussed, the USOC and its NGBs are required to adopt, apply, and enforce IOC and IF rules that determine or affect American athletes' eligibility to qualify for, or participate in, Olympic or other international sports competitions. For example, the USOC and NGBs must comply with the IOC Charter's athlete eligibility requirements and antidiscrimination provisions protecting athlete participation opportunities. They also must comply with CAS awards resolving issues concerning the eligibility of American athletes that arise in connection with the Olympic Games or in disputes with an IF or WADA. Arbitration before the CAS generally is the agreed forum for resolving eligibility disputes between a U.S. athlete and the IOC or an IF.

The The New York Convention on the Enforcement of Foreign Arbitration Awards, 9 U.S.C. §201 et seq., a treaty to which the United States is a party, requires U.S. courts to recognize and enforce valid foreign arbitration awards, including CAS awards that the USOC, an NGB, or athletes are parties thereto. In *Slaney v. IAAF*, 244 F.3d 580 (7th Cir. 2001), the Seventh Circuit held that a valid foreign arbitration award precludes an American athlete from relitigating the merits of an eligibility dispute in a U.S. court. The court concluded that "[o]ur judicial system is not meant to provide a second bite at the apple for those who have sought adjudication of their disputes in other forums and are not content with the resolution they received." *Id.* at 592. Moreover, a U.S. court may be unable to provide effective relief to an American athlete whose eligibility to participate in sports competition is adversely affected by an IOC or IF rule or decision because its judicial authority is not binding on foreign sports governing bodies outside its jurisdiction. See, e.g., *Michels v. USOC*, 741 F.2d 155, 159 (7th Cir. 1984) (noting that an IF "can thumb its collective nose" at the USOC and ask the IOC to disqualify the entire U.S. Olympic weightlifting team if the USOC placed an athlete suspended by the IF on the team).

Problem 14-1

Andy is a junior at Aquatic State University and the National Collegiate Athletic Association (NCAA) champion in the 100-meter butterfly swimming event. In the recently completed Olympic Trials conducted under the auspices of United States Swimming, Inc. (USS), he finished fourth in this event, only 0.01 second behind the third-place finisher. He failed to make the United States Olympic team because only the top three finishers qualify for this event. Andy believes that the winner of this event used an "illegal kick" during the race and should have been disqualified. He promptly filed a complaint with the USS race officials overseeing this event, which was rejected within one hour after the race ended. The USS's governing body denied his appeal. Andy sues the USS, the USOC, and the IOC and seeks a court order enabling him to participate in the upcoming Olympic Games, which will be held in the United States, as a member of the United States Olympic team in this event. Is he likely to be successful?

COURT OF ARBITRATION FOR SPORT

A. Overview

KEY TERMS
- CAS Ad Hoc Division
- CAS appeals arbitration
- CAS ordinary arbitration
- Code of Sports-Related Arbitration
- Court of Arbitration for Sport (CAS)
- De novo arbitral review
- International Council of Arbitration and Sport (ICAS)
- Lexsportiva
- Swiss Federal Tribunal

There are potential jurisdictional problems as well as inherent difficulties with attempting to apply a specific country's laws to the rules and enforcement activities of international sports organizations such as the IOC and the numerous IFs whose governing authority is exercised worldwide. Courts generally do not provide an ideal forum for resolving Olympic and international sports disputes and are understandably reluctant to regulate athletic competition by judicial decree, but a rising tide of disputes generated the need for an independent international tribunal with final and binding authority to resolve them.

In 1983, the IOC established the CAS, which is based in Lausanne, Switzerland, and subject to Swiss law. The CAS was formed to resolve legal disputes in sports quickly and inexpensively. Its creation recognizes the need for international sport's governance to be uniform and protective of the integrity of athletics competition, while also safeguarding all athletes' legitimate rights and adhering to fundamental principles of natural justice. The CAS "provides a forum for the world's athletes and sports federations to resolve their disputes through a single, independent and accomplished sports adjudication body that is capable of consistently applying the rules of different sports organizations. . . . " Richard H. McLaren, *The Court of Arbitration for Sport: An Independent Arena for the World's Sports Disputes*, 35 Val. U. L. Rev. 379, 381 (2001). It is "a unifying institution that can help deliver sport back to its origins . . . [and] ensures fairness and integrity in sport through sound legal control and the administration of diverse laws and philosophies." *Id.*

Despite its designation as a "court," CAS is actually an arbitral tribunal. CAS arbitrators have legal training and recognized competence in the field of sport and/or international arbitration. Like other arbitral bodies, CAS jurisdiction is dependent on the parties' written agreement to submit their dispute to CAS for final adjudication. Courts will enforce a written agreement to arbitrate before CAS, which bars litigation arising out of the subject dispute in a judicial forum. The IOC and all Olympic IFs have agreed to CAS jurisdiction. By rule, the IFs require their respective member NGBs and athletes to submit all disputes with the IF to CAS arbitration.

In 1994, the structure and operation of the CAS were modified in several major respects to make it independent from the IOC and more efficient. The International Council of Arbitration and Sport (ICAS), a group of 20 high-level jurists, was created to oversee the CAS and appoint its members, thereby removing these roles from the IOC's auspices. The IOC and other international sports organizations continue to fund the operations of ICAS and the CAS, but they do not govern or administer either organization. The ICAS administers the basic operations of the CAS and manages its funds, and its president also serves as the CAS president.

Currently, there are approximately 300 CAS arbitrators (including 30 from the United States) representative of the world's continents, and they are appointed by the ICAS for four-year renewable terms. They must have legal training and knowledge of sport, be fluent in either English or French (the two official languages of the CAS), be objective and independent in their decisions, and adhere to a duty of confidentiality.

The CAS *ordinary arbitration procedure* is used to resolve sports-related commercial disputes such as sponsorship contracts, television rights to sports event, and contracts between athletes and their agents. These proceedings usually are confidential and private and do not result in the publication of an award by the CAS.

The CAS *appeals arbitration procedure* is used to resolve appeals from final decisions of sports federations (requiring the exhaustion of all available internal administrative remedies) involving matters such as doping, discipline for misconduct, athlete eligibility issues, or competition results. Each party selects one arbitrator, and the president of the Appeals Arbitration Procedure appoints the third arbitrator who serves as the president of the panel. CAS rules provide for these cases to be decided within three months after the case file is transferred to the CAS panel handling the case, and they generally result in a published award.

The CAS Ad Hoc Division operates at the site of each Olympic Games to provide for expedited resolution of all disputes arising during the Games or during a period of ten days preceding the Games Opening Ceremony (e.g., nationality requirements or doping violations). All disputes are resolved by a panel of three arbitrators from a pool of CAS arbitrators specifically chosen by the ICAS for the Olympic Games. Their decision, which must be written and provide reasons, generally must be rendered within 24 hours of the filing of a request for CAS adjudication. See generally Richard H. McLaren, *Introducing the Court of Arbitration for Sport: The Ad Hoc Division at the Olympic Games*, 12 Marq. Sports L. Rev. 517 (2001).

The Code of Sports-Related Arbitration (Code) governs the organization, operations, and procedures of the ICAS and the CAS. See *http://www.tas-cas.org/en/arbitration/code-procedural-rules.html*. In any CAS proceeding, all parties may be represented by counsel. The parties must follow the CAS's procedural rules and time limits for bringing claims as set forth in the Code. In both appeals arbitration and Ad Hoc Division proceedings, CAS panels independently decide the parties' dispute on the merits.

A CAS arbitration award resolves the subject dispute, orders appropriate relief (including damages and allocation of costs), and is final and binding on the parties. CAS panels frequently cite and rely on prior awards. CAS arbitration awards are creating a body of Olympic and international sports law, a so-called *lex sportiva*. See generally James A.R. Nafziger, International Sports Law at 48–61 (2d ed., Transnational 2004). Matthieu Reeb, the CAS secretary general, publishes digests of CAS Ad Hoc Division and appeals arbitration awards, and there is an index and database of nonconfidential CAS awards on the CAS website at *http://www.tas-cas.org*.

The CAS currently has branches in New York City and Sydney, Australia. Regardless of its physical location, the "seat" of all CAS arbitrations is always considered to be Lausanne, Switzerland. This ensures uniform procedural rules for all CAS arbitrations, which provides a stable legal framework and facilitates efficient dispute resolution in locations convenient for the parties.

A CAS award may be challenged before the Swiss Federal Tribunal, Switzerland's highest court, under the Swiss Federal Code on Private International Law of December 18, 1987. However, Article 190(2) of the Code provides only very limited grounds for vacating an arbitration award such as incompetence or irregularity of the arbitration panel; if the award is outside the CAS's jurisdiction or did not decide a claim; if the parties' rights to be heard and treated equally were violated; or if the award is incompatible with Swiss public policy. See *Matuzalem v. FIFA*, 4A_558/2011 (1st Civil Court, March 27, 2012) at 6 (CAS "substantive adjudication of a dispute violates public policy only when it disregards some fundamental legal principles and consequently becomes completely inconsistent with the important, generally recognized values, which according to dominant opinions in Switzerland should be the basis of any legal order"). Because a CAS award is a foreign arbitration award (i.e., it is always a Swiss award, regardless of where the CAS arbitration occurred), it may be judicially confirmed and enforced by a U.S. court pursuant to the New York Convention treaty.

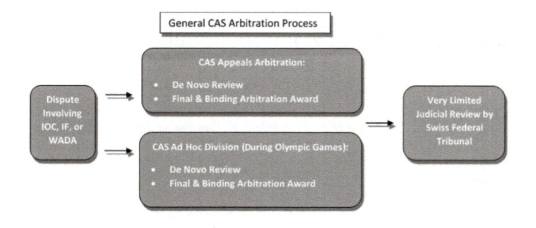

B. Disputed Competition Results

During the 2004 Athens Olympics, American Paul Hamm came from twelfth place to win the gold medal in men's all-around gymnastics when he earned scores of 9.837 in both the parallel bars and the high bar, the competition's final two events. However, judges incorrectly deducted one-tenth of a point from the start value of South Korean gymnast Yang Tae-Young's parallel bars routine. Because of this error, Yang received a lower score for his routine. Yang's final overall score was 0.049 point behind Hamm, which resulted in his winning the bronze medal rather than the gold medal.

The Korean Olympic Committee (KOC) protested the start value attributed to Yang's parallel bars routine because it was lower than he had previously received for the same routine in the gymnastics team and qualifying competitions. Acknowledging this error, the International Gymnastics Federation (FIG) suspended the three judges responsible for incorrectly determining the start value of Yang's routine.

The IOC refused to issue duplicate gold medals to both Hamm and Yang, as proposed by KOC and the USOC. However, IOC president Jacques Rogge stated that the IOC would respect a request by FIG to correct the error in Yang's score and to reallocate the medals for the men's all-around gymnastics competition. FIG, however, refused to change the competition results or award a duplicate gold medal to Yang because a timely protest on his behalf had not been made to the appropriate official in charge of the competition's judging.

FIG subsequently attempted to send a letter to Hamm stating that Yang was the "true winner" of this event because of the judges' scoring error. FIG's letter suggested that Hamm's voluntary decision to return his gold medal would be regarded "as the ultimate demonstration of fair play by the whole world." The USOC rejected FIG's proposal and refused to forward the letter to Hamm.

In the following case, Yang and the KOC petitioned the CAS to correct the judging error and to rule that Yang was entitled to receive the gold medal in the men's all-around gymnastics competition.

Yang Tae Young v. International Gymnastics Federation

Arbitration CAS 2004/A/704, Award of October 21, 2004

Panel: The Hon. Michael Beloff (England); Mr. Dirk-Reiner Martens (Germany); Mr. Sharad Rao (Kenya).

[Editors' note: In gymnastics, an individual competitor's score is awarded by a combination of start values based on the degree of difficulty in a particular routine and on execution as determined by FIG's Code of Points. The primary purpose of this Code is to provide an objective means of evaluating gymnastics exercises, and each gymnast "has the right [t]o have his performance judged correctly, fairly, and in accordance with the stipulations of the Code of Points."

Unlike sports such as diving, an evaluation of the start value of a gymnastics routine is not made before its performance because gymnasts will frequently modify a planned routine in response to competitive circumstances or will fail to execute a planned element. The judges' assessment of start values is in part subjective and in part objective. Elements that make up start values, such as a *belle* or a *morisue,* are objectively identified. Whether any element has been fully performed is a matter of subjective judgment. In this case, the three judges responsible for determining the start value of Yang's parallel bars routine erroneously characterized a belle as a morisue, giving him a start value of 9.9 rather than 10. Video analysis confirmed that Yang's start value should have been 10.]

The extent to which, if at all, a Court including CAS can interfere with an official's decision is not wholly clear. An absolute refusal to recognize such a decision as justiciable and to designate the field of play as *"a domain into which the King's writ does not seek to run"* in Lord Atkin's famous phrase would have a defensible purpose and philosophy. It would recognize that there are areas of human activity which elude the grasp of the law, and where the solution to disputes is better found, if at all, by agreement. It would contribute to finality. It would uphold, critically, the authority of the umpire, judge or referee, whose power to control competition, already eroded by the growing use of technology such as video replays, would be fatally undermined if every decision taken could be judicially reviewed. And, to the extent that the matter is capable of analysis in conventional legal terms, it could rest on the premise that any contract that the player has made in entering into a competition is that he or she should have the benefit of honest "field of play" decisions, not necessarily correct ones.

Sports law does not, however, have a policy of complete abstention. In *Mendy v. AIBA,* where the challenge was to a referee's decision to disqualify a boxer for a low blow (CAS OG 96/06), the CAS ad hoc Panel accepted jurisdiction, even over a game rule, but considered it inappropriate to exercise it. It said:

> [T]he referee's decision, is a purely technical one pertaining to the rules which are the responsibility of the federation concerned. It is not for the ad hoc Panel to

review the application of these rules. This restraint is all the more necessary since, far from where the action took place, the ad hoc Panel is less well-placed to decide than the referee in the ring or the ring judges. The above-mentioned restraint must be limited to technical decisions or standards; it does not apply when such decisions are taken in violation of the law, social rules, or general principles of law, which is not the case in this particular instance. . . .

In short, courts may interfere only if an official's field of play decision is tainted by fraud or arbitrariness or corruption; otherwise although a Court may have jurisdiction, it will abstain as a matter of policy from exercising it. . . .

While in this instance we are being asked, not to second guess an official but rather to consider the consequences of an admitted error by an official so that the "field of play" jurisprudence is not directly engaged, we consider that we should nonetheless abstain from correcting the results by reliance of an admitted error. An error identified with the benefit of hindsight, whether admitted or not, cannot be a ground for reversing a result of a competition. We can all recall occasions where a video replay of a football match, studied at leisure, can show that a goal was given, when it should have been disallowed (the Germans may still hold that view about England's critical third goal in the World Cup Final in 1966), or vice versa, or where in a tennis match a critical line call was mistaken. However, quite apart from the consideration, which we develop below, that no one can be certain how the competition in question would have turned out had the official's decision been different, for a Court to change the result would on this basis still involve interfering with a field of play decision. Each sport may have within it a mechanism for utilising modern technology to ensure a correct decision is made in the first place (e.g., cricket with run-outs) or for immediately subjecting a controversial decision to a process of review (e.g., gymnastics) but the solution for error, either way, lies within the framework of the sport's own rules; it does not licence judicial or arbitral interference thereafter. If this represents an extension of the field of play doctrine, we tolerate it with equanimity. Finality is in this area all important: rough justice may be all that sport can tolerate. . . .

There is another and powerful consideration, well articulated on behalf of Hamm. Had the competition been on one apparatus only, i.e., the parallel bars, then the conclusion that the judging error led to a disarray in the medal positions would follow as night follows day. (We put on one side the contention . . . that Yang had the benefit of the error—a failure by AB Judges to deduct points for a gymnastic fault exceeding the stipulated number of pauses during his exercise. . . .) But the event was not a single apparatus event, but an all around one.

After the parallel bars, there was one more apparatus on which the competitors had to perform, i.e., the high bar. We have no means of knowing how Yang would have reacted had he concluded the competition in this apparatus as the points leader rather than in third position. He might have risen to the occasion; he might have frozen (his marks on the high bar were in fact below expectation and speculation is inappropriate.) So it needs to be clearly stated that while the error *may* have cost Yang a gold medal, it did not necessarily do so. . . .

There are two victims of this unusual sequence of events, Hamm and Yang. Hamm because, as he eloquently explained, a shadow of doubt has been cast over his achievement in winning the sport's most prestigious prize. Yang because he may have been deprived of an opportunity of winning it. Both Hamm and Yang are superb athletes at the pinnacle of their sport: neither was in any way responsible for the Judge's error: each has comported himself with dignity which this controversy has subsisted. Nonetheless the Court of Arbitration is not Solomon: nor can it mediate a solution acceptable to both gymnasts or their respective NOCs. CAS must give a verdict based on its findings of fact viewed in the context of the relevant law.

For the reasons set out above, we dismiss this appeal.

NOTE

Governing body legal duty to follow competition rules. Even if rules provide that athletics governing body's final determination of competition results is not appealable, "CAS will always have jurisdiction to overrule the Rules of any sport federation if its decision making bodies conduct themselves with a lack of good faith or not in accordance with due process." Arbitration CAS Ad Hoc Division (O.G. Athens 2004) 009, *Hellenic Olympic Committee and NikolaosKaklamanakis v. International Sailing Federation*, award of August 24, 2004. The CAS has ruled that a sports governing body must comply with and consistently apply objective criteria established by its rules such as time or points earned by competition results when selecting athletes for a team or event.

Problem 14-2

During the 2002 Olympics, by a 5-4 judges' decision, a Russian pairs figure-skating team won the gold medal despite making a few technical errors, while the silver medalist Canadian team skated flawlessly. Shortly thereafter, the French competition judge claimed that the French skating federation president had pressured her to vote for the Russians. Based on a recommendation from the ISU, the IOC's executive board voted to also award gold medals to the Canadian team. Because there was no evidence of any Russian involvement in the matter, the Russian team members were permitted to keep their gold medals. (Note: Although the French judge later recanted her accusation, the ISU suspended her and the French federation president for three years plus the 2006 Olympics. This scandal also led the ISU to change its methods of judging skaters' performances.) If the IOC had allowed the initial competition results to stand, should the Canadian team have prevailed in an appeal to the CAS?

C. Doping Violations and Sanctions

 • Principle of proportionality
• Strict liability
• Therapeutic use exemption (TUE)

1. Strict Liability Standard, Clear Notice Requirements, and Proportionate Sanctions

As a policy matter, CAS has upheld a sport's governing body's adoption and use of a strict liability standard (i.e., liability without any personal fault) for doping offenses. In *USA Shooting and Q. v. Int'l Shooting Union (Quigley)*, Arbitration CAS 94/129, Award of May 23, 1995, in Matthieu Reeb, *Digest of CAS Awards 1986–1998* (1998) at 187, the CAS stated:

> It is true that a strict liability test is likely in some sense to be unfair in an individual case, such as that of Q., where the athlete may have taken medication as the result of mislabelling or faulty advice for which he or she is not responsible — particularly in the circumstances of sudden illness in a foreign country. But it is also in some sense "unfair" for an athlete to get food poisoning on the eve of an important competition. Yet in neither case will the rules of the competition be altered to undo the unfairness. Just as the competition will not be postponed to await the athlete's recovery, so the prohibition of banned substances will not be lifted in recognition of its accidental absorption. The vicissitudes of competition, like those of life generally, may create many types of unfairness, whether by accident or the negligence of unaccountable persons, which the law cannot repair.
>
> Furthermore, it appears to be a laudable policy objective not to repair an accidental unfairness to an individual by creating an intentional unfairness to the whole body of other competitors. This is what would happen if banned performance-enhancing substances were tolerated when absorbed inadvertently. Moreover, it is likely that even intentional abuse would in many cases escape sanction for lack of proof of guilty intent. And it is certain that a requirement of intent would invite costly litigation that may well cripple federations — particularly those run on modest budgets — in their fight against doping.

Id. at 193.

In *Quigley*, CAS stated that doping rules must provide clear notice to protect athletes' legitimate expectations. It explained that if a strict liability test is adopted, "it becomes even more important that the rules for the testing procedure are crystal clear, that they are designed for reliability, and that it may be shown that they have been followed." Moreover, "as a general matter, if breaches of specific requirements laid down by a federation for the testing procedure are sufficiently material as to call into question the validity and correctness of the positive result, any athlete would be entitled to have that federation's decision overturned." The CAS panel ruled that the athlete, who tested positive for a banned stimulant in medication prescribed by a physician for bronchitis while competing in a skeet shooting competition in Egypt, did not commit a doping violation because the IF rule defined doping as the use of a banned substance "with the aim of attaining an increase in performance." The language of this rule did not clearly articulate a strict liability standard for doping offenses.

The CAS Ad Hoc division for the 2000 Summer Olympics in Sydney, Australia, upheld clearly defined IOC strict liability doping rules requiring Romanian gymnast Andreea Raducan to forfeit her gold medal in the women's individual all-around competition in artistic gymnastics. She tested positive for pseudoephedrine, a banned substance, after taking a cold and flu tablet prescribed by the Romanian gymnastics team doctor on the day she competed in this event. CAS ruled that this doping violation justified the stripping of her gold medal "as a matter of fairness to all other athletes." Raducan did not challenge the identity or integrity of her urine sample or the validity of its analysis, but she pointed out a discrepancy between the recorded total volume of her collected urine sample (62 ml) and that which arrived at the laboratory (80 ml in the A sample, and 20 ml in the B sample). The CAS ruled that "the minor irregularity revealed in the record showing the volume of urine taken cannot reasonably be considered to have affected the results of what is a valid test." It also rejected her claimed defenses that pseudoephedrine impaired (rather than enhanced) her athletic performance, that heavier athletes would not produce positive test results if taking the same dosage of the drug as she did, and that she is a 16-year-old minor who should not be found guilty of doping under these circumstances. Arbitration CAS Ad Hoc Division (O.S. Sydney 2000) 011, *Andreea Raducan v. International Olympic Committee (IOC)*, award of 28 September, 2000, in CAS Awards-Sydney: The Decisions Delivered by the Ad Hoc Division of the Court of Arbitration for Sport During the 2000 Olympic Games in Sydney (2000), at 111.

In *Chagnaud v. FINA*, Arbitration CAS 95/141, Award of April 22, 1996, CAS stated that sports governing bodies "should make allowance for an appreciation of the subjective elements in each case" in order to determine "a just and equitable sanction." Rather than a fixed minimum sanction for all doping offenses (e.g., a two-year suspension), the CAS panel expressed its preference for "a sliding scale of suspension periods depending on the degree of fault of the athlete." Applying this principle of proportionality, it reduced a swimmer's suspension from the two-year period provided by FINA's rules to approximately 13½ months because her coach mistakenly gave her a tablet, which she did not know contained a banned substance, shortly before an event.

QUESTION

Do you agree with the CAS panel's *Andreea Raducan* decision? (Note that Olympic athletes have the ability to seek prior approval to take a needed medication, a therapeutic use exemption (TUE) process not utilized by Raducan.)

2. Interpretation and Application of the World Anti-Doping Code

KEY TERMS
- International Convention Against Doping in Sport
- No fault or negligence
- No significant fault or negligence
- U.S. Anti-Doping Agency (USADA)
- World Anti-Doping Agency (WADA)
- World Anti-Doping Code (WADA Code)

On November 10, 1999, the World Anti-Doping Agency (WADA), an international collaborative effort between governments and sports organizations to combat doping in sport, was established in Lausanne, Switzerland. Its purpose is to promote harmonization and equity for athlete drug testing as well as to establish common and effective minimum standards for doping controls, especially for out-of-competition tests, and uniform sanctions for doping.

On March 5, 2003, at the World Conference on Doping in Sport held in Copenhagen, Denmark, almost 80 national governments (including the United States) and all of the major international sports federations approved the first World Anti-Doping Code (WADA Code). This code seeks to harmonize regulations regarding anti-doping across all sports and all countries of the world. It is described as "a core document that will provide a framework for anti-doping policies, rules and regulations within sport organizations and among public authorities."

The WADA Code, which became effective on January 1, 2004, establishes a uniform system of drug-testing procedures and fixes sanctions for violations, which may be reduced in "exceptional circumstances" if the athlete bears "no fault or no negligence" or "no significant fault or no significant negligence." Virtually all international sports federations now have adopted and implemented the code, which applies to their respective NGBs and athletes. Two revised versions of the WADA Code became effective on January 1, 2009, and January 1, 2015, respectively.

In July 2008, the U.S. Senate ratified the International Convention Against Doping in Sport adopted by the United Nations Educational, Scientific, and Cultural Organization on October 19, 2005, which is based on the WADA Code. On August 4, 2008, shortly before the Beijing Olympics began, President George W. Bush signed the treaty's instrument of ratification. Countries must ratify this treaty to be permitted to host future Olympic Games. It is important to understand that the NCAA and U.S. professional sports leagues and their respective athletes, which are not members of an international sports federation or currently directly regulated by the federal government, are not automatically subject to the WADA Code. In accordance with federal labor law, doping regimes for unionized professional sports leagues are established by collective bargaining. See Chapter 12. However, all U.S. athletes must agree to comply with the WADA Code as a condition of competing in the Olympic Games or other international sports competitions governed by it.

The U.S. Anti-Doping Agency (USADA) was formed in 2000 and is an independent private anti-doping agency for Olympic sports in the United States. USADA, which is not subject to the control of the USOC, currently provides drug education, conducts drug testing of U.S. athletes, investigates positive results, and recommends charges and sanctions for violations. Its website is *http://www .usantidoping.org*. USADA handles the initial adjudication procedure that an IF requires its U.S. member NGB to undertake when a U.S. athlete tests positive for a banned substance. See generally Travis T. Tygart, *Winners Never Dope and Finally, Dopers Never Win: USADA Takes over Drug Testing of United States Olympic Athletes*, 1 DePaul J. Sports L. & Contemp. Probs. 124 (2003).

Applying the IF's rules (which are based on the WADA Code), a USADA review board considers written submissions to determine whether there is sufficient evidence of doping to warrant a hearing. If so, USADA proposes doping charges and sanctions against the athlete that are consistent with the IF's rules. If the athlete does not accept USADA's proposed sanction, he or she may request a hearing before an AAA panel (a right provided by the ASA), whose members are also U.S. CAS arbitrators. In the AAA arbitration proceeding, USADA and the athlete are adverse parties. The IF may observe the proceeding or participate as a party. The athlete, the IF, or WADA may appeal the AAA arbitration award to the CAS, whose decision is final and binding. (This is a unique procedure that applies only to AAA doping awards because an arbitration award generally cannot be appealed to and reconsidered by another panel of different arbitrators.) For example, in a widely publicized case, an AAA panel upheld a USADA doping charge against Floyd Landis, the winner of the 2006 Tour de France bicycle race, based on a French laboratory's finding of exogenous testosterone in his urine. Although Landis proved that the French lab deviated from the international standards for laboratory analysis, USADA proved to the comfortable satisfaction of the panel that the lab's departure from the standards did not cause the positive test results. *USADA v. Landis*, AAA 30 190 00847 06 (Sept. 20, 2007). The CAS rejected Landis's appeal of the AAA award.

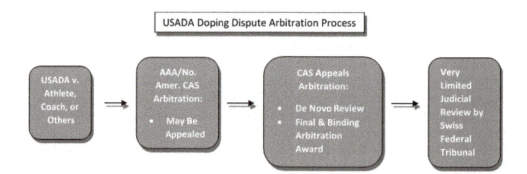

USADA Doping Dispute Arbitration Process

USADA v. Athlete, Coach, or Others → AAA/No. Amer. CAS Arbitration: • May Be Appealed → CAS Appeals Arbitration: • De Novo Review • Final & Binding Arbitration Award → Very Limited Judicial Review by Swiss Federal Tribunal

Armstrong v. Tygart, 886 F.Supp.2d 572 (W.D. Tex. 2012) arose out of USADA's July 2012 charges that Lance Armstrong, although he had not tested positive for a banned substance, had committed several antidoping rule violations and had been involved in a doping conspiracy with five others that began in January 1998 and continued until he retired from cycling in 2009. It sought to invalidate all of his competition results from August 1, 1998 (including his seven Tour de France cycling titles) to the present and to impose a lifetime period of ineligibility for future competitions sanctioned by sports governing bodies that are signatories to the WADA Code.

The court rejected Armstrong's allegations that the USADA arbitration procedures violated his federal constitutional due process rights and concluded that "the USADA arbitration rules, which largely follow those of the American Arbitration Association (AAA), are sufficiently robust to satisfy the requirements of due process." *Id.* at 584. Observing that "Armstrong is asking a court of the United States to decide matters which are designed to be resolved by, and with direct input from, members of the international community," the court stated, "[F]ederal courts should not interfere with an amateur sports organization's disciplinary procedures unless the organization shows wanton disregard for its rules, to the immediate and irreparable harm of a plaintiff, where the plaintiff has no other available remedy. To hold otherwise would be to turn federal judges into referees for a game in which they have no place, and about which they know little." *Id.* at 586.

Thereafter, Armstrong refused to participate in the USADA arbitration process, and USADA imposed the foregoing sanctions.

The following case provides an example of how the CAS has interpreted and applied the "exceptional circumstances" provisions of the WADA Code, which must be proven by an athlete to justify a reduction in the standard sanction for a doping offense.

Guillermo Cañas v. ATP Tour
Arbitration CAS 2005/A/951, Revised Award of 23 May 2007

Panel: Ms Maidie Oliveau (USA); Mr Christopher Campbell (USA); Mr Yves Fortier (Canada)

[Editors' note: Guillermo Cañas is a tennis professional from Argentina who has been a member of the ATP Tour since 1995 and a member of the ATP's Player Council since 2004. The respondent, ATP Tour, is a not-for-profit membership organization composed of male professional tennis players and tournament organizations. The ATP sanctions tennis tournaments and provides league governance and support to its member tournaments and players.

Cañas provided a urine specimen during an ATP-sanctioned tournament in Acapulco, Mexico, on February 21, 2005. He tested positive for hydrochlorothiazide (HCT), which is identified in the ATP Rules under "S5. Diuretics and Other Masking Agents as a Prohibited Substance." The ATP Anti-Doping Tribunal determined that Cañas committed a "Doping Offense" by having HCT present in his body and imposed a two-year period of ineligibility on him.

Cañas claims that he ingested Rofucal, a medication containing HCT, which he received from tournament personnel after requesting that a prescription from the tournament doctor to treat congestion be filled and instead received a prescription intended for the coach of another participant in the tournament, Mr. Carvallo. He claims that the HCT was present in his urine as a result of taking the medication intended for Mr. Carvallo.]

Under the ATP Rules, since a Prohibited Substance was present in the Player's specimen, there is a Doping Offense. The only issue to be determined is what are the *Consequences* based on this Doping Offense.

The burden of proof shifts to the [Cañas] under ATP Rules, K.3.b. to establish by a balance of probability: first how the prohibited substance entered his system; and second, that he bears *No Fault or Negligence*, or in the alternative *No Significant Fault or Negligence*, for the Doping Offense in order for the two years period of ineligibility to be eliminated or reduced.

With respect to the first requirement of how the Prohibited Substance entered his system, Appellant established that he ingested Rofucal delivered to him by Tournament staff. . . .

Once the Panel accepts that Appellant has met his burden of proving how the Prohibited Substance entered his system, the question of his level of fault or negligence needs to be determined.

Appellant is responsible for the presence of the Prohibited Substance in his specimen. He is an experienced professional athlete, active in the ATP Player Council and fully aware of the risks of doping, as evidenced by his testimony and the fact that he carries the ATP wallet card with the list of Prohibited Substances with him.

He took the medication he received with no review whatsoever of the contents of the box, even though he knew that the medication had been through several hands before being delivered to him. . . .

Appellant relied blindly on the system set up to take care of him at the Tournament site, assuming that it was foolproof. This is clearly negligent. The Player has a duty of utmost caution after visiting the Tournament doctor, when actually ingesting medications. It would have been normal for him to rely on the trustworthiness and knowledge of the Tournament doctor if the doctor had handed the medications to him but any professional athlete these days has to be wary when, as in this case, he receives medications which, he knows, have gone through several hands. Thus, ATP Rules M.5.a (which allows Player to establish *No Fault or Negligence*) is not applicable to the Appellant's case. . . .

The Appellant's case is next reviewed under the provisions of ATP Rules M.5.b (which allows Player to establish *No Significant Fault or Negligence*). . . .

It is the degree of negligence which is at issue pursuant to the criteria established in the ATP Rules. The definition of *No Significant Fault or Negligence* requires the Panel to look at "the totality of the circumstances."

The following factors weigh in the Appellant's favor: Appellant was at a Tournament sanctioned by the Respondent, where as a star player, he had every expectation that his visit to the Tournament doctor . . . would be the safest possible way for him to obtain medical treatment for his condition. There was no use of this or any other Prohibited Substance in any competition other than the one in respect of which the specimen was obtained. The reason for Player's ingestion of the substance was clearly medical. A mistake in the delivery of the medication was made not by Appellant or anyone working for him, but rather by the Tournament employees. . . .

Taking into account these factors, the Panel believes that the present case is substantially different from the typical doping case and qualifies as "exceptional." Appellant has established that he bears *No Significant Fault or Negligence*, allowing for the period of *Ineligibility* to be reduced by no less than one-half of the minimum period of *Ineligibility* otherwise applicable (ATP Rules M.5.b.), which in this instance is two years. . . .

Based on the provisions of ATP Rules M.5.b., the Panel must determine the actual period of ineligibility to be imposed on Appellant. . . . [T]he period of ineligibility can range between one and two years. In deciding how this wide range is to be applied in a particular case, one must closely examine and evaluate the athlete's level of fault or negligence. . . .

The following factors weigh against the Player in determining his level of fault or negligence: He did not list the medications on the doping control form he completed during the Tournament. He took the medication he received with no review whatsoever of the contents of the box, even though he knew that the medication had been through several hands before being delivered to him. At the hearing held before the Tribunal, Player was unable to recall whether he took pills or liquid but he now recognizes Rofucal as the medication he took. He is an experienced professional tennis player, active on the Player Council and aware of the risks inherent in the ingestion of unknown substances.

Under the circumstances, he could have at least made the effort to double check the prescription he was given against the medication he received or at least paid attention to the medications he was taking and read the label. . . .

Weighing all of the factors in favor of and against the Appellant identified above, the previous CAS decisions with respect to medical prescriptions and the totality of the circumstances, the Panel is unable to give the Player the maximum reduction in the period of ineligibility. Thus, the Panel determines that Player's period of ineligibility will be reduced by nine months, from two years to fifteen months. . . .

In accordance with ATP Rules L.1., Appellant's results obtained at the Tournament shall be disqualified, including forfeiture of any medals, titles, computer ranking points and prize money. . . .

QUESTIONS

Do you believe the *Cañas* CAS reached a fair result? Why or why not?

NOTES

1. "Exceptional circumstances." As illustrated by *Cañas*, the existence of "exceptional circumstances" under the WADA Code establishing "no fault or negligence" or "no significant fault or negligence" for a doping violation is necessarily a fact-specific inquiry to determine the reasonableness of an athlete's action (or inaction) to ensure that he or she does not ingest or use a banned substance.

It is very difficult (but not impossible) for an athlete to be able to prove "no fault or negligence" for a doping offense. In *ITF and WADA v. Richard Gasquet*, Arbitration CAS 2009/A/1926 & 1930, award of December 17, 2009, the CAS determined that a professional tennis player's positive urine test for a small amount of cocaine more likely than not resulted from kissing a previously unknown woman in a nightclub multiple times. The panel concluded, "[U]nder the given circumstances, even if the Player exercised the utmost caution, he could not have been aware of the consequences of kissing a girl who he had met in a totally unsuspicious environment. It was simply impossible for the Player, even when exercising the utmost caution, to know that in kissing Pamela, he could be contaminated with cocaine. The Player therefore acted without fault or negligence." It observed that "the [ITF Anti-doping] Programme cannot impose an obligation on an athlete never to go out to any restaurant or nightclub where he might meet an attractive stranger whom he might later be tempted to kiss. This would be an unrealistic and impractical expectation that should not be imposed on athletes by sanctioning bodies in their endeavors to defeat doping."

An athlete also may have difficulty proving "no significant fault or negligence" for a doping violation, which is necessary to justify a reduced sanction from the fixed minimum. In Arbitration CAS Ad Hoc Division (O.G. Athens 2004) 003, *Torri Edwards v. International Assn. of Athletics Federations and USA Track & Field*, award of August 17, 2004, the CAS upheld an American female sprinter's two-year suspension for testing positive for the banned stimulant nikethamide, which prevented her from competing in the 2004 Athens Olympics. Edwards's chiropractor gave her a package of "Coramine Glucose" tablets purchased in Martinique (where the event was being held) that contained nikethamide, which she ingested. Edwards claimed that "exceptional circumstances" justified reducing or eliminating her two-year suspension pursuant to IAAF rules. Rejecting Edwards's appeal, the CAS ruled:

> [T]he Appellant's chiropractor had access to the box of "Coramine Glucose" which stated the substances contained in the tablet (including nikethamide) and to the leaflet which even contained a warning for athletes. . . . To ignore these facts was at a minimum negligence on the part of the chiropractor and such negligence must be attributed to the athlete who uses him in supplying the athlete either a food source or a supplement. It would put an end to any meaningful fight against doping if an athlete was able to shift his/her responsibility with respect to substances which enter the body to someone else and avoid being sanctioned because the athlete himself/herself did not know of that substance.

2. Exclusivity of WADA Code sanctions. The CAS has determined that sports governing bodies that are signatories to the WADA Code are prohibited by contract from imposing sanctions for doping violations in addition to those prescribed by the code. See *USOC v. IOC*, CAS 2011/O/2422 (2011) (invalidating IOC rule precluding any person sanctioned with a suspension of more than six months for a doping violation on or after July 1, 2008, from participating in the next Olympic Games after expiration of the suspension); *British Olympic Association (BOA) v. WADA*, CAS 2011/A/2658 (2011) (invalidating BOA bylaw declaring any British athlete previously found guilty of a doping offense to be permanently eligible to represent Great Britain in the Olympic Games).

DEVELOPING INTERNATIONAL ISSUES

At present, the globalization of professional sports leagues is more a concept than a reality. Even so, sports leagues and associations around the globe nevertheless must grapple with an increasing array of issues that transcend national borders. The business and legal struggles relate in large part to the movement of professional athletes from one country to another, but other international sports ventures are underway, assuring that legal problems will follow close behind. A few truly global sports events exist today (e.g., the Olympic Games, soccer's World Cup), but most international sporting events are regional transnational competitions (e.g., Pan-American Games), continental events (e.g., the UEFA Champions League, an annual European soccer championship), or country-versus-country competitions in various sports. However, our intent is not to denigrate the importance of these significant athletic competitions. Rather, it is to caution that the internationalization — much less the globalization — of professional team sports has not yet arrived, but North American professional leagues may leap boldly forward in a few short years. For example, NBA Commissioner David Stern has expressed interest in creating a European division of NBA clubs, and the NFL is considering the possibility of having a club based in London.

In the meantime, it is not too soon to consider briefly some of the legal ramifications arising out of the movement of athletes across national borders and the potential expansion of U.S. professional sports leagues into foreign markets. *Union Royale Belge des Sociétés de Football Association, Royal Club Liégois, and Union des Associations Européennes de Football (UEFA) v. Jean-Marc Bosman (Bosman)*, Case C-415/93 (European Court of Justice, December 15, 1995), provides an excellent illustration of the complex intersection of the competing interests of players, domestic professional sports clubs, national governing federations, and international sports governing bodies. The facts giving rise to the *Bosman* case are as follows.

The Fédération Internationale de Football Association (FIFA) organizes and exercises plenary authority over the governance of football (i.e., soccer) at the world level. Professional and amateur football clubs belong to the national governing federation in their respective countries and must comply with its rules. National federations are members of FIFA and the confederation for their continent; the Union of European Football Associations (UEFA) is the European confederation for football.

FIFA and UEFA regulations, which are incorporated into the rules of the European national associations, govern the movement of football players between clubs. These regulations are applicable to player transfers between clubs in different European Union countries or clubs belonging to the same national association within a European Union country. Pursuant to these regulations, when a player is transferred between clubs, his new club is required to pay his former club a transfer fee to compensate for the former club's development and training of the player. If the two clubs disagree as to the amount of the transfer fee, it is to be determined by a UEFA board of experts based on a predetermined formula. A transfer fee was required to be paid even if the player's contract with his former club had expired. The former club's national association must issue an international clearance certificate before a player is eligible to play for his new club.

Jean-Marc Bosman, a professional footballer of Belgian nationality, was employed from 1988 by RC Liège, a Belgian first division club, until his contract expired on June 30, 1990. Thereafter, he entered into a one-year contract with US Dunkerque, a club in the French second division. US Dunkerque agreed to pay RC Liège a compensation fee of BFR 1.2 million for the temporary transfer of Bosman for one year payable on receipt of Bosman's transfer certificate issued by the Belgian national football federation to its French counterpart. The contract between the clubs also gave US Dunkerque the option for full transfer of Bosman for the payment of BFR 4.8 million. Both contracts between US Dunkerque and RC Liège and between US Dunkerque and Bosman were subject to the condition that the Belgian transfer certificate be sent to the Belgian national football federation in time for the first match of the season. RC Liège, which had doubts as to US Dunkerque's solvency, did not request that the Belgian transfer certificate be issued, which precluded Bosman from playing for US Dunkerque and obtaining his contractually agreed salary.

One of the claims Bosman alleged was that the FIFA and UEFA transfer rules are illegal under European Union law and sought damages for his lost earnings caused by the result of the application of the transfer rules. Specifically, he asserted that these transfer rules violated a treaty provision guaranteeing workers the freedom of movement among European Union member countries to obtain employment.

The European Court of Justice (ECJ) ruled that the transfer rules constitute an obstacle to freedom of movement for professional football players. It rejected the contention that the transfer rules are justified by the need to maintain financial and competitive balance between European football clubs and to create an incentive for clubs to identify and train young football players. The ECJ explained:

> As regards the first of those aims, Mr Bosman has rightly pointed out that the application of the transfer rules is not an adequate means of maintaining financial and competitive balance in the world of football. Those rules neither preclude the richest clubs from securing the services of the best players nor prevent the availability of financial resources from being a decisive factor in competitive sport, thus considerably altering the balance between clubs.
>
> As regards the second aim, it must be accepted that the prospect of receiving transfer, development or training fees is indeed likely to encourage football clubs to seek new talent and train young players.
>
> However, because it is impossible to predict the sporting future of young players with any certainty and because only a limited number of such players go on to play professionally, those fees are by nature contingent and uncertain and are in any event unrelated to the actual cost borne by clubs of training both future professional players and those who will never play professionally. The prospect of receiving such fees cannot, therefore, be either a decisive factor in encouraging recruitment and training of young players or an adequate means of financing such activities, particularly in the case of smaller clubs. Furthermore, as the Advocate General has pointed out, the same aims can be achieved at least as efficiently by other means which do not impede freedom of movement for workers. . . .

Finally, the argument that the rules in question are necessary to compensate clubs for the expenses which they have had to incur in paying fees on recruiting their players cannot be accepted, since it seeks to justify the maintenance of obstacles to freedom of movement for workers simply on the ground that such obstacles were able to exist in the past.

Id. at ¶¶ 107–113.

Fifteen years after *Bosman*, the ECJ continues to invalidate sports league rules that constitute an obstacle to freedom of movement by European professional athletes whose contracts have expired if the challenged rules do not actually further a legitimate objective or require more than is necessary to achieve such a purpose. In *Olympique Lyonnais SASP v. Olivier Bernard and Newcastle UFC*, Case C-325/08 (European Court of Justice, March 16, 2010), the court ruled that the required payment that a soccer player must make to the club that trained him before being permitted to sign his first professional contract with another club is illegal if not reasonable in relation to the training costs incurred by that club.

NOTES

1. North American leagues in foreign countries. At present, U.S. professional sports leagues such as the NHL, NBA, MLB, and Major League Soccer (MLS) have clubs only in the United States and Canada. In addition to cultural differences in business practices and currency valuation, there is a host of complex legal issues to consider if a sports league operates in multiple countries. For example, as discussed in Chapter 12, Canadian labor law is largely provincial rather than national as in the United States. In light of the ECJ's *Bosman* ruling, it is important to recognize that how a U.S. professional league's labor issues would become more complicated if it established a division or satellite league in two or more countries that are part of the European Union.

2. North American league agreements with International Federations. For example, the NBA's agreement with the international governing body for basketball (the International Basketball Federation, or FIBA) requires recognition by all concerned parties that an existing player contract will be respected and not interfered with during its term, which had significant implications during the 2011 NBA lockout. Such agreements seek to stabilize the process by which players move from a club in one country to one in another country.

3. NHL agreements with European hockey leagues and federations. After the NHL settled its negotiations with the NHLPA and entered a new CBA in 2005, it signed a new player transfer agreement with the International Ice Hockey Federation (IIHF), the governing body for international ice hockey for all national federations, later that same year. The agreement established regulations for the transfer of European players to the NHL; however, the Russian Federation declined to enter into the agreement, and its players were therefore subject to different rules when negotiating with NHL clubs. The player transfer agreement with the IIHF expired following the 2006–2007 season, and although a new agreement was reached for the 2007–2008 season, it was terminated after one year.

Since the 2009–2010 season, the NHL has executed player transfer agreements on an individualized country-by-country basis instead of on the basis of an overarching agreement with the IIHF. The NHL currently has agreements in place with countries such as Sweden, Finland, Slovakia, and Germany. These player transfer agreements require the NHL to pay a development fee to the individual federations for the right to sign their players while under contract — approximately $225,000 per player.

The NHL does not have a player transfer agreement with Russia. However, the NHL and the Kontinental Hockey League agreed for the 2011–2012 and 2012–2013 seasons that they will cooperate regarding disputed player contracts. Russian players (and players coming from other countries not subject to a player transfer agreement) are subject to the defected status provisions of the CBA. Essentially, these provisions permit an NHL club to extend its negotiation rights indefinitely for an NHL drafted player whose rights reside with that NHL club. In contrast, a club's negotiation rights for a player subject to a player transfer agreement would expire after two years.

4. Anticipating international play and expansion. Some U.S. leagues have already addressed the possibility of international play and possible international expansion by negotiating with their players association some of the ground rules by which this may occur. Consider, for example, the following provisions in the latest MLB collective bargaining agreement:

- [I]f a Major League franchise is awarded to a city outside the United States and Canada, then championship season, All-Star, Division Series, League Championship Series and World Series games played in that city by such franchise shall not be considered international play.
- In furtherance of joint efforts to develop the sport internationally, the [MLBPA] and the Office of the Commissioner, on behalf of the Clubs, agree to (i) meet regularly to ensure continued collaboration and cooperation and (ii) keep the other informed regarding all contemplated or planned International Play.

See 2012 MLB CBA, Article XV, Section K.

Glossary

Academic progress — a student-athlete's movement toward the timely completion of a baccalaureate or equivalent degree measured by several variables, including an evaluation of the student's cumulative grade point average (GPA), earned academic credit, and the maximum time necessary for the student-athlete to complete his or her declared major.

Academic Progress Rate (APR) — a metric created by National Collegiate Athletic Association (NCAA) legislation that gives a real-time snapshot of the academic progress of individual teams at member institutions.

Adhesion contract — a contract, usually between two parties of unequal bargaining power, offered on a take-it-or-leave-it basis that limits another party's acceptance to the terms written therein, all of which must be accepted for a contract to be formed.

Agent — a party acting in the interest and under the direction of another, the principal.

Anticompetitive effects — for the purposes of antitrust law, an adverse effect on market competition (which usually affects the price, quantity, or quality of goods or services) caused by the reduction or elimination of competition among entities that otherwise would engage in economic competition absent an agreement not to do so.

Anticybersquatting Consumer Protection Act of 1999 (ACPA) — a federal law to prevent cybersquatting, the unauthorized act of registering another's trademark as an Internet domain name; the act provides a trademark owner with the right to bring suit against a defendant for bad-faith registration or for use of an identical or confusingly similar domain name.

Arbitrary and capricious — a standard of review used by courts in determining whether the decision of a private association, such as a sports governing body or a league commissioner, should be invalidated; generally requires showing that the body or individual acted in an unreasonable or irrational manner.

Assault — a tort in which an actor intends to cause harmful or offensive contact or an imminent apprehension of such contact with the person of another and the other is actually put in such imminent apprehension.

Assumption of risk — a tort law doctrine whereby an individual who voluntarily participates in an activity assumes the risk of any injury that occurs as a result of such participation.

Athletic events not copyrightable — the Copyright Act of 1976 provides that only "original works of authorship fixed in any tangible medium of expression" within one of eight statutory categories of "works of authorship" are subject to copyright protection; athletic events are not within any of these categories, and, unlike movies, plays, or television programs, they are not "authored" because they are not predetermined or scripted events.

Attempted monopolization — a violation of §2 of the Sherman Act whereby an entity with 50 percent or more of the relevant market has engaged in unlawful predatory conduct intended to exclude a rival business entity from the market through means other than fair competition on the merits.

Boosters — any representative with an interest in the athletic success of a university; generally, these people have made some financial donation to the school, employed student-athletes, or volunteered time to the athletic program.

Breach of contract — a legal claim premised on the assertion that a party to a contract has failed to sufficiently fulfill its contractual obligations or promises such that the aggrieved party has or will suffer damages as a result of the breach.

Buyout — a provision of a coaching contract designed to dissuade a coach from prematurely terminating his or her employment at an institution by requiring the coach to pay a specified amount, determined in pre-contract negotiations, in the event that the coach breaches an existing employment contract with a team.

CAS Ad Hoc Division — an on-site process used to resolve legal issues and disputes that arise within ten days prior to or during the Olympic Games and other international or transnational sports events on an expedited basis.

CAS appeals arbitration — an alternative dispute resolution process used to resolve appeals from the final decisions of sport federations, usually involving competition results or doping, disciplinary, or eligibility issues, and competition results.

CAS ordinary arbitration — an alternative dispute resolution process used to resolve disputes relating to legal relations between parties such as contractual disputes involving sponsorships, media rights, and agent contracts.

Catastrophic injury insurance program — an insurance compensation program developed by the National Collegiate Athletic Association (NCAA) that provides for the payment of insurance benefits to student-athletes, student coaches, student managers, student trainers, and student cheerleaders who are catastrophically injured while participating in certain activities that are defined as covered events in the program.

Charitable immunity — a tort law doctrine under which an educational facility may be absolved from liability for the negligent actions of its employees because of its charitable purpose.

Civil Rights Restoration Act — an act by Congress designed to restore certain civil rights that have been limited by the courts or others.

Clearly erroneous — a standard of review whereby the appellate courts will uphold (not reverse) a trial court's factual determination unless the higher court firmly and unquestionably determines that the lower court mistakenly found that a particular fact was present.

Clustering — the intentional concentration of student-athletes in a specific field of study.

Code of Sports-Related Arbitration — codified rules that govern the operations and procedures of the International Council of Arbitration for Sport (ICAS) and the Court of Arbitration for Sport (CAS).

Collective bargaining agreement (CBA) — the agreement reached between the players' labor union and a professional sports league clubs' multiemployer bargaining unit concerning wages, hours, and other terms and conditions of employment; the CBA is binding on all parties to the agreement, including the league, its member clubs, and current and future players.

Commissioner "best interests of the game" authority — an often-broad contractual grant of authority from league clubs to their commissioner to make decisions and take appropriate action to further the league's best interests and integrity of the game; this power may give the commissioner sole discretion in certain aspects of league governance (i.e., investigation of game fixing, betting, other forms of corruption, and other disciplinary matters).

Committee on Infractions (COI) — a group of individuals drawn from National Collegiate Athletic Association (NCAA) member institutions and other sources that hears cases involving major violations of NCAA rules.

Common law — case law or legal precedent developed by decisions of judges rather than via legislation.

Compensable event — a Workers' Compensation Act requirement stipulating that, for an injured employee to receive available benefits, the injury sustained by that employee must be an accidental injury that arises out of and in the course of employment.

Competition on the merits — for the purposes of federal antitrust law, the lawful ability of all business entities, including those with monopoly power (e.g., the nation's only major professional league for a sport), to compete fairly against other producers of a similar product for the patronage of consumers.

Competitive advantage — a theory under which certain athletes will be prevented from participating in interscholastic or intercollegiate athletics because their participation will give them an unfair (or competitive) advantage over other competitors.

Competitive balance or luxury tax — a tax, established by the league collective bargaining agreement (CBA), that is paid to the league by a team that exceeds a maximum amount with its annual aggregate player salaries; it is intended as a means of maintaining competitive balance among league clubs by creating an economic disincentive for wealthier clubs to acquire the best players by paying them salaries that lower revenue clubs cannot afford to pay.

Competitor's privilege — the allowable level of competition within the law (e.g., one agent is allowed and expected to be competing for the clients of another agent).

Complainant — a person or organization that takes legal action against another; a person that files a complaint with an administrative or enforcement agency.

Compliance — generally, the following of or conforming with legal requirements or rules; in the context of sports law, the following of rules set forth by the National Collegiate Athletic Association (NCAA), such that each member institution has a compliance department whose main purpose is to make sure each athletic program is following NCAA rules.

Confidentiality — a decree or agreement to keep discussions or rulings out of the public; any information that needs to stay private will be deemed confidential.

Conflict of interest — a situation where an individual is confronted with a scenario that may provide personal gain while causing detriment to another, to whom a duty is owed.

Consideration — something of legal value that is exchanged between the parties to a contract; an essential element of an enforceable contract.

Contract — a promise or set of promises for the breach of which the law gives a remedy, or the performance of which the law in some way recognizes as a duty.

Contract law — a body of state law that governs the agreed terms of the legal relationship between parties (e.g., terms and conditions of employment between a club and player).

Contract of hire — a contract that binds an employer to pay compensation to an employee who performs services, sets forth the place to perform such services and work to be performed, and sets the compensation for the performance of the work.

Contract rationale — a theory advanced by student-athletes in Fourteenth Amendment litigation asserting that the athlete's university scholarship constitutes a contract that gives rise to a property interest of which the athlete cannot be deprived without due process of law.

Contributory negligence — a tort law doctrine whereby a plaintiff may be barred from recovering for damages resulting from the defendant's negligence if the plaintiff has contributed in any way to his or her own harm.

Cooperation — a determining factor used by the National Collegiate Athletic Association (NCAA) when imposing sanctions; schools that cooperate with the NCAA in its investigation tend to receive lesser punishments than those schools that choose not to cooperate.

Copyright Act of 1976 — a federal law that grants the copyright owner the exclusive right to use and authorize others to use copyrighted material in one of five statutorily defined ways, including the right to publicly perform an audiovisual work such as the broadcast of a sports event.

Copyright infringement — the infringing use of another's copyrighted work without consent of the copyright owner; for example, by the unauthorized public performance of the broadcast of a sports event.

Court of Arbitration for Sport (CAS) — a Lausanne, Switzerland–based private international arbitration tribunal that adjudicates sports-related disputes, primarily those involving Olympic sports.

Curt Flood Act of 1998 — a federal statute that limits the broad scope of baseball's common law antitrust immunity by providing Major League Baseball (MLB) players with the same rights as other professional athletes such as football, basketball, hockey, and soccer players to challenge anticompetitive restraints affecting the terms and conditions of their employment on antitrust law grounds.

Decertification — a formal process requiring at least 50 percent of a professional sports league's players to vote to decertify the union in a National Labor Relations Board (NLRB)-supervised election.

Declaratory and injunctive relief — an early resolution of the rights of the parties under a contract or statute.

Defamation — a false statement of fact about a person with the requisite level of fault (at least negligence) made to a third party that harms one's reputation; can be either an oral (slander) or a written (libel) statement.

Deference — a term often used by courts to describe their belief that professional determinations by educational institutions and sports governing bodies should be given significant weight in determining whether those acts should be found to violate the law.

De novo arbitral or judicial review — a form of review pursuant to which a court or arbitration tribunal resolves a legal dispute on its merits without providing any deference to resolution by a sports governing body, league, or commissioner; this differs from traditional judicial review, whereby a court will invalidate an action or decision by a sports governing body, league, or commissioner only if it is arbitrary, capricious, or irrational.

Dictum — a view expressed by a judge in a decision that is not necessary to deciding the issue before the court.

Disassociation — an action taken by a university to end a booster's ties to a university; usually occurs after a booster is found to have committed a National Collegiate Athletic Association (NCAA) violation.

Discretionary function — a function or task that requires an individual to exercise his or her own personal deliberation or judgment (i.e., examining facts, weighing options, or reaching an independently reasoned conclusion).

Disparate impact — indirect discrimination by a rule or law against a group or class of people.

Disparate treatment — direct or intentional discrimination against a person, group, or class of people.

Due process — the principle that the courts must procedurally and substantively respect the legal rights of parties before them.

Duty of care — the responsibility legally assigned to one for the protection of another against some harm or injury because of the nature of the relationship that exists between them or because the actor engaged in some risk-creating conduct that brought the harm into existence.

Duty of good faith — a term implied in all contracts that requires honesty in fact and the observance of reasonable commercial standards of fair dealing.

Economic rationale — a theory advanced by student-athletes in Fourteenth Amendment litigation asserting that the athlete retains a property interest, which arises from training for a lucrative career as a professional athlete, of which the athlete may not be deprived without due process of law.

Educational malpractice — professional negligence premised on an educator or institution's failure to provide the educational services that are reasonably expected of such educator or institution.

Eighth Amendment (cruel and unusual punishment) — language in the Eighth Amendment to the U.S. Constitution that has been interpreted to prohibit imposing a punishment on a condemned person that is considered to be unacceptable because of the excessive measure of pain, suffering, and humiliation inflicted on that person.

Employment at will/at-will employment — an employment contract that allows the employer to discharge the employee without cause, for any or no reason, and without a hearing allowing the employee to contest the termination; the employee may also leave his or her employment relationship for any or no reason and not be held in breach of contract.

Entwinement — a legal theory expounded by the Supreme Court to determine whether a private actor or association is sufficiently engaged in public activity or with government entities to be deemed a state actor for constitutional purposes.

Equal accommodation — under Title IX, changes made to allow equal athletic participation opportunities, treatment, and benefits for men and women.

Equal protection — the commitment to equal treatment by the states (i.e., government) of persons within their jurisdiction, as embodied in the Fourteenth Amendment to the U.S. Constitution.

Equal treatment — having the same privileges, opportunities, and burdens as others (under Title IX, the opportunity for male and female athletes to have the same quantity and quality of athletic participation opportunities, equipment, training, competition, etc.).

Exclusive bargaining representative — after the players have selected a union that is certified by the National Labor Relations Board (NLRB), the union has the exclusive authority to collectively bargain with the league's multiemployer bargaining unit on the players' behalf.

Exculpatory agreement — a contractual provision in which one party agrees to fully or partially absolve another from a legal liability that could potentially arise from the use of products or services offered by the party seeking to be absolved from liability.

Express contract — a contract where the mutual assent arises from the words exchanged between the parties to the contract.

Faculty athletics representative (FAR) — a member of the faculty at an National Collegiate Athletic Association (NCAA) institution who acts as the liaison between the academic and athletic departments of the university and as the university's representative for the NCAA and athletic conference; the faculty member may not serve in any capacity in the athletic department.

Failure to bargain in good faith — the breach of a statutory duty imposed by the National Labor Relations Act on both the league's multiemployer bargaining unit and the players' union to meet at reasonable times and to confer in good faith regarding wages, hours, and other terms and conditions of employment; it is not an unfair labor practice or an act of bad faith for either side to take a hard-line stance in collective bargaining.

Fair Labor Standards Act (FLSA) — a federal law that is administered by the U.S. Department of Labor, which requires employers to pay covered employees who are not otherwise exempt at least the federal minimum wage and overtime pay of one-and-one-half-times the regular rate of pay; it provides exemptions for employees employed by certain seasonal and recreational establishments.

Felony reckless manslaughter — a form of manslaughter where a person was aware that his or her conduct created a substantial and unjustifiable risk that another person's death would result, but consciously disregarded such risk in a manner constituting a gross deviation from the conduct of a reasonable person in the same situation.

Fiduciary — a person granted power over the interest of another; also describes the nature of a relationship in which such a duty is owed.

Fiduciary duty — a legal duty of allegiance and loyalty that a party in a position of trust owes to another person or entity (e.g., principal-agent, member of board of directors-corporation), which requires the former to make decisions and put the interests of the other above one's own personal interests.

First Amendment — a provision of the U.S. Constitution that protects freedom of religion, speech, association, and expression; it limits the scope of federal and state law creation and protection of intellectual property rights (e.g., trademarks, copyrights, right of publicity).

Foreseeability — the likelihood that some discernible future consequence will result from present conduct, behavior, or events.

Fourteenth Amendment — a provision of the U.S. Constitution that prohibits the states from making or enforcing any law that abridges the privileges or immunities of U.S. citizens or deprives such citizen of life, liberty, or property without due process of law.

Free agency restrictions — collective bargaining agreement (CBA) terms that establish when and how a player whose contract has expired becomes a "free agent," which typically means the player may sign a contract with another league club; in most leagues, a player must have played in the league for an agreed minimum number of seasons before becoming eligible to be a free agent.

Full and effective accommodation — under Title IX, an educational institution's provision of a sufficient number and range of athletic participation opportunities that fully satisfies the interests and abilities of the disfavored gender.

Gender equity — managing an athletics program in a manner that treats male and female athletes fairly by providing similar benefits and burdens for both.

Good faith and fair dealing — a requirement that the parties, in contracting and related contexts, deal with each other in a forthright and honest manner.

Hearsay — a common objection made by a lawyer to testimony offered by a witness that is based on what that witness has been told by another, not based on his or her own knowledge.

Horizontal restraint — for purposes of antitrust law, an agreement among direct competitors that reduces economic competition among them (e.g., agreeing to fix prices or to limit output of goods or services that are purchased or produced).

Illegal exclusionary conduct with anticompetitive market effects — For the purposes of §2 of the Sherman Act, anticompetitive action other than fair competition on the merits by a business entity intended to exclude or prevent a business rival from competing in the market for the patronage of consumers.

Illegal per se — for the purposes of antitrust law, an agreement that has clear anticompetitive effects without any offsetting procompetitive justifications, which is deemed to be an unreasonable restraint of trade as a matter of law that violates §1 of the Sherman Act.

Impasse — a deadlock in the collective bargaining process that is usually temporary; prior to impasse, the courts have determined that a league is required to adhere to the terms of the expired collective bargaining agreement (CBA), and after impasse, the league's multiemployer bargaining unit may unilaterally implement new mandatory terms of employment if the proposals have been offered to the players' union and bargained in good faith prior to impasse.

Impermissible benefits — any benefit provided to a prospective student-athlete, current student-athlete, or student-athlete's friends and relatives that is not also available to the general public or general student body.

Implied contract — a contract where the mutual assent or apparent agreement arises from the conduct of the parties to the agreement.

Implied-in-fact — terms of a contract or promise, which are gleaned from the parties' words or conduct, even though not literally expressed by them.

Indefinite duration — a contractual relationship without a specified duration.

Informed consent — a tort law doctrine under which a physician will be held liable for an intentional or negligent failure to provide a patient with full disclosure of material information regarding the patient's medical condition or potential consequences of proposed treatments for such condition.

Infraction — any violation of a National Collegiate Athletic Association (NCAA) rule.

Infractions Appeals Committee (IAC) — a group of individuals drawn from National Collegiate Athletic Association (NCAA) member institutions and other sources that hear appeals of decisions rendered by the Committee on Infractions.

Inherently distinctive mark — a mark that is arbitrary or coined in connection within the goods or services that it identifies (e.g., "Miami Dolphins" for an National Football League (NFL) team).

Initial eligibility standards — National Collegiate Athletic Association (NCAA) academic requirements that an entering freshman must have attained in order to be eligible for athletics-related financial aid, practice, and intercollegiate competition during the student's first year; pursuant to such standards, the freshman must have registered with the NCAA Initial-Eligibility Clearinghouse, completed a minimum grade point average (GPA) in a defined number of "core courses," and attained a certain minimum score on either the SAT or ACT.

Injunctive relief — a court order requiring a party to do or refrain from doing some act.

Injury by accident — a Workers' Compensation Act requirement that an injured employee provide proof that the injury that he or she sustained was caused by an identifiable yet unexpected event.

Input market — for the purposes of antitrust law, products or services (e.g., players, coaches, and playing facilities) necessary to produce a product or service sold to consumers (e.g., athletic competition such as National Collegiate Athletic Association (NCAA) football or National Basketball Association (NBA) basketball).

Intentional injury exception — when an employee suffers a work-related injury as a result of an intentional tort perpetrated by the employer or at the employer's direction, the applicable state workers' compensation law is not a bar to a common law tort action for damages.

Intentional tort — a civil wrong that results in harm to another by an act knowing, willfully, or purposefully committed by the actor.

Intermediate scrutiny — a standard of review that requires gender-based distinctions to be substantially related to and in furtherance of important government objectives.

International Convention Against Doping in Sport — an international treaty based on the World Anti-Doping Code, pursuant to which countries that are its signatories commit to combat sports doping.

International Council of Arbitration for Sport (ICAS) — a Lausanne, Switzerland–based organization that consists of 20 international jurists whose role is to oversee the Court of Arbitration for Sport (CAS), including appointment of its members and promulgation of the Code of Sports-Related Arbitration (which governs the operations of the CAS).

International Federation (IF) — a nongovernmental organization (NGO) recognized by the International Olympic Committee (IOC) that functions as the worldwide governing body for a single sport or group of sports.

International Olympic Committee (IOC) — an international, not-for-profit, nongovernmental organization (NGO) based in Lausanne, Switzerland, which serves as the supreme governing body of the Olympic Movement.

Investigation — an evidentiary inquiry that occurs once the National Collegiate Athletic Association (NCAA) enforcement staff has become aware of a possible major infraction of rules at an institution; it involves conducting interviews both off campus and on to determine if there is enough evidence to move forward with a full investigation or if the investigation should be dropped because no major violation has occurred or there is a lack of information.

Invitee — an individual who enters another's premises for the purpose directly or indirectly connected with the business dealings of the possessor or an individual invited to enter or remain on the land as a member of the public for a purpose for which the land is held open to the public.

Jock majors — fields of study that allow student-athletes to more easily satisfy institutional and National Collegiate Athletic Association (NCAA) academic requirements without substantially interfering with their eligibility to compete in intercollegiate athletics.

Just cause — a reasonably legitimate reason for engaging in certain conduct such as terminating an employee.

Lack of institutional control — a finding by the Committee on Infractions (COI) that an institution engaged in a major violation that occurred in part because of a failure on the part of the member institution to exercise adequate oversight of or control over its intercollegiate athletics program.

Lanham Act — a federal law that prohibits infringement of trademarks and service marks by their unauthorized usage that creates a likelihood of consumer confusion.

Law of private associations — a body of state law governing the legal relationship among members of a private association (e.g., National Collegiate Athletic Association (NCAA) universities and professional sports league clubs), which requires the parties to comply with the terms of the association's charter and bylaws, provide procedural due process, act in a rational and consistent manner, and comply with applicable public laws; courts generally will only intervene in the affairs of a private association if it fails to comply with these requirements.

Law of the shop — in the context of a professional sports collective bargaining agreement (CBA), the requirement that a player disciplinary system provide players with advance notice of prohibited conduct and potential discipline.

Lex sportiva — the developing body of Olympic and international sports law jurisprudence created by sports arbitration awards rendered by the Court of Arbitration for Sport (CAS).

Liberty interest — an interest, such as free speech or the right to vote, that is well recognized and protected regardless of how it is defined by a state; liberty interests may also include interests created by state statutes, regulations, and ordinances.

Likelihood of confusion — the unauthorized use of a trademark or service mark in a manner that creates likely consumer confusion regarding the source, affiliation, endorsement, or sponsorship of a product or service; such conduct violates the Lanham Act and similar state laws.

Limited duty rule — a tort law doctrine that holds that if a spectator at a sporting event or a sports participant voluntarily partakes in an inherently dangerous activity, there is no legal duty to protect or warn such spectator or participant about the common, frequent, and expected inherent risks of that activity.

Liquidated damages provision — a provision of a contract that includes a good-faith estimate of the loss to a nonbreaching party in the event of the other party's breach of their contract.

Lockout — a lawful means of economic pressure that a professional sports league may use in an effort to convince the players' union to agree to its proposed collective bargaining agreement (CBA) terms; during a lockout, the league's players are precluded from playing games or participating in other club activities and are not paid their respective salaries.

Major infraction — any violation of National Collegiate Athletic Association (NCAA) rules that is not secondary in nature; these violations usually give a school a substantial advantage, either through recruiting or on the field, and can subject a school to severe punishment.

Malpractice — a tort in which a professional such as a doctor or lawyer is held civilly liable for his or her failure to render proper services as a result of negligent, reckless, or criminal conduct constituting a deviation from an established industry standard of care.

Mandatory subjects of bargaining — wages, hours, and other terms and conditions of employment; if either the players' union or the league's multiemployer bargaining unit requests bargaining on these issues, the other side must bargain in good faith, and the National Labor Relations Board (NLRB) resolves disputes regarding whether particular issues constitute a mandatory subject of collective bargaining.

Manslaughter — the unlawful killing of one person by another without malice aforethought.

Ministerial function — a function or task that becomes mandatory given the circumstances and does not allow for personal discretion or judgment (e.g., reporting an athlete's use of performance-enhancing drugs or benching a player who is no longer eligible because of poor academic performance).

Misappropriation — the unauthorized use of another's intellectual property for commercial or other gain that causes harm to its owner.

Monitoring — a National Collegiate Athletic Association (NCAA) member institution's responsibility to be aware of possible violations occurring on its campus; a gross lack of monitoring can lead to a "lack of institutional control" charge and severe penalties.

Monopolization — a violation of §2 of the Sherman Act whereby an entity with 70 percent or more of the relevant market has engaged in unlawful predatory conduct intended to exclude a rival business entity from the market other than by fair competition on the merits.

Monopoly power — in economic terms, the ability to charge a supracompetitive price (i.e., price higher than in a competitive market) or to exclude competitors through predatory conduct; for practical purposes, control of 70 percent or more of the relevant market (properly defined in terms of product or service and geography) based on consumer demand constitutes monopoly power.

Multiemployer collective bargaining unit — the exclusive collective bargaining representative for the league's member clubs, which has the authority to bind all clubs to the terms of agreements reached with the players union.

Mutual assent — the objective willingness of parties to be bound by the terms of an agreement usually manifested through the process of offer and acceptance.

National Collegiate Athletic Association (NCAA) — a national association of public and private universities that promulgates and enforces rules designed to regulate intercollegiate athletic competition among its members.

National governing body (NGB) — the national governing body for a particular sport recognized by the country's national Olympic committee and that is a member of the corresponding International Federation (IF) for the sport.

National Labor Relations Act (NLRA) — also known as the Wagner Act, the NLRA was enacted by Congress in 1935 and establishes the basic legal framework that governs the relationship between labor and management; it provides workers with the ability to unionize, collectively bargain, and engage in strikes and picketing to advance and protect their interests.

National Labor Relations Board (NLRB) — a federal administrative agency that enforces the federal labor laws by policing the process of unionization and collective bargaining, including adjudication of claims of unfair labor practices.

National Letter of Intent (NLI) — an agreement between a student-athlete and an institution in which the athlete agrees, for a minimum of one year, to attend the institution named in the document.

National Olympic Committee (NOC) — the governing authority for Olympic sports within a country, which is recognized by the International Olympic Committee (IOC).

Negative injunction/negative injunctive relief — an equitable remedy that a court has the discretion to grant for breach of contract when money damages are not an adequate remedy to compensate the nonbreaching party for harm suffered; although a court generally will not order a party to render the contractually agreed services, it may order the breaching party (e.g., a player) not to provide services to another club until the existing contract expires.

Negligence — a tort law cause of action that requires the plaintiff to prove by a preponderance of the evidence that (1) the defendant owed a duty of care to the plaintiff; (2) the defendant breached that duty by failing to exercise reasonable care under the circumstances; (3) the defendant's failure to exercise reasonable care is the actual and proximate (foreseeable) cause of the plaintiff's injury; and (4) the plaintiff has suffered some compensable damage, such as a loss of wages, as the result of the defendant's negligent conduct.

No fault or negligence — a defense that justifies imposing no sanction for a doping violation it requires proof that an athlete did not know or suspect, and could not reasonably have known or suspected even with the exercise of the utmost caution, that he or she used or was administered a banned substance.

Nondisclosure — a failure to relay information that may be required because of the legal nature of some relationships.

Nonstatutory labor exemption — a broad, judicially created exemption, which immunizes the terms of a collective bargaining agreement (CBA), as well as all restraints on the labor market for players' services from antitrust challenge, so long as there is an ongoing collective bargaining process between the players' union and a professional sports league.

No significant fault or negligence — a defense that justifies a reduced sanction for a doping violation, which requires proof that an athlete's fault or negligence in connection with a doping violation, when viewed in the totality of the circumstances, was not significant in relation to the doping violation.

Offer — a promise to do or not to do something conditioned on the other party's promising to do or to refrain from doing something in return.

Olympic Charter — the codified principles, rules, and bylaws that govern the Olympic Movement and Olympic Games.

One academic year in residence — a National Collegiate Athletic Association (NCAA) regulation whereby a student-athlete is required to spend one academic year (usually one contiguous fall and spring semester) enrolled full time at a specified institution in order to participate in the institution's intercollegiate athletics.

Order to show cause — a determination by the National Collegiate Athletic Association (NCAA) that a coach or staff member should be prevented from fulfilling coaching or other responsibilities for a designated period of time.

Organizing Committee for the Olympic Games (OCOG) — the legal entity responsible for conducting and funding the Olympic Games in the host city.

Output market — for purposes of antitrust law, products or services produced and sold to consumers (e.g., athletic competition such as National Collegiate Athletic Association (NCAA) football or National Basketball Association (NBA) basketball).

Patent law — a federal law that grants exclusive intellectual property rights to inventions that satisfy the statutory requirements of novelty, nonobviousness, and utility (e.g., the Arena Football League (AFL) obtained a patent for its unique system of playing indoor professional football).

Penalties — punishments that are generally determined on a case-by-case basis to fit the violation that occurred; in the sports law context, schools will often get scholarship reductions or public reprimands but rarely bowl and television bans; the most severe penalty is the "repeat offender" punishment, also known as the "death penalty," in which the National Collegiate Athletic Association (NCAA) orders the complete shutdown of a program for a given period of time.

Performance-enhancing drug — any drug used to improve performance during a sporting event; in many cases, drugs used for the purpose of improving performance that create health risks to the user or others are deemed a violation of antidoping rules.

Performance incentive — a benefit in excess of salary or wages promised to an individual and conditioned upon the individual's achievement of an expressed goal of the institution or organization promising the benefit.

Perquisites — a privilege, gain, or profit incidental to an employment in addition to regular salary or wages, especially one expected or promised.

Prima facie — the basic elements necessary to prove a legal point or to find that a violation of the law has occurred.

Principal — the party whose interests are paramount in the principal-agent relationship (e.g., the athlete in the athlete–sports agent relationship).

Principle of proportionality — a legal principle requiring that the sanction for a doping violation be proportionate to the violation, taking account of all of the relevant circumstances, particularly an athlete's degree of culpability.

Privacy interest — under the Fourth Amendment limitation on searches and seizures, courts often seek to protect parties from having their person or belongings (privacy) searched without establishing sufficient cause for doing so.

Procedural due process — a constitutional limitation on government or state power that mandates that a certain amount of process or procedure (notice and hearing) must be afforded by a party.

Procompetitive effects/justification — for purposes of antitrust law, a defense claiming that a challenged restraint's positive economic effects (e.g., the production or maintenance of a brand of athletic competition desired by consumers, or the enhancement of its quality) offsets its anticompetitive effects and is a reasonable restraint that does not violate the Sherman Act.

Promise — a commitment by a person to do or not to do something in the future.

Promissory estoppel — a doctrine that provides for the enforceability of a promise based on the promisee's justifiable and detrimental reliance on such promise, despite the nonexistence of an otherwise enforceable contract.

Proper supervision — the use of ordinary care as a reasonable person under the circumstances by one to whom an authoritative role is assigned, especially in the management of others.

Property interest or right — a legal entitlement to ownership in tangible property such as money, personal property, and real estate, or intangible property such as intellectual property, a special skill, etc.

Qualified immunity — a tort law doctrine under which an employee may be absolved from negligence occurring in the scope of his or her employment if such negligence results from the exercise of a discretionary act rather than a ministerial act.

"Quick look" rule of reason — in comparison to the per se rule of illegality, a case-by-case, fact-specific method of antitrust analysis used to weigh the anticompetitive and procompetitive effects of a restriction to determine whether on balance it is predominately anticompetitive (unreasonable and illegal under the Sherman Act) or predominately procompetitive (reasonable and legal under the Sherman Act); in contrast to the full rule of reason, the "quick look" rule of reason is applied when a restraint has clear anticompetitive effects (usually evidenced by adverse effects on price or output) that are not offset by procompetitive justifications that cannot be achieved by other, less restrictive means.

Reckless conduct — conduct by an actor that creates a substantial and unjustifiable risk of harm or injury to another.

Repeat offender — any school that commits a major infraction within five years of having committed another major infraction; the violations do not have to occur in the same sport at a school for that school to be deemed a repeat offender, and a repeat offender is subject to severe penalties, including the "death penalty."

Reserve clause — a contractual term that restrains the labor market for a player's services by giving his or her current club perpetual rights to a player's services, even after the expiration of his or her contract.

Restitution rule — a measure of damages, sometimes referred to as *unjust enrichment*, that requires the breaching party to restore any benefits received to the party conferring those benefits.

Retaliation — to deliberately harm a person in response to some action that person has taken (or something that person is perceived to have done).

Right of publicity — a state law right created by either statute or common law that protects an individual's name, likeness, and persona from unauthorized commercial use.

Right to control — a test employed by courts to determine the nature of an employment relationship; it examines whether the employer possessed the right to control the manner, means, and details of the worker's performance.

Rule of reason — in comparison to the per se rule of illegality, a case-by-case, fact-specific method of antitrust analysis used to weigh the anticompetitive and procompetitive effects of a restriction to determine whether on balance it is predominately anticompetitive (unreasonable and illegal under the Sherman Act) or predominately procompetitive (reasonable and legal under the Sherman Act); in contrast to the "quick look" rule of reason, the full rule of reason requires a jury to determine disputed issues of material fact and the plaintiff to plead and prove that the relevant market (e.g., National Collegiate Athletic Association (NCAA) football or National Basketball Association (NBA) basketball) is restrained by the challenged conduct and to consider more complex economic analysis.

Salary cap — the annual maximum amount that a club may spend for aggregate player salaries, which is determined by the league's collective bargaining agreement (CBA).

Satisfactory progress — a National Collegiate Athletic Association (NCAA) regulation that requires student-athletes to declare a major early during their college tenure and complete a substantial amount of the coursework for their major within a specified period of time.

Scholarship rationale — a theory advanced by student-athletes in litigation asserting that a loss of an athletic scholarship deprives the athlete of benefits that result from being awarded a scholarship in exchange for athletic participation.

Search and seizure — a Fourth Amendment term covering an examination or search of a premises (business, residence, or vehicle) or person.

Secondary infraction — any violation of National Collegiate Athletic Association (NCAA) rules that is inadvertent or accidental and does not provide the school with a substantial recruiting or competitive advantage; while secondary violations merit less severe penalties, a culmination of several secondary violations may constitute a major violation, creating exposure to potentially more severe penalties.

Secondary meaning — acquired when the consuming public associates a descriptive trademark or service mark with a particular product or service (e.g., "Warriors" as the name of a National Basketball Association (NBA) franchise).

Sexual harassment — unwelcome words or actions of a sexual nature, or on the basis of gender, that bother or threaten a person or the quality of the person's experience in school or the workplace.

Sherman Act §2 — a provision of federal antitrust law prohibiting monopolization and attempted monopolization.

Single economic entity defense — a defense to an alleged violation of §1 of the Sherman Act asserted by a professional sports league, which asserts that the league and its member clubs collectively constitute a single economic entity that creates a single product that none of them could make separately; therefore, their collective decisions and conduct is not covered by §1, which encompasses only concerted action between and among economic competitors.

Sovereign immunity — a tort law doctrine that precludes a party from bringing a suit against the sovereign government without the government's consent; thus, a public educational institution acting as a subsidiary agency of the state may be absolved from tort liability for negligent acts of its employees, such as coaches, athletic trainers, and administrative personnel, who cause injury to an athlete.

Special relationship — an affiliation between two or more individuals, premised on trust and confidence, that gives rise to a legal duty of care owed to the subservient or dependent members of the affiliation (i.e., between a coach and his or her student-athletes).

Speech rights (freedom of speech) — those rights of speech and expression protected by state and federal (and international) constitutions and declarations of rights.

Standing — the requirement in constitutional law that a party demonstrate sufficient connection with or harm from the action challenged to justify that party's participation in the case.

State action/state actor — for the purposes of the Fourteenth Amendment to the U.S. Constitution, a concept that is used by courts to determine whether the rules and decisions of a private entity or organization (e.g., a sports governing) is sufficiently governmental in nature to be subject to federal constitutional limitations and requirements.

State constitution — state constitutions and declarations of rights limit government power within the individual states and provide specific rights to persons within those states.

Statement of Financial Assistance — an agreement between a student-athlete and a college or university in which the granting institution agrees to extend financial aid to the student in exchange for the student-athlete's agreement to participate in intercollegiate athletics on behalf of the institution; financial assistance may cover costs, including tuition, fees, room, board, and books, associated with enabling a student-athlete to participate in the educational process of the institution.

Statutory labor exemption — an antitrust exemption created by two federal labor statutes that provides a labor union with immunity from antitrust liability for its unilateral efforts to further its members' (e.g., players) economic interests by unionizing, engaging in the collective bargaining process, and striking or picketing; it also immunizes the activities of multiemployer collective bargaining units (e.g., the representative of a league's clubs) from antitrust challenge.

Strict liability — liability without any personal fault; for doping offenses, this means that an athlete is liable for a doping violation based on the mere presence of a banned substance in his or her body, regardless of whether he or she intended to take a banned substance or was negligent (i.e., failed to use reasonable care to prevent a doping violation).

Strike — a lawful means of economic pressure that a players' union may use in an effort to convince a professional sports league to agree to its proposed collective bargaining agreement (CBA) terms; during a strike, the players refuse to provide services to their respective clubs, which forces the clubs not to play games or to hire replacement players (most of whom are not major league caliber).

Subpoena — a writ issued by a court or government agency requiring a party to testify or produce certain evidentiary material.

Substantial proportionality — under Title IX, a very close (within 1 to 2 percent) relationship between the ratio of male and female students in the undergraduate student body and the ratio of male and female student-athletes.

Substantive due process — a constitutional limitation on government or state power to enact or enforce substantive legislation or regulation that infringes on a general or unenumerated (not specifically included constitutional) right.

Suspicionless — a term used to describe searches (drug tests) permitted by courts even when there was no individualized suspicion of wrongdoing (drug use).

Swiss Federal Tribunal (SFT) — Switzerland's highest court, which has the jurisdiction to review Court of Arbitration for Sport (CAS) arbitration awards, which is rendered on very narrow procedural and substantive grounds.

Ted Stevens Olympic and Amateur Sports Act (Amateur Sports Act, or ASA) — a federal law that provides the legal framework for regulating Olympic sports in the United States and grants the United States Olympic Committee plenary governing authority; it also provides the U.S. Olympic Committee with the exclusive right to use and license others to use all of the Olympic marks within the United States and prohibits their unauthorized usage "for the purpose of trade, to induce the sale of any goods or services, or to promote any theatrical exhibition, athletic performance, or competition."

Temporary restraining order — a short-term order designed to protect a party while the court is considering whether it should issue an injunction in a case.

Termination for cause — the justifiable discharge of an employee that is based on certain provisions or terms of the contract existing between the employer and the discharged employee.

Therapeutic use exemption (TUE) — an exemption granted by an antidoping organization that permits an athlete to take prescribed medication containing a banned substance for legitimate health reasons.

Third-party beneficiary — a party in contract law who may assert rights under the contract, even though she or he was not a party to the original contract, on the ground that the party was an intended beneficiary of the contract.

Trademark Counterfeiting — the intentional and unauthorized use of a mark on a product that is known to be "identical with, or substantially indistinguishable from," a federally registered mark, which creates a likelihood of consumer confusion regarding its source, affiliation, endorsement, or sponsorship.

Trademark Dilution Revision Act of 2006 (TDRA) — a provision of the Lanham Act that protects the unauthorized use of a "famous mark" (e.g., "America's Cup") from dilution by blurring or tarnishment.

Trademark/service mark — a name, logo, or other symbol that identifies a product or service.

Trademark/service mark infringement — the unauthorized use of a name, logo, or other symbol that creates a likelihood of consumer confusion regarding the source, affiliation, endorsement, or sponsorship of a product or service.

Transfer rules — regulations promulgated and enforced by athletic associations to limit the ability of a student-athlete to participate in interscholastic athletics after the student moves from one school to another.

Unauthorized public performance of copyrighted work — the violation of federal copyright law by the unauthorized display of a copyrighted work "at a place open to the public or at any place where a substantial number of persons outside of a normal circle of family and its social acquaintances are gathered" (e.g., the interception of a broadcast sports event and its unauthorized streaming over the Internet).

Unethical conduct — a finding by the National Collegiate Athletic Association (NCAA) that a coach, administrator, or staff member failed to act with honesty and integrity.

Unfair competition — the unauthorized use of another's intellectual property (e.g., a trademark) that causes a likelihood of consumer confusion.

Unfair labor practice — conduct by either a league multiemployer collective bargaining unit or a players' union during the collective bargaining process or otherwise that violates the obligations or rights established by the National Labor Relations Act (NLRA).

Uniform Domain Name Dispute Resolution Policy (UDRP) — a policy that provides a trademark owner with the right to arbitration as a means of remedying the unauthorized use of its trademark as an Internet domain name.

Uniform or standard player contract (UPC) — the standard form agreement between a player and his or her team, the terms of which (as well as the parties' contractual freedom to amend or modify them) are established by the league's collective bargaining agreement (CBA).

United Nations Convention on the Recognition and Enforcement of Foreign Arbitral Awards, 9 U.S.C. §201 (New York Convention) — an international treaty, to which the United States is a party, that provides a procedure for national courts to recognize and confirm valid foreign arbitration awards; a national court is empowered to vacate a foreign arbitration award only on very limited grounds.

United States Anti-Doping Agency (USADA) — an independent, nongovernmental antidoping agency for Olympic sports in the United States, which provides drug education, conducts drug testing of U.S. athletes, investigates positive results, and prosecutes doping violations.

United States Olympic Committee (USOC) — the organization that governs the Olympic Movement in the United States; it has exclusive authority over all Olympic sports and athletes in the United States.

Vacation of records — a punishment levied by the National Collegiate Athletic Association (NCAA) against schools for using ineligible players, whether they were deemed ineligible at the time of the game or retroactively determined to be ineligible; the institution or coach may not be credited with any victories during the time frame of using an ineligible player (though any losses are still counted), and all the player's stats and accomplishments are also no longer credited.

Voluntary participation — the willful, knowing, and purposeful involvement of an individual in an activity without the coercion or influence of another.

Waiver rule — a process by which an interscholastic or intercollegiate athlete may seek to be relieved from limitations on participation on the grounds of fairness (to the athlete).

Warrant — a judge's order acknowledging sufficient cause to permit law enforcement officers to engage in a reasonable search.

Workers' compensation law — a statutory system of administrative benefits established by state law that provide a method whereby workers are able to obtain compensation and medical expenses for work-related injuries or diseases.

World Anti-Doping Agency (WADA) — an international agency based in Lausanne, Switzerland, that is the product of a collaborative effort between governments and international sports organizations to combat sports doping, which promulgates the World Anti-Doping Code (WADA Code).

World Anti-Doping Code (WADA Code) — antidoping regulations and rules created by the World Anti-Doping Agency (WADA) that aim to create a uniform system of rules and sanctions for doping violations applicable to all competitive sports played throughout the world, particularly Olympic sports.

Table of Cases

Principal cases are indicated by italics.

Index